Authoritarian El Salvador

RECENT TITLES FROM THE HELEN KELLOGG INSTITUTE
FOR INTERNATIONAL STUDIES

Scott Mainwaring, series editor

The University of Notre Dame Press gratefully thanks the Helen Kellogg Institute for International Studies for its support in the publication of titles in this series.

Carlos Guevara Mann
Political Careers, Corruption, and Impunity: Panama's Assembly, 1984–2009 (2011)

Gabriela Ippolito-O'Donnell
The Right to the City: Popular Contention in Contemporary Buenos Aires (2012)

Susan Fitzpatrick-Behrens
The Maryknoll Catholic Mission in Peru, 1943–1989: Transnational Faith and Transformation (2012)

Barry S. Levitt
Power in the Balance: Presidents, Parties, and Legislatures in Peru and Beyond (2012)

Sérgio Buarque de Holanda
Roots of Brazil (2012)

José Murilo de Carvalho
The Formation of Souls: Imagery of the Republic in Brazil (2012)

Douglas Chalmers and Scott Mainwaring, eds.
Problems Confronting Contemporary Democracies: Essays in Honor of Alfred Stepan (2012)

Peter K. Spink, Peter M. Ward, and Robert H. Wilson, eds.
Metropolitan Governance in the Federalist Americas: Strategies for Equitable and Integrated Development (2012)

Natasha Borges Sugiyama
Diffusion of Good Government: Social Sector Reforms in Brazil (2012)

Ignacio Walker
Democracy in Latin America: Between Hope and Despair (2013)

Laura Gómez-Mera
Power and Regionalism in Latin America: The Politics of MERCOSUR (2013)

Erik Ching
Authoritarian el Salvador: Politics and the Origins of the Military Regimes, 1880–1940 (2013)

For a complete list of titles from the Helen Kellogg Institute for International Studies, see http://www.undpress.nd.edu

AUTHORITARIAN
EL SALVADOR

Politics and the Origins of the Military Regimes,
1880–1940

ERIK CHING

University of Notre Dame Press

Notre Dame, Indiana

Copyright © 2014 by University of Notre Dame Press
Notre Dame, Indiana 46556
www.undpress.nd.edu

Manufactured in the United States of America

Library of Congress Cataloging-in-Publication Data

Ching, Erik Kristofer.
Authoritarian El Salvador : politics and the origins of the military regimes,
1880-1940 / Erik Ching.
pages   cm. — (From the Helen Kellogg Institute for International Studies)
Includes bibliographical references and index.
ISBN 978-0-268-02375-1 (pbk.) — ISBN 0-268-02375-1 (paper)
1. El Salvador—History—Revolution, 1932. 2. El Salvador—
History—1838–1944. 3. Authoritarianism—El Salvador—History.
4. Military government—El Salvador—History—20th century.   I. Title.
F1487.5.C54   2013
972.8405'2—dc23
2013030743

To **JACK** *and* **DAVID**

CONTENTS

TABLES

ACRONYMS AND ABBREVIATIONS

AGN	Archivo General de la Nación, San Salvador, El Salvador
AGS	Archivo de Gobernación Sonsonate, El Salvador
AMI	Archivo Municipal de Izalco, El Salvador
AMJ	Archivo Municipal de Juayúa, El Salvador
AMS	Archivo Municipal de Sonsonate, El Salvador
ARENA	Alianza Republicana Nacionalista (Nationalist Republican Alliance)
CN	Colección de Nulos
FA	Fondo Alcaldía
FO	Foreign Office
FRTS	Federación Regional de Trabajadores Salvadoreños (Regional Federation of Salvadoran Workers)
FWTP	Frederick William Taylor Papers, UCLA Dept. of Special Collections
IFC	Ismael Fuentes Collection
MG	Ministerio de Gobernación
ORDEN	Organización Democrática Nacionalista (Nationalist Democratic Organization)
PB	"Pre-Burn" Collection
PCN	Partido de Conciliación Nacional (National Conciliation Party)
PCS	Partido Comunista Salvadoreño (Communist Party of El Salvador)
PND	Partido Nacional Democrático (National Democratic Party)
PRO	Public Record Office, London, England
PRUD	Partido Revolucionario de Unificación Democrática (Revolutionary Party of Democratic Unification)

RG	Record Group
RGASPI	Russian State Archive of Social and Political History, Moscow, Russia
SI	Sección Indiferente
SRI	Socorro Rojo Internacional (International Red Aid)
SS	Sección Sonsonate
SSV	Sección San Vicente
USNA	United States National Archives, Washington, DC
WNRC	Washington National Record Center, Suitland, Maryland

ACKNOWLEDGMENTS

Any project in the works as long as this one will invariably accumulate much indebtedness. As I take this opportunity to consider the debts I have accrued along the way, I find it personally humbling and professionally eye-opening to realize the amount of support from individuals and institutions that is necessary to bring a project like this to fruition. Researching, writing, and revising are solitary efforts, but they only occur because of highly collective networks of support.

In a reverse chronology, I open with those who most recently helped to make this possible. The first is my home institution, Furman University, which granted me a yearlong sabbatical award for 2011–2012 that made time available for the final round of revisions. Since completing the initial version of this manuscript as a dissertation at the University of California, Santa Barbara, in 1997, I have worked steadily but intermittently over the years on revising it into a book. Meanwhile, I was drawn into various other projects on Salvadoran history. In fact, I was embarking on yet another of those for my sabbatical when Scott Mainwaring, editor of the series in which this book is being published, contacted me to tell me he had been working on a new study in comparative politics, and El Salvador was one of his cases. He suggested I submit my work to the University of Notre Dame Press. As a result, I directed a portion of my sabbatical leave towards completing the revisions to this project. I would like to thank Scott for his support and for encouraging me to set aside another new endeavor and focus on this one.

The research for this project was done under the auspices of various institutions and organizations. The Albert J. Beveridge Grant for Research in the History of the Western Hemisphere from the American Historical Association funded my exploratory trip to the Salvadoran archives. The subsequent yearlong trip was made possible by a Fulbright grant, which also included trips to Moscow and London. The writing of the initial version of this study, my dissertation, was done with grant support from the history department and the graduate division at UC Santa Barbara, and from the Academy for Educational Development.

All of the publication projects that I have undertaken since arriving at Furman have informed this project and made it better and more contextualized. Thus, the research endeavors for those projects are somewhat synonymous with this one. Fulbright, once again, supported an extended research trip to El Salvador in 2005, and the Research and Professional Growth Committee at Furman has funded multiple short-term trips to El Salvador since my arrival in 1998. A grant from the Associated Colleges of the South's (ACS) Faculty Renewal Program funded a research trip to El Salvador. Follow-up research in Moscow was made possible by the ACS's Global Partners Project–Central Europe and Russia Task Force.

My participation on Furman's Latin America study abroad program has also been a valuable asset to this project. Between 2004 and 2012, it kept me returning to El Salvador more or less annually. While my mission on those programs was to teach students, the necessity of creating opportunities for them provided me with many unexpected contacts and research threads that I later followed on my own.

I extend special thanks to Hector Lindo-Fuentes, my coauthor on *Modernizing Minds in El Salvador* and *Remembering a Massacre in El Salvador*. He has been with me since the start of my graduate career and has been a continual sounding board and source of support. So too has Knut Walter, historian of El Salvador, whom I first met on my initial research trip to El Salvador in 1993. I would not have made it this far without the two of them.

I would also like to thank other scholars, most of them Salvadoranists, who have helped me along the way as collaborators, commenters, sounding boards, or research companions, including Aldo Lauria-Santiago, Virginia Tilley, Michael Schroeder, Carlos Gregorio López Bernal, Paul Almeida, Jeff Gould, Ellen Moodie, Brandt Pederson, Alfredo Ramírez, María Eugenia López, Aldo García Guevara, Rafael Lara-Martínez, Carlos Henríquez Consalvi, Leigh Binford, Bob Holden, Henrik Rønsbo, Jan Suter, Patricia Alvarenga Venutolo, James Mahoney, Héctor Pérez Brignoli, and René Aguiluz. Thanks also to members of my dissertation committee—Sarah Cline, Fernando López Alves, and Robert Collins—and to Gerald Horne, formerly of the Black Studies Department at UCSB.

My fellow historians in the history department at Furman University have been as much friends as colleagues. They have created a nurturing professional environment and have been nothing but encouraging, oftentimes picking up the slack when I was abroad, on family leave, or cloistered away in my office. They have provided me with intellectual insights and stimulated many ideas and concepts that have contributed to this study and to the others I have worked on. I am grateful to be part of their community. Many of my non-historian colleagues here at Furman have been equally helpful in an interdisciplinary context.

The two anonymous reviewers who evaluated the manuscript for UND Press offered excellent suggestions. Reviewer #1, in particular, provided the most comprehensive review I've ever seen, or written, for that matter. I am particularly appreciative of that reviewer's attentiveness to and support for the manuscript. The acquisitions editor at UND Press, Stephen Little, has been gracious and encouraging throughout the publication process. I thank Kellie Hultgren for her careful work in copyediting. I am especially grateful to designer Brian Faulkenberry of Furman University's Marketing Department for creating and revising the maps for this book.

A historian is utterly reliant on archives and thus equally dependent upon archive and library staffs. I've been invariably impressed by the staff members I have worked with across multiple continents, but especially those in El Salvador, who labor under adverse conditions but who have always been gracious and eager to assist me. The staff members at the national archive (Archivo General de la Nación, or AGN) in El Salvador, in particular, have had to endure me on multiple occasions, but especially for that long year in 1994 and 1995 when I was a fixture in the building nearly every day, from opening until closing. Our physical surroundings were less than ideal, and the archive was still in something of a shambles, but they patiently negotiated me as they went about their business of bringing order to the chaos around them. So, to Miguel Angel, Isabella, Maria Eugenia, Luís, Mauricio, Sebas, and some others whom I am undoubtedly overlooking, I extend my heartfelt thanks. I also would like to acknowledge the adept assistance of Svetlana Rosenthal in the Comintern Archive in Moscow, Russia. She was gracious and accommodating. Also, the library staff at Furman University has been nothing but supportive in helping me with my seemingly unending requests for arcane and hard-to-find sources over the past fifteen years.

Aldo Lauria-Santiago, Patricia Alvarenga Venutolo, and I utilized the archives in El Salvador at a distinct moment, the late 1980s and early 1990s, when the archives were opened to the public for the first time and the staff members were still taking stock of the monumental task of ordering and protecting the nation's documentary patrimony. Still, they granted us gracious and liberal access to the materials. Without that liberal access, this project would never have been possible. As I describe in more detail in the introduction, I was able to sift through every page of documentation in the Gobernación collection, along with other collections in national, regional, and municipal archives. A strength of this project is the extent to which its conclusions are based on a comprehensive survey of the extant documentary record. Access to the materials is now more strict and controlled, as it should be. But without a similar degree of access, especially in the absence of detailed indices and high levels of organization in the collections, recreating this research would be, I believe, next to impossible, especially for a solitary researcher.

I would like to thank Jack Bermingham and David Rock, my undergraduate and graduate advisors respectively. Jack triggered my desire to teach, and he has since supported me more times than I can count. David never planned to have a Salvadoranist under his tutelage, but he endured me patiently and supported me avidly. In recognition, I dedicate the book to them.

I would not be writing these words without family and friends. As to the latter, most of them would not care one way or the other if I mention them in writing, so for the sake of simplicity, I will simply say, thanks, you know who you are. As to the former, my parents Harriette and Woody, my sister Nissa, and my in-laws Matt and Carol and Rob and Jaime have been there to help out so much, I cannot even begin to do them justice in words. And last but not least, my wife Cathy and my children, Anders and Halle: they are my foundation of support, and, naturally, they had to deal with my self-sequestering more than anyone else.

* * *

Small portions of chapters 6, 7, and 8 have been published previously, and they reappear in the present work with permission of the respective publishers:

"In Search of the Party: Communism, the Comintern and the Rebellion of 1932 in El Salvador." *The Americas* 55, no. 2 (1998): 204–39. Reprinted with permission of *The Americas*.

"Indians, the Military and the Rebellion of 1932 in El Salvador," by Erik Ching and Virginia Tilley, *Journal of Latin American Studies* 30, no. 1 (1998): 121–56. Reprinted with permission of Cambridge Journals.

Material from *Modernizing Minds in El Salvador: Education Reform and the Cold War, 1960–1980,* by Héctor Lindo-Fuentes and Erik Ching, © 2012, is used and reprinted by permission of the University of New Mexico Press.

Material from "Patronage and Politics under Martínez, 1931–39: The Local Roots of Military Authoritarianism in El Salvador," by Erik Ching, from *Landscapes of Struggle: Politics, Society and Community in El Salvador,* edited by Aldo Lauria and Leigh Binford, © 2004, is used and reprinted by permission of the University of Pittsburgh Press.

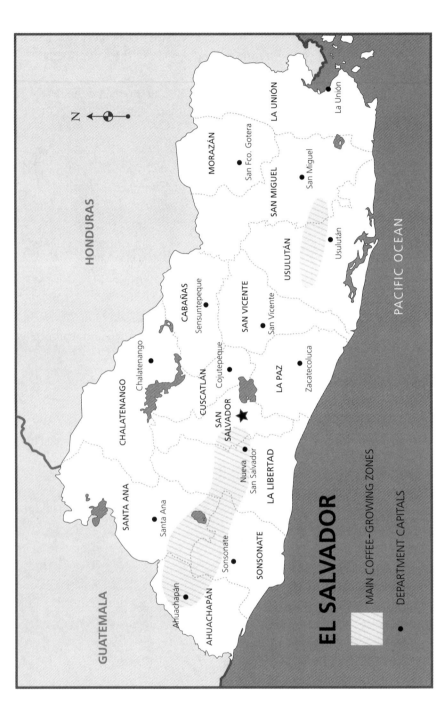

Map 1. El Salvador's Fourteen Departments and Their Capital Cities (Contemporary)

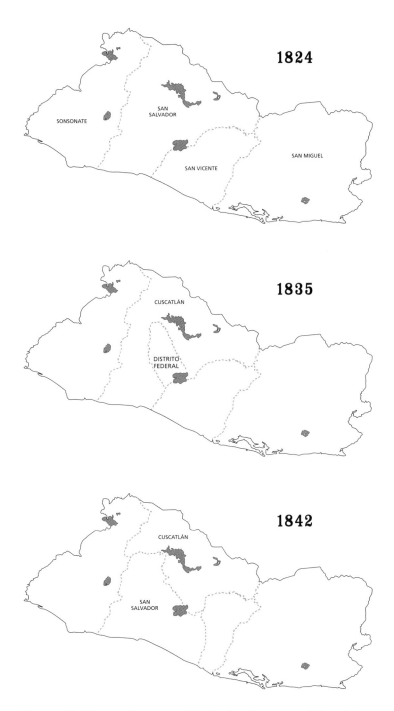

Map 2. The Historical Evolution of El Salvador's Departmental Boundaries

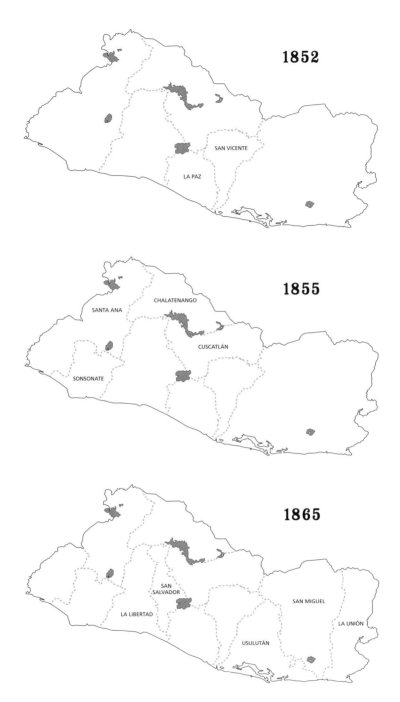

Map 2. continued

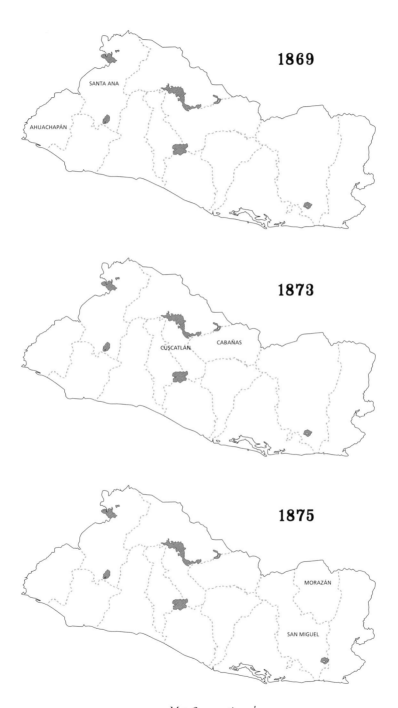

Map 2.   *continued*

INTRODUCTION

On December 2, 1931, El Salvador's civilian president, Arturo Araujo, was deposed in a quickly executed military coup. He was replaced by his vice president, General Maximiliano Martínez.[1] At the time, the 1931 coup seemed unexceptional. El Salvador and its neighboring countries had experienced plenty of coups, and many military officers had served as president. In hindsight, the 1931 coup was a watershed in Salvadoran history. Arturo Araujo had been elected in a relatively free and fair election, the first of its kind in El Salvador. Sixty years would pass before democracy returned to El Salvador. Unbeknownst to anyone at the time, the Martínez regime would usher in five decades of dictatorial military rule, the longest run of uninterrupted military rule in Latin American history. That series of military regimes was followed by twelve years of devastating civil war between 1980 and 1992. Not until after the war did democracy return to El Salvador, and only then because the war caused the military to be restructured and the political system to be reformed.

The Martínez regime exemplifies an authoritarian tradition in El Salvador. He was a stern, esoteric man, and his adherence to theosophy garnered him the nickname *El brujo* (the witch or sorcerer). He ended the nascent experiment with democracy and used state power to violently suppress popular dissent. The most extreme example of his regime's repressive character came in response to a peasant uprising in the western zones of the country in January 1932, just six weeks after he came to power. During the uprising, peasant rebels attacked roughly one dozen townships, killed approximately one hundred people, and damaged a variety of businesses and residences owned by local elites. In response, government soldiers swept through the western countryside, killing untold thousands of people, sometimes in highly orchestrated mass executions. The killings of 1932 would prove to be one of the worst episodes of state-sponsored repression in modern Latin American history. In various ways, the events surrounding General Martínez's rise to power and the 1932 uprising exemplify El Salvador's well-earned reputation as a nation long on authoritarianism and short on democracy.

The compelling and tragic events of the late 1920s and early 1930s in El Salvador inspired questions that led to this study. What were the origins of the Martínez regime? How did the political system operate during his reign? Did it resemble past regimes? Was there indeed a democratic interlude prior to Martínez, and if so, how did it function? What were the causes of the 1932 uprising, and how did the events of 1932 affect the consolidation of the regime under Martínez, as well as the military-led regimes that succeeded him?

I have grouped my responses to those questions in the following five arguments. First, politics in El Salvador was indeed defined by a long-standing system of nondemocratic authoritarianism that dates to the earliest days of the republic, but which took full form with the rise of the coffee economy and state centralization in the late nineteenth century. The system was characterized by a complex series of patronage-based alliances that functioned according to a set of informal rules that every political actor understood, but which were never codified. This system of nondemocratic authoritarianism was challenged between 1927 and 1931 under the leadership of President Pío Romero Bosque. He and a coterie of state bureaucrats attempted to change the informal rules by directing the system away from patronage and towards a more genuine democracy. That reform initiative resulted in the election of Arturo Araujo in 1931. The regime of General Martínez overturned those reforms and returned to the structures and practices of the pre-Romero era. Therefore, continuity is the first and foremost theme advanced by this study. The military regime that began in December 1931 was rooted in the structures and practices of the liberal dictatorships prior to 1927.

El Salvador's nondemocratic political system exhibited some highly paradoxical traits, including a vigorous and regular electoral process with high voter turnout, and a political discourse that celebrated democracy, freedom of suffrage, and individual liberty. A second claim of this study is that a fundamental disconnect existed between what political actors said and what they did, between their rhetoric and reality, between the formal legal codes and the informal rules of how politics was actually practiced. Out of these paradoxes emerged a distinct political culture of authoritarianism that became a determinant variable in setting the parameters by which Salvadorans practiced politics. Thus, an extension of this second argument is that culture matters in explanations of how and why El Salvador's particular political system came to exist. El Salvador's material conditions may or may not have predisposed it towards authoritarianism, but its inhabitants' decisions, practices, and habits mattered. The era of President Romero Bosque offers a particularly revealing window on how the informal rules functioned. He advocated for genuine democratic reforms, and his actions prompted local political actors, accustomed to the traditional practices, to bombard the central government with requests for clarification. Why were the ministry's officials rejecting the usual practices, and why did they seem to be changing the meaning of the terms *democracy* and *freedom of suffrage*?

As one might expect, the unequal relationship between landed elites and their laborers served as a foundation for patronage relations and the attendant patron-client relations. But class inequality was not the sole inspiration for nondemocratic political practices. A third argument of this study is that peasant communities employed the same exclusionary practices as their elite counterparts. The number of cases available to support this claim is not extensive, but those cases that do exist show peasant communities manipulating local polling stations just as their elite rivals did. Not surprisingly, those elections tended to produce unanimous results in favor of the peasants' candidates, even though their members constituted the overwhelming majority of the voting population and presumably would have won the elections, had they been conducted freely and fairly. These discoveries suggest that nondemocratic practices were deeply entrenched in Salvadoran society and political culture. They also show that peasants and poor people participated in the construction of their nation's political systems. Elites may have set the terms of debate, in part by crafting the laws that governed political procedures, but poor people pursued their interests through the extant systems. Nonelites therefore took part in the normalization of nondemocratic authoritarianism in El Salvador.

A fourth argument of this study operates along a similar vein: long-standing conflicts existed between indigenous peasant communities and ladino (non-Indian) elites throughout the western highlands for control over local political office. Once again, these political conflicts took place between rival patronage-based networks, not necessarily between poor advocates of democratization and elite adherents of nondemocratic authoritarianism. The conflicts came to a head just prior to the 1932 uprising, in the midst of the Romero reforms, the Martínez coup, and the growing impact of the Great Depression. These revelations about local political conflicts suggest the need for a revisionist interpretation of the 1932 uprising, rooting its causes in long-standing local affairs and the organizational autonomy of peasant communities, rather than the traditional version that stresses the organizational impetus of the Salvadoran Communist Party. The rebellion demonstrated poor people's ability to press their demands and force the existing system to acknowledge their needs. The succession of military governments after 1932 dutifully placed the needs of common Salvadorans at the center of political rhetoric, even though their actual policies paled in comparison to it. The 1932 uprising demonstrated the risks associated with violent insurgency for the long-term interests of peasants and poor people. The rebellion enflamed elites' passions and made them more reactionary and resistant to change, hallmarks of their actions in subsequent decades.

Finally, the government's response to the 1932 uprising created a model that all successor military regimes would follow. The Martínez regime used violence on a colossal scale to beat back the threat of an autonomous peasantry; as part of that process, it returned the political system to its pre-reformist norm, but with an even more intensified centralization of power in the central government. But it also insisted that reform, or at least the idea of reform, was an essential counterpart to repression and political authoritarianism. Regime bureaucrats sought an ordered and stable society, one in which economic production could proceed unabated. They realized that dead and rebellious peasants did not made good workers. As a result, they adopted a strategy in which they repressed when they felt it necessary and closed down the abbreviated democratic opening, but simultaneously called for social reforms as a way to prevent rebellion. In particular, they identified one source of the problem as unscrupulous elites who exploited workers and thus created fertile ground for communist agitation. Such calls for reform were accompanied by the standard rhetorical appeals to democracy and free suffrage. This reform/repress dichotomy was fully evident in the response to the 1932 uprising, which suggests that the uprising represented a key moment in the shaping of military rule in El Salvador. Even though the Martínez regime did little to implement reforms, it set a precedent on which its successors would expand. For better or worse, the combination of reform and repression became the standard strategy of military governance for fifty years.

The relevance of these five arguments can be further clarified by placing them in the broader context of Salvadoran historiography. The nature of military rule in El Salvador and the corresponding relationship between landed elites and the military have been the topics of much academic discussion. A prevailing narrative posits that landed elites and the military formed a united front. The elites surrendered control over the offices of government in exchange for security. To that end, the military became the Praetorian Guard of the landed elites (primarily coffee growers), and military officers were allowed to enjoy whatever privileges came with officeholding. In exchange, those officers guaranteed that elites were free to organize their economic affairs as they wished. The military's brutal response to the peasant uprising of 1932 seemed to embody that arrangement, as did the many subsequent episodes of state repression of the working poor. Political scientist William Stanley summarized this relationship succinctly in the title to his 1996 study of El Salvador: *The Protection Racket State*.[2]

The present study more or less sustains that argumentative thread, but stresses the need to look at it with a nuanced eye. Too easily we can fall into a rigid interpretive frame that implies that the relationship between landowners and military officers was seamless. In fact, it was fraught with complexities. Neither the military nor the elites operated as unified blocs. Each was characterized by internal divisions and messy political rivalries, some merely personal or opportunistic, and others that were ideological and based on differing visions of the country's future. When those complicated assemblages of elites and officers met in the political arena to make policy and determine the personnel of government, the prospects for complexity increased exponentially. Certainly, conservative officers found common cause with conservative elites, and together they could form a formidable political bloc. But challengers abounded, and sometimes they bonded over an alternative ideological vision, even over a shared belief in the need for social reform. Sometimes loyalty to institution trumped ideology, as when soldiers, for example, banded together and adhered to the internal rules of the armed forces, regardless of other stakeholders' interests.

Ironically, the esoteric authoritarian General Martínez highlights this need for nuance. He may have repressed without quarter and defined economic development as export-agricultural production led by landed elites, but he also raised the call for reform and demonstrated an evolving relationship with elites. Not the least example of this complexity was his government's attempt to end the system of plantation-owned stores and stop the elites' customary practice of paying workers in coupons rather than legal currency. Even if he failed in that particular attempt, and even if the overall byproducts of his reform program were modest, Martínez created the unprecedented expectation that government, with its capacity for autonomous action, was obligated to look out for common people. And even if elites did not find themselves overly threatened by Martínez's policies, they feared that future regimes (military or civilian) might be worse. Indeed, Martínez's successors followed his lead, even if they disavowed his name, and pursued reforms more aggressively, eventually implementing a land reform, an act that elites would never forget and never forgive. However much elites might have benefitted from military rule, many of them became highly suspicious of military leaders' commitment to their priorities of economic libertarianism and the sanctity of private property. If nothing else, this study seeks to demonstrate that the foundational years of military rule in El Salvador demonstrate the need for a nuanced approach.

A second, parallel historiographical debate is the role of El Salvador's poor or "subaltern" peoples in the making of their nation's history. It is safe to say that until the latter half of the twentieth century, they were largely absent from historical narratives. Due in no small part to the surge in popular mobilization in the 1960s and 1970s, progressive intellectuals looked to rectify this absence. One of the initial contributions came from the famed poet and activist Roque Dalton. In two brief historical surveys published in the early 1960s, *El Salvador* and *El Salvador: monografía*, both of which remain in print today, Dalton challenged the prevailing narratives that withheld critiques from elites and denied agency to subaltern actors. Subsequent studies built on Dalton's foundation and consolidated a subaltern counternarrative of national history. The present study shows the value of that counternarrative. Admittedly, the system of patronage and clientelism that prevailed in the nineteenth and early twentieth centuries worked to the long-term benefit of elites and the detriment of the working poor. After the attempt to create a more genuinely democratic system failed in 1931, Martínez returned to past political patterns and rested his system of governance on patronage-based, hierarchical class relations. In the Martínez system, local elites served as municipal political leaders and workers and peasants constituted the rank and file. But peasants and the working poor were not absent from the process. They bargained constantly with elites and in the process shaped the manner and way in which Salvadoran history unfolded. Not the least act of "bargaining" was the 1932 uprising. Thereafter, few, if any, leaders in El Salvador dared rule without at least paying lip service to the need for social reform. And whatever motived the eventual enactment of reforms, particularly the land, banking, and export reforms after 1979, be it conviction or expediency, the mobilized demands of poor people were largely responsible for making them happen.[3]

Nevertheless, one of the distinguishing features of El Salvador, at least compared to some other countries in Latin America, is the absence of a clearly defined moment in the nineteenth century when plebian masses, either urban or rural, articulated their definition of civic republicanism and sought to insert that definition into the national body politic. Scholars who have conducted research in Mexico, Colombia, Peru, Chile, and Argentina, for example, have found evidence of these moments.[4] Whether the failure to do so in El Salvador reflects an actual difference from these other countries, the peculiarities of the documentary record or the distinctiveness of the scholars who have done research in it can be debated.

Regardless, for the time being, El Salvador seems to represent a distinct case.

As should be evident, this study's point of departure is politics and elections. The political arena was the space in which Salvadorans negotiated with one another over their society and its future. Elections were revelatory moments in the process. No political leader in El Salvador, whether dictator or democrat, served in office without the sanction of an election, however fettered the voting might have been. Even though El Salvador has been typified by authoritarian and dictatorial politics throughout its modern history, it was also the site of vigorous electoral activity. Elections happened with great regularity, and many people turned out to vote. At some level, these electoral proceedings were political theater, or "civic ceremonies," as Peter Guardino describes them in Mexico.[5] But they were essential to proving a leader's ability to rule. Getting lots of people to the polls and then controlling the electoral outcome proved that a candidate deserved to hold office. And similarly, when politics turned violent, a leader's ability to enact violence was meant to be understood, in the words of historian Robert Holden, "by its witnesses, victims, and perpetrators alike as a demonstration of fitness to rule."[6] By examining political activities and elections, the present study seeks to show how the political system functioned and thereby contribute to an understanding of the nation's enduring authoritarianism.

This study begins in earnest in the late nineteenth century, when the liberal oligarchic state consolidated in conjunction with the rise in coffee exports. Thus, the background is one of state centralization and its highly paradoxical nature. A strong state made possible the modern military authoritarian regime that began with Martínez in 1931, but as the historian and theorist Charles Tilly observes, almost no democratic system in the world has come into existence in a society characterized by a weak state.[7] Indeed, it was only after the Salvadoran state became stronger and more centralized in the late 1920s that a democratic process emerged. And it was only with the power of the newly centralized state that Martínez destroyed the fledgling democracy. An understanding of how the Salvadoran state centralized in the late nineteenth and early twentieth centuries and what that process meant to the day-to-day practice of politics is therefore essential to answering questions about the persistence of authoritarianism in El Salvador. The study looks at the early and middle nineteenth century as well, but selectively, seeking out general patterns. The primary objective is to arrive at the pivotal moment in the late 1920s and early 1930s with a contextualized and explanatory eye.

The study is defined by its distinct sources. Most of the evidence consists of documents from Salvadoran archives, especially the national archive, the Archivo General de la Nación (AGN). I first went to the AGN in 1993, shortly after the civil war ended and just a few years after its doors were opened to the public for the first time.[8] I have since returned numerous times. Its collections are of mixed usefulness for a study of politics. Some potentially key collections, such as military records and presidential papers, are not housed there. They have either been destroyed or stored secretly elsewhere. Also, the AGN holds almost no records after the 1940s, when ministerial offices moved out of the National Palace to disparate new locations throughout the capital. Furthermore, records for the period prior to 1889 are scant, because the original archive burned down that year.

Nevertheless, the AGN holds many useful documents for the study of politics between 1890 and the 1940s, especially the papers of the Ministry of Government (Ministerio de Gobernación, or MG), the main body of sources for this study. That collection contains correspondence between the local, departmental, and national levels of government and includes substantive material on elections and political affairs. The collection consists of roughly five hundred archival boxes and one hundred and fifty bundles (roughly equivalent to another three hundred and fifty boxes) for the years 1889 to 1944. The materials are organized only by year, and documents relating to politics are intermixed with all other correspondence. The only way to find relevant information is to sift through the entire collection one page at a time. Indeed, my goal was to get through every box and bundle of documentation, which was a challenge, but thanks to generous access granted by the staff of the AGN, along with the use of a portable photocopier, I accomplished my goal and sifted through every dusty and mold-ridden page. In doing so, I gained a comprehensive overview of the extant documentary record.

I wanted to move further back into the nineteenth century to see if the patterns I was finding after 1890 had precedents. At first this seemed an impossible task, owing to the lack of documentation. Fortunately, the

AGN contains the papers of Gobernación San Vicente (the office of San Vicente's departmental governor). These materials had been stored in San Vicente and thus were not lost to the fire of 1889, and they also survived the 1936 earthquake that destroyed much of San Vicente City. The records date back to the 1840s and contain correspondence between the ministry of government, the departmental governor, and municipal political officials. In addition to those materials, the AGN holds sixteen file drawers of documents that were pulled from the embers of the 1889 fire; they offer further evidence of politics in the early decades of the nineteenth century. I also traveled to the municipal archive of Sonsonate City, which at that time contained records from as early as the 1790s, including invaluable electoral data dating back to the 1820s, when the very first elections were held in El Salvador. This discovery prompted me to seek out materials in other municipal archives throughout the western region, and while their collections were nowhere near as extensive as that of Sonsonate, they did provide valuable evidence.

In addition to archives in El Salvador, I consulted archives in the United States (State Department records), England (the papers of the Foreign Office), and Moscow (the archive of the Comintern). The latter shed particularly valuable insight on the events surrounding the 1932 uprising, in the form of correspondence between El Salvador's fledging Communist Party, the Comintern, and the Comintern's regional office, the Caribbean Bureau in New York City.[9]

The Gobernación records constitute the main body of evidence for this study, and like any source, they are particular. They reside in a hybrid place between the public and private spheres. They were not intended to be circulated publicly, unlike newspapers or broadsides, which are printed with the intent of informing a public community, swaying opinion, and contributing to Habermas's "rational-critical public debate."[10] But neither were they the closed correspondence of a small group of individuals operating in an institutionalized structure, as were the letters and reports exchanged between the Salvadoran communists and the Comintern. Admittedly, some of the Gobernación records are like the Comintern materials, but most of them are the consequence of very public events, such as elections, the results of which were often published in publicly circulated newspapers. Furthermore, the individuals participating in the Gobernación correspondence were not necessarily close affiliates in a closed bureaucracy. They were often separated by vast distances—geographical, professional, and social—and the participants in the correspondence did not necessarily know one another, nor did they depend upon one another for their professional future. In fact, sometimes the authors were rivals. Thus, their correspondence is as much a reflection of a public political process as a closed, intrastate "community of discourse."[11]

Consequently, the Gobernación records allow the pursuit of a variety of research tracks. They can reveal something of the hidden transcripts of the subaltern voice, through the petitions contained therein, although they are not as effective at doing so as, for example, the sources Ricardo Salvatore employed to look at the *paysanos* of Buenos Aires, or as the artisanal newspapers that James Wood used to study Santiago's semi-urban plebeians.[12] The Gobernación materials can illuminate the ways people communicated with one another about politics, both as confidants and as strangers. But normally their discourse was not intended for the public sphere, and so when I sought to better understand the ways they dialogued publicly about democracy and politics, I turned to more public, albeit less abundant, sources, such as periodicals and newspapers.

Introducing El Salvador

El Salvador followed the general chronological pattern of the rest of Latin America. It achieved independence from Spain in the 1820s and then entered into an extended period of political instability and economic malaise. A global economic downturn that lasted until the latter nineteenth century adversely affected all of Latin America, with few countries able to find buyers for their products. Peru was an exception, with its supplies of bird guano, which were used to make fertilizer. El Salvador also produced a crop that retained market validity: indigo, a blue dye derived from a plant that had been grown there since precolonial times. Regardless, the mid-nineteenth century was a challenging time for all of Latin America, El Salvador included.[13]

An economic revival began in the 1870s and 1880s in the form of an export boom that lasted until the Great Depression in the 1930s. During that boom, almost every country in Latin America experienced a rapid surge in North American and European markets for its primary commodities. El Salvador's crop was coffee, indigo having been displaced by other sources (British India) and the development of synthetic dyes. Coffee took over as the nation's main export crop by the 1870s and went on to dominate the Salvadoran economy. By the 1920s it accounted for as much as 90 percent of the nation's export revenues.[14] Throughout Latin America, the export boom grew economies and stabilized politics, but it also resulted in economic inequity and political dictatorship. El Salvador was no exception, and a small group of elite families came to control the lion's share of wealth and power.[15]

The inequities accompanying the export boom eventually prompted calls for reform throughout Latin America. Beginning in the early twentieth century, most Latin American countries witnessed a rising tide of labor activism and reform-oriented political movements. The Mexican Revolution of 1910 to 1940 and the reform movement in Uruguay under President José Batlle are just two of the more well known, albeit diverse, examples. In El Salvador the reform movement was delayed and short-lived, taking the form of a brief democratic opening between 1927 and 1931 and a peasant uprising in 1932. But following the pattern of many other countries in which the onset of the Great Depression had triggered reactionary responses, El Salvador witnessed the coup that brought General Martínez to power, resulting in a thirteen-year dictatorship.[16]

Depression-era dictators like Martínez found it difficult to weather the wave of democratization that swept across Latin America with the Allied victory in WWII. In many countries, new leaders came to power through democratic elections or mass-based populist movements, pushing the conservatives and reactionaries back.[17] The demise of General Martínez in 1944 provides a typical example. He was undone by a rising tide of a popular discontent that culminated in a general strike.[18] It appeared that El Salvador might reinvigorate its moribund democracy of 1931 and join other countries undergoing democratization, like neighboring Guatemala. But a reactionary countercoup put a quick end to that prospect and ushered in another four years of dictatorial military governance.

Nevertheless, El Salvador experienced its own version of populist reformism. Even though military officers continued to control government, each successive regime touted the cause of social reform more than its predecessors had. The conservative regime of 1944 to 1948 fell in a coup to a group of young, reformist officers who portrayed themselves as defenders of the common person and enemies of unscrupulous elites. Ultimately, the "revolutionaries" were more talk than action, and they refused to democratize, but they followed the continental pattern after WWII of appealing to the masses and legitimizing the calls for justice and reform. They fell from power in October 1960 to a combined civil-military movement that promised to advance the cause of reform even further.[19]

The consolidation of the Cold War and the victory of the revolutionaries in Cuba in 1959 polarized Latin America and reinvigorated the conservative right, which associated reformism with communism and advocated an increased use of violence to defend itself from enemies at home and abroad. This growing polarization resulted in seizures of power by militaries or conservative movements, which threw reformists and populists out of office. With few exceptions, almost every country in Latin America came to be controlled by an anticommunist military dictatorship. Some examples include the ouster of President Jacobo Arbenz in Guatemala in 1954, the coup by General Augusto Pinochet against President Salvador Allende in Chile in 1973, and the Argentine military's seizure of power in 1954 and then again in 1976.

In El Salvador, the post–Cuban Revolution backlash came in the form of a military coup in January 1961 that ousted the civil-military reformers of October 1960 and accused them of being communists. The new leaders followed the pattern of attributing popular demands for change to communism.[20] They used violence and intimidation to quell the so-called communist threat, and they stayed in power through massive voting fraud in the presidential elections of 1972 and 1977. They also perpetrated increasingly brutal acts of violence in the countryside in hopes of quelling mass organization. But they also tried to maintain popular support by appealing to the reformist spirit of their predecessors. And they pursued modernizing reforms more aggressively, hoping to stave off looming financial ruin by diversifying the economy and creating jobs for the swelling mass of landless laborers. They opened up the political system to proportional representation in the 1960s, enacted a massive education reform in 1968 designed to boost school enrollment and train students for an emergent industrializing economy, embarked on widespread infra-structural improvements, and eventually tried to enact a land reform in 1976. Their strategy failed, and the increasing polarization culminated in the civil war of 1980 to 1992.[21] Not every country in Latin America expe-rienced a full-scale civil war like that in El Salvador, but most every nation experienced a conservative backlash against reformism in the 1960s and 1970s, defined by state-sponsored terror and a corresponding radicaliza-tion of opposition.

El Salvador followed many Latin America–wide patterns, and thus questions about its history of authoritarianism can be answered in part by comparing it to other Latin American case studies. But Latin America exhibited tremendous diversity, and any generalizations need to be placed within the context of distinctiveness. As a case in point, El Salvador wit-nessed, as mentioned previously, both the longest run of interrupted mili-tary rule (1931–1979) and one of the single most violent acts of state-sponsored repression (the massacre of 1932). El Salvador thus had much less experience with populist reformism than the rest of Latin America. Whereas almost every country in Latin America had experienced at least one extended left-leaning or progressive government, El Salvador had sus-tained next to none. Basically, the political right has ruled El Salvador throughout its modern history.

In addition, El Salvador is the smallest country in Latin America, a situation that has had multiple consequences. One of these is a high popu-lation concentration. Even in the early twentieth century, few vacant areas existed in El Salvador. The countryside was heavily cultivated and densely populated, and so too was it highly deforested. In the western hemisphere, only Haiti is more deforested than El Salvador. Another consequence of El Salvador's small size was a distinct experience with state centralization. The debates between centralists and federalists that were so important to other nations in Latin America mattered less in El Salvador. And once the state did centralize, the potential for regional factionalism was not great.

The economy of El Salvador was one of the most monocrop in Latin America. With as much as 90 percent of its export revenues derived from coffee by the late 1920s, El Salvador relied on a single crop for economic survival more than most any other country. Even with economic diversifi-cation in the 1940s and 1950s, in the form of cotton production and some modest industrialization, coffee continued to predominate. El Salvador's modest land area also meant that its coffee plantations were distinct. Whereas coffee growers in Brazil, for example, could move on to new land once their current land deteriorated, no such option existed for Salvadoran growers. A large coffee plantation in Brazil might be many thousands of acres in size, whereas in El Salvador plantations approaching one thousand acres were rare. Consequently, growers in El Salvador became some of the most efficient in the world. Nevertheless, control over El Salvador's coffee economy and the wealth that derived from it remained highly exclusive. El Salvador was not Costa Rica or Venezuela, where smallholders thrived.[22] In El Salvador, a small handful of people owned most of the nation's arable land and controlled the processing and marketing of coffee. The remaining majority of the population either worked for them or barely survived on tiny plots of marginal land.

Another distinct feature of El Salvador's economy was its limited degree of foreign investment. Most of the major economic units in El Salvador, especially its coffee plantations, were owned by Salvadorans. There was no United Fruit Company, as in neighboring Guatemala, Honduras, and Costa Rica. Nor was there a substantial immigrant presence in the coffee economy, as with the Germans in Guatemala. Admittedly, some immigrants came to El Salvador and made a fortune in coffee and commerce, such as the Hills and the Dukes, but they married into well-established Salvadoran families and became part of the traditional Salvadoran elite.[23] When hard economic times hit in El Salvador, there were no foreign multinational corporations to target; instead it would be Salvadoran versus Salvadoran.

With regard to its ethnic identity, El Salvador once again offers a distinct case. It is common to hear Salvadorans describe their nation as the most mestizo in Latin America. Indeed, the indigenous presence in El Salvador declined significantly over time, more so than in most other countries that had large indigenous populations at the time of independence. Statistics relating to ethnic identity are invariably vague and difficult to come by, but at the time of independence El Salvador's indigenous peoples may have comprised a near majority of the population. By the turn of the twentieth century, their proportion had declined to roughly 20 percent, and by the mid-twentieth century it had probably fallen below

10 percent. By that time Salvadorans commonly claimed that their country had no indigenous people at all. The causes of the decimating decline in indigenous identity are manifold and complex, but they resemble continental patterns. Assimilationist pressures and discriminatory practices in both the public and private sectors made it difficult for indigenous people to retain their identity from one generation to the next. These pressures were particularly intense in the late nineteenth and early twentieth centuries, amidst rapid economic expansion and state centralization. The decline in indigenous identity may have been more precipitous in El Salvador than in other countries, but it was part of a broader pattern. Nevertheless, El Salvador stands in contrast to its neighbor Guatemala, where the proportion of indigenous people never dropped below 50 percent. Even if indigenous peoples were under great pressure in El Salvador, the issue of ethnicity and ethnic relations played decisive roles at key moments in the nation's history. A case in point is the 1932 uprising. The geographic center of that uprising, the western highlands, was a demographic center of indigenous people, and most of the municipalities that experienced significant rebel activity were disproportionately indigenous.[24]

Finally, as with any nation, El Salvador's distinct geography shaped its socioeconomic history. As mentioned previously, El Salvador is a small country, approximately one hundred fifty miles long and sixty miles wide. It runs from Guatemala in the west to the Gulf of Fonseca in the east, and from the Pacific Ocean in the south to the Honduran border in the north.[25] For those readers not familiar with Salvadoran geography, a visualization exercise might be useful. Imagine El Salvador as a series of three steps climbing out of the Pacific Ocean and ending in Honduras. The first step is the coastal plain, which sits roughly at sea level and is anywhere from a few hundred yards to twenty miles wide. The second step is the central plateau, which sits at approximately two thousand feet above sea level and is roughly thirty miles wide. It is defined by a string of roughly one dozen volcanoes or volcanic upwellings that reach elevations as high as seven thousand feet. The third step is a mountain range that runs more or less the entirety of the Honduran border. The typical elevation of the range is four thousand to five thousand feet above sea level. El Salvador has one main river, the Lempa, which begins in the far northwest and runs east until it reaches the middle of the country, where it takes a sharp turn and runs straight for the Pacific Ocean. The once wild river has been restrained by a series of three dams that were constructed between the 1940s and 1970s, but the lower end of the system, the so-called Bajo Río Lempa, still experiences seasonal flooding.

El Salvador has few natural resources beyond its fertile soil and the labor of its people. Invariably, the country's economic history, and the developmental programs that policymakers have pursued, revolved around agriculture. The hot, low-lying coastal plain is suited to growing tropical products like sugar, cotton, and fruit, and subsequently it has played a relevant role in the nation's economic history. A significant portion of the nation's population has lived there. By contrast, the mountain range along the Honduran border is comprised of nutrient-poor, rocky soil and thus has been the poorest and least densely populated of El Salvador's three steps. The middle step, the central plateau, has been the economic and demographic center of Salvadoran history. Most of El Salvador's largest cities are located there. During the colonial era and in the early nineteenth century, indigo was grown on the relatively flat floor of the plateau in the eastern region of country, in what are today San Miguel and San Vicente departments. But starting in the late nineteenth century, when the coffee economy took off, El Salvador's volcanic upwellings offered some of the best coffee-growing lands in the world. There are three main coffee-growing areas: the western highlands situated at the intersection of Sonsonate, Ahuachapán, and Santa Ana departments; the central highlands around the San Salvador volcano and the cities of San Salvador and Nueva San Salvador (now Santa Tecla); and the highlands in the east, around Usulután. The latter was something of an agricultural frontier when the coffee economy emerged. The two western regions, by contrast, were densely populated, especially by indigenous people living on communal land that they had inherited from the Spanish crown. The privatization of those lands in the 1880s and their entrance into the marketplace for coffee cultivation was a defining moment in Salvadoran history.

Theorizing Democracy in El Salvador

Most people in El Salvador have lived most of their lives under authoritarian regimes. In this regard, El Salvador is something of a symbol for most nations, because democracy has been the exception rather than the rule in modern history. Scholars and practitioners alike have asked count-less times about what variables cause a society to democratize. It would be foolish to try to understand El Salvador's experience without drawing upon the wisdom contained in the vast and sprawling literature on demo-cratic theory. Fortunately, some studies have synthesized the debates and placed them in a Latin American context, which helps to elucidate the Salvadoran case.

Before moving into those debates, it is necessary to define the key terms in use here: *democracy* and *authoritarianism*. For the sake of sim-plicity, the present study follows the lead of Paul Drake in his historical overview of democracy in Latin America. He focuses on elections and electoral competition and adopts what he calls a "binary, minimalist defi-nition." He defines a democratic society as one in which political leaders are chosen in relatively free and fair elections and the civil liberties of the citizenry are generally respected. In contrast, an authoritarian society is one in which those conditions are absent, where leaders come to power arbitrarily, militarily, or through elections that are not free and fair, and in a societal context in which civil liberties are not respected. The term *au-thoritarian* is sometimes associated narrowly with the military regimes of the latter twentieth century, but following Drake's lead, the term is used more broadly here as being roughly synonymous with "dictatorial" and "nondemocratic."[26]

From these definitions it then follows that the term *democratization* refers to the process by which a society transitions from authoritarianism to democracy. It also stands to reason that societies can exhibit degrees of democratization, whereby a highly democratic society would allow "broader suffrage, hold more honest elections and protect more civil liber-ties" than its more minimally democratic counterparts.[27]

It is widely accepted among scholars of political theory that poverty, inequity, and societal factionalism hinder democracy and promote au-thoritarianism. So if a society is generally poor, or its extant wealth is di-vided unequally, or its citizens are deeply divided by ethnicity or religion, then the sense of collective trust necessary to build a lasting democracy will be absent. This material/structural explanation for the origins of de-mocracy is exemplified by a study coauthored by an economist and a po-litical scientist, Daron Acemoglu and James Robinson, who aptly titled their work *Economic Origins of Dictatorship and Democracy*.[28] Drake has made a general observation about Latin America that advances a similarly materialist approach, pointing out that the former core area of the Spanish empire, roughly the highland spine stretching from Mexico through Central America into the Andes, has been less democratic than regions on the colonial periphery, such as Chile, Argentina, and Uruguay. Drake explains this divergence by referring to Latin America's material/economic history, in which the former core areas had large indigenous populations and the people who set up the governments and economies in those areas wanted access to labor. They gained it through racial hierarchies and highly coercive practices during both the colonial era and modern nationhood after independence. Comparatively speaking, peripheral areas exhibited less divisiveness because they were settled later in the colonial era for reasons other than the exploitation of native labor.

Central Americanists have employed a similar comparative argument to explain the divergent political outcomes on the isthmus.[29] In fact, Central America provides something of a laboratory for studying democratization because its five nations share similar histories and a close geography, yet they have produced divergent political systems. Costa Rica emerged as a relatively stable and functioning democracy, while its neighbors remained entrenched in authoritarianism. Some Central Americanists explain this divergence with an argument similar to Drake's comparison between core and peripheral areas of the Spanish empire. According to this explanation, Costa Rica was part of Drake's colonial periphery because it had a minimal concentration of indigenous peoples and so, despite being settled early in the colonial era, it remained a small and insignificant outpost of the Spanish empire. By comparison, the rest of Central America, and especially El Salvador and Guatemala, had large indigenous populations and became more important economic centers based on the exploitation of local labor.

By the nineteenth century, Costa Rica was still poor and relatively isolated, but it avoided the intense social hierarchies and racial hostilities of its neighbors. So when the export boom came along and Costa Rica emerged as a coffee producer, like its neighbors El Salvador and Guatemala, it did so differently, in a manner that was less coercive or conflictive.

Subsequently, political leaders in Costa Rica could direct precious financial resources towards things other than war that would pay a return on their investment, like education. By contrast, leaders in El Salvador and Guatemala felt they had to invest in the military to preserve the coercive mechanisms that made their distinct methods of production possible.

These comparative arguments reveal that El Salvador exhibited many of the structural variables that promote authoritarianism rather than democracy. Compared to some of the larger core areas of the Spanish empire—Mexico and Peru, for instance—El Salvador was an impoverished and marginal place, and it did not have the opportunity to create a highly educated population or a strong economic foundation. Throughout its history, most of its people have been poor and illiterate, living a precarious hand-to-mouth existence in the countryside. At the time of independence, for example, El Salvador was a nation of roughly 250,000 people with a miniscule professional class consisting of around two dozen lawyers, doctors, and pharmacists. By 1930 it was a nation of 1.5 million, most of whom were still uneducated rural dwellers. But compared to Costa Rica, El Salvador was a core area of the colonial enterprise, and so it entered independence facing the legacies of colonialism—coercion and racial hierarchy—akin to those in Guatemala, Mexico, and Peru. When El Salvador entered nationhood it possessed, as historian Héctor Lindo-Fuentes put it, "weak foundations" for economic and political modernization.[30]

Arguably, El Salvador's best chance to avoid authoritarian underdevelopment was during the coffee era in the late nineteenth and early twentieth centuries, when spectacular profits from agriculture could have been invested in broader and more sustainable development initiatives. However, that did not happen, and by the 1950s the window of opportunity was closing. By then, El Salvador's structural problems were fully evident to anyone who cared to see them. The nation's population was exploding, its agricultural frontier had all but disappeared, it relied on imported oil for energy, and its economic survival hinged on fickle international markets for agricultural commodities. Even if the political will had existed in the 1950s and 1960s to enact massive structural reforms, which it did not, avoiding long-term economic catastrophe would have been difficult. In hindsight, El Salvador would have had to have invested the surplus wealth from coffee differently, in a manner akin to Costa Rica. But in order to do so, the country needed a sense of common purpose and well-developed system of democratically based exchange; tragically, neither of those existed.[31]

Charles Tilly's study of democracy illustrates the challenges that a place like El Salvador faced in creating a more inclusive system. Tilly identifies three preconditions for democracy or, as he calls them, three "democracy-promoting causal mechanisms." First, networks of trust and confidence that operate on a personal or local level have to be integrated into the national public arena. In other words, a society has to build collective trust, and its people have to cease operating as autonomous islands where trust exists only within isolated communities of family or friends rather than in the collective, national enterprise. Second, public politics has to be isolated from economic inequality. This means that either the inequity of a society needs to be reduced, or politics has to find a way to operate outside it. Lastly, local centers of autonomous power, such as warlords, patronage networks, or local militias, have to be eliminated. A strong, homogenizing state creates a situation in which all citizens find themselves bound together in a collective enterprise, rather than dedicating their loyalty to local power centers that weaken collective consciousness. Tilly emphasizes that democracy movements almost never emerge in nations with weak states; a strong state is a necessary precursor to democratization.[32]

When Tilly's analysis is applied to El Salvador, we see that only one of his democracy-causing mechanisms existed there by the late 1920s: a strong state that eradicated regional bases of autonomous power. The emergence of that one mechanism helps explain the short-lived democratic experiment that culminated in the election of Arturo Araujo in 1931. But the failure of the other two categories helps explain why democracy failed to withstand the military coup of December 1931.

A society's material conditions may predispose it towards democracy or authoritarianism, but they are not destiny, nor do they eradicate variation within categories.[33] Take the examples of Mexico and Peru. Carlos Forment, a historian of nineteenth-century Latin American politics, shows that Mexico and Peru exhibited great variation in democratic potential. Forment acknowledges that both countries were authoritarian and followed the predictable path of former core areas of the Spanish Empire.

But Forment shows that public life in the two societies was vastly different, and therefore their potential for democracy diverged. He focuses on the presence of civic associations—clubs and organizations—and the existence of print culture, such as newspapers. He shows that Mexico had a robust and vigorous civic-associational life and an active print culture, whereas Peru's were moribund. Forment believes that the presence of civic associations is important because just as the renowned theorist of democracy Alexis de Toqueville argued many decades ago, civic associations make democracy more likely. When citizens practice democracy locally or gather to discuss plans for their association, they are much more likely to demand democracy in public politics. According to Forment, Mexico possessed a greater potential for democracy than Peru, and thus if Mexico failed to achieve democracy, some other contingent variables must be blamed. One such contingency, according to Forment, was foreign invasion—first by the United States in the 1840s and then by France in the 1860s.[34]

One implication of Forment's study is the decoupling of political practices from socioeconomic structures. If Mexico and Peru were roughly alike in their structures, yet divergent in their civic-associational lives, then perhaps their distinct cultures or praxes of politics functioned independently and guided those nations' respective histories. This study offers similar potential, to the extent that it suggests that El Salvador's political practices preceded the onset of the coffee economy in the late nineteenth century. There is little doubt that the distinct nature of El Salvador's coffee economy and the distribution of the rewards of coffee growing contributed to the authoritarian practices of the twentieth century. But if the political practices preceded coffee, then either the material explanation needs to be pushed back earlier into El Salvador's history, or the explanatory variable is less material and more cultural/discursive. Perhaps El Salvador's coffee economy was determined by its politics and not vice versa.[35]

Many scholars agree with Forment's claim that international pressure can be an important contingency in promoting either democracy or authoritarianism. If a powerful foreign government, such as the United States or the United Kingdom, creates incentives for a Latin American nation to democratize, then it is possible that democratic movements will be invigorated. By the same token, if powerful foreign governments tolerate authoritarianism, then democracy's prospects diminish. In the case of

El Salvador, the United States was the main foreign power in the region, and it tended to encourage authoritarianism. It stood on the side of democracy in the 1920s under the auspices of the 1923 Washington Treaties, which called for diplomatic recognition to be withheld from any government that came to power in a nondemocratic manner. Accordingly, the United States withheld recognition from Martínez after the December 1931 coup. But when faced with Martínez's obstinacy, it was unwilling or unable to do anything, and eventually it recognized the Martínez government in 1934. Arguably, it even bolstered Martínez by tolerating his harsh response to the 1932 uprising in the name of anticommunism. By contrast, the United States promoted democratic reforms in neighboring Nicaragua at roughly the same time in the early 1930s, ironically in the midst of a U.S. military occupation.[36]

Another explanation for democratization revolves around the timing and nature of elite factionalism and mass-based mobilization. Political scientist Deborah Yashar has contributed to this arena with a comparative study of Guatemala and Costa Rica in the mid-twentieth century. She isolates the variables of elite unity and mass demands to argue that when a society's elites factionalize at the same time that a mass movement coalesces, then democratization will likely occur. If either variable transpires independently, change is unlikely.[37] Acemoglu and Robinson advance a similar claim in *Economic Origins of Dictatorship and Democracy*. In response to the question "Why does a nondemocratic elite ever democratize?" they answer, "Because the disenfranchised citizens can threaten the elite and force it to make concessions."[38] This analysis can be usefully applied to El Salvador. A modest variation of elite division and mass demand occurred in the late 1920s and early 1930s, promoting the brief process of democratization, but neither variable was sufficiently robust to sustain democracy, and thus authoritarianism returned in the military coup of 1931.

To summarize, scholars of politics have identified variables that tend to promote either democracy or authoritarianism. Some of those variables are long-term structures, while others are short-term contingencies. Some are domestic, and others foreign. El Salvador possessed few of the variables that promote democratization. Its structures put it on a path towards authoritarianism, and when countervailing contingencies favored democratization, they were insufficient to create lasting change.

Democratic Discourse and the Informal Rules of Politics

Following the definition of democracy provided by Drake, a democratic election is one in which multiple candidates present platforms to a voting population and the members of that population go to the polls of their own volition and choose their preferred candidate. By that definition, democratic elections have almost never occurred in El Salvador. Instead, elections were highly managed affairs with more or less predetermined outcomes and unanimous or near-unanimous results. On some occasions only one candidate ran, but on many occasions multiple candidates competed, or at least wanted to compete, and so the challenge for the eventual victor was to control the polling stations and make sure that voting went his way. Candidates employed a variety of tactics to achieve that goal, many involving some degree of physical coercion or violence. The dominant candidate often used violence to fend off rivals and secure control of the polling station, and his rivals responded with violence in desperate attempts to dislodge him.

Even though elections in El Salvador were not democratic, any study of them needs to acknowledge two overwhelming paradoxes: 1) that elections occurred constantly and oftentimes with large turnouts; and 2) they were accompanied by an unrelenting democratic discourse that celebrated free suffrage, liberty, and individual will. Even in a small country like El Salvador, the scale of these paradoxes is mind-boggling. El Salvador had between 200 and 248 municipalities at any given moment in its modern history. Elections for municipal officials and legislative deputies occurred every year or every other year, depending on the particular time period, and elections for national officials (congressional representatives and president) occurred every two or four years. Thus, during El Salvador's first century of independence, literally tens of thousands of people oversaw something like twenty thousand elections and produced untold thousands of pages of politically based documentation, much of which ended up in archival storage. Furthermore, most of those people lived in small, highly intimate communities in which they and their families interacted with one another constantly. The documentary record reveals that all those people in all those places over all that time consistently violated the formal, written rules of politics and adhered to an informal, unwritten code typified by patronage and clientelism. Similarly, all of those people over all of that time and space employed democratic-sounding language to describe what they were doing, even though there was little or nothing democratic about their practices.

Any scholar who takes stock of that situation cannot help but ask how the system functioned so consistently over time. How did political actors from one generation to the next learn the informal, unwritten rules? And if political actors were aware that they were betraying the formal, written rules of politics, would a researcher not expect to see the façade fall away at some point in the documentation? Would political actors not at some point speak to one another more frankly about what they were doing and reveal their understanding of how the system really worked? And given that elites were invariably concerned about mass autonomous action, why would they employ such an egalitarian-sounding discourse and codify electoral rules that stressed democracy and liberty?[39]

Maybe these questions and their corresponding paradoxes can be easily explained. After all, elections were highly managed affairs, so the fact that they took place regularly and with high turnouts might be insignificant; elites might have controlled them and forced poor retainers to come to the polls and vote according to their orders. By extension, the democratic discourse might have been empty rhetoric, a language that powerful people used to mask their nondemocratic practices. Even if such a discourse risked inciting the masses' desire for equality, El Salvador was hardly unique in this regard. As the historian Florencia Mallon writes in her study of nation-state formation in Mexico and Peru, elites in both of those countries sought to "construct nation-states around hegemonic national-democratic discourses."[40]

Even a wave of revisionist scholarship that has revealed the existence of genuinely democratic practices in nineteenth-century Latin America agrees that those explanations might suffice.[41] For example, the historian Jorge Myers, who studied elections and political language in nineteenth-century Argentina, found a vigorous "discourse of Republic [that] became the single legitimate medium of public expression after 1820."[42] Yet he contends that democratic and republican "principles could be proclaimed which not only were simultaneously being violated but whose violation was explained away in terms which the dominated could expose only through an arduous process of class-specific resemantization." In other words, Myers says that rich, powerful people could create an exclusive system of rule by building up an explanatory system that celebrated democracy and individual rights and that was difficult for poor masses to challenge. Myers goes on to say that "what was being proclaimed as a principle for all could be understood from the vantage point of the dominators as in fact applicable only to the ruling few." Recognizing the modern-sounding political discourse that accompanied elections in Argentina, he concludes that "revolutions in political language can take place without concomitant political revolutions. Thus we have to look closely at the language they used and how they coded it to make sense to themselves in their social context."[43]

Another historian of nineteenth-century Argentina, Hilda Sábato, operates in a similar vein as Myers, but in the broader context of electoral practices in nineteenth-century Latin America as a whole. She first acknowledges the predominance of elections: "Throughout the nineteenth century, in most areas of Latin America, elections to choose local, regional and national representatives, both direct and indirect, were held regularly and very frequently—in many places, several times a year. They were the prescribed way to political office."[44] Like Myers, Sábato recognizes that those elections were often accompanied by a vigorous, modern-sounding political rhetoric that hailed democracy, citizenship, and freedom of choice. But she says that the newly emerging concept of a "modern citizen" overlapped with more traditional colonial or even precolonial concepts— pueblos, *comunidades,* and so on. She goes on to say that "the concept of modern representation was too abstract to be rapidly accepted by vast sectors of the population."[45]

These arguments by Meyers and Sábato offer reasons why we need not take too seriously the paradoxes of Salvadoran elections. Their studies allow us a couple of options: either Salvadoran elites believed that whatever they were doing actually constituted democracy, or elites understood the dilemmas they were facing and consciously employed a democratic-sounding rhetoric to mask their authoritarian practices. But Myers, Sábato, and other like-minded scholars see the situation in more complex terms. As one example, Drake confronts the conundrum in his survey of politics and elections in Latin America. He too observes the existence of the parallel universes of formal, written political rules and informal, unwritten political practices, or what Drake calls "custom."[46] He readily acknowledges the challenge to understand how the two systems operated side by side over long expanses of time and across vast geographic spaces. In his search for an answer he turns to the field of study known as social institutionalism or discursive institutionalism.[47] Scholars operating in those arenas contend that once certain practices get up and running, they carry an autonomous momentum that can be difficult to divert. Certain practices become the accepted norm; they become ingrained into the cultural and social milieu, such that political actors simply could not conceive of the world working any other way. In the words of one institutionalist scholar, "compliance occurs in many circumstances because other types of behavior are inconceivable; routines are followed because they are taken for granted as 'the way we do these things.'"[48] "Hence the naturalness of the lie," declares Holden, "for without the constitutional disguises that made it possible for political authorities to claim a purely legalistic but spurious legitimacy, the hard patrimonial core of politics could scarcely have survived."[49]

Two scholars of contemporary Latin American politics, Gretchen Helmke and Steven Levitsky, have come to similar conclusions in their attempts to document and understand the parallel existence of formal and informal institutions. They define informal institutions as "socially shared rules, usually unwritten, that are created, communicated and enforced outside officially sanctioned channels." They contend that the existence of informal rules is often "less a product of actor design than the (often unintended) consequence of a particular historical experience that creates certain socially shared expectations." Helmke and Levitsky recognize the difficulty of studying informal institutions that do not exist in writing and can be documented only by observing them in practice. They describe the diverse methods that political scientists have employed to resolve this dilemma in the contemporary era, with one of the principal methods being simply a closely detailed "ethnographic" case study. The present work is an example of that method. It is historical, rather than contemporary, but it shows how the informal rules in El Salvador functioned by studying the imprint they left on the documents that Salvadorans used to conduct their day-to-day political affairs.[50]

Aspiring political actors in El Salvador were exposed only to the informal rules of politics, and they came to believe that elections were managed affairs that one described with a democratic-sounding language. They accepted that norm and acted accordingly. In the process, they failed to see contradiction in either the use of democratic-sounding language amidst nondemocratic practices or in the adherence to informal rules that failed to correspond to the formal, written rules. If they did not see those contradictions, then it is not likely that they would have talked about them as such in their written documentation. If most of the politically active population accepted those rules as normal, abided by them, and passed them down from one generation to the next, then anyone with an alternative vision who sought to change the system would have confronted an overwhelming weight of institutionalized practice or "custom." That is precisely what happened in El Salvador in the period between 1927 and 1931, when a new president, Pío Romero Bosque, tried to reform the electoral system.

Another way of describing the situation is that El Salvador exhibited a distinct political culture of authoritarianism. Following the lead of scholars like Peter Guardino and Consuelo Cruz, political culture is defined here as "discourses and practices characterizing politics," which are "neither monolithic nor static."[51] They are created by humans interacting in a social arena, and while culture may be stubbornly resistant to change, and while its existence may not even be apparent to the subjects who are acting it out, it is mutable in the hands of human actors. Thus, regardless of a society's structural or material predispositions, culture can be an autonomous and causal variable.

In her comparative study of political rhetoric in Costa Rica and Nicaragua, Cruz provides compelling evidence that political culture plays a role in guiding a society towards a particular political outcome. Cruz begins her comparison at the customary starting point—defining Costa Rica as democratic and Nicaragua as authoritarian. But Cruz then breaks with the standard materialist argument and insists that those outcomes were not predetermined by geographic, ethnic, or economic history. Instead, she insists that the extant political cultures in each society (i.e., the way that Costa Ricans and Nicaraguans came to see themselves and define their societies) contributed to the creation of their divergent polities. Specifically, she says that there is "no fixed rule as to which comes first," cultural or material structures.[52]

Cruz digs into the documentary record as far back as the early colonial period to reveal that the people who lived in the lands that would become Costa Rica and Nicaragua defined themselves distinctly. Costa Ricans possessed a "high-worth collective identity," whereas Nicaraguans had a "low-worth collective identity." This divergence meant that Costa Ricans, and particularly elite Costa Ricans, defined their population, and especially their poor people, as inherently meritorious. When they created laws, they did so to protect people and release their productive capacity. By comparison, Nicaraguan elites considered their people flawed and so created laws to control them. One of the many consequences of these divergences was different expectations for leadership. In Costa Rica, good leaders were defined as those who tried to meet the needs, expectations, and welfare of the whole of the population and who set aside personal political interests. In Nicaragua, leadership was seen more pessimistically; it was widely accepted that leaders would surrender to personalistic disputes without much concern for the general welfare.

Ironically, Cruz reveals that Nicaragua's political system was more electoral than Costa Rica's: more elections occurred in Nicaragua, and they began at an earlier date. But Cruz insists that what counts are the policies that political leaders implemented, regardless of how they came to power. Even though political leaders in Costa Rica avoided electoral accountability more than their Nicaraguan counterparts, they were more "democratic" in their policymaking. Building upon Cruz's foundation, I contend that El Salvador was more like Nicaragua than Costa Rica.

Both Guardino and Cruz insist that in the study of political cultures, actors' internal and private thoughts matter less than their actions and statements. It is next to impossible to determine what people actually thought based on our extant documentary record. But that is beside the point, Guardino says, because "public statements and practices are in fact what actually define political culture, which is ultimately about what people say and do rather than what they think."[53] He goes on to say that "for understanding political culture and how it changed over time, people's private beliefs are strangely irrelevant." Cruz concurs, saying that "the analyst need not be concerned with the sincerity of the actor(s), but rather with the blunt question: Are their actions consistent with their words? In the crudest terms, do they adhere, do they deliver?"[54]

I agree with them, and throughout this study I focus on what people said and did. But at the same time I cannot help but pose the question: What were political actors in El Salvador really thinking when they praised democracy and practiced authoritarianism? Were all those people in all those places who conducted all those elections over all those years duping themselves? Were they aware of the paradox, but somehow unable to articulate it in their correspondence with one another? Were they ignorant of the paradox? Were they subject to the hegemonic power of a small coterie of rich actors who pulled the strings from behind the scenes? Again, I recognize that these questions are somewhat beside the point, to say nothing of being too grandiose to engage in a meaningful way here. Fortunately, other scholars of Latin American political history have posed them, and it is worth looking at how they responded.

In his study of nineteenth-century politics and elections in Argentina, Myers notes a paradox similar to that discussed here—political actors employed a highly sophisticated political rhetoric that appealed to all of the modern republican principles, even though their elections were highly managed, nondemocratic affairs designed to meet the interests of a select few. He acknowledges that sometimes those elite actors employed democratic discourse "with out and out cynicism and a brutal disdain for ethical criteria." But he also contends that they "frequently fervently believed" in what they were saying and would have "invoked them [the values of the democratic discourse] . . . even when their immediate functionality" had expired.[55] Myers finds himself compelled to ask if those actors truly believed what they were saying. In response to that question he draws upon the work of Paul Veyne, a French scholar of ancient Greece and Rome, who responded to the question of whether the ancient Greeks truly believed in their gods with "an ambiguous and reticent . . . yes and no." In other words, Myers is unsatisfied with a traditional "functionalist" explanation that political leaders in nineteenth-century Argentina were aware of the contradictions between their rhetoric and their practices and thus their language was an intentional smokescreen. Like Drake, Myers finds himself advocating for a sort of institutionalist explanation whereby the difference between intentional, conscious action collapses with more long-standing norms of conduct that actors accept as the proper order of things.

It is for this reason Myers chooses to focus on the "ambiguity and complexity of this phenomenon, on the frequent opacity of its effects . . . and on the manner in which an ideological postulate elevated to a position of centrality in the constitution of all public discourse, could not but disperse—prismatically—into a dazzling array of simultaneous meanings and effects."[56]

Another edifying example is provided by the U.S. South in the nineteenth century. Many southern planters employed a highly republican-sounding political rhetoric that touted democracy and freedom of choice. All the while, of course, they presided over a highly unequal society, both before and after emancipation. A British traveler to the United States in the 1820s astutely observed such traits among southern planters: "Look at them at home; you will see them with one hand hoisting the cap of liberty, and with the other flogging their slaves."[57] Various scholars of the nineteenth-century United States have discussed the intense intellectual and ideological compartmentalization that existed in the minds of southern elites to allow them to employ their liberal rhetoric so wholeheartedly, fully believing what they were saying, while living in a situation that they fully understood to be contradictory.[58] Of course, the issue of race was a key variable in that compartmentalization, which was not the case in El Salvador. Nonetheless, the U.S. South thus provides another example of contradictory rhetoric and reality residing side by side.

In El Salvador, a massive disconnect existed between the language of politics and the practice of politics, and between the informal and formal rules of politics. At the very least, documenting the existence of that disconnect and showing its functional existence over time goes a long ways toward explaining why El Salvador has had such a long and enduring tradition of authoritarianism and why prodemocracy advocates have faced such overwhelming hurdles in trying to implement reforms, even into the twenty-first century.

Structure of the Book

The book is divided into eight chapters and follows a broadly chronological pattern, although the first four chapters are organized somewhat thematically as well. Chapter 1 sets out the rules of politics in El Salvador in both their formal and informal guises. The formal rules—that is, the letter of the law—include the constitutionally defined laws governing politics and elections, as well as the specific rules relating to the methods by which voting was supposed to occur. These formal rules stated that El Salvador was a democratic republic in which popular will was to be expressed through free elections that would determine public officeholding. The informal rules reveal the ways in which Salvadorans actually practiced elections and how those practices often stuck to the letter of the law, but fundamentally subverted the spirit of the law as it related to democracy.

Chapter 2 shows those practices in action in a series of case studies of national-level politics in the nineteenth century. The limitations in source material prevent the presentation of a seamless narrative of nineteenth-century politics, but the available documentation allows for the reconstruction of some distinct cases between 1845 and 1894. They stand as metaphors for the whole. The cases reveal that politics consisted of regionally based patronage empires constantly jockeying with one another for position. The leaders of those miniature empires relied on the support of allies in the municipalities who could deliver the political capital necessary to sustain them. That capital included votes primarily, but also soldiers, money, food, and war material when things turned violent. The chapter remains focused on the national level, leaving the details of network building at the municipal level to the next two chapters.

Chapters 3 and 4 shift the focus from the national to the municipal level. Chapter 3 looks at the methods that municipal-level political bosses employed to build their networks. The traditional disparity between landed elites and their laborers was one mechanism that allowed for the creation of a political network. But it was hardly the only one. Family and ethnicity were other methods. And military officers, who might not have had much personal wealth, could also be effective political players.

Chapter 4 then builds off the methods examined in chapter 3 and shows how local networks competed with one another for control over local office in municipal elections. The second half shows how the emergence of a more powerful and centralized state shaped the local networks. In the past, national-level political actors were merely regional strongmen who had cobbled together fragile coalitions with other regional strongmen. Now, whoever sat in national-level office presided over a powerful entity that was less susceptible to attack. In this new structure, instead of trying to replace one patronage network with another, everyone operated within the confines of a single network that controlled the state.

Chapter 5 begins a succession of four chapters that adhere to a more strict chronological flow. This first chapter looks at the Meléndez-Quiñónez dynasty, which brought the system of centralized authoritarianism to its highest level to date. The chapter looks at the strategies and tactics used by the members of the Meléndez and Quiñónez families to control elections, illustrating that patronage and patron-client networks continued to define political activity, even with the increasing centralization of state authority. It takes as its main example a pair of aspiring political actors who felt alienated from the Meléndez-Quiñónez machine and tried to take their presidential aspirations outside the established norm by organizing independent political bases, similar to campaigns of the nineteenth century. They learned quickly and brutally that such endeavors had serious consequences.

Chapter 6 is dedicated to the administration of Pío Romero Bosque (1927–1931) and especially to Romero's democratic reform program. It examines Romero's tactics and the insurmountable obstacles that he faced in trying to inject a genuinely democratic spirit into electoral practice. Romero Bosque ultimately failed in his endeavor, but the documentary record of his efforts provides an invaluable look into the heart of the political system.

Chapters 7 and 8 focus on the first of the modern military regimes under General Martínez. Both chapters examine the formative period of 1931 to 1940, but each chapter analyzes a distinct aspect of Martínez's rule. Chapter 7 looks at politics. Martínez's regime turned back the clock on Romero Bosque and reinvigorated the patronage system as it had functioned under Meléndez-Quiñónez. Chapter 8 looks at social policy. The rebellion of 1932 prompted the military to appreciate the need for social reform, or at least the need to appear supportive of the idea of reform. This chapter delineates the ideology behind the reforms and details the specific policies pursued by the Martínez regime. One byproduct of this study is a realization of the complex relations that existed between economic elites and the military-led governments in twentieth-century El

Salvador. Martínez's reform program might not have threatened elites greatly, but it clearly antagonized them. It began a decades-long process through which elites remained suspicious of military leaders in office, believing that those leaders' commitment to laissez-faire capitalism was constantly in flux even as the elites avidly welcomed the military's coercive opposition to independent labor organizing, especially in the countryside.

CHAPTER 1

THE RULES

Formal and Informal

Leaders of newly independent nations throughout the Americas in the late eighteenth and early nineteenth centuries faced the challenge of determining what type of governing system best suited their societies. Regardless of the examples of the United States' break from Great Britain and of Spain's former colonies, national leaders in what came to called Latin America tended to equate independence with liberalism and modernism, but feared the extension of liberty to the masses of society. Hence, they often ended up living in complex, paradoxical systems, hybrid societies of sorts. They touted the merits of equality and structured their societies as republics in which popular elections determined officeholding, and yet they operated under a different set of informal rules that constrained freedom and concentrated authority. El Salvador was one of these new nations, and its tendency to fall into this pattern resembled that of its neighbors.

This chapter looks at the formal and informal rules that governed political life in El Salvador. The formal rules were officially laid down in constitutions and ordinances, and they explained how elections were supposed to work and how politics was expected to transpire. The informal rules were the ways in which people actually behaved when they did politics and conducted elections. The informal rules tended to stick to the letter of the formal rules; after all, people voted, and political leaders took office only after having won an election. But the informal rules diverged substantially from the spirit of the law. If the basic premise behind the concepts of popular will and freedom of suffrage was that individual voters had the right to select their leaders from a range of options without duress or coercion, then democracy was fleeting throughout the first century of El Salvador's existence.

The following vignette from the vice presidential election of 1895 is presented as a metaphor for the broader whole of politics and elections in El Salvador. Most of the remaining evidence in this chapter will be drawn from the nineteenth century in order to set up the next chapter's series of chronologically ordered case studies.

The Vice Presidential Election of 1895

The vice presidential election of 1895 left behind some of the most detailed records of any election in El Salvador. The records consist of municipality-by-municipality voting results, as well as a slew of telegrams and reports exchanged between the municipal and national levels, including some rare communiques between candidates and their local electoral activists. This cache of evidence reveals how national-level patronage networks and the accompanying electoral system functioned at a particular moment in time.

The 1895 vice presidential election occurred in the wake of a coup d'état led by General Rafael Gutiérrez (1894–1899) that overthrew President Carlos Ezeta (1890–1894). In the subsequent presidential election, Gutiérrez ran unopposed and won by a margin of 61,080 votes to 91—in other words, by the typically unanimous or near-unanimous result of an unrivaled political boss.[1] However, Gutiérrez had below him two powerful allies, Prudencio Alfaro and Carlos Meléndez—the latter would go on to hold the presidency in 1913. In the meantime, both Alfaro and Meléndez had played lead roles in Ezeta's overthrow, but only one of them could become vice president. Gutiérrez apparently decided not to choose between his two aspiring underlings and instead allowed them to battle it out in an election. Alfaro won the contest with 38,006 votes to Meléndez's 18,792, with the remaining 4,000 votes being divided up between four lesser candidates.

Those results make it appear that the election was genuinely competitive, and indeed at some level it was. Candidates faced off, voters from across the country cast votes, those votes were tallied up, and a winner was declared. But more revealing than the final result is the manner in which voting was conducted at the municipal level. Records reveal that voting within each municipality was not very competitive; in most cases it was decided by unanimous or near-unanimous results, and patronage networks were clearly in operation. The election was built around the practice of each candidate contacting powerful allies in the department capitals who in turn called upon subordinate political bosses in the municipalities. The municipal bosses were expected to control the polls in their towns and prevent affiliates of the rival candidates from doing the same. A close election such as this one, between two powerful political players such as Alfaro and Meléndez, would normally have ended in bloodshed, just as the rivalry between Generals Gutiérrez and Ezeta had. Fortunately, in this case, the presence of an undisputed superior authority, General Gutiérrez, ensured a peaceful process.

Alfaro's point man in Sonsonate Department was Abrahán Rivera, a prominent landowner and a rising political boss in Sonsonate City.[2] In the following letter, Rivera informs Alfaro of his success in Sonsonate Department on election day.

> Dr. don Prudencio Alfaro
> My dear friend:
> As we expected, in this department, with the exception of Izalco and Armenia, where there was imposition of comandantes working on behalf of other candidates, our triumph has been complete: The great majority has voted in our favor. In Nahuizalco, which is the toughest municipality in terms of elections, we have won with almost unanimity. At the last minute they had changed the comandante with the intention of altering the voting in favor of Pérez, but in the end this comandante could do nothing on account of the efficient work of Colonels Marcelo Brito and Lucas Peñate and of don Abrahán Guerra who have carried the day like true champions. In Juayúa, which is another important village, our triumph is complete. Colonel Tadeo Pérez [no relation to candidate Pérez] took the baton and aided us with great fortitude. In San Julián and the other coastal villages we have triumphed splendidly due to the cooperation of don Dionisio

Herrera and the Señores Chinchilla and de León. In all the municipalities surrounding this city [Sonsonate] I have had very good agents
at work, such that you won almost by unanimity. In this population
where there has been the most work of the Melendistas, I have put a
close watch on these rabbits [*conejos*] . . . so that despite the great
amount of work that was being done on behalf of Meléndez, we reduced their supporters to an insignificant number.

Abrahán Rivera, Sonsonate, January 16, 1895[3]

Rivera's letter offers a rare and vivid description of a patronage-based political network in action. In his letter, Rivera lists each local subaltern by
name and describes how they neutralized the local affiliates of the rival
candidates. As Rivera points out, his allies reigned supreme in all but two
of the department's fourteen municipalities. Final returns from the election confirm his claim. Excluding those two outliers, Izalco and Armenia,
Alfaro won the department by a combined total of 2,565 votes to 65.[4]

Complete returns from the 1895 election provide a nationwide view
of the monopolization of polling stations and demonstrate that what
transpired in Sonsonate was typical. Voting occurred in all 248 municipalities in the nation. In 176 of these municipalities the victorious candidate won with more than 95 percent of the vote, including 96 municipalities where voting was unanimous. Alfaro's network dominated seven
of the fourteen departments (La Paz, Usulután, San Miguel, La Unión,
Morazán, Ahuachapán, and Sonsonate), winning them by a combined
total of 20,320 to 2,574. To his detriment, Meléndez controlled only two
departments by comparable margins, San Vicente and Cabañas: 4,931
votes to 600. In the remaining five departments (Cuscatlán, Chalatenango, Santa Ana, San Salvador, and La Libertad) the two candidates split
the departmentwide vote evenly, but voting at the municipal level was
starkly divided. Cuscatlán Department provides a clear example. Alfaro
and Meléndez each took 50 percent of the vote, but in thirteen of the department's seventeen municipalities the victorious candidate won with
more than 94 percent of the votes, including six municipalities that were
decided by unanimity (see table 1.1). A similar result is found in Chalatenango Department, where Alfaro received just over 4,000 votes and Meléndez just under 3,000, a relatively even split. In twenty-seven of Chalatenango's thirty-five municipalities victory was attained with at least 91

percent of the votes. Unfortunately, the historical record does not contain detailed letters from affiliates in other departments comparable to Rivera's correspondence from Sonsonate. It can be safely assumed that in each of those departments, men like Rivera were diligently working on the behalf of Alfaro or Meléndez in the same way that Rivera was doing in Sonsonate. When Alfaro assumed the office of vice president, he knew that he owed those departmental bosses something for their support, or that he had burned through some of the political capital that he had accrued previously.

Table 1.1   Voting in Cuscatlán Department, Vice Presidential Election, 1895

Municipality	Alfaro Votes	Alfaro %	Meléndez Votes	Meléndez %
El Carmen	0	0	278	100
Tenancingo	12	5	222	95
Aguacayo	66	79	18	21
Santa Cruz Analci	0	0	120	100
Cojutepeque	13	3	345	97
El Rosario	0	0	151	100
Guayabal	29	11	238	89
San Pedro Perulapán	825	97	30	3
San Cristobal	98	59	68	41
Santa Cruz Michapa	11	6	169	94
Suchitoto	795	76	248	24
San Ramón	0	0	176	100
Oratorio de Concepción	127	99	1	1
Monte San Juan	0	0	366	100
San Rafael	482	98	8	2
Candelaria	8	3	241	97
Perulapía	166	100	0	0
Totals	2,632	49.5%	2,679	50.5%

Source: Asamblea Nacional, "Elección de 1895," AGN, MG, unclassified box.

In those departments where voting was divided evenly, neither candidate's network achieved departmentwide supremacy; there were no equivalents to Sonsonate's Abrahán Rivera. Instead the candidates settled for as many municipalities as their subordinates could muster. In a recurrent scene, one municipality provided near-unanimous support for one candidate, while a neighboring municipality, sometimes located just a few kilometers down the road, produced an equally complete victory for a rival candidate. Overall, the results of the 1895 election highlight the golden rule of politics in El Salvador: to win an election, a network had to monopolize voting.

The 1895 election also reveals the democracy-laden discourse that accompanied these nondemocratic procedures. Carlos Meléndez was supported in his electoral bid by the newspaper *La Verdad,* based in the city of Nueva San Salvador. Unfortunately, no copies of that newspaper are known to have survived. But we know something of the claims made in *La Verdad* because after the election, Alfaro's supporters responded to them in a pair of lengthy editorials in the government's official newspaper, *Diario Oficial.* It seems that Meléndez did not take his defeat in stride. Although he had supported General Gutiérrez during the 1894 coup, he broke with him after his failed bid to become vice president. Shortly after the election, Meléndez's supporters (and probably Meléndez himself), launched a vigorous public relations campaign in the pages of *La Verdad,* claiming that the past elections for both president and vice president had been done fraudulently and against popular will. In the words of the *Diario Oficial* editorialists, *La Verdad* claimed that "there had been no liberty in the elections," the "victorious candidates for the executive offices had been imposed," and thus the "new government was illegal."[5]

Gutiérrez's supporters in *Diario Oficial* responded to those claims in multiple ways. First, they dismissed *La Verdad* on ideological grounds, accusing it of being "a clerical, Catholic newspaper" opposed to liberalism. Then they discredited the claims of electoral imposition in the vice presidential election by showing the departmentwide results that they touted as proof that multiple candidates received votes.

In the *San Salvador Department* Alfaro received 4,543 votes; Meléndez received 2,696.

Santa Ana. – Pérez 1,901. Alfaro, 1,210. Regalado, 432.

La Libertad. – Meléndez, 2,752. – Alfaro 1,001. Regalado, 472.

Sonsonate. – Alfaro 3,645 – Pérez. 590 – Meléndez, 188 – Hurtado, 177.

San Vicente. – Meléndez, 3,170 – Alfaro, 260.

Ahuachapán. – Alfaro, 2,635 – Meléndez, 2,634.

La Paz. – Alfaro, 3,334 – Meléndez, 408.

Usulután. – Alfaro, 3,096 – Meléndez, 270.

Chalatenango. – Alfaro, 4,278 – Meléndez, 2,750.

Armed with that evidence, the authors insisted that "only a losing candidate blinded by party loyalty" could fail to see "that the numerical results prove that an imposition under such circumstances was impossible." Thus, they summarized, "the election for the vice president . . . has been free."[6]

Defending the presidential election was more of a challenge because, after all, Gutiérrez had been elected by unanimity without an opponent. The authors in *Diario Oficial* explained that "the unanimity is the result of the prestige of the April [1894] Revolution, the respect its leaders have shown for public liberty, and the honor demonstrated by the Provisional Government." Thus, the authors concluded that the executive officers' right to govern had been established by "the Salvadoran people freely exercising their right to vote in the most recent elections."[7]

In many and diverse ways, the vice presidential election of 1895 symbolizes the nature of electoral politics in nineteenth- and early twentieth-century El Salvador. First and foremost, it reveals that a lot of people voted in elections. Assuming that widespread ballot stuffing did not swell the numbers of voters, the more than sixty thousand votes cast represented at least 40 percent of eligible voters.[8] That is a lot of people physically making their way to a polling station on election day, especially considering that a sizeable portion of those people who did not vote were probably supporters of the recently ousted Ezeta network and thus would not have been allowed to vote. If nothing else, the high turnout indicates that political leaders took elections seriously. However predetermined the outcome may have been, as in the case of Gutiérrez's presidential election, or however managed the voting was at any given polling station, such as during the vice presidential contest between Alfaro and Meléndez, political leaders needed their rule sanctified by an election, and they wanted people showing up on election day to legitimize the process.

Another characteristic revealed by this election is the absence of political platforms, policy proposals, or ideological vision. The candidates made no apparent attempt to explain themselves to voters or appeal to their particular interests—or, at least, no evidence survives to indicate that they did. Instead, the election consisted simply of two powerful national-level political actors lining up allies in municipalities to control voting at polling stations. Whatever means national political bosses employed to build alliances at the local level, and however local political bosses constructed their networks in the municipalities, be it coercion, persuasion, or both, they put them to work on election day by getting voters to the polls in support of the national-level boss.

The fact that voting occurred in the municipalities, under the purview of municipal authorities, provided the raw material for building the complex webs of patronage that bound local, regional, and national actors together. In fact, the electoral machinery used in national elections, such as voter registration lists (examined in more detail below), had been in action just a few weeks prior in municipal elections. Thus, the ability to deliver votes for a national-level politician was a direct continuation of delivering the same for oneself or one's allies in a recent municipal election.

The success of national-level candidates hinged upon the capabilities of worthy and dutiful allies at the departmental and municipal levels, men like Abrahán Rivera in Sonsonate City. It is not clear what Rivera received from Alfaro for his successful efforts in Sonsonate. Perhaps Rivera was repaying a debt to Alfaro. Perhaps he received a government position in San Salvador. Perhaps he simply accrued political capital for his own battles in Sonsonate—assurance that a future petition from him would receive a favorable review at the national level. The available evidence does not reveal enough about Rivera's career to say for certain, but unless he was somehow exceptional, he is likely to have applied one or another of these options.

Finally, the vice presidential election of 1895 shows that a rhetoric of democracy accompanied elections. Both Meléndez and Alfaro appealed to the principles of popular will, free suffrage, and democratic liberty to justify their assessments of the election. No one disparaged democracy. Rather, they accused one another of failing to live up to the high standards of democratic freedom, despite the fact that both of them followed the same nondemocratic procedures during the election. Neither side allowed opposition voters to cast ballots in areas where their allies controlled the polls. In most every municipality, voting was decided by unanimity or near unanimity. Each candidate wanted to control polling stations and maximize the number of votes in his favor while limiting or eliminating votes for his rivals. Even if Meléndez's supporters in *La Verdad* had exposed the fallacies behind their opponents' statistical defense in *Diario Oficial* by insisting that municipal-level results proved that Alfaro's allies had prevented Meléndez's supporters from voting, their case would have been no stronger, because they had done the same thing. Nevertheless, everyone employed a common rhetoric of democratic liberty.

These generalized comments will be fleshed out in greater detail in the coming pages. Suffice it to say for now that the vice presidential election of 1895 provides a revealing introduction to the complex and sprawling nature of politics in El Salvador in the nineteenth and early twentieth centuries. I will now back up in chronology and show the formal electoral rules that had been put in place in the decades leading up to that moment in 1895.

The Formal Rules of Politics in Republican El Salvador

In 1821, after nearly three hundred years of Spanish colonial rule, Central America declared its independence. This break with the colonial motherland came without war, but it occurred within a distinct context of social inequality. A small minority of the population, the creoles (American-born Spaniards), had championed the cause of independence and intended to master the new order. They constituted less than 10 percent of the total population of Central America, and an even smaller proportion in El Salvador, yet they believed that they were the rightful heirs to Spain's authority.[9] They justified this claim on the grounds that they were the only people in Central America qualified to govern, because the remaining 90 percent of the population consisted of Indians, Africans, and mestizos, whom the creoles considered to represent the regressive features of American society. The creoles assumed that these dark-skinned and mostly illiterate masses should not be allowed to participate freely in politics, because they would surely use political power to the detriment of the creoles and society as a whole.

The daunting task of building a new nation from the disparate remnants of the former Spanish empire was not unique to the creoles of Central America. Throughout Latin America, creoles struggled to give form to their nationalism and determine the type of government that would best serve their interests.[10] Naturally, intense debates ensued, with one of the most common divisions occurring between so-called conservatives and liberals. The former wished to retain much of the old colonial order, whereas the latter wished to transform society in ways consistent with more modern-looking structures. With the exception of a handful of radical liberals, who drew inspiration from events like the French Revolution and called for mass empowerment, most conservatives and liberals shared concerns over mass political action. Whatever structures they hoped to put in place in their newly independent nations, they wanted to be able to maintain control.

The process is well symbolized by the inveterate liberal creole Simón Bolívar, the "Liberator," who vanquished Spain's colonial armies and then faced the task of building a nation in the region known as Gran Colombia. Bolívar steadfastly believed that the structures of government in Britain, France, and the United States were models of modernity and progress, and especially of nationalism, but he rejected for his own land what he considered to be those nations' excessive commitment to liberty.[11] Bolívar held the conviction that he and his fellow creoles were in conflict not only with Spain, but also with the masses, or as he put it, "we are disputing with the natives for titles of ownership."[12] Bolívar sought to create a government in which liberty and democracy would be hailed, but curtailed. "All should not be left to chance and the outcome of elections," Bolívar said famously before the Congress of Angostura in 1819, "the people are more easily deceived than is Nature perfected by art. . . . Absolute liberty invariably lapses into absolute power."[13] Bolívar adopted measures to make government exclusive, like a hereditary senate, with a powerful executive.[14] Similar concerns shaped the foundations of government in Central America.[15]

The creoles of Central America did not waver in their belief that the masses should be hindered from participating in politics, although they disagreed as to what type of government would best suit their needs. Some conservative creoles remained loyal to the idea of a monarchy and hoped for the establishment of an empire, if not the return of the Spanish crown. Other creoles, however, favored a form of republicanism, a government run by elected representatives. Parallel to and part of this conflict between monarchism and republicanism was a debate between federalists and centralists. Centralists wanted the five former intendancies of the Kingdom of Guatemala (now the five independent republics of modern Central America) to be consolidated under a single dominant regime. Federalists believed that the traditional animosity between the distinct regions demanded the creation of a federal government that would grant each province autonomy over its own affairs.[16]

The supporters of republicanism and federalism prevailed, although local conservatives, especially in Guatemala, initially held the upper hand and supported Central America's incorporation into the Mexican empire under Agustín Iturbide. That empire collapsed in 1823, freeing the new leaders of Central America to frame a constitution the following year to formalize the institutions of their new government, the United Provinces of Central America. The resultant charter of 1824 reflected the diverse motives that inspired it. It abolished slavery and rejected the idea that citizenship depended upon one's continent of origin in favor of the more modern concepts of place of birth and naturalization.[17] It outlined a federal republic and heralded the virtues of representative democracy: "the government of the Republic is popular, representative and federal."[18] It established popular elections as the method of transferring political power and separated the government into three branches: legislative, executive, and judicial. In short, it established democratic republicanism as the normative order, but democracy was a more worrisome prospect than republicanism.[19]

The charter of 1824 limited mass participation by making all elections indirect, a tactic adopted from Spain's Cádiz Constitution of 1812. Historian of Mexico Peter Guardino says that the Cádiz Constitution was not designed to encourage competitiveness. It was built around the notion of individuals working in corporate communities, such as guilds, who would send enlightened leaders to represent their interests at the governing level.[20] The Central Americanist historians Mario Rodríguez and Jordana Dym concur, pointing out that the Cádiz Constitution served as a model for Central America's 1824 constitution. Voting lists from some of the first elections in El Salvador in the 1820s and 1830s, found in the municipal archive in Sonsonate City, reveal the functioning of indirect elections. Voters cast their votes for *electores* (electors or delegates), who then voted for the actual candidates on their behalf. The distance between the common voter and the candidates increased with the scale of the election. In municipal elections the selection of electors occurred in one round, meaning that connection between voter and candidate was relatively close. But in elections for the offices of president, vice president, and representatives to the federal congress, the selection of electors occurred in three rounds. Only in the first round did the common voter participate, and with each successive round, the number of electores grew smaller. By the final round of voting the electores and candidates were far removed from the common voter and had little accountability. Other tactics that limited the power of the common person included literacy and wealth requirements for officeholding. Thus, as Rodríguez acknowledges, the first government of Central America appealed to the principles of liberalism and democracy, but functioned more akin to a monarchy.[21]

Although the creoles from the various regions of Central America agreed about the need to curtail mass empowerment, they failed to settle their own provincial rivalries. Just as the creoles of Paraguay, the Banda Oriental (Uruguay), and Upper Perú (Bolivia) defined true independence as liberation from both Spain and Argentina, the creoles of each Central American region considered their participation in the United Provinces to be almost as stifling as colonization by Spain. The rivalry between El Salvador and Guatemala was particularly intense. El Salvador produced many agricultural commodities, especially indigo, and the infamous merchants of Guatemala sought to control the marketing of those goods. El Salvador in turn resisted the Guatemalan monopoly, considering it a continuation of Spain's mercantilist economy. Similar rivalries raged between all the provinces, and soon the peace of independence gave way to chronic warfare and instability. By 1839 conditions had deteriorated so badly that when John Lloyd Stephens, the roving ambassador from the United States, arrived on the scene he was unable to locate a functioning government. "After diligent search," he wrote to his superiors in Washington, "no government found."[22]

Although the demise of the federation was associated with widespread disorder, in El Salvador the transition from federation to republic revealed a degree of continuity. It did not incite a revolutionary change in power; rather, the same men who had represented El Salvador in the federation assumed the reins of leadership in the new nation. A few of these men were Eduardo Vega, José Campo, and Vicente Gómez of Sonsonate, and Gerardo Barrios of San Miguel. They and others like them had participated in federal politics and went on to hold the highest-ranking offices in the new national government.[23] These men brought to El Salvador the same political philosophy that had predominated in the federation, namely a belief that government should be representative, and that democracy was a heralded principle, even though its actual practice was disconcerting.

Despite their suspicions about democracy, the initial leaders of El Salvador set important precedents for mass political participation in the country's first constitution of 1841. They established representative democracy as the governing standard and eliminated some of the restrictions on mass participation in the 1824 constitution. The 1841 charter divided the powers of government into executive, judicial, and legislative branches. It made popular elections determinant for all officeholding. It made suffrage universal for all men over the age of twenty-one, regardless of ethnicity, literacy, or wealth. "All political power emanates from the people," it reads, "the base of the electoral system is the population." It retained indirect voting for municipal elections, which in some rural precincts enhanced the power of large landowners because the boundaries of voting precincts often coincided with the borders of haciendas. However, the 1841 charter made national elections direct, even though national-level candidates still had to meet wealth requirements. Deputies and senators to the National Assembly had to prove possession of 500 and 4,000 pesos respectively, and the president and vice president had to own at least 8,000 pesos each. An individual who was elected deputy for Santa Ana District in 1849 had to resign his office because he did not "meet the constitutional requirements of possessing 500 pesos' worth of capital, and moreover, the money which he claimed as his actually belonged to his mother."[24] The 1841 constitution did not establish wealth restrictions for municipal officials, although some municipalities created their own wealth-based requirements for officeholding. In Sonsonate City and San Vicente City, for instance, candidates for local office had to qualify as "*hacendados y propietarios*" (landowners).[25]

Each constitution that succeeded the original charter in 1841 enhanced the electoral power of the citizenry. The constitution of 1864 abolished wealth requirements for national officeholders, and the constitution of 1872 discontinued indirect elections at the municipal level. All of these extensions of electoral liberty were retained in the final constitution of the nineteenth century, which was ratified in 1886. Thus, by the 1870s, legally speaking, the political system of El Salvador was wide open. All adult males were enfranchised, all elections were direct, and no restrictions on officeholding existed. Notably, this steady advance of legal rights occurred regardless of the ostensible ideological orientation of the constitutions' authors, because the constitutions of 1872 and 1886 were drafted by so-called liberals, and those of 1841 and 1864 were drafted by so-called conservatives.

This degree of electoral freedom in El Salvador's legal codes contrasts with some other examples in Latin America, such as Colombia. Mass suffrage was codified in Colombia in 1853, in part because elites desperately needed mass support in their incessant battles with one another. Recognizing this, the masses bargained for legal rights. Liberal elites in particular were willing to extend voting rights to them in exchange for their support against conservatives. But by the 1870s and 1880s, elites on both sides of the spectrum came to worry about the degree of mass empowerment. During the so-called Regeneration period that began in the 1870s, and then specifically in the new Colombian Constitution of 1886, elites banded together and retracted some of the electoral privileges they had granted in the 1850s.[26] Similarly, in Nicaragua in the early 1880s voters still had to qualify as a "citizen" to be allowed to vote and hold political office, and to achieve citizenship a person had to own at least 100 pesos.[27]

In El Salvador the opposite occurred. Restrictions codified in the early years of the federation and republic steadily fell away with each successive constitution, so that by the 1870s no restrictions remained. The reasons for this divergence are speculative. El Salvador witnessed plenty of intra-elite factionalism and infighting, and elites drew upon mass support for their respective conflagrations, but that factionalism was more personal than ideological, so perhaps elites shared opinions about the legal code and no faction felt the need to suddenly retract the actions of their pre-decessors. Research has shown with some definitiveness that Salvadoran elites tended to share a generalized liberal ideology. Even though they sometimes framed their disputes with one another in the standard conser-vative/liberal rhetoric of the day, the fact remains that most of them were basically liberals. This unity of ideology was caused in no small part by a shared animosity for Guatemala, where a more ideologically driven con-servatism held sway throughout much of the nineteenth century.[28] Per-haps the masses in El Salvador simply managed to keep the pressure on elites longer and more effectively than their Colombian counterparts. Or perhaps the Salvadoran masses had never put a degree of pressure on their elites comparable to that imposed by the Colombian masses, so the Salva-doran elites did not fear codifying mass political participation. Whatever the cause of the divergence, the comparison between El Salvador and Co-lombia highlights the former's advance of mass electoral rights and the latter's retraction of them.[29]

Still, El Salvador's elites were concerned about autonomous mass ac-tion, and thus it is curious that they were so willing to advance a modern-looking electoral code. In facing this conundrum, Salvadoran elites were hardly unique in the context of nineteenth-century Latin America. Re-search on other nations reveals a constant tension among nineteenth-century elites wishing to participate in cutting-edge forms of nation-state formation, which often meant embracing liberal principles, while still protecting themselves from the vagaries of autonomous mass action. Elites throughout Central America were clearly aware of foreign models and the broader ideological trends relating to the language of republican democ-racy. As just one example, Costa Rican elites included elements of France's Declaration of the Rights of Man in their state constitution of 1824.[30] It also seems apparent that elites in El Salvador, like their counterparts in Colombia and Mexico, believed that potentially disruptive mass action could be curtailed through educational discipline. In Colombia, for ex-ample, Cerbeleón Pinzón drafted a primary-school text in 1864, *Cate-cismo repúblicano para instrucción popular,* to inculcate the masses with respect for social order. He wrote the text after mass suffrage had been granted in the 1850s, intending, in the words of historian James Sanders, to "discipline the masses, teach them their responsibilities and duties, so that they would not interpret their new rights in too radical a manner, [and] know their place behind liberal leaders."[31] Similar catechisms appeared in other Latin American nations.[32] In El Salvador a comparable text, *Cartilla del ciudadano* (Catechism of citizenship), was written in 1874 by the liberal man of letters Francisco Galindo. It became a required text in schools. In it Galindo distinguished between the "people" (*el pueblo*) and "rabble" (*el populacho*), identifying the former as the foundation of the nation and the latter as a social problem.[33]

Nevertheless, some features that limited voter freedom remained in place in El Salvador's electoral system. The main one was oral voting.[34] The secret ballot was not established in El Salvador until the Constitution of 1950, meaning that until then all voting was conducted orally and in public. (Incidentally, female suffrage was granted in that same charter in 1950.) On election day voters gathered at the assigned polling station and awaited the formation of the electoral board (*directorio*). Once the board had been formed, voters filed before its members and announced their vote, which was written on a tally sheet (*pliego*) by a board official. Voters were dismissed without being allowed to verify their vote. A North American resident in El Salvador in the early twentieth century once bore witness to oral voting: "There is no secret ballot," he wrote to his wife, "but there are 15 clerks who take down the wishes of the voters in their books as the ballot is passed around the table. The voter simply states who he wishes to vote for, publicly, and the clerks make the record."[35] The tally sheets that have survived into El Salvador's national archive offer physical evidence of this system at work. An examination of them reveals that each contains only one style of handwriting, that of the board member who recorded the votes.

Elections in El Salvador occurred frequently. Municipal councils were elected every year, as were representatives to the national congress. Presidential elections occurred every two years until the 1864 Constitution and then every four years thereafter. All of these elections were highly regimented affairs that functioned more or less in the following manner. Voting for all elections took place in the municipality and was overseen by municipal officials. Voting in municipal elections lasted one day, usually the first or second Sunday of December. Voting for national elections lasted three days and occurred roughly three weeks later, during the first or second weekend of January. In the month leading up to an election, voters were required to register their names in the registration book (*libro de registros*) that was located in the municipal hall (*cabildo*), which naturally was under the control of the reigning municipal council. The registration book was used on election day to cross-check voters for eligibility, and that same registration book was used for both municipal elections and national elections.

At 8:00 a.m. on the morning of an election, the reigning municipal officers gathered in front of the municipal hall to oversee the selection of the electoral board, which was to be comprised of at least four of the town's residents. The electoral board was chosen by a vote of whomever happened to be standing in front of the municipal hall at that early hour. Once the electoral board had been chosen, its members sat down behind a table inside the municipal hall and proceeded to accept people's votes, starting at 9:00 a.m. Voters filed before board members, announcing their name and their vote. If the board members determined that a voter was eligible in the registration book, they recorded his vote on a tally sheet. Voting ended at 5:00 p.m., and the results were either carried physically or telegraphed (once that became available) to the departmental governor's officer for counting and verification.[36]

At the local level, candidates competed for four offices—alcalde, regidor, síndico, and juez de paz. The alcalde (mayor) was the municipal executive who presided over council meetings, made political appointments, ruled on such things as disputes over land and water, and controlled the municipal police. He appointed the *alguaciles* (sheriffs) who patrolled the *cantones* (neighborhoods or precincts) and rural areas outside the municipality. Regidores (council members) supervised administrative affairs and stood in for the alcalde in case of his absence. Each municipal council had at least two and as many as ten regidores, depending on the size of the municipality. The síndico oversaw financial affairs and monitored municipal employees. The juez de paz (justice of the peace) administered local justice.[37]

At the national level, candidates competed for the office of president and vice president and for seats in the legislative congress. All other national-level government offices were appointed by the president, including cabinet positions, judgeships, and departmental governorships. El Salvador stands out from larger countries in Latin America in that it did not have state governments and therefore did not have state-level legislatures or elections. Instead, El Salvador was divided into departments, which were administrative subunits of the national government. Departmental officials (particularly the departmental governor and the departmental military commander) were appointed by the president or the commanding military officer (who, most of the time, were one and the same). El Salvador had four departments in 1824 (Sonsonate, San Salvador, San Vicente, and San Miguel), and by 1875 it had its modern-day equivalent of fourteen departments (see map 2). Even though elections occurred at only two levels—municipal and national—the department was an important component of the political system because its officers (the governor and military commander) presided over affairs throughout their departments and represented important intermediaries between the local and national levels.

Electoral nullification was an important legal procedure in El Salvador that was designed to ensure adherence to electoral law. Each constitution stipulated that elections could be nullified if they were proven to have been conducted irregularly. The decisive question, of course, was who decided the meaning of *regular* and *irregular?* The answer to that question will be explored in greater detail in forthcoming chapters. Suffice it to say that the rules of electoral nullification were quite explicit. If evidence existed that voting for any election ran contrary to the stated laws, then officials at the departmental and national levels had the authority to nullify the election. Initial nullification requests were sent by a complainant at the municipal level to either the departmental governor or the minister of government in San Salvador. If those higher officials needed further evidence, they had the authority to send an investigative team to the municipality to produce a written report. The team could interview local residents, and if necessary, relevant witnesses could be called into the offices of higher authorities to provide testimony. If a victorious candidate was found guilty of misdeeds, his election was nullified and a replacement election was scheduled for a later date. Evidence shows that nullifications were a common feature of elections. El Salvador's national archive contains more than three hundred complete nullification cases between 1889 and 1936, as well as surviving documentation from a few dozen more cases for the period prior to the 1889 archive fire. Many other nullification procedures, for which there are no surviving records, are mentioned in peripheral documents, suggesting that the actual number of cases was even greater.[38] As will be shown in the following pages, these nullification requests, which serve as the court cases of politics, provide valuable evidence into the nature of electoral procedures.

In summary, the letter of the law in El Salvador called for the creation of a representative democracy. Since the beginning of the republic, there had been few restrictions on voting, and whatever restrictions were in place steadily evaporated throughout the nineteenth century. Elections occurred frequently and at regularly scheduled intervals. And, as we are about to see, voters went to the polls. Victorious candidates assumed office, and nobody held office without the sanctity of an election. Some elections were highly competitive, such as the vice presidential election of 1895. Almost every election, competitive or not, tended to follow the letter of the law. But at a deeper, more fundamental level, they deviated from the spirit of the law as it related to democracy and individual liberty. Voting did not reflect the opinions of autonomous individuals selecting from a range of alternative platforms and ideologies. Instead, voting reflected political networks' abilities to monopolize polling stations and ensure that whoever came to the polls voted accordingly.

The Informal Rules of Politics in Republican El Salvador

What compelled people to seek and hold political office in El Salvador? This is a sprawling question that can draw upon a morass of theories about human behavior. I will avoid that mess and stick to the basics. First, it should be pointed out that some people did not want to hold political office. A broadly accepted truism in El Salvador is that elites preferred to avoid politics and looked down on political officeholding as a dirty business that got in the way of making money.[39] To the extent that such a belief actually existed, it seems to have been a twentieth-century phenomenon; in the nineteenth century many elites held office, in part because the accumulation of private wealth often depended upon public policy or public favors. Furthermore, throughout much of the nineteenth century, the long midcentury economic downturn had circumscribed opportunities for private profit in the marketplace. Public officeholding was often a route of ascent, even if the government's treasuries were meager and frequently plundered. People sought political office for diverse reasons: some were driven by highly selfish desires, while others felt called by altruism and hoped to improve society. Regardless of motive, people pursued political office to make policy and wield power, and anyone who wanted to get anything done had to have influence in the public sphere of government. Even if a person did not want to hold office himself, he wanted to be allied with someone who did.

At the local level, municipal officers presided over such things as land and water disputes, judicial rulings, the registration of births, deaths, and marriages, and various other factors of residents' daily lives and livelihoods. The central government was weak and somewhat powerless throughout much of the nineteenth century, and municipal officials enjoyed a lot of latitude. In addition, municipal officials oversaw voting for national elections, and thus, inevitably, they were drawn into national-level political affairs.

Much the same can be said for national-level officials. Political office at the national level bestowed upon its holders various powers and responsibilities in the judicial, economic, and social arenas, including such areas as pensions, infrastructure, taxes, and education, to name just a few. Whatever compelled aspirants to pursue national-level office and affect policies in one or more of those arenas, be it personal aggrandizement or altruistic service, no political actor launched or succeeded in a career without creating a network tied into broad-based alliances at the departmental and municipal levels. Those alliances are the main focus of this book.

The foundation of political power at the municipal level is the subject of chapters 3 and 4. In those chapters I look at local elections and the ways in which municipal-level political players built up their networks and used them to control polling stations and fend off rivals. For now, it is enough to note that one of the most common methods of building a local political network was for local power players (usually elite landowners) to unite and acquire a group of loyal underlings, or clients, who could be enlisted on election day to do their bidding. The economic disparity between landowners and laborers was a basic mechanism that allowed for the accumulation of clients. But it was hardly the sole route to building a local network. As we will see, family ties and ethnic bonds, among other factors, transcended economic disparity and allowed people to create networks at the local level. In fact, some municipal-level political bosses, especially in impoverished areas of the country, were quite poor relative to their counterparts in other areas of the country, but they remained politically relevant because of the votes they presided over, especially if they happened to live in densely populated zones.

At the national level, political players succeeded or failed depending on their ability to build political networks out of disparate departments and municipalities. The strength of any one person's network determined his ability to succeed in both electoral politics and warfare. My main contention is that politics in El Salvador and the building of these political networks operated according to an informal set of rules revolving around patronage. Scholars of Latin America have long recognized the existence of patronage in politics, but as historian Luis Roniger points out, only recently have they begun to study it systematically.[40] Early works on patronage tended to describe it in the limited context of caudillismo, the notorious "leaders on horseback" who were as much plundering bandits as political officials, who rewarded their supporters with stolen booty acquired through military adventurism.[41] Later studies have taken a more nuanced approach, endowing patronage with more subtlety and flexibility. They demonstrate that the typical patron was a local landowner and political official who came to power through an election—albeit a rigged one—and who distributed payoffs in the form of appointments and jobs rather than riches gained through plunder.

The institutions of caciquismo in Mexico and coronelismo in Brazil have attracted scholarly attention and inspired substantive and enlightening studies of patronage and patronage networks. The cacique and the coronel functioned in roughly the same manner in their respective nations as in El Salvador; they were local- or regional-level political bosses who presided over their immediate patronage networks and who tapped into broader networks at the national level, which in the case of Mexico were led by powerful caudillos. Ultimately, the power base of a cacique or a coronel was the body of local clients or retainers he could count on to provide votes or to serve as soldiers in support of higher-level political allies.[42] El Salvador did not have terms that were used regularly in political parlance, although occasionally powerful political patrons were referred to as *jefe* (boss) or *cacique,* and sometimes as *notables* (notable persons). From this point forward I will use the term *political boss* to refer to these political actors at both at the municipal and national levels.

A brief case study from the municipality of Chalchuapa (Santa Ana Department) in 1919 makes clear how the power of appointment could be used to influence an electoral outcome. The incumbent alcalde's political network hoped to extend its tenure in office for another year, but it faced a stiff challenge from a rival network. The alcalde feared that his alguaciles were not going to support him in the election, even though he himself had appointed them. Why the alguaciles might have shifted loyalties remains unclear. Regardless, the alcalde put the powers of his office to work by dismissing all of them a few days prior to the election and appointing new ones, with the understanding that they would arrest opposition supporters. One of the appointees testified that the alcalde "told us that he was sure that in receiving our new appointments we would work to ensure the victory of his candidate."[43]

When analyzing these patronage alliances and their attendant patron-client relations at the local level, we must keep in mind their complexities and the need for nuance in describing them. As Justin Wolfe, a historian of nineteenth-century Nicaragua, insists, we must avoid "simplistic notions of caudillo politics . . . [in which] local elites controlled the masses through patronage and coercion and deployed them like pawns in political demonstrations, strikes, and regional uprising."[44] As Wolfe and many other scholars of Latin American political history reveal, mass actors demonstrated the capacity for autonomous thought and action.[45] However hierarchical a system might have been, and however effective elite actors were at creating a hegemonic norm that benefitted them, the masses were capable of interpreting affairs from their perspectives and seeking satisfaction of their defined interests. Thus, political alliances between elites and commoners involved some form of negotiation, just as did the alliances between the elites themselves. Returning to the vice presidential election of 1895 as an example, the national-level political player, Prudencio Alfaro, bargained with regional bosses like Abrahán Rivera in Sonsonate, who bargained with municipal bosses throughout Sonsonate Department, who in turn bargained with the masses of voters who cast their votes at the polls on election day. Each of those interactions had a history, whether personal or institutional. Most political actors lived in close proximity to the people with whom they practiced politics, and their political relationships were intimately tied into all other social interactions. The history of those interactions and the ways in which individual actors remembered them constituted the raw material of political relationships. Although the sources surviving in the Salvadoran documentary record tend to be bureaucratic rather than personal, offering limited insight into these on-the-ground realities, they still reveal something of the complexity of people's interactions. At the least, they demonstrate the need to keep these complexities in mind as we read of them.

At the foundation of their political empires, bosses traded to other bosses the services of their local networks in return for favors, such as appointment to political office, assistance in political battles, and favorable rulings from higher authorities in legal disputes, among many other forms of favor and payback. One common form of patronage reward, especially in the nineteenth century, was military promotion.[46] A local official once described a patronage relationship as being *"en servicio"* (in service) to someone else. He noted that in his jurisdiction patronage was commonly used to influence judicial outcomes. Certain criminals, he claimed, never received punishment because well-positioned allies secured lenient rulings from the police and judges.[47]

Patronage knit disparate bosses together into powerful political machines that propelled their leaders into office by controlling elections and fighting off rivals. Patronage networks resembled political parties in that they were mechanisms of political ascent, and occasionally these networks were even referred to as *partidos* (parties). But they differed from any modern concept of political parties. They did not offer platforms or political agendas, nor did they compete for popular appeal. Instead they were highly personalistic, typically hierarchical units designed to monopolize voting, control public office, and militarily resist rival networks when necessary.

The nomenclature of networks reflects their makeup. They did not bear distinct names beyond those of their reigning bosses. A network led by a Meléndez, for instance, was referred to as the *Melendistas*; another, led by a Rivera, was called the *Riveristas*. The names changed with changes in leadership. Not until the 1920s, and then only at the national level, were attempts made to form political parties. During the nineteenth century political actors referred to party names only in the application of the terms *liberal* and *conservative* to political factions, as in the "liberal party" or the "conservative party." These were not official parties, but rather labels used to disparage opponents and justify one's own aspirations based on hyperbolic accusations.[48] Networks grew and contracted over time as new patronage deals were struck and old ones were broken. However, networks tended to remain stable over time. It was not uncommon for a political actor to maintain some of the same patronage alliances throughout his entire political life.

Broadly speaking, the system in El Salvador functioned in the following manner. At the municipal level, political bosses accumulated retainers or clients and marshaled them to ascend the heights of local power. Accomplishing this task meant fending off local rivals, perhaps through the use of violence, in order to control the annual municipal election. Once in charge in his municipality, a boss entered into patronage relations with larger political networks at the departmental and national levels. One of the key assets available to a local boss in negotiations with outsiders was the votes of his municipality, something that outside aspirants desperately wanted. Similarly, when political affairs turned violent and national-level bosses needed resources for combat, local bosses served as the conduit for the precious commodities of men, food, money, and war material. It was the local boss's duty to generate votes and resources in his municipality at the behest of his larger patrons. In return he hoped to either climb the ladder of politics or receive support from powerful outsiders in political conflagrations at home.

At a certain level, national-level bosses were simply successful municipal-level bosses. They typically came from wealth and had a local power base (their land, and a stronghold of friends, families, and retainers at either the municipal or regional level) that they could rely upon when needed. But rarely, if ever, was that personal base alone sufficient to propel a political aspirant to the heights of national office. For that, aspirants needed allies, lots of them, capable leaders in dozens of disparate municipalities who could produce the votes and resources necessary to advance a political career.

Building Pyramids

The extent of popular participation in elections in nineteenth- and early twentieth-century Latin America is a point of historiographical debate. Received wisdom holds that elections during those years were characterized by an extremely restricted franchise in which elites excluded the popular sectors either through formal laws or informal practices. Revisionists challenge this assumption by offering evidence of a broader franchise and even genuinely democratic practices.[49] A similar debate raged in the 1960s and 1970s about U.S. colonial history.[50]

The revisionist line holds great promise, because it brings new evidence to light and employs revealing theoretical frameworks, such as those that grant agency to subaltern actors. But the revisionist line does not seem to describe the Salvadoran case very well. In El Salvador, elections tended to be all or nothing. The goal of political activity was to eliminate the opposition, control the polling place, and monopolize voting. Competing networks did not share the spoils of government, and political opponents did not sit together on the same municipal council.

The traditional route of ascent from local to national politics lay through the National Assembly. Historian Alain Rouquié's definition of the state as "the place for transactions and bargaining between locally propertied groups," applies literally to the National Assembly in El Salvador.[51] The three dozen or so members of the assembly were regional strongmen who held their positions at the behest of their political networks. They arrived in San Salvador looking to form alliances with other bosses in hopes of building ever-larger pyramids, and whoever assembled the largest networks could compete for the ultimate political prize, the presidency.

Each member of the assembly had a bargaining chip to offer potential allies: the resources of his local network. When he or his allies needed a certain electoral result, he had to be able to generate the needed votes from his local affiliates. When political disputes turned violent, he had to produce soldiers, money, or war material. As a result, each member of the assembly waged political battles on two fronts: at the national level, where he struggled to sustain his alliances, and at the local level, where he had to guard against the machinations of opponents at home, who were busy seeking out alliances with other national-level patrons. In this way, national politics comprised of a series of constant and crisscrossing inter-actions between local, departmental, and national levels. Although many local conflicts had nothing to do with national politics, some local po-litical battles grew directly out of national-level disputes, and in turn most national conflicts were fought out in the municipalities.

Since the road to national power lay through the National Assembly, political actors who aspired to national-level office usually launched their careers in their own legislative precincts by winning election as a represen-tative to the assembly. Until 1883 the assembly consisted of two houses, the chamber of deputies and the senate. Each senator and deputy was elected from his respective parish (*parroquía*). The senator's parish was known as a circle (*círculo*), which consisted of up to thirty thousand in-habitants, and the deputies' parishes were called districts (*distritos*), which had no more than fifteen thousand inhabitants. The largest municipality in each parish was designated as the capital (*cabacera*) and served as the administrative center. The total number of parishes in the nation hovered around four dozen, accounting for the roughly three dozen deputies and one dozen senators. Each department typically had two circles consisting of two or three districts, each of which contained roughly six munici-palities.

In 1883 the administrative system changed slightly. The new consti-tution that year (one of many in the 1880s that finally culminated in the durable charter of 1886) abolished the senate, leaving only the chamber of deputies (that is, the National Assembly) as the sole legislative body. Each deputy to the assembly was elected in departmentwide elections rather than by individual parishes. Each department elected three depu-ties, for a total of forty-two members in the assembly. This system re-mained in place until after World War II.

Prior to the changes of 1883, the parish was the first step of the po-litical ladder beyond the municipality. Parish politics gave a local politi-cian his first opportunity to form extramunicipal alliances. He and the bosses of the other five or six municipalities in his district or circle had to elect one deputy or one senator to the national legislature. Each boss wanted the votes of the other members' municipalities, and each hoped to use his own votes as leverage to extract favors from his counterparts or to influence the choice of candidates.

The reigning bosses of the parish capital were the main arbiters of electoral power. They were usually prominent landowners, and since the capital was the largest city in the area, its bosses had at their disposal the greatest number of votes. Moreover, the capital was the administrative center of the parish and served as the site of vote counting, meaning that the other municipalities had to send their ballots to the capital to be tallied, giving the bosses of the capital even more influence. A typical example of the vote-counting orders that went from the capital to outlying municipalities reads, "the vote counters of . . . each voting district are to arrive at the municipal hall of this municipality at twelve o'clock noon, next Sunday the fourteenth of this month, bringing with them the *pliegos* [ballots] . . . in order to effect the counting of the votes."[52]

The election of 1870 in the parish capital of Izalco reveals a typical example of the ability of local bosses to dominate affairs. Of the offices to be chosen that year, and of the four positions to be filled on the electoral council, all but one of were filled by Izalqueños (see table 1.2). The election also reveals the relationship between land, family, and politics. Two families, Barrientos and Castillo, both prominent landowning clans, accounted for three of the four elected positions, as well as the president of the directorio.[53]

Table 1.2 Assembly Elections, Izalco Parish, December 1870
(each official's municipality of origin is listed in parentheses)

Senator:	Mariano Fernández (n.a.)
Substitute Senator:	Ramón Barrientos (Izalco)
Deputy:	Benigno Barrientos (Izalco)
Substitute Deputy:	Aristides Castillo (Izalco)
Members of Directorio:	Ramón Barrientos, President (Izalco)
	Antonio Menéndez (Izalco)
	Manuel Díaz (Izalco)
	Faustino Quiñónez (Izalco)

Source: Junta Electoral, San Julian, December 6, 1870, AGN, FA, Box "#2.2"; and Junta Electoral, Izalco, December 6, 1870, AMS, Box "Elecciones, 1870–9."

Deputies and senators typically ran unopposed and won their offices by unanimous vote. All of the candidates in the 1870 election in Izalco, for example, won by unanimity. Electoral results from other times and places reveal similar results. The deputy from Santa Ana District, for example, won his election in 1841 with 127 unanimous votes. The deputy of Sonsonate District won his election in December 1841 with 320 unanimous votes, and in October 1842, the deputy from Sonsonate District won with 307 unanimous votes.[54] But congressional elections differed from municipal elections in that the dominant bosses of the capital city did not physically control each polling station, and as a result, their ability to control voting in each municipality depended upon the strength of their patronage ties and the fortitude of their local allies. When adversaries of the reigning bosses in the capital came to power in an outlying town, voting could be contested.

The deputy election of 1883 in Atiquizaya District offers a typical example of a contested parish election (see table 1.3). Four of the district's five municipalities unanimously supported Rafael Guerrero, the candidate put forth by the Atiquizaya bosses. But officials in one outlying municipality, Apaneca, opposed Guerrero and gave all 141 of their votes to an alternative candidate. Although Guerrero won the election and went on to San Salvador as the deputy from Atiquizaya, his ability to build patronage alliances at the national level was weakened by Apaneca's opposition because he could not guarantee the unanimous vote of his own parish.

Table 1.3   Deputy Election, Atiquizaya District, December 30, 1883

Municipality	Candidates, and Votes Received	
	Rafael Guerrero	Domingo León
Atiquizaya	381	0
El Refugio	83	0
San Lorenzo	121	0
Turín	97	0
Apaneca	0	141

Source: Junta Electoral, Atiquizaya, December 30, 1883, AGN, MG, Box "1882, 1884, 1886, 1887, 1888."

Sources do not reveal the motivations behind Apaneca's defiance. But the range of possibilities is limited. Either the bosses of the reigning network in Apaneca disagreed with the choice put forth by the leaders in Atiquizaya, or they were acting in concert with national-level opponents of those leaders. Whatever the case, the election illustrates the functioning of national-level politics during the nineteenth century. Each municipality typically voted unanimously according to the dictates of the reigning local network. And if one network fell to another, then the candidate and his attendant voters changed, but the results were the same—unanimity or near unanimity. The goal of politics was not to sway voters and allow for a competitive franchise, but rather to create patronage alliances that could control voting.

Each January, during assembly elections, aspiring bosses across the nation grappled with one another for dominance in their respective parishes. Each parish boss wanted to get himself or one of his immediate allies elected to the assembly and thus in position to broker deals with bosses from other parishes and departments throughout the country. Parish bosses usually had to negotiate with their respective department capital first and thus could not broker deals independently at the national level. Even before 1883, when parishes controlled the selection of deputies and senators, the departmental capital still had a lot of power. It had its own senator and deputy, giving it control over as much as one-third of the department's allotment of congressional representatives. In addition, bosses in the department capital were usually its most prominent landowners and had family and land spread throughout the department, giving them at least some influence over outlying parishes. After 1883 the department capital held an even greater tactical advantage, because its officials oversaw the selection of all three of the department's deputies to the National Assembly.

The department capital was also in a privileged bargaining position because it housed two powerful officials appointed at the national level, the departmental governor and the departmental commander (*comandante*), both of whom had wide jurisdiction. The governor, as the departmental executive, ruled on everything from electoral irregularities to land disputes and labor contracts. The commander presided over the departmental garrison, organized the militia, and commanded the military patrols. The same person often held both positions, giving him tremendous latitude. When one or both of them allied with the reigning political network in the departmental capital—meaning that the president in San Salvador had chosen them from that network—they facilitated the political unification of the entire department. When either the governor or commander was not allied with the reigning political network in the department capital, politics took on a more freewheeling quality, rife with conspiracies and frequent violent clashes. Regardless, parish bosses typically acquiesced to the department capital, recognizing that it was better to be a subordinate member of a powerful network than the leader of an inconsequential network.

Departmental capitals produced most every major player in national-level politics. In the first decades after independence these players included Rafael Campo and Vicente Gómez of Sonsonate; Doroteo Vasconcelos, General Inocente Marín, and General Indalecio Miranda from San Vicente; General Gerardo Barrios and General Joaquín Guzmán from San Miguel; and Francisco Dueñas and Manuel Gallardo from San Salvador (La Libertad). In the latter decades of the nineteenth century, new people from other departments rose to prominence, such as General José María Rivas of Cuscatlán, General Francisco Menéndez of Ahuachapán, and Rafael Zaldívar and General Tomás Regalado of Santa Ana, to name just a few. The emergence of political players from departments like Ahuachapán and Santa Ana reflected the surge in coffee production, turning those once marginal areas into economic and political powerhouses.

The major political bosses typically migrated back and forth between their home capital and the national capital in accordance with their political fortunes. The standard route of ascent began in the department capital with service on numerous election councils and in various municipal offices. Then, once a boss had positioned himself atop the hierarchy of the department capital, he got elected to the National Assembly, giving him an opportunity to build alliances at the national level. If he proved adept at political deal-making at the national level and took advantage of opportunities when they presented themselves, and if he received the full electoral and material support of his home network when he needed it, he had the chance to ascend to higher offices, such as judgeships, the cabinet, the vice presidency, or the presidency. In the event that he came to hold one of these high-ranking offices but found himself ousted from power in a military action or a reversal of electoral fortune, he simply returned to his home capital and reentered municipal politics. In the event that his defeat was further compounded by an ouster from his position in the departmental capital, he simply retreated one step further to his private estate, where he and his allies awaited an opportunity to resume political activity. In the worst-case scenario, he was forced into exile, leaving his political and economic fortunes behind.

The political career of Rafael Campo, an important political player from Sonsonate City in the early decades of the republic, illustrates the ups and downs of politics and the movement to and from the national capital. In 1840 Campo served as an elector in the annual municipal elections in Sonsonate City. In the next two years he was elected to the assembly as a deputy. He also was a presidential candidate in 1842. In 1843 he returned to Sonsonate and held the position of regidor on Sonsonate's municipal council. The available sources do not reveal his political activities over the next ten years, but in 1856 he achieved what he had failed to do in 1842: he became president of the republic. When his two-year term ended in 1858, he returned to Sonsonate and temporarily retired from politics. When his national-level rival, Gerardo Barrios of San Miguel, ascended to the presidency in 1860, Campo remained in Sonsonate but kept a low profile, serving only one time in municipal politics— as an elector in 1862. In 1863 Campo joined the rebellion against Barrios led by Francisco Dueñas. Campo was among those who arrested Miguel Saizar, Barrios's departmental governor in Sonsonate City. Dueñas set up a provisional government in Sonsonate and named Campo minister of foreign relations. Later that same year, Campo was selected to serve as first designate to the president. In the years 1864, 1865, 1868, and 1869 Campo was back in Sonsonate City, serving on electoral councils. When General González ousted Dueñas in 1871, he chose Campo as a designate to the president, presumably as a conciliatory move to subdue the opposition. Apparently the tactic failed, because one year later Campo was forced into exile in Nicaragua, suspected of plotting against the González government.[55] The archival trail of Campo's career ends there, but it maps the path of a political boss as he maneuvered through the twists and turns of patronage-based political activity.

Throughout the nineteenth century, national politics followed to a great extent the rise and fall of alliances between departmental networks. For instance, in the mid-1840s San Vicente and San Miguel were allied against Sonsonate and San Salvador. By the late 1850s, after some turnovers at the departmental level, San Vicente allied with Sonsonate against San Salvador and San Miguel. During the early years of nationhood, San Miguel, San Vicente, San Salvador, and Sonsonate constituted the main seats of provincial power. By the latter half of the nineteenth century, their predominance had been usurped by the upstart coffee-producing departments of Santa Ana and La Libertad, and to a lesser extent Ahuachapán and Usulután. The indigo-producing regions of San Miguel and San Vicente waned, as did Sonsonate, which was a minor coffee producer in comparison to its neighbors. Cuscatlán was an important department throughout the nineteenth century. In the first half of the century it was an indigo producer, and even though its economic importance declined in the second half of the nineteenth century, it remained politically relevant because it was the home of a highly skilled boss, General José María Rivas, who made the department a powerful force despite its declining economic fortunes. The remaining departments of Chalatenango, La Paz, Cabañas, Morazán, and La Union were of marginal importance in national politics.

The departmental governor stood at the center of these interdepartmental conflagrations. As liaison between the local and national levels, he participated in most political conflicts. Fortunately, governors, unlike presidents, tended to leave behind copious records that shed light on the wrangling. In almost every case, presidents chose their governors and commanders from the pool of political bosses in the department capital rather than from outside the department, a fact that reflects the weakness of central authority in the nineteenth century. Like feudal barons in medieval Europe, who presided over their estates as if they were their personal patrimony rather than the monarch's property, political bosses in departmental capitals considered the positions of governor and commander to be theirs, and seldom did the national government have the power to resist them. The constitution of 1841 even stipulated that the president had to choose his governor from a list of candidates sent to him by officials in the departmental capital, effectively giving them control over the selection process.[56] Presidents often disobeyed the rule by ignoring the list, but they did not go outside the department to make their selections until the twentieth century, when a stronger central state gave them the power to do so.

Presidents used their power of appointment to reward allies and punish enemies. They might not have appointed outsiders to departmental positions, but neither did they appoint members of an opposition network from within the departments. This practice had reasons both practical and political. Practically, presidents wanted governors whom they could trust to carry out their orders. Politically, they used appointments as patronage rewards to strengthen ties to a department. Because a president almost assuredly came to power with the support of a fraction, if not a minority, of the nation's departmental capitals, his gubernatorial appointments often were drawn from weaker local factions. In these cases, the governor presided over a hostile department and held the difficult position of being an intermediary between his patron on the one side and local opponents on the other. Even in departments where the reigning network in the capital solidly supported the president, and where the governor was drawn from that network, one or two municipalities likely belonged to the opposition and tried to make life difficult for the governor. Fortunately for historians, these conflicts tended to generate revealing evidence into how politics functioned, as we will see in forthcoming chapters.

Battling for the Presidency: The Pinnacle of Politics

The presidency was the ultimate goal of political activity, and conflicts over presidential succession exemplified the political system. Bosses who ascended to the presidency were those who had assembled the most stalwart networks. Because elections were the cornerstone of presidential succession, election day was the moment when a boss solidified his claim to power by demonstrating his ability to better his opponents in the art of electoral control. The network that monopolized a majority, if not all, of the polling stations in the country was the victor. Violent clashes between competing networks commonly preceded elections. These clashes came in the form of coups d'état or protracted wars that sometimes lasted months and occasionally involved armies from neighboring states.

Although the presidency changed hands fifty-eight times between 1841 and 1898, and thirty-three different people held the office (see table A1 in the appendix), the situation is less complex than it appears because only thirteen transfers took place between rival patronage networks (see table 1.4). The transfers listed in table 1.4 omit minor shuffling within a dominant network, as well as instances in which rivals held office only for a few days. Table 1.4 lists only substantive changes, when a reigning network succumbed to a competitor, or to its own internal divisions.

Each network listed in table 1.4 ascended to the presidency because of its ability to establish political dominance, but opponents were always present. Certain municipalities, if not entire departments, opposed the dominant network. The typical problem facing each president was his inability to centralize power permanently, even in the wake of military victory. Opponents waited for the right moment to strike, usually with the approach of an election, hoping to knock the incumbents out of power. Allies of a sitting president also looked to elections expectantly, hoping to be chosen as successor. In some cases, a president shunned all comers and attempted to remain in power—a move that usually required the drafting

Table 1.4   Main Transfers of Power between Rival Networks at the National Level, 1841–1903

1841–1844	Francisco Malespín, Juan Lindo, Escolastico Marín
1844–1851	Joaquín Eufrasio Guzmán, Eugenio Aguilar, Doroteo Vasconcellos
1851–1854	Francisco Dueñas
1854–1856	José María San Martín
1856–1858	Francisco Dueñas, Rafael Campo
1858–1863	Gerardo Barrios, Joaquín Eufrasio Guzmán
1863–1871	Francisco Dueñas
1871–1876	Santiago González
1876–1885	Rafael Zaldívar
1885–1890	Francisco Menéndez
1890–1894	Carlos Ezeta
1894–1898	Rafael Antonio Gutiérrez
1898–1903	Tomás Regalado

of a new constitution exempting them from the standard prohibition against consecutive terms. However, changing the constitution was risky business. Not only did it exacerbate the opposition, it also turned allies into rivals by frustrating their hopes of rising in the political ranks.

Because copious evidence exists for the 1895 vice presidential election, it is an informative case study. But as a metaphor for nineteenth-century politics, it may not be ideal due to the late date at which it occurred. How much did the 1895 election reflect earlier electoral patterns, such as those of the 1840s and 1850s? The absence of equally comprehensive electoral documentation for earlier years, most likely burned in the fire of 1889, makes it difficult to answer this question. But partial data from municipal and departmental archives indicate that the monopolized voting of 1895 mimicked prior electoral patterns.

For example, in the presidential election of December 1841 (one of three presidential elections held that year), multiple candidates participated in the election, suggesting that no single boss was able to establish unmitigated supremacy. But when a candidate won a particular voting district, he tended to do so unanimously.[57] In Sonsonate City, where voting was conducted in the rural cantones, results were unanimous in four of the city's six cantones, while four different candidates each won at least one cantón each (see table 1.5).

Similarly, in the election of August 1841, Juan Lindo won all 183 votes from Atiquizaya District. In December 1843, the municipality of San Antonio reported all 77 of its votes in favor of Jacinto Huezo, while the neighboring cantón of Sonzacate gave all 50 of its votes to Eugenio Aguilar. In a later election, December 1853, the municipality of Santa Catarina Masahuat cast all 100 of its votes for José María Silva, who was one of many candidates running in that contest.[58] This admixture of results suggests strongly that when multiple networks competed for power at the national level in the 1840s and 1850s, each local boss fell in line behind his particular patron and endeavored to produce a unanimous result in his favor.

By contrast, unanimous results at the national level occurred only when one network dominated, meaning it had eliminated its rivals through negotiation or force. The election of Gutiérrez in 1895 offers one such example. The election of 1891 offers another. It was held in the wake

Table 1.5   Results from Sonsonate City, Presidential Election of December 1841

Voting District	Candidate	Votes	% of Total
Santo Domingo	Antonio José Cañas	43	100
San Antonio	Manuel José Arce	23	100
Nahuilingo	José Mariano Campo	56	100
Barrio del Angel	Pedro Arce	29	100
Barrio el Sur	José Mariano Campo	22	47
	Pedro Arce	19	40
	Manuel José Arce	9	19
Barrio el Norte	José Mariano Campo	26	38
	Juan José Guzmán	17	25
	Antonio José Cañas	14	20
	Pedro Arce	5	7
	Manuel José Arce	4	6
	three others	1 each	4

Source: Junta de Elección, Sonsonate, May 11, 1841, AMS, Box "Elecciones, 1840–9."

of General Carlos Ezeta's successful coup against President Menéndez in 1890. Ezeta won the election by a margin of 52,342 votes to 19, with his brother, General Antonio Ezeta, gaining the vice presidency by an almost identical margin.[59] In another example, Francisco Dueñas ran unopposed in the election of 1852 and then commented on the "unanimous voice of the citizenry" that had put him in office.[60] In the election of 1864, Dueñas again ran unopposed, this time after forcing Gerardo Barrios from power in a military invasion from Guatemala. Partial results from that election suggest that Dueñas's victory was appropriately unanimous. He won Sonsonate Department by a margin of 1,442 votes to 20. All twenty "opposition" votes went to Dueñas's close allies, including Rafael Campo of Sonsonate and Manuel Gallardo of Nueva San Salvador.[61]

In sum, although nineteenth-century electoral returns are incomplete, they show a recurrent pattern. When a single network went unchallenged, voting was unanimous; when multiple networks competed, local affiliates produced unanimous results at the municipal level in favor of their national-level patron.

The Discourse of Democracy

Electoral contests were accompanied by a specific discourse, a unique language of politics in which both incumbent and challenger recited certain words and phrases as part of their participation in an election. The discourse was laced with appeals to democracy and references to the value of electoral liberty. Political actors celebrated the principles of democracy, freedom of suffrage, and popular will. They did so not only in their internal correspondence, but also in public pronouncements. Furthermore, they did so without regard for their supposed ideological differences. Liberals and conservatives alike employed the discourse of democracy with equal verve. A few examples here will suffice to illustrate broader patterns, with more examples appearing in the pages ahead.

One example comes from the national level in the late 1840s and early 1850s, during the transition from the Guzmán-Aguilar-Palacios network to the Dueñas network. The former held power between 1844 and 1851, and the latter for the next three years, between 1851 and 1854. (See table 1.1 above, and table A1 in the appendix.) The Guzmán-Aguilar-Palacios network was "liberal," whereas the Dueñas network was "conservative," making this a particularly clear example.[62]

As historians Lowell Gudmundson, Héctor Lindo-Fuentes, and Sajid Herrera have pointed out, the terms *liberal* and *conservative* mattered little in El Salvador in terms of actual ideological differences. Editorialists and spokespersons used the labels to disparage one another, as we saw above in the case of the 1895 vice presidential election, when supporters of the victor, Prudencio Alfaro, dismissed the newspaper that supported their rival as "clerical and Catholic." The members of the Guzman-Aguilar-Palacios network identified themselves as liberal and referred to their rivals as "conservative men" who wanted to discredit El Salvador's "liberal institutions."[63] But the more central purpose of criticizing their rivals was to hail their own commitment to democracy. As just one example, Isidro Menéndez, the famed jurist and priest of liberal political persuasions, delivered a speech in the National Cathedral in September 1848 celebrating the "expression of the enlightened and free will of the great majority of the population, which is the basic foundation of any political association."[64] Similarly, the lead editorial in the government's official newspaper (then named *La Gaceta*) in August 1849 accused conservatives of being retrogrades who believed that "liberty, democracy and republicanism are worthless phrases." The editorial went on to claim that those "absolutist" enemies would be beaten back by the "irresistible force of people's opinions." It then hailed the United States as a model for the world because its "democratic institutions march forward steadily," proving to the world that "the ideas of liberty and equality are not utopianisms, but realizable goals."[65]

A few weeks later, various editorials in *La Gaceta* celebrated the liberty of the recent election to choose a new president, the successor to Doroteo Vasconcelos. That election was in fact a classic example of an insignificant shuffle within a reigning patronage network. Nevertheless, one editorial opened by disparaging conservatives as "enemies of popular, republican and constitutional systems, and of everything democratic." Even though none of those rivals had competed in the election, editorialists proceeded to proclaim that conservatives' failures in the most recent elections proved El Salvador to be guided by "the people" and "popular institutions."[66] Another editorial hailed the elections as having chosen the president "according to the will of the majority of Salvadorans," which "presage[s] peace and progress for the nation."[67]

When the government then changed hands from the "liberal" Guzmán-Aguilar-Palacios network to the "conservative" Dueñas network, the discourse remained unchanged. Admittedly, an occasional editorial appeared in the pages of *La Gaceta* cautioning Salvadorans against untried and untested new methods based on "utopian, impractical theories"— which was code for liberalism. But Dueñas and his allied spokespersons continued to celebrate progress and democracy with the same enthusiasm as their predecessors. Even though Dueñas had come to power in a nondemocratic manner, and he and his allies remained in power through equally nondemocratic means, he hailed the "popular vote" that put him in the presidency once again in 1853.[68] Shortly thereafter, the lead editorial in *La Gaceta* celebrated the "representative system" for guaranteeing "personal liberty" and for being guided by "people's demands."[69] Just two weeks later, the president of the National Assembly took the closing of that year's congressional session as an opportunity to describe public opinion as the "sure guide of representative governments." Dueñas, too, spoke upon the assembly's closing, describing the congressional body as the "organ of public opinion."[70]

A similar example is provided by the rhetorical expressions of Luciano Hernández, an intellectual and military official who held various high-ranking posts in both the second reign of the "conservative" Francisco Dueñas (1863–1871) and the subsequent "liberal" regime of Rafael Zaldívar (1876–1885). During the Dueñas era, Hernández wrote that "popular suffrage, the independence of the three branches of government and a free press . . . constitute the essence of a republican, popular and representative system." A few years later he wrote, "This government affirms to the population and to the popular opinion in general that the institution of direct representation is the most explicit guide for the protection of the social wellbeing that we enjoy by virtue of nature." He continued, "The collective will of the nation is the most powerful executor of the laws that protect our justice, peace, liberty and labor."[71]

A few examples from the municipal level further reveal the discourse of democracy that accompanied political activity in El Salvador's patronage system. In 1866 the loser of an election in San Vicente City accused the victor of "supplanting the greater portion of the voting . . . which is counter to free suffrage in a Republican country." In 1874, in Atiquizaya (Ahuachapán Department), an opposition network described the tactics of the incumbents as "counter to the values of majority rule." In 1892 a member of a defeated network denounced the victors because they "prevented us from giving our free vote for the person that we wanted to elect." And in 1925, in the village of San Cristobal (Cuscatlán Department), the challengers described themselves as "free citizens" who were upholding "the just principles of the law [against] . . . a small group of poorly intentioned citizens trained in the art of control."[72]

In the midst of a political system dominated by patronage and clientelism, these references to democracy seem out of place until they are cast in the proper context. The references to democracy originated in the constitutions and the corresponding formal rules. Those rules declared El Salvador to be a democratic republic in which mass opinion reigned supreme. The egalitarian language was appropriated by challengers, but given new meaning. Their appeal to democracy was not meant to create a genuine democracy. Rather, challengers appealed to democracy as a way of demanding that the incumbent network step aside.

A political conflagration in the coffee-producing municipality of Alegría (Usulután Department) in the early twentieth century illustrates the actual meaning of democratic discourse. The election pitted Ramón Bautista, the challenger, against Alonzo Iglesias, the incumbent. On the eve of the municipal election of 1927, Bautista accused Iglesias of planning to monopolize the election in the same manner that he had for the prior decade. "Iglesias has acted like an oligarch for the past fourteen long years," claimed Bautista, "employing the military and civil powers at his disposal to threaten humble workers whose only crime was having triumphed legally in the elections." Bautista pressed on, saying that "[if] things continue in this way, freedom of suffrage is a myth. . . . We only ask for liberty for a free people able to vote for whom they wish."[73]

At first glance, Bautista's denunciation suggests that the 1927 election revolved around class-based conflict—an elite was denying free suffrage to local masses who wanted to select someone else as their public representative. Indeed, Iglesias was a wealthy coffee grower who had monopolized municipal government since at least 1921. Upon further inspection, the story becomes more complex, because Bautista was as much an elite political boss as Iglesias. Bautista too was a landowner. On his finca "Santa Clara" he grew coffee and raised cattle. Moreover, he was the head of a patronage network that had traded power back and forth with Iglesias's network for the previous forty years. Since the 1890s, Alegría had known only the rule of Bautista or Iglesias. Now, in 1927, after Iglesias had held power for the past decade, Bautista believed that it was his turn to hold power once again, but Iglesias was refusing to step aside, which prompted Bautista to denounce him as an antidemocratic oligarch. Bautista eventually won the election of 1927. In succeeding years, he conducted politics in the traditional manner. Either he or his son, or a loyal subordinate, controlled political office. This pattern went on until 1937, when Iglesias regrouped his forces and regained control of the municipal government yet again.[74] The events in Alegría illustrate how the democracy-laden discourse of the challengers grew out of long-standing conflicts between competing bosses.

According to the informal rules, all political bosses hailed democracy and declared themselves defenders of popular will. But a slight variation in the rules occurred when incumbents responded to challengers' accusations of nondemocratic conduct. It was at that moment that incumbents occasionally vilified democracy. When they did so, they characterized democracy as a depravity, accusing the challengers of stirring up the masses and risking mob rule, which would destroy the lives of all honest citizens. An example of this variant of political discourse is provided by the incumbent network in the municipality of San Rafael (Cuscatlán Department) during the election of 1895. The incumbent referred to the challenger in the following terms: "For more than one year this individual of pernicious character . . . has tried to ensure in the local elections the triumph of candidates that do not correspond in any way to our social and political interests, because they [the candidates] are comprised of the ignorant class, with all of their Machiavellian seductions, hoping to dictate their will upon the public and social interests of this municipality."[75] Most political bosses shared this view of democracy, regardless of whether they were challenger or incumbent. But within the peculiar confines of the Salvadoran political system and its informal rules, only incumbents discredited democracy in that manner. It was their way of telling challengers to abandon their bid for power.

Incumbents sometimes employed a variation of this strategy by accusing challengers of acting immorally by looking to alter the status quo. For example, in 1845 the governor of San Vicente chastised a municipal-level political boss for allying with a rival network seeking to oust the incumbents: "Your actions can only be taken as contrary to the current administration . . . and therefore will include you amongst those who are of immoral principles and against the decent customs of the nation. . . . It is your responsibility to defeat the sources of discord, to procure the unity of your village, to not confuse gossip with true patriotism, and to avoid individuals with whom it is not proper to associate."[76] And in 1895, the governor of San Miguel Department demanded that a rival network "refrain from advancing political licentiousness" and engaging in acts of "immorality . . . and indecency."[77]

*   *   *

The vice presidential election of 1895 is a revelatory moment in the history of politics in El Salvador because its uniquely comprehensive documentation survived into the archival record. As for the election itself, there was nothing particularly unique about it—a fact that allows it to stand as a metaphor for the broader whole of electoral politics in nineteenth- and early twentieth-century El Salvador. In it we see an impressive adherence to a formal system of procedures in which multiple candidates competed in elections for which many people turned out to vote—at least 40 percent of the eligible electorate. The results show that it was a reasonably competitive race between the two main candidates, Prudencio Alfaro and Carlos Meléndez. But the voting results, when studied in close detail, reveal clearly that a set of informal rules was in play. Elections were highly managed affairs in which whoever controlled voting in the municipalities produced unanimous or near-unanimous results in favor of their particular candidate. The key to electoral success at the national level was thus to cobble together alliances with as many municipalities as possible and then use the political capital of those municipalities to beat back rivals. In peaceful electoral contests that capital came in the form of votes, whereas in violent clashes it took the form of soldiers and war material. But even if the outcomes of an electoral contest were predetermined by a violent clash in which only one network was left standing, no political leader assumed office without first proving his ability to produce an election in his favor. That paradoxical adherence to the letter of democracy while following a practice of authoritarianism defined political life in El Salvador.

CHAPTER 2

NATIONAL-LEVEL NETWORKS IN CONFLICT IN THE NINETEENTH CENTURY

El Salvador was not Brazil, where independence from Portugal came with intact political institutions and a centralized government. When Napoleon invaded the Iberian Peninsula in 1807, the Portuguese monarchy fled to Brazil and brought with it a complete government. Prominent Brazilians might have resisted the arrival of the monarchy as a threat to their resident authority, but as historian Richard Graham points out, Brazilians of wealth and property accepted the new situation, because "if forced to choose between liberty and order, the propertied chose order."[1] Elite Brazilians placed a high premium on stability because of their reliance on slavery, believing that even minor disruptions in society might lead to something horrific like the Haitian Revolution.[2]

Over the next eight decades, Brazil was characterized by a stable political system. Two emperors held power for the seventy years between independence and the formation of the first republic in 1889. The emperor was the undisputed central authority, and beneath him were the National Congress and presidents of the states, who in turn presided over regional and municipal authorities. The entire system was held together by a vast and intricate network of patronage in which superior authorities had the power to appoint, and subordinates offered services in hopes of receiving appointment. A local juror once referred to the system as the "Great Pyramid."[3]

Politics in El Salvador was also based upon patronage, but under different circumstances than in Brazil. Like Mexico and Colombia, El Salvador lacked central authority at the outset of independence.[4] When Central America gained its independence from Spain in 1821, a centralized administration failed to emerge. The federal government collapsed under the weight of insolvency and regional rivalries between its leaders. Thus, although independence had come without the warfare that ravaged much of the rest of Spanish America, peace soon collapsed into incessant battles that exacerbated the already desperate financial situation. Between 1824 and 1842 El Salvador participated in forty interstate battles, second only to Guatemala's fifty-one.[5] Following the collapse of the federation, instability reigned in El Salvador. State institutions were born defunct, and no single political group could generate sufficient strength to consolidate authority. Instead of one great pyramid, the political system of El Salvador consisted of numerous little pyramids, distinct patronage networks that battled one another for control over the central state—however decrepit and insolvent it may have been.

Making sense of nineteenth-century politics in El Salvador can be a challenge. The government changed hands frequently, and distinctions between administrations can be difficult to discern. The presidency changed hands forty-two times between 1841 and 1861 and an additional sixteen times between 1861 and 1899 (see table A1 in the appendix). Even when the long regimes of Francisco Dueñas (1863–1871) and Rafael Zaldívar (1876–1885) are included in the calculation, the average administration lasted just over one year.[6] However, this turnover becomes more intelligible when it is examined in the context of patronage alliances. Many people held the presidency, but they belonged to only a handful of political networks, and much of the turnover in office resulted from inconsequential shuffling within individual networks. The number of actual transitions between rival political networks was small, as was the number of people who held positions of genuine leadership in those networks.

What follows is a series of vignettes showing patronage-based political networks operating at the national level in the nineteenth century. Limitations in the documentary record prevent the construction of a seamless narrative of nineteenth-century politics. But records allow for this series of substantive glimpses into seven distinct moments, starting with a case study from San Vicente Department in 1845 and ending with a coup in 1894. Additional information provides a look at José María Rivas, a regional strongman from the region around Cojutepeque, and at the political battles over departmental boundaries. The chapter focuses on the national level, leaving analysis of the details of network building at the municipal level to the next two chapters.

Sensuntepeque, 1845

The first example of patronage-based politics derives from discord in San Vicente Department in 1845, a year of great political instability. The regime of Francisco Malespín had been overthrown after much war and bloodshed, and General Joaquín Eufrasio Guzmán of San Miguel was in power. Most of San Vicente Department, including San Vicente City, supported Guzmán.[7] Guzmán faced a variety of actual and potential conspiracies, and he looked to consolidate his regime by bolstering the army and infusing money into the national government's coffers. He ordered each department to contribute resources to that cause. In San Vicente's case the price was two hundred men and 5,000 pesos. The governor of San Vicente sent out circulars to the alcaldes: "The Supreme Government has ordered this department to recruit 200 men to augment the forces which sustain the territorial integrity and public liberties of El Salvador. The following distribution has been established for each municipality; the men are to be present in this city by the last day of the present month."[8] Depending on any given town's size, it was expected to produce between four and thirty men. All sixteen municipalities in the department, with the exception of one reticent municipality, supported Guzmán and sent the soldiers to San Vicente City carrying declarations of adhesion to the governor. The defiant municipality was Sensuntepeque, which refused to send its allotment of twenty-five men.[9]

Sensuntepeque's opposition is odd, given that it was the birthplace and political stronghold of Doroteo Vasconcelos, a major political player from the department and an ally of Guzmán. But in 1845, Sensuntepeque was run by an opposition network led by Comandante Santo Cuellar, who was allied with General José Escolástico Marín, another major player in San Vicente Department who had been president of the republic on two occasions in 1842.[10] Just after Sensuntepeque received the orders to produce the twenty-five soldiers, Guzmán's fears seemed confirmed; a cache of weapons, including two canons, had been uncovered in the house of one of Marín's allies in San Vicente City.[11] The governor referred to Marín as "*el faccioso*" (the factional one) and "the enemy of the nation."

The language that the governor used to castigate Cuellar and his fellow bosses in Sensuntepeque exemplified interpatronage conflict: "Despite the warnings that I have directed at Comandante Cuellar, you continue working in a contrary manner, which will force me to use whatever measures are necessary to ensure the tranquility and well-being of the Salvadoran people. As you are my subalterns [*subalternos*] and functionaries [*funcionarios*], I will not tolerate any act of disorder, to say nothing of subversion against this government that I represent."[12] The governor was informing the officials of Sensuntepeque, in no uncertain terms, that he expected them to recognize his authority and follow his orders. His discourse established hierarchy, himself as the departmental executive, the officials of Sensuntepeque as his underlings. The terms *subalterno* and *funcionario* were standard words used by upper-level bosses when communicating with those they perceived as inferiors.

Shortly after the arrival of the governor's threat, Sensuntepeque capitulated and sent the twenty-five men to San Vicente. In less than two weeks, however, most of the recruits had deserted, prompting yet another conflict with the governor. He ordered Cuellar and his cohorts to round up the deserters: "The soldiers have committed the unforgivable crime of deserting the army, and as it is probable that they have returned to that village, I order you to take active measures to capture and return them here."[13] The municipality's sluggish response to the request, combined with its continued alliance with Marín, incited yet another denunciation from the governor: "Your continued association with Marín can only encourage plots against the actual administration and aid enemies of the State, as well as involve yourselves in immoral acts against the good customs of the people. . . . It is your obligation to resist the motives of discord and work for unity in your region and not confuse true patriotism with scandals that are in no way convenient to facilitate."[14] In this letter, the governor once again employed the archetypal language of patronage disputes. He defined Sensuntepeque's opposition as "immoral" and "discordant," terms that would be used constantly over the next one hundred years as bosses denounced one another. Unfortunately, the remaining portions of the governor's logbook are lost, and thus the outcome of the conflict of 1845 is unknown. Nevertheless, the evidence is sufficient to expose interpatronage battling. The governor was presiding over a department that was uniformly behind him except for one municipality, Sensuntepeque, which became a focal point of conflict.

Aguilar/Palacios, 1846

Another glimpse into the workings of a patronage network in action comes from the tumult over the presidency in 1846. As we saw in the prior case study, in the aftermath of the fall of Francisco Malespín in 1844, Joaquín Guzmán of San Miguel assumed the presidency to complete Malespín's term. In February 1846, in a typical example of minor shuffling within an incumbent patronage network, Senator Fermín Palacios succeeded Guzmán and served as interim president while the National Assembly elected a Guzmán ally, Eugenio Aguilar, to serve as president for the term of 1846 to 1848. But apparently Palacios did not take kindly to the approval of Aguilar as Guzmán's successor, because for reasons not made clear by the available evidence, he teamed up with Bishop Jorge de Viteri y Ungo and overthrew Aguilar in a coup four months later. The coup took Aguilar by surprise, but he and his allies quickly organized themselves. José María San Martín, a prominent political figure in San Salvador and an ally of Aguilar, contacted Doroteo Vasconcelos, then governor of San Vicente, who fired off letters to allies in San Miguel and Cojutepeque (Cuscatlán Department). "Our President was forced to surrender power to Senator Fermín Palacios," wrote Vasconcelos, rallying the troops. "It is urgent that we oppose these fatal and sad results . . . we must openly support the legitimate President."[15]

A notable ally in San Miguel was Gerardo Barrios, who was then serving as departmental commander and who was also Guzmán's son-in-law. A few days after sending out his letters, Vasconcelos received confirmation from Barrios and the others and sent a letter back to San Martín, announcing the readiness of the alliance. Messengers were exceptionally busy during crises such as these, running correspondence back and forth between departments, since the telegraph was not yet available. Vasconcelos addressed San Martín as "the Jefe who commands our forces." He wrote, "I say with anticipation that in the Department of San Miguel, as in that of 'La Paz' and in that which I command, we disavow whatever individual comes to power by way of unconstitutional means."

Backed by these supporters, Aguilar launched a countercoup that forced Palacios to step down. Bishop Viteri y Ungo fled into exile in Honduras. The return of Aguilar incited yet another countercoup, this time by one of Malespín's brothers, who invaded El Salvador with a small army from Honduras. But Barrios and others repulsed the invasion.[16] Aguilar remained in office for the duration of his term and then handed power off to Vasconcelos, who stayed in office until 1851.

San Vicente City, 1852

Six years later, in 1852, another political confrontation broke out in San Vicente Department, providing further insight into interpatronage rivalries. The president at the time was Francisco Dueñas, who came to power despite the opposition of most of San Vicente Department, which remained an ally of Guzmán and his cohorts in San Miguel. Dueñas's gubernatorial appointment in San Vicente City faced the difficult task of supervising a uniformly hostile department. It was exactly the opposite of what a previous governor had faced in the 1845 case study above, when the entire department was loyal to him and the president, with the exception of the lone municipality of Sensuntepeque. In 1852, San Vicente City was under the control of the Vasconcelos family. The governor referred to the municipal council of the city as "*el partido de oposición*" (the opposition party).[17]

Dueñas suspected the Vasconcelos clan of organizing a rebellion from San Vicente, so he instructed his governor to bolster the barracks in San Vicente City by recruiting troops from other municipalities. The governor ordered each municipality in the department to send horses and soldiers "to the central plaza of this city to support the forces of the national government."[18] Not surprisingly, most of the municipalities ignored the request, and the few soldiers who did arrive quickly deserted. The governor put a five-peso bounty on the head of each deserter, but none of the municipalities responded to the reward. The governor then raised the bounty to fifteen pesos, and still none of the municipalities complied. "None of the deserters have been captured," he wrote, "[owing to] the inertia of the Alcaldías of this department, principally the officials of this city [San Vicente], who have rejected my repeated requests."[19] The emerging dispute between the governor and the municipal council of San Vicente took on a curious spatial element in that their offices were located just a couple of blocks from one another, and messengers for the opposing sides must have crossed paths as they carried the correspondence back and forth between the offices.

As the municipal elections of 1852 approached, the governor hoped to oust the Vasconcelos clan, and the tactic he chose was accusing the Vasconcelos-dominated municipal council of improprieties. In October he detailed a litany of inappropriate behavior and abuses, such as failing to maintain the city's infrastructure and absconding with municipal funds. The accusations were typical of the criticisms that networks used in their attempts to nullify rivals. Normally, someone other than the governor would submit the initial denunciation, leaving him in a position to appear as a neutral judge. But in this case the governor took it upon himself to write the denunciation. Whether or not the accusations were true is impossible to determine and effectively irrelevant; all that matters for our present analysis is that they gave the governor the pretext on which to demand the removal of the council's members.

The governor continued to berate the municipal council in a series of reports, and he also began mentioning his power to disband the council. But before he acted on this threat he found a new angle of attack. In late October he accused Dolores Hernández, one of the municipality's regidores, of stealing a horse from his hacienda. The governor demanded

Hernández's resignation. Again, the truth of the governor's denunciation is impossible to determine, although Hernández denied the charge and refused to step down. The remainder of the council supported him and took their appeal to the Supreme Court, whose members must have opposed Dueñas, because it ruled in Hernández's favor and ordered the governor to withdraw his request for the regidor's resignation. The governor's lengthy response to the court stands as a testament to nineteenth-century politics. He informed the court that the president of the republic is the "Jefe Máximo" and authority originated with him, not the court. He insisted that both the court and the governor are servants to the president, just as the members of San Vicente's municipal council are subalterns to him. He claimed that everyone's duty is to obey the orders of their superiors: "If the officials of San Vicente were allowed to abide by the Court's ruling, no subaltern employee would comply with the orders of the Executive. For this reason, a basic tenet of public authority is the Executive having all necessary independence to guard his employees for faults or excesses which they might commit in the exercise of their positions. . . . All of this seems basically fundamental enough for me to contend that the Court has no authority to command me without prior declaration from the Senate."[20] The governor's appeal to the senate reflected the fact that it was safely under the control of Dueñas and his network.

The governor's response to the court portrayed a political order that every patronage boss hoped for, one in which he held the presidency and all power flowed downward from him. It was not until well into the twentieth century that such a condition came to exist in El Salvador. Until then, networks reigned only temporarily, unable to consolidate authority and facing constant acts of subterfuge on the part of opponents. The 1852 case from San Vicente City is an example of the everyday forms of political conflict in mid-nineteenth-century El Salvador. Functionaries of the incumbent network kept a vigil for rebellious activities and worked constantly, if rarely successfully, to undermine their rivals' political base.

Barrios, 1859–1863

The conflict surrounding the ascent and reign of Gerardo Barrios (1859–1863) provides another example in which patronage alliances are evident.

Barrios had been a major political player from San Miguel Department throughout the preceding two decades, but 1857 marked the moment at which he began his climb to the top of the political hierarchy. In that year, Barrios returned to El Salvador after serving as a commander in the army dispatched to Nicaragua to fight the American filibuster William Walker. On June 7, 1857, Barrios landed his forces, numbering around 1,500 men, at the port of La Libertad. The president at the time was Rafael Campo of Sonsonate, a Barrios adversary. Barrios sent word to Campo that he intended to bring his victorious army to the capital city, which at that time was located in Cojutepeque because San Salvador had been destroyed in an earthquake in 1854. Campo and other high-ranking officials distrusted Barrios, suspecting that he would use his army to seize power. One of Campo's allies during the tumult was Ramón Belloso, who had been the main commander of the Salvadoran troops in Nicaragua. Belloso and other members of the officer corps accused Barrios of treason, and on June 10 Campo relieved Barrios of his command and named himself chief of the Expeditionary Army. Barrios responded by proclaiming himself to be in rebellion against the government and began marching his army toward Cojutepeque.

In the meantime, Campo had been preparing for battle. He had placed Colonels Ciriaco Choto and Juan Choto, both of Sonsonate, in charge of organizing the capital's defenses. They drew soldiers and supplies from their home region as well as from Santa Ana, an allied department. A military clash seemed inevitable, had it not been for the timely interjection of José María San Martín, who negotiated a deal between the opposing chiefs. The specifics of the deal are unknown, but they probably revolved around the question of who would succeed Campo after his term expired in January 1858. On June 13 Barrios turned command of his army over to Campo, and on June 20 Campo announced that the conflict had been resolved. He made specific mention of "the recruits, most of them volunteer soldiers, sent by Sonsonate and Santa Ana Departments," to defend the national government.[21]

When Campo stepped down in 1858, Barrios and his allies were the principal beneficiaries. Miguel Santín del Castillo became president. He was born in San Vicente and owned family properties there, but as a young man he had moved to San Miguel and become a nominal ally of Barrios.[22] The vice presidency went to Joaquín Guzmán, Barrios's father-in-law and his closest ally. The position of first designate to the president went to one of Campo's allies, Lorenzo Zepeda of Sonsonate. Barrios became second designate to the president and also the minister of foreign relations.

In June 1858 Santín stepped down temporarily from the presidency. His departure was ostensibly due to illness, but it probably had more to do with politics and the looming conflict over the location of the new national capital in either San Salvador or in the new city of Nueva San Salvador (now Santa Tecla). Barrios assumed the presidency and held it until September 1858, when Santín returned. Relations between Santín and Barrios dissolved shortly thereafter, for reasons that remain unclear. Santín likely suspected Barrios of harboring designs on the presidency. For whatever reason, he ordered Barrios to retire his post as commander of the army. Barrios agreed to resign on the condition that Santín resign from office as well. In January 1859 they both stepped down, arranging for the National Assembly to choose the next president. Barrios, who was serving as a senator from San Miguel, proposed his father-in-law, Joaquín Guzmán. Santín had since formed an alliance with Sonsonate and opposed Guzmán, knowing full well that he and Barrios were virtually the same.

The National Assembly became center stage for the debate over Santín's successor. Representatives from each departmental network had to choose sides. San Miguel, San Salvador, and Santa Ana supported Barrios. Sonsonate, San Vicente, and Cuscatlán backed Santín, as did the bosses of Nueva San Salvador, dissidents from San Salvador Department.[23] Manuel Gallardo described the conflict in his memoirs. He was then serving as a deputy from Suchitoto District in Cuscatlán Department. It was only his first year in the assembly, but he was president of the Chamber of Deputies and thus held an important tactical position in the coming vote. He wrote of the intense lobbying to which he and the other deputies were subject. "Barrios constantly demanded that I side with him," he wrote.[24] Barrios ultimately prevailed, despite Gallardo's opposition, because he had accumulated enough allies in the assembly to get Guzmán elected president and also to pass a resolution declaring Santín and his allies to be in open rebellion. The bulk of Santín's supporters, including Francisco Dueñas and the Choto family, fled into exile in Guatemala. Guzmán then retired from office six weeks later, allowing Barrios to become president.[25]

Barrios assumed the presidency on March 9, 1859, and remained in office for most of the next four years. It was a time of heavy conflict, owing to the bitter political environment. Barrios invested most of his time and energy in preparing for war with the exiles, who had allied with Rafael Carrera in Guatemala and were preparing to join Carrera's invasion of El Salvador. Needing to bolster his defenses, Barrios initiated a broad mobilization campaign to recruit soldiers and accumulate supplies. One of his first acts was to seize the lands and properties of the exiles and sell them off to allies. As one of the nation's wealthiest people, Dueñas had much to lose, including two exceptionally fertile plantations outside Nueva San Salvador, "El Espino" and "Santa Elena," as well as numerous urban properties in San Salvador.[26]

Barrios then ordered each department to produce soldiers, money, and war material. Barrios's gubernatorial appointees oversaw the collection. Fortunately, many of the letters and communiqués between the governors and the national government have survived. They depict a constant shuffling of troops, the collection of loans, both forced and voluntary, the transfer of mules and supplies, and the mobilization of militias.[27] Just as in San Vicente in 1845 and 1852, those regions loyal to Barrios readily furnished the mandated resources, while opposing departments balked, becoming points of never-ending conflict for the regime.

The example of Sonsonate is edifying. The department was a center of opposition to Barrios, and its strategic location close to the Guatemalan border ensured that it would be an important region in the coming war. As all the main families of Sonsonate were opposed to Barrios, he was forced to choose a relative nobody, Miguel Saizar, as his governor. Only once in the previous two decades had Saizar been involved in politics in Sonsonate City, and then only as an elector in a municipal election. Saizar was aware of his fortune in being promoted to one of the more important offices in the country and endeavored to please his patron. He sent a constant stream of letters to San Salvador, laden with optimistic assessments. He wrote of Sonsonate's readiness to face the invasion, condemned the low moral character of the opposition—whom Saizar called the *"culebras"* (snakes)—and heralded the greatness of the Barrios regime. But a closer reading of the correspondence reveals that Saizar faced unending problems.

Saizar failed to subdue the opposition or produce resources for Barrios's army. None of the local landowners willingly gave money, and all of them resisted Saizar's attempts at forced loans. Whereas the governors of other departments were generating thousands of pesos in revenue, Saizar managed only a few hundred. Landowners refused to surrender their laborers for militia training, and Saizar's recruiting agents repeatedly returned to Sonsonate from the surrounding environs empty-handed. One of these agents, who had been sent to recruit around the port city of Acajutla, reported that his "efforts were in vain." He also wrote of "the necessity of procuring a jail for this miserable village in order to hold the recruits."[28] Of the conscripts that Saizar did obtain, many deserted and most of the rest were needed in Sonsonate to guard against conspiracies and sabotage by local opponents.

Despite Sonsonate's resistance, Barrios assembled a sizable army, but not one strong enough to hold off the Guatemalans and the Salvadoran exiles. They invaded El Salvador from the west in March 1863. Barrios's forces were pushed steadily back toward San Salvador. In June, Barrios received a fatal blow when one of his main commanders, Santiago González, changed sides. He and his entire army of four thousand men joined the invading force. By September, Barrios's army had been driven all the way back to the capital city. The invasion culminated in October with the siege of San Salvador, forcing Barrios and the remnants of his army to flee to the east. Dueñas became the next president, his second stint in that role.[29]

Over the next two years Barrios was to be found in Costa Rica and Nicaragua, plotting the overthrow of Dueñas. In 1865, the first element of his plan was put into action in San Miguel. General José Trinidad Cabañas, Barrios's brother-in-law, seized the municipal plaza in San Miguel. Dueñas sent an army under the command of Santiago González and Indalecio Miranda of San Vicente to defeat the rebellion. They did so and executed Cabañas in the process. Barrios was later arrested in Nicaragua. The Nicaraguan government agreed to extradite him to El Salvador on Dueñas's promise that he would not be harmed, but Dueñas had him executed anyway.

Barrios is commonly portrayed by students of Salvadoran history as a martyr of Carrera's expansionist aims and Dueñas's treasonous acts. A case for this argument can be made. More relevant to the present discussion, however, is how the rise and fall of Barrios symbolizes the pattern of internal Salvadoran politics. Barrios was the classic nineteenth-century political player. He was a military commander, landowner, and political boss. He first rose to power in his home base of San Miguel and went on to hold numerous civil and military posts at both the national and departmental levels. His political network was built upon a solid foundation of family ties. His two closest allies were his father-in-law, Joaquín Guzmán, and his brother-in-law General Cabañas. He had made a career participating in and negotiating alliances between departmental networks. He rose to power on the strength of his alliances, and he fell because his opponents had the capacity to form bigger, stronger alliances, in this case with an outsider, Carrera of Guatemala.

Juntas de Notables, 1876 and 1890

When a single network dominated, its leading members faced the difficult task of selecting the one person from among their ranks who would serve as president. Unless they could reconcile members' competing aspirations peacefully, intranetwork conflict became a real possibility. If a reigning network succumbed to an internal power struggle, it became vulnerable to attack by rivals and thus faced the prospect of losing power entirely. We saw in the previous chapter that in 1895, the dominant network led by General Gutiérrez used an election to settle the competition over the vice presidency between Prudencio Alfaro and Carlos Meléndez. This approach was viable for a vice presidential election because Gutiérrez was an undisputed authority figure and kept political passions in check. But in presidential elections there was often more than one aspirant and no such authority to ensure order. On at least two occasions, once in 1876 and again in 1890, the members of the dominant network sought to negotiate a peaceful solution to internal debates over presidential succession by organizing *Juntas de Notables,* meetings of the leading members of the network designed specifically to select the next president.

The Junta of 1876 was held in the wake of the overthrow of General Santiago González (1871–1876), who himself had come to power in a coup against Francisco Dueñas (1863–1871). González precipitated his own political demise by trying to stay in power for an additional term. In the election of 1876 he ensured that his close ally Andrés Valle was victorious and then took for himself the positions of vice president and commander in chief of the army. His actions were typical political behavior, and so too was the appearance of an opposition movement.

González might have been able to hold off the inevitable opposition if it had remained solely domestic in nature, but his and Valle's days in power came to a sudden close when their relationship with President Justo Rufino Barrios of Guatemala soured. In February 1876, at the beginning of Valle's term, González and Barrios allied in opposition to the García regime in Honduras. Their alliance deteriorated when González refused to support Barrios's plan to invade Honduras. Barrios went ahead with the movement against García anyway; it failed miserably, causing a rapid deterioration in relations between González and Barrios. In April war broke out between Guatemala and El Salvador. Barrios got the better of González by invading El Salvador from two directions, east and west, pinching González's troops in between. After two weeks of fighting, González sued for peace. Barrios agreed to withdraw if González and Valle would resign from office and allow their opponents to conduct a Junta de Notables to select the next president. The junta was held in Santa Ana in late April. One of the participants was Manuel Gallardo, who referred to the event in his memoirs, saying that the participants settled on two main candidates, Rafael Zaldívar of Santa Ana and General Indalecio Miranda of San Vicente. According to Gallardo, Barrios found both of them acceptable, but Zaldívar won the day because he received a strong endorsement from the president of Costa Rica, with whom Zaldívar had formed a close relationship while working in Costa Rica as a professor during the González administration.[30]

The second Junta de Notables was held in 1890 at the behest of President Francisco Menéndez. He had come to power in 1885 in a coup against Zaldívar (1876–1885), who had served an unprecedented nine years in office. The purpose of the junta was to choose Menéndez's successor. Menéndez invited approximately two dozen of his closest political allies, among them Francisco Castañeda of La Paz Department, who later wrote a book about the Menéndez presidency in which he described the Junta of 1890. Castañeda wrote that the assembled participants negotiated for the better part of one day before voting. The results of the vote appeared in the *Diario Oficial*.[31] Four persons received votes, three of whom were members of González's cabinet. The top recipient, Julio Interiano, received fourteen votes, while the other candidates received one or two votes each. Following the junta, Interiano and Menéndez began mobilizing their local allies to conduct the customary one-sided election.

Ironically, the junta did not achieve its basic goal, which was to maintain the cohesiveness of the network by facilitating negotiations among its leading members. The junta members had chosen Interiano, but one of the other candidates felt slighted. He was General Carlos Ezeta, the commander of Santa Ana, and one of Meléndez's supporters in the coup of 1885. Ezeta wanted the presidency, and having not received it in the junta, he decided to take it by force. He launched a rebellion in June 1890 that toppled the Menéndez government. Menéndez himself was killed during the storming of the presidential palace. In a later declaration of victory, Ezeta referred specifically to the "conspiratorial . . . Junta de Notable" that had excluded him.[32]

The two Juntas de Notables, despite their differing outcomes, shared a common goal: keeping the reigning network in power by allowing its principal members to meet and negotiate presidential succession. In this, the juntas exemplified nineteenth-century politics by disregarding the masses and excluding rivals.

The Coup of 1894

Transfers of power between rival patronage networks seldom occurred peacefully. Of the thirteen shifts in power listed in table 1.4, at least nine involved some form of violent act, either a coup d'état or a prolonged war. Countless other unsuccessful plots were launched as well. These violent grabs for power were built upon the same foundation of interdepartmental alliances as any other political activity. The plotters were departmental bosses who, for one reason or another, decided that the incumbents had to be forcefully evicted from office. Typically, it was when incumbents decided to retain the presidency for an additional term that the opposition grew impatient and responded with violence. The plotters fostered alliances with strongmen from other departments. Sometimes these strongmen were appointees of the incumbents, such as departmental commanders willing to betray their current patron in hopes of retaining or surpassing their position under the new regime. If the solicited strongmen were out of power, they joined the coup in hopes of being appointed governor or commander, or to some other position. The standard procedure for overthrowing a president was for the main instigator to initiate an assault by either seizing control of the barracks in his home department or launching an invasion from a neighboring country. His allies in each department then launched smaller plots in order to neutralize the regime's local affiliates. If enough departments sided with the rebels and the main assault force possessed sufficient strength, the president and his allies had no choice but to resign, flee, or face death. After taking power, the new leaders doled out rewards to their supporters in the form of money, promotions, and offices.

The coup of 1894 left behind a particularly rich vein of evidence revealing the manner in which such overthrows were carried out. That coup, which ousted General Carlos Ezeta, originated in Santa Ana under the leadership of General Rafael Gutiérrez. He was supported by roughly four dozen landowners from the region, who are referred to as "the Forty-Four." The coup succeeded not only because of Gutiérrez's strong support in Santa Ana, but also because of the fortitude of his allies in all the departments except one, Morazán. Sonsonate Department provides a typical example of what transpired. Gutiérrez's main ally there was the departmental commander, Carlos Zepeda. Before Gutiérrez even had time to send troops to Sonsonate, Zepeda had arrested Ezeta's main supporters. When the Expeditionary Army eventually did arrive, its commander, General Joaquín Bran of San Miguel, sent the following report to Gutiérrez:

> Comandante Carlos Zepeda has put at my disposition the prisoners Manual Godoy, Isaac Rivas, Rito Amaya, Rosendo Ferrera, Delfino Berrios, Enrique Baxter, Antonio Castellanos, Ambroico Méndez and Marcelino Echeverría. They, as well as Dr. Francisco Galindo, are being detained under the authority of the Provisional Government that you now control. We are at your orders. We have a column of cavalry, 1,000 infantry and all of the artillery from the east. . . . In San Miguel I have named General Carlos Tiberio Avilez as interim Governor and Comandante. He has worked energetically to reorganize the authorities of the municipalities of that region. In Gotera [capital of Morazán Department] General Juan

Bran has been named Governor and Comandante, but he is being threatened by General Escalón, who has proclaimed against your Government.[33]

For whatever reason, General Pedro José Escalón, the departmental commander in Morazán, remained loyal to the doomed Ezeta government. During the coup he took approximately two hundred and fifty men and fled into the nearby mountains. They began stealing mules and other supplies from the local population in preparation for a protracted resistance campaign. Back in Sonsonate, General Bran recognized the problems that Escalón could pose. He was well armed and well supplied, and he was operating close to the refuge of the Honduran border. Bran instructed Governor Avilez in San Miguel to avoid antagonizing him and to send a commission to negotiate for Escalón's surrender. Avilez did so, and within one week he had secured Escalón's support. The terms of the deal are not known, but Escalón's capitulation suggests that he got what he wanted.[34]

One by one, Ezeta's departmental allies fell. Those who were not defeated either surrendered or fled, as did Ezeta himself. One of Gutiérrez's commanders reported the surrender "of Colonels Ayala and González who have placed themselves and their soldiers at my command in order to avoid an effusion of blood."[35] Gutiérrez's new governor in Usulután reported that the former governor fled with 3,000 pesos from the government's coffers.[36]

In the wake of his success, Gutiérrez faced a financial crisis. Demands for cash were pouring in from his allies across the nation, but Ezeta had left behind an empty treasury. Gutiérrez's commanders had promised payment to their troops, and now they were anxious to appease them. The jefes of Sonsonate, for instance, requested 5,000 pesos in order to pay off their "army of liberation."[37] The commanders in San Miguel reported that "our funds are exhausted and we are unable to pay the departmental garrison nor can we attend to the payment of the forces of General Andino."[38] Other allies expected Gutiérrez's government to cover loans imposed by Ezeta during the coup of 1890.[39] Lacking funds, Gutiérrez turned to the only remaining source of ready cash: private loans. Some allies were willing to make loan arrangements with the government. The new commander of San Miguel claimed that in light of the financial difficulties of the new regime, some merchants in San Miguel "are prepared to enter into loan negotiations."[40] But in opposition departments, the government had to resort to forced loans. The governor of La Paz was ordered to squeeze 6,000 pesos out of his department.[41]

Gutiérrez also rewarded allies with military promotions. Sergeant Andrés Carballo was promoted to the rank of lieutenant for "service lent during the most recent revolution."[42] Four years earlier, Carlos Ezeta had employed the same tactic, but to a much greater extent. He doled out no fewer than thirty-two promotions to officers above the rank of captain for their "valor and defense of the nation in the Revolution of June 1890."[43] In sum, military overthrows functioned according to the same patronage principles as any other political activity. Interdepartmental alliances were the backbone of a boss's support, and he was expected to reward his allies in the event of success.

José María Rivas—Symbol of a Weak State

Each nineteenth-century president faced the common challenge of staying in power despite the weakness of the state over which he presided. Office-holders did not possess a sense of belonging to an institution of government; rather, they saw themselves first and foremost as members of their respective patronage networks. Presidents rose to power on the backs of their networks and stayed in power only so long as they maintained their allies. The timely defection of one or two well-placed allies could tip the balance in favor of an opponent and ensure a successful coup. Barrios learned this lesson in 1863 when González defected. Presidents looked to prevent such betrayals, as well as to eliminate pockets of opposition throughout the country. We saw evidence of this in the municipality of Sensuntepeque in 1845, in San Vicente Department in 1852, and in Sonsonate Department between 1860 and 1863. But the limits of the state precluded a president from consolidating authority. If he invested the resources necessary to eliminate one rival, he faced the likelihood of being attacked from behind by another opponent, if not by one of his allies.

The career of General José María Rivas epitomizes the dilemma of nineteenth-century presidents and illustrates the weakness of central government.[44] Rivas was a major political player from Cuscatlán Department who drew much of his support from the local indigenous population. Rivas apparently generated loyalty among the local people by portraying himself as their benefactor as well as their military commander. Francisco Castañeda claimed in his 1893 book that Rivas inherited his high status in Cuscatlán from his family, especially his father, who had also been a military man and a political player in the department.[45]

Rivas rose to national prominence in the early 1860s, when he organized resistance throughout Cuscatlán Department to President Barrios's attempts to conscript soldiers there. Rivas and his followers skirmished constantly with Barrios's recruiting patrols until 1863, when Barrios was faced with the inevitable invasion from Guatemala and then attempted to turn Rivas into an ally. He named Rivas governor of Cuscatlán and allowed him to keep his forces under arms. Rivas accepted the position but later turned on Barrios during the siege of San Salvador and joined the invading army. One of the few handwritten documents by Rivas that has survived into the historical record discusses the events of 1863. It is a testimony by Rivas on behalf of one of his officers, who was requesting a military pension in 1875. Rivas wrote, "Lieutenant Juan José Martínez was under my command during the campaign of 1863 which ended in the siege of the Capital against General Gerardo Barrios."[46] For his betrayal of Barrios, Rivas received again, this time from Francisco Dueñas, the governorship of Cuscatlán. Thereafter, Rivas embarked upon a twenty-five-year political career of supporting the current administration only to betray it to its successor.

In 1870 Rivas joined Santiago González in the overthrow of Francisco Dueñas and again was rewarded with the governorship of Cuscatlán. Rivas retired temporarily to his agricultural properties, and it is not known what role, if any, he played in the transition from González to Zaldívar in 1876. But under Zaldívar, Rivas once again held the governorship of Cuscatlán. In 1885 he sided with General Menéndez in the overthrow of Zaldívar and again became governor of Cuscatlán.[47] No doubt by this time sitting presidents kept a wary eye on Cojutepeque and its fickle governor.

In 1888 Rivas revolted against Menéndez, apparently because Menéndez refused to choose him to fill a vacancy in the vice presidency.[48] The revolt failed, but Rivas was allowed to remain in Cuscatlán. Rivas revolted yet again in 1890, this time because Menéndez refused to appoint him governor and commander of Cuscatlán.[49] Menéndez sent Generals Carlos Ezeta and Horacio Villavicencio to subdue the rebellion, which they did, but they failed to capture Rivas, who fled to Honduras. Cuscatlán remained in such a state of disarray that Menéndez had to cancel elections in the region, and so the department went without representation in the National Assembly that year.[50]

Flush from their defeat of Rivas, Ezeta and Villavicencio turned on Menéndez and ousted him in the coup of 1890.[51] Upon assuming power, Ezeta believed that Guatemala intended to invade El Salvador, so he and his brother, General Antonio Ezeta, and Villavicencio positioned the army along the Guatemalan border. While mobilizing for war, Ezeta suspected Villavicencio of plotting a coup, so he had his brother attack him and chase him into exile.

Rivas took advantage of the crisis in Ezeta's command. He telegraphed Ezeta, offering to come to Santa Ana and join the defense against Guatemala if Ezeta would reinstate him as governor of Cuscatlán. Ezeta accepted the offer. Rivas assembled an army of three thousand and set out for the Guatemalan border. Upon arriving in Nueva San Salvador, however, Rivas revolted and occupied the poorly defended capital city of San Salvador. Now Ezeta had hostilities on two fronts, the Guatemalans to the west and Rivas to the east. Having no choice but to regain control over the capital, Ezeta sent his brother back to San Salvador at the head of an expeditionary army. He retook San Salvador, captured Rivas, and executed him, bringing to a sudden close his nearly thirty years of political intrigue. Fortunately for the Ezetas, the Guatemalans withdrew from the border, unable to take advantage of the strife inside El Salvador because of their own domestic political problems.[52]

Rivas was repeatedly appointed governor and commander of Cuscatlán Department despite his track record of betrayal and broken alliances. In that regard, Rivas symbolized the limits of central authority. Presidents could not control him, nor could they ignore him. One of his detractors referred to his political empire as "six thousand armed Indians in Cojutepeque that constitute a state within a state . . . an independent republic within the Republic of El Salvador."[53] Each president in succession bought off Rivas by giving him command of Cuscatlán, but in so doing each mortgaged his own future. To his credit, Rivas was an adroit political player. He had an uncanny ability to detect coming regime changes, and he repeatedly joined the winning side.

The Politics of Space

El Salvador's geography did not lend itself to vastly different and widely separated patronage empires. El Salvador is a small country, smaller than most states in Mexico or Argentina, where thousands of miles of territory, mountain ranges, and deserts might separate political strongholds. Admittedly, transportation in El Salvador could be slow, due to poor roads, especially during the rainy season, and thus even short geographical distances could be effectively isolating. This fact was evident even in the 1920s. Frederick William Taylor, the North American agricultural expert hired as a consultant by the Salvadoran government, noted in 1924 the difficulty of reaching various cotton plantations in San Salvador Department owing to the lack of roads and the need to wade swelling steams.[54] Nevertheless, throughout the nineteenth and early twentieth centuries, El Salvador's political system was not characterized by vastly differentiated regional areas. Rather, political bosses fought over the seemingly innocuous jurisdictional boundaries that separated municipalities, districts, and departments. These boundaries were much more than mere administrative divisions; they demarcated political empires.

The more territory a boss had under his authority, the more resources and votes he had at his disposal. As a result, space was a heavily politicized commodity. Bosses sometimes struck at their rivals by manipulating jurisdictional boundaries. At the same time, opposition factions within certain jurisdictions sometimes were anxious to divide the jurisdiction and lay claim to their own political destinies.

The political importance of space is evident in the conflagration described above between Sensuntepeque and the governor of San Vicente in 1845. Sensuntepeque was a district capital. One of the municipalities under its jurisdiction, Dolores, was controlled by a rival network loyal to the governor and President Guzmán. As the conflict between the governor and Sensuntepeque heated up, the bosses in Dolores requested that they be allowed to secede from Sensuntepeque District and join the district

headed by San Vicente City. The governor saw the proposal as an opportunity to weaken the power of his adversaries and expressed his support for
the idea:

> I have received the Act celebrated in your municipality requesting that the
> Supreme Government allow the village to separate from Sensuntepeque
> and fall under the authority of San Vicente. It is very sensible to solicit
> separation given the conditions of discord. You share my desire to guard
> and conserve order in the department . . . and foster security and defense
> as a single family of one opinion sharing the same sentiments. I will
> present your request to the Supreme Government.[55]

Although it is not known how the national government responded to the
proposal, the request itself, in conjunction with the governor's response to
it, illustrates the politicized nature of jurisdictional borders. A similar process was at work in San Vicente in 1852. The governor was bemoaning the
close alliance between the jefes of Santo Domingo and his adversaries in
San Vicente City, but he took solace in noting that at least Santo Domingo "belongs to the parish of San Sebastián," which was controlled by
the governor's allies.[56]

One of the more renowned political disputes over space occurred with
the relocation of the capital city in 1858. The original capital of San Salvador had been destroyed by an earthquake in 1854. The municipality of
Nueva San Salvador was founded in 1854 on lands just to the south of the
San Salvador volcano as the site of the new capital.[57] In the meantime, the
offices of government had been relocated to Cojutepeque in Cuscatlán
Department. When the time came in 1858 to either return the capital to
San Salvador or establish it in its new home in Nueva San Salvador, the
political implications of the decision became apparent. Although the two
cities were located just a few kilometers apart, and both were located in
San Salvador Department, each was controlled by a different political network. Nueva San Salvador was the stronghold of Francisco Dueñas and
his allies. San Salvador was the stronghold of Dueñas's long-standing rivals
José María San Martín and Eugenio Aguilar, among others. The selection
of one city or the other as the capital would result in financial and political
gain for the corresponding network. The bosses of Nueva San Salvador

wanted to cut into the traditional power of their counterparts in San Salvador. The bosses of San Salvador wanted to preserve what they already had invested. Under the direction of Interim President Gerardo Barrios, the government returned to San Salvador, delivering a strong blow to the Dueñas faction. Not surprisingly, Barrios and Dueñas became staunch enemies.[58]

Even before the conflict over the capital had developed, Dueñas had indicated his desire to break away from San Salvador. The decision of 1858 only intensified that desire, but his plans had to wait until after the Barrios administration was destroyed. In 1865, once he had come to power, Dueñas joined forces with Manuel Gallardo, who had recently moved to Nueva San Salvador and begun to plant coffee there, to carve the department of La Libertad out of the western half of San Salvador (see map 2). Gallardo became a political fixture in the new department, serving numerous terms in the National Assembly and holding a variety of posts on the municipal council of Nueva San Salvador, the new departmental capital.[59]

Not only did Dueñas bolster his own political clout by creating La Libertad, he also struck at Barrios's power base by breaking up the mighty department of San Miguel. When Dueñas came to office in 1863, San Miguel was by far the largest department in the nation, comprising the entire western third of the nation. Whereas every other department comprised only two or three districts, San Miguel had six.[60]

The same year that La Libertad was created, Cabañas launched his failed insurrection in San Miguel. Following the defeat of Cabañas, Dueñas carved up San Miguel and created two new departments in the process, Usulután and La Unión. Now Dueñas had more patronage to distribute, in the form of governorships and commander posts, and San Miguel was no longer the threat it once was. The combined impact of the division of the department, the deaths of Barrios and Cabañas, and the demise of indigo as a cash crop resulted in the steady dwindling of San Miguel's political influence.

* * *

National-level politics in nineteenth-century El Salvador consisted of multiple patronage-based networks at the regional level battling one another for control over the national government. The fortunes of any one network rested on the durability of its alliances. When those alliances held, the leaders of that network had the capacity to seize control of the state and hold onto it for some time. When those alliances were weak or tenuous, the network's leaders either failed to gain control of the national government or held it only temporarily.

Political incumbents at the national level countered their aspiring rivals in various ways. One way was to build alliances with dissident networks at the municipal level in the rivals' home region(s), thereby forcing them to deal with local affairs rather than direct their undivided attention at dislodging the incumbents from national office. Similarly, rivals sought to weaken the incumbents by mobilizing opposition in their home regions. One example is provided by the case of San Vicente Department in 1845, in which the entirety of the department stood behind President Guzmán with the exception of one municipality, Sensuntepeque, whose political leaders allied with the opposition. Seven years later, the national government had shifted to a new political network under the control of President Francisco Dueñas, presumably leaving almost all of San Vicente Department opposed to the national government (with the likely exception of the network in Sensuntepeque, unless something there had changed in the interim—available sources do not provide an answer). And so it went, back and forth, throughout most of the nineteenth century: patronage-based networks jockeying for position, rising and falling on their leaders' abilities to build and sustain alliances. The case study of General Rivas from Cojutepeque further illustrates the need for such allies. He excelled at building alliances with rising political networks and then betraying them at just the moment when a strong rival was on the rise and ready to seize power.

CHAPTER 3

BUILDING NETWORKS
AT THE LOCAL LEVEL

The last two chapters focused on jockeying at the national and regional levels, but those supramunicipal networks rested on a foundation of municipal-level alliances. This chapter turns to the municipal level, looking into the means by which municipal-level political actors built up their local political empires. As will be shown, wealth inequality and the corresponding system of clientelism was one basis for their expansion. But it was hardly the only one. Family, militarism, and ethnicity were other variables. The primary goal of any local political network was to win the annual municipal elections and then, by choice or by fiat, to enter into alliances with regional- and national-level political players. This chapter looks at how local networks were built, and the next chapter will show how they operated.

At the end of the last chapter, we left our national-level chronology at roughly the year 1900. The bulk of the evidence for this chapter also draws from the nineteenth century, but some looks ahead to the twentieth century. The twentieth-century evidence is used specifically to support this chapter's themes, and I avoid linking it to the national-level chronology, which will reappear at the end of chapter 4 and feature especially in chapter 5.

Clientelism

Clientelism is by definition hierarchical, and the accumulation of clients normally occurred in those places where social inequality was most pronounced—on rural land. In many cases in Salvadoran history, patrons were landowners, and clients were the laborers from their properties. In 1873, for example, one local patron referred to the clients of his rivals as "the employees of the haciendas of Méndez and Córdova."[1] On another occasion, an observer captured the essence of municipal politics when he described partisan differences as "local clashes which occur in all municipalities, where the most powerful [*el más pudiente*] surround themselves with elements of the proletarian class and exercise pressure over these most weak individuals [*las más débiles*]. Out of this is born the opposing bands and from these emerge local clashes."[2] A foreign traveler in El Salvador noted that "the hacendado leads his retainers to the polling-booth and sends or restrains them from partaking in revolutions."[3]

The terms that political actors in El Salvador used to refer to patrons and clients reflect their relative social status. Clients were called *obreros, jornaleros,* or *mozos,* common terms denoting a laborer or a person of inferior social standing. Patrons were referred to as *jefe* or *cacique* (boss or chief), and sometimes as *notables* (notable persons). The government's lists of local landowners were called *listas de notables* (lists of notable persons).

Clients constituted political capital. They were the foundation upon which a patron built his political empire. He used his clients either to support his own bid for office or to bolster an ally's candidacy and accumulate patronage in the process. Depending on the circumstances, clients were used either as voters or fighters. When a patron went unchallenged on election day, meaning that his control of the polling station was secure and his rivals had conceded to him, he simply sent his clients to the polls and claimed victory at the end of the day. When rivals refused to back down and persisted with their challenges, clients were converted into fighters, and violent clashes between rival patronage factions ensued.

Because the patron-client relationship was inherently hierarchical, economic inequality was an important raw material in its evolution. The emergence of the coffee economy thus assumes special importance in El Salvador's development, because coffee advanced social differentiation. In some coffee-producing countries throughout Latin America, peasants responded to market opportunities and excelled in coffee production.[4] This was not the case in El Salvador, where credit was a major impediment to smallholders, as was access to quality land.[5]

Coffee inspired the privatization of the communal lands in the 1880s and 1890s. The incentive to privatize land extended from the potential profit in coffee and the ascendance of liberalism, which held that land was more productive in private rather than communal hands. Before the initial privatization decree was handed down in 1881, communal and state-owned (*baldío*) land accounted for more than half of all property in El Salvador, and on that land resided an extensive and thriving peasantry. Within two decades, virtually all the communal and state-owned lands had been transferred to private owners.

The privatization process worked to the long-term detriment of the peasantry, although research reveals that its demise was more drawn out than scholars had initially believed. Some land speculators and prospective coffee barons took peasant communal lands, but mostly they titled properties that had been lying fallow. Much of the cultivated land was turned over to the peasant producers who were working it at the time. The privatization decrees gave preference to people already using the land, allowing both Indian and ladino (non-Indian) peasants to employ legal channels to title communal holdings.[6]

It took decades for the injurious consequences of the privatization process to become fully evident. Most of the peasant plots were too small to support successive generations of family members. As the population grew, competition for land became acute. With each passing year more members of peasant households had to leave the land either seasonally or permanently in search of paid work. Some made their way to urban areas; many simply turned to the coffee plantations, searching for either wages or land to plant subsistence crops as *colonos* (sharecroppers). Coffee also accelerated land concentration by increasing the value of land. Some smallholders sold off their plots to speculators and larger landowners. Historian Aldo Lauria-Santiago, who first subjected the privatization process to the scrutiny of archival evidence, describes the contradiction that privatization meant for the peasantry: "Thus at the same time that the process created a peasantry with clear control over the lands it possessed, it also opened the door for the eventual impoverishment of the participants and certainly the potential for proletarianization or landlessness for those who did not participate in it."[7] In sum, the coffee era in El Salvador was characterized by advances in inequality and, as we will see in the coming pages, clientelism followed in kind. But the existence of clientelism did not depend solely on inequality in production, a point that becomes evident when we look at the era before coffee.

Inequality was not the predominant feature of pre-coffee El Salvador. Research on agricultural production during the period 1840 to 1880 reveals that the export sector was limited, peasants had access to land, and many large estates sat stagnant or suffered decline. At the turn of the nineteenth century, El Salvador had approximately four hundred plantations/haciendas, accounting for roughly one-third of all land in the nation. Some of these estates were not even in production. An estimated fifteen thousand people, out of an approximate national population of two hundred and fifty thousand, resided on the estates as workers and renters. A portion of these tenants had only superficial economic ties to landlords, and as a result they were less susceptible to the political machinations of the elites. Thus the potential pool of clients was small.[8]

Indigo was the main export crop during the pre-coffee era, and while haciendas produced some of it, smallholder production predominated. The peculiar nature of indigo production allowed smallholders to produce a high-quality crop that could compete with the big estates.[9] With access to land and a viable export crop, peasants were not forced to depend upon the estates for land or wages. The result was a market that favored laborers, with estates facing chronic shortages of workers.[10] Lauria-Santiago, once again, summarizes the situation:

> The colonial inheritance of El Salvador included a few large and many medium-size haciendas, but these were never able to fully incorporate or functionalize the peasantries with which they came into contact. . . . A successful and expanding sector of small producers—Indian and Ladino communities, independent *labradores,* squatters and peasant tenants—

began to emerge in response to the diverse opportunities offered by local and international markets. . . . The pre-1880 changes produced an independent and dynamic peasant and smallholder economy that competed effectively with hacienda production—which was itself limited by the scarcity of cheap labor, capital, and other barriers to elite-led economic development.[11]

In short, the disparity between landlord and peasant was less pronounced in the pre-coffee era.

Nevertheless, clientelism was a feature of pre-coffee Salvadoran politics. In the first place, distinct points of inequality existed in the system of production, despite the relative independence of the peasant sector. For example, in 1852 a group of peasants went to the alcalde of Tepetitán (San Vicente Department) requesting that he aid them in their negotiations with nearby haciendas. The peasants came, noted the alcalde, "owing to the small amount of communal land they have available to grow products of primary necessity, requesting this office to see if the owners of the haciendas 'San Isidro' and 'Cobo' could rent them land in order to plant their crops." The alcalde surmised that the landowners would reject the offer because "they are dedicating their lands to the production of tobacco."[12]

A shortage of credit gave large landowners a decided advantage. Banks were virtually nonexistent, so large landowners typically possessed the lone sources of credit from fortunes built decades or centuries earlier. Smallholders, particularly the indigo growers, had to turn to the large estates for loans. Estate owners used this opportunity to assert control over the marketing of indigo. As José Fernández reveals in his study of indigo production, large landowners dominated the indigo economy by controlling marketing and credit.[13] Fernández ended his examination in the early nineteenth century, but additional evidence suggests that his description of indigo production applies to later periods as well. In the words of the governor of San Vicente in 1855, "The production of indigo is controlled largely by the owners of the large haciendas who speculate in the crops produced by small cultivators, who produce a better crop than the larger growers."[14]

Large landowners also used credit to circumvent the depressed labor market. Records from Sonsonate Department from the 1860s and 1870s indicate that landowners extended cash loans to peasants in exchange for labor. The loans normally ranged in amount between one and three dozen pesos and signified between a few weeks' and a few months' worth of work. Peasants occasionally used the system to their advantage by incurring debts and running off.[15] The archives, especially the municipal archive in Sonsonate, contain many cases relating to the punishment of rural dwellers who reneged on their deals. The government recognized the debts as a legal contract, and in the event that deserters were captured, they were subjected to the judgment of governing officials. Normally they were ordered to fulfill their obligations to the landowner and then perform additional labor on public-works projects. One of the verdicts reads, "A decision against José María Musún, unmarried, day laborer [*jornalero*], resident of Izalco, 28 years old, for having deserted his finca "La Trinidad" on February 12, 1878, given that he was in debt service to his *patrón* Fernando Cerén for ten pesos, he is sentenced to fifteen days of public works and is ordered to repay his ten pesos obligation to Cerén."[16] A lack of comprehensive data prohibits a detailed study of the labor market and the role of debt in securing laborers. But the existence of many dozens of these court cases from one department over a limited period of time suggests that they were an important part of the system of production, and that landowners used debt in order to gain access to and exert control over labor in the absence of an advanced export economy.[17] Thus, pre-coffee El Salvador offered pockets of inequality that created the potential for patron-client relations. They would become more commonplace during the coffee era.

The oral vote ensured that any given political boss knew how his clients voted. To the extent that a patron could coerce a person, he could control his franchise. A local official once commented on the impact of oral voting: "There is here a coffee grower who intends to ensure that the local authorities of this village and of the village of California are persons at his command. . . . This coffee grower, as he has done on numerous other occasions, is capable of falsifying the elections . . . by bringing the *mozos* and coffee cutters from his properties and from the surrounding jurisdiction to vote as he commands."[18]

The oral vote facilitated client accumulation. It allowed a boss to identify people as prospective clients and, by virtue of his ability to know their vote, conscript them into his service. Certainly laborers, or persons who were economically subservient to the boss, were most susceptible to conscription. But the oral vote allowed a boss to make a client out of any person who could not stand up to him, or who was not already in the service of another boss. This coercion sometimes occurred on a personal level, but it also took place on a village-wide level. One common tactic was for a boss and his main retinue of followers to patrol the municipality prior to an election and order the population to vote for its candidates. In 1903, for example, the incumbent bosses in San Antonio Masahuat (La Paz Department) were accused of "going about three days prior to the election, abusing their authority and practicing force over the citizenry . . . threatening those who did not obey them with imprisonment in the cuartel [barracks]."[19] Another common ploy was to post a gang of thugs outside the municipal hall on election day. Their presence delivered an unmistakable message to anyone thinking of voicing support for opposition candidates. To the extent that the perpetrators of these schemes went unchallenged by other bosses, they controlled the franchise of an entire village.

Not only did the oral vote allow an individual boss to gain and control his clients and exclude the clients of his rival, it also allowed bosses in general to hinder autonomous action by the masses. Bosses competed with one another for office, but they agreed on one axiom: independent political activity on the part of the masses threatened social order. Peasants and smallholders not under the command of a political boss had difficulty coming to polls autonomously and independently; to have done so was tantamount to social revolution. Sometimes this meant that elections were small affairs with only a few participants. But bosses cared more about who voted and under what circumstances voting occurred than the number of votes cast. In short, the oral vote was a crucial tool allowing the powerful to control the suffrage of the less powerful and keep political power securely in their possession.

The patron-client relationship was hierarchical and often based upon coercion; however, it also could be based upon paternalism and negotiated exchange. This was, in part, because the power of the patron was not without limits. As sociologist Anthony Giddens points out, "no matter how imbalanced they [power relations] may be . . . actors in subordinate

positions are never wholly dependent, and are often very adept at convert-
ing whatever resources they possess into some degree of control over the
conditions of reproduction of the system."[20] Historian Patricia Alvarenga
Venutolo gives empirical weight to Gidden's observation in her study of
violence in rural, western El Salvador. She reveals that landowners recognized the limits of their hegemony over the countryside, even if they sometimes exceeded it with abusive behavior toward their workers. Alvarenga
Venutolo shows that landowners avoided traveling alone outside their
properties for fear of being ambushed by workers.[21] It is also likely that
fear of widespread mass revolt, to say nothing of actual episodes of insurrection, served as a constant reminder to patrons of the need for restraint
in their relations with subordinates.[22]

Some instances of patron-client interaction were based upon positive
rewards. Bosses may have had no choice but to offer rewards for support.
Others with more limited hegemony may have astutely recognized that
voluntary supporters were both easier to control and more dependable.
The rewards they doled out varied from the material to the social. Bosses
occasionally threw parties on the eve of an election and distributed food,
money, or liquor to the members of their network. One local boss observed that his rival was "putting to work the power of money and *guaro*
[liquor]."[23] Although clients did not have a choice in these elections, material rewards eased the process. Clients who demonstrated extended loyalty
received greater material rewards, such as promotion within the boss's
clique or to higher status on the estate, perhaps as an administrator. Luis
Cotera of Santa Lucia (San Vicente Department) stands out as an example
of a midlevel client. In 1852, Cotera at once worked as the administrator
for a local hacienda, served as alcalde in the municipality, and held the
rank of second lieutenant in the local militia. Virtually every political boss
wore multiple hats: landowner, military officer, and elected official. Cotera
represented the subordinate version of each. He was not a landowner, but
he was far from being a *mozo*.[24]

Some bosses encouraged loyalty not only through material rewards,
but also by tapping into the regional, ethnic, or national identities of their
followers. A classic example of this type of relationship is offered by General José María Rivas of Cojutepeque. As seen in the previous chapter,
Rivas was the undisputed political boss of Cuscatlán Department throughout most of the second half of the nineteenth century. His base of power

lay in the indigenous population and his ability to field a formidable armed force from amongst them. The bond of loyalty between Rivas and his supporters remained strong even when rivals chased him into exile. Research suggests that Rivas inherited some of his political empire from his father, another strongman from the region, and built it up by casting himself as a benefactor to his followers and appealing to their ethnic identity.[25]

The limited documentary record prevents a detailed examination of the relationship between General Rivas and his followers in Cuscatlán. It can only be assumed that the relationship typified the complexities of nineteenth-century patronage-based politics. Rivas and his followers must have been involved in continual negotiations with one another, and the inevitable factionalisms and complexities within the indigenous population of the region most likely played into those negotiations. Lauria-Santiago has shown that factional divisions existed in the communities of indigenous peasants in and around the municipality of Izalco in western El Salvador in the latter half of the nineteenth century, especially after coffee began to dominate the local economy. He shows that alliances were made between indigenous communities throughout the western region and powerful political bosses at the national level who were seeking men and resources. The limited evidence of those alliances suggests that some sort of negotiated bargaining occurred. Lauria-Santiago claims that the national strongmen appealed to their local allies by drawing upon "corporate, ethnic, personalistic, ideological, regional, national and even extra-national" appeals.[26] Research from other national settings, such as Peter Guardino's studies of Oaxaca and Guerrero in Mexico, and James Sanders's examination of the Cauca region in Colombia, shows that El Salvador would have been an extreme outlier had it avoided the bargaining that went into the construction of patron-client political relations elsewhere. Perhaps Rivas had a relationship with his followers in Cuscatlán that bore some resemblance to the relationship that Guardino documented between highland indigenous communities in Oaxaca and urban elites in Oaxaca City. If so, then in exchange for lending Rivas their support, the communities gained autonomy, and Rivas had to maintain influence at the national level in order to protect that autonomy, to say nothing of preserving his position as a regional caudillo or strongman.[27]

The lack of evidence makes any conclusions about the day-to-day functioning of politics in El Salvador's pre-coffee era tentative. I am not trying to stake out a contrarian claim versus those scholars who have advanced the political autonomy of the peasantry during the pre-coffee era, either in El Salvador or in other Latin American case studies.[28] One of those scholars, Ricardo Salvatore, offers a revealing description of the problems with the traditional arguments in his study of the "*paysanos*" of Buenos Aires in the mid-nineteenth century: "they served to locate the subaltern in a particular, convenient site: a subordinate, contradictory, almost impossible location, devoid of agency."[29] In fact, I have argued for the need to interpret rural events, such as the 1932 insurrection in western El Salvador, through the lens of peasant autonomy.[30] And the events of 1932 occurred well after peasant and indigenous communities had been subjected to decades of intensely transformative pressures from the expanding coffee economy. In the pre-coffee era, when they had access to large tracts of land and the pressures of export-led production were modest, peasants undoubtedly had a material base from which they could interpret their world and act accordingly. Lauria-Santiago advances precisely that claim in his study of land and politics in nineteenth-century El Salvador, which he based largely on records relating to land and property transactions.[31] Furthermore, we have the case of the wave of indigenous rebellions in the late 1820s and early 1830s, highlighted by the Aquino rebellion of 1831 to 1832. Even if we know little about those events, they certainly reveal a peasantry acting autonomously.

Nevertheless, El Salvador does not seem to have experienced a definitive moment when peasants and plebians articulated a version of civic republicanism and injected it into the broader body politic. In other words, El Salvador seems to stand distinct from what Sanders shows us to have occurred in Colombia's Cauca region in mid-nineteenth century, or what Cecilia Méndez shows for the Huanta region of Peru in the 1820s, or what James Woods shows to have happened in the peri-urban environs of Santiago de Chile in the 1840s and 1850s, or that Salvatore demonstrates in regard to the Argentine *paysanos* in the 1850s. Admittedly, El Salvador's distinctiveness in this regard may be due to a lack of evidence, perhaps on account of the national archive fire in 1889. Or perhaps it is due to my reliance on a particular kind of evidence, primarily Gobernación records, whereas Sanders and Salvatore rely on petitions, court cases, and military files, among other records, and Woods employs the newspapers that Santiago's artisanal plebes produced. Perhaps future research will prove my claim wrong.

At the least we can draw a couple of conclusions from El Salvador's extant documentary record: first, that the foundations of the patron-client system were being laid down in the pre-coffee era; and second, that clientelism was not static, but rather was fluid and came in different forms, ranging from the coercive to the reciprocal. Common to all patron-client relations was personalism. Clients promoted the political careers of their patrons, whether that person was a local or an outsider, and whether they knew him personally or not; the patron may or may not have distributed rewards in return for their support. In the absence of organized efforts to direct the system towards a more egalitarian end, the system worked in the long run to bestow political power upon a small handful of people.

Family and Patronage

Family was a bedrock of patronage politics. Family members built economic empires together, passed their wealth on to one another through inheritance, and entered into politics to defend their mutual interests. Fathers and sons did business together, and business often translated into politics. When brothers, uncles, and brothers-in-law entered the fray, a single family could assemble a substantial political force. Granted, family ties were not synonymous with political alliances. In El Salvador, as in any society, families had their internal disputes and personality conflicts. But for the most part, family and politics reinforced one another, because in a society where the formal rules of politics seldom applied, family relations offered political security.

The governor of San Vicente Department revealed the interrelationship of family and politics in the aftermath of the 1852 municipal elections, which took place after Francisco Dueñas became president. As we saw in the previous chapter, Dueñas rose to power despite the opposition of most of San Vicente Department, including the leading political network in San Vicente City. Dueñas's gubernatorial appointee in the department despised the municipal council that came to power in San Vicente

City in 1852 because its members were close familial relations of his arch-
enemy, Doroteo Vasconcelos, a major political player from San Vicente
Department who twice had been president. The new alcalde in San Vicente was Faustino Vasconcelos, Doroteo's brother. One of the regidores,
Jacinto Artiga, was married to the Vasconceloses' sister and, according to
the governor, was "one of the most notorious political actors in the city."
The governor also noted his displeasure with the electoral results in a
nearby municipality because "its officials have family ties with San Vicente
City and they all exchange friendly communications."[32]

Although commenting many years later, the individual in a prior
chapter who referred to patronage as being *en servicio* to another person,
and who noted that local criminals often got off due to their patronage
ties, also affirmed the importance of family to patronage relations. "The
authors of crimes," he wrote, "are the same authorities, or are their family
members, who are ordered to investigate the crimes. . . . The guilty party
turns out to be a cousin, uncle, godfather, or close friend of the father
of the investigator."[33] The alcalde of a neighboring municipality commented that "the realm of justice requires reformation, because as it func-
tions these days, connections of friendship and family allow innocents to
be condemned and true criminals to be absolved."[34] While these last two
comments were made with regard to judicial affairs, they still reveal the
importance of family to matters of local power.

Blood relations were the most durable form of political alliances, and
father-son teams were a common feature of political life. In the following
pages we see that the right-hand man to General Rivas in Tacuba was his
son, Dr. Rafael Rivas Jr. In Atiquizaya (Ahuachapán Department), a
father-son team ran the town throughout most of the 1870s. The father
was Agustín Piñeda, an aspiring coffee grower. When Piñeda lost to a rival
network in 1874, he had his son break into the municipal hall and steal
the voting lists.[35]

When patronage ties went beyond the immediate family, they typically consisted of no more than two or three distinct families. For example, in Jiquilisco, a coffee-growing municipality in Usulután Department, the dominant patronage network in the 1890s consisted of three
families. The departmental governor described them as "a party [*partido*]
of three well-to-do [*acomodadas*] families that has tenaciously controlled

this municipality for many years in order to preserve their large landholdings and cover up their many misdeeds [*pilladas*] which they have committed."[36]

Political alliances not based on blood typically revolved around marriage. Sons of a patron often married the daughters of his allies. The municipality of Juayúa offers a good example of this aspect of politics. In the late nineteenth century, a group of three aspiring families, Mata, Cea, and Salaverría, joined political forces and in time became bound by marriage. A Cea son married a Salaverría daughter, and another Salaverría daughter married a Mata. In the 1910s a Honduran immigrant, a wealthy doctor by the name of Máximo Jerez, married into the Salaverría family, garnering himself not only a large coffee finca, but repeated positions on the municipal council.[37]

Municipal elections and municipal councils often took on distinctly familial overtones. In Ahuachapán City in 1887, the alcalde and síndico were brothers, and one of the regidores was their nephew.[38] Similarly, in Juayúa in 1891, the alcalde and síndico were brothers and one of the regidores was their brother-in-law.[39] Familial collusion of this sort was illegal and provided opponents with an opportunity to submit denunciations. One of these denunciations, from the village of Chinameca in 1911, noted that the municipal secretary was the son-in-law of the alcalde, and together "they are building a true dictatorship in this municipality."[40] In Izalco, in 1920, the alcalde incurred the wrath of his rivals by hiring only his own family members for positions in the municipal office.[41] The recurrence in the historical record of these types of denunciations against nepotism indicates that a close relationship existed between family and politics.[42]

The incomplete results from three municipal elections in turn-of-the-century Santo Domingo de Guzmán (Sonsonate Department) demonstrate the links between family and politics. The elections occurred in 1896, 1900, and 1901 respectively, and each was controlled by a single patronage network dominated by a select few people bearing an even smaller number of surnames. In the election of December 1896, two surnames, García and Pérez, account for five of the six positions on the municipal council (see table 3.1). In the next election for which records are available, December 1900, the same two surnames account for eight of the eleven positions on the council and the directorio combined. Similar names appear in the election of December 1901. In total, for the three elections only seven surnames are listed, and four of them predominate: Pérez, García, Vásquez, and Ramírez. Although it is not certain that those persons who bore the same surnames were related, in a small village like Santo Domingo it was highly likely, and thus the results from table 3.1 suggest a strong interrelationship between family, patronage, and elections.

Table 3.1   Municipal Officials, Santo Domingo de Guzmán, 1896, 1900, 1901

Municipal Council	Members of Directorio
(December 1896)	
A) Bacilio Vásquez	n.a.
R) Irene Pérez	
R) Laureano Pérez	
S) Luis García	
J) Mauricio García	
J) Eleno Pérez	
(December 1900)	
A) Riviano Ramos	P) Aniceto García
R) Irene Pérez	VP) Máximo García
R) Macario Pérez	E) Pedro Ramos
S) Gabriel Pérez	E) Guillermo Ramírez
	Se) Wenceslas García
	Se) Luis García
(December 1901)	
A) Bacilio Vásquez	P) Aniseto García
R) Catarino Ramírez	VP) Luis García
R) Laureano Pérez	E) Fidel López
S) Aniseto Vásquez	E) Hermenejildo Sánchez
	Se) Fidel Ramírez
	Se) Atiliano Pérez

Source: Juntas de Elecciones, Santo Domingo de Guzmán, 1896, 1900, and 1901, AGN, MG, SS, Box "Política 1890–1899, 1900–1908."

Key: A) Alcalde, R) Regidor, S) Síndico, J) Juéz, P) President, VP) Vice President, E) *Escrutador,* Se) Secretary

Just as politics was a family affair, so too was it a gendered affair in which women rarely participated openly. Since women could not vote, they were not sought out as clients. Nor did rich women function publicly as political bosses. It is clear from lists of landowners and financial elites that some women possessed substantial amounts of land and wealth. For example, in 1893 the government compiled a list of the most important landowners in La Libertad Department. The list contains fifty-nine names and estimates their combined worth at more than four million colones. Three of the people listed are women who account for more than 300,000 pesos, or roughly 8 percent of the total.[43] Another example of a rich woman is the widow of Agustín Regalado, who as of 1926 owned more than one thousand manzanas of cultivated coffee land in Sonsonate Department, making her one of the largest coffee growers in the nation.[44] Nevertheless, these well-off women rarely translated their wealth into political power, at least in an overt way. In none of the available records is there an indication that women operated as political bosses. Rich women might well have directed political empires from behind the scenes, presumably through male facades, but if these instances occurred, they were not evident in the historical record.

One isolated instance occurred in 1909, when a woman from a small municipality in San Salvador Department denounced a political network and requested an election nullification.[45] It was common practice for political networks to use their most humble members to submit denunciations in order to give the *solicitudes* (solicitations) more validity. Peasants and day laborers typically submitted the initial denunciations or nullifications, and then the patrons or landowners entered as witnesses to corroborate their clients' stories. Given the unprecedented nature of the case from Santiago, it would appear that, for whatever reason, the network took this strategy to a distinct level and had a woman sign the *solicitud*. Notwithstanding this example, the principal role of women in politics appears to have revolved around the construction of patronage alliances through wedlock. The main political duties, such as accumulating clients, negotiating patronage deals, and fighting it out on election day, were performed by men. We are therefore left to assume the diverse and manifold ways in which women maneuvered behind the scenes and negotiated the gendered hierarchy of Salvadoran politics in the same way that poor laborers negotiated the class hierarchy.

The home, as the stronghold of a family's empire, often took center stage in political drama. It provided seclusion from the prying eyes of rivals and also served as a symbol of a boss's power over his clients. Bosses frequently held political meetings in their homes.[46] Normally these meetings were private affairs that took place amidst great secrecy, but on occasion they spilled out into the public arena. In 1891 in the village of Lislique (La Unión Department), for instance, a network had been gathering regularly in the house of one of its adherents to plot strategy for the forthcoming election. During one of the meetings, the participants decided to conduct a "pre-election vote," the results of which, not surprisingly, resulted in a victory for the network's candidates. After the vote the ballot-casters spilled out into the street, shouting slogans such as "the candidates to be elected have already been decided upon." Such manifestations continued to emerge from the house on a daily basis as election day drew near.[47] In 1899 in Santa Clara (San Vicente Department), a boss's home served as the site of a similar "pre-election" vote. The incumbent network, led by the landowning Bonilla-Artiga family, gathered in the Bonilla house and held a private vote amongst its adherents. The following day, the leaders brought the results to their opponents, informing them that any who did not accept the results would have to face the weapons stockpiled in the Bonilla home.[48]

Not only was the family home a base of operations, it also provided sanctuary. For instance, in 1897 in the village of Uluazapa (San Miguel Department), an opposition network gained a tactical advantage in the central plaza during the municipal election, forcing the electoral board to abandon the municipal hall and continue the election from the front doors of its members' homes.[49]

The Military and Politics

In his study of the relationship between the military and state-building in nineteenth and early twentieth-century Central America, historian Robert Holden insists that we refrain from drawing a continuum between military and civilian rule, as if they were either/or options. With his argument exemplified by the phrase "armies without nations," Holden contends that the difference between combative civilians and political officers was minimal.[50] In a political system in which power sometimes emanated from the barrel of a gun, military men automatically possessed political capital. They had access to weapons and could draw upon alliances with other officers. They also were trained in the art of conscription, finding the accumulation of soldiers to be akin to, if not synonymous with, the accumulation of clients. Officers also often enjoyed a reputation for violence, which facilitated a successful career in politics.

Each of El Salvador's constitutions prohibited active-duty officers from participating in politics. But recurrent denunciations of politically active officers suggest that the rule was ignored. "Military service," read one of these denunciations in 1849, "is incompatible with local office-holding, therefore, conduct new elections throughout Cuscatlán Department due to members of the army being elected as alcaldes and regidores."[51] "Active duty" was a vague status, particularly during the nineteenth century, when the central government was too weak to enforce order on its supposed employees. Active duty meant that one received a government salary, but the government was constantly in arrears, and the source of one's salary varied greatly. Sometimes payment came from government coffers, but at other times it was doled out by a patron from resources that had been either donated or extracted forcibly from local elites. Rank, too, was a rather haphazard designation. High rank might have been the product of years of military training and service, or it might have reflected nothing more than an impromptu promotion given out by an embattled general or president seeking to augment his beleaguered forces. Rank typically corresponded to the level at which one participated in politics. Generals involved themselves in national politics, while colonels and lesser officers participated in municipal politics. Most political bosses held some form of military rank and carried the title of their rank with them throughout their lives. Most officers were in a semipermanent state of retirement, waiting to respond to the call of a patron, while in the meantime busying themselves with their own financial and political affairs.

Officers took part in local politics to varying degrees. At the lowest level, an officer served as the gun-toting enforcer of a local patron. One boss rose to power in La Unión City in the 1890s "by way of the armed forces," as his opponents referred to the assistance he received from the local commander.[52] In municipalities lacking a permanent military force, bosses went outside the municipality to search for military allies. In 1895, a boss in Apopa (San Salvador Department) found an ally in the commander of the Policía Montada (the mounted police), the roving precursor to the National Guard. The boss was Juan Merino, a local landowner, who was challenging the incumbent network led by Jose Duque, also a prominent landowner. On the morning of the election the commander rode into the municipality and watched as Duque's network monopolized the election of the electoral board, selecting Duque as president. To the astonishment of Duque's followers, the commander arrested Duque and removed him from the municipality.[53]

The difficulty of an enforcer's task depended upon the intensity of the local rivalry. The commander of the Montada had an easy time of it in Apopa. In contrast, in 1914 the commander of Santa Elena (Usulután Department), Vicente Bolaños, found himself caught up in a heated conflict. Bolaños worked on behalf of the Lozano family, which owned numerous properties around Santa Elena. The Lozanos faced some determined challengers, and Bolaños reasoned that the best strategy was to deny them access to the municipal hall. The night prior to the election, he occupied the central plaza and posted armed guards at each of its four entrances. On the morning of the election the opposition gathered a few blocks away and prepared to storm the municipal hall. Bolaños and seven of his men rode out on horses to engage the challengers and met them two blocks away from the plaza. Bolaños and his men fired guns into the air, scattering the charging opponents. To deter further raids, Bolaños set up a machine gun in the middle of the plaza. Not surprisingly, a member of the Lozano family, Pablo Lozano, was elected alcalde without further interruption.[54]

Officers aspiring to be more than mercenaries built their own networks. Military men were fortunate in that they did not have to be rich in land to be successful in politics. Colonel Tadeo Pérez of Juayúa is an example of a military officer who was neither a landowner nor a member of a wealthy family, and yet became a prominent political force in the village during the 1880s and 1890s. Pérez gathered a few clients of his own and formed an alliance with one of the village's lesser coffee-growing families, the Mendozas. Together they challenged the dominant network run by the Mata-Cea-Salaverría alliance. On two occasions, in 1886 and 1891, Pérez and Mendoza bettered the dominant group in the municipal elections.[55]

Another example of a landless military officer making it big in local politics is General Rivas of Tacuba. When Rivas retired in the 1910s, he was landless and arrived in Tacuba with only his family, some guns, and, most important, a ruthless sense for politics. Rivas allied with the local police chief and a few landowners, including Leopoldo Cuenca and Francisco Morán, and assembled a substantial network. Rivas and his allies ran the town during the 1910s and 1920s. Cuenca, for instance, served as alcalde for a total of five years during this period. Rivas himself did not hold office, choosing instead to convert his newfound political clout into financial gain. He became the village's leading merchant in sugar and milk and took up residence in a large house near the center of town. General Rivas demonstrated how a career in the military could be transformed into political and economic success.[56]

If a landless officer could succeed as a political boss, a military man with property had an even greater advantage. Propertied officers had ready-made patronage networks. From their lands they received wealth and clients; from their families they gained political allies; and from their military careers they drew experience. Colonel Hipólito Balibrera of Jucuapa (Usulután Department) exemplifies a landed military officer engaging in politics. In the late nineteenth century, Jucuapa had become a relatively important coffee-producing municipality where some two dozen families had planted almost two thousand manzanas of coffee. Balibrera owned one coffee plantation. Although he had political aspirations, he faced a formidable opponent, a powerful alliance of four landowning families: Castillo, Hidalgo, Castro, and Araujo. But Balibrera was a man of many hats. As a family patriarch, landowner, and military officer, he possessed all the requirements for success in politics. Balibrera assembled a patronage network consisting of his family members and the clients from his properties and made a power grab in the election of 1897. The ensuing conflict was intense. Balibrera won the initial election, but his opponents managed to oust him and force another election. Balibrera then won the second election, only to be forced from office yet again. His opponents assumed office in May 1898, but Balibrera convinced the regidores to retire from office and forced the municipal council to disband.

The intensity of the conflict in Jucuapa is revealed in the discourse employed by Balibrera's opponents. They accused him of unleashing the political will of the proletarians, a denunciation typical of an incumbent network when faced with a formidable challenger. "Colonel Hipólito Balibrera," claimed his opponents, "has put the ignorant people in a state of disorder and in that is threatening the principle of authority and public order." Unfortunately, a lack of documents prevents us from learning the ultimate results of the 1897 election. Regardless, Balibrera demonstrated that propertied military officers could be tough political players.[57] As landowner, political aspirant, and military officer, he was a prototypical political boss.

Ethnicity and Politics

In regions with substantial indigenous populations, political networks commonly developed along ethnic lines. Indigenous peoples, or Indians, as I will refer to them hereafter, were rarely allowed to hold municipal office or function as political bosses, partly because of racism and prejudice, but also due to class divisions. Indians were, for the most part, peasants and laborers rather than hacendados and finqueros, and as such served as clients and subalterns instead of alcaldes and regidores. In certain municipalities, however, they competed directly with the ladinos and even controlled municipal government. In these instances, Indians proved to be equally as adept in controlling voting and monopolizing government offices.

Statistics remain in dispute as to the percentage of Indians in El Salvador's population across time. Figures have ranged from a low of 5 percent to a high of 30 percent for any given time period after independence. The disparities in numbers are caused in part by the lack of consensus as to what constitutes Indian identity, as well as a basic problem of poor record-keeping. In recent research, George Lovell and Christopher Lutz indicate that in 1807 Indians accounted for more than 30 percent of the total population of El Salvador. Virginia Tilley has conducted extensive research on Indian demographics in the late nineteenth and early twentieth centuries by surveying birth records to determine the ethnic classification of newborns. She concludes that at the turn of the twentieth century Indians accounted for roughly 10 percent of the population and held steady at that rate until the 1950s, when municipalities ceased denoting ethnicity. Tilley's research also confirms that the western departments contained the greatest proportion of Indians. In 1900, the departments of Sonsonate and Ahuachapán were roughly 50 percent Indian. The department of San Salvador was close behind, and the departments of La Libertad, Cuscatlán, La Paz, and Morazán contained lesser but significant percentages.[58]

Most Indians lived in distinct communities (*comunidades*) that served as the political, religious, and economic foundation of Indian life. The communities were by-products of the colonial era, when Indian and Spanish societies were separated formally into a *república de los indios* and a *república de los españoles*.[59] The Indian townships resided alongside the official municipalities. For instance, the municipality of Izalco in Sonsonate Department consisted of the formal municipality controlled by ladinos and two Indian communities, Asunción Izalco and Dolores Izalco.[60] Although subject to the formal laws of the nation, Indian communities were semiautonomous in their political and economic affairs. They selected their own political and religious leaders. The economic base of the community was its communal lands, potentially large tracts that in most cases had been granted to the Indians by the Spanish crown. These lands were the official domain of the community, and access to them was governed by community leaders.

The political and social life of Indian communities in El Salvador has not been studied extensively, but available evidence allows for a rough sketch.[61] Rodolfo Cardenal has conducted research in church archives and summarizes what Indian communities looked like in nineteenth-century El Salvador. The *cofradía* (a Catholic brotherhood) was the heart of the community, guiding the spiritual and political life of its members. The ranking men of the community held the positions of authority in the cofradía. The highest of these positions was the alcalde, followed by the regidor, the mayordomo, and finally the alguacil. Each position came with certain religious and political responsibilities. The officeholders conducted the administrative affairs of the community, including taxation and the allocation of resources, and also presided over the religious icons (*ima-genes*), processions, and festivals. Wealth determined one's rise up the ladder, for the more important the position, the more financial responsibilities it placed upon its holder. A high-level official, for instance, hosted the annual religious festival, an event that required an outpouring of food and drink at his expense.[62]

Evidence suggests that communities used some form of election to determine which of their members would occupy positions of authority. Each year the communities had to submit the names of their new officials to the national government. The language of these requests indicates that the officials were elected. The Indian community of Juayúa submitted a typical request in 1867: "The Community of Indians [*Común de Indígenas*] of the village of Juayúa, or better said, the persons who possess its communal lands, announce the election of the following, for alcalde. . . ."[63] Evidence also suggests that only high-ranking male members of the community voted in these elections. For instance, in 1888 the two Indian communities of Izalco each had to elect a *juez partidor,* the individual who would represent the community during the privatization of its communal lands. In both cases, the documentation refers to those persons allowed to vote as the "*individuos más caracterisados* [*sic*]," a phrasing commonly used to refer to senior, well-established persons, suggesting that the remaining members did not vote.[64] Whatever method was used, it is clear that Indian and ladino officialdom were separate from one another; Indians ran their communities, and ladinos governed the formal municipality.

We do not know enough about the history of indigenous communities in El Salvador to know the extent of the impact on their identities of new national laws, such as the constitutional extension of citizenship to all adult men and the privatization of communal lands. In cases of indigenous communities in other countries, it is evident that those two legal developments significantly affected indigenous peoples' ability to preserve their identity. The former challenged the traditional hierarchies of office-holding in communities, which were usually based on age. Constitutions that made all people equal before the law suddenly put young Indian men on an equal footing with their elders and produced simmering intracommunity rivalries.[65] Similarly, the abolition of community-managed property took away the main material foundation of community identity and eliminated one of its most important bureaucratic responsibilities—managing the land and controlling access to it. But as Justin Wolfe, a historian of nineteenth-century Nicaragua, points out, indigenous identity did not depend wholly on control over land or specific religious obligations. Admittedly, those things could greatly facilitate the survival of indigenous identity, but ultimately, like any other identity, indigenous self-conceptualization was based on how individual people chose to see themselves.[66]

In the case of El Salvador, it is apparent that despite the privatization of communal lands in the 1880s, indigenous community identity survived and thrived throughout the first three decades of the twentieth century. In at least two specific cases, Indians crossed the political borders of their community and challenged ladinos for direct control over a municipality. The cases are from Nahuizalco and Cuisnahuat between 1880 and 1930. Both municipalities are located in Sonsonate Department, and both had populations that were nearly 90 percent Indian.[67]

Nahuizalco

Nahuizalco is located northwest of Sonsonate City at the base of the coffee highlands in Sonsonate and Ahuachapán Departments.[68] The village has indigenous origins and has existed since at least the time of the conquest; it has long been recognized as a core of El Salvador's Indian population. It is a sizable village that typically accounted for at least 10 percent of the entire population of Sonsonate Department. In the year 1858 its population was just under 5,000; by 1900 it was 9,000; and in 1913 it was roughly 14,000. Of 2,319 males living there in 1858, 2,284 were listed as "*jornaleros,*" which in the language of that day meant peasant agriculturists. Although the statistic fails to distinguish between adults and children, it reveals the degree to which smallholding predominated the village's economy. When the privatization decrees were handed down in the 1880s, community members received titles to much of the communal land, and smallholding continued to prevail, although a few ladino-owned coffee plantations and cattle ranches emerged as well. A government survey of Nahuizalco in 1913 took note of the emergence of the coffee fincas and cattle haciendas and noted that Indians were working on them. But the survey also noted that "one of the circumstances that most contributes to the development and well-being of this district [*comarca*] is the manner in which the rural property is divided up; here each inhabitant possesses a piece of land where he grows his subsistence crops." Such evidence portrays Nahuizalco as a predominantly Indian village in which Indians retained a substantial economic presence despite the privatization decrees and the emergence of ladinos.[69]

The archival evidence of Nahuizalco's political history begins in the year 1884 with a rebellion. On the night of October 5, as many as two thousand Indians attacked the town and killed the municipal officials, leaving only the priest alive, and then burned the municipal hall, the archives, and the home of a local ladino who was described as being the "greatest oppressor" of the Indians. The rebels killed more than two dozen people, all of them ladino. After suppressing the revolt and returning the ladinos to power, the government launched an investigation and eventually executed ten people for leading the revolt.[70] The rebels' motives are unclear, but their actions reveal intense animosity between Indians and ladinos, as well as the fact that in 1884 ladinos controlled the municipal council. Just over one year later, however, in the elections of 1885, the Indians gained control of the council and held on to it for the next eighteen years.

The Indians rose to power in Nahuizalco in 1885 probably as a result of the overthrow of President Rafael Zaldívar (1876–1885) in May of that year. The coup against Zaldívar was led by General Francisco Menéndez, who went on to serve as president until 1890. Menéndez was aided in the coup by a number of other generals, including General Rafael Gutiérrez, who, according to reports from the U.S. consul, led a force of Indian soldiers from Nahuizalco.[71] If that is true, we can only assume that some interesting negotiations went on between the indigenous people of Nahuizalco and General Gutiérrez. The unfortunate lack of documentation prevents us from knowing what they said to one another and the promises that might have been made between them. But available evidence suggests that 1885 was not the first time that the indigenous inhabitants of Nahuizalco had been recruited in support of a national-level political conflagration. Witnesses to the rebellion of 1884 testified that some of the rebels were dressed in militia uniforms, suggesting a preexisting linkage between local forces and national-level political players.[72] It is likely that the Indians were given control of the municipality in December 1885 in exchange for their service to the coup leaders.

It is notable that Nahuizalco's Indians make their appearance in the political record in the mid-1880s, at roughly the same time that the privatization decrees were being implemented. A lack of evidence prevents us from knowing if privatization inspired Nahuizalco's Indians to rise up in rebellion in 1884, or ally with Gutiérrez in 1885, or seek control of the municipal government. But some the coincidences are noteworthy. After all, prior to privatization, the Indians would have had little need to bother with municipal government. They would have lived in a functioning community with control over a vast communal property, so municipal government might have been a distraction. But after privatization, it is possible that Indians decided to enter into municipal politics in hopes of being able to use the powers of local government to protect themselves and prevent their ladino rivals from taking the advantage.

It is amidst these events that an Indian by the name of Nicolas Lúe became alcalde in Nahuizalco in December 1885. For the next seventeen years the Indians retained control of the municipal council. Some of the Indian surnames that predominate in the lists of municipal officials are Lúe, Tepas, Lipe, Cumil, Nolasco, and Córtez (see table 3.2). A pair of nullification requests from 1887 and 1894 suggest that the Indians were divided into at least two competing factions, because both requests were submitted by Indians in denunciation of other Indians.[73] Unfortunately, a lack of documentation prohibits the reconstruction of the rival networks, and the steady turnover in office makes it impossible to identify the principal leaders of each network or to trace the evolution of their political relations. In their study of ethnic politics in the region, historians Jeff Gould and Aldo Lauria-Santiago also noted these intra-Indian divisions and suggest that they reflected economic differentiation as a result of the expansion of coffee. They suggest that some of the more prosperous Indians may have thrown their lot in with ladinos, believing that their interests and prospects would be better protected under ladino leadership.[74] Regardless of means, however, it is clear that between 1885 and 1903, Indians controlled municipal government.

Table 3.2   Election Results in Nahuizalco during the Years of Indian Rule, 1885–1901 (partial results)

December 1885	*December 1886*	*December 1887 (annulled)*
A) Nicolás Lúe	A) José María Arias	A) Manuel Hernández
	R) Isidoro Tepas	R) Francisco Cortéz
	R) Hipólito Campo	R) Juan Cerén
	R) Nazario Lúe	R) Isidrio Cortéz
	R) Juan Crúz Merío	R) Candelario Lipe
	S) Cipriano País	S) Francisco Crúz

May 1888 (replacement)	*December 1889*	*December 1890*
A) Isidoro Pérez	A) Matías Beltrán	A) Manuel Hernández
R) Pedro Pérez	R) Jesús Hernández	R) Francisco Cortéz
R) Norbeto Lúe	R) M. Merío	R) Santiago Blanco
R) José Hernández	R) Nazario Cumil	R) Catarino Cortéz
R) Norbeto Rafael	R) Rosalio Hernández	R) Cresencio Quinteros
S) Juan Ramos Hernández	S) Norbeto Crúz	S) Manuel Ortíz

December 1891	*December 1893*	*December 1895*
A) Santiago Nolazco	A) Andrés Martínez	A) Ruperto Martínez
R) Serapio Galicio	R) Manuel Esquina	R) Demetrio López
R) Enrique Cortéz	R) Yanuario Esquina	R) Candelario Lipe
R) Leandro Juárez	R) José Nolazco	R) Antonio Lúe
R) Ascencio Cerén	R) Juan Pérez	R) Francisco Cortéz
S) Saturino Arias	S) Feliciano Pérez	S) José María Hernández

December 1896	*December 1900*	*December 1901*
A) José María Tepas	A) Indalecio Cortéz	A) Rúperto Martínez
R) Leandro Juárez	R) Gerónimo Cortéz	R) Eulojio Tesorero
R) Manuel Tesorero	R) Esteban Pérez	R) Salvador Milan
R) Manuel Valentín	R) Victoriano Rafael	R) Simon Lipe
R) Estanislao Lipe	R) Nicolás Merced	R) Pataleon Pérez
R) José Ramos Hernández	R) Juan Cena	R) Encarnación Ortíz
R) Norberto Lúe	R) Albino Elena	R) Buenaventura Páis
S) Norberto Guzmán	S) Norberto Guzmán	S) Lorenzo Pérez

Source: Libro del Gobernador, Nazario Salaverría, Sonsonate, June 1885 to January 1886, AGN, MG, unclassified box; Juntas de Elecciones, Nahuizalco, AGN, MG, SS, Box "Política 1890–1899, 1900–1908."

Key: A) Alcalde, R) Regidor, S) Síndico

Throughout the first decade of Indian rule, the ladinos of Nahuizalco kept a low profile. They did not challenge the Indian councils in the annual elections, unless they were surreptitiously working through factional Indian allies. But in the election of 1896 the ladinos emerged and publicly challenged the Indians for control over municipal government. The ladinos were led by the Brito family and in particular Eduardo Brito, the family patriarch. Brito was an aspiring cattle rancher, and he and his family came to own two sizable plantations in Nahuizalco. The Britos allied with another ladino family, Valdés, whose principal representative was Sebastián Valdés, owner of the plantation "Santa Teresa." The Valdés family too was emerging as a prominent landowning clan, eventually possessing five plantations in the region.[75]

A local citizen of Nahuizalco described the political battle of 1896 in plain terms, although his sympathies were with the Indians: "During last Sunday's elections for local authorities in this village, some [*algunos cuántos*] ladinos attempted to elect as Alcalde Sebastián Valdés; but the people, that is the Indians, rejected said individual and instead chose the Indian José María Tepas as Alcalde and other Indians for the remaining posts. Those persons who supported the candidacy of Valdés are dissatisfied and are working to nullify the elections contrary to the will of the people."[76] The ladinos did not find allies at the national level to support them in their bid to oust the Indians from the municipal council. The president at the time, General Rafael Gutiérrez, was the man who had mobilized Nahuizalco's Indians in 1885, and so it appears that the ladinos did not have a sympathetic ear in the current administration. The government rejected the ladinos' nullification request and allowed the Indians to remain in power. But the mere existence of the nullification attempt foretold ongoing Indian/ladino rivalries. If it is true that the Gutiérrez government rejected the petition because its local allies were in power in Nahuizalco, then we would have a classic example of repayment of a patronage favor.

The ladinos made a second grab for power in 1901, and although they failed once again, they made a show of strength. The notable feature of the election was the dramatic increase in voting among the Indians. In prior elections, the number of Indian voters ranged between a low of 52 (in the election of 1890) and a high of 187 (in the election of 1895). But in 1901, Indians cast 651 votes. The victorious Indian candidates won with 649 votes apiece, demonstrating their capacity to control virtually all of the voting. But the ladino candidates were not excluded entirely: Eduardo Brito received one vote for síndico. His ability to ensure that even this single vote was recorded in his favor reflects the growth of his political clout. Moreover, the sudden surge in the overall number of voters suggests that the Indians considered the ladinos to be a genuine threat and decided to rely upon their strength in numbers. The increase also may reveal a diminution of intra-Indian factionalism. In either case, the near unanimity of the election indicates that the Indians excluded the ladinos from voting and knew how to conduct elections according to the informal rules of politics.[77]

In the election of 1903, the ladinos finally prevailed over the Indians by seizing control of the polling station and preventing their adversaries from voting. Eduardo Brito was elected president of the electoral board, and a member of the Valdés family, Arcadio Valdés, was elected alcalde. The seven other people elected to the municipal council along with Valdés were Martín Hernández, Eulalio Guzmán, Ambrocio Pérez, Andrés Mauricio, Pedro Crúz, Eulalio Tadeo, and José Zacapa. Some or all of them might have been Indian—at least some of the surnames suggest that they were. But none of them appear in corroborating documents that would allow either their ethnicity or their political loyalties to be traced. None of them had been in office during the prior eighteen years of Indian rule. If they were Indians, they were likely estranged from the Indian hierarchy and shifted their alliances to the ladinos in hopes of climbing the political ladder. Regardless, the ladinos controlled the election of 1903. The results of the next election (1904) are not known, but the election of 1905 resulted in yet another ladino victory. Sebastián Valdés was elected alcalde, and another Valdés and a Brito served on the electoral board.[78]

The results of the next eighteen elections are not known, but it appears that Indians successfully competed in them. A local observer commented in 1926 that Indians "almost always are in control of this Municipality."[79] In 1923 Indians were in power and were confronted by the ladinos, led by Rodolfo Brito, the heir to Eduardo Brito's political empire, and Antonio Contreras, Rodolfo's nephew. They convinced some members of a nearby National Guard post to assist them in preventing Indians from entering the polling place during the election. Antonio Contreras was elected alcalde, but he was later forced from power in a nullification process; this suggests once again that the Indians had managed to build loyalties with national-level power players.[80] The stakes of the 1923 election were high because the government of President Alfonso Quiñónez Molina had changed the tenure of municipal office to four years, so whoever got control of the council in 1923 would hold it until 1927. The documentation suggests that the next four years were tumultuous, with ladino and Indian representatives moving into and out of municipal office. A document from September 1926 states that the alcalde was an Indian by the name of Pedro Rodríguez, but five months earlier a letter written by three ladinos, evidently estranged from the Brito-Contreras network, states that the national government had made a mistake by allowing Brito and Contreras to return to power, because they mistreated Indians.[81]

Evidence of local politics in Nahuizalco in the 1920s and 1930s reveals much about politics at the national level and thus could be reserved for later chapters, but I have presented the evidence here because it highlights the ongoing ethnic basis of political network building at the municipal level. With the ascension of Pío Romero Bosque to the presidency in 1927, the Indians had an opportunity to regain control of the municipal council once and for all, because the Romero government emphasized genuinely democratic procedures, and by virtue of their overwhelming numbers the Indians had a great advantage. Indeed, Indians won the municipal election of December 1927, but the Brito clique did not surrender power easily. Rodolfo Brito contended that the victor, Pedro Mendoza, was illiterate and demanded that his election be annulled; illiterate people were not legally allowed to hold public office. The Romero government investigated the denunciation and eventually ruled in Brito's favor, despite the advice of the military commander of Sonsonate Department, who wrote that "it is better to have four thousand content Indians rather than four content ladinos, who have used the municipal offices only to swindle the Indians."[82]

Thereafter, Nahuizalco became a hotbed of ethnically based political conflict. Whichever group was in power, Indians or ladinos, the other barraged the national government with a continual string of denunciations and nullification requests.[83] The denunciations arrived not only at election time, but in the interim as well. In one of these interim nullification requests, submitted by the ladinos in 1930, members of the Brito family charged Pedro Mendoza, then serving on the municipal council—despite his illiteracy, it would seem—with drunkenness, another charge that if proven true made one ineligible for public office. Mendoza defended himself by saying that Brito's request was "motivated by nothing more than bitterness over their loss in the last election."[84] The government, however, ruled that Mendoza was a drunkard and nullified his election.

Overall, the Indians failed to regain control of the municipal government after 1927, except for one instance in the election of December 1929. The ladinos were powerful beyond their numbers. They possessed significant financial resources and controlled the municipal police. The ladinos also had other elements in their favor. The Romero government, while supportive of democratic ideals, was far removed from the local complexities of Nahuizalco. Government authorities probably harbored the same stereotypical attitudes about Indians used by Nahuizalco's ladinos in their denunciations. Such bias probably made it easier for national-level officials to believe that Mendoza was a drunk, whether he was or not. The Romero government was also overwhelmed by the multitude of nullification requests pouring into San Salvador at the time. Government officials found it difficult to find the time to conduct proper investigations, and in a pinch it was easier to enforce the status quo, which in Nahuizalco after 1926 meant favoring the ladinos. However, in one notable exception, the government's lack of knowledge actually worked to the advantage of the Indians. In the election of December 1929 the ladinos won the initial election, but in an ironic twist, the Indians charged the victor, Rodolfo Brito, with drunkenness and demanded that his victory be nullified. In response to the Indians' request, the national government dispatched the deputy departmental governor (the regular governor was occupied with other nullification requests), who was so busy with his own backlog of cases that he abandoned all hope of discovering whether or not Brito actually was a drunk and ruled in favor of the Indians simply because "they presented more witnesses than the opposition."[85] Notwithstanding this one example, such capriciousness rarely benefited the Indians, and by the municipal election of January 1932 they had run out of patience.

The municipal elections that took place in January 1932 had been postponed from the original date of December 1931 because of political tumult at the national level, which will be described in later chapters. The timing was propitious, because throughout the western region, Indian communities were mobilizing for an armed insurrection, and the day of the election almost coincided with the day of the planned revolt. In the election one slate was led by a member of the Brito family, Francisco Brito, while the other slate was headed by an Indian, Pablo Cruz. When it came time to vote, the ladinos seized control of the municipal hall and allowed Indians to vote, but recorded their votes in favor of Brito. The Indians protested and demanded a nullification. They sent their initial request to the governor of Sonsonate on January 16. Nullifications normally required two months to be processed, and decisions seldom arrived in less than four months. Although the Indians knew this, they wanted immediate action. Four days later, on January 20, having received no response, the Indians sent another letter to Sonsonate requesting a response to their petition, but still no word came back. They sent yet another petition the following day. The failure to act on the third request, they warned, would have grave consequences: "Certainly it was not your intention to forget our petition, nor is it normally obligatory to respond in such short time, but failure to transmit even a verbal acknowledgment of our petition is now a threat to the social order."[86] No response arrived, and on the next day Nahuizalco was taken over by armed peasants.

Cuisnahuat

The municipality of Cuisnahuat offers another case in which Indians participated directly in municipal politics. Cuisnahuat was a remote, medium-sized village located in the eastern part of Sonsonate Department, close to the border with La Libertad Department, in what was then known as the "balsam coast." It was an agricultural village dedicated primarily to the production of subsistence crops, although during the nineteenth century it had also produced balsam wood. An 1858 agricultural survey by the departmental governor reported that the "majority of the land is uncultivated and comprises highland forests and virgin mountains. . . . The principal occupation of the inhabitants is the cultivation and exploitation of balsam." The governor also took note of the predominantly Indian makeup of the population: "The language or dialect used by the inhabitants is Nahuat. . . . Generally the men dress in nothing more than the *calzoncillo* and *camisa de manta* and the women in a skirt [*refajo*] of typical fabric and a wrap [*tapadera* or *toalla de madapollan*]." The population of the village in 1858 was estimated at 750. In 1903 it had risen to 3,235, which qualified it as the sixth largest in the department. By the 1920s the agricultural production of the village was still predominated by smallholders, and only three properties of medium size were identified officially as haciendas. A government survey in 1913 reported that "the patrimony of the inhabitants consists of the cultivation of cereals and the exploitation of some balsam. There are no haciendas or fincas of great importance, and the rural property is in the hands of the Indians."[87]

The archival evidence of Cuisnahuat's political history begins in the year 1885 with the Indians already in control of the municipal council. It is not clear when or how the Indians originally ascended to power, or if they did so in the same apparent manner as Nahuizalco's Indians in 1885—in alliance with a powerful national-level political player. Regardless, Cuisnahuat's Indians controlled all but one election over the fifteen-year span between 1885 and 1900. It appears that the Indians were not divided, as were their counterparts in Nahuizalco, because each municipal council and electoral board was dominated by individuals who had held posts in past years. Juan Inocente Martínez, Albino Clara, Bernardino Ramírez, and Luís Hernández were among the principal Indian leaders (see table 3.3). Politics in the village was divided along ethnic lines, ladinos on one side, Indians on the other. In 1900 the Indians lost power to the ladinos after a bitter campaign. The ladinos held the municipal council for the next two years until the Indians succeeded in ousting them. The Indians then held the council for at least the next five years.

Land was at the center of the political conflict in Cuisnahuat, as is evident in the election of 1900. The ladinos won the election, and the Indians submitted a nullification request. Fortunately, both sides of the dispute provided long explanations of their positions. The Indians were represented by Albino Clara, the standing alcalde, and Bernardino Ramírez. They accused the ladinos of enlisting the services of armed men who used force and violence to ensure a ladino victory: "The armed men

Table 3.3 Municipal Councils in Cuisnahuat, Sonsonate Department, 1885–1899 (partial results)

December 1885 (Indian)	*December 1886 (Indian)*	*December 1887 (Indian)*
A) Damian Hernández	A) Luís Hernández	A) Bernardino Ramírez
R) Juan Incocente Martínez	R) Ignacio Coreto	R) Jesús Leonardo Carías
R) Coronado Ruis	R) Monico Augustín	R) Marcelo Santos
S) Margarito Pintín	S) Juan Antonio Zosa	S) Luis Conce

December 1888 (Indian)	*December 1889 (Indian)*	*December 1890 (Ladino)*
A) Juan Incocente Martínez	A) Juan Inocente Martínez	A) Antonio Chacón
R) Manuel Constante		R) Oracio Espinoza
R) Felix Hernández		R) Jesús Leandro Gómez
S) ? Flores		S) José María Rivas

December 1891 (Indian)	*December 1893 (Indian)*	*December 1896 (Indian)*
A) Luís Conce	A) Juan Inocente Martínez	A) Albino Clara
R) Prudencio Valenica	R) Remigio Flores	R) Norberto Crúz
R) Pedro Guerra	R) Francisco Ramírez	R) Inocente Augustín
S) Romualdo Bardales	S) Simon García	S) Perfecto Constante
(Directorio)	(Directorio)	
Bernardino Ramírez	Bernardino Ramírez	
Narcisco Hernández	Fidel Hernández	
Damian Hernández	Perfecto Constante	
Macario Reyes	Luís Hernández	
Venancio Hernández		

December 1899 (Indian)

A) Albino Clara

Source: Libro del Gobernador, Nazario Salaverría, Sonsonate, June 1885 to January 1886, AGN, MG, unclassified box; and Juntas de Elecciones, Cuisnahuat, AGN, MG, SS, Box "Política, 1890–1899, 1900–1908."

Key: A) Alcalde, R) Regidor, S) Síndico

were working on the behalf of José María Hernández, who is the principal representative of the ladinos, who have recently arrived in this region and have taken the best land away from the Indians. The ladinos want to gain control of the positions of local authority for themselves, as they did in 1891, which resulted in the loss of protocol in the Municipality, for they used up all the municipal funds for their own purposes and distributed the greater portion of the lands to themselves."[88]

The ladinos responded to the Indian denunciation in kind:

Since many years ago, the number of ladinos in this region has been increasing and suffering from the dictatorial attitude of the Indians in regard to the holding of municipal office. They have contempt for everything outside their primitive customs and their idolatrous and immoral habits, and they reject everything that is progressive. They beat their children and have no respect for the property of people outside their community. We present the following list of complaints:

1) If there is a complaint against a jornalero, the Indian Alcalde instead orders the arrest of the solicitor.

2) They spend the municipal funds in the bar.

3) Five or six caciques dominate the rest of the population and do not want any power to go to the ladinos for fear of losing their power. . . .

8) The Indian Alcalde Luis Hernández used municipal funds to purchase property for himself, and contrary to the law, forced ladinos to pay a tax [canon].

9) It is the only village in the nation that is governed solely by Indians.[89]

These denunciations reveal that both the Indians and the ladinos proffered the same complaints: the monopolization of land and political power by the other group.

The ethnic clash over land is revealed in the case of the hacienda "Tonalá." In 1890, a local ladino by the name of Juan Mathé complained to the national government that Indians were squatting illegally on portions of Tonalá. The hacienda had been measured by the national government and purchased by Mathé in the year 1888, the same year that the communal lands of Cuisnahuat were measured and privatized. The Indians claimed that Tonalá was part of their communal domain and that Mathé had no right to title it for himself. That Tonalá became the center of a legal dispute would not have surprised anyone familiar with the agricultural report of 1858, because in that report the Indians' ties to Tonalá are made clear. During his visit to Cuisnahuat in 1858, the governor interviewed some of the older villagers (*ancianos*), who informed him that their ancestors originally had lived in the "lands of Tonalá" but were moved in the early eighteenth century to what is now Cuisnahuat due to the flooding of the Río Grande. The ancianos claimed that the Spanish crown (*autoridad regia*) granted their lands to them as ejidos, or communal lands, but that the titles had since been lost. Mathé claimed that the lands of Tonalá were state-owned *baldio* land and that he had purchased them legally from the government. The ministry of government investigated, ruled in favor of Mathé, and instructed the municipal council of Cuisnahuat, which at the time was controlled by Indians, to respect Mathé's rights and assist him in preventing incursions. The council agreed to abide by the government's decision but continued to refer to Tonalá as the "alleged" *baldio* land. Regardless of who held the legitimate claim to Tonalá, the conflict reveals that the Indian leadership held the conviction that ladinos were benefiting at their expense.[90]

It is evident that certain ladinos held substantial portions of Cuisnahuat's land wealth. Juan Mathé is one clear example. On an 1897 list of village inhabitants, only one person is categorized as a *notable,* a ladino by the name of Francisco Lemus who had served on the ladino-controlled council of 1901. Only ladinos appear on lists of the principal cattle ranchers in the village. Of these, Francisco Recinos served on the 1901 council, and Antonio Chacón served on the 1901 council and also the ladino-controlled council of 1890. At the same time, certain Indians possessed disproportionate amounts of land. A list of the principal agriculturists in the village contains nine names, three of which are Indian: Bernardino Ramírez, Albino Clara, and Anastacio Hernández, three of the four main Indian political leaders in the region. Ramírez also owned one-third of a nearby hacienda. It is not clear how these Indians accumulated their landholdings. It is likely that they followed the pattern set by wealthy Indians in almost every other community: they or their families had gained access to extra portions of communal land prior to the era of privatization and then acquired titles to the land during the privatization process.[91] Unfortunately, lack of evidence prevents us from knowing how these wealthier Indians legitimized their wealth and continued to curry favor among their poorer brethren. Presumably they relied on traditional indigenous cultural mechanisms, such as the age-based hierarchy within the cofradía.[92]

The Indian and ladino elites of Cuisnahuat employed identical tactics to gain political power. They controlled the polling station, elected themselves to the electoral board, excluded one another's supporters from voting, and put themselves in office. In the election of 1900, for example, the ladinos controlled the polling station and refused to allow Indians to vote. They even went so far as to state in the official election report that "the greater part of the Indian citizenry did not participate [*no concurrió*] in the election despite being registered to vote."[93] In clear violation of the formal rules, but in keeping with the tradition of monopolized elections, both Indians and ladinos elected persons to the municipal council who also had served on the electoral board. For example, in the election of 1900, José María Hernández served on the board and was also elected síndico. In the election of 1901, Antonio Quintanilla, Francisco Lemus, and Antonio Chacón held positions on the board and were elected to the council. In the election of 1903, Bernardino Ramírez was elected alcalde after having served on the board. When the ladinos reported their electoral results, they did not indicate if voting was unanimous, and although the Indians recorded "opposition" votes in 1903, only members of their network received these votes (see table 3.4). The results of the election of 1903 exhibit the typical voting pattern in which a single political network monopolized the election. One of the candidates (Chacón) who lost the position of alcalde proceeded to win the office of regidor, while another candidate who lost the position of regidor won the office of síndico. A curious feature of the election of 1903 is the inclusion of Chacón, a ladino, on the Indian-controlled council. Either this represents a rare case in which a member of the opposition was given a position on a municipal council as a concession, or Chacón had joined forces with the Indians. Unfortunately, the available evidence does not make clear what transpired. Regardless, Chacón's involvement does not undermine the point that the Indians controlled the election.

In short, the two competing factions of Cuisnahuat looked very much like any traditional patronage network. Both of them were run by a handful of local elites who employed the traditional tools of electoral manipulation to gain power; they monopolized voting and distributed the spoils

Table 3.4 Election Results, Cuisnahuat, Sonsonate Department, 1900, 1901, 1903 (partial results)

Municipal Council	Votes Cast	Members of Directorio
December 1900 (Ladino)		
A) Apolinario Rivas	n.a.	José María Hernández
R) Adolfo Cierra		Francisco Lemus
R) Justo Rodríguez		
S) José María Hernández		
December 1901 (Ladino)		
A) Antonio Quintanilla	n.a.	Antonio Quintanilla
R) Antonio Chacón		Francisco Lemus
R) Francisco Recinos		Antonio Chacón
S) Francisco Lemus		Indalecio Sierra
December 1903 (Indian)		
A) Bernardino Ramírez	154	Bernardino Ramírez
Anastacio Hernández	19	Antonio Chacón
Antonio Chacón	1	Vicente Chacón
R) Antonio Chacón	166	Román Jacinto
Regimio Flores	6	Fidel Hernández
R) Isidoro Martínez	68	
Crisanto Barrera	1	
S) Crisanto Barrera	173	
Remigio Flores	1	

Source: Juntas de Elecciones, Cuisnahuat, AGN, MG, SS, Box "Política, 1890–1899, 1900–1908."

Key: A) Alcalde; R) Regidor; S) Síndico

of office among themselves. Ethnicity did not alter the functioning of patronage-based politics, but simply gave it a unique look. If anything, ethnicity made political bosses' lives easier, because the supporters were motivated by their ethnic identities. Nevertheless, the bosses were the principal beneficiaries. Democracy was no more apparent within the ethnically based networks than in any other patronage alliance.

* * *

Local political networks were built on diverse foundations. Oftentimes they revolved around the stereotypical patron-client relationship of a landed elite and his dependent laborers. The elite sought to have his clients do his bidding. But the clients wanted something too. Even if their bargaining position was limited because of their economic vulnerability, their interactions with the patron were a relationship, and like any other relationship, it was complicated and open to negotiation. We have little direct evidence of those relationships, but we can surmise that they were complex. If nothing else, this chapter shows the diversity of the foundations of local political networks, particularly in the case of ethnicity. In municipalities with significant indigenous populations, as in the cases of Nahuizalco and Cuisnahuat, ethnic bonds provided a basis for political recruitment. Powerful, ethnicity-based political networks in both municipalities battled for control over municipal office with rival ladino networks that were similarly united along ethnic lines. These ethnic networks demonstrated an impressive adherence to the informal rules of politics. Even though the indigenous majority was likely to win any election in which people voted unencumbered, the indigenous networks practiced politics in the same manner as their ladino counterparts, by controlling the polling stations and restricting the franchise to their supporters.

CHAPTER 4

MUNICIPAL ELECTIONS AND MUNICIPAL AUTONOMY, CA. 1880-1930

The last chapter showed how local political networks were built. This chapter looks at what those networks did on election day to gain control of municipal office. It looks at the nature of the challenge between rival networks, the tactics they used in their attempts to control voting, and the ways they used violence and the nullification process in support of their bids for office. All of this was highly regimented, and yet it all functioned according to informal rules that everyone understood and accepted as the normal way of doing things.

This is a good moment to remind ourselves of the frequency of elections in El Salvador, as well as their intimate settings. In its first century of existence, El Salvador experienced something in the range of twenty thousand elections, involving tens of thousands of electoral overseers and candidates and hundreds of thousands of voters. Most of those elections took place in small communities, such as those described in the pages below, where most every political player knew everyone else involved in the process. Whatever happened in any one election would be remembered and carried over into the next one—to say nothing of its impact on interpersonal and professional relationships in the interim. Even in the larger urban areas, anyone with political clout knew everyone else of relevance. Given that elections for national offices occurred in the municipalities, and that they were run by the municipal authorities who had come to power in municipal elections just one month prior, the municipal setting was ground zero for all political affairs in El Salvador.

This chapter is divided into two interrelated parts that transition into the national narrative in the next chapter. The first part sticks closely to the details of electoral battles at the municipal level. The second part begins by returning to the national level, showing how relations between the municipal and national levels changed from the early twentieth century onward with the consolidation and centralization of state power. Throughout most of the nineteenth century, regional- or national-level political networks had limited ability to control electoral happenings in the nation's municipalities, and even sometimes in their own strongholds. But slowly and steadily, starting around 1900, that began to change as the power of the central state grew. National-level authorities began to impose their will more readily, and in response municipal-level officials defended themselves with the concept of municipal autonomy.

Local Elections

Once a local political boss assembled a network of supporters (clients, strategic allies, friends, family, ethnic kinsmen, and so on), he was ready to contend for power in the annual municipal elections. These elections represented precise moments when the strength of politician and network were put to the test. At stake was control over the municipal government and all the rewards that officeholding brought, including the opportunity to build or reinforce alliances with more powerful political actors outside the municipality.

Months of planning and preparation had to come together on election day if a network was to stand victorious at the end of the day. It had to control voters, secure the support of any necessary allies, and outmaneuver opponents. Most important, a network had to control the polling station. Elections were contested affairs, but voting was not. Candidates competed with one another for control over the polls in order to monopolize voting. A network gained control of the polls either physically, by occupying the polling station on the morning of the election, or metaphorically, by ensuring that the officials who conducted the election were allies.

Like the national-level elections examined in the preceding chapters, municipal elections were decided by overwhelming margins, and usually by unanimity. This was the case in both indirect elections prior to 1872 and direct elections thereafter. The multitude of voting records scattered throughout Salvadoran archives stands as evidence.[1] In Nahuilingo (Sonsonate Department), the municipal council that came to power in 1840 did so with all nine electoral votes in its favor.[2] The village of Santa Clara (San Vicente Department) reported, as the results of its election of 1843, "the eight electors have gathered . . . and have elected, by a unanimity of votes, Señor Coronado Panameño as Alcalde."[3] In Sonsonate City in 1864 the municipal officials were elected "by a unanimity of votes."[4] In Nahuizalco in 1908, the Junta de Elecciones reported that "in the act of voting by the citizens of this municipality for the officials to serve in the next year, it has resulted that the following persons were elected by a unanimity of 454 votes each."[5]

In the event that voting in an indirect election did not go according to the plans of the dominant network, the leaders of the network simply canceled it and held additional rounds of voting. During the election of 1854 in San Miguel City, the dominant network canceled voting three times because some of the electors voted for other candidates. On the fourth round, the dominant network reined in the dissenters and obtained the desired unanimous results.[6]

Results from the election of 1883 in the village of Ataco (Ahuachapán Department) are indicative of the overwhelming majority that was achieved in the absence of unanimity. A total of 106 votes were cast, and all of the candidates obtained more than 90 percent of the votes (see table 4.1). Local electoral officials often did not even bother to record the opponents' votes in such lopsided contests. They dismissed the tiny minority of opposition votes in terms similar to those used in 1889 by the president of the electoral board in Ishuatán (Sonsonate Department): "Other candidates received votes for said offices, but in numbers so insignificant that . . . the citizens listed above are elected."[7] Although dominant networks preferred to eliminate their opponents from an election, occasionally, either as a concession or as part of a negotiated deal, the dominant network allowed its rivals to cast some votes. The danger in such gestures became apparent when the opposition refused to accept its predetermined defeat and sent large numbers of voters to the polls. The dominant network then had to take drastic action in order to preserve its victory. Such an event occurred in a municipal election in the port town of Acajutla (Sonsonate Department) in the late 1880s. The dominant network allowed its rivals to cast some votes but then discovered that it was losing the election. Voting was canceled and, in the words of the departmental governor, "various disturbances" broke out.[8]

Allowing the opposition to participate in an election was the exception to the rule. In almost all cases where more than one candidate received votes for the same office, each candidate belonged to the same political network. The candidate who lost the election for one office typically won a different office in that same election. The results from the municipal election of 1849 in the village of Guadalupe (San Vicente Department) illustrate this phenomenon (see table 4.2). The election was indirect, and Guadalupe was a small village, so only ten electores participated—for the

Table 4.1   Election Results, Ataco, Ahuachapán Department, 1883

Position	Candidate	# of Votes	% of Votes
Alcalde	Isidro Rivas	101	95
	Andrés Avelino	4	4
	Sesario Vicente	1	1
Regidor #1	Baleriano Enriques	96	91
	Lucas Gómez	10	9
Regidor #2	Juan Secundino	104	98
	Lucas Gómez	1	1
	Baleriano Enriques	1	1
Síndico	Sinecio Juares	104	98
	Domingo Carlos	2	2

Source: Junta Electoral, Ataco, December 17, 1883, AGN, MG, Box "1882, 84, 86, 87, 88."

sake of comparison, in that same year more than fifty electores participated in the election in the larger municipality of Sonsonate City.[9] The
election offers a typical example of an election that was dominated by a
single network. Multiple candidates received votes, but all of them were
members of the same network, and the losers of one office simply won different offices. Bentura Cornejo lost the position of alcalde but won regidor
#1, and Ignacio Parada lost regidor #2 but won the office of síndico.

The results from the municipal election of 1886 in Juayúa (Sonsonate
Department) offer a similar case (see table 4.3). The election was direct,
which explains the large number of votes relative to Guadalupe in 1849,
but the results are similar. Multiple candidates received votes for each office, but all of the participants were part of the same political network, and
each of the four regidores had lost at least one other office in that same
election.

The evidence does not make clear whether the results in tables 4.2
and 4.3 show members of the same patronage network competing with
one another for office, or if the winners were predetermined by the upper

Table 4.2   Municipal Election, Guadalupe, San Vicente Department
December 1849 (Indirect Voting)

Office	Candidate	# of Votes
Alcalde	Ciriaco Piñeda	7
	Bentura Cornejo	2
	Rafael Morales	1
Regidor #1	Bentura Cornejo	9
	Rafael Morales	1
Regidor #2	Liverate Aguilar	9
	Ignacio Parada	1
Síndico	Ignacio Parada	6
	Apolinario Platero	4

Source: Junta Electoral, Guadalupe, December 16, 1849, AGN, MG, SSV, 1849, unclassified box.

Table 4.3   Municipal Election, Juayúa, Sonsonate Department,
December 1886 (Direct Voting)

Office	Candidates (Number of votes in parentheses)
Alcalde	Tadeo Pérez (163); Ramón Mendoza (25); Adolfo Cea (24)
Regidor #1	Ramón Mendoza (158); Felipe González (25); Margarito Mata (11)
Regidor #2	Luciano Siete (133); Luciano Mendoza (28); Felipe González (23); Román Mendoza(12)
Regidor #3	Luciano Mendoza (85); Luciano Siete (33); two others with less
Regidor #4	Margarito Mata (90); Luciano Mendoza (24); two others with less
Síndico	Isidoro Josa (135); Zeferino Alfaro (72)

Source: Junta Electoral, Juayúa, December 1886, AGN, MG, SS, Box "Política, 1890–9, 1900–08."

echelons of the network. One possibility is that the leading bosses of a network did not want to alienate their underlings by choosing one over another, and thus allowed them to compete for office, just as occurred in the vice presidential election of 1895. The danger in allowing genuine competition was the possibility of rivalries developing within a network. Regardless, the results in tables 4.2 and 4.3 reveal a single political network doling out the spoils of office to its own members. Overall, tables 4.1, 4.2, and 4.3 emphasize the golden rule of politics in El Salvador: electoral victory required the monopolization of polling stations.

The Nature of the Challenge

The system of patronage-based politics promoted a monopoly on office-holding, but the system also functioned best when it allowed for some turnover. Political bosses out of power had to feel that they would be given a fighting chance to oust the incumbent and take their turn in office. If an opposition boss was perpetually denied access to power, he might take his bid outside the system by turning populist and trying to tap into the political will of the masses. Richard Graham describes a similar process at work in Brazil: "Since some who deemed themselves worthy of power would inevitably not hold it, their protest must be accommodated if it were not to threaten stability. A means had to be devised that would assure them that their time would come."[10] While exclusive, political office had to be shared.

The formal rules of municipal elections, which remained basically unchanged between 1840 and 1940, were designed to safeguard the system by encouraging turnover in office.[11] The rules stipulated that elections were to occur annually and that municipal officials could not be elected to consecutive terms. During the early years of the republic, officials had to remain out of office for two years before regaining their eligibility; it was later changed to one year.[12] The rules also prohibited family dynasties. Municipal officials who shared four degrees of consanguinity were not allowed to serve together. In some cases this restriction was applied to members of consecutive councils. The rules also forbade municipal officials from campaigning on the behalf of future candidates, thereby limiting their opportunity to use official powers to boost allies. Finally, the rules stipulated that all eligible voters were required to both register and vote. This provision was designed to prevent incumbents from restricting the franchise to their supporters. Granted, all of these rules were ignored to varying degrees, but not so much as to threaten the long-term survival of the system. Political powerbrokers recognized that the best insurance against losing power permanently was to give up power temporarily. In some cases, challengers had to wait up to a decade before coming to power, but invariably the incumbents stepped aside.

The Tactics of the Challenge

In order to ascend to power, a challenger ultimately had to beat the incumbents at their own game by assembling a body of clients and supporters, building alliances with other political bosses, and controlling the machinery of the election. If an election was uncontested, meaning that opposition networks deferred to a single, dominant network, voting was a routine process. The dominant network controlled the electoral board and allowed only its voters to appear before the board members on election day. When opponents persisted with their challenge, voting became disordered, because only one network could claim victory at the end of the day.

Opponents could launch a challenge at any stage of the electoral process. The first opportunity was during the period of registration, when every voter was supposed to make his way to the municipal hall and register his name in the registration book (*libro de registros*). The incumbent municipal officials supervised the registration book and sometimes used their power to discriminate against rivals. Registration officials in the municipality of Jayaque (La Libertad Department) in 1890 mysteriously disappeared whenever opponents arrived to register. "The Alcalde and his Municipal Secretary," accused the opposition, "refuse to do it [register us], making excuses and retiring at the moment we arrive to inscribe ourselves."[13] In the village of Yoloaiquín (Morazán Department), the alcalde arbitrarily altered the rules of registration in order to disqualify his opponents. The names of voters customarily were carried over from one year's registration book to the next, but in 1889 he ordered that voters now had to come to the municipal hall to register anew. Of course, he conveniently failed to inform his opponents of the change. On election day only the supporters of his network were registered.[14]

When municipal officials resorted to devious tactics, opponents resorted to similar measures. In the municipality of Jocoro (Morazán Department), for instance, the incumbent network refused to allow its opponents to register throughout the late 1870s and early 1880s. By election day of 1885, the opponents had run out of patience. They sent a group of their adherents posing as voters into the municipal hall. When they arrived before the election table, they pulled out weapons, grabbed the registration book, and tried to run off with it. A fight ensued, and in this case the opposition lost.[15]

Notwithstanding these examples, the registration book was not the ideal place to engage in electoral manipulation, because if a political deal was struck just prior to the election, a network might discover that it had excluded its own supporters. Moreover, the registration list was the official registry of the municipality, and officials used it for non-electoral purposes, such as tax collection and labor recruitment. So limiting the population's ability to register could prove counterproductive once the election was over.

When election day arrived, the selection of the election board offered the next opportunity for conflict. As with the registration book, the incumbent network held an advantage because the current municipal officials supervised the selection of the electoral board. It was up to the opposition to position its supporters in front of the municipal hall at the appropriate hour and force the officials to accept its slate of candidates for the board. It was precisely at this moment, 8:00 a.m. on the morning of an election, that opposing networks faced off. The leaders of each network took this opportunity to survey the strength of one another's forces and decide whether or not to persist in the bid for power. The victor stood to gain municipal power; the loser risked losing the support of his allies and sometimes even his life.

The election of 1911 in the city of Santa Ana offers a case in which one network decided to acquiesce. Two networks contested for power in the election. The incumbents were led by the Ayalas, an important coffee-growing family. The challengers were led by General Medina, also a coffee grower. Medina positioned his supporters in front of the municipal hall at 8:00 a.m. in preparation for the selection of the electoral board. Looking out over the plaza, the incumbents determined that Medina had enough supporters to control the board, so they decided to forgo the election and appoint their own board. Shortly after eight o'clock, a member of the incumbent group stepped out of the municipal hall and informed the crowd that an electoral board had been chosen and voting could commence. When Medina and his followers realized what was happening, Medina and two of his allies went into the municipal hall to negotiate. But the incumbents refused his overtures, and after a few minutes he returned empty-handed. Believing that the incumbents had the strength to defeat him if things turned rough, he withdrew his supporters from the plaza and accepted defeat.[16]

Networks employed a variety of tactics to secure control over the selection of the electoral board. In particular they took advantage of possession of the municipal hall. For instance, in the election of 1874 in

Atiquizaya (Ahuachapán Department) the incumbents initially invited representatives of the opposition onto the board but then ousted them at the last minute. "All was going well," claimed members of the opposition, "until we were told to leave and a new board was formed. When we tried to reclaim our positions the door of the municipal hall was closed before us. As a result the candidates supported by the Alcalde won."[17] In 1903 in Chinameca (San Miguel Department) the alcalde canceled two board elections because the opposition controlled them.[18] In 1891 in Juayúa (Sonsonate Department) the incumbent network lost the election for the electoral board, so the alcalde "tore the tally sheets in half . . . and declared Adolfo Cea President of the Directorio."[19] Incumbents and challengers alike frequently tried to outdo their rivals by simply waking up earlier. On numerous occasions, the leaders of a network arrived to the municipal hall at 8:00 a.m. only to discover that a rival network had turned out hours earlier to select an electoral board.[20]

The importance of controlling the board became evident once voting began. The members of the board had the power to change or ignore votes as they saw fit. In 1891 in Chapeltique (San Miguel Department), the board members appeared to be accepting votes from each of two contending networks; however, they actually recorded opposition votes in favor of their candidates.[21] Similarly, in Mercedes (La Paz Department) in 1908, the board members allowed opposition voters to enter the municipal hall, but when they arrived before the election table they were allowed only to give their name while their votes were recorded according to the desires of the board members.[22] Networks also engaged in more universal forms of electoral fraud, such as having their supporters vote more than once and bringing in voters from neighboring municipalities.[23]

Another method that networks occasionally used was forming a second electoral board in another part of town and setting up a parallel election. In 1899 in San Miguel City, for example, the opposition network successfully controlled the electoral board, but when the incumbents surrendered the municipal hall, they took the registration book with them and conducted their own election on the other side of town. Each group filled out separate tally sheets and submitted them to the departmental government for verification. The challengers claimed to have received precisely nine hundred votes, whereas the incumbents listed six hundred votes.[24] A similar process took place in the village of Santiago de María (Usulután Department) in 1927, when two evenly matched networks faced off in the election. The local police chief described the event: "At twelve o'clock today two Directorios conducted voting for the election of municipal officials. For the position of Alcalde, one Directorio recorded 754 votes in favor the candidate Don Augustín Gotuzzo; also recording one vote for Don Raúl Avila and another vote for Dionisio J. Guerrero. . . . The other Directorio . . . recorded for the position of Alcalde a total of 644 votes, all in favor of Raúl Avila."[25] It was up to national-level authorities to sort out these messes (and in these two particular cases, the government's decisions are not known).

Elections tested the power of a boss and his network. He could boast of his importance and lay claim to leadership in the municipality, but until he proved his status in the public arena, his claims meant nothing. He had to demonstrate his capacity to monopolize the machinery of the election, control the actions of his own supporters, and simultaneously thwart the aspirations of his rivals. Whoever successfully performed these tasks secured political office.

Election Nullifications

If a network tried all of these various tactics and still found itself losing an election, it had one last chance to avoid defeat: request that the election be nullified due to irregularities. As mentioned previously, each constitution in El Salvador made provisions for elections to be nullified if they were proven to be irregular. The decisive factor, of course, is who decided the meaning of *regular* and *irregular*. Initial requests for nullification were sent by supplicants in the municipality to either the departmental governor or the minister of government in San Salvador. Those officials had the power to send investigators to the municipality to accumulate evidence. If a victor was found guilty of misdeeds, his election was nullified and a replacement election was scheduled for a later date. Ostensibly, the nullification procedure existed to prevent electoral manipulation by giving candidates the right to have opponents investigated for illegal practices. Such investigations were supposed to be conducted by neutral outsiders. Like most political procedures, however, the nullification process was subverted according to the informal rules of politics. Local bosses submitted nullification requests in order to solicit the aid of powerful bosses outside the municipality in their local conflagrations. Whether or not outsiders responded to local pleas depended upon a variety of circumstances, notably the importance of the municipality and the political indebtedness of the official who received the request. The goal of the people who submitted the request was clear: force the victors out of office.

Nullifications were a recurring element of local political battles. As mentioned previously, El Salvador's national archive contains more than three hundred complete cases between 1889 and 1936, as well as a few dozen more cases for the period prior to 1889.[26] Many other nullification procedures, for which there are no surviving records, are mentioned in peripheral documents, suggesting that the actual number of cases was even greater. During particularly intense conflicts, local networks utilized the nullification process repeatedly. In Izalco, for example, the election of 1890 resulted in three nullification requests, and the election of 1900 produced five.[27]

In order to file a nullification, a supplicant had to denounce the victors by providing a summary of their offenses. These denunciations varied greatly in content. Some of them described seemingly real events, while others contained pure fabrications. Determining the difference requires a careful reading of the documentation. Nullification requests based on real events tend to contain detailed and well-documented information that can be corroborated by other evidence. By contrast, fabrications are thin in detail and speak in general terms, such as "disturbances occurred in the past election" and "the officials imposed themselves during the election."[28]

Many of the fabricated accusations avoided altogether the events related to elections and concentrated instead on personal attacks and character assassination. One common form of personal denunciation was to accuse a person of being a drunkard. A nullification from Santa Rosa (La Unión Department) reads, "The Alcalde, the First Regidor, the Second Regidor, the Third Regidor, and the Síndico are drunks . . . and therefore I submit this request for nullification."[29] Other commonly used accusations included gambler, vagrant (*vago*), crazy person (*loco*), and the all-encompassing "dishonorable."[30] Victors countered by seeking out "honorable" persons to testify on their behalf. An investigator once based his judgment on the "honor" of the witnesses. He wrote, "I consider the witnesses that came to the defense of the accused to be . . . of more robust morality than those who corroborated the denunciation; therefore, I declare the nullification void."[31] Of course, the quality of one's honor lay in the eyes of the beholder, and more often than not it increased in direct proportion to political and economic clout. When a nullification request was rejected, the vanquished politician had few alternatives but to wait until the next election and hope his own patronage alliances remained strong enough to survive the interim.

One set of circumstances that invariably resulted in nullification was when the victor of an election used the name of a superior official without his permission. In 1897, in the village of Ishuatán (Sonsonate Department), the victorious network won the election by announcing that its candidates were the official candidates of the governor and whoever did not vote for them would be sent to the army barracks in Sonsonate City. In fact, the governor did not support the particular candidates, and when he became aware of the situation he nullified the election immediately.[32]

In summary, nullifications were an extension of the competition between patronage networks. They reveal one manner in which the formal rules of politics were subverted to the needs of patronage and clientelism. The defined reason for the nullification process was to prevent electoral fraud, but in practice it was just another weapon in political actors' arsenals, allowing them to turn to more powerful outsiders when all other methods had failed.

Electoral Violence

Violence was a recurrent feature of elections.[33] In a political system based on hierarchy and coercion, the difference between a monopolized election and a violent grab for power was small. When an election turned violent, the inherently coercive nature of the political system ascended to its ultimate level, physical force. Whoever could physically beat his opponent into submission was rewarded with control over the municipal government. In most social contexts, the emergence of violence indicates a lack of order and a breakdown in social norms. But in El Salvador, political actors recognized that violence was possible, if not likely, in any given electoral exercise. Whether or not an election turned violent depended upon a variety of circumstances, not the least of which was individual personality and preference for settling differences through force. But the likelihood of politics turning violent was also predictable. Electoral violence typically occurred when the competing networks were evenly matched. A political boss who was clearly inferior did not initiate violence for fear of losing his life, to say nothing of the election, and dominant networks found no reason to push an already defeated opponent into a reckless act of self-defense. But when rivals of equal strength faced off and neither group capitulated, the consequences could be fatal.

Violence came in degrees, beginning with the threat of using it. A boss who hoped to control a forthcoming election often threatened his opponents with violence if they challenged him. Threats could be delivered directly, from one person to another, or indirectly by way of the rumor mill. During an electoral conflict in San Miguel City, a presiding official got the rumor mill churning by proclaiming, according to the testimony of another official, "in the presence of other persons that on the day of the election he intended to place guards before the municipal hall with orders to incarcerate [the opposition] in order to impede the participation of the supporters of Gerardo Barrios."[34] The more notorious a boss's reputation, the more likely it was that his threats would have the desired effect. It was up to the recipient of a threat to either surrender or stand his ground. In 1848 in Ahuachapán City, an opposition network came to power by way of a threat. In the days leading up to the election, a rumor circulated that the town would suffer violent retribution if the incumbents did not step aside and allow the newcomers to take power. The incumbents gathered their followers in the central plaza on the morning of the election, but they withdrew upon the arrival of the challengers, who rode into town on horseback, established themselves in the municipal hall, and declared themselves the victors.[35]

If verbal threats failed, political bosses resorted to display. In San Antonio Masahuat (La Paz Department), for example, the election of 1903 saw the alcalde and his allies standing in the doorway of the municipal hall, holding machetes. They permitted their clients to enter but chased away the supporters of their opponents.[36] In 1907, the alcalde of Mercedes employed a similar form of intimidation, but his weapon of choice was a loaded revolver.[37] In Juayúa in 1911, the leaders of one network had its members patrol the municipality with machetes and guns to intimidate opponents. A member of the opposition described one of the armed patrols as "a band of dragons" who threatened potential voters by telling them to "watch out when you leave your homes, because we have orders to ensure the victory of Mauro Salaverría."[38]

If threats and displays proved ineffective, political bosses raised the stakes. For instance, in Rosario de Mora (San Salvador Department) in 1911, a gang of forty men arrived at the municipal hall on the morning of the election, shortly before voting was to take place for the electoral board. The leader of the gang, Teodoro Segovia, was allied with Natividad Murcía, a landowner and head of the opposition network. The alcalde rejected Segovia's request to participate in the selection of the electoral board. Segovia responded by dragging the alcalde out of the municipal hall and beating him in public view. He then oversaw the voting, which resulted in his election as president of the electoral board. In the actual election, Murcía was elected alcalde and Segovia was chosen as first regidor.[39]

The beating of municipal officials was a recurrent feature of the local politics. For example, General Rafael Rivas employed this tactic during his rise to power in Tacuba (Ahuachapán Department) in the 1910s. From his hideout in the surrounding mountains, he launched numerous raids into town. On most of these forays he simply rode through town shooting his pistol into the air, humiliating his political opponents. On one of his raids, however, he dragged the síndico out of the municipal hall and whipped him in the center of the municipal plaza.[40] The beating of a municipal official indicated a coming regime change, because the ability to drag an official out of his office and pummel him in view of his supporters signified both the official's weakness and the strength of his opponents.

The election of 1897 in San Sebastián (San Vicente Department) illustrates what could occur when two evenly matched networks refused to back down. One of the networks was run by an alliance of three families, Rosa, Rivas, and Abarca, that had held power between 1891 and 1894. The other network was led by José María Ayala and had been in power since 1894. On the eve of the election of 1897, the Rosa-Rivas-Abarca

network believed that the time for its return to power had come and demanded that Ayala step down, but Ayala refused. On the morning of the
election a dozen members of the Rosa-Rivas-Abarca network, armed with
pistols and machetes, appeared in front of the municipal hall and insisted
that the election board be placed under their control. Ayala responded by
ordering the chief of police, Pedro Rivas (no relation to the Rivas network), to disarm the supplicants. Upon hearing the order, the armed men
drew their weapons and opened fire. One of Ayala's followers fell dead on
the spot. Ayala and the remainder of his allies fled into the municipal hall
with the attackers in hot pursuit. Two more of Ayala's men were killed in
a hallway and another was killed further inside. Ayala too was shot, but
only wounded. The man who shot Ayala was Geronimo Abarca, whom
Ayala had replaced as alcalde in 1894. A counterattack by Ayala's men expelled the assailants from the municipal hall and brought the melee to a
close, but the Rosa-Rivas-Abarca network went on to win the election.[41]

After the fatal events of December 1897, the opposing networks in
San Sebastián returned to politics as usual. Over the next two decades
they traded power back and forth every three years or so. The violent
clash of 1897 did not rupture the political system, but functioned instead
as part of the ongoing ebb and flow of power transfers. The case of San
Sebastián highlights an important feature of politics in El Salvador: bosses
considered violence to be another, albeit more intense, form of political
negotiation.

As the State Grows, the Municipalities Decline

The production of coffee, the expansion of state revenues, and the professionalization of the military were three mutually reinforcing elements of
state centralization. Coffee generated the wealth, some of which ended up
as state revenues, which in turn allowed the state to expand its bureaucracy
and professionalize the military. Coffee exports from El Salvador began in
earnest in the 1860s and expanded steadily during the succeeding decades.
In 1864 El Salvador exported a mere 5,000 quintales of coffee. In 1870,
exports had risen to 59,000 quintales; by 1881 they were 145,000 quintales; and by 1890 they were up to 330,000 quintales.[42] The monetary

value of exports grew as well, a reflection not only of increased production, but also of the steady growth in the price of coffee on the world market. During the 1860s the average annual value of coffee exports from El Salvador was 204,000 pesos. During the 1870s it was 1,136,000 pesos; in the 1880s it was 2,754,000 pesos; and in the 1890s it was 5,729,000 pesos.[43]

The state benefited from the coffee economy primarily by way of import duties. Export duties were virtually nonexistent, so profits from coffee sales abroad paid for imported goods and their corresponding taxes. Import duties eventually became the single largest source of government revenue. Between 1850 and 1870, when coffee production was still in its infancy, state revenues remained stagnant at around US$1 million per year. As coffee production increased in the 1880s, revenues rose to an annual average of roughly US$4 million per year. By the turn of the century, the annual average was up to US$8 million. In 1912 revenues reached an all-time high of nearly US$15 million.[44]

Historians and contemporaries alike noted the impact this new money had on the expansion of the state bureaucracy. Héctor Lindo-Fuentes describes the various public sectors that were financed by the new wealth, including the education and judicial systems, transportation, communication, and credit institutions.[45] In 1901 the minister of the interior took note of the rapid expansion of the state, referring to it as "the process of cementing together the institutions . . . of our country."[46]

By far the largest recipient of the newfound financial resources was the army. A modern, highly organized military was a constant desire of nineteenth-century presidents who wanted to bolster their regimes and extend their authority. Conscripted soldiers assembled by local patronage allies performed poorly on the battlefield and dispersed as soon as the fighting was over, if not sooner. Presidents wanted professional armies ready to defend their regimes against enemies both foreign and domestic. As a result, government planners made military professionalization a priority. Gerardo Barrios is commonly credited with initiating the first efforts to professionalize the army. He introduced new war material and brought in foreign advisors. His successors continued his programs, writing a new military code and creating an officer training school, the Escuela Politécnica, which was often staffed by foreign advisors.[47]

The scope of military professionalization expanded rapidly in the 1880s and 1890s. Successive presidents centralized military command, increased the number of permanent soldiers, and established new army posts throughout the country. The soldiers in these posts patrolled their immediate regions and enforced order. They also oversaw the organization of the militia by enlisting and training local men every Sunday. Patricia Alvarenga Venutolo found evidence suggesting that by 1892 there were more than sixty thousand militia members, while the regular army had three thousand permanent soldiers.[48] Another facet of the professionalization schemes was the creation of elite military units. The first of these, the Policía Montada (mounted police), was created in 1889 to patrol the countryside, enforce vagrancy laws, and guard against criminal activity. This modest force of a few dozen men was replaced in 1912 by a much larger and more ambitious entity, the Guardia Nacional (national guard). The Guardia was trained by Spaniards who modeled it after their own Guardia Civil. It rapidly became the preeminent military unit in the nation, while also garnering a reputation for brutal tactics. Guardia units were better trained and better equipped than the regular army, and their members received higher pay—as much as three times the salary of a regular soldier. The first Guardia patrols operated in the western coffee departments with fewer than four hundred troops. By the 1920s the number of guardias had risen to nearly one thousand and posts had been established in all fourteen departments.[49]

The growth and expansion of the military has long been a focus of scholars of turn-of-the-century El Salvador, who see in it the seeds of El Salvador's modern authoritarian state. For them, the military served as the Praetorian Guard of the coffee barons, making El Salvador safe for coffee, capitalism, and the growing maldistribution of wealth.[50] This perspective is accurate to the extent that it reflects one role that the military played in Salvadoran history. However, the military played another role as well, one less commonly discussed in the historiography, that of disciplining local elites. Military posts sat on the frontline of state centralization, and the soldiers manning these posts often had to subdue local patronage networks and bring stubborn political bosses into the fold of the centralizing system. Michel Gobat found the Nicaraguan Guardia Nacional to play a similar role, albeit under the direction of U.S. military commanders who were trying to rein in regional strongmen as part of their occupation strategy.[51]

Political centralization was at once the most sought after and the most elusive goal in the pre-coffee political arena. Presidents longed to be the supreme patronage-giver, able to control each and every election throughout the nation. But as we saw in previous chapters, administrations in the nineteenth century were hindered by the weak and destitute government over which they presided. Whoever held the presidency did so at the head of a coalition of patronage alliances that was only slightly—and usually temporarily—more powerful than its adversaries. Each patronage network controlled the elections in its region, and for the most part it elected whomever it wanted, both for municipal offices and seats on the National Assembly.

After the establishment of the coffee economy, ruling networks found themselves in charge of an increasingly powerful institution in the form of the national government. With more money and resources at their disposal, ruling networks were better able to control elections and consolidate their political authority. A trend emerged after 1880 in which the national government and the political bosses who controlled it (oftentimes high-ranking officers themselves) increasingly influenced local elections in ever-larger portions of the nation. Slowly but surely, the numerous patronage networks were being consolidated under the authority of the national government.

A symbol of the emerging trend came in 1885, when the government of President Francisco Menéndez attempted to draft a new constitution. Menéndez's opponents in the assembly constantly resisted his efforts and ultimately managed to block most of the changes he wished to insert. Instead of bending to their will, Menéndez simply dissolved the assembly and sent the opposition deputies home. He then waited until the following year to reassemble the legislature, after he could ensure the election of more supportive deputies.[52] The byproduct was the constitution of 1886.

Another symbolic event was the coup of 1898. For the next three decades, presidents came to power as the hand-chosen successors of the sitting president. General Tomás Regalado held office until 1903, when he chose Pedro José Escalón to succeed him. Escalón remained in power until 1907, when he and a coterie of allies agreed to select General Fernando

Figueroa as the successor. Figueroa stayed in office until 1911, when he passed power to his vice president, Manuel Araujo. Araujo was assassinated in 1913, evidently for reasons unrelated to the issue of presidential succession. Because Araujo's vice president had recently resigned, the first designate, Carlos Meléndez, came to power, beginning what would become thirteen years of uninterrupted rule by members of the Meléndez-Quiñónez family.[53] The U.S. chargé summarized this electoral system in 1910, on the eve of the presidential election of 1911: "popular suffrage is but a fiction. . . . That the official candidate will be elected in 1911, is according to general opinion, a foregone conclusion."[54]

The peaceful and controlled nature of these power transfers after 1898 did not mean that opposition had suddenly disappeared. After the coup by Regalado in 1898, for example, the comandante of San Miguel, Horacio Villavicencio (who had intended to launch his own coup in 1898 but had been beaten to the act by Regalado), mobilized his allies and, judging from the influx of reports and denunciations arriving in San Salvador from across the nation, relentlessly harassed Regalado's supporters.[55] Regalado tolerated this activity for a brief while, but he suspected Villavicencio of plotting a coup. He sent General Manuel Rivas, a relative and political disciple of José María Rivas of Cuscatlán, to San Miguel to dispense with Villavicencio. Rivas took San Miguel without a shot, and Villavicencio fled the country.[56]

Opposition existed during other administrations as well. In 1906, a variety of political aspirants opposed the selection of General Figueroa as the successor to Escalón. General Luis Barahona was the most powerful of them, but his attempt to challenge Figueroa in the election was forestalled when Figueroa threw him in jail and cracked down on his supporters. Shortly thereafter, Manuel Rivas organized a revolt that was defeated by troops loyal to Figueroa.[57] Prudencio Alfaro (the victor in the 1895 vice presidential election) organized a revolt against Figueroa in June 1907. He gathered a small group of supporters in Nicaragua and sailed to the port of Acajutla, where they were quickly defeated by local officials loyal to the government. In 1911 Alfaro was organizing yet another revolt when police agents uncovered his plans and ambushed him at his hideout near Santa Ana City.[58] When President Araujo was assassinated in 1913, many people accused Alfaro of masterminding the operation, which he vigorously denied in a rambling, vindictive defense.[59]

These examples of opposition constitute just a sampling of many smaller coups and conspiracies. Taken together, this multitude of examples indicates that there was never a shortage of aspirants to the presidency prepared to resort to desperate measures to attain the highest office. But the notable feature of all the conspiracies after 1898, excepting Villavicencio's apparently widespread machinations, is their limited and local nature, as well as their absolute weakness vis-à-vis the army. The power of the central government was reaching impressive heights.

Further insight into the workings of this increasingly centralized political system appears in a U.S. State Department memorandum from the U.S. embassy in El Salvador regarding the forthcoming presidential election of 1911. The memo revolves around a conversation between the current president, Figueroa, and H. P. Garthwaite, an American then serving as director of a mining corporation in El Salvador. Garthwaite was playing the role of intermediary between President Figueroa and the U.S. embassy on the delicate topic of presidential succession. Figueroa was looking for the United States' reaction to his possible choices for his successor, knowing that whoever he chose was assured to be the next president. Figueroa told Garthwaite that he was leaning towards Tomás Palomo or Francisco Dueñas and against Manuel Enrique Araujo, because the latter had supposedly made too many promises to a clique of coffee growers. In hindsight, we know that Araujo ended up as the candidate and became the next president. We also know that Palomo and Dueñas, who were close allies and relatives, remained powerful, albeit frustrated, political actors for the next two decades, throughout the Meléndez-Quiñónez years (1913–1926) and the reformist Pío Romero Bosque era (1927–1931). Unable to break through as the chosen successor in 1910 or in the years thereafter, Palomo eventually took his quest for the presidency outside the established system. He challenged Alfonso Quiñónez Molina for the presidency in 1919 by mobilizing an independent base and trying to gain enough local supporters to guarantee control over polling stations on election day in 1920 and secure his victory. He continued to be supported by Dueñas, as well as various other wealthy families. Palomo's strategy in 1919 was reminiscent of the era before political centralization, and indeed it resulted in a variety of violent clashes between his and Quiñónez's local allies, which are detailed in the next chapter. It was exactly the kind of scenario that Figueroa wanted to keep in the past. For whatever reason, he chose Araujo and managed to keep Palomo and Dueñas at bay, allowing for an orderly, predictable election.[60]

It is not evident from the State Department's correspondence whether the United States had a preferred candidate from among Figueroa's options or if it influenced his decision making in any way. But in this particular memo on Garthwaite's conversation with Figueroa, the U.S. embassy seems to have asked Figueroa, naively, why he would not allow the election to be conducted freely and fairly, that is, by refusing to choose an official candidate and simply guaranteeing order and allowing multiple candidates to compete for the office. According to Garthwaite, Figueroa responded by saying that "this would be impossible and would result in the appearance of a crowd of candidates who would bring about great disorders." Figueroa apparently went on to say that any victor from such a competition "would undoubtedly be a demagogue of the worst type."[61] If the content of that memo accurately reflects what Figueroa said, then two insights can be drawn from it. The first insight is that Figueroa was speaking as a classic patronage boss, but within the context of a recently centralized system. The worst prospect for such a political leader would be a return to a decentralized era in which elections were competitive, not in the traditional sense of candidates competing for popular support by trying to sway public opinion, but rather in the marshaling of patronage alliances throughout the country to control polling stations on election day. Such competition typically resulted in high levels of violence. Figueroa did not want that.

The second insight relates to Figueroa's reference to "demagoguery." Although Figueroa did not elaborate upon his meaning, it implies that he was concerned about the prospect of autonomous action on the part of Salvadoran masses, who would select a populist candidate with reformist tendencies. On the one hand, such a comment can be interpreted from the perspective of traditional political discourse in a patronage-based political system. Political bosses customarily disparaged democracy when they were the incumbents, and challengers used a democracy-laden rhetoric to accuse them of monopolizing power, even though they themselves had no genuine democratic pretenses. In this case, Figueroa and his allies represented the incumbency, and any who challenged them would be described as populist demagogues. On the other hand, it is possible that

Figueroa was genuinely concerned about autonomous mass action, although there were few examples in El Salvador's recent history to suggest that such a prospect loomed. Still, El Salvador was going through economic and social change at the time, and perhaps Figueroa was musing on the prospect that such changes might have political ramifications. Under the impact of the coffee economy, El Salvador's demographic profile was becoming more complex. The rural population was in flux as a consequence of the privatization process that began in the early 1880s, and the urban population was growing and coming to include a nascent urban working class and a small but growing middle class. Perhaps Figueroa recognized that these new demographic sectors were less susceptible to the traditional system of patronage-based politics and thus represented the prospect of an alteration of the political system, as countries such as Mexico, Argentina, and Uruguay were coming to discover.[62] Unfortunately, the extant documentary record does not make clear Figueroa's understanding of the situation, nor does it further clarify the meaning of his words to Garthwaite in late 1910. Regardless, his noteworthy comments offer insight into El Salvador's centralizing political system in the early twentieth century.

Figueroa's comment occurred in a private sphere of closed correspondence between political confidants. A few years later, a rare but noteworthy diatribe against democracy would appear in the public sphere in the form of an editorial essay. The author was a prominent lawyer by the name of Alfonso Reyes Guerra, and his piece was published in 1913 in a small but reasonably influential periodical dedicated to arts and letters, *El Ateneo de El Salvador.* The piece is rather long, consisting of five published pages divided into four sections. The ostensible inspiration for Reyes's work was debates in international political circles at the time over the merits of the secret ballot. Reyes staunchly opposed secret voting, and in the process of explaining why he makes a variety of strongly disparaging comments about the prospect of autonomous mass action and its threats to a genuine and real democracy. In Reyes's words, universal suffrage expressed through secret voting "not only results in a rude and detestable absurdity that runs contrary to the wise laws that are designed to perfect humanity, but also stagnates and falsifies Democracy." Echoing Figueroa's rhetoric about demagoguery, Reyes claimed that the secret vote "is a

flattering incentive to vanity and the instincts of the masses; it has promoted and will promote destabilizing demagogues." Reyes went on to
claim that unfettered mass opinion in the form of the secret vote contra-
dicted genuine liberties because it generated instability and threatened the
social order. As evidence for his claim, he cited cases of voter fraud in the
United States under the system of secret voting.[63]

Yet again, the extant historical record does not allow us enough evidence to further explore the reasons for Reyes's highly public denunciation
of universal suffrage and the secret ballot. He makes a brief reference to
unnamed political figures in El Salvador who supposedly wanted to reform the constitution to allow for secret voting. If this was so, then Reyes's
essay might represent the rare voice of elite, established El Salvador publicly fretting over the empowerment of the masses. Regardless of Reyes's
intentions as an author, his piece certainly could have been read that way.
However, it is also possible that his diatribe was simply part and parcel of
the standard political discourse of centralized, patronage-based politics,
disparaging democracy as a way of undermining challengers to the incumbents. We do not know enough about Reyes and his political affiliations to
determine which of these options is more likely. But the appearance of his
antidemocratic discourse in a publicly circulated periodical in 1913 is a
notable and rare occurrence.

The Rise of "Municipal Autonomy"

The most revealing evidence for political centralization originates at the
local level. Beginning in the late 1880s, the archival record offers many
examples of the national government's attempts to influence local politics,
especially voting procedures in municipal and assembly elections. For example, in 1892 the departmental commander of Usulután wrote to the
minister of government to remind him that "probably due to your busy
schedule, you have not yet informed me as to who should be elected
Deputies for the next Assembly." The commander went on to list the
various aspirants who had already announced their candidacies, under-
scoring the importance of receiving the minister's prompt directive in
order to avoid factional disputes.[64] In 1896, the "Jefe Político" (governor)
of La Paz Department submitted to the municipalities under his jurisdic-

tion a letter on the behalf of the national government that contained a list of persons whom the government wanted to be elected in the forthcoming municipal elections. At least one of the municipal councils, that of San Juan Nonualco, rejected the proposed candidates, saying that while they were honorable men, the council would stick with its initial choices.[65] The responses of the remaining municipalities in the department are not known, nor is the government's reaction to San Juan's resistance, but the mere existence of the list reveals an attempt by the national government to centralize the process of electing local officials.

The national government also looked to influence other municipal offices, especially that of municipal secretary. Each municipality had one secretary, who was appointed by the municipal council. His duties were administrative, the most important being recording the proceedings of the weekly council meetings in the *libro de actas,* the official registry of the municipality. The secretary also monitored the volumes of paperwork that were produced during the course of an administration. Traditionally, the secretary was the one official who retained his position from one election to the next, so new secretaries were appointed only when the prior one had retired, died, or left office in search of another position. The secretary thus represented a point of continuity in municipal government and was likely to be well informed in local political affairs. Officials in the national government looked to control the position of secretary and began exerting pressure on municipal councils to appoint certain persons to the post. In 1895, for example, the municipality of La Ceiba (Chalatenango Department) found itself in conflict with the minister of government who, operating through the departmental governor, had rejected the council's choice for a new secretary because the candidate had not been approved by the national government. La Ceiba's municipal council responded to the rejection by pointing out that the national government had no constitutional right to reject the council's decision.[66] Unfortunately, the outcome of this case is unknown.

National officials attempted to force the municipality of Nahuizalco (Sonsonate Department) to alter its choice for secretary in 1899. The national government wanted Francisco Burgos to hold the position, but the council appointed a different candidate, prompting the national government to levy a twenty-five-peso fine on each member of the council for "having disobeyed the order that was given to them . . . by the Supremo

Poder Ejecutivo."[67] Like the council in La Ceiba, the Nahuizalco council referred to its constitutional right to choose its own secretary. The result of this conflict is not known either, but the willingness of both La Ceiba and Nahuizalco to resist the national-level directives suggests that they did not fear repercussions. Nevertheless, these two cases reveal the growing desire of the national government to influence local affairs. In time, local officials would be unable to resist.

The national government delivered its orders to the municipal level through a chain of command that ultimately ended with the local military post. The president and his immediate advisors worked through the minister of government, who passed orders on to the departmental governors, who in turn sent commands to the alcaldes and municipal councils. When the local officials ignored the governor, he and his superiors turned to their sole representatives at the local level, the military commanders and the Guardia Nacional posts. It is here that the professionalization of the military assumed special importance. In prior decades, local military officials had taken orders from their patronage networks, and oftentimes the alcalde and the local comandante were the same person, or at least belonged to the same political network. But towards the turn of the twentieth century, thanks to the professionalization programs and the creation of new army posts and military units, the chain of command was centralized, and local military officials increasingly took their orders from their superiors in the national government. Granted, this too was an uneven and drawn-out process. As we saw in prior chapters, military officials continued to engage in various forms of political subterfuge during the late nineteenth and early twentieth centuries. But the dynamics of political activity were changing, however gradually.

One sign of this change was the emergence of new forms of conflict between the local and national officials. Local officials, particularly the municipal council and the local police, began to clash with units of the army and Guardia Nacional. These conflicts frequently regressed into violent encounters between police officers and soldiers. Police officers were local residents employed by the municipal council, whereas soldiers and guardias were paid by the national government and likely came from far-away regions. Elites at the local level held highly ambivalent views about the expansion of armed forces under the auspices of the national government. They supported the army when it enforced vagrancy laws, protected against theft, and prevented peasant uprisings, but they viewed the arrival of a military post with suspicion, knowing that its soldiers obeyed orders from superiors outside the municipality. Whenever a new military post was established in a municipality, it brought with it new potential for conflict.

The case of the village of Tecapa provides a vivid example of the kind of conflict that sometimes erupted when a new military post was established. Tecapa was an important coffee-growing municipality in the department of Usulután. Until 1889, it did not have its own military post; instead it shared one with two neighboring municipalities, Estanzuelas and El Triunfo. Leading officials in Tecapa had had only a few encounters with soldiers from that post because patrols came through the village infrequently. In 1889, however, as part of its plan to expand the number of command posts and promote the organization of militia units, the military high command in San Salvador decided to place a military post in each of the three municipalities. The military explained its decision by referring to "the slow development of the militia in the District of Jucuapa [in which Tecapa was located], and . . . the various responsibilities of the Alcaldes which prevent them from effectively performing additional duties as the Comandantes."

The municipal council of Tecapa opposed the plan vehemently. In its response to the military, it professed that "we have corresponded always with the standing militia regulation, although it seems convenient to suspend said measure given the great damage that it causes the agricultural industry, which consists here of the production of coffee. . . . All hands are needed to harvest this precious fruit." The council was quick to point out that coffee production was the foundation of the nation's wealth—"[it] enriches our country"—and that hindering its collection would have far-reaching consequences: "the loss of these exports would destroy the glorious advantages which are enjoyed by families, municipalities in the form of revenues, and the same goes for the national government." The council considered the proposed division to be part of a broad program of military expansion in the region, noting that "already we have seen many times in other municipalities the fatal consequences of military preponderance." The council provided another, revealing reason for why they did not want the military to place a post in their municipality: "Conflicts inevitably exist between Local Comandantes and Alcaldes when these positions are filled by distinct persons."

The military command rejected Tecapa's request, prompting the alcalde of Tecapa to send a last plea in which he denounced the proposed commander, Second Lieutenant Vicente Mejía, as a politically biased adherent of a former president who would engage in partisan politics in the municipality. The alcalde then suggested to military officials that if they insisted on establishing a post in the municipality, at least they should select a local person as commander, such as "Captain Isidoro Castillo, who is accepted by the population and does not signify a threat." The high command rejected these proposals, and the post was founded with Mejía as its commander.[68]

The military's intransigence proved to be its demise in Tecapa. Three weeks after the command post was established, "a group of armed people" destroyed it, according to sparse reports arriving in Usulután City.[69] The perpetrators of the attack were not identified. Regardless, the destruction of the post symbolizes the degree to which the expansion of the military clashed with local interests. The members of Tecapa's municipal council captured the essence of the emerging conflict between the local and national levels. The council members understood that their adversary was not a traditional patronage boss swooping down to incorporate their municipality into his political network. Rather, their adversary was something new and formal, something that had been witnessed in other municipalities and had resulted in, as the council members put it, "fatal consequences." The council members referred to this new adversary as "military preponderance," but what they essentially were describing was the consolidation of political and military power under the central state.

The clash at Tecapa in 1889 presaged many similar clashes throughout the country between local officials and the emerging national state. In one municipality after another, local landowners and municipal officials expressed dissatisfaction over the arrival of military troops. Like the council in Tecapa, landowners commonly complained about the military drawing laborers away from the plantations for militia training and public-works projects. One such letter was sent by the owner of the hacienda "La Mizata" near Teotepeque in La Libertad Department. The owner appealed to the secretary of state as a fellow landowner:

The *colonos* of my Hacienda want to leave because the Local Comandantes in the region continually demand from them certain services, such as guarding the place known as "Bocana de Mizata" at night. . . . I approach you in confidence, because you too have owned a hacienda and know the difficulties of maintaining servants and *mozos* in regions which are located far from a village, even without the local Comandantes who arrive at all hours to assign these ridiculous obligations.[70]

Similar letters arrived from other landowners, such as Vicente Sol, a major coffee grower in the region of Santa Tecla.[71]

Notwithstanding these examples, local authorities most commonly manifested their opposition to the expanding national government and its new military posts by employing the principle of "municipal autonomy." A cornerstone of liberal ideology (to the extent that liberalism existed as a unified ideological construct) was the rejection of centralized government as something akin to monarchy. Liberalism called for decentralized government that consisted of, as the authors of a study on liberalism in Latin America put it, "independent branches linked together to prevent dominance of one [branch]."[72] Liberal ideologues worldwide, and in El Salvador too, considered the independence of the municipality to be a basic element of decentralized government. Each of El Salvador's constitutions called for the "independence of the municipality."[73] Liberal spokespersons heralded municipal autonomy as a key element of government. Francisco Castañeda, who held various governmental positions during the liberal administrations of the 1880s and 1890s, wrote in 1893 that "the independence of the municipality signifies the triumph of liberty over the hated centralization of government . . . sustaining the sovereignty of the nation, as in *e pluribus unum* of the Americans."[74] El Salvador's minister of the interior wrote in his annual report of 1901 that municipal governments "are the basis of our republican government and have functioned in the past year with all the independence that the laws bestow upon them."[75] Historian David Bushnell points out, however, "the extent to which the liberals [across Latin America] by frequent violation of their stated principles established a strong nation-state."[76] This was the case with the notorious liberal Porfirio Díaz in Mexico, as one example, and also with the succession of liberal regimes in El Salvador after 1880.

References to municipal independence rang hollow to officials at the municipal level in El Salvador because they believed they were experiencing a general diminution in their freedom. In the process of rejecting orders from their departmental governor, who had submitted to them a list of candidates for the next election, the members of the municipal council of San Juan Nonualco appealed to "our political constitution which guarantees for us in Article 117 our freedom to choose whoever we believe will encourage the aggrandizement and progress of this population."[77] A similar, if less formal, appeal to municipal autonomy was made by the municipal authorities in Mejicanos (San Salvador Department) after they arrested a man running through the town and brandishing a gun. The police in Mejicanos charged him with illegally carrying a firearm in public. The man turned out to be David Castillo, a security agent working for the ministry of government, who was in pursuit of a fugitive. Castillo presented his credentials from the ministry and even had the minister send a telegram to Mejicanos ordering that he be released and that his firearm be returned. But the municipal secretary ignored the orders, telling Castillo, according to the subsequent police report, that "Ministers have no jurisdiction in the village and they [the municipal officials] are not obliged to obey any orders from any Minister, and only will attend to the rule of law."[78]

Whether implicit or explicit, this appeal to municipal autonomy lay at the core of what became an epidemic of clashes between local officials and the military representatives of the national government. In many of these examples, as in the case of Tecapa, the selection of the local military commander was the point of contention. Local officials preferred to have someone in the post who was known or subservient to them. The governor of Ahuachapán, for example, informed the minister of government in 1891 of "the reemergence of discord between the Local Comandante and the Municipality [municipal council] of Apaneca which, as is typical, has resulted in dissension between them and a disobedience of my orders." The governor attempted to ease the dispute by appointing a new commander and "threaten[ing] the Municipal Council." But ultimately he had to confess that he failed to resolve the problem, as evidenced by two local citizens who, under the charge of the alcalde, continued to engage in "grave activities" against the military post.[79]

In her study of rural violence in El Salvador, Alvarenga Venutolo cites newspaper accounts of eight violent clashes between municipal police and military units in five cities over a six-year period starting in 1906.[80] A common point of contention in these conflicts was the local military commanders' service as the political arm of the national government. A member of the municipal council of Oratorio de Concepción (Cuscatlán Department), for instance, denounced the local commander for refusing to allow the council's preferred candidates to receive any votes in the municipal election.[81] Another letter from a member of the municipal council of Cojutepeque (Cuscatlán Department) noted that the departmental commander sent out orders to the local commanders in each municipality telling them whom to support in the elections.[82] Similar denunciations arrived from municipalities across the country, such as San Rafael (La Paz Department), Santa Ana City, Berlín (Usulután Department), Tenancingo (Cuscatlán Department), and Juayúa (Sonsonate Department). The case of Tacuba, discussed above, is another example.[83] In each of these cases, the plaintiffs requested that a military post be removed from the village because its members had meddled in local political affairs.

When local officials lacked an explicit reason to demand the removal of a military post, they used whatever example of military intransigence they could find. An accusation against a guardia for raping a girl in the municipality of San Martín (San Salvador Department) prompted the alcalde of that municipality to request that the Guardia post be disbanded for fomenting "social discord."[84] The municipal council of Jiquilisco (Usulután Department) also demanded that its local Guardia post be disbanded, but it provided no specific reason, stating simply that the municipality was doing well economically due to coffee production and that the Guardia was "counterproductive to the social interests of this locality." It insisted that municipal police could handle local affairs.[85]

Rarely, if ever, did the national government remove military posts at the behest of local officials. But some high-ranking military authorities took into account the problems that could arise out of conflicts with local power holders. In 1915, for instance, the departmental commander of San Vicente Department recommended to the minister of war that the army not follow through with its plan to establish a military post in the municipality of Verapáz. "I am of the opinion that a detachment of the army should not be posted in Verapáz," stated the commander, "because . . . it will not create harmony between military and civil authorities, because in that village they [the civil authorities] always have sought to nullify, even abolish the military."[86] Such accommodating sentiments from high-ranking officials, however, were rare. More often they pressed forward with whatever they wanted to do.

A revealing case is provided by General Rafael Rivas, the famed jefe of Tacuba in Ahuachapán Department. In the 1910s, General Rivas retired from the military and took up residence in that remote village, where he built for himself a small political empire. Rivas appears to have earned the genuine support of much of the local population and used that support to resist challenges to his authority. Rivas's most persistent opponent was the local Guardia Nacional post. The dispute between Rivas's network and the Guardia lasted for many months and occasionally reached violent propor-tions. The Guardia ultimately gave up due to its near-complete lack of support from the local population, which refused to turn on Rivas. In ac-cepting failure, the commander of the Guardia wrote to his superiors that "The people here belong to him [Rivas] body and soul and will not say anything against him; everyone here tells us that General Rivas and his son are their *padrinos* [protectors/godfathers] and that they hold him in the greatest esteem and owe him great gratitude."[87]

One incidence of conflict between the Guardia and General Rivas's political network occurred on October 11, 1921, when a pair of national guardsmen on patrol came across twenty of Rivas's supporters lounging on a street corner. The men were drinking, and one or more of them was in a state of stupor. The guardias interrogated the men, asking them if they "had a license to be in public in such a condition." Unsatisfied with the responses, they arrested one of the more obstinate individuals. Dr. Rafael Alfonso Rivas, General Rivas's son, who served as liaison for his father and spent much time fraternizing with his father's followers, was in a nearby building. He overheard the evolving conflict and stepped into the fray, refusing to allow the guardias to depart with their prisoner. Accord-ing to Guardia reports, Rivas told them that "while the men did not have the required license, he had given them the necessary guarantees and told them that they were allowed to go about [*andar*] at whatever hour they preferred." Rivas then proclaimed that if the guardias did not withdraw he "would demonstrate his importance . . . by raising the village [*pueblo*] up against them." The guardias retired and, in their report, described Dr. Rivas as "the son of the Caudillo."[88] The incident of October 11 represents a moment in which the proverbial captain of a local patronage network stood up to the state's military force—ironically his father's former profession.

In sum, the steady expansion of the central state precipitated conflicts with local power holders who manifested their concern in various ways. They ignored the state's orders regarding elections and appointments; they appealed to the principle of municipal autonomy; they clashed with local commanders and members of the Guardia Nacional. While they scored some victories along the way, they ultimately lost the war as the central state expanded steadily.

*   *   *

Municipal elections remained consistent with the patterns of political behavior in El Salvador discussed in past chapters: officers formed electoral boards, voters passed before the boards' members, votes were announced and recorded on tally sheets, and the results were ultimately sent off to the departmental governor's office or to the ministry of government in San Salvador. But this superficial adherence to the formal rules of politics was accompanied by a much more complex series of informal practices that saw municipal-level actors employing a wide array of tactics to control voting and win local elections.

These municipal-level electoral battles were highly paradoxical affairs, in that they were at once parochial events that occurred in relative isolation and events of central importance to national-level politics. Whoever controlled voting at the municipal level determined how voting would transpire in national-level elections. And national-level candidates desperately wanted those votes.

Until roughly the turn of the twentieth century, the ability of any one national-level political network to control affairs in the municipalities was limited to the reach of its patronage-based alliances. At any given moment, an incumbent faced hostile regions where municipal authorities did what they wanted to do, albeit in accordance with their respective political alliances. Starting around 1900, with the growth in state power, the areas that remained outside the reach of the sitting network declined steadily. One way that local actors tried to resist this growing national authority was to appeal to municipal autonomy. Such appeals were little more than the vestiges of a political system in a stage of transition. As we are about to see, the consolidation of the central state did not change the fundamental structure of politics; it merely altered its manner of functioning.

THE NETWORK OF THE STATE

Meléndez-Quiñónez, 1913–1926

On the eve of the presidential election of 1898, General Tomás Regalado overthrew President Rafael Gutiérrez in a quickly executed coup d'état. To participants and onlookers alike, the coup seemed a routine exercise. The insurgent was a one-time ally of the president who had grown impatient with Gutiérrez's refusal to relinquish power and his plans to rig the forthcoming election to remain in office. Over the preceding five decades, the nation had witnessed countless such events, so many that the process seemed normal and the names of the participants hardly memorable. There was no indication that this one was any different. But unbeknownst to everyone, the coup of 1898 would be the last time a sitting president was cast out of office in a violent overthrow by a rival until December 1931. The coup of 1898 holds real and symbolic importance as a forecast of the coming change in the functioning of politics in El Salvador.

At the turn of the twentieth century, El Salvador was in the midst of a centralization of political authority and a manifold increase in the powers of the national government. As in the rest of Latin America, this process of centralization was fueled by the onset of the industrial revolution in Europe and the United States and the consequent increase in demand for primary materials produced by Latin American nations. In the case of El Salvador, coffee was the sole product competitive on the international market. It brought unprecedented amounts of wealth, which gave the country both the means and the motivation to increase the size and powers of the state. Prospective coffee growers needed new public services, such as banks to provide investment capital, roads and railroads to deliver their crops to port, and security forces to protect private property and enforce vagrancy laws. Planters also needed a safe climate for investment—incessant warfare and political instability did not encourage business ventures. These initiatives were beyond the scope of the individual growers and the local governments over which they presided; they were endeavors of national proportions, which only a government of equal extent could undertake.

It is tempting to assume that the centralization of the state necessitated the demise of patronage and clientelism. How could the state "institutionalize," as Robert Williams describes the process of state growth, if political bosses continued to hold sway in the municipalities and serve their respective networks rather than the central government?[1] Richard Graham engaged this dilemma in his study of nineteenth-century Brazilian politics. He contends that patron-client relations are not necessarily "superseded by the inevitable triumph of an impersonal and universalistic 'rational' bureaucracy." Instead, the Brazilian state "advanced the interests of the propertied principally by reproducing and maintaining the patron-client system itself."[2] A similar process was at work in El Salvador.

The growth of central authority in El Salvador reinforced patron-client relations. The national government became the supreme patronage network and subsumed the factionalism of the individual networks. Local bosses retained their clients and monopolized voting in the municipalities, but now they did so on behalf of the state and whoever happened to be presiding over it. This process of centralization was prolonged and uneven. It lasted roughly four decades between the mid-1880s and the mid-1920s, the period in which coffee became the undisputed engine of the Salvadoran economy. The long duration of the process reflects not only external variables, namely the growth of the international coffee market, but also internal processes, especially the resistance to state centralization on the part of some local political bosses. Although most local elites saw the growth of the state as economically advantageous, some considered it a threat to their power because they would almost certainly have less voice in the national state than they had in their local political empires. This erosion of local authority was the price of national stability, and some bosses accepted it more grudgingly than others. Those who resisted gave rise to new modes of conflict and a political discourse that celebrated local autonomy.

The mercurial process of state centralization culminated during the administrations of Jorge Meléndez (1919–1923) and Alfonso Quiñónez Molina (1923–1927). They were brothers-in-law and close political allies who created the Partido Nacional Democrático (PND), the National Democratic Party. Contrary to its name, the PND was neither democratic nor a political party. It was, however, national in scope. It was the first patronage network to achieve national dimensions. Meléndez and Quiñónez disallowed political activity outside the confines of the PND and, with only a few exceptions, placed the local political networks under their authority. It was during this period that El Salvador finally constructed its own version of Brazil's "Great Pyramid." The present chapter picks up the story of national politics in the 1910s, with the ascension to power of Carlos Meléndez, who assumed the presidency after the assassination of Manuel Enrique Araujo in 1913.

Meléndez-Quiñónez, 1913–1919

Under the administrations of the Meléndez and Quiñónez families, the state reached its most centralized status to date. Carlos Meléndez was the first member of the family to serve as president. He came to power in 1913 to complete the final two years of Araujo's term. Meléndez was then elected to his own four-year term in 1915. He was succeeded in 1919 by his brother, Jorge Meléndez, who was followed in 1923 by his and Carlos's brother-in-law, Alfonso Quiñónez Molina. Quiñónez and Carlos Meléndez, the eldest of the three, were seasoned politicians; both had held numerous political and administrative posts since the late nineteenth century. Both had served at least twice on the municipal council of San Salvador. Carlos Meléndez had been a major player in presidential politics in the 1890s and 1900s, including competing with Prudencio Alfaro in the vice presidential election of 1895.[3] By contrast, Jorge Meléndez was a political novice, having remained aloof from politics and dedicated himself to agricultural pursuits. The presidency was the only political post he would ever hold.

The Meléndez and Quiñónez families were fabulously wealthy and owned vast tracts of land, especially in the vicinity of San Salvador. An agricultural census from 1929 reveals that Jorge Meléndez owned more than half of the land around the municipality of Soyapango, to the east of San Salvador, the centerpiece of which was the sugar plantation "Prussia."[4] Together the families owned sixteen plantations throughout San Salvador Department.[5] The families owned a few coffee plantations but made most of their money off sugar. In fact, the Meléndez family was the largest sugar producer in the nation.[6] North American and European chroniclers who traveled to El Salvador in the 1910s and 1920s and had the opportunity to meet members of the two families commented on their vast wealth and the foreign schooling of their children. A Briton by the name of Arthur Ruhl arrived in El Salvador in 1927 and described his visit with Jorge Meléndez:

> I visited the electric-light and power plant in which he is interested, in the hills just outside the capital, and drove thence out to his country house and sugar plantation. The spacious and entirely modern villa, with its gardens and magnificent view, was just the place in which a similarly well-to-do English family would prefer to spend most of their time. . . . There was a sugar-mill, the storage sheds of which were piled high with the fragrant new sugar, corn, and coffee, vegetables and fruits of all sorts, some 500 peasants were regularly attached to the estate, while 200 more came for the coffee picking.[7]

Frederick William Taylor, the American agronomist, wrote to his wife after a visit to some of Jorge Meléndez's plantations, "Melendes [*sic*] is a very wealthy man with all sorts of activities going on. . . . They do things at his places on a very large scale. He expects about 10,000 sacks of coffee this year, and great lot of sugar."[8]

When Carlos Meléndez entered office in 1913, he looked to formalize the political control of the state. To this end he founded the "Club Melendista," a pseudopolitical party that he intended to use as a mechanism to regulate elections at the local and departmental levels. Local political aspirants were supposed to receive approval from the club before being allowed to run in an election. The idea was that each municipality would have a local branch linked to a central committee in San Salvador through intermediary branches in the departmental capitals. The system functioned to a certain degree. In 1914, for example, the committee secretary of the club in Sensuntepeque, the main club for Cabañas Department, submitted a letter to the central committee that contained the names of candidates to be approved for the forthcoming municipal elections. The secretary assured the committee that each of the candidates had been chosen in their local clubs and that they were "loyal Melendistas."[9] That same year, the alcalde of El Refugio (Ahuachapán Department) received from the departmental governor the name of the candidate who was to be elected in that municipality. The alcalde, however, did not approve of the candidate and asked the central committee to reconsider, saying that there is another person in the municipality who better represents the "soul of the Melendista party."[10] This particular request is interesting, because it reveals an attempt by a local political official to maneuver within the emerging system. He opposed the candidate proposed at the national level, but he recognized the necessity of working within the Club Melendista. In doing so he demonstrates the extent to which political success required approval from the central authority.

The central committee of the Club Melendista had to guard against opponents posing as supporters. In 1913 the governor of San Vicente, for example, received from the municipality of Apastepeque a warning that "the President of the Directorio and the candidate for Alcalde proclaimed to be Melendistas, but in actuality are Barahonistas [an adversary of Meléndez]."[11] In January 1915, the U.S. chargé included in his report to Washington a description of the municipal elections of 1914, noting the extensive violence that had accompanied voting in rural and outlying areas.

These disturbances took place among Melendistas, so-called. The political intriguers, unwilling to come out into the open and announce their candidacies, or to declare themselves in favor of another, produced political division by causing several aspirants who pretended to be of that party to run for the same office. This split the Melendista party in some places and resulted in the election of a few municipal officers who are not now favorable to Don Carlos Meléndez or in sympathy with his aspirations, and, in effect, these "Alcaldes" selected are nothing but his political opponents. It is not thought, however, that these officers can amass such force or voting power as to endanger the success of Meléndez at the poles [*sic*] and it is believed that after the elections are over and the inauguration has taken place, even these will see it to their advantage to change their attitude and be friendly. No one would pretend to say that the elections were free but just how the pressure was exercised it was not easy to determine.[12]

The chargé's description reveals two things: the main political force in the nation was the Club Melendista, and opposing factions were trying to gain office under its aegis. The report indicates that there was opposition, but that it was unwilling to present itself as a coherent movement due to almost certain failure. The chargé's description provides evidence of the degree to which the process of political centralization had been successful.

Despite these and other examples of the Club Melendista's involvement in politics, Meléndez failed to get the club operating on a fully national scale.[13] The club existed only in certain regions, and even there it often operated informally. Still, the creation of the club constituted an important political step. It represented a president attempting to formalize political centralization and to name the emerging political pyramid. Moreover, the Club Melendista was the precursor to the PND, which would be structured in much the same manner but would function on a more comprehensive scale.

Carlos Meléndez and his familial successors, Jorge Meléndez and Alfonso Quiñónez Molina, saw themselves as architects of a single centralized network. They interpreted the political stability of the two prior decades as the result of centralization, and they took advantage of opportunities to draw contrasts with the factionalism of earlier eras. Carlos Meléndez offered such an assessment in a speech in August 1914, on the occasion of resigning the presidency to his vice president, Alfonso Quiñónez Molina, in order to qualify for the election of 1915. The constitution stipulated that candidates for the presidency could not have been president for at least six months prior to an election. The law supposedly encouraged turnover in office, but just as in officeholding at the municipal level, the formal rules seldom held sway over informal guidelines. Meléndez got around the spirit of the law by giving power temporarily to

Quiñónez. In his speech Meléndez defended this controlled succession by comparing it to the instability of the nineteenth century. He referred to the transition as "a phenomenon of high moral significance [that has] filled me with proud hopes and once more caused me to understand that the Salvadoran people are an honorable, industrious, and peaceful people, and that they were tired of military meetings, riots of the populace, and of revolutions of political bosses, which has happily all done its time, thanks to the good sense of the common people and to the high moral level of the other social classes."[14] Three years later, Jorge Meléndez employed a very similar discourse to laud his brother's government. In a booklet entitled *Economic Orientations of President Meléndez,* he proclaimed that the Meléndez administration was the culmination of the victory of "civilized government" over caudillismo:

> Why would capitalists risk their money by investing it in a transport business, for example, when in the morning General X, jefe of a revolutionary band, expropriates it? Why would they put their money into useful enterprises when just as quickly it is extracted by an exaggerated tribute decreed by some irresponsible government born in the clamor of gunfire? . . . It is necessary that politics be guided along a path that little by little dispenses with the gangrene of personalism, the primordial cause of our instability.[15]

Both of these proclamations contain significant doses of liberal rhetoric, and they are barely distinguishable from such classic liberal edicts as Sarmiento's *Civilization and Barbarism.* But the Meléndez brothers were not simply extolling a general political ideology; they were announcing El Salvador's passage from the factionalized patronage of the nineteenth century to a system of centralized patronage under their command in the twentieth century.

The Presidential Election of 1919

When Carlos Meléndez's term was drawing to a close, two candidates emerged as his most likely successors. One of them was Alfonso Quiñónez Molina, his vice president; the other was Tomás Palomo, who had held two ministerial posts under Meléndez: government and hacienda. Palomo was Meléndez's personal physician and a close family friend. Precedent called for Meléndez to select one of these two men and then put his political machine to work to ensure the candidate's victory on election day. In an act reminiscent of his 1895 vice presidential campaign, Meléndez refused to choose between the two men and left the issue of succession to be settled by them. Meléndez did not reveal—at least, in any source that has survived into the historical record—why he chose that route. Available sources suggest that he balked at the unsavory prospect of choosing between two loyal and powerful allies.[16] Either way, the ensuing electoral campaign was an intense and revealing episode in the political evolution of El Salvador. One important consequence of the campaign was the formation of the PND. Fortunately, we have two highly revealing views of the election: reports from the U.S. legation in San Salvador, which took a special interest in the contest, and the memoir of Enrique Córdova, the minister of war who witnessed the events as they unfolded.

The campaign between Quiñónez and Palomo began in earnest around the middle of 1918. Both candidates targeted the municipal elections of December 8 as a crucial moment in the campaign; whoever could control the most municipalities would be able to monopolize the greater portion of the voting in the presidential election five weeks later, between January 13 and 15. Quiñónez was a formidable opponent. His wealth, his lineage, and his years in office, not to mention his current position as vice president, endowed him with a great number of contacts and allies. But Palomo was no political novice. As minister of government and hacienda, he too had built up a coterie of alliances, and he was closely related to the Dueñas family, one of the wealthiest and most influential at the time. Furthermore, President Figueroa had seriously considered Palomo as his successor in 1910 before settling on Manuel Araujo. Both candidates initiated their organizational activities by calling upon allies in the municipalities and the departmental capitals to prepare to control the polling stations. In this regard as well, the election resembled the vice presidential election of 1895, except for one major difference: in 1895 there was an undisputed leader who kept electoral passions in check.

Because both candidates were well-positioned government officials, the apparatus of the state, and especially the military, a potentially crucial pillar of support in political tussles, became a point of dispute. Palomo invested much effort in building alliances with military officers, and by all available accounts he was successful in convincing many of them to join his cause. Enrique Córdova commented repeatedly in his memoir on Palomo's support in the military. As just one example, Córdova wrote that "it must be remembered that the majority of the Departmental Comandantes . . . were active supporters of Palomismo. . . . As a result of the Comandantes' support for Palomo, the Quiñónez movement accused him of impositions, and the truth is that many impositions were committed, but they were not the exclusive work of the Comandantes, the greater part was carried out by the security forces of Hacienda, who obeyed the direct orders of the Minister of Hacienda, Palomo."[17] The U.S. chargé, too, noted the military's support for Palomo. In one of his reports to Washington he included a description of a political clash in San Miguel: "A heated discussion, terminating in a scuffle, took place a few days ago at San Miguel and was stopped by General Calderón, the Governor, who, being a strong Polomist [*sic*], arrested ten of the Quiñónes [*sic*] participants and sent them to the Capital for trial."[18] This split within the military would prove to be an enduring legacy of the 1919 election.

It was in the midst of the heated electoral campaign that Quiñónez founded both the PND and the Liga Roja. The PND was a political machine, and the Liga Roja was a paramilitary organization. As will be shown in the next section, the Liga was organized parallel to the PND; local commanders of the Liga were the same local political bosses allied with Quiñónez through the PND, and its rank and file were the clients of these bosses. Córdova wrote of the Liga, "don Alfonso, in order to assure his succession at the appropriate time, organized the Liga Roja, an assault force [*cuerpo de asalto y gritos*] that worked at all costs for the imposition of its Jefe, discrediting the Government and alarming that sector of the population not allied with Quiñónez."[19] Needless to say, the potential for electoral violence under these circumstances was high.

The municipal elections of December 8 arrived amidst this growing political tension. Córdova stated that on the day before the election he received numerous telegrams from across the nation describing the rapid mobilization of Quiñonista and Palomista factions. "Very early on the eighth of December," Córdova wrote, "I sent out groups to monitor the two parties and they informed me that here in San Salvador Quiñónez had the majority of the city's laborers, but Palomo had a great number of campesinos which had been brought into the city from the fincas of the Dueñas family, of Guillermo Meléndez [a brother of Carlos Meléndez who had sided with Palomo], and of the Vilanova family."[20] The elections were particularly violent, with very few votes being cast. Opposing bands simply battled one another for control over the polling stations. The U.S. legation placed the initial estimate of casualties at one hundred killed and two hundred wounded, but it later determined that the actual numbers were much higher (no precise figure was given).[21] Quiñónez was the overwhelming victor, at least according to Córdova and the U.S. legation.[22]

A document from the municipality of Nahuizalco in Sonsonate Department offers a glimpse into the level of violence and discord that accompanied the electoral season of 1918/1919. The document comes from a rare source in El Salvador, a private collection of personal papers belonging to Ismael Fuentes (1878–1934), the former secretary general of Quiñónez's electoral campaign. Fuentes is a bit of an enigma. He was orphaned at a young age, and his parentage is uncertain, which at the time in El Salvador was usually an insurmountable hurdle to social climbing. But he received an education in the military academy and married well, into the Palomo family, thereby becoming a cousin of the Dueñas family.[23] Yet, for whatever reason, he rejected Palomo's candidacy and joined forces with Quiñónez. The document in question is a report to Fuentes from the head of Quiñónez's party in Nahuizalco detailing the clashes that occurred between the Quiñonistas and the Palomistas in the four months leading up to the municipal election in December 1918.

According to the author of the report, both factions were large and strong in Nahuizalco, although the Palomistas had the advantage of being supported by the soldiers stationed in the village and seemingly also by the departmental garrison in Sonsonate City. The first major conflagration occurred in September 1918 as both sides began gearing up for the election. Members of the two political clubs seem to have crossed paths, and a melee ensued that involved many dozens of people. In the end, sixty-three Quiñónez supporters were arrested and sent to the military barracks in Sonsonate City. Tensions presumably remained high for the next four months, but the author skips ahead to the night before the election to describe the return to violence. That night, a leading Palomista and some soldiers apparently passed by Quiñónez's election headquarters and opened fire on the building. The following morning, according to the author, approximately 1,500 Quiñóñez supporters were standing outside the municipal hall, waiting to vote. A group of heavily armed Palomistas showed up and announced that the election was canceled. The ensuing clash devolved into an extended shoot-out that resulted in many deaths. The author identified by name forty-one Quiñónez supporters who were killed and another twelve, including himself, who were wounded. He does not mention how many, if any, casualties the Palomistas suffered. The author claimed that some of the casualties came from a group of Quiñónez supporters who had taken refuge in a church, but the Palomistas pulled them out after shooting down the door.[24]

The violence that accompanied the 1918 municipal elections followed the customary patterns of patronage-based politics. When two evenly matched bosses faced off without a superior authority to constrain the conflict, high levels of violence ensued. Although Palomo was an underdog relative to the powerful machine that the Meléndez-Quiñónez family had built, he managed to assemble a formidable force, particularly with his support from segments of the military. As a comparative example, the exact opposite had occurred in the 1895 vice presidential election. Even though two powerful bosses, Carlos Meléndez and Prudencio Alfaro, had competed with one another for the prize of the vice presidency, a superior official, General Gutiérrez, reigned undisputed above them and kept the violence in check.

Quiñónez likely would have gone on to win the presidency had it not been for an unexpected development. On December 11, just three days after the municipal elections, Carlos Meléndez became sick. All available sources describe his ailment as an "attack of paralysis," which was probably a stroke or a heart attack. The paralysis struck him twice in three days and eventually resulted in his death the following year. In the meantime, he was unable to remain in office. On December 21, during a momentary recovery, he turned the presidency over to Vice President Quiñónez. Quiñónez found this ascent to the presidency a mixed blessing. On the one hand, Palomo immediately withdrew from the race, citing the conflict of interest in having his opponent sitting in the presidency.[25] On the other hand, Quiñónez technically was disqualified from running for president, because he was holding the office within the six-month window prior to the election. Suddenly, El Salvador had no candidates for president.

In this vacuum, Jorge Meléndez emerged as the PND's candidate. According to Córdova, Quiñónez initially asked Francisco Martínez Suárez, the secretary of foreign affairs, to run, but he rejected the offer.[26] Quiñónez then apparently considered running himself, despite his ineligibility. On either December 31 or January 1, he had his minister in Honduras ask the U.S. legation in Tegucigalpa to contact the State Department to inquire if the United States would recognize him if he were elected president. It is not known how or even if the State Department responded to the inquiry, but Quiñónez abandoned the notion and turned to his novice brother-in-law, Jorge Meléndez, announcing him as the PND candidate less than one week before the election.

In yet another odd turn of events, a political novice by the name of Arturo Araujo announced that he would challenge Meléndez in the election. Araujo was an enigmatic figure. He was a wealthy landowner from the region of Armenia in Sonsonate Department who had attended university in England, received an engineering degree, and become something of an Anglophile. He married an English woman and admired greatly the British Labour Party. Upon his return to El Salvador he began cultivating a prolabor reputation. He reportedly paid his workers more than the average daily wage and provided them with housing and medical care. In 1918, at a national meeting of artisans in Armenia, which he had helped to organize, he was given the title "Benefactor of Workers."[27]

Meléndez and Quiñónez did not take kindly to Araujo's sudden entrance into the race. Although they announced that he would be allowed to participate freely in the election, they made sure that he would receive almost no votes. First, they ordered their subalterns in the municipalities to prevent Araujo supporters from voting. Then, in a seeming attempt to humiliate Araujo, they arranged for a third person who was not even a candidate in the election to receive more votes than Araujo. This person was Pío Romero Bosque, then chief justice of the Supreme Court. Evidence of these manipulations is found in telegrams from local officials acknowledging receipt of their orders from San Salvador. For example, the alcalde of San Sebastián wrote, "I understand your telegram referring to the voting in favor of Dr. Romero Bosque; I have communicated it to the Directorio in order that it be put into effect."[28] The alcalde of Verapáz informed his departmental governor that "today at one o'clock in the afternoon, I instructed the Directorio to adjudicate votes in favor of Pío Romero instead of Jorge Meléndez."[29] The U.S. chargé reported that "it was carefully planned that Dr. Pío Romero Bosque should receive the second greatest number of votes and accordingly voters were sent by the Melendez-Quinonez [sic] party to cast their votes for Dr. Bosque." The chargé went on to describe a particularly explicit case of fraud that, unbeknownst to him, was standard practice: "Mr. Salvador Sol, a leading Quiñonista, visited three towns with two hundred men from his plantation who registered their votes in the three places."[30]

The final results from the election had Meléndez receiving 166,441 votes, Pío Romero Bosque 4,370 votes, and Araujo 1,022 votes.[31] Quiñónez was elected vice president, and Romero was selected as minister of war. The minister of foreign affairs was Juan Francisco Paredes, who, according to the U.S. legation, had served as the "chief of the Quiñonista party" in his home region of Ahuachapán.[32]

Incensed over the results of the election, Araujo spent the next year planning the overthrow of the Meléndez government. In March 1920 a gun battle broke out between his supporters and government troops on his hacienda "El Sunza" outside Armenia. Reports from the U.S. legation indicate that the government discovered Araujo's conspiratorial activities and sent two dozen guardias to his plantation to arrest him. Araujo's supporters held the guardias at bay long enough for their leader to flee to Honduras, where in the coming weeks he assembled between three hundred and one thousand men.[33] In May he crossed into El Salvador and seized the town of Arcatao in Chalatenango Department and attacked two military stations in the surrounding region. The Meléndez government responded quickly to the invasion by requisitioning automobiles in the capital and sending troops to the border. Araujo was defeated again and returned to Honduras, where he remained quietly until 1923, when the Quiñónez government allowed him to return to his agricultural pursuits in Armenia.[34]

As for Ismael Fuentes, he continued to work for Jorge Meléndez's election after Quiñónez's forced withdrawal in late 1918. As a result of

Mélendez's victory and his loyal service, Fuentes was awarded a series of diplomatic posts in Spain and Uruguay. Some of the letters in his personal correspondence are from lower-ranking Quiñonista activists throughout the country who claimed to have served him and the PND during the election and were hoping to enlist Fuentes's support in some personal or professional matter before he left the country and his influence waned.[35] It is apparent from some of these letters that Palomo supporters continued to suffer the consequences of their candidate's loss. A letter from a Quiño-nista in the town of San Francisco dated late March 1919 informs Fuentes that Palomistas continued to languish in jail.[36]

In sum, the period 1913 to 1919, which began with the ascension of Carlos Meléndez and ended with the election of Jorge Meléndez, illus-trates the extent to which the centralized political system of the early twentieth century was a proverbial new wine in an old bottle. Voting re-mained under the control of political bosses, who had simply been brought under the aegis of a centralized authority. When this authority dissipated, as it did in 1918 when Carlos Meléndez refused to choose his successor, the system broke down into its constituent parts and operated very much as it had in the nineteenth century, with interpatronage rivalries vying for votes and political office.

The PND, the Military, and the Liga Roja, 1919–1923

Following their victory in the election of 1919, Jorge Meléndez and Al-fonso Quiñónez Molina worked to consolidate their authority and expand the PND. Their basic goals mirrored those of the Club Melendista: pre-vent political factionalism and create a single pyramid of patronage in which they were the ultimate authorities. As one local PND affiliate put it, the enemy was *"políticos independientes,"* local bosses who engaged in poli-tics without party affiliation.[37] Another local affiliate referred to outsiders of the PND simply as "the enemy. . . . It is necessary to stop all of their intrigues; the enemy always is the enemy."[38]

The structure of the PND resembled that of its many predecessor networks. It was hierarchical and highly centralized. The party was headed by "our grand, noble and illustrious Jefe," who was usually Alfonso Quiñónez.[39] He presided over the national committee, which monitored the departmental committees, which in turn watched over the municipal chapters known as "clubs." The party was indistinguishable from the government. The minister of government sat on the national committee, departmental governors conducted the business of the departmental committees, and alcaldes presided over the municipal clubs. Patronage governed the relationships between the various levels. High-ranking bosses had the power to appoint, and low-ranking bosses hoped to be appointed. The success of the system required obedience to one's superiors, as is suggested by the following description from a local affiliate: "The Constitution of the party is obliged to aid us mutually, each one of us is to sustain the other, whether as individuals or as part of the general association, in all that relates to our political and social life; but in order to have this mutual aid and the protection of the party, it is necessary to be honorable, sincere and faithful to our principles and to our *Jefes Supremos,* the foundations of the edifice."[40] In other words, mutual progress would result only when individuals properly served their superiors.

An interesting aspect of the PND is the extent to which its discourse resembled that of patronage networks from the nineteenth century. For instance, in 1921 the governor of Ahuachapán referred to the political activities of a local faction operating outside the jurisdiction of the PND as "anti-patriotic conduct . . . sordid and perverse work of a certain diabolical spirit that seeks to break apart the Great Party [*el Gran Partido*]."[41] The canon of any patronage network defined unity as patriotic and moral, whereas opposition was immoral and traitorous. Such discourse was consistent with political language used throughout the preceding decades, suggesting continuity between the PND of the 1920s and its predecessor networks.

Ismael Fuentes's archival collection reveals that political insiders employed this same language in their private correspondence with one another. The collection contains personal letters that Fuentes received during his time in Spain from various high-ranking figures in the PND and well-positioned government officials, including President Meléndez and Vice President Quiñónez. Such personal correspondence is a rare source in El Salvador. Some of the letters were handwritten, and the authors used the informal "tu" in addressing one another; they also discussed a variety of personal and family matters that did not appear in customary government communiques. Invariably, the authors turned to the subject of politics, and one might expect that in doing so they would let down their guard and speak frankly about their nondemocratic tactics. After all, Fuentes had spearheaded the PND's electoral endeavors in 1918, and both he and his correspondents possessed intimate knowledge of the methods employed to secure victory. But, in fact, they retained the standard discourse of democracy, describing their activities as legal and based on the principles of freedom and liberty. As just one example, in a letter dated November 5, 1919, President Meléndez refers to their political adversaries as "false patriots" and "eternal enemies of legality" who "overflow with political passion" and create a "bitter situation" through their "desperate struggle." By contrast, Meléndez describes himself and his allies as pursuing "patriotic ideals," in part through their support of a "free press."[42]

Aspirants to political office had to receive approval from the PND in order to be elected, as illustrated in the following letter, in which the governor of Chalatenango Department informs the minister of government of problems with a municipal election.

> The candidacy of the municipal authorities approved by the Committee of the Partido Nacional Democrático and recommended in particular by the Superiors of the Party, so that they [the candidates] would triumph without alteration in the election of the 11th in this municipality, did not come to be victorious as I had instructed the Alcalde, for the Secretary, Héctor Trujillo, rejected the referred candidacy and organized another at his convenience. . . . In this matter I request instructions as to what to do.[43]

When local affiliates solicited high-ranking members (that is, the people who held the power to appoint), they were quick to make reference to the services they had performed on behalf of the party. For example, one solicitor wrote in his letter to the minister of government, "You are well aware of my role in the most recent electoral struggle and of my loyalty to the Democratic [PND] cause, for I am actually the *vocal* of the Comité Central of the Partido Nacional Democrático of this municipality."[44] Another solicitor pointed out that he was "the President of the

Club Quiñonista and had been one of the first to enlist and work for the party," especially during "the electoral imposition of 1918–1919."[45]

When local political factions outside the organizational realm of the PND refused to desist in their attempts to gain municipal office, Meléndez and Quiñónez turned to coercion, which in some instances meant the military. In the municipal elections of 1920, for example, Jorge Meléndez learned of two municipalities in San Miguel Department in which the PND candidates were not being put into office by the local electoral boards. He ordered two detachments of soldiers to the region to ensure that the proper candidates won.[46] During that same election, Pío Romero Bosque, as minister of war, informed the minister of government that "the Alcalde of San Fernando (Chalatenango Department) has directed to me a communication containing information that a group of individuals belonging to a contrary band is attempting to use force to make prevalent their ideas in the next election for local authorities; I have directed to the Departmental Comandante orders to take whatever measures are necessary to avoid such friction in the cited population."[47] One difficulty for the PND arose when these local disputes had nothing to do with broader political issues and instead grew out of conflicts between members of the same faction. For example, in 1922 a police agent reported the emergence of a political fight between members of the same municipal council in the village of Chilamatal (La Libertad Department). The agent reported that the source of the factionalism was a debate over who would receive the greater share of revenues from the selling of licenses to vendors for the annual Easter celebrations.[48]

Conflicts with the Military

Despite these two examples of Meléndez's reliance upon the military to undermine a local faction, the split that emerged within the military during the election of 1918 remained a lingering problem. Enrique Córdova, the minister of war who had commented extensively on Quiñónez's relations with the military in 1918, indicated that after the election sectors of the military remained actively opposed to the Meléndez government. "For a period of time," he wrote, "there was a mutiny in the cuarteles every fifteen days."[49] Córdova's comment seems slightly exaggerated in hind-sight, but still it reflects his opinion that relations between Meléndez and some sectors of the military were strained. Three generals, in addition to General José Tomás Calderón (mentioned above), appear in the archival record as being opposed to Meléndez. They are Generals José María Per-alta and Juan Amaya, who had led Araujo's invasion from Honduras in May 1920, and Armando Llanos, the commander of the military school.

The military's opposition to Meléndez grew partly from a combina-tion of support for Palomo and opposition to Meléndez's policies.[50] In the post–World War I economic crisis of 1919, for instance, the government, suffering from a deficit in revenues, decided that it would deal with the fiscal crisis by placing army salaries in arrears. The U.S. chargé noted in early 1920 that "the army . . . has become dissatisfied because of delay of the payment of the troops and reorganization of the Guardia Nacional, a branch of the police force, which has robbed the army of many of its du-ties and supplanted them in importance."[51] The chargé later noted that even the salaries of the National Guard were in arrears.[52] Another indict-ment of Meléndez came from General Salvador Peña Trejo. In his 1964 memoir about the military coup of 1931, Peña Trejo discussed his mem-ory of military affairs in the 1910s and 1920s and identified 1918, the year of the electoral conflict between Quiñónez and Palomo, as decisive. Until that year, he claimed, the military had been paid on time and in full, but under Meléndez and Quiñónez army pay often went into arrears, and even when soldiers were paid, they often received only half their due.[53]

Meléndez exacerbated his strained relations with the military in 1920 when he announced his intention to reform the military to limit its influ-ence on both government and society. He aired these ideas in the annual presidential address before the National Assembly in February. "For a long time, and in accordance with unwise custom," Meléndez said, "the Army has been the arbiter of social destiny in our country. My desire—and in this I am intelligently supported by my colleagues in the Government—is for this noble institution to fulfill its duty in terms which are called for by the Constitution and the culture of the Republic. To this end, without neglecting military and tactical training, there has been undertaken in-tense work to turn the military corps more into centers of learning and general enlightenment."[54] Meléndez also proposed that the system of military justice be reformed so that the military would be more accountable to civilian courts, and he called for the creation of a civilian commission to devise a new system and submit it to the assembly for approval. These were bold proposals, and although there is no evidence that Meléndez followed up on them, their pronunciation certainly did not win him support in the military.

Shortly after Meléndez's speech, General Llanos resigned as director of the military school, citing as his reason for leaving the government's failure to pay the military cadets.[55] But Meléndez considered Llanos to be a "Palomista" whose resignation was motivated by broader political issues and ordered him to be exiled. Llanos was escorted by armed guards to the port of Acajutla, where he was shipped to Costa Rica. The U.S. chargé met with Meléndez as Llanos was being escorted away and reported the following conversation: "The President informed me that they [Llanos and General Julio Salinas, Llanos's predecessor] were against the Government and could not be relied upon. He further said that he was considering the closing of the Polytechnic School [military school] and sending a number of men to the United States to be educated as officers. He said that they were disloyal and untrustworthy."[56] Two months later a barracks revolt broke out in San Salvador, coinciding with Araujo's invasion from Honduras. Troops loyal to Meléndez quickly suppressed the revolt but failed to catch the officer who had instigated it, allowing him to flee to Honduras and join Araujo.[57]

In 1922, two military coups broke out against the Meléndez government. The first occurred in February in the military school. All sixty-three cadets marched out of the school and set up barricades at strategic points of transit to the campus. According to reports from the British legation, the cadets ambushed troops loyal to the government and caused as many as fifty casualties. None of the other barracks in the capital joined the revolt, and the cadets were suppressed in one day. Meléndez closed down the school in the wake of the revolt, and it was not reopened until 1926 under President Quiñónez. The second rebellion broke out in May among soldiers of the Sixth Infantry barracks in San Salvador. Approximately one-half of the four hundred soldiers in the barracks participated. They gained control of the fort at approximately 1:00 a.m. on May 22 and were joined by Dr. Valle, a politician whom Meléndez had exiled in 1921. The rebels apparently declared Valle to be president and commander in chief of the army. The revolt ended when the rebels failed to capture a second barracks (Zapote) that was situated closer to the center of town. Immediately after the rebellion, the British minister met with Meléndez, who told him that 160 of the 200 rebels escaped and the rest had been either captured or killed.[58]

This amalgamation of evidence relating to Meléndez's difficulties with the military does not suggest that Meléndez faced a complete breakdown in the military chain of command. But it does show that some individuals and groups in the military were dissatisfied with his regime and also that he was aware of their opposition. The degree of conflict between Meléndez and the military was unprecedented in the forty or so years since 1880, when the process of professionalization had begun.

The Liga Roja

It was within the context of these hassles with the military that Meléndez and Quiñónez created a paramilitary organization, the Liga Roja. Scholars initially saw in its violent and authoritarian methods a symbol of the Meléndez-Quiñónez era as well as the military regimes after 1931. In particular, it struck them as something of a precursor to the paramilitaries of the 1960s and 1970s, such as the Organización Democrática Nacionalista (ORDEN, the Nationalist Democratic Organization), that were set up to oppose the growing wave of rural mobilization. Unfortunately, many of these initial studies were forced by sheer paucity of evidence to include only generalized descriptions of the Liga. The opening of the Salvadoran archives has brought new evidence to light and promoted a revisionist interpretation, although the total amount of evidence relating to the Liga remains modest. The revisionist line describes the Liga as a semipopulist organization, one created by the Meléndez-Quiñónez political machine but comprised of poor people who made the Liga their own and who used it to mobilize against the system of injustice in El Salvador.[59] If that argument is correct, it would represent one of those precious historic moments when subaltern actors acted autonomously and bargained with elites to achieve something for themselves. The circumstances surrounding the Liga's creation lend credence to this approach, because they are consistent with other case studies in which subalterns found negotiating space. The Liga was created in the midst of intra-elite battles that prompted one faction, Meléndez-Quiñónez, to reach out to new actors to counterbalance its loss of a monopoly over the military.[60]

While the revisionist argument is plausible, the available evidence does not support it very well. Instead, the evidence suggests that the Liga Roja remained more a direct paramilitary arm of the Meléndez-Quiñónez political machine, and when Quiñónez disbanded it in 1923, he appears to have been more concerned with local elites using it to advance their sectarian interests at the cost of the central state, rather than rural masses using it to challenge the fundamental structure of the system. Admittedly, these two arguments do not have to be mutually exclusive. Just as a revisionist argument has shown the complexity of the paramilitary organization ORDEN in the 1960s and 1970s, it is possible that even if the Liga Roja remained an elite-directed paramilitary entity, subalterns found bargaining space within it.[61] I do not believe that the evidence is sufficient to show the nature of the relationship between Liga leaders and rank-and-file members. Nevertheless, in the absence of new materials, I find that the strength of the revisionist claim is limited.

Some of the first reports of Liga activity appeared in the newspaper *Diario del Salvador* in the waning months of 1918, as the electoral conflict between Quiñónez and Palomo intensified. The reports describe violent clashes in various municipalities between branches of the Liga and supporters of Palomo. Interestingly, many of the Palomistas in the reports were military personnel, either local commanders or military patrols actively defending the Palomo camp (thus providing further evidence of Palomo's success in gaining the support in some sectors in the military).[62] References to Liga activity continue to appear over the next four years, especially during electoral periods (although municipal elections came less frequently after 1920, when Meléndez and Quiñónez changed the duration of municipal officeholding from one to two years).

The close association between the Liga Roja and the PND is made evident by the numerous requests from local affiliates and aspiring officeholders, who anxiously referred to themselves as members of both the PND and the Liga. In Yayantique (La Unión Department), a group of people submitted a nullification request for the election of December 1921 in which they referred to their candidate as the "President of our local Club and Jefe of the Liga Roja."[63] From the municipality of Mejicanos, located just outside San Salvador, a letter to Jorge Meléndez arrived in January 1920, informing him that the PND had won the recent election but was being challenged by an opposing faction. The author of the letter encourages Meléndez to act in defense of the victors, who are "faithful members of your party," and one of whom "belongs to the Liga Roja."[64] In 1921 in the municipality of Chilanga (Morazán Department), the two political factions facing off in the municipal election both claimed to be the local representative of the Liga Roja. The government had to send out an investigative team to determine which faction was genuine.[65] In 1921 the secretary of the Santa Ana chapter of the Liga defined its role as sustaining the "initiative of our governing patriot, Don Jorge Meléndez, upheld by the Great Partido Nacional Democrático and the Liga Roja, which in its abundance now exists throughout the entire country, and which recognizes as its illustrious jefe, Dr. Alfonso Quiñónez Molina."[66]

The Liga Roja was particularly active in 1922 in defense of Alfonso Quiñónez Molina's bid for the presidency against Miguel Molina. Local Liga chapters organized a variety of public processions to demonstrate support for Quiñónez. One of these demonstrations was staged in San Salvador on December 10, 1922, and was described in a local newspaper. "The marchers," reads the article, "were lined up in perfect order, subject to the discipline of their various jefes, for the Partido Nacional Democrático is not an unruly and incoherent mob . . . but an organized conglomeration of men that moves as an army, obedient to the orders of their captains . . . that great meeting of men moved harmoniously as battalions that would pass review in a military parade. It was a brilliant spectacle."[67] When Quiñónez resorted to violence against Molina in late 1922—as will be shown below—the Liga Roja took the lead in the repression.

The recurrent and public presence of the Liga Roja drew the attention of the U.S. and British legations, both of which were taking an increased interest in political affairs.[68] The officers in the legations provide a number of revealing descriptions of the Liga, noting that its members wore a uniform that resembled the military's and bore a distinctive insignia of a bleeding machete.[69] In January 1922 the British Minister learned that members of the Liga Roja in Sonsonate City were harassing the Salvadoran employees of the local branch of the British-owned Salvador Railway Co. He went to Sonsonate and reported that upon "arriving at Sonsonate, I saw Mr. Wilson and the other British subjects who stated that since the arrival of the Red League, the town had been in a turmoil, that bands of men, members of the Red League, most of whom were intoxicated, had made demonstrations against the foreigners, and had roamed the town, smashing and looting houses, uttering cries of 'death to the foreigners.'"[70] The diplomatic officers were quick to point out that the rank and file of the Liga was drawn from the lowest classes of society. A report from the U.S. legation reads, the "Red League [is] composed principally of illiterate Indians and the most degraded elements of the population."[71] This reference to Indians may reveal actual indigenous membership in the Liga, but it cannot be taken literally, because legation officers often used the term to refer to anybody who appeared to be a peasant.

Nevertheless, the rank and file of the Liga Roja was indeed comprised of laborers and peasants from the rural areas. They were incorporated into the Liga not independently, but rather through the local political bosses and landowners allied with the PND. The U.S. chargé offered one of the most revealing descriptions of the manner in which Meléndez and Quiñónez gathered many hundreds of Liga members into the capital in December 1922 for a crackdown on the opposition. "The Red League," he wrote, "appears to be organized somewhat on the lines of the ancient feudal system, various land owners being expected to furnish their respective quotas. Mr. Salvador Sol, formerly minister to the United States, for instance, supplied the government with two hundred men from his estates, and other persons have sent larger numbers."[72]

Although the Liga Roja was a key pillar of the Meléndez-Quiñónez regime, the documentary record provides surprisingly few names (around one dozen) of local Liga jefes and even fewer names of the rank and file. This precludes a comprehensive look at the social and regional makeup of the Liga. But the few available examples represent a wide geographical cross-section of the nation and paint a suggestive portrait. They indicate that the local jefes of the Liga were either landowners or municipal officers under the PND, or both. Salvador Sol, for instance, was a member of one

of the major coffee-growing families. He owned two haciendas in Sonsonate and ten urban properties in San Salvador.[73] In the village of Nahuizalco, a newspaper story on the Liga identified Rodolfo Brito as a
principal figure in the local Liga chapter.[74] He was a ladino and a member
of the landowning Brito family that was at the forefront of the campaign
to wrest control of the municipal government away from the Indians, as
discussed in chapter 3.[75]

In Nueva Concepción (Chalatenango Department), the two jefes of
the Liga Roja were the brothers Francisco and Rubén Parrilla. They were
the largest landowners in the region, and although Nueva Concepción was
not located in a coffee-growing region, it did produce large amounts of
primary crops and cattle, as well as some sugar, and it had a mine. The
Parrilla brothers owned three of the region's eighteen haciendas, on which
they raised cattle and grew sugarcane. They had three sugar-processing
mills, one of which was operated by hydraulic rather than animal power,
and they owned the sole mine. Francisco Parrilla had served as an alcalde
for the PND in 1921.[76] In Yayantique (La Unión Department), the person
who identified himself as "Jefe of the Liga," Domingo Guzmán, owned
one of only twelve haciendas in the region. Although Yayantique was a
relatively poor, corn-growing municipality, Guzmán was a rich man and a
major landowner by local standards.[77]

The leader of the Liga Roja in Chalchuapa (Ahuachapán Department) was Carlos Portillo. His status as a Liga jefe was mentioned in a
1930 newspaper article that reported on his electoral activities. Chalchuapa was one of the major coffee-growing municipalities in the nation,
and the Portillo family was one of the municipality's biggest growers, owning three coffee plantations.[78] In the municipality of Colón (La Libertad
Department), a political conflagration in 1929 resulted in the identification of Isidoro González and Alberto Guadrón as former leaders of the
Liga Roja. The accusation came from their political opposition, so it must
be taken in perspective, but both González and Guadrón had served on
the municipal council under the PND for five years (1922–1927). They
were also prominent landholders in the region, owning coffee-growing
land around the area of El Jabalí, which is located on the side of the San
Salvador volcano opposite the capital city.[79] A very similar political dispute
took place in the municipality of Tenancingo (Cuscatlán Department) in

1929. Elías Barriere was identified by his opponent as being the former jefe of the Liga Roja in the village. Barriere had served as síndico for the PND in 1923. He also was a one of the few large landowners in the region. The municipality was not a major agricultural producer, and it had only five haciendas, but Barriere owned one of them.[80] In sum, this amalgamation of evidence relating to the identity of Liga jefes is not exhaustive, but it is suggestive. It indicates that Liga jefes were local elites, and that the organizational structure of the Liga ran parallel to that of the PND. In light of such information, the Liga appears to have been more a militarized wing of a political/patronage network than a populist organization.

One of the more intriguing pieces of evidence is a reference to the Liga's composition in Izalco (Sonsonate Department). It appeared in one of the main daily newspapers at the time, *Diario del Salvador,* in the midst of Quiñónez's quest for the presidency in 1922.[81] The reference identified two of the Liga's jefes in Izalco as José Feliciano Ama and Felix Turish, and declared that the village had 965 affiliates behind them. Izalco had a large indigenous population, and Ama and Turish were both local indigenous leaders. So the fact that Quiñónez and the PND would choose indigenous leaders to head the local branch of the Liga Roja would seem to challenge the claim made above that the Liga was not a populist organization. Indeed such evidence carries that potential.

However, such evidence can also be used to support a patronage-based argument. Quiñónez and the PND wanted something out of Izalco—votes, mainly—which Ama and Turish could potentially deliver. In return, Ama and Turish wanted outside support for their local affairs, presumably defense of indigenous issues in disputes with local ladino elites. By allying with Ama and Turish, Quiñónez ran the risk of alienating local ladinos, just as allying with the ladino Rodolfo Brito in Nahuizalco ran the risk of alienating the politically active indigenous community in that municipality. It is not clear why Quiñónez and the PND chose the ladino minority in Nahuizalco and the indigenous majority in Izalco, but such was the curious nature of patronage-based political deal making in El Salvador.

Regardless, the affiliation with the indigenous community in Izalco did not necessarily promote the cause of democracy. As we saw in the case

of Nahuizalco in chapter 3, whenever the indigenous community participated in electoral conflicts with the local ladino population, it did so in
roughly the same nondemocratic manner as its ladino rivals. It was consistent with the structure and function of patronage-based politics for a local
power player, in this case an indigenous community, to seek out alliances
with powerful outsiders to promote local causes. We have little record of
the local political activity of the indigenous people in Izalco under Ama's
leadership. But the evidence shows him reaching out to Quiñónez, the
PND, and the Liga Roja. We know nothing about what Ama and his followers might have garnered from their support for Quiñónez, but the pact
was part of an emergent pattern of alliance-seeking by Ama. As we will see
in the next two chapters, Ama again reached out to a powerful outsider in
1929, in the run-up to the 1931 presidential election. That outsider was
the candidate Alberto Gómez Zárate, who had been a loyal functionary of
the Meléndez-Quiñónez network and whose candidacy most advanced
elite interests. Notably, Ama chose not to ally with Arturo Araujo, the
prolabor populist from just down the road in Armenia. And when Gómez
Zárate lost the election to Araujo, Ama shifted his alliance to yet another
outsider, the Communist Party, in the municipal elections in late 1931
and eventually in the run-up to the uprising of January 1932.[82] All of this
evidence shows a local power player, in this case an indigenous leader from
Izalco, making alliances with powerful outsiders regardless of ideological
orientation, in a traditionally patronage-based manner, with both parties
hoping to get something out of their relationship with one another. The
first evidence we have of Ama playing that role was with Quinónez and
the Liga Roja.

Alfonso Quiñónez Molina disbanded the Liga Roja after he won the
presidential election in January 1923. The U.S. chargé reported in July
1923 that "the Liga Roja, so far as the public knows, has been very largely
dissolved."[83] Again in 1925 he wrote that "the so-called Liga Roja, which
was of material assistance to the party at the time of the last elections has
been dissolved and no longer exists."[84] Little evidence exists to explain why
Quiñónez dissolved the organization that had been such an important
part of his and Jorge Meléndez's political empire. One argument claims
that it was because the peasants who comprised the Liga were acting autonomously, and Quiñónez feared the prospect of a social revolution.[85] It
seems more likely that the emergent independence of the Liga reflected

machinations of local elites who were looking to use it to regain some of their lost autonomy. The U.S. chargé wrote in 1923 that the leaders of the Liga "were greatly disappointed at not obtaining the political plum they had hoped for as the result of their efforts during the elections, and there is a chance of considerable trouble arising from this disorderly element should conditions seem to give them a chance for making trouble."[86]

A 1923 case relating to the Parrilla brothers in Nueva Concepción reveals the extent to which an elite-led, local branch of the Liga acted independently from the PND. In September 1923, the national government received reports that politically motivated violence had erupted in Nueva Concepción. The government sent a military patrol of twenty-five soldiers to the village; upon arriving, they discovered that the municipal council, consisting of the Parrilla brothers and their allies, was holed up in the municipal hall and the local commander was threatening to arrest them. The commander of the newly arrived patrol allowed the council to leave the municipal hall and then conducted a series of interviews to learn what had transpired. He concluded that the Parrilla brothers, upon receiving word that the national government intended to bypass them in the forthcoming municipal election of December 1923, had mobilized the local chapter of the Liga to attack the army post—the most immediate representative of the national government. The local commander repelled the attack and cornered the Parrilla brothers inside the municipal hall.[87] If this case from Nueva Concepción is at all representative of broader processes at work, it suggests that by reining in the Liga, Quiñónez was sealing a crack that had developed in his political empire.

Quiñónez, 1923–1926

In January 1922, President Meléndez had a pair of extended private conversations with a member of the U.S. diplomatic corps. The summary of those conversations, which the officer provided in a memo to the State Department, offers a penetrating look into the structure of the PND and the political system as it functioned in El Salvador at the time. The diplomatic officer believed that Meléndez considered him a friend and confidant, and thus he assumed that Meléndez was speaking with him openly and frankly. The officer opined that Meléndez embraced his friendship because he felt isolated from many of his fellow countrymen, owing to his political inexperience and the strong opposition of many powerful families, especially Tomás Palomo and his many allies, including the Dueñas family. The officer even claimed that Meléndez felt alienated from his brother-in-law, Alfonso Quiñónez Molina, because the latter was such a "silent and uncommunicative person that although they both lunched together daily with his mother, he was not in his brother-in-law's political confidence and knows little of his plan or actions." In hindsight, the officer's assessment of Meléndez seems naïve. In particular, he seems incapable of recognizing that Meléndez, notwithstanding any feelings of genuine friendship that he might have had for the officer, probably hoped to achieve a diplomatic goal by speaking with him. In particular, it seems apparent that Meléndez wanted to assure him that his regime shared the United States' democratic values and that the forthcoming presidential elections were not going to cause instability in the region. In order to prove the latter claim, Meléndez described the manner in which his brother-in-law had put the necessary components in place to dominate the forthcoming elections without disturbances or violence. In the officer's words:

> He [Meléndez] went on to say that Dr. Quiñónez had worked steadily and for years with all sorts of people, that he was the titular and real head of the Partido Nacional Democratico [sic], and that through this and through the work of the Liga Roja . . . he had built up so strong a personal following that even if the next elections were absolutely free and open to all, he would be elected. He said he was getting in the hands of the party all the minor jobs and offices of importance and prestige such as local alcaldes, chiefs of police and justices, who could be depended upon to work for the success or their party and incidentally themselves.[88]

In other words, Meléndez was revealing the manner in which a highly centralized patron-client network advanced the cause of one of its leaders through the use of political appointments and paramilitary intimidation.

Indeed, as Meléndez predicted, Alfonso Quiñónez Molina won the presidential election of January 1923 as the candidate of the PND, but the process did not go as smoothly as predicted. Rumors floated about for many months that some Palomista supporters would rally around a member of the Dueñas family to challenge Quiñónez, but in the end Quiñónez's opponent turned out to be Miguel Tomás Molina, a lawyer, a landowner, one-time minister of government under Meléndez, and a cousin to Quiñónez. It is not clear why someone of such pedigree and position would challenge Quiñónez rather than join him, but such was the complicated nature of a highly centralized patron-client system, as Palomo's candidacy four years earlier had also demonstrated. Perhaps Molina felt slighted by the system. It is also possible that Molina was motivated by a mild commitment to political reform, a precursor to Pío Romero Bosque, who would launch full-fledged democratic reforms four years later. The British chargé was not a big fan of Molina but described him nonetheless as "a hard-working and conscientious man [whose] absolute honesty and integrity are never questioned."[89] Molina insinuated his belief in the need for popular will into his public discourse. One of his party's political broadsides reads, "Governments cannot and should not be divorced from Public Opinion. They need its force, which is like a solid social base upon which they can allow themselves to engage in direct political action. . . . El Salvador needs a Government with Public Opinion."[90] Molina's reference to "public opinion" sounds like any other political challenger who appealed to democracy to challenge an incumbent. If this was Molina's intention, his use of the term seems vague and mild in comparison to the explicit appeals to democracy made by prior political bosses in the same position. What is notable about Molina's discourse is that he presented it publicly, in the form of a broadside that was handed out and posted on walls in San Salvador. Previously, such appeals had tended to remain in internal documents exchanged between political functionaries. Nevertheless, it was the traditional role of challengers within the patronage system to use a democracy-laden discourse against incumbents, especially those who had been entrenched in power for some time.

Molina appealed directly to workers, who were in an embryonic stage of organization. In another of its broadsides, Molina's party wrote on the so-called worker question. "Frankly speaking," it reads, "here we do not have a true struggle between capital and labor; but this does not mean that we should ignore the well-being of that social class that lives by working with its muscles. . . . If we study the concern of workers, we will see

that many abnormalities exist, principally: THE LACK OF ORGANI-
ZATION; THE LOSS OF TIME; and THE ABSOLUTE ABSENCE
OF PROTECTIVE LAWS [caps in original]."[91] It also was highly uncommon for a candidate to make such appeals to the working class as a political force.[92] In short, regardless of his ultimate intentions in the election,
Molina had broken some long-standing taboos on proper political behavior.

The distinctiveness of Molina's campaign might explain why Quiñónez took Molina's challenge seriously, even though the extent of Molina's support was localized. Molina did not begin his campaign in earnest
until two months prior to the election, giving him very little opportunity
to organize. Also, because Meléndez and Quiñónez had changed the term
of municipal officeholding to two years in 1921, there were no municipal
elections in December 1922 around which Molina could mobilize support, as Palomo had done in 1918. Moreover, Meléndez had placed the
entire nation under a state of siege, which disallowed political rallies. Molina and his top-ranking aides complained incessantly to the U.S. legation
about their inability to engage in electoral activity owing to surveillance
and harassment from the government.[93] Evidence of the level of surveillance is found in a letter from a local PND affiliate in the municipality
of Verapáz, informing the upper echelons of the party about the activities
of Molina's supporters: "Until today in my jurisdiction there has been no
work carried out in favor of the cause of the Constitutionalists [Molina's
party]. My fellow citizens are affiliates of the Partido Nacional Democrático . . . with the exception of 15 who were Palomistas . . . and now are
affiliated with the party of Dr. Miguel Tomás Molina. By way of post I
will send to you the names of these persons who are adverse to Dr. Quiñónez Molina, the actual Jefe of the Nation."[94] In his broadsides, Molina
accused the government's security forces, especially the Liga Roja, of re-
pressing his supporters.[95] Ultimately, Molina's campaign was confined to
greater San Salvador and a few departmental capitals.

Meléndez and Quiñónez tolerated Molina's campaign until December 25, the day when Molina organized a political rally in downtown San
Salvador. What took place that afternoon came to be known as the Christmas Day Massacre. One eyewitness to the event was the British chargé,
who subsequently wrote a lengthy report. He said the procession was
comprised of men, women, and children who made their way through

downtown, waving banners and signs in support of Molina. At around 4:00 p.m., police officers, soldiers, and especially members of the Liga Roja, whom the chargé identified by their conspicuous bleeding-machete insignia, began firing into the crowd. The demonstrators fled in all directions while security forces shot, clubbed, and slashed. The chargé himself ran into a phalanx of five national guardsmen who fired their guns over his car.[96] More than one hundred people were hospitalized during the crackdown, and dozens were said to have been killed. Molina and ten of his closest advisors took asylum in the Spanish embassy.[97] His followers were subject to ongoing repression by the security forces in the following days. One of the most notorious incidents was the arrest and eventual execution of Alberto Escalante, a young artisan who was president of the San Vicente chapter of Molina's party. The perpetrator of the crime was Rosendo "Chajazo" Barahona, a guardia who was operating under the orders of General Calvo, commander of the Guardia Nacional. Why Escalante was singled out for murder was never determined. But the incident generated an enormous amount of press five years later, when the Romero government tried to bring the perpetrators to justice. Barahona's menacing look and scarred face provided appropriately compelling newspaper photos to accompany the accusations.[98]

A few days after the massacre, Jorge Meléndez met with the U.S. chargé, who reported the following discussion: "In a recent conversation with me, President Meléndez has expressed great regret that the circumstances do not permit an unrestricted political campaign such as is conducted in the United States. He has stated that the temperament of the Salvadoran people renders absolute freedom of elections, as prevails in more enlightened nations, impossible in this country, where truthfully, he says, the electorate is unable to exercise the franchise intelligently."[99] In expressing this disregard for democracy, Meléndez offered the classic discourse of an incumbent political boss. Further insight into his character was revealed one year later, when he reportedly entered the bar at the International Club and ordered drinks to toast the events of Christmas 1922.[100]

On January 5, 1923, Molina issued a statement from exile telling his supporters to boycott the election.[101] Quiñónez went on to win the election unanimously, receiving 178,000 votes.[102] Pío Romero Bosque was elected vice president and was also chosen as minister of war. The actions taken by Meléndez and Quiñónez in the election of 1923 reveal the degree to which politics had become centralized. They also suggest that Meléndez and Quiñónez had learned a lesson during the election of 1919, namely that the opposition could not be allowed to mount an organized challenge.

Politically speaking, the next four years under Quiñónez were uneventful in that he simply extended the political order under the PND. To facilitate this process, he had the term of municipal office extended to three years for half of the municipal council, with the other half to be replaced after two years. The documentary records relating to the elections of 1923 and 1925 indicate that they were similar to earlier elections under the PND. Aspirants had to receive approval from the PND hierarchy, and while there was a degree of negotiation and jockeying for position between local aspirants and the upper echelons of the PND, ultimately the central committee set the slate of candidates. The following samples of letters illustrate the broader process. In the first one, a group of local elites asks the minister of government to select a new alcalde for their municipality.

> Quezaltepeque, September 25, 1923
> Señor Minister of Government,
> Señor: under your authority and as good citizens of this village, we come to denounce the bad acts of the municipal authorities. . . . For these abuses you should suspend said functionary. Those listed below, Señor Minister, plead [*le rogamos*] that for the next term you name us an Alcalde that is honorable, progressive, and of the people, one that has neither ambitions or bad faith.[103]

A second letter from a local candidate in El Cármen (La Unión Department) expresses fear that his opponents are plotting against him. He tries to convince the national committee that his credentials in the PND are sound.

> October 9, 1923
> Sr. Minister of Government
> I am aware that in recent days . . . there occurred a meeting in the house of don Nicolás Canales . . . with the object of misinforming against me

before your authority to the effect that my candidacy would not be approved for Alcalde in the next election. My candidacy has been put forth by the PND Club of this population and by the Departmental Committee for your approval. It is my honor to make clear to you that all of the individuals who denounce me are persons who only are trying to denigrate this honorable population, being contrary to our party as well as the good propositions of our constituted government.[104]

Another typical example originated in the election of 1925 in El Refugio (Ahuachapán Department), in which President Quiñónez himself named the candidates who had received his approval: "So that it will take place, I am informing you that the Central Committee of the Partido Nacional Democrático has approved the following candidates for El Refugio: 2nd Regidor, Moisés Jiménez, and Síndico, Juan Martínez."[105] These examples indicate the extent to which political centralization had become formalized.

Measuring Continuity in the PND

Lists of municipal officials provide valuable evidence into the nature of officeholding at the local level. These lists reveal whom the PND appointed and the extent to which PND leaders relied upon a select few people to hold municipal office. In order to measure this continuity most effectively, we would need complete electoral results for all of the PND-era elections (1918, 1919, 1920, 1921, 1923, and the partial election of 1925). Unfortunately, such complete evidence does not exist. Instead, we have complete records for every election in all fourteen departments for the years 1921, 1923, and 1925, and records from only two departments, Ahuachapán and San Vicente, for one additional year, 1920. Thus, evidence exists for the four consecutive elections for only two departments, but the results are revealing.

I posed two questions of that evidence. First, did any official serve in more than one administration, and if so who, and in what years was he elected? Second, did anybody bearing the same surname serve in more than one administration, and if so, in which years? A summary of these inquiries is presented in table A2 in the appendix. The results reveal that in ten of the twelve municipalities in San Vicente Department at least one official served in multiple administrations. In all twelve of the municipalities at least two people bearing the same surname served on different municipal councils.

The evidence from Ahuachapán Department offers almost identical results. The municipality of Tacuba was excluded from the analysis, owing to the peculiar influence of General Rafael Rivas, as was discussed earlier. In eight of the department's eleven remaining municipalities, at least one person served in multiple administrations. And of those eight municipalities, all but one of them had at least two people serving in multiple administrations. In all eleven municipalities in Ahuachapán, at least two different surnames showed up in multiple administrations.

This evidence suggests that the PND was a closed political network that relied upon the same few people to hold office at the municipal level. When it is recalled that political networks did not allow adversaries to serve with them on the municipal councils, the continuities in table A2 in the appendix serve as a testament to the exclusive nature of officeholding under the PND. Essentially, the same political network at the local level was sanctioned by the PND and held office for the duration. Admittedly, the evidence of the surnames is inconclusive, functioning as a rather blunt tool to measure political relationships. Family ties were of crucial importance to political alliances, but the evidence does not prove that people bearing the same surname were actually related or were necessarily allies. But given the limited number of politically active persons in these municipalities, especially the less populated ones, the evidence is highly suggestive.

*   *   *

El Salvador experienced some significant changes during the first three decades of the twentieth century. The economy grew dramatically and became increasingly dependent on coffee. In the realm of politics, the chaotic transitions of the nineteenth century, the consequence of multiple patronage networks competing with one another, came to an end. Coup plotting did not come to end, but successful coups did. Politics was still undemocratic and based on patronage. Violence and intrigue continued to accompany elections. But transitions between regimes became more stable and predictable. As the state centralized and the powers of the national government increased, the network that happened to have control found itself with an unprecedented ability to exert authority over rivals at the local and regional levels. The process of centralization reached its apogee during the Meléndez and Quiñónez era in the late 1910s and 1920s. The multiple and competing pyramids of patronage that had dotted El Salvador's political landscape during the preceding decades had been replaced by a single, central pyramid. Political bosses who hoped for any real chance of political ascent now worked within the one existing network rather than trying to overthrow it and replace it from outside.

We know little about the two challengers for the presidency, Tomás Palomo in 1918 and Miguel Molina in 1922. But Molina at least, and possibly Palomo as well, signaled a potential shift in the political winds from a system based on patronage, personalism, and controlled elections to one that was more modern, party-based, and even democratic in orientation. Regardless of whether those two aspirants actually embodied those virtues, something was afoot in El Salvador in the mid-1920s. When the last member of the Meléndez-Quiñónez dynasty left office in early 1927, El Salvador was about to experience something unprecedented: a genuine attempt at democratic reform.

CHAPTER 6

FACING THE LEVIATHAN

*Pío Romero Bosque and the Experiment
with Democracy, 1927–1931*

The presidential election of March 1927 arrived amidst the usual speculations: Who would President Quiñónez Molina choose as his successor?
Would someone challenge him? Would there be violence? Quiñónez Molina exacerbated the incertitude by providing no hints about his preference. "The Presidential situation remains the same," wrote the American
agronomist Frederick William Taylor to his family in late 1926, "only
seven weeks to the election and no announcement of candidates."[1] Quiñónez Molina's hesitation seems to have been inspired by his desire to get
himself reelected. To do so, however, he would have had to circumvent the
constitutional prohibition against a president serving consecutive terms in
office, regardless of whether or not he resigned six months prior to the
coming term. The president tried to have a new constitution written that
would allow for reelection. In July and August 1926 he called for the formation of *cabildos abiertos,* town-hall meetings in which the general population theoretically discussed and then voted upon proposed changes to
the constitution. But only a handful of municipalities actually held the
cabildos, and Quiñónez Molina quickly abandoned the idea. Such a move
would have generated some degree of domestic opposition. But according
to reports from the U.S. legation, it was the international context that

concerned Quiñónez Molina the most. He reportedly failed to get the U.S. legation to promise recognition if he were to proceed.[2] According to the Washington Treaties of 1923, the United States would grant recognition only to those governments in Central America that achieved power by legal means. Although an altered constitution was technically legal, it did not inspire confidence in the U.S. State Department for future political stability in El Salvador. And so, as the year 1926 wound to a close, Quiñónez Molina turned to his vice president and minister of war, Pío Romero Bosque. Nobody stepped forward to challenge him, and he won the election of January 1926 by the customary unanimous result.

By all indications, Romero Bosque was going to carry on the centralizing tradition of Meléndez and Quiñónez and defend the political monopoly of the PND. But all was not as it appeared. He broke with the old ways and initiated a series of political reforms designed to foster genuine democracy. Those reforms were as unprecedented as they were unexpected, and the road to reform was not an easy one. Romero Bosque faced a leviathan, an established political system that had been functioning for more than eight decades according to rules quite contrary to democracy. Entrenched political bosses stood to lose if the reforms were implemented, and not surprisingly, they resisted them. Although his ultimate goal of creating democracy in El Salvador did not come to fruition, what Pío Romero Bosque accomplished in four years is nothing short of remarkable. The capstone of the reforms was the presidential election of 1931, in which Arturo Araujo was elected to office in a mostly free and fair democratic process. The reforms, however, had much less success at the municipal level, where the logistical problems of monitoring electoral procedures in roughly 240 municipalities were monumental. Needless to say, it was much easier to directly appoint 240 political bosses and give them carte blanche to maintain local order than it was to ensure 240 democratic elections, which meant investigating the multitude of complaints and denunciations that such elections invariably generated.

The goal of the present chapter is twofold. The first goal is to document the Romero reforms. While prior scholars have noted the uniqueness of the Romero Bosque years, lack of documentation has prevented them from detailing the actual process of the reforms, the context within which they were enacted, and the extent to which Romero Bosque was committed to them.[3] Second, and more importantly, this chapter will use the reforms as a window into the core of El Salvador's political system. These years represented a rare moment in Salvadoran history when the state acted autonomously as a neutral third party beholden unto nothing other than a political ideal.[4] Romero Bosque and his associates invested time and energy in investigating political developments in the municipalities, and the resulting documentation sheds an unprecedented degree of light on the traditional system of politics.

The Unlikely Reformer

Pío Romero Bosque's credentials as a political insider were impeccable. He had entered government in the early 1890s as a deputy in the National Assembly. Shortly thereafter he received a law degree from San Salvador's National University and was appointed to a series of provincial judgeships. In 1899 he was made a judge on the Supreme Court, after which he held a succession of high-ranking government posts, including minister of government (1903–1907), chief justice of the Supreme Court (1904–1919), minister of war (1919–1927), and vice president (1923–1927).[5] Romero Bosque was a landowner, although not nearly at the level of the Meléndez-Quiñónez family. He qualified as a *notable* in his home department of La Paz, owning two haciendas: "Nahualapa," near Santiago Nanualco in La Paz Department, and "El Rosario," on a hilltop outside San Salvador in the cantón of Planes de Renderos.[6] The latter property produced coffee.[7] He had important family connections, a crucial asset for any political career. His daughter was married to Julio Mejía, whose father, Federico Mejía, was minister to the United States between 1907 and 1913. The Mejías, in turn, were intermarried with the Dukes, one of the richest and most powerful families in the nation.[8]

Romero Bosque could not have retained his numerous high-ranking offices without having supported the electoral machinations and intrigues required by the project of state centralization. As minister of government in the Escalón administration (1903–1907), he was the point man for all political and electoral affairs; unfortunately, the archival record for these years is too lean to produce an explicit link between him and such activities. There is, however, direct evidence from Romero Bosque's tenure as minister of war in the 1920s linking him to the defense of the PND. For example, a document from December 1921 reveals that he ordered the local comandante of San Luis de la Reina (San Miguel Department) to ensure the victory of local PND candidates who were being challenged by an outside faction.[9]

Even before Quiñónez Molina had chosen him as his successor, Romero Bosque had developed a reputation with the U.S. legation as a yes-man for the president. The U.S. chargé noted in 1925 that he was the president's closest advisor.[10] The chargé later described him as "weak and irresolute" and as a "kindly old gentlemen who has never done anyone any special harm."[11] Romero Bosque contributed to this impression with a speech delivered in December 1926 upon receiving the nomination from Quiñónez Molina and the PND. As reported by the U.S. chargé, he promised to defend the political status quo: "Dr. Pío Romero Bosque declared . . . that he took an oath to support the Party's program. He said that his one ambition would be to continue the efficient policies and methods of administration which President Quiñónez had so effectively carried out during the past four years."[12] After the election, a legation officer referred to Romero Bosque as a man "of no particular force, and with probably no superfluous amount of backbone."[13] The chargé opined that Quiñónez Molina chose Romero Bosque precisely for his supposed weakness, so that he could run things from behind the scenes.

If Pío Romero Bosque seems an unlikely candidate to carry out a campaign of democratization, why did this career insider abandon his political heritage and take up the banner of reform? Unfortunately, a substantiated answer to this question remains elusive, because crucial documentation, such as Romero Bosque's presidential and personal papers, is missing. But some speculation is possible. First and foremost, it is not uncommon for political reformers to emerge from within authoritarian regimes. They tend to be driven by diverse motives, some more selfish than others. For example, politicians who reach a glass ceiling within an existing system might find that reformism is the only way to advance their own careers. Another argument—one of the most common, in fact—focuses on the emergence of mass mobilization. When an authoritarian-style regime is faced with a sudden surge in mass action, it can respond in one of two ways: reform or repression. While many regimes have resorted to repression, many others have chosen reform. Scholars have discovered that advocates of reform within exclusive regimes often constitute a tiny minority of high-ranking officials who use their positions and skills to ward off their authoritarian associates.[14] They typically believe that reforming the system is the only way to save it, because a failure to reform will incite the masses, who are likely to take much more if they revolt. Notably, Romero Bosque once explained the reform program as the progeny of a select few people at the national level in a speech before the National Assembly in 1930, saying that "happily, the national interests have now been confined to a select . . . group, who under all circumstances show their attachment to the best causes of the country."[15]

This approach has found resonance with scholars of El Salvador, who have examined Romero Bosque's democratization and suggested that he adopted political reform at least partly in response to a surge in worker radicalism and/or mass mobilization in the 1920s.[16] That argument has promise. The growth of the coffee economy changed El Salvador's social composition. Cities had grown and so too had their middle and working classes. An organized labor movement began to coalesce in the 1920s, most notably in the form of the Federación Regional de Trabajadores Salvadoreños (FRTS, Regional Federation of Salvadoran Workers), which was founded in 1924. The union expanded steadily throughout the rest of the decade, although it tended to remain highly urban in orientation. In 1928 a radical wing emerged within the FRTS and took control in 1929. The radicals eventually went on to form the Partido Comunista Salvadoreño (PCS, the Communist Party of El Salvador) in 1930.[17]

A variant of this argument is that Romero Bosque's reformism emerged from a more explicit political necessity. As will be demonstrated below, shortly after coming to office Romero Bosque broke ties with his predecessor, Alfonso Quiñónez Molina, and thereby alienated the powerful PND political machine and all of its local adherents. Without a parallel organization to support him, Romero Bosque faced isolation, a weak position from which to resist the conspiracies that every president faced. In casting about for a new base of support, he might have turned to the newly emergent middle and working classes of the urban areas, especially in San Salvador. But in order to appeal to them, he had to offer them something different—reformism and democracy. In their study of politics in the late 1920s as a prelude to the 1932 uprising, historians Jeff Gould and Aldo Lauria-Santiago advance this argument. It is also supported by case studies from other countries, in which politicians who wish to build a coalition must deal with urban constituencies differently than their rural counterparts, because the urbanites, including the urban poor, are not subject to the same types of dependencies as rural workers and peasants.[18]

The political explanation for Romero Bosque's reforms is plausible, and so too is the argument that his reforms were a response to a rise in mass mobilization. But the latter argument rests on shakier evidence. Romero Bosque embarked upon his reformism immediately upon assuming office, before the radical labor movement had emerged. At the time, the government had good relations with the existing labor organizations, including the FRTS, which was then receiving a government subsidy. As late as January 1929, the national government was still sending an annual Christmas card to the union.[19] There is not much evidence to suggest that a groundswell of popular demand for democracy had arisen in the years or months preceding Romero Bosque's arrival in office. People at the local level, elites and commoners alike, were not expecting democratic reforms, and as will be shown, once the Romero Bosque administration initiated the reforms, locals of all stripes found themselves bewildered by them.

If nothing else, the Romero reforms reveal the importance of state centralization to the story of Salvadoran politics. Reform was possible because the state had become empowered, and because the traditionally decentralized system of patronage-based politics of the late nineteenth century had been consolidated into a single unified system by the mid-1920s. Those developments gave someone like Romero Bosque the capacity to carry out a reform program, regardless of the motivations behind it.

One thing is certain about Romero Bosque's approach to political reform: he was committed to seeing it through. An indication of his genuineness comes, ironically, from one of his most vehement detractors, Manuel Andino. In 1930 Andino, who by his own admission was a political opponent of Romero Bosque, wrote a book on the presidential campaign of 1931. The book's stated purpose was to prove that Romero Bosque's plan was a farce and that his reformism was nothing more than a

concealed attempt to remain in office for another term. For all his postur-
ing, however, Andino failed to provide any examples of misdeeds or evidence that Romero Bosque had designs on continuing beyond his term.
The book reads more as a testament to Romero Bosque's successes.[20] Another endorsement comes from Enrique Córdova, one of the candidates in
the election of 1931. Disappointed over his loss, and suspicious that
Romero Bosque might have somehow aided the victor, Arturo Araujo,
Córdova nonetheless wrote that "no one can deny that don Pío . . . gave
ample guarantees to all the parties, and the elections of that period proved
to be a process that was democratic, instructive, and realized in peace despite the existing laws which were insufficient by themselves to guarantee
freedom of suffrage."[21]

The Romero reforms would prove highly similar to a democratic experiment taking place in neighboring Nicaragua at roughly the same time,
under the auspices of U.S. occupation. As revealed impressively by the research of historian Michel Gobat, the United States decided that one of
the best strategies for long-term stability in Nicaragua was to centralize
the power of the national government by breaking the power of regional
strongmen, and that one of the most effective ways to accomplish that
goal was to hold genuinely democratic elections. The logic behind the
U.S. plan was that democratic procedures would work against the regional
caudillos and make both the electorate and the newly elected officials loyal
to the centralizing process. Gobat shows that in fact the Nicaraguan Guardia Nacional, which, ironically, would become notorious for serving as the
armed enforcer of the long-standing Somoza family dictatorship, was created by the United States expressly for the purpose of promoting this
democratic process. According to Gobat, the United States and the Guardia took the task seriously, even placing a marine in charge of every polling
station to ensure that irregularities did not occur. Not surprisingly, the
United States' efforts produced mixed results. How could they not, when
the marines at the polling stations barely spoke Spanish? Nevertheless, one
of the freest elections in Nicaraguan history resulted in the election of José
Moncada as president in 1928.[22] In El Salvador, Romero Bosque played
the role of the United States, and as we are about to see, he too enlisted the
military to support his reformist agenda. Although there is no evidence to
suggest as much, it seems plausible that part of the inspiration for the

Romero reforms was a desire to curry favor with the United States, given its democratization program in neighboring Nicaragua.

Breaking with Quiñónez

The first sign that something original was afoot with Romero Bosque was the rapidity with which he broke ties with his predecessor. Quiñónez Molina had remained very close to the seat of power in Romero Bosque's government. He was the official head of the PND, and he held the position of first designate to the president, which placed him second in line to the presidency behind the vice president, Gustavo Vides, who had also been handpicked by Quiñónez Molina. (Vides served as minister of finance during the Quiñónez administration.)[23] But just as many battles start small and grow in size, so too did the conflict between Romero Bosque and Quiñónez Molina. The conflict began with two minor political appointees, the undersecretaries of *fomento* (development) and public instruction, Marcos Letona and Salvador Rivas, who had retained their offices at Quiñónez Molina's insistence. One month after taking office, Romero Bosque forced Letona to resign and accused Rivas of appropriating money earmarked for schools; Rivas also resigned.[24] Quiñónez accused Romero Bosque of reneging on his promise, and according to various reports the two had heated verbal exchanges, one of which took place in Romero Bosque's office and ended in Quiñónez being escorted out by security guards.[25] The U.S. chargé opined that the attacks on the undersecretaries were "simply part of the campaign to do away with the Quiñónez influence."[26]

Soon the conflict turned to Quiñónez himself. In April, Romero Bosque lifted the state of siege that had been maintained throughout Quiñónez's presidency.[27] Press censorship and the ban on public demonstrations disappeared, and the students of the National University immediately took to the streets to protest Quiñónez's position as first designate to the president. They marched before the National Assembly, the National Palace, and even Quiñónez's private home. Romero Bosque addressed one of the rallies, saying in reference to Quiñónez's position, according to reports from *Diario Latino,* that "it seems that such an appointment is unconstitutional. . . . I always will be with the people, upholding and defending their rights."[28] In June a debate erupted in the National Assembly between Quiñónez's and Romero Bosque's supporters over whether or not a former president legally could serve as first designate.[29] The issue was resolved a few days later when Quiñónez resigned and took his family into exile in France. The U.S. military attaché claimed that some high-ranking military officers pressured Quiñónez to leave in retribution for past transgressions against the military.[30]

Shortly after Quiñónez departed, Romero Bosque began to chip away at the Meléndez-Quiñónez reputation. His government opened an investigation into the murder of Alberto Escalante. As mentioned in the prior chapter, Escalante, the president of the San Vicente chapter of Miguel Molina's political party, had disappeared during the crackdown of December 1922. The trial that resulted from the investigation became a highly publicized event that lasted more than two years. Transcripts of the trial were published in the newspapers, and Meléndez himself, as well as his minister of government, Arturo Argüello, had to testify, as did many dozens of other people, including General Calvo, the former director of the Guardia Nacional, who supposedly oversaw the Christmas Day repression. Escalante became something of a martyr, and when his remains were returned to San Salvador from the site near the Guatemalan border where he had been killed, a large public demonstration took place, led by Escalante's widow. Escalante's burial site became something of a symbol of past government oppression. One of the candidates in the 1931 presidential election, for example, organized a rally there to open his campaign.[31]

Quiñónez's departure foretold his declining influence in Salvadoran politics, but he did not surrender without a fight. In December 1927, he and Jorge Meléndez organized a coup against the Romero government. The available documentary sources, including the memoir of Enrique Córdova, newspaper accounts, and intelligence reports from the U.S. legation, offer almost identical versions of the events, with much of the evidence coming from the testimonies of participants arrested after the coup.[32] According to these sources, the coup proceeded more or less as follows: Jorge Meléndez was the principal organizer and financier. In the weeks leading up to December, he enlisted the support of some of his and Quiñónez's former allies, including Federico Kreitz, who was chief of police under Quiñónez and, according to one source, a one-time jefe of the Liga Roja. Kreitz was joined by Colonel Juan Aberle, chief of the army's machine shop, and Major Manuel Noguera, deputy chief of police. Meléndez also assembled as many as five hundred so-called peones and armed them with machetes. These workers included laborers from Meléndez's many haciendas, including the main one, "Prussia," as well as other peasants who had been recruited from outlying areas, even as far away as Honduras. Kreitz had been in charge of assembling the peones and arming them.

The plan was for Aberle and Noguera to gain control of the barracks of the First Infantry and the police headquarters in San Salvador and then quietly depose Romero Bosque. At the same time, the workers from Prussia would be trucked into the capital to create a diversionary disturbance. At the appointed time on the morning of December 6, Aberle and Noguera presented themselves before the chief of police, Colonel Leitzelar, and informed him that a military junta had elected Aberle as president and Noguera as chief of police. Leitzelar demanded confirmation from the commander of the First Infantry, General Carmona, who was supposedly a coup supporter. But when asked to confirm Aberle's claim, Carmona balked and said he knew nothing of the coup. An identical scenario played out with the second-in-command of the barracks. Aberle then surrendered to Leitzelar, who took him and Noguera to Romero Bosque in the National Palace. Upon being presented to Romero Bosque, Aberle made one last effort to gain the presidency. He told Romero Bosque that a military junta had elected him president, and that if Romero Bosque resigned peacefully, he and his family would be guaranteed safe passage out of the country. Romero Bosque had the two conspirators arrested, and within forty-eight hours they had been court-martialed and executed by firing squad. The workers from Prussia never arrived in the capital.

In the aftermath of the coup, more than one hundred people were arrested, including Kreitz, General Carmona, and a number of middle-level military commanders and government bureaucrats whose names came up as affiliates of the conspirators. Among those arrested were a large number of the laborers from Prussia. Jorge Meléndez managed to avoid arrest. He had been on his hacienda "Valencia" during the coup, and upon hearing reports of its failure, he started walking towards Honduras. One of his associates went to the U.S. legation and asked if Meléndez could receive asylum, but the U.S. chargé denied the request. Meléndez arrived in Honduras twenty days later, after what must have been an eventful overland journey. He eventually ended up in Costa Rica, where he invested in the sugar industry.[33]

The failure of the coup had many implications. It brought the Meléndez-Quiñónez influence to a decided end and left Romero Bosque unquestionably in charge of the government. In February 1928, from his post in exile in Paris, Quiñónez had a conversation with a former U.S. chargé in El Salvador in which he summarized the break between him and Romero: "You know, of course, that we are no longer friends with Romero Bosque. We were old friends. He was in my government. I helped him greatly. But we have nothing to do with each other now." During the conversation, Quiñónez did not admit to organizing the coup, but he expressed sympathy for it and condemned Romero Bosque for executing Aberle and Noguera.[34]

The failed coup also sheds light on Romero Bosque's complex relations with the military and the decisiveness that he could exhibit in dealing with potentially rebellious officers. The execution of Aberle and Noguera was a bold move that delivered an unmistakably clear message to anyone thinking of future conspiracies. Another example of Romero Bosque's ability to deal with the military came in April 1928, when a group of military officers demanded that an active-duty officer be placed in the position of subsecretary of war. Thinking that the officers were planning a coup, Romero Bosque gathered them together and told them, "If you do this, I warn you that you had better shoot me first, for if you do not, I shall shoot all of you."[35] As will be further revealed below, Romero was a skilled negotiator with the military, and the support he received from some of the highest-ranking officers was crucial to the success of his reformism.

The First Experiment: The Municipal Elections of December 1927

Romero Bosque first signaled his intent to initiate reforms in a speech in June 1927, shortly after Quiñónez left for France. He proclaimed in the speech that he would "cede to the will of the citizens. . . . [W]e all know that if the evolution of a nation is slow and gradual, great schisms will not be opened up in the political sphere, because there will not be confusion in the determinant forces. I present this truth in order to make clear at this time the importance of the work that we should undertake to achieve success in our political and administration organization."[36] Two phrases stand out in this speech. The first is "ced[ing] to the will of the citizens," his first hint at democracy. The second is the insistence on "slow and gradual" change. It is not clear whether Romero Bosque had a detailed plan mapped out for his reforms, but his language indicates that he saw reform as a drawn-out process. As it turned out, he used each successive election, starting with the municipal elections of December 1927, to push his reformist agenda a bit further.

In the months following his June speech, Romero Bosque issued a series of strongly suggestive hints that the elections of December 1927 would be democratic, or at least that candidates would not be imposed by the government. Romero Bosque did not issue anything resembling an official decree. Rather, he presented his intentions to particular people who then passed on the news by word of mouth and in statements made to newspaper reporters. It is not clear why Romero Bosque chose this circuitous route to disseminate his plans, but it probably had something to do with his conception of a "slow and gradual" process. The first example was an editorial in *Diario del Salvador* in August. The commentary began with a description of the existing political system and then explained how life under Romero Bosque would be different:

> Our administrative corruption is such that the alcaldes, all the way down to the most insignificant pueblos, have been imposed by superior authority, and we have arrived at such a state of corruption that there is no such thing as a municipality of the people. . . . But the current jefe of the Executive office, Pío Romero Bosque, assures us that there will not be any imposition: that the ominous epoch, in which a President immersed himself in anything and everything, is over. We will be left free to make use of our rights and choose our own municipality.[37]

Two months later an anonymous editorialist from the municipality of Guazapa wrote that "we are standing on the verge of a significant date" when impositions would end, "the time when the instigators of intrigues and false patriots will have to recede to the background until they can find their civic dignity."[38] The U.S. chargé reported that Romero Bosque told him in the course of conversation that he desired the forthcoming municipal elections to be democratic.[39] Not all reactions to the hint of change were positive. One editorialist in *Diario del Salvador* argued that Romero Bosque's intentions were misplaced, because the Salvadoran populace was not prepared for democracy. But even this negative editorial reveals that people were aware that change was afoot.[40]

Romero Bosque officially disbanded the PND in September and announced that candidates would not be allowed to invoke the name of the PND when campaigning for office. The closest thing to an official pronouncement on the elections was an interview that Manuel Mendoza, Romero Bosque's minister of government and a close political associate, gave to the newspaper *Diario Latino* on November 25, 1927. Mendoza said that "first the main goal is to guarantee the freedom of the vote, that is the main job. . . . This government does not favor any candidates anywhere; the government's interest is simply in guaranteeing liberty."[41]

Based on petitions that arrived in San Salvador, news of Romero Bosque's reformist agenda was making its way out to distant municipalities. A political aspirant from Alegría (Usulután Department), for instance, began a petition by saying that, "I am animated by the demonstrations that the Supreme Jefe of the Nation and his faithful associates have made in regard to their firm proposal in favor of liberty so that the people can exercise freely and amply their right of Suffrage."[42] Another petition from the village of San Julián (Sonsonate Department) began, "I have confidence in the proclamation of Señor Pío Romero Bosque, and rapidly is the day arriving in which we will choose the Municipality that will guide us in the coming year, and respectfully we ask if really there will be liberty to choose a Municipality that is at the service of the people?"[43] A correspondent from San Sebastián (San Vicente Department) wrote that "the declarations of the Government that the elections will be entirely free have been received with great applause."[44]

The message was getting out, but some local political players interpreted it in ways contrary to Romero Bosque's intention. They either ignored it or found it to be nothing more than an oddly explicit form of traditional patronage-based discourse. "Have not these same promises," a skeptical editorialist mused, "been songs in the mouths of all past Presidents?"[45] Although Romero Bosque was the incumbent, he still presided over a political network created by his predecessor, and thus his appeals to democracy easily could have been interpreted as nothing more than a message to PND affiliates that a change in nomenclature was forthcoming. As the day for the elections drew near, the usual mass of petitions flowed into the National Palace from local partisans seeking recognition as the official candidates and assistance in assaults on their rivals.

A political faction in Armenia (Sonsonate Department), for example, informed Romero Bosque that "we have decided to sack the current Alcalde, Don Emetrio Torres, in the next election. . . . We ask that you change the Comandante Local . . . and that if we continue with this indicated plan in your favor you send us a military troop on the day of the election."[46] In Atiquizaya (Ahuachapán Department), a local group created the Pío Romero Bosque Patriotic Club, and under its title, submitted to the government a slate of candidates for approval.[47] Another letter arrived from the municipality of San Agustín (Usulután Department) in which the author asks Pío Romero to "adjust his list" to include their desired candidates.[48] A political faction in the municipality of Ishuatán (Sonsonate Department) appealed to the government on the grounds that its members had been responsible for generating votes for Romero Bosque in the presidential election of January 1927, whereas their rivals had failed to even turn out to vote.[49] The list of examples goes on.[50]

Many of the solicitors demonstrated an impressive capacity to couch their requests in the democracy-laden rhetoric that they thought Romero Bosque wanted to hear. A faction from San Pedro Puxtla (Ahuachapán Department) suggested that since "everyone in the village" already supported them, the government actually would "comply with the principle of free suffrage" by making their candidates official.[51]

Romero Bosque had to contend with this skewed sense of democracy among both local political players and high-ranking members of his bureaucracy. A prime example of the latter is Horacio Villavicencio, governor of San Vicente and the former governor of San Miguel under Quiñónez. In November 1927 he submitted a report, at Romero Bosque's request, on the political situation in San Vicente City. Villavicencio used the report as an opportunity to demonstrate his ability to play the political game according to his interpretation of Romero Bosque's rules. He opened the report with a lengthy denunciation of past political procedures: "The system of managing the municipalities has been a disaster, for them, for the Government, and for the President. Always has been employed the weapon of intrigue, causing the disgrace of the villages; it is difficult to imagine the lack of progress of the villages owing to the fact that they have been run by incompetent persons. . . . I have been a witness to this in San Miguel." He then professed his loyalty to Romero: "I am a faithful and enthusiastic servant of my fatherland, and of you, for your elevated position as Jefe of the Nation, and for your personal character." Finally, when Villavicencio got around to describing politics, he informed Romero that three different factions had emerged in San Vicente City, and that one of them should receive the government's support because its members "are friends of your government" and its principal leaders "are personal friends of yours."[52] If Romero Bosque was going to encourage democracy in San Vicente, he first was going to have to get his governor to understand what he meant by it.

In his November interview with *Diario Latino,* Mendoza mentioned these partisan requests for government recognition and assistance. His interviewer wrote that "the Minister described . . . some people who have asked the Minister when they can expect the arrival of the instructions, saying that the 'boys' [*muchachos*], that is to say the servants of certain interests, are ready to obey the Government's orders." Mendoza said that "I have told them that no instructions are coming and that this government is going to guarantee impartiality."[53]

As the day for election drew near, perhaps the single greatest problem for Romero Bosque was the plethora of candidates that came forward to compete in the elections. The U.S. chargé observed that "in some districts where alcaldes are being elected there are as many as five or six candidates, all of whom are presumed to be running on independent or free tickets."[54] Unless Romero Bosque's bureaucracy had the capacity to monitor every municipal election in the nation, which it did not, the likelihood of violence was high. If the prior eight decades of electoral history provided any hint as to what was forthcoming, it was that various factions would jockey for position and then, on election day or the evening before, they would violently rush to gain control of the municipal hall. Surely memories of the violence in 1918 were fresh in Romero Bosque's mind. The fact that the Meléndez-Aberle-Noguera coup occurred just ten days prior to election day further exacerbated the possibility of violence.

Romero Bosque responded to this foreboding situation with an exceptionally pragmatic approach. He recognized that genuine popular participation was impossible, so he settled for an alternative option of so-called conciliation candidates. Roughly two weeks prior to the election, he instructed the governors and commanders of the departments, as well as the local commanders, to inform the various factions in each municipality that none of them would be allowed to win the election. Rather, they had to come up with a slate of candidates agreeable to all. In his November interview, Mendoza said that "we are studying the possibility of finding conciliation candidates; this is mediation, not intervention."[55] The governor of Usulután reported on his progress. He was having success in most of the department's municipalities, but in Jiquilisco the candidates were being obstinate. He wrote, "Yesterday I interviewed Eugenio Flores, Fabio Guerrero, and Federico Castro, the three candidates for Alcalde in the municipality of Jiquilisco, and I tried to encourage them to come to an agreement in the way of conciliation in order to avoid the consequences of a battle between the three parties, but it has not been possible yet."[56]

Newspaper reports commented prodigiously on the process of "conciliation," as it came to be known. "Motivated by the demands of the governor's office to form a fusion of candidates," reads one of the reports from Chalchuapa (Ahuachapán Department), "we have learned that don José María Escancilla is prepared to unite, and others are prepared to do so as well."[57] In a taped interview (a very rare historical source in El Salvador) from sometime in the 1960s, General Antonio Claramount Lucero recalls the election of 1927. He was then serving as departmental commander in Usulután, and he recalled gathering candidates together to get them to settle on compromise candidates. He said that the process was reasonably successful in preventing a breakdown in social order; during the elections, he recalled, only two people died and ten were wounded throughout the department, whereas in the past, under such circumstances dozens of people were killed.[58] Even Horacio Villavicencio of San Vicente got in on the process. In one report he wrote, "I understand your circular. I am endeavoring to meet with the diverse groups that have put forth candidates. . . . I will report as soon as possible as to the progress . . . of forming a single slate of candidates."[59]

In those municipalities where conciliation was achieved, candidates won their elections by unanimity. "Today at 12:00," reported the director of police from Atiquizaya, "the Directorio handed over to the Municipality 42 tally sheets [*pliegos*] containing 1342 unanimous votes . . . having been elected the slate of candidates that I had reported to you previously."[60] Such elections hardly reflected popular suffrage, but they were generally peaceful and they represented the first step on Romero's difficult road to reform. In those municipalities where government authorities failed to achieve conciliation, local factions settled their differences in any number of ways. As General Claramount Lucero noted above, some of them resorted to violence. In the village of Santiago de María (Usulután Department), the two political factions conducted two distinct elections.[61]

Measuring the Transition in 1927

From the elections of 1927 we have a complete list of the municipal officials from San Vicente Department and a list of the alcaldes in Ahuachapán Department. It is possible to compare this data with the lists from 1920 to 1925 to gain a rough idea of the extent to which the Romero reforms shifted political officeholding away from the PND stalwarts who had monopolized it. I posed two questions: First, did the municipal officials serve under any of the PND administrations that came to power between 1920 and 1925? Second, did any people bearing the same surname serve in any of those administrations? The results appear in the appendix in table A3.

In San Vicente Department, in nine of the twelve municipalities at least one of the municipal officials elected in 1927 had served in an administration under the PND. And in eleven of the twelve municipalities at least one person bearing the same surname had served in a PND administration. The results from Ahuachapán are similar, although with only the names of the alcaldes, the data is less complete. (Tacuba was excluded once again for reasons relating to General Rivas, as discussed in the prior chapter.) Only one of Ahuachapán's eleven municipalities had an alcalde elected in 1927 who had served in a PND administration, and in five out of the eleven municipalities people bearing the alcalde's same surname had served under the PND.

As mentioned in the last chapter, this data, especially the surnames, allows for an imprecise but nonetheless valuable examination of political continuities. The results suggest that Pío Romero Bosque had limited success in effecting a shift in political power at the local level. Members of local networks formerly affiliated with the PND retained their hold on power. However, it is notable that some municipalities experienced a complete break with the past, especially San Vicente City, in which not one person, or even one surname, carried over from the administrations of 1920 to 1925.

The Ongoing Process: Investigations, Enlisting the Military

During an interview with a reporter from *Diario del Salvador* in June 1929, Romero Bosque gave this response to a question about the forthcoming municipal elections of December 1929: "During my administration there have been two stages of liberty, and in this, the latter one, the Salvadoran populace is demonstrating its spirit of order and discipline, as is characteristic of cultured people."[62] This comment suggests that Romero Bosque saw his reform campaign in two stages separated by the two-year gap between the elections of 1927 and 1929. The first stage consisted of his battles with Meléndez and Quiñónez, and the municipal elections of December 1927. The second stage encompassed the flurry of elections beginning with the municipal elections of 1929, which were followed by another round of municipal elections just one year later because in 1928 Romero Bosque had returned the duration of municipal officeholding to one year. The culminating moment would be the presidential election in January 1931.

Broadly speaking, a prevailing feature of Romero's reform movement was its reliance on the existing legal framework. Romero did not pass new laws; rather, he looked to enforce the current laws in both letter and spirit. He sought to pull the political system out of the mire of peculiar interpretations and traditions that had led it to operate according to the informal guidelines. Romero constantly presented his reforms in the context of their legality. Seldom did he discuss his vision of a democratic El Salvador without referring to "*la Ley*" (the law). "Complete liberty inside of the legal established order," he stated in the June 1929 interview when asked about his vision of the future. "I will oppose political hierarchy to the greatest extent possible, but always within the law."[63]

This dependence on the existing legal system meant that Romero Bosque had to confront some limitations to reform. Among other things, it meant that voting remained oral, which was one tool of political coercion. In 1930, one of the U.S. diplomats in El Salvador, Raymond Leslie Buell, observed that "there is no provision for secret ballot . . . and until a new electoral law . . . provides for the secret ballot, there can be no guarantee of a fair election."[64] Interestingly, in April and May 1927, the Romero government tried to revise the constitution and even went so far as to draft portions of a new charter that called for the secret vote.[65] For unknown reasons, the revision failed. But at least the attempt meant that some of the highest-ranking members in the administration, maybe even Romero Bosque himself, recognized the seriousness of the issue. In an interview in November 1927, Minister of Government Manuel Mendoza stated that "our electoral laws need reforming; the secret vote inspires the greatest confidence in electoral acts."[66] Still, nothing came of it, and the secret vote was not installed until 1950.

Nevertheless, Romero Bosque and his associates worked diligently to encourage some form of democratic practices. His strategy was straightforward. He surrounded himself with a coterie of loyal, like-minded bureaucrats who used the powers of the state to enforce the electoral laws. Of these bureaucrats, by far the most industrious and the closest to Romero Bosque was Minister Mendoza. Virtually every order relating to political or electoral affairs that emerged from San Salvador between 1927 and 1931 came from either Romero Bosque's or Mendoza's desk. They worked long hours and produced a voluminous amount of paperwork in the process. The greatest weapon at their disposal was the dual process of investigation and nullification, which created the ability to enforce a new political agenda. But of course this meant that they had to investigate the seemingly infinite number of denunciations and alleged misdeeds that emerged from any given election cycle, which required enormous amounts of time, energy, and manpower, more than Romero Bosque and Mendoza had at their disposal.

Each investigation required that a state official travel to the respective municipality, take testimony, and accumulate evidence of alleged wrongdoing. Usually the investigators were the departmental governor, the deputy governor, the departmental commander, or another person somehow affiliated with the ministry of government. After evidence was collected, the case went before the departmental governor, who was allowed to rule on clear-cut cases. But in more complicated cases, or if the governor's decision was challenged, it went to San Salvador to be reviewed by Mendoza or Romero Bosque.

We can see from table 6.1 that the number of nullification proceedings increased dramatically during the Romero Bosque era. The annual average number of nullification proceedings between 1919 and 1923 was less than nine, whereas between 1927 and 1930 it was more than thirty. Also of interest is the increased length of each proceeding. Between 1918 and 1923, the average number of pages of each investigation was twenty, whereas between 1927 and 1930 it grew to more than forty. The bulk of any given investigation was dedicated to testimony from witnesses and participants, so this surge in paperwork serves as a rough indication that the Romero administration conducted more thorough investigations.

In 1928, the Romero government also introduced a new process of electoral investigation. Instead of waiting until after the election, the ministry of government now conducted investigations prior to the election in hopes of addressing problems before they could result in misdeeds. Before the municipal elections of 1929, the ministry conducted an impressive sixty-eight of these inquiries, meaning that it investigated almost one third of all the municipalities in the nation during this three-month span. Another fifty-eight of these investigations were carried out prior to the elections of December 1930. This meant an enormous amount of work for Mendoza and his assistants.

In some of the investigations, fraud and irregularities were obvious, and thus a ruling was easy. But in most cases, clarity proved elusive, and it was within the context of these difficult investigations that the Romero government confronted its enemy in all its grandeur. Romero Bosque and Mendoza quickly discovered that in most cases, neither the group submitting the denunciation nor the group being denounced was conducting politics according to the official rules. Instead, all parties were

Table 6.1　Nullification Proceedings Conducted by the Ministerio de
Gobernación, 1913–1930

Year	Number of Proceedings	Average Number of Pages per Proceeding
1913	2	n.a.
1914	3	n.a.
1915	2	n.a.
1916	2	n.a.
1917	2	n.a.
1918	3	9
1919	8	22
1920	8	20
1921	9	13
1923	9	15
1925	1	10
1927	34	40
1929	40	46
1930	22	52

Source: Records of nullification contained in AGN, CN.

Note: Only proceedings that were complete were included in the tabulation of pages per proceeding.

engaging in some form of electoral manipulation and using the nullification process as an excuse to invite a more powerful ally to come to their rescue. Romero Bosque and Mendoza often found themselves in the difficult position of not being able to rule in anyone's favor, effectively surrendering the election to the traditional practices. In his interview in November 1927, Mendoza commented extensively on the difficulty of the investigative process.

> It is difficult to guarantee [the freedom of the vote] given the many petitions and *solicitudes* that arrive on my desk. The sheets for and against a candidate are mostly exaggerations of either his virtues or his defects; nevertheless this is all part of the process. I also am receiving constant denunciations against candidates who supposedly have judicial processes

pending against them, or for their involvement in vice or prostitution. All of these have to be studied as well. . . . Particularly important are the denunciations from small villages, where this class of civil struggle can provoke genuine armed conflicts between the participants.

Mendoza then described some of the traditional tactics: "One way is to move voters from one place to another to vote two or three times according to the interests of the powerful individuals whose service they are under and who exercise control over various municipalities. Another way is to introduce clandestinely fictitious lists of voter registrants, persons who exist only in the minds of the persons who put the list there."[67]

A few examples of investigations highlight the general process. Take for instance the case of Jiquilisco (Usulután Department) in the election of December 1927. Shortly after the election, a group of people supporting the candidacy of Gregorio Chávez for alcalde requested nullification on the grounds that the incumbents had intimidated them with threats of violence. Chávez presented witnesses who claimed to have overheard members of the municipal council telling him that if any of his supporters came to vote "they would be sorry." The members of the electoral board offered a different story, claiming that it was Chávez who threatened violence. According to them, in the weeks leading up to the election Chávez purchased all of the machetes from the local stores to arm his supporters. He then spread the rumor that "blood would flow" if his opponent, Guerrero, was elected. The municipal council consequently ordered the local commander to patrol the streets to protect the citizenry, not to intimidate the opposition.

In response to this charge and countercharge, the departmental governor traveled to Jiquilisco to conduct an investigation, one of many proceeding simultaneously in his department. He accumulated almost sixty pages of testimony from local citizens and then returned to his office in Usulután to make a decision. After two weeks of deliberation he ruled that Guerrero's election should be nullified, citing testimony from persons who corroborated Chávez's account. Guerrero appealed, so the case was sent to Mendoza in San Salvador. The minister reluctantly reversed the governor's decision because both sides had an identical number of equally reliable witnesses, which precluded a definitive resolution.[68]

The case from Jiquilisco provides an example of the most frequent problem that Romero Bosque and Mendoza faced in the investigative process: exactly contrary accounts based on a similar number of witnesses who appeared to be equally reliable. Confronted with this dilemma, and overwhelmed by the number of cases in their dockets, governors often based their decisions on seemingly bizarre or discriminatory foundations. In response to a nullification request from the municipality of Nahuizalco (Sonsonate Department), for instance, the governor ruled in favor of one side simply because it presented more witnesses.[69] In another case from Ataco (Ahuachapán Department), the governor ruled against one side because its witnesses were "for the greater part illiterate laborers, whereas those for the other side are mostly artisans and agriculturists, who for their improved social position and education have a greater sense of their responsibility in testifying."[70]

To reach a definitive conclusion in any of these investigations, the government needed a combination of physical evidence, a capable investigator who could trip up untruthful witnesses, and a large investment in time and human resources. An example of a successful case comes from Santa Maria (Usulután Department), where the governor found that two of the witnesses for one side gave conflicting testimonies, proving that they had fabricated their stories. But getting to this point required dozens of interviews.[71] In another case, from the municipality of Tecoluca (San Vicente Department), the governor discovered that one group had pasted the names of some of its voters into the registration book after the election had taken place.[72] In these cases the evidence was clear and the rulings were easy.

Another case from Jiquilisco illustrates the government's enormous commitment of time and resources to ensuring some degree of long-term stability in a municipality. After the conflict in the 1927 election, partisan differences remained intense and flared up as the election of 1929 approached. The ministry of government launched two pre-electoral investigations in the municipality in response to accusations of wrongdoing. This, however, was not enough to prevent one side from submitting a nullification request after the election. The government then launched another investigation that dragged on for six months and resulted in the nullification of the election. A supplemental election scheduled for June 1930 incited still more allegations of misdeeds, bringing yet another government investigation. This time both Pío Romero Bosque and Manuel Mendoza got involved. They exchanged dozens of letters and telegrams with people in Jiquilisco in hopes of settling the myriad disputes. The June election finally satisfied all sides, and no more denunciations arrived from the village until the next election, just six months later.[73] The case offers something of a success story in that at one point all sides finally accepted the results of an election. But getting to that point required no less than five government investigations and the personal involvement of the president. And Jiquilisco was just one village in a nation of more than two hundred and forty municipalities. The process of building sustainable democratic institutions was indeed long and difficult.

Local partisans who simply refused to abide by the government's rulings raised the specter of violence. In the municipality of San Miguel de Mercedes (Chalatenango Department), for instance, the government nullified the 1929 election of Anastasio Hernández as alcalde. The past municipal council was to remain in office until a supplemental election could be held at the end of January. But when the former council members attempted to return to their offices on the morning of January 1, they were confronted by Hernández and approximately eighty of his followers armed with shotguns and machetes. Four people were killed and two more were wounded in the ensuing violence before a group of soldiers and guardsmen arrived from Chalatenango City.[74]

This case from San Miguel de Mercedes suggests the important role that the military played in the Romero reforms. Like his predecessors, Romero Bosque ultimately turned to the military to control belligerent local bosses. His motives were different; he was using the military to defend electoral liberties rather than to impose political appointees, but the principle remained the same. Violent opposition by local strongmen was met with military force. Thus, a crucial aspect of the reform program was Romero Bosque's ability to enlist the support of the military.

Pío Romero Bosque and the Military

Romero Bosque had developed a solid working relationship with many high-ranking military officers during his eight-year tenure as minister of war (1919–1927), even though he served under Presidents Meléndez and

Quiñónez, who had an antagonistic relationship with some sectors of the military. In 1925, the U.S. chargé said that he believed that the military officers' conflicts with Quiñónez and Meléndez actually helped Romero Bosque, because they found him to be their sole ally in government: "Dr. Romero Bosque [is] supported by numerous army officers," claimed the chargé in 1925, "who, as the Department has previously been informed, are almost all hostile in secret to Dr. Quiñónez on account of the contemptuous way in which he treated them while in office."[75] U.S. legation officers opined that one of Romero Bosque's greatest assets upon entering office in 1927 was his good standing in the military. "He [Romero Bosque] is unquestionably very popular in the Army," observed the chargé in 1926, when rumors of Romero Bosque's candidacy began to circulate.[76] The same chargé noted after the inauguration that "the mighty army group . . . have been closely associated with the new President for some years, during his tenure as Minister of War, and apparently have been led to believe that with his induction into office they would be able to reap ample reward for the efficient and enthusiastic support they gave his candidacy for president. In fact, without their support it is extremely doubtful that he would ever have been considered by Dr. Quiñónez as his successor."[77] In his memoir, General Peña Trejo credited Romero Bosque with doing a great deal to enhance military discipline and training during his tenure as minister of war and also noted that as president, Romero Bosque reversed the policies of his predecessors by paying the military promptly and in full.[78]

Romero Bosque demonstrated a great capacity for flexibility in his relations with military officers. He punished and threatened at the same time that he cajoled and rewarded. Examples of the former include his willingness to execute two military officers and arrest many others for participating in the attempted coup of 1927. He rewarded Colonel Leitzelar for his loyalty during the rebellion by promoting him to brigadier general. We also saw in 1928 Romero Bosque's ability to take a strong verbal stance with officers he suspected of plotting against him. But he acceded to these same officers by appointing an active-duty officer, General Andrés Menéndez, to serve as undersecretary of war.

A similar act of acquiescence came later in 1928, when the investigation into the murder of Alberto Escalante implicated two high-ranking officers, including General Calvo, the former director of the Guardia Nacional. Romero Bosque suddenly issued an unconditional amnesty for both officers.[79] In the aftermath of that decision, Romero Bosque may well have questioned his support for freedom of the press, because the ire of many people over the amnesty was aired out in the newspapers. Escalante's widow wrote a letter that made the front page of *Diario Latino*. In it she castigated Romero Bosque for impeding the investigation into two persons who appeared to have been involved in the murder of her husband.[80] Romero wrote a weakly worded response in which he stated that he "always tried to do his best and to do justice while in office."[81] A barbed editorial from Enrique Córdova referred to the amnesty as being "entirely politically motivated."[82]

In his relations with the military Romero Bosque employed a strategy of divide and rule, taking advantage of the division between older officers who had ascended through the ranks and younger upstarts who had graduated from the military school. His new undersecretary of war, Menéndez, was a classic example. He began his career as a lowly private in 1889 and steadily climbed the ladder to become a colonel in 1915 and finally a general in 1920.[83] Some other examples of older officers who were close to Romero and supported him were Colonel Salvador Castaneda Castro, governor of Cuscatlán; General Maximiliano Hernández Martínez, director of the military school, which had been reopened in January 1927 under the new name of Escuela Militar; General Antonio Claramount Lucero, commander of Usulután; General José Trabanino, president of the Círculo Militar (the officer's club); and General José Tomás Calderón, the commander of San Miguel, who in 1930 would be charged with assembling the government's prodemocracy booklet, "Free Suffrage."

According to comments from the U.S. legation and from Pío Romero Bosque himself, the president used military promotions and appointments to keep officers in check. "He has changed several military commanders suspected of engaging in such [political] activities," noted the U.S. chargé in April 1930. "In the matter of Army promotions," the chargé later stated, "he [Romero Bosque] has advanced those, presumably, who will best serve him. The nominations are said to have been made individually and, after having been confirmed by the Assembly, are retained by the President for signature until he sees fit to release them, so holding the advancements in his own hand."[84] In a 1934 interview, Romero Bosque looked back upon his relations with the military and said, "as you know, my success in keeping the country at peace for four years was largely due to the fact that I never allowed any of the Generals too much foreground, never trusted a single one of them, and constantly shifted them from one post to another."[85] Unfortunately, the documentary record does not reveal which commanders were changed, when they were changed, or for what reasons.[86]

Romero Bosque's calculated dealings with the military paid off when he needed support for his reforms. General Trabanino delivered a speech in September 1929, on the occasion of becoming the director of the Círculo Militar, in which he first denounced past military interventions in politics and then declared the military's support for Romero Bosque: "In the past . . . the Armed Forces have not guaranteed the free exercise of the rights of the citizenry, but have violated the Constitutional liberties. But if to err is human, so too is it human to forgive. If our blame is large, so too should be our amends. And it is in this moment, in which our Government has promised to respect the liberties bestowed by the Magna Carta, that the army will fulfill its mission by recognizing these words."[87] Trabanino's speech paved the way for an even more substantive declaration of support from the military. In November 1930, on the eve of the 1930 municipal elections and the 1931 presidential election, the military issued a manifesto to the nation signed by more than six hundred officers, essentially every officer above the rank of sergeant. The signatories claimed that the manifesto was the first time in history that the armed forces had addressed themselves directly to the people of El Salvador and that the importance of the coming elections merited such a groundbreaking event. The manifesto declared the military's support for Romero Bosque's policies in the forthcoming elections, and it delivered a promise that the military would not support particular candidates and instead would defend constitutional liberties.[88] The following day the national police issued a similar declaration.[89] Proclamations such as these do not necessarily translate into reality on the ground, as low-ranking officers can manipulate orders to their liking and high-ranking officers can harbor ulterior motives. But certainly the proclamations were unprecedented, and they suggest that Romero Bosque had gained some degree of military support. The military would prove to be a valuable asset in the elections, especially in the presidential election of 1931. Romero Bosque used armed units to maintain order, thereby creating a stable environment in which his officials were better able to monitor electoral procedures.

Elections, 1929–1931

Romero Bosque's pragmatism seems to have been in play during the elections for deputies to the National Assembly in January 1928. It appears he sacrificed any pretense of democracy in those elections, hoping to focus on the next round of municipal elections. The archives in El Salvador contain very little information on 1928 deputy elections, and press coverage was equally thin. According to reports from the U.S. legation, Romero Bosque withheld the pretense of democracy in both this election and the following deputy elections in January 1929. With regard to the elections of 1928, the U.S. chargé wrote that "It may be of interest to the Department to know that the [deputy] elections passed off in a very tranquil manner. As a matter of fact they were an absolute farce, all the candidates elected in accordance with the wishes of the present Government."[90] The elections of January 1929 elicited the following comment in an editorial in the newspaper *El Dia:* "Year by year El Salvador has what is called the election of deputies. The custom is old. And just as old as this simulation of elections is the custom of criticizing the Government for the system for which we are all to blame."[91] Apparently both elections were carried out in the traditional manner: the government selected a set of candidates after negotiating with local elites. It is not clear why Romero Bosque held out this double standard for municipal and deputy elections. One possibility is that he did not want to place the power of impeachment in the hands of potential enemies.

For the electoral span starting with the municipal elections of December 1929 and ending with the presidential election of 1931, however, Romero Bosque employed new strategies and sought to install genuine democratic procedures. Principal among these procedures was mixed electoral boards. The traditional method of electing the board from the municipality at large on the morning of the election was tantamount to allowing the dominant faction to monopolize it. Romero Bosque believed that this system could be improved if at least one representative from each political faction sat on the board. Starting with the election of December 1929, he ordered his departmental governors and commanders to assemble lists of the registered candidates in each municipality and then, one week prior to the election, gather these candidates to decide upon the electoral board.[92] One major roadblock to this process was factions that refused to participate in the process. A telegram from the governor of Sonsonate reported that in six of the department's fourteen municipalities at least one faction had refused to participate. In most cases, the reluctant groups were the dominant ones that had the most to lose by sharing seats on the boards. The problem usually was rectified when the government told them that if they did not participate, they would be excluded from the election altogether.[93]

A variation on the mixed electoral boards was separate boards. Instead of one polling station with representatives from each faction, a distinct board was created for each party and accepted votes only from its own supporters. Other parties were allowed to post one or two observers around the tables of their competitors to watch for irregularities. Usually this tactic was applied in larger municipalities where many people voted and the potential for clashes between rivals standing in the same line was much greater. The practice was used widely during the presidential election of 1931.[94] In San Salvador, for instance, the ministry of government drew up a detailed map of the city with exact locations for each party's polling station.[95]

The government also sought to increase its presence in outlying municipalities during elections. This came in the form of observation teams, usually military units. "The country will be an armed camp," predicted the U.S. chargé on the eve of the municipal elections of 1929.[96] General Peña Trejo claimed in his memoir that "Pío Romero Bosque ordered many officers of the army to pass through the principal populations of the republic in the capacity of observers and coordinators . . . and in the event of electoral disturbances to maintain order and guarantee freedom of suffrage." Peña Trejo also identified himself as being one of the seven army officers to staff the office of general inspector of the army, which was charged with overseeing the military's electoral observation teams.[97] Another tactic to increase the government's presence in the municipalities was employed on the eve of the presidential election of 1931. Departmental governors gathered together party representatives from each of the municipalities and endeavored to instill in them an understanding of the government's insistence that electoral rules be obeyed.[98]

The government also looked to establish more direct contact between the local and national levels. This process usually was conducted from the offices of Pío Romero Bosque and Manuel Mendoza. For his part, Romero Bosque issued explicit declarations of his and his government's intentions for the elections. "The elections will be free," declared the *Diario Oficial* in July 1929 in reference to forthcoming elections.[99] In the same month Romero Bosque wrote in regard to the presidential elections of 1931 that "the Salvadoran people will select freely their future President without recommendation of imposition of any kind."[100] In November 1929, Romero Bosque sent a declaration to every municipality in the nation, informing them that "the Government has no official candidates in any part of the country and is firmly committed to guaranteeing the right of free suffrage."[101] In April 1930, Romero Bosque wrote a detailed six-page memo about his intentions for the future presidential election. The memo was distributed throughout all levels of the state bureaucracy, and it is summarized in one sentence: "I make this formal call to our patriotism that in this next step to resolve the political problem of the presidential succession, that we be ready to support, in any way possible, the form that this process takes, as a reflection of our prudence and a confirmation of our preparation for a democratic life."[102]

Mendoza oversaw much of the day-to-day correspondence with the municipalities. His letters and telegrams to and from the countryside reveal that many local factions still did not understand, had not heard about, or chose to ignore the reforms. A political aspirant in San Vicente City, for instance, wrote to Pío Romero Bosque in March 1930 requesting support for his political faction. He prefaced his request by pointing out that "I have been your unconditional supporter since before the Salvadoran people chose you to direct the destiny of the nation, and when in 1926 they conducted the election, I, full of enthusiasm, brought out 600 votes in this city; I was joined by General don Teodor Avila, who at that time was Comandante of this Department."[103] If nothing else, that letter is a revealing testimony to the traditional manner in which past elections had been conducted. A similar letter arrived from the village of Panchimalco (San Salvador Department). The ministry of government had sent a telegram to the village requesting that a list of the candidates for the forthcoming municipal elections be submitted so that mixed electoral boards could be formed. The author took the telegram as an opportunity to recommend official candidates, and instead of submitting lists of the various candidates, he submitted to Mendoza "the following names of persons worthy of fulfilling the position of municipal authorities" and then wrote that "we ask that with your authority you give them the help that they deserve."[104] To this request, and many others like it, Mendoza responded, "In regard to your telegram recommending specific citizens as candidates in the coming term . . . I say to you that not in this population, or in any other population in the Republic have I given such orders or recommendations of this manner."[105]

From the municipal elections of December 1929 we have a complete record of the officials elected in Ahuachapán Department. I asked the same questions of these records as I did of the records from 1927: Did any of the officials elected in 1929 serve under any of the PND administrations that came to power in 1920, 1921, 1923, or 1925? Did any persons bearing the same surname serve in any of those administrations? The results are compiled in the appendix in table A4. They reveal that the rate at which power shifted power away from PND stalwarts in 1929 was similar to that of 1927. In three of the department's eleven municipalities there were no direct carryovers of officials from the PND. Interestingly, these same three municipalities (El Refugio, San Lorenzo, and Turín) appear in the data from 1927 (table A3) as also having no ties to the PND. This suggests that in those villages where the PND was pushed out of power, it stayed out.

The Presidential Election of 1931

The presidential election of 1931 was a major event that generated many expectations and large amounts of documentation. It was to be an innovation, and Romero Bosque saw it as the capstone of his four-year tenure and perhaps of his entire political career. His memo of April 1930 took a philosophical tone when he wrote that "[if] this fourth year of work . . . results in an era of peace and liberty, we will have won for ourselves a decisive victory."[106] The municipal elections of December 1930, and even the deputy elections of the preceding January, were warm-ups for the 1931 presidential elections. The presidential candidates used them to mobilize support and to test their capacities to generate votes. Local candidates began to operate under the banner of their respective national parties, which often worked on the behalf of their local partisans by submitting denunciations and solicitations to the national government.[107] Rather than discussing these preliminary elections in any detail, I will focus here on the election of January 1931, for it serves as a metaphor for the entire period from 1929 to 1931.

Six candidates ran in the election.[108] They were Alberto Gómez Zárate, who had held a series of positions under Meléndez and Quiñónez and was serving as minister of war under Romero Bosque until he resigned to participate in the election; Enrique Córdova, who was working privately as a lawyer; General Maximiliano Hernández Martínez, who resigned as director of the military school for the election; General Antonio Claramount Lucero, who resigned as commander of Usulután for the election; Arturo Araujo, who had been engaged in private business affairs since his failed coup attempt in 1920; and Miguel Tomás Molina, the challenger in the 1922 election who had since been working in the private sector.

The electoral campaign was a peculiar affair in that it fostered a genuine sense of competition, but generated virtually no real differences between the candidates, with the exception of Arturo Araujo and his Partido Laborista (see below). All of the candidates campaigned with varying degrees of vigor. They canvassed the nation to drum up support, deliver speeches, and organize local chapters of their respective parties. But the platforms on which they ran are virtually indistinguishable from one another and are notable for their banality and vagueness. They made imprecise promises of financial integrity and administrative responsibility, but beyond that said very little. All of the candidates seemed to want to avoid being identified with any one particular sector of society. This vagueness was noticed by both U.S. and British diplomatic officers, who were keeping a close eye on the election and found it strange that no one stepped forward as the candidate of the coffee planters.[109]

The one exception was Araujo, who ran on a decidedly partisan platform geared toward the working masses. Just as he had done in 1920, Araujo ran under his Partido Laborista (Labor Party) and presented himself as the workers' candidate. Two of Araujo's more renowned supporters were Alberto Masferrer, the widely respected philosopher and semisocialist, and Felipe Recinos, the former director general of the FRTS, who had been expelled from that organization in February 1930 when the radical faction took control of the union. One of the Partido Laborista broadsides was an "Open Letter Directed to the Salvadoran Workers and Campesinos" that pitched Araujo as a "true friend of the working class . . . who knows their [the workers'] sufferings, the precarious situation in which they live, and who listens to their anguished voices."[110] This same message was delivered constantly in speeches by Araujo and representatives of his party. One of Araujo's campaign workers stated, in a June 1930 speech in the town of Guazapa, that "Araujo is a millionaire who has redistributed part of his capital to the workers and campesinos."[111] By targeting labor as the core of his support, Araujo obviously was banking on the government's ability to create an electoral environment in which workers would indeed be able to freely turn out to the polls.

It appears that one tactic used by Partido Laborista organizers to drum up support was to promise land redistribution. Araujo denied publicly that he sanctioned such an idea, or that his functionaries were even making such promises, but three separate sources suggest otherwise.[112] The first is a report in the newspaper *El Espectador,* founded by Manuel Andino in 1930 specifically to report on the electoral campaign. An article in a June 1930 issue described Araujo's organizers in the municipality of Quezaltepeque (Chalatenango Department) making promises of land redistribution.[113] A second source is internal documentation from the Communist Party that contains reports from outlying party cells mentioning the activities of the Partido Laborista and its promises of land redistribution. This issue was especially important for the PCS because its leaders believed that such promises could undermine their organizational efforts.[114] The final source is the memoir of General Peña Trejo, in which he writes that followers of Araujo promised that their candidate would "redistribute the great plantations of the rich among the campesinos in order that they can plant agricultural products."[115]

The two front-runners in the election were Araujo and Gómez Zárate. The competition between them captured the real and symbolic issues at stake in the election. While Araujo was chasing the labor vote, Gómez Zárate was running an intense, if demure, campaign that looked to appeal to everyone and offend no one. Of the six candidates, Gómez Zárate was the most closely associated with the remnants of the PND and the legacy of Meléndez and Quiñónez. Araujo recognized this and endeavored to undermine Gómez Zárate by invoking unsavory memories of the Meléndez-Quiñónez years, such as the Christmas Day massacre of 1922.[116]

Lists of party affiliates in Sonsonate, San Vicente, and San Salvador Departments reveal that Gómez Zárate did indeed have a disproportionate number of supporters among those people who had served under the PND, but he certainly was not the only candidate to have former PND officials holding positions in local party branches. The data from Sonsonate and San Vicente consist of complete lists of the seven-member electoral boards for the local elections of December 1930 that show the party affiliation of each member. The data from San Salvador Department comes from the municipality of Nejapa and consists of lists of people who held positions on the executive councils of the local wing of each of the national parties. I compared the names on these lists with the names of the officials who had served on municipal councils between 1920 and 1925. Out of 257 names listed in the documentation, only 16 had held office between 1920 and 1925 (see table 6.2). Of these 16, 8 belonged to Gómez Zárate's party, 4 to Araujo's, 3 to Córdova's, and 1 to Claramount Lucero's. (Martínez and Molina had not yet declared their candidacies at this point.) This information suggests that the national candidates formed alliances with anyone in the municipalities willing to support them, and thus even Araujo had former PND officials in his party.

One week before voting was to begin on January 11, a curious alliance emerged between Arturo Araujo and General Maximiliano Hernández Martínez. The latter abandoned his campaign to become the vice presidential candidate under the Partido Laborista. This alliance took the remaining candidates by surprise, as Araujo and Martínez had shown no prior degree of association. Presumably, each saw in the other an opportunity to

Table 6.2   Local Affiliates of Candidates in the 1931 Election Who Had Served on Municipal Councils under the PND between 1920 and 1925

Alberto Gómez Zarate's Affiliates

Rubén Ceferino Ceceña, Armenia (Sonsonate)
Pedro Martínez Cuéllar, Sonzacate (Sonsonate)
Antonio Rodríguez, Nahuilingo (Sonsonate)
José Calvo Díaz, Izalco (Sonsonate)
Francisco Rivas Alfaro, San Sebastián (San Vicente)
Raúl Gómez, Santo Domingo (San Vicente)
Manuel Esquivel, Nejapa (San Salvador)
Pedro Esquivel Jr., Nejapa (San Salvador)

Arturo Araujo's Affiliates

Santos Hernández Morán, Cuisnahuat (Sonsonate)
Manuel Vega Ruíz, Izalco (Sonsonate)
Cecilio Jovel, Nejapa (San Salvador)
Doroteo Flores, Nejapa (San Salvador)

Enrique Córdova's Affiliates

Jorge Mazzini, Sonsonate City (Sonsonate)
Vicente Herrera, Nahuilingo (Sonsonate)
Fernando Novao, Nejapa (San Salvador)

Antonio Claramount's Affiliates

José Angel Colindres, San Antonio del Monte (Sonsonate)

Sources: List of Directorios for Sonsonate Department, January 27, 1931, AGN, MG, SS, Box "Política, 1930–9"; "Nomina de las personas que integran los Directorios de Elecciones en el Departmento," San Vicente, December 1930, AGN, MG, SSV, 1930, Box 6; List of persons who comprise local branches of national-level political parties in Nejapa, Department San Salvador, in Benjamín Arrieta Rossi, Governor of San Salvador Department, to Minister of Government, July 4, 1930, AGN, MG, unclassified box.

advance his own position. Martínez had been making a poor showing in the election and was sure to lose. By joining a front-runner like Araujo, he had a good chance of becoming vice president. For his part, Araujo gained a high-ranking and well-connected military officer who might facilitate relations with the military. If this was Araujo's motive, it backfired on him, because he would be ousted in a military coup in December 1931 and Martínez would succeed him as president. But for the time being, the deal seemed mutually beneficial.

In the days leading up to the election, and during the three days of voting, hundreds of complaints arrived in the national capital in the form of telegrams describing every sort of electoral manipulation. Judging by the number of responses that Mendoza sent out, he must have slept very little during those days. He sent out a continuous stream of orders, threats, and inquiries to local officials accused of engaging in fraudulent acts.[117] A typical example of Mendoza's response was sent to the alcalde of Izalco on January 9: "I have been informed that you are trying to impose a candidate. Abstain from this illegal act, for the elections should be practiced freely by the citizens, and the functionaries are obliged to observe the strictest impartiality. If you persist you will be responsible for the disorders that will occur and the actions which will be taken against you."[118] Given the sheer volume of complaints, some irregularities must have taken place. But not one complaint contained reports of violence, and all of the candidates accepted the results of the election.

The U.S. chargé summarized the election in the following glowing terms: "During the elections, the order, and real freedom of voting, which existed throughout the entire republic is well worthy of praise."[119] More than 200,000 votes were cast, with the following rounded-off results: Araujo, 101,000; Gómez Zárate, 64,000; Córdova, 32,000; Claramount Lucero, 16,000; and Molina, 4,000. Because Araujo did not have an outright majority, the election went to the assembly. Córdova gave the votes of his deputies to Araujo, who thus became the official winner and succeeded Romero Bosque in March 1931. Shortly after assuming office, Araujo issued a manifesto to the nation that stated, "I cannot be indifferent to the cause of the workers for they constitute the great majority in the ranks of the party which has raised me to power. I am loyally linked to these as well as to all persons who are truly desirous of bettering the conditions of labor."[120]

* * *

In October 1929, a man by the name of Luís Silva took the presidential elections of 1931 as an opportunity to write a lengthy editorial on democracy and the Romero reforms. Such an editorial was not an uncommon occurrence in El Salvador during the period from 1927 to 1931, because the question of democracy generated much public discussion, and with the lifting of press censorship, newspapers were a natural outlet for debate.[121] Silva's article, however, is particularly noteworthy for its insightful analysis. He wrote in response to a prior editorial that had hailed Pío Romero Bosque for bringing democracy to El Salvador. Silva shared that author's enthusiasm for popular suffrage and applauded Romero Bosque's efforts as well, but he cautioned against ill-placed optimism. He first pointed out the manifest difficulties in trying to reshape a political system riddled with people accustomed to and experienced in the practices of imposition and patronage. Silva took the issue a step further by insisting that "liberty" was not a gift bestowed upon a nation by a president, but rather a right that emerged from within a nation itself and that would survive only with the dogged determination of a populace committed to tolerance of differing opinions.

Silva got to the heart of the issue by portraying democracy not as an event, but as a process. His interpretation draws parallels to the contemporary notion of social capital, a term that refers to the "features of social organization, such as trust, norms and networks," that facilitate "voluntary cooperation . . . reciprocity [and] civic engagement."[122] As a public good, social capital is a commodity that enhances social and political interaction. As more people in a society trust one another and believe that the rules of society, both de facto and de jure, are legitimate and will be enforced judicially by the government, the more willing they are to invest themselves in the functioning of that society. Social capital, in this sense, is self-reinforcing. The longer it exists, the more ingrained it becomes, and the more entrenched are the norms that make institutions such as a democracy possible.

Romero Bosque was building social capital. He used the powers of the state to enforce a new set of rules that he hoped would serve as the foundation for the development of better institutional norms. Araujo's victory, especially in light of the prolabor agenda on which he ran, stands as a testament to Romero Bosque's efforts. What would have happened had the Romero reforms been allowed to proceed is, naturally, speculative and outside the realm of the present study. As the next chapter shows, however, that question is moot, because the nascent democratic system came crashing down in December 1931 in a military coup that would usher in five decades of uninterrupted—and decidedly nondemocratic—military rule.

CHAPTER 7

POLITICS UNDER THE MILITARY REGIME, 1931-1940

The Araujo government lasted only ten months. It arrived amid cautious optimism about a new political process and left in ignominy, in a military coup during the first week of December 1931. In the confused aftermath of the coup, Araujo's vice president, General Maximiliano Hernández Martínez, assumed the presidency, ostensibly to complete the remainder of Araujo's term (1931–1935). Martínez (who went by his maternal name) completed that term and stayed in office for another nine years, including a second term (1935–1939), and the greater part of a third, six-year term (1939–1945). He was forced from office in 1944, shortly before the subservient National Assembly was to elect him to another six-year term that would have left him in office until 1950.

The Martínez era constitutes a crucial period of transition between the patronage-based dictatorships of the nineteenth and early twentieth centuries and the modern military regimes of the latter half of the twentieth century. It was hardly the first time that an officer had sat in the president's chair in El Salvador, but there was something new about the Martínez era: a ranking officer in a professionalizing, centralizing army was in charge of the government, and several of his high-ranking counterparts held key offices. The military did not formally take control of the state as an institution and rule it like the "bureaucratic authoritarian" regimes in

Brazil, Chile, and Argentina during the 1960s and 1970s. But Martínez began five decades of intertwined relations between military officers and governance in El Salvador. The distinct subculture of military politics would become state politics, and once officers got hold of public office, a whole new route for career enhancement became available to them. In addition to climbing the ranks inside the military, they now had government positions at their disposal, and they were not anxious to give them up. The longer an officer held the presidency, the more young officers took it for granted that their range of future career options would include political office. Between officers' expectations, civilian elites' tolerance of them serving in government, and the masses' inability or unwillingness to prevent it all from happening, military governance in El Salvador proved to be highly durable. Eventually it would take twelve years of civil war (1980–1992) to amend the system and dislodge the officers from power.

This chapter and the next describe that inaugural military regime. Both chapters limit themselves to the period from 1931 to 1940, when Martínez consolidated his hold on power. The second chapter is devoted to social policy and the regime's relationship to the peasant rebellion of January 1932. The present chapter examines politics and shows how Martínez reversed the Romero reforms and returned politics to the highly centralized patronage system that had operated under the PND. Under Martínez, politics once again functioned as a pyramid in which the national government was the supreme dispenser of power and position. Martínez changed the name of the official political party to the Partido Nacional Pro-Patria, but for all intents and purposes the system functioned as it had as the PND under Meléndez and Quiñónez—though more efficiently, in no small part because Martínez enjoyed a secure monopoly over the tools of coercion.

The political system under Martínez will be examined here at both the local and national levels. At the national level, Martínez guarded against opponents, both real and imagined, and constantly fought off rival officers who wanted to oust him and often attempted coups in hopes of assuming his position atop the pyramid. (This pattern of military politics would become commonplace over the next fifty years.) At the local level, Martínez and his fellow administrators sought out loyal bosses who could monopolize polling stations and produce votes for the government's candidates, including the annual slate of deputies for the National Assembly, and for Martínez himself during his repeated bids for the presidency. Local power players jockeyed for position within the ranks of Pro-Patria, and those who received the party's blessing were allowed to hold sway over their localities. Elections became, once again, highly managed affairs with unanimous or near-unanimous results.

Salvadoran elites found much to fear in the late 1920s and early 1930s: the democratization plans of Pío Romero Bosque, the populist reformism of Arturo Araujo, the economic collapse of the Great Depression, and a radicalized peasantry that rose up in rebellion in January 1932. With General Martínez at the helm, they slept easier at night. They got security, control over their municipalities, and a government that avidly supported export-oriented agriculture. But as will be demonstrated in the following pages, they had to make a Faustian bargain to get those things—even if they did not fully realize they were doing so at the time. Along with security came the military as an institution, and its members did not always share the elites' commitment to the freewheeling laissez-faire capitalism that had allowed them to accumulate unprecedented amounts of private wealth. The military would emerge as an advocate of social and economic reforms, and its members would blame so-called unscrupulous elites for El Salvador's problems. Even as the military maintained a strict vigilance over the masses' autonomy and crushed any signs of independent organizing, they would press the cause of social reform in both rhetoric and practice. The social reformism of the Martínez regime may have been mild, but it set precedent, and some of Martínez's policies were enough to give elites the jitters. As we will see in the next chapter, they were only partially successful in resisting the Martínez government's desire to change the way they did things on their own properties.

From Araujo to Martínez

Araujo entered office at an inauspicious time, when the Great Depression was beginning to have a markedly negative impact on the nation's financial situation. Between 1929 and 1932, the value of Salvadoran coffee dropped from US$16.70 per quintal to US$7.50 per quintal.[1] Coffee exports dropped accordingly, from 120 million pounds in 1931 to 87 million pounds in 1932, and imports followed suit, plummeting from US$17.8 million in 1929 to US$5.1 million in 1932, causing a corresponding reduction in customs revenues.[2] Already in 1930, the U.S. and British legations were commenting on the government's foreboding financial situation.[3] They reported that the government was borrowing heavily from Salvadoran banks and accumulating a sizable internal debt. Furthermore, the government could not secure an external lender due to a lack of collateral. The main source of revenue, customs duties, was already accounted for: 70 percent of customs duties went towards interest on the 1922 loan, while the remaining 30 percent was being disbursed by the U.S. customs agent, Mr. Renwick, to Salvadoran banks in payment for interest on the floating debt.[4] In October 1930 the British chargé reported that "the financial situation is serious, the [internal] loan raised in August for US$200,000 is depleted. The school teachers have not been paid for six months."[5]

By 1931 the financial situation was only growing worse, and Araujo had the added problem of meeting not only normal state expenditures, but also his constituents' expectations. Immediately after his victory in January 1931, Araujo was swamped with petitioners and position-seekers arriving at his home and later at his office in search of work or land.[6] The British chargé noted that, to its detriment, "the new administration has found no solution to its most pressing problems, namely where to find money for current expenses."[7] According to the U.S. legation, by May 1931 the floating debt had risen to more than US$1.5 million from just US$400,000 not six months prior. In April the government put before the National Assembly a proposal to contract an external loan of up to US$2 million. In doing so, the government ignored the advice of its own Consejo Económico, a group of private citizens including some of El Salvador's leading financiers, such as Rodolfo Duke, that had been appointed by the government to analyze the financial situation. It had concluded that further loans were unwise.[8] In July the National Assembly nevertheless approved the loan proposal. Finding a willing lender, however, was difficult, and thus the loan remained in limbo. Nevertheless, the mere possibility of incurring yet another loan generated a groundswell of opposition, especially among people such as the university students, who associated loans with selling out the nation to foreigners. The week after the assembly made its decision, university students organized a demonstration. Although the government forbade the march, some nine hundred students turned out, and a violent confrontation ensued between the marchers and the Guardia Nacional. An undetermined number of students were wounded, and as many as thirty were arrested.[9]

At the same time that the government was proposing to solve its financial strain with a foreign loan, it was drawing up a budget for the fiscal year 1932 that was almost guaranteed to alienate powerful interest groups. One proposal, for instance, set aside one million colones (approximately US$500,000, or 8 percent of the total budget) to purchase agricultural properties at market price to be divided up and then rented out to landless workers at below market value. Alberto Masferrer, the renowned man of letters and advocate for social reform, held a seat in the National Assembly under Araujo's Partido Laborista and was the main proponent of this plan.[10] Another proposal was to streamline the military by eliminating those officers who drew salaries but did not perform actual duties. The government actually attempted to implement this plan in August 1931, but seven of the targeted officers informed the government that they would not accept the proposal, and the government backed down.[11]

Ultimately it was the financial crisis, Araujo's handling of it, and his strained relationship with the military that led to his political demise. In August, desperately short of funds, the government suspended military pay, demonstrating that it was either unaware of or unwilling to learn from the example of the Meléndez government in 1919, that failure to pay military salaries was a recipe for intrigue. According to the memoir of Salvador Peña Trejo, shortly thereafter the eventual leaders of the December coup began plotting against Araujo. Three months later, on the night of December 2, the coup began with a machine-gun assault on the presidential palace. Most of the barracks in the capital supported or at least ignored the rebellion, leaving only the Presidential Guard to defend Araujo. Overwhelmed and facing defeat, Araujo and a core group of supporters and government officials fled the capital. Most of them escaped unharmed, with the exception of Minister of Finance José Espinosa, who was killed in crossfire. Araujo fled to Nueva San Salvador, where he hoped to organize a counterassault. But upon arriving there he discovered the barracks to be in a state of disarray and generally opposed to him. He then retreated to Santa Ana, where he was joined by a few hundred supporters. Despite this display, Araujo concluded that his chance for success was nil, and on the morning of December 4 he turned over the presidency to the first designate and fled into Guatemala.[12]

In the confused aftermath of Araujo's departure from the capital, the main conspirators, eleven midlevel officers, formed a military directorate and assumed control of the executive's powers. Two days later they turned power over to the vice president, General Martínez, who supposedly had been jailed on the first day of fighting. Martínez's ascent to the presidency has generated much historiographical debate. Some writers claim that he actually was a coconspirator and that his arrest was fabricated in order to give him legitimacy as president. Others accept the story of his arrest and suggest that the coup was indeed hatched by the lower-ranking officers who were embittered over the issue of pay.[13] After reading the archival documents in the Ministerio de Gobernación, I concur with Knut Walter's assessment of the debate, that the documentation is too inconclusive to determine Martínez's role one way or the other.[14] The issue is somewhat irrelevant, because either side of the argument shows Martínez to have been, above all, a shrewd political player who constantly placed himself in the right place at the right time to achieve a rapid climb up the political ladder, from director of the military school in 1930 to president just fifteen months later.

Much has also been written about Martínez's atypical religious and philosophical beliefs. He was a theosophist who believed in reincarnation. He also was a teetotaling vegetarian who ascribed to *cromoferapia,* or cure by colors. He is said to have stored bottles of colored water in the sun for medicinal purposes and to have prescribed them to friends as cures for a variety of ailments. One of the more biting and at the same time engaging descriptions of Martínez comes from a Canadian journalist with a self-declared leftist bent who interviewed Martínez in 1944. The journalist claimed to have cut the interview short because it was a struggle to maintain composure in the face of Martínez's ramblings, but he nevertheless concluded that Martínez was a "powerful personality."[15] Indeed, for all his eccentricities, Martínez proved to be an extremely adroit leader. He adopted strict economic measures to bring the government's revenues into line, and he had a skill for staying in power by crushing his enemies and rewarding his followers, to the point that he eliminated the opposition and fostered loyalty among his core supporters. Martínez's political personality was characterized, according to the British chargé, by a carefully balanced use of the "iron hand" and the "velvet glove."[16]

Martínez certainly assumed office in the midst of a volatile political situation in which numerous pressures bore down upon him. The issues that demanded his immediate attention, beyond the selection of a new government, were elections and finances. Municipal elections were scheduled to occur less than one week after he became president, and elections for deputies to the National Assembly were to occur four weeks after that. The financial situation remained chaotic and promised to grow only worse. Meanwhile, opponents, both actual and potential, were to be found on all sides. Among them were power-hungry military officers, as well as supporters of Romero Bosque's now beleaguered reforms. One of the more formidable opponents was the U.S. government, which by the end of December had concluded that Martínez's rise to power violated the Washington Treaties of 1923, and thus his regime would not receive diplomatic recognition. The U.S. dispatched a special envoy, Jefferson Caffery, to El Salvador in hopes of pressuring Martínez to resign.[17] In addition, Martínez faced an increasingly radical peasantry in the western coffee-growing departments; they would rise up in a massive rebellion during the third week of January 1932, just six weeks after he became president. All of these problems were exacerbated by Martínez's lack of an organized political machine that he could use to consolidate his hold on power. El Partido Nacional Republicano, the small political party that had sponsored his candidacy in 1930 and early 1931, had withdrawn its support in June 1931 when he joined with Araujo.[18] Nor could Martínez look to the remaining laboristas for support, because they considered him a traitor. The fact that Martínez stayed in power amidst these myriad challenges is a testament to his political capabilities.

Upon taking office, Martínez first relied upon the velvet glove in hopes of assuaging the opposition. One of his first tasks was to select his cabinet and make a variety of other high-ranking appointments. Martínez was careful to give these positions to representatives of certain stakeholders. For example, the three highest-ranking leaders of the coup were given posts: Colonel Joaquín Valdés as minister of war; Captain Manuel Urbina as chief clerk to the president; and Colonel Osmín Aguirre as chief of police. Martínez balanced this younger and potentially rebellious military presence with two trusted older officers, General Salvador Castaneda Castro, who was given the key post of minister of government, and Colonel José Ascensio Menéndez, who became the undersecretary of war. Martínez had a core group of civilians in his government, including Miguel Angel Araujo, a well-known lawyer, as minister of foreign affairs.[19] The position of minister of finance also went to a civilian, but it was left vacant until Martínez decided to promote Araujo's undersecretary of finance, Pedro Fonseca, to the position in the interim. In February 1932, Martínez replaced Fonseca with Miguel Tomás Molina, who lent credibility to the government because of his well-known prodemocracy stance.[20] Martínez left lower-level officials in their places, both in the capital and in outlying regions, proclaiming after appointing his cabinet that "all other appointments remain unchanged for the present."[21] The U.S. chargé observed that Martínez "has thus far dismissed from office very few of his [Araujo's] appointees."[22] Laboristas in the security forces, however, were not tolerated. In Santa Ana seven police agents were dismissed because of their affiliation with the Labor Party.[23]

The Martínez government portrayed itself as an agent of conciliation rather than of repression and division. On December 8, 1931, General Castaneda Castro distributed a nationwide memo in which the new government presented itself to the nation. The memo stressed the government's commitment to "harmony, personal liberties, and the preservation of private property." And, in words quintessential to Martínez, the memo described the government's determination to "instill a sentiment of love for El Salvador" among the populace.[24] The government also declared its commitment to electoral liberties and announced that all political parties, including the communists and the laboristas, would be allowed to participate in the forthcoming municipal elections.[25] In the ensuing weeks government spokespersons repeatedly used the term *democracy*. For example, in one of his many circulars, Castaneda Castro announced that "the civil and military authorities of this government will lend guarantees to all persons who support . . . the democratic institutions of the nation."[26]

While the government presented its friendly face to the public, behind the scenes it monitored potential adversaries. Principal among them
were former members of the Romero Bosque government and the candidates of the 1931 presidential election. One week after assuming power,
Martínez gathered the four remaining candidates from the election (Miguel
Molina, Alberto Gómez Zárate, Antonio Claramount Lucero, and Enrique Córdova) into his office and attempted to get them to proclaim their
support for his government. Molina responded to this call, accepting the
position of minister of finance, and so too did Gómez Zárate, who ordered his constituents to support the government's slate of candidates in
the deputy election of January 1932.[27] In return Gómez was appointed
chief justice of the Supreme Court, a position he held for the duration of
Martínez's years in office. Enrique Córdova did not support Martínez, and
as a result he was placed under police surveillance. In his memoir he writes
of police agents arriving at his house shortly after the meeting with Martínez. He also describes the experience of Manuel Mendoza, Romero
Bosque's minister of government, who gave up sleeping at home because
of threats and harassment from the security forces. Both Córdova and
Mendoza withdrew from public life and kept low profiles.[28] Claramount
Lucero did not come out in support of Martínez, but he temporarily remained politically active, especially for the 1931 municipal elections, as
will be shown below.[29]

However, it was not civilian politicians, but rather his cohorts in the
army that Martínez needed to watch most closely. Civilian politicians had
little hope of challenging the weaponry of a military regime without a
mass demonstration of popular support, whereas a military officer needed
only weapons, some loyal soldiers, and a bit of timing and luck to overthrow the government. The December coup proved this point, and it was
the leaders of that coup whom Martínez distrusted the most. They were
young, dissatisfied, upwardly aspiring, and had proven their willingness to
carry out martial plots. At the military school they had shared the same
instructor, the Chilean General Carlos Ibañez del Campo. Martínez knew
that loyalty to instructor and generation were some of the strongest bonds
between officers; the same principle ultimately would lead him to rely
upon officers of his own generation. Martínez initially sought to divide
the plotters. After giving the three highest-ranking officers positions in his
government, he dispatched the remaining eight conspirators to remote

and inconsequential posts in outlying regions.[30] He soon disposed of the other three as well, and throughout his tenure in office, conflicts with rebellious officers constituted one of his main preoccupations.

One of the more pressing concerns for Martínez was the forthcoming elections, scheduled for December 13, 1931 (municipal elections), and January 12, 1932 (deputy elections). Thousands of municipal officials and the forty-two deputies of the assembly were to be elected, and the infant Martínez regime was not in a strong position to control the process. Martínez approached the situation pragmatically. He recognized that under the circumstances, obedient deputies were more important than subservient alcaldes, because the assembly would be grappling with some decisive issues, including Martínez's ongoing presidency and the nation's financial affairs. Martínez concentrated his efforts on the deputy elections and left the municipalities more or less to their own devices.

For the municipal elections, the government issued an order stating that neither violence nor disorder would be tolerated.[31] Reports from local officials about the potential disturbances, especially in the western region, with its increasingly mobilized peasantry, prompted Martínez to postpone the elections from their scheduled date of December 13 to January 3, 1932. In some areas of the west, elections were pushed back yet again, until the first week of February.[32] But in most of the nation, the municipal elections took place on January 3. They generated the standard amount of denunciations and accusations of wrongdoing. Notably, the authors of these *solicitudes* recognized the political shift in San Salvador and adjusted their discourse accordingly. They appealed to the military by identifying their opponents as laboristas or as "adherents of Araujo." A candidate in San Julián, for instance, wrote in his solicitation that his adversary is "an active laborista" and that if the government would help him get into office, he would serve as its "loyal sentry" against Araujistas in the region.[33]

It appears that the government did not respond to these requests and simply let the electoral conflicts run their course. Martínez did, however, follow through with his promise to allow the PCS to participate in the elections, and the communist slate in San Salvador ran a very close third, although repression of suspected communists in the countryside continued.[34] Comprehensive results from the elections are not available, so it is impossible to determine whether one particular party dominated the elections. But reports from the U.S. legation, as well as descriptions in *Diario Latino,* indicate that Claramount Lucero's party made a strong showing, notably winning San Salvador.[35]

The deputy elections of January 12 to 14 were decidedly more predetermined. The military submitted slates of candidates to each department and did not allow competition. General Castaneda Castro signaled the government's intent for the election when, two weeks prior to the election, he asked the U.S. State Department if it would accept his interpretation of the word "electing" as referring only to popular elections for president and not for deputies.[36] Apparently the State Department did not even bother to respond to the inquiry. The resultant electoral farce is revealed in the following telegram, sent from the alcalde of San Julián to the governor of Sonsonate, confirming that the electoral board was changed in accordance with the government's orders: "I understand the content of today's telegram in which I am ordered to substitute in the organization of the Directorio for the deputy elections, Rafael Agueda for Atilio Martelli and as Secretary Jesus Peña for Manuel de Leon."[37] After the election, the U.S. chargé reported that "the official returns indicate that the entire membership of Congress will be composed of deputies backed by and favorable to the Martínez regime and there will apparently not be any opposition group in the new Assembly."[38] The newspaper *Diario Patria* described the elections as "the adoption by the new government of the old procedures which discredited the exercise of suffrage amongst us."[39]

The military's control of the deputy elections was an important step in consolidating its hold on power. However, just one week after the elections, the government was confronted with perhaps its single greatest challenge, the peasant rebellion of January 1932. Late in the night of January 22 and early in the morning of January 23, peasants rose up in rebellion throughout El Salvador's four westernmost departments. In a matter of three days they gained control over roughly one dozen municipalities, including the important and populous townships of Nahuizalco, Izalco, and Juayúa in Sonsonate Department. Local military units were overwhelmed, and at first the rebellion seemed a potentially mortal blow to a regime already standing on the brink of collapse. However, the government's response to the rebellion ended up bolstering Martínez. The government sent reinforcements to the west on the morning of the twenty-fifth, and these troops unleashed a reign of terror over the peasant population. In roughly two weeks' time, military units killed untold thousands of people throughout the western countryside. The military assault is known simply as *la matanza,* "the massacre." Although crucial issues about the matanza remain obscure, such as who ordered the killing and the precise motives behind the orders (for instance, we do not know if Martínez specifically ordered the brutal response), the aftermath of the slaughter left no question as to who was in charge of El Salvador—Martínez and the military. Even U.S. Secretary of State Henry Stimson lamented in his personal diary that "the man [Hernández Martínez] who is president and who is the only pillar against the success of what seems to be a nasty proletarian revolution . . . we are unable to recognize under the 1923 rule."[40]

The 1932 uprising would prove to be a major event in Salvadoran history, and its legacy continues to affect the nation to this day. The uprising and the government's response to it will be discussed in greater detail in the next chapter. Suffice it to say for now that the uprising played a major role in shaping Martínez's strategy of governance. Among other things, it incited a reformist rhetoric that placed working people's interests at the forefront of government discourse. It also allowed Martínez to construct a sizeable police state that would become the backbone of his thirteen-year rule.

After the rebellion, the Martínez government capitalized on its enhanced position by directing its attention to the financial situation, another potential source of destabilization. The government slashed spending, cut interest rates by 40 percent, and placed a moratorium on all operations with interest for four years. In a bold move, the government also ceased all payments on the 1922 loan, thereby allowing most of the customs duties to pass directly into the government's coffers.[41] Martínez used part of that revenue to keep the military paid promptly and fully.[42] In summary, by the second quarter of 1932, the Martínez government had weathered the worst of the storm and was on its way to consolidating its hold on power.

Consolidating Power

Martínez adopted a political strategy in which he first secured control over San Salvador and then extended his authority outward to the rest of the nation. As long as the outlying municipalities did not become breeding grounds for coups or opposition movements, Martínez was willing to ignore them while he guarded against conspiracies in San Salvador and in the military barracks. Martínez initially focused his suspicion on two of the three remaining architects of the 1931 coup, Colonels Aguirre and Valdés. Rumors of conspiracy swirled around them, although it is not clear whether they actually plotted against Martínez. The U.S. chargé, William J. McCafferty, suggested that "Martínez intends to secure complete control of the army by breaking the power of the young military officers and placing older and more dependable army officers in charge of military posts."[43] Aguirre was the first to go. He reportedly moved against Martínez shortly after the rebellion of 1932. The actual timing and nature of Aguirre's alleged conspiracy are not known, but the British minister noted in May that Aguirre's plot had been stifled and that he had been demoted from the chief of police to the governorship of Cuscatlán Department (where he remained until 1944).[44] Colonel Valdés was not as lucky as Aguirre. In July 1932 he was reported to have attended a drinking session with some fellow officers, including the governor of La Libertad. During the revelry some disparaging remarks were made about Martínez, and rumors of a coup began to circulate. Martínez responded by removing Valdés as minister of war and dispatching him to Spain on a "special mission," otherwise known as diplomatic exile. Valdés remained in political obscurity for the remainder of the Martínez regime.[45]

Martínez's problems with uppity young officers did not end there; in fact, they were just beginning. In November 1932 a group of young officers in San Miguel reportedly rose up and tried to seize the barracks. The conspirators were jailed, but their ultimate punishment is not known. Martínez denounced the revolt as a "communist plot," an accusation he would use many times in the coming years to denounce conspirators.[46]

Martínez's political strategy is evident in the municipal elections of December 1932 and the deputy elections of January 1933. Just as he had done with the elections the prior year, he ignored the municipal elections and concentrated instead on the deputy elections. The government intervened only in those municipalities where electoral violence had occurred or was expected. This intervention closely resembled that of Romero Bosque in 1927; government officials brought the rival factions together and got them to settle on a compromise candidate.[47]

Comprehensive results from the deputy elections have survived. They reveal that the government's slate of candidates ran virtually unopposed and won their elections unanimously. In only 4 of the 235 voting districts did a second slate of candidates appear on the ballot. It is not clear if this slate actually constituted organized opposition to the government, or if the government simply allowed some additional supporters to appear on the ballot. In either case, none of the second slates received more than eleven votes, and each of them lost by an average of 99.9 percent of the vote.[48]

To further bolster his regime, Martínez built up the intelligence wing of the security forces. An undetermined number of police agents were converted into spies and placed at the disposal of dependable officers and governors. The ranks of this intelligence apparatus were augmented by civilian collaborators, known as the *orejas,* or "ears," of the government. Some orejas were employed formally, such as the schoolteacher in Sonsonate Department who doubled as a spy and submitted reports to the military.[49] Most civilian informants, however, were incorporated informally. Here, the military relied on its ability to cultivate an environment of suspicion and intrigue, such that people would be willing to come forth with any information that might garner them a financial reward. The labor organizer and Communist Party member Miguel Mármol described the effectiveness of the orejas. While trying to stay out of the government's clutches after surviving the matanza of 1932, he was able to avoid the uniformed officials, but he found it nearly impossible to determine who might be an informant for the police. It was an oreja who eventually fingered him in 1934.[50] In another example, a Palestinian shopkeeper, Jorge Abullarde, encountered the oreja system in June 1933 at a small social gathering of "friends." Abullarde voiced his criticisms of the Martínez government, and the next day he found himself in jail, accused of conspiring to overthrow the government.[51] The experiences of Mármol and Abullarde lend credence to the assessment by the British minister stating that "all persons opposing the government are known and closely watched and have had little opportunity to act, especially since Colonel Joaquín Valdés, minister of war, was sent into exile."[52] The governor of Sonsonate, Colonel Julio César Calderón, later referred to some "secret agents" under his authority and their intelligence-gathering missions, which had been operating for a number of years.[53]

In July 1933, political tensions increased rapidly when Martínez announced his intention to run for president for the term of 1935 to 1939. This decision was a reversal of his earlier promise to leave office after the completion of Araujo's term. Although Martínez did not address specifically the issue of competition, observers rightly assumed that he planned to run unopposed. The British minister, for instance, commented that "no organised opposition would be tolerated, and the term 'elections' is a recognised euphemism." The minister also sarcastically added that "the time-honored procedure in such cases was not to be neglected."[54] Martínez's decision to run alienated the prodemocracy sector. Miguel Molina, for instance, resigned as minister of finance in protest.[55] Molina was left in relative peace after his resignation, but other suspected advocates of democracy received less benign treatment. Manuel Mendoza, for instance, suffered an increase in police vigilance. Twice he appealed for a reprieve, promising that he was not opposing the government, but his appeals brought no relief.[56] Pío Romero Bosque and Antonio Claramount Lucero were exiled after Martínez accused each of them of organizing "communist sedition." Claramount Lucero was sent to Guatemala in August 1933, and Romero Bosque went to Costa Rica in December of the same year. It appears that both of them were exiled for trying to organize campaigns to challenge Martínez in the election. In an interview with the U.S. military attaché in Costa Rica, Romero Bosque denied that he had plotted against Martínez and claimed that his exile was a product of his supporters trying to get him onto the ballot. Claramount Lucero too was reported to have been mobilizing his supporters.[57]

Martínez's decision to run was a prescription for military revolt because it dashed the hopes of many an officer who wanted to become president. Romero Bosque commented on this problem during his interview: "this very military organization may prove Martínez's undoing. In building up the army to the point he has, placing high-ranking army officers in most of the positions of power and trust, and incidentally lucrative, he has also awakened more than one dormant ambition."[58] According to the U.S. chargé, Martínez was sufficiently worried: "It has been quite evident during the past few weeks that the Martínez Government feels considerable nervousness . . . and is taking every precaution against subversive activities."[59] Martínez responded to the potential for armed rebellion by ordering his security forces to round up suspected opponents of the regime, civilian and military alike. The U.S. chargé commented on a rumor that discontented army officers associated with civilian plotters had been imprisoned and possibly executed.[60] Miguel Mármol noted in his testimony to Roque Dalton in the late 1960s that during his tenure in prison in 1934, his fellow prisoners included a "group of cavalry officers" and "some young officers accused of being partisans with General Claramount."[61] The British legation reported in 1934 that "within the army a certain amount of discontent lingers, particularly among junior officers who, under former governments, were able to hold many positions at once and draw several salaries. This is no longer possible and officers who in the past might have drawn 300 Colones per month now receive as little as 60 after deducting taxes, contributions, etc."[62]

Martínez's problems with the military peaked in late January 1934, when an attempted coup was discovered. Among the accused conspirators was General Castaneda Castro, the minister of government and a trusted confidant of Martínez. By the government's account—the only version currently available—Castaneda Castro confessed to his involvement in the coup. He supposedly planned to bring a new political party to power, one that would take government away from both the military and the poor and give it over to wealthy planters.[63] Such a denunciation sounds suspicious because it promoted Martínez's image as a populist (see next chapter) at the same time that it denounced Castaneda Castro. Whether Castaneda Castro participated in the coup remains uncertain. The U.S. chargé described him as a man of "Presidential timber," an opinion Castaneda Castro evidently shared, judging from the fact that he briefly assumed the presidency in 1944.[64] However, it is possible that Castaneda Castro had no involvement in the coup. The British minister noted that Martínez used the coup "as a good excuse to get rid of many troublesome individuals by deportation."[65] Martínez might have fabricated Castaneda Castro's participation in an effort to eliminate a potential rival. Either way, Castaneda Castro was arrested, jailed, and placed on a list of "political enemies" that Martínez kept.[66] He remained in jail for a few weeks and was then released, only to be exiled to Panama in 1935 for allegedly participating in another plot.[67] One of the conspirators from the January 1934 coup, a Mexican lawyer, died in prison. The government claimed that he committed suicide, but as the British minister noted, "it is believed he was killed, but nothing could ever be proved."[68] Such actions suggest that Martínez intended to have nothing to stand in his way of reelection. As Romero Bosque put it, "if Martínez wishes to re-elect himself, there is no power on earth to stop him, because through the ponderous military organization he has built up he controls the country absolutely."[69] According to the British minister, "nothing short of assassination can prevent him from being reelected in January, 1935."[70]

Pro-Patria

In July 1933, shortly after announcing that he would run for president in 1935, Martínez founded the Partido Nacional Pro-Patria (the National Party of the Fatherland). Pro-Patria was created under the guise of Martínez's political party for the campaign, but in actuality it became his patronage network, the heir to the PND, which Martínez would use to consolidate political control throughout the nation. In addition to leading the charge on Martínez's campaign, Pro-Patria controlled the selection of municipal officials and deputies. In the immediate sense, of course, controlling municipal elections and winning the election of 1935 were two sides of the same coin. Martínez needed loyal supporters in the municipalities who could monopolize voting and guarantee his victory in 1935.

The supreme council (Consejo Supremo) of Pro-Patria was established in San Salvador in July 1933 and charged with building the party into a nationwide institution. In August its members outlined an efficient organizational structure that closely resembled that of its predecessor, the PND. Pro-Patria chapters (called "delegations") would be established at the departmental, municipal, and cantonal levels. Like the PND, Pro-Patria was indistinguishable from government. Martínez controlled the supreme council, governors oversaw the departmental delegations, and alcaldes monitored the municipal delegations. The departmental and municipal delegations consisted of an executive committee (*directiva*) of up to two dozen persons and an unlimited number of members. Cantonal delegations consisted only of rank-and-file members.[71]

Pro-Patria grew exponentially because each delegation was expected to organize the level immediately below it. The supreme council oversaw the formation of the fourteen departmental delegations. Affiliates from the departmental delegations then traveled to the outlying municipalities to oversee the formation of municipal delegations, whose members in turn ventured out to organize cantonal delegations. Indeed, this strategy showed demonstrable results. Although we have comprehensive data for only one department (Sonsonate), Pro-Patria's dramatic growth in that region is evident. By October 1933, municipal delegations had been founded in nine of the department's sixteen municipalities, and by June of the following year delegations existed in all eleven municipalities. At least seven of the sixteen municipal delegations had cantonal delegations; the other nine probably did as well, but we lack the corresponding lists. By October 1934, Sonsonate Department had nearly 10,000 card-carrying members, with an additional 6,500 members waiting for *carnets* (membership cards) to arrive from the capital. Two months later the total number of affiliates had risen to almost 20,000. Without corresponding lists from the rest of the nation, it is impossible to say if Pro-Patria's rate of growth in Sonsonate was exceptional. But it is clear that Pro-Patria chapters were being established nationwide, and in time they were to be found in virtually every corner of the country. As just one indicator of the degree to which Pro-Patria expanded, the government assembled a commission in 1940 to conduct a thorough survey of all the "societies, organizations, and clubs in the nation." The commission concluded that "in almost all the populations, there does not exist any society except for the subcommittee of the Partido Pro-Patria."[72]

Pro-Patria delegations mirrored local social hierarchies. The municipal delegations, and especially the executive committees of these delegations, were dominated by local elites, the same people who hoped to serve on the municipal councils. In contrast, the cantonal delegations, as well as the rank and file of the municipal delegations, consisted of commoners—day laborers, peasants, and in the western regions, Indians. It was Pro-Patria's objective not to exclude commoners, but rather to incorporate them into the ranks of the party in order to control their franchise. Pro-Patria wanted to place the voting power of the nation under its direct authority.

The municipality of Nahuizalco offers an exemplary case of the structure of a Pro-Patria delegation. The municipal delegation had 29 members, and the 17 cantonal delegations had a combined total of 283 members. The municipal delegation was dominated by the same socially prominent ladinos who had controlled Nahuizalco's political scene since 1923: Brito, Magaña, Olivares, Aguirre, and Mejía. In contrast, the 283 members of the cantonal delegations consisted of peasants, not one of whom appears on lists of Nahuizalco's landowners or moneyed citizenry.[73] Recognizably Indian surnames permeate the cantonal membership lists, including Lúe, Galicia, Crúz, Tépaz, Cúmet, Zetino, Shúl, and Campos. If we include other surnames common to Nahuizalco's Indians, such as Pérez, Cortés, and Hernández, it is safe to estimate that Indians accounted for well over 70 percent of Pro-Patria's membership in Nahuizalco.

The delegation of Sonsonate City followed a similar pattern. The executive committee consisted of thirty-five of Sonsonate's most prominent persons, including the president of the committee, Lisandro Larín, who had served as governor of Sonsonate Department under Pío Romero Bosque and as the alcalde of Sonsonate City on two occasions.[74] Another member of the committee was Héctor Herrera, who owned at least four haciendas in the vicinity of Sonsonate and had also served as national auditor under Martínez in 1932.[75] In contrast, the regular members of Sonsonate's municipal delegation consisted mostly of day laborers. Unfortunately, we have only four of the seventeen pages of the list of regular members, but the surviving pages contain the names of 119 people, 82 of whom are listed as jornaleros, or day laborers. Of the remaining thirty-seven names, only two are listed as *agricultores* (landowning farmers), while the rest are listed as some type of artisan. Data from other municipalities in Sonsonate follow the pattern set by Nahuizalco and Sonsonate. From Juayúa, for instance, we lack the lists of the cantonal delegations, but have the list of the municipal delegation, which reads like a who's-who of the region's coffee growers, including Máximo Jerez, Secundino Mata, Francisco Villacorta, Maximo Rauda Salaverría, Vicente Magaña, and Jesús Cea.[76]

Pro-Patria was thoroughly bureaucratized. Officials kept detailed membership lists, each member received a *carnet,* and the head of each delegation had to submit frequent reports detailing his group's activities and spending.[77] The party was very hierarchical as well, placing great importance on service to one's superiors. An indication of this is found in the party charter, which read, "In order to establish discipline, order and unity of action in the work of the Partido . . . the Cantonal Delegations will know only of the activities of the Local Delegation; Local Delegations of the Departmental Delegation; and the Departmental Delegations of the Supreme Council."[78] In some municipalities women's committees were formed, presumably for propaganda and organizational work, since women still were not allowed to vote.[79] The amount of work that an individual had to perform as part of his or her membership in Pro-Patria varied with the membership level. Officers on the executive committees had more responsibilities than regular members, and members in the bigger cities had more activities to attend to than members in the cantones. The average member in a cantonal delegation was expected to perform some nominal organizational work, turn out for the occasional conference or parade, and, most importantly, show up on election day.

During the municipal elections of December 1933, Pro-Patria swung into action and began gaining control over the nation's electoral process. Roughly six weeks prior to the election, Martínez informed each of his fourteen departmental governors that the municipal officials about to be elected must first meet the approval of Pro-Patria. He instructed the governors to make use of their contacts in the municipalities to produce a list of three potential candidates for alcalde from each municipality. These names were to be forwarded to San Salvador, where the supreme council would make the final decision. The goal of this process, according to the circular, was "to choose persons that most meet the needs of the nation, the department and the Partido Nacional."[80] The circular opens a window onto how the patronage system functioned under Pro-Patria. Although Martínez and the supreme council had the final say on who would be elected, it was the departmental governor and people at the local level who assembled the original list. Thus, up and down the various administrative levels, there were favors to be given and received and patronage to be dispensed.

This process is revealed in further detail by a letter from Guillermo Barrientos, a political jefe in the municipality of San Julián (Sonsonate Department), who wrote to a member of Pro-Patria's departmental delegation in Sonsonate City. Barrientos had been given the task of finding candidates in the municipalities of San Julián, Cuisnahuat, and Ishuatán.

Obviously this was a highly enviable responsibility, for it gave Barrientos the power to determine whose names were sent on to the next level for approval. Once Barrientos had settled upon the candidates, it was in his interest to see that they got elected, and so in his letter he lobbied on their behalf: "These persons are the best that we could hope to find for being in agreement with the aspirations of the National Party; for this reason I encourage you to have a prompt interview with the Governor, putting before him this list of names." Barrientos also noted in his letter that the process of selecting candidates had generated opposition amongst those factions he had passed over: "There is no lack of persons in these places, motivated by one reason or another . . . who want to undermine our sincere efforts and change these names."[81] This last comment by Barrientos predicted the multitude of requests that would pour into the departmental capitals and the national capital from local political factions looking to convince the government to change its slate of candidates.

It is interesting to note that from the list of the sixteen final candidates for Sonsonate Department, only one of them had supported Martínez during the election of 1931. Of the fifteen remaining candidates, nine had supported Gómez Zárate, one was a Molinista, and four are identified as having been neutral. This list reveals the issue mentioned above, that Martínez lacked a foundation of supporters when he came into office in 1931. The list also reveals the reward that Gómez Zárate, and by extension his followers, received for his support of the Martínez regime.[82]

The Election of 1935

As the presidential election of January 1935 drew near, it became increasingly evident that Martínez's victory was virtually guaranteed. He had exiled, arrested, or placed under surveillance all potential challengers, and most of the military was firmly under his control. Moreover, the municipal elections of 1933 and 1934 had given Martínez two opportunities to place people in municipal office who were beholden to him and his party and thus would associate their political survival with producing favorable results on election day. A unanimous victory in the election was Martínez's goal. The election was not a rote exercise of political protocol, but rather a public demonstration of Martínez's power, proof of his capacity to serve as the supreme political boss. The more votes he could generate, the more he proved that superiority.

For the election to qualify as an actual demonstration, however, people had to get out and participate in it. Predetermined elections tended to generate apathy. The assembly elections of January 1932 reportedly drew only 379 voters in the entirety of San Salvador during three days of voting.[83] For the election of 1935, the government devised a series of tactics to get people out to the polls. Government employees were informed that they had to vote. One week prior to the election they received their orders: "you are obligated to make use of their right to vote by turning out at the electoral polls in the next elections."[84] The Pro-Patria delegation in Sonsonate City put forth an innovative idea to generate votes. Its members reasoned that a simplified voting process would encourage greater participation and therefore stated, "This Delegation presents to the Supreme Council the idea that each citizen, upon presenting himself at the electoral urns, only need show his respective party *carnet* to cast his vote." But simplifying the vote was not likely to generate more voters, since the process was already quite simple. Sonsonate's delegation eventually settled on a more time-proven method of drawing people to the polls: bribery. "This Delegation has decided that on the eve of the election, we will entertain the public with a movie in the early evening and then invite everyone to a designated place at three o'clock in the morning for coffee, tamales and bread, so that they will be gathered together and organized to go to the electoral urns when they open in the morning."[85] The national government followed Sonsonate's lead, agreeing that a satiated citizen was more likely to vote. It offered its own idea for largesse: during the election, electricity and water would flow without the customary daily rationing.[86]

A few days before voting began, governors directed the municipal officials to confirm their orders as to who was to be placed on the directorios and which persons were to receive votes as deputies (assembly elections took place simultaneous to the presidential election). One governor's orders read, "Serve instructions to the Alcaldes to ensure that no variations are reported in the election of the Directorios from those names which have been sent to them by the Supreme Council of the Pro-Patria Party."[87]

The alcalde of one municipality acknowledged his orders for the deputy election: "I understand which candidates should be elected as Deputies."[88]

When the election finally arrived, the performance came off without a hitch. According to the government's statistics, 77 percent of registered voters cast their ballots during the election, a 20 percent increase over the 1931 election.[89] Whether this many people actually voted is not known. If not, members of the various electoral boards preserved the facade with steadfast determination. Throughout the three days of voting they submitted daily and sometimes twice-daily reports describing the progress of the election and the throngs of citizens turning out to vote. The commander of Cabañas Department provided a typical report: "Throughout Cabañas Department elections for supreme authorities are being conducted in the greatest of order. Voting is unanimous in favor of the noble cause postulated by General Maximiliano H. Martínez. . . . People are providing a civic and patriotic demonstration. We expect complete success."[90] Juayúa reported that "The number of votes recorded to date is 1,214, being the number recorded today 394. All voting is being gathered with total spontaneity in complete calm. All the citizens have come to vote freely."[91] The final tally counted 329,555 votes unanimously in support of General Martínez. The British minister offered the following summary of the election: "The election itself, on the 13th to the 15th January, was the usual farce. There was no other candidate, but the people were nevertheless urged to record their votes. . . . The elections for the National Assembly [also] took place, all the candidates elected . . . being Martínez men. There is no Opposition."[92]

Local Politics under Pro-Patria, 1935–1939

During the term from 1935 to 1939, local political affairs continued to be governed by the same policies that had been employed in the municipal elections of 1933 and 1934. Pro-Patria remained the political machine, and local officials had to receive approval from the party in order to hold power in the municipality. Local Pro-Patria delegations assembled the preliminary lists of candidates, which were sent to the departmental level and ultimately to the national level for approval.

Just as before, local people who had gained the confidence of the departmental governor, or of some other high-ranking party official, had tremendous power to determine candidates. One of these people was Gabino Mata Jr., a cattle rancher and coffee grower in the municipality of Juayúa (Sonsonate Department). A series of letters between Mata and the governor of Sonsonate, Julio Calderón, reveals the process by which candidates were settled upon. Mata owned land in Nahuizalco, and the governor often solicited his advice for that township as well. In one letter, for instance, Mata recommended the candidate Rafael Renderos for the position of alcalde in Nahuizalco. Mata revealed that he and Renderos had been exchanging letters for a period of time, and as a result of these exchanges, he had decided to support Renderos. "I have chosen in Renderos," wrote Mata, "a person who knows to perform his duties to the satisfaction of those who are most able to appreciate his work." This is simply another way of saying that Renderos would be a loyal party man and a dutiful follower of Mata and, by extension, of the governor. Mata then made a suggestion about the deputy election: "At the same time . . . permit me, Señor Governor, to recommend that Alfredo Schlesinger of Juayúa be substituted for Ricardo Vilanova for the position of Deputy."[93] Just a few days later, Renderos decided to take an administrative position in San Salvador, and thus Mata and the governor had to come up with another candidate. The governor sent a note to Mata asking him what he thought of Rodolfo Brito, to which Mata responded, "In regard to the slate that you have mentioned for Nahuizalco with the candidate Rodolfo Brito . . . I have no doubt that he will follow the patriotic ideals of our current order of things."[94]

If local bosses wanted to change the slate of candidates, they had to convince the Pro-Patria hierarchy to approve alternates. "Those signed below," reads one petition to the minister of government, "come to request: that in this population a seemingly very valid rumor is running that Héctor Córtez Alfaro has been proposed before your authority as the individual who should exercise the *jefatura* of the municipality in the next period; we consider him to be an unworthy person for the greater portion of this village. . . . We sincerely ask of you that whichever other person would be given the *jefatura* of the municipality will have our respectful sympathy and adhesion."[95]

In such negotiations, the current members of Pro-Patria had an exponentially better chance of convincing the departmental- or national-level officials to side with them. There appears to have been a very close parallel between those persons who held municipal office and those persons who were card-carrying members of Pro-Patria and who held positions on the local executive committees. For instance, in the municipality of Izalco in 1939, of the ten persons who made up the municipal council, five of them held positions on the executive committee of Pro-Patria; of the remaining five, three had immediate family members on the committee.[96]

Once the upper echelons of Pro-Patria decided whom they were going to sanction in the municipalities, they sent to the governor the names of those persons. In the following telegram, the subsecretary of government instructs the governor of Ahuachapán to install a particular slate of candidates in Ahuachapán City.

> December 2, 1937
> Governor, Ahuachapán
> You are informed that the superior authorities have approved definitively the following personnel for that Municipality:
> Alcalde, Dr. José Morán
> Regidores from numbers one to eight: Alfonso Salaverría, Marco Antonio Vásquez, Dr. Miguel Angel Chacón, Prof. Vicente Morales Durán, Rogelio Alvarez, José Ignacio Tobar, Juan Gertrudis Herrera, Rubén Antonio López,
> Síndico: Dr. Juan Padilla
> It is recommended that this list not be altered.
> Hermogenes Alvarado h., Subsecretary of Government[97]

The chosen candidates then brought their clients out to the polls to complete the electoral process. Pro-Patria kept fairly complete results for municipal elections after 1935, and the data from these elections show that unanimous voting was the norm. In a typical example of the kind of report that was sent to San Salvador from a locality after an election, a local boss from Guazapa (San Salvador Department) wrote after the municipal elections of 1937 that "voting has been closed with seven hundred twenty (720) voters in favor of Alcalde Joaquín Mayorga Melara. . . . The most complete order reigned."[98] The reports contained only the number of votes cast, for there was no reason to mention opposition unless a rival faction had attempted to force its way into the process.[99] Another of these reports stated that "by unanimous votes the following persons have been elected. . . ."[100] In the event that dissenting votes were recorded, the recipient was another member of Pro-Patria, and he seldom received more than a handful of votes. For example, in San Martín (San Salvador Department) in the election of 1937, precisely 351 votes were cast. Two of the candidates received 351 votes, and the other four candidates garnered only 350 votes. The four dissenting votes were cast in favor of the president of the election board.[101]

On occasion, a local boss mustered up the courage to challenge the slate approved by Pro-Patria. For example, in 1937 in the village of Jucuarán (Usulatán Department), Lupario Rivera tried to muscle his way into municipal office. Such activity did not escape the notice of Pro-Patria's hierarchy, and as soon as Rivera began to assemble his clients, local Pro-Patria affiliates fired off a telegram to the supreme council detailing Rivera's activities. Rivera was subdued, and for his attempt to operate outside Pro-Patria he was denounced as an "immoral person in every sense," the archetypal denunciation of factitious bosses.[102] When challengers such as Rivera emerged, the government responded decisively. "You are informed," reads one example, "that the Minster of War has instructed the Local Comandante, Major Antonio Calvo, to establish whatever obstacle is necessary to prevent the subversive elements from challenging the candidacy of Carlos Salazar Barrientos, a person of good and ideal character."[103]

If Pro-Patria had the power to change local bosses, it seldom did so. This fact was determined by comparing the names of persons elected as alcalde over a succession of three elections: 1937, 1939, and 1941 (after 1935, elections took place every other year).[104] We have complete lists of all the municipal officials elected in 1937 and 1939 and a list of only the alcaldes elected in 1941. I compared three departments, Sonsonate, Ahuachapán, and San Miguel. I chose Sonsonate because the corresponding documentation from *Sección Sonsonate* of the AGN allows me to include some additional information. I chose Ahuachapán for the sake of maintaining continuity with the tables in the prior chapter. For this same reason, I intended to choose San Vicente as well, but it was missing from the data of 1941, so I substituted another eastern department, San Miguel, in its place. In addition to comparing the names of the alcaldes, I also compared the names of the remaining municipal officials to determine if there were additional linkages between the successive administrations, such as persons who were elected in multiple years or who bore the same surname and were elected multiple times. As I mentioned in the preceding chapters, a shared surname does not mean that two people necessarily were related, or that they were political allies, but it is quite likely. The point of looking for these additional linkages was to fill any gaps that might open when comparing only the office of alcalde. The data can be found in table A5 in the appendix, with the additional linkages identified in a paragraph below the lists of alcaldes.

The results of the comparisons reveal that in thirty-seven of the three departments' forty-eight municipalities, Pro-Patria selected the same person to serve as alcalde in at least two of the three elections. Of the remaining eleven municipalities, where the alcalde was different in each of the three elections, the data reveal that in all but one of them, there was at least one additional linkage. This information suggests that Pro-Patria relied upon the same coterie of local political players to run municipal affairs. The party had no need to alienate powerful local bosses, so long as they got out the vote for Pro-Patria and ran local affairs in an acceptable manner. This relationship worked in reverse as well; as long as the army did not threaten the concerns of the local bosses, such as private property or the system of clientelism, they had no reason to resist a government controlled by the military.

There is also some indication that the political networks that Pro-Patria relied upon had been there continuously since the 1920s. For instance, in the municipality of Nahuizalco (Sonsonate Department), we saw in chapter 3 that the ladinos led by Rodolfo Brito and his cousin Antonio Contreras managed to oust the Indians in 1926. We see that in 1937 and 1939, Brito and his cronies are still in power in Nahuizalco. And this sense of continuity under the military is particularly evident in the case of neighboring Juayúa, an important coffee-producing village.

Data from Juayúa reveal consistency in municipal authority throughout the 1920s and 1930s. In table 7.1 we see that the same bosses who directed the municipality prior to the military regime continued to serve under Pro-Patria. To fully appreciate the information contained in table 7.1, we should understand, first and foremost, that all of the individuals listed were members of the same patronage network. This particular network was run by a powerful alliance of coffee growers led by the Mata and Salaverría families, in conjunction with Máximo Jerez and Emilio Redaelli. Mata and Salaverría were well-established, intermarried families that had been living in Juayúa since at least the 1860s. They were the pioneers of coffee production in the town and by the 1920s owned numerous agricultural properties. Máximo Jerez was a doctor from Honduras who emigrated to Juayúa in the 1910s and married into the Salaverría family. He received from Salaverría a large coffee finca and became a close political ally of the Salaverría-Mata network. Emilio Redaelli was an Italian immigrant who owned a smaller coffee finca and worked as a coffee merchant for the local coffee processing plant owned by B. Daglio, another Italian. Redaelli was a close associate of Jerez and would be killed by rebels during the insurrection of 1932.[105]

As can be seen in table 7.1, the Mata-Salaverría-Jerez-Redaelli network dominated politics in Juayúa throughout the 1920s and 1930s. Máximo Jerez served in municipal government on four occasions (1923, 1931, 1937, and 1939), Redaelli served twice before he was assassinated (1923 and 1929), and members of the Mata family appear repeatedly (1923, 1933, 1937, and 1939). Alongside these bosses were subordinates, men who were not property owners but who made a career out of holding municipal office on behalf of the dominant bosses. Vicente Rivera was one of these subordinates; he served in office four times (1925, 1931, 1937, and 1939). Similarly, Epigmeñio Hidalgo (1931, 1937, and 1939) and Ezequiel Quintanilla (1921, 1923, and 1929) each served in office three times. These last three men were essentially clients, but of a different sort, with more responsibilities and better rewards than the field laborers brought in once a year to cast votes.

National Politics, 1935–1939

Just as in municipal politics, Martínez adopted the same policies for national-level politics between 1935 and 1939 as he had employed

Table 7.1   Municipal Officials Elected in Juayúa, 1921–1939 (partial results)

December 1921
A) Miguel Mendoza (C)
R) Francisco Villacorta
R) Vicente Rivas (C)
R) José Martín Josa (C)
R) Ezequiel Quintanilla
R) Concepción Molina
R) Rafael Murillo
S) José Cruz Peñate (C)

December 1923
A) Emilio Redaelli (C)
R) Humberto Mata (C,c)
R) Ezequiel Quintanilla
R) Carlos Martínez Cea
R) Roberto Downie
R) Joaquín Olivares
R) Rafael Molina
S) Máximo Jerez (C,c)

December 1925
R) José Martín Josa (C)
R) José Cruz Peñate (C)
R) Pedro Beltrán (C)
S) Vicente Rivera

December 1929
A) Emilio Redaelli (C)
R) Francicso Rivas Cortes
R) Rafael Molina
R) Ezequiel Quintanilla
R) Rafael Murillo
R) Concepción Molina
R) José Angel Valladeres
S) Máximo Rauda Salaverría (C)

December 1931
A) Máximo Jerez (C,c)
R) Vicente Rivera
R) Alvaro Díaz (C,c)
R) Justo Zamora
R) Rafael Borja
R) Moisés Menéndez
R) Aurelio Mejía
S) Epigmeńio Hidalgo

December 1933
A) Gabino Mata, Jr. (C,c)

December 1937
A) José Agilberto Mata (C)
R) Máximo Jerez (C,c)
R) Vicente Rivera
R) Moisés Menéndez
R) Juan Felipe Quintanilla
R) Juan Antonio Magaña (C)
R) Antonio Linares
S) Epigmeńio Hidalgo

December 1939
A) José Agilberto Mata (C)
R) Máximo Jerez (C,c)
R) Vicente Rivera
R) Moisés Menéndez
R) Juan Felipe Quintanilla
R) Juan Antonio Magaña (C)
R) Alvaro Díaz (C,c)
S) Epigmeńio Hidalgo

Source: Listas de propietarios, 1912, 1917, 1926, Departamento Sonsonate, AGN, MG, unclassi-fied boxes; Listas de administraciones municipalies, Juayúa, 1921, 1923, 1925, 1929, 1931, 1934, 1937, 1939, AGN, MG, unclassified boxes; and the Libro de Actas de Juayúa, Archivo Municipal de Juayúa (AMJ).

Note: Elections were held every two years between 1921 and 1929; the election of 1925 replaced only a fraction of the 1923 slate. Between 1929 and 1935, elections were held annually. After 1935, elections returned to every other year.

Key:
C: coffee grower (at least 10 manzanas planted)   A: Alcalde   S: Síndico
c: cattle rancher   R: Regidor

between 1931 and 1935. He sought to preserve his position on top of the political pyramid by monitoring potential rivals and eliminating known rivals, especially the ever-impatient junior officers. All the while he was positioning himself to get elected to yet another term in 1939.

The intelligence network remained the backbone of Martínez's regime. He rightly understood that his impressive showing in the 1935 election was the result of his unfettered use of the regime's coercive powers. He looked to his intelligence apparatus to preserve that control. Shortly after the election of 1935, Martínez issued a decree stating that the government would tolerate no internal dissension. The decree came in response to university students' criticism of the government's decision to exile a dissident journalist. The decree claimed that internal enemies, including communists, were conspiring against the government: "The public already knows of the strong and thoughtless campaign which elements devoted to violence and disorder are undertaking against the Supreme Government. . . . That campaign has reached dangerous extremes." The government then invoked the memory of 1932 to justify an unmitigated response: "As will be remembered, the tremendous events of 1932 began in the same way. The press . . . with the only desire of gaining illegitimate popularity is fanning the bonfire of discord. But things can not follow the path that they are trying to pursue. . . . The public authorities are resolved to maintaining peace and social tranquility, imposing suitable corrective measure on the transgressors of the law and enemies of the internal order of the nation."[106] The decree was, in essence, a justification for expanding the scope and scale of the intelligence apparatus. Virtually every identifiable organization or social group fell under some form of surveillance. Occasionally the archival records offer a hint of the brutal side of this intelligence machine, such as the report from a comandante of the Guardia who informed one of the departmental governors that fifteen subversives had been "arrested and interrogated."[107]

A principal target of the government's surveillance was the students at the National University. Their proclivity for progressive politics earned them a reputation as dissidents, a somewhat deserved accusation. Miguel Mármol reported in his memoir that the students were at the forefront of efforts to rebuild the Communist Party in the latter 1930s.[108] In February

1932, Martínez had suspended the university's autonomy in order to "prevent by all legal means possible the University Institution from being converted into a center of political and antisocial propaganda."[109] The following year five students were suspended for periods ranging from one month to three years for their participation in a supposedly radical student organization, the Asociación General de Estudiantes Salvadoreños (AGEUS, General Association of University Students).[110] By 1935 the opposition between the students and the military had grown more intense. In June 1935, the student newspaper, *Opinión Estudiantil,* criticized the government for its tendency to denounce any idea that challenged its own views as being "communist." Martínez shut down the newspaper and exiled the editor.[111] It was the exile of that editor that had sparked the controversy leading to the military's decree. Martínez then introduced a spy network into the university. The spies monitored student meetings and transcribed student conversations. Even a meeting held for the seemingly innocuous purpose of choosing the color of the university's Olympic banner attracted undercover surveillance. The notes from that surveillance list both the student participants and the content of their comments.[112]

Martínez's distrust of the students emanated from his apprehension over intellectuals in general. Military leaders considered intellectuals a cause for concern because they were, by strict definition, not landowners and thus "proletarians." But whereas the countryside proletarians (campesinos) were dangerous on account of their ignorance, the intellectual proletarians, as "professionals of written thought," were capable of "molding national opinion," as was claimed by a book put out by the military surveying El Salvador's intellectual community. The book also reveals that military leaders believed that El Salvador's intellectuals were, on the whole, "marked [by] socialist tendencies." Thus intellectuals were closely watched, and a detailed record was kept of their activities. More than one of them ended up on Martínez's list of political enemies. Hugo Lindo, for instance, was on the list. At the time he was a young, apolitical poet whose public activities amounted to publishing a book of poems and working for the newspaper *Diario de Hoy.*[113]

The military kept track of many different groups. In addition to documenting intellectuals, Martínez assembled extensive lists of merchants, professionals, and wealthy people.[114] The list of wealthy people offers an impressive demonstration of the military's ability to gather information. The list is broken down by municipality and contains not only the names of well-to-do individuals, but also, in some cases, an estimation of their capital worth. Martínez was nothing if not informed.

Junior military officers remained the most immediate threat to Martínez's political survival, and they continued to launch coups against him. The first coup after the election took place in October 1935. The conspirators, a group of noncommissioned officers, tried to seize control of the artillery barracks in central San Salvador, but troops loyal to Martínez subdued the revolt and placed the conspirators in jail. The motive behind the revolt is unknown, although the government denounced it as "communist" sedition. Most of the prisoners remained in jail until August of the following year, when a war council (*Consejo de Guerra*) absolved them and sent them into exile. Also implicated in the coup was General Salvador Castaneda Castro, providing Martínez with the pretext to exile him to Panama.[115]

A second coup broke out in October 1936. It was centered in the Fifth Infantry Regiment in Santa Ana and was led by Lieutenant Rodolfo Bhaños. Evidently spies had infiltrated the conspiracy during planning, and thus the government was ready for them. Implicated along with Bhaños were his brother, his father, and another civilian. As was customary, the government denounced the coup as a "communist" conspiracy. According to the U.S. chargé, the coup had more complex origins. Trustworthy informants told him that the coup was financed by wealthy citizens from Santa Ana who had heard rumors that Martínez intended to amend the constitution to allow himself to be reelected in 1939. Hoping for a more subservient president, they sought to oust Martínez before it was too late. Martínez had Bhaños executed by a military firing squad two weeks after his arrest. Bhaños's brother received a sixteen-year prison sentence, and the remaining prisoners reportedly were released.[116] This decisive response suggests that Martínez indeed saw the coup as a serious affair.

In addition to suppressing coups, Martínez continued to eliminate his military rivals by the time-proven method of banishing them to overseas posts. One of the principal rivals, Colonel José Arturo Castellanos, suffered this fate in 1937. Castellanos was believed to be a leader of the junior officers. While on a weapons-buying mission in Europe, he was ordered to report to Liverpool, England, and assume the position of consul to Great Britain. According to the British minister in San Salvador, "the appointment is undoubtedly due to the desire to keep out of Salvador a too ambitious officer."[117]

In January 1939, a third coup attempt was uncovered just hours before it began. The coup would have been centered in the military barracks opposite the Presidential House. Apparently one of the conspirators phoned a warning to an acquaintance in the barracks, who then informed his superiors. The prisoners included some high-ranking officers: Colonel Julio Calderón, former comandante of La Libertad; General Leitzelar, retired chief of police; and Colonel José Ascencio Menéndez, former undersecretary of war. Menéndez, the identified leader of the coup, was suspected of trying to fulfill his "presidential aspirations." It was ironic that Martínez did not denounce the coup as a communist conspiracy, because it was the first coup to have actually solicited the support of the nascent Communist Party.[118] Menéndez was exiled to France, and the remaining conspirators were sent to Mexico.[119] Thus, as in his first term, Martínez's road to the next election was lined with the dashed hopes of his junior officers.

The presidential election of 1939 presented Martínez with a decidedly more precarious legal situation than had the election of 1935. In 1935, Martínez had circumvented the constitutional restriction against consecutive terms in office by claiming that his first term was actually Araujo's. In 1939 there was no such loophole, and thus the constitution would have to be amended if Martínez hoped to remain in office. The draft of the new constitution of 1939 preserved most of the content of its 1886 predecessor, with the notable difference to be found in article 92, which addressed presidential elections:

> As demanded by national interest, the citizen that will be elected President in March of the current year . . . according to this Constitution will be elected by the Deputies of the National Assembly, who are absolved this one time from applying the incapacity of Article 94 [forbidding reelection].[120]

For good measure, the updated article 92 also extended the presidential term from four to six years.

Ratification of a new constitution was a two-stage process that began in the municipalities and ended in a constitutional convention. The new constitution first had to be approved by the *cabildo abiertos,* the town-hall meetings at which the general populace theoretically voted on the proposed changes. If the changes passed the cabildos, they would appear before a constitutional convention comprised of forty-two popularly elected delegates, three from each department. The cabildos were scheduled to take place in July 1938, and Martínez turned to Pro-Patria to ensure that the process ran smoothly.[121] It seems as though Pro-Patria did not even bother having the populace vote during the cabildos, for there is no record of voting or any mention made of the voting process. Instead, Pro-Patria delegations organized public conferences and rallies, accompanied by plenty of food and fanfare, and then reported their region's unanimous support for the new constitution. Many of these reports from the municipal delegations have survived. An archetypal example is provided by the delegation of Usulután City: "Pro-Patria Delegation was opened last night amidst fevered regalia. Last night conferences were held in the central plaza and a reception was given in the Central Hotel. Today the conferences continue with the goal of holding the public session of the *cabildo abierto*. In unison the citizens agree with our patriotic ideals."[122] In this manner was Martínez's new constitution approved, clearing his path for reelection.

Martínez decided to have himself elected in 1939 by the National Assembly rather than by popular vote, which suggests that he was aware of growing opposition to his political monopoly. Whereas in 1935 Martínez had placed great emphasis on the election as a grand exhibition and had used it to display his power and his supposed popular support, in 1939 he limited that exhibition to the deputies of the National Assembly. Perhaps Martínez felt that the *cabildos abiertos* offered a sufficient exhibition. Moreover, further demonstrations of "popular" support were described by various Pro-Patria delegations, which continued to organize parades and rallies right up to the eve of the election in the assembly.[123] Evidence suggests, however, that the Martínez government was becoming wary of its opponents. Martínez knew that his self-serving motives were not as universally well received as the Pro-Patria delegations liked to report. In Santa Ana, for instance, the government faced subversive propaganda campaigns throughout the month of October 1938, in the form of broadsides plastered nightly onto public walls, calling for Martínez's resignation. One of these broadsides, signed by a group calling itself the Civilian-Military Association, proclaimed, "It is time that the head of this [constitutional] pact be convinced that the devotion to democracy in El Salvador is a tangible fact. General Martínez should not stain our fatherland with fresh blood. He should respect the prevailing Constitution. He should avoid causing the people of El Salvador to remain downtrodden forever."[124]

Perhaps the force behind the propaganda campaign was the same group of individuals rumored to have backed Lieutenant Bhaños's coup in Santa Ana in 1936. Either way, the propagandists were never captured. In addition to the propaganda campaign, Martínez was confronted with blatant dissent in his own government. In October four of his subsecretaries resigned en masse in protest of his coming third term. They included Manuel López Harrison, Hermogenes Alvarado, David Rosales, and Colonel José Ascencio Menéndez, the subsecretaries of public works, government, public instruction, and war, respectively.[125] Of the four, only Rosales managed to stay off Martínez's list of political enemies. And Colonel Menéndez, as was mentioned above, conspired to overthrow Martínez three months later. The government's concern over the flurry of opposition was more evident in December, when the National Assembly voted to maintain the state of siege, citing that "in regards to the reelection, in addition to its supporters, there are also those who oppose it."[126] Whether this resistance drove Martínez to limit his reelection vote to the National Assembly remains uncertain. At the least, it explains why, in October 1938, Martínez took the unprecedented action of fining the alcaldes of Tejutepeque and Jutiapa fifty colones each for failing to follow orders regarding the forthcoming assembly elections.[127] Martínez could afford no furtive opposition in the new assembly. The presidential election itself was a highly secretive affair. Martínez refrained from public pronouncements, and the government did not even announce the results of the voting.

Martínez's Discourse of Democracy

Shortly after securing his bid for another term as president, Martínez was confronted by an unexpected challenge, the onset of World War II. Like most of the rest of Latin America, El Salvador had little choice but to side with the United States and join the Allied cause, regardless of its leader's interests. The problem for Martínez was how to generate popular support for a prodemocratic, antitotalitarian foreign policy without animating demands for genuine democracy at home. This same challenge had beset political actors in El Salvador for decades, namely how to tout democracy in a nondemocratic system without causing it to fall apart under the weight of its own paradox. Martínez attempted to resolve this problem with a public relations campaign designed to clarify his regime's position on democracy and the war. The cornerstone of this campaign was a series of weekly radio addresses that Martínez delivered to the nation between 1940 and 1943. In them, Martínez celebrated the concept of democracy but worked diligently to define it as a personal issue, rather than a public or civic good. Democracy, he insisted, existed philosophically in one's own mind, not in the public arena of government.

The radio was an effective way of reaching large segments of the Salvadoran population. No statistics exist as to how many Salvadorans had radios and therefore what percentage of the population could have tuned in to Martínez's broadcasts. But radio was becoming one of the principal forms of mass communication, especially in nations with high illiteracy rates, and it is safe to assume that at least some portion of the Salvadoran population had access to a radio. Those whom the radio could not reach heard the message via Pro-Patria. Martínez had each of his addresses transcribed, copied, and sent out to Pro-Patria officials throughout the country, who were then expected to make the contents known to their populations. The goal was to spread Martínez's message as widely as possible.

Martínez opened his public relations campaign in October 1940, even before the United States had officially entered the war. He delivered his first speech before a group of party functionaries and followed that up with a radio address to the nation three days later. A summary of the address was sent to the Associated Press in New York. The main message of both speeches was an explicit defense of democracy. In the first address, Martínez described the defense of democracy as a sacred act:

> If the Salvadoran population is disposed to sacrifice itself to defend its democracy with all of its mental, spiritual and religious faculties, if it were disposed to do that, it would comply with the most sacred duty for the

fatherland, for its home and for humanity, and if it were disposed to do that, it would find in me a captain willing to protect these ideas mentally and spiritually for the people of El Salvador and for the entire world. . . . I want the whole world to understand that in my words and in my mind I know the meaning of the word *politics*.[128]

In the second address, Martínez defined El Salvador as a democratic country and insisted that its population unite in the defense of democracy.

We have to become politically involved because it is through political involvement that we address our economic, social, health, educational and infrastructural problems . . . and now more than ever those with consciousness among us must become politically involved because the nations of Latin America, El Salvador included, have lived democratically and that democracy is in grave danger. . . . We have a cause that is more powerful and more brilliant than the totalitarian nations, and that cause is democracy, and we must defend it.[129]

After this initial appeal to democracy, Martínez began the long and arduous task of trying to limit the public's conceptualization of democracy to an idea rather than a political structure. His argument consisted of three parts, or as he called them "logics" (*lógicas*): people are mental beings; democracy is a mental construct; and a democratic society is a conglomeration of individuals sharing those mental constructs. Martínez did not present these three logics together in any one speech or as a coherent and formal program. Rather they were themes that recurred in his addresses, without a specific order.

Martínez advanced his idea that human beings were primarily mental rather than physical beings in various forms. Sometimes he made the case explicitly, such as in his statement that "man is a mental being." Other times he was less explicit, such as when he defined humanity by its "spiritual sentiments," or when he referred to people's internal guide: "This simple word that we call consciousness is one that spiritual men have accepted, maintained, respected and loved. This consciousness is man's guide."[130]

Extending his definition of people as mental beings, Martínez considered individual merit and personal success or failure to be determined by mental state rather than accomplishments. Egoism was the worst mental state possible, and Martínez believed that most of the world's problems originated with egotistical people. Martínez denounced egoism in almost every one of his addresses. In one example, he said, "The current world is full of an egoist philosophy, which has originated with people, but which has no benefit to humanity, because the egoist man works first and foremost on his own behalf, for himself, and for his immediate family, and when he adds his fellow nationals to that list, then his nation confronts other nations, and the most powerful nation becomes that one which is comprised of men hungry to take over other people."[131]

The opposite of egoism was altruism. "It is necessary to develop an altruist philosophy," said Martínez in one address, "a philosophy based on truth that clarifies man's purpose on earth and that allows him to pursue that mission in accordance with the divine plan, with a pure mind and pure emotions."[132] Altruistic men are "happy, loving men," he insisted, they are cultured leaders dedicated to service. "If man would believe in service instead of being served, then humanity would change. The bad spirits would be directed towards new paths."[133]

Martínez situated his definition of democracy within these notions of egoism, altruism, and personal merit. Democracy was an internal phenomenon, a personal philosophy based in the "good sentiments" of the population:

> And if it is said that democracy is deeply philosophical, the reason is very simple. What is pursued by democracy? Democracy seeks out a better world, and for this it is necessary to fill oneself with deep thoughts, and the liberty that comes with awakening consciousness can only be achieved by people who live in a pure democracy that allows different men and women of that country to develop themselves amidst deeply moral principles.[134]

> In my understanding, when there are good sentiments in the people of a country, then this country wants to live in harmony with itself. This harmony promotes the establishment of democracy.[135]

Martínez defined democratic liberty similarly. It too was internal, existing in individuals' thoughts. If a person believed in liberty, then that person was democratic, and by extension, a democratic society was one in which its citizens did the same.

> Democratic countries have freedom of thought, and this freedom is the only thing that can awaken the world from its nightmare.[136]

> The highest aspiration is self-determination, as defined by people having liberty, but those people also want a government, and as a result they will have freedom of thought. That freedom of thought is democracy.[137]

> Now then, why are we democratic? Why do we see ourselves as such? Why does democracy constitute part of our spiritual base and why does democracy become implanted in our personalities? The man that today is full of vice must improve himself tomorrow. Democracy's guide is consciousness, and democracy permits mental liberty; it comes tomorrow to kill the killer that is our personality today, which is why democrats must preserve this as a gift, but with a sense of liberty that is healthy.[138]

> If we consider closely what we mean by democracy; a populace that aspires to the highest good is democratic.[139]

Implicit in these constant references to democracy as a mental state is the idea that democracy does not exist in the public sector or in political structures. Martínez rarely spoke about specific government programs. But when he did, his references to them were vague, layered with appeals to concepts like "order" and "tranquility." For example, in one address Martínez said, "This country that is truly democratic, whose citizens' lives develop harmoniously within, what does it have to offer? Order, peace, tranquility, work and a better way of life."[140] In another example, Martínez was careful to limit expectations on what a democratic government can accomplish: "A well-conceived democracy does not create new worlds, it seeks the well-being of those who live in it. A democratic government does not say to the industrialist, 'I am going to lower your labor costs, I am going to improve your condition'; to the rural landowner, 'I am going to protect your property'; to the worker, 'I am going to give you land.' This type of democratic government offers nothing but demagoguery."[141]

On one occasion Martínez described a democratic government in more effective terms, but such a government had to limit people's mental liberty in order to prevent social chaos, because chaos arose from an excess of liberty. He said, "We have to constrain man's liberty, because too much mental liberty can result in extraordinary excesses, much more grave than the criminal acts that our laws currently prohibit. Why? Because people do not have a well-developed sense of discernment and oftentimes we sink down to perverse levels that run counter to our relational lives."[142]

Martínez's distinct religious views inspired some of his views on democracy. Specifically, Martínez subscribed to theosophy, a philosophical/religious framework based in Buddhist and Brahmanic traditions that adhered to pantheism and a belief in reincarnation. Martínez rarely made specific reference to his religious views. Rather, he remained more broadly philosophical. His addresses were highly theoretical in tone, and when he spoke about political matters, such as El Salvador's position in World War II, he normally presented them in the context of reflections about human nature or the meaning of life. Martínez designed his addresses more as educational exercises than as political statements. He seemed to fancy himself a philosophical leader of the nation. In one address, for example, he presented his ten rules for achieving happiness and satisfaction. They included, among others, "Know yourself; Love those around you as you love yourself: Be careful of what you say; Monitor your instincts; Guard your thoughts; Use your talents."[143]

Martínez made direct reference to his religious views on only one occasion. He dedicated the greater part of an address in February 1941 to a discussion of the teachings of Jiddu Krishnamurti (1895–1986), a theosophist spiritual figure of Indian descent who resided in the United States. Martínez credited Krishnamurti with his ideas about egoism, altruism, and democracy, explaining that "Krishnamurti wants people to live forever by perfecting their thoughts and feelings so that one day, not long from now, this infinite life will be achieved; we will achieve it when we all understand that we are brothers who internally desire to give ourselves to one another, and this highest accomplishment will be, gentlemen, the concept of democracy."[144] Thus, Martínez's religious views and his desire to interpret the world philosophically provide one context for understanding his definition of democracy as a mental state. But Martínez's religion may simply have endowed his discourse with a particular flair, because his discussion of democracy can also be understood in the traditional context of patronage and clientelism. The supreme patron, the president, was defining his patronage network, the nation, as democratic. Such an act was a well-established pattern of the informal rules of politics—hail democracy, but structure the system so that mass expression of opinion is curtailed. In this regard, the transcripts of Martínez's radio addresses from the early 1940s might be seen as nothing special. But in fact, those transcripts are a rare and precious source, because they reveal the incredibly elaborate ways in which one particular supreme patron tried to control the meaning of democracy in the public's mind.

*   *   *

In his interview from exile in 1934, Pío Romero Bosque expressed his thoughts on Martínez's intention to run in the election of 1935: "I established an innovation, whether the people will allow a return to the old methods remains to be seen."[145] Romero Bosque's comment captures the essence of the Martínez regime as a rejection of the Romero reforms and a return to the prior political system. When Martínez came into power in December 1931, he found the system of patronage and clientelism still largely intact, despite Romero Bosque's efforts to eliminate it. Martínez defended the system and operated it in the classic sense of a political pyramid. Martínez placed himself and his immediate associates atop the pyramid, and through his political machine, the Partido Pro-Patria, he presided over a vast network of patronage that controlled municipal offices, the seats in the National Assembly, and ultimately the presidency. This chapter has illustrated the continuities between Pro-Patria and its predecessors, particularly the PND under Presidents Meléndez and Quiñónez, and thereby suggests that the military authoritarianism present after 1931 was already in place when Martínez came to power.

CHAPTER 8

POPULIST AUTHORITARIANISM, 1931-1940

In the late nineteenth and early twentieth centuries, El Salvador's economy grew rapidly under the influence of coffee. This expansion created more opportunities for some Salvadorans, but most of the rewards from coffee went to a small portion of the population. For most Salvadorans, coffee signified the decay of society and community rather than economic opportunity. In conjunction with this economic expansion, the population grew but the amount of available land diminished. The shortsighted nature of the privatization decrees of the 1880s and 1890s was becoming apparent by the 1920s as more peasants faced proletarianization. The need was great for a political system that could respond to their problems and give society as a whole an arena in which to resolve issues in a productive and peaceful manner. But the political system remained exclusive. The growth of the state and the centralization of power consolidated rather than disbanded the system of patronage and clientelism. It was a recipe for disaster.

In the 1920s, a few forward-looking people recognized the developing crisis and became convinced that reforms had to be enacted. It seems that Pío Romero Bosque was one of these individuals. He instituted a program of democratic reform that sought to give political voice to a greater portion of the nation's population. The failure of his program, in conjunction with the onset of the Great Depression, lit the fuse of a bomb. In January

1932 the explosion came in the form of a massive peasant rebellion in the western departments. The revolt occurred just six weeks after the military coup that brought General Maximiliano Martínez to power. The military reacted to the rebellion with violence on a colossal scale. Troops descended upon the western region and killed thousands of people in a few days. As the last chapter demonstrated, in conjunction with this repression, the Martínez regime adopted a reactionary political agenda, overturning the reforms of the Romero years and returning to the system that had prevailed previously.

Notwithstanding their violent response to the rebellion and their reactionary politics, many military leaders took the rebellion as a warning sign, an indication that the long-term health of society required some change. To that end, they embarked upon a reform program that sought to uplift rural workers by shielding them from the impersonal forces of the market and defending them from the abuses of certain landowners. The program was limited in its objectives and ultimately had only minimal impact on the rural poor. But the reforms left an important legacy. As one component of Martínez's governing strategy, the reformist agenda set a precedent upon which his successors would expand in coming years. The reforms also had a significant impact on certain groups, such as Indians in the western departments.

One revelation of this chapter is that El Salvador's poor, subaltern actors inserted their needs and demands into the public arena. The uprising failed to deliver a coherent message or a specific series of demands, and it is impossible to know whether military leaders would have embraced the idea of reformism in the absence of a peasant uprising. But it is evident that military leaders linked their reformism to the 1932 uprising. They had killed rural poor people by the thousands, and they continued to resist autonomous rural mobilization, but they interpreted the uprising as a sign that the peasants were disgruntled and that if nothing was done to alleviate their suffering, then future uprisings remained a possibility.

This chapter also demonstrates the Faustian bargain that elites made with the military in the wake of the 1932 uprising. They got something they wanted from Martínez: security and an avid supporter of export-led production based in privately owned estates. But in trade they got military rulers who were not necessarily beholden to them, who had their own particular perceptions and ideologies. The Martínez government's reform program may not have been very stout, but it was the first shot in a long battle between elites and the military, part of their tense marriage of convenience. As just one example of that tension, this chapter shows how hard elites had to fight against the government's plan to abolish plantation-owned convenience stores and the prohibition against paying laborers in coupons (*fichas*) rather than legal currency.

The Uprising of 1932

For all their lasting legacy, the events of 1932 lasted only a short time. The actual rebellion took place over three days, with rebels controlling most of the occupied towns for less than forty-eight hours. The exception was the remote municipality of Tacuba in Ahuachapán Department, which was under rebel control for three days. After recovering from the initial surprise, soldiers from Sonsonate City and Ahuachapán City regained control of the occupied towns even before the main reinforcement column arrived from San Salvador on January 25. Those reinforcements then swept through the countryside, murdering people by the thousands, sometimes in highly orchestrated mass executions. The slaughter lasted roughly two weeks. And then, just as quickly as it had come, the army withdrew from the western region, leaving behind the same number of troops in each town that had been there before. The repression was horrifying and brutal, but short-lived. El Salvador has dealt with the legacy of those events ever since. As the famed poet Roque Dalton once wrote, all Salvadorans "were born half-dead in 1932."[1]

The events of 1932 have been amply narrated elsewhere, so I need not repeat that exercise here. Instead, a few brief references will be adequate to provide a sense of the scale of events. Initial reports of certain "disturbances" occurring in the western departments began filtering into the national capital in the late hours of January 20.[2] Over the next three days more telegrams and reports arrived, depicting a situation that was rapidly spinning out of control: one in which local military posts were overwhelmed and municipalities were falling to peasant insurgents. The reports reveal that late in the night of January 22 and early in the morning on January 23, rebels launched a series of coordinated attacks throughout Sonsonate, Ahuachapán, and La Libertad Departments. Sonsonate Department saw the most fighting. The military barracks in Sonsonate City were assaulted, and rebels seized control of roughly half a dozen municipalities in the area, including the important and populous towns of Izalco, Nahuizalco, and Juayúa. A later telegram described the events: "Communist hordes have caused great damage in the municipalities of Izalco, Juayúa, Salcoatitán, Nahuizalco and Sonzacate. The Municipal Buildings of Nahuizalco, Salcoatitán and Sonzacate were all burned, destroying the archives. The contents of the vaults were stolen. In Juayúa and Izalco, the rebels caused considerable damage, they burned records and parts of the archives."[3] Given the extent of the reports, it is surprising how few people the insurgents killed—fewer than one hundred by the time the entire rebellion had been brought to a close.

The military's reinforcement column left San Salvador by train on the afternoon of January 24, but it was delayed by sabotage on the rail lines. It arrived in Sonsonate the next morning. By that time troops from the barracks in Sonsonate and Ahuachapán had regained control over the occupied towns and ended the rebellion. Opposition from the poorly armed rebels had evaporated before the military's firepower. At that point the retributions began. The well-fortified and fast-moving military units swept through the insurgent regions one village at a time, killing peasants both indiscriminately and in highly orchestrated mass executions. Only a few eyewitness reports of the massacre survive. One of the more poignant accounts comes from a North American missionary who was living in the municipality of Juayúa at the time. He survived the rebellion behind the locked door of a house in the center of town and then witnessed the summary executions. "All day long, and this lasted for several days," he wrote, "we could hear the shots in the plaza as the work of execution went on."[4] A Canadian naval officer who traveled to San Salvador from Sonsonate on the twenty-fifth reported:

> During this trip many dead bodies of Indians were observed along the railway lines specially [sic] around Sonsonate. It was also noticed that nearly everyone walking about carried a small white flag which they waved continually to show they were not red; many residences also had large

white flags displayed in a conspicuous place. It is doubtful whether these white flags influenced the troops patrolling the country, as one body was observed lying dead with the white flag still in his hat.[5]

Another eyewitness account comes from El Salvador's Communist Party (PCS). Although persecuted and standing on the brink of collapse, the central committee sent one of its members, "Comrade M," to the western zone on a reconnaissance mission. "M" made the following report:

> Mass arrests took place. In the evening the jails were vacated, the prisoners were taken to the surrounds of the city of Sonsonate, mass shootings took place. The bodies were left exposed on the streets. . . . Entire villages abandoned by our comrades were reduced to ashes by the government troops. . . . Our comrades were hanged by the tens and their bodies remained hanging for a few days. Suspicious elements were arrested. Emergency decrees were put into effect by the government. . . . No village was left [untouched], no finca, no plantation. Executions took place of all suspicious elements, not sparing women and children."[6]

From these and other accounts of the repression, it is evident that the military responded to the rebellion quickly, harshly, and relentlessly.

As quickly as the military put down the rebellion, it stopped the massacre and vacated the western region. A similar scenario played out in each of the once-occupied municipalities: a military unit arrived, regained control of the township, returned the local authorities to power, and departed shortly thereafter, leaving behind the same number of troops that had been stationed in the town prior to the rebellion.

The mixed responses from local officials in the wake of the rebellion make evident the military's rapid departure. The officials initially thanked the military for saving them from the rebels. Officials in Izalco wrote, "In the name of the Izalqueño people, we send our most express gratitude to the Constitutional President of the Republic, General Maximiliano Hernández Martínez, for the opportune dispatch of troops to this city, when it was under the control of the communist bandits."[7] But gratitude quickly gave way to trepidation as the military units departed. In Tacuba, for example, the military remained only two days, between January 25 and 27. The alcalde of Tacuba responded to the sudden withdrawal by protesting to the departmental governor, "We have been liberated by way of the [military's] energetic persecution, but without having been left with a military detachment sufficient to maintain the regained territory, nor to continue the persecution. . . . The communists are numerous and are waiting in ambush, and at any moment will launch a surprise assault."[8] Most of the municipalities were not vacated as quickly as Tacuba, but in the coming days all underwent a similar experience.

Local officials in some municipalities attempted to convince the military to stay longer, or at least to leave behind more soldiers. Only a few municipalities succeeded in doing so, and they had to assume all financial responsibility for the soldiers, including their salaries and daily necessities. Juayúa was granted an additional military detachment, but in return the government decided to relocate Juayúa's post of the Guardia Nacional. Upon being informed of the plan, the alcalde of Juayúa pleaded for the guard post to remain: "The Guardia is essential to the peace and tranquility on the fincas and in the countryside of this region. . . . Without the Guardia the agricultural work will be subjected to the crimes of bad elements still in the mountains. Juayúa contributes more than 200 million colones to the nation and has demonstrated high patriotism at every opportunity. We help the Government and are currently paying a detachment of soldiers that is also part of the national defense, and we consider it just that you do not abandon our interests."[9] The military's response to the plea is not known, but the appeal demonstrates the extent of the military's withdrawal from the west.

Instead of leaving its own forces behind, the military created a paramilitary force called the Civic Guard (Guardia Cívica).[10] Civic Guard units were established in each municipality and local "patriotic" citizens were enlisted to serve in their ranks. Participation in the Civic Guard was voluntary, and all costs, including uniforms, weapons, and rations, were incurred by the local community; members of the Civic Guard received no pay. To finance these costs each municipality formed a Comité de Defensa Social (social defense committee), which solicited donations from local citizens. The initial task of the Civic Guard was to dispose of the thousands of bodies left in the wake of the massacre.[11] Ultimately, the main duty of the Civic Guard was to serve as the eyes and ears of the military, patrolling the villages, especially at night, and reporting evidence of further rebel activity.[12]

The military's rapid withdrawal from the west signified the national government's intent to put a quick and formal end to the massacre. The military's decision to avoid the use of prolonged and overt repression is evident in the case of Huizúcar, a predominantly Indian village located roughly ten kilometers to the south of San Salvador.[13] On the night of January 29, armed rebels from the area stormed the municipal plaza and attempted to seize control of the municipal hall, but were thwarted by the timely arrival of military units.[14] As elsewhere, the military departed the village shortly after restoring order. Two weeks later the rebels again attempted to destabilize the local government, this time by sending a written denunciation to the national government accusing the ladino mayor, Vicente Platero, and the entire municipal council of opposing the military regime. Upon receiving a copy of the denunciation, Platero sent his own letter to the capital, in which he identified the solicitors as "the same individuals who had participated in the seditious uprising." The departmental governor launched his own investigation and concurred with Platero, recognizing the strange turn of events that now had the rebels presenting themselves as allies of the military in order to denounce the local government. "Those who denounce the Alcalde of Huizúcar," noted the governor, "are contrary to our government and its institutions, having already manifested their sentiments during the communist sedition. . . . They are full of bad intentions and threaten to introduce disorder and anarchy."[15] But the national government responded to the affair in Huizúcar by instructing Platero to "not take into account their denunciation"; in other words, simply ignore them.[16] No further military campaigns were launched around Huizúcar, or in any other municipality for that matter.

The military's nonreaction in Huizúcar and its rapid demobilization in the entire western region are emblematic of its overall approach to the countryside after of the massacre. Military leaders believed that the long-term stability of the countryside depended on reform rather than repression. They based this belief upon a specific interpretation of the rebellion and its causes. According to this interpretation, the rebellion was caused not by communism, but by the incessant poverty and oppression that peasants endured in their daily lives in the countryside. Granted, the rebels were constantly referred to as "communists" by newspaper reporters, local officials, military spokespersons, and subsequent writers alike. But military leaders believed that the communists were few in number and that their role in the rebellion had been limited to organizing. For instance, the military kept an ongoing list of persons suspected of belonging to the PCS. As of October 1931 the list contained only 340 names, and more than 70 percent of those named came from San Salvador. Notably, Sonsonate Department had fewer than twenty-five members.[17] Communist Party documents in the Comintern Archive in Moscow, Russia, corroborate the military's figures almost exactly. A member of the party's central committee who testified before the Comintern's New York office, the Caribbean Bureau, in late 1932, reported that by the end of 1931 the party had four hundred members, almost three hundred of whom resided in San Salvador, and only eighteen of whom were based in Sonsonate Department.[18] In his first public address after the rebellion, Martínez provided the following interpretation of the role of the communists: "When this country was suffering from the effects of a depressed economic situation, the Communists, enemies of peace and the Fatherland, endeavored to throw the Republic into the most tremendous disorganization. With idealistic aspirations for improvements in favor of the champions and workers in general, the Communists took advantage of those peoples' simple-mindedness . . . and convinced them to rise up against the constituted authorities and the leading classes of society; the Communists promised them a radical change in the institutions under which they live."[19] Martínez and other military leaders might be suspected of falsely minimizing the extent of communist influence simply to dismiss peasant revolutionary sentiment and to affirm national unity. But Communist Party documents in the Comintern Archive reveal, in the words of party leaders themselves, that the party was wracked by confusion and disorganization in the months leading up to the rebellion.[20] In their reports to New York and Moscow, party leaders described a situation in which the party was dealing with a variety of internal conflicts, especially the lingering sentiment of what some party leaders referred to as "bourgeois" values amongst the cadres. For more than one year after it was founded in March 1930, the party invested much of its time and energy in searching for "bourgeois reformists" in its ranks and educating its members in Marxist ideology. When the party finally turned to organizing in the west in the middle of 1931, it confronted a host of problems that limited its capacity to build contacts with the western masses, especially the issue of ethnicity. The PCS consisted almost exclusively of urban ladinos, whereas the rural regions of the west were predominantly Indian.[21] Military leaders were probably not aware of the party's internal problems, but they seem to have believed that the organized left was not the primary cause of the insurrection. Rather, they interpreted the communists' ability to organize as a consequence of social conditions, and thus the way to avoid future rebellions was to address those conditions, not simply attack the organized left.

Interpreting 1932

Contemporary military leaders' complex interpretations of the uprising stand in contrast to long-held assumptions in historiography. Since the onset of the modern historiography of 1932, which more or less begins with the 1971 publication of *Matanza,* the seminal study by the North American historian Thomas Anderson, received wisdom has held that communism was the main cause of the 1932 uprising.[22] The basic premise of this argument, which has been labeled "communist causality," is that the origins of the rebellion are to be found in the organized left, including the Communist Party, its affiliated labor union, the Federación Regional de Trabajadores Salvadoreños (FRTS, Regional Federation of Salvadoran Workers), and its sister organization, the Socorro Rojo Internacional (SRI, International Red Aid). All of these organizations had their origins in urban areas, mainly San Salvador, among the nascent urban working class that had begun to emerge as a demographic and social force in the 1910s and 1920s. According to communist causality, the urban-based radicals targeted the western countryside and its rural population for organizational mobilization starting in the late 1920s, once they had gotten their own affairs in order. To that end, they sent organizers out to the western region, including the famed Salvadoran activist Farabundo Martí, who headed up the SRI but was on close working terms with the Communist Party. On account of the skills and diligence of organizers like Martí, and the receptivity of the western masses due to their miserable living conditions, the prospect of armed rebellion emerged. The decision to move forward with the rebellion and its subsequent organization rested with the leaders of the radical left. Supposedly, they planned the rebellion, decided upon its strategy and timing, and delivered their directives to the western masses. One of the supposed reasons for the failure of the rebellion is that the organizational center of the radical left fell apart in the critical days leading up to the proposed start. A main cause of this collapse was the arrest of Farabundo Martí in San Salvador and the subsequent seizure of a cache of homemade bombs and detailed plans. His arrest threw the organizational infrastructure into disarray, and when the day of the uprising arrived, the masses were more or less left to their own devices.[23]

Anderson's *Matanza* is a foundation of the communist-causality narrative, but another decisive contributor was the testimonial of Miguel Mármol. The young shoemaker from the environs of San Salvador got involved with the FRTS in the 1920s and went on to be one of the co-founders of the Salvadoran Communist Party in 1930. He was in El Salvador during the events of 1932, survived the massacre (barely), and went on to take a leadership role in the Communist Party. In 1967 he met up with the famed Salvadoran poet and communist activist Roque Dalton in Prague. Mármol was returning from a trip to the USSR, and Dalton was in exile for political activity in El Salvador. Their chance encounter led to Mármol telling Dalton his life story, which Dalton recorded in a series of handwritten notes and then turned into a five-hundred-page testimonial that was first published in Costa Rica in 1972. Even though it was not published in El Salvador until many years later, Mármol's testimonial had a tremendous impact on popular understandings of 1932. It was a harrowing page-turner that placed the events of 1932 at the center of Marmol's life. The book contributed to the solidification of communist causality by making the Communist Party and its affiliated activists, such as Farabundo Martí, primary actors in the uprising. After all, Mármol was a Communist Party member, and he told his story from his own perspective, which revolved around the activities of the party and party leaders' decisions leading into the uprising.[24]

The communist-causality approach found a receptive audience in El Salvador in the 1970s because of the country's growing political polarization. The militant left and its supporters were primed to embrace communist causality because they were organizing for revolution in El Salvador. A communist-causality reading of 1932 provided precedent for contemporary endeavors, in which urban radicals were trying to mobilize the population, including rural workers. Roque Dalton himself embraced militant revolution; not coincidentally, he was working on the final draft of *Miguel Mármol* as he was preparing to return to El Salvador and join one of the nascent guerrilla organizations. Similarly, the right was equally ready to embrace communist causality because it too found precedent in it for contemporary activities. The story of communists organizing an insurrection in 1932 but being trounced by the Salvadoran military, along with armed civilian paramilitaries, was an ideal prologue for the right's counterinsurgency activities.

Another reason that communist causality had such argumentative power is that the range of sources available to scholars at the time was exceedingly thin, and those sources that did exist referred ubiquitously to the rebels as communists. While, in hindsight, those sources can be read against themselves in opposition to communist causality, the simple fact that the word *communism* appeared in them so frequently seemed to confirm interpretations found in *Matanza* and *Miguel Mármol*. Hence, even a new study in the 1990s described the uprising as communist and the radical organizations as becoming "hegemonic" in the west.[25]

One of the first alternatives to the communist-causality approach was provided by Costa Rican historian Héctor Pérez Brignoli. In the early 1990s he reinterpreted the extant documentary record as showing that the uprising was more like an indigenous village riot from the colonial era than a modern insurrection led by a militant left. His effort lacked the substantiation of new archival evidence, but it represented a significant step in opening up the interpretive environment.[26]

The appearance of new evidence in the 1990s and 2000s pushed the interpretive debate about 1932 further. The main elements of this new evidence consist of four bodies of material: archival documents from El Salvador that become available for the first time in the late 1980s; the correspondence between the PCS and the Moscow-based Comintern, which was housed in a Moscow archive and became available for the first time after the collapse of the Soviet Union; a series of nearly two hundred interviews with aged residents and their family members in western El Salvador, conducted by a team of researchers under the co-direction of North American historian Jeff Gould in the late 1990s and early 2000s; and the personal papers of Roque Dalton, including his original handwritten notes from the interview with Miguel Mármol, which the Dalton family had in Cuba and began to make available to selected researchers in the mid-2000s.

All of these new materials have enhanced significantly the breadth and depth of our knowledge about the events of 1932. Unfortunately, when it comes to interpreting the causes of the uprising, the motives of the insurgents, and the specific manner in which it was organized, the lacuna in source materials persists. Even the interviews done under Gould's guidance, which form a substantive basis of *To Rise in Darkness,* the study of 1932 he coauthored with Aldo Lauria-Santiago, are limited in this regard. As Gould and Lauria-Santiago point out, of the nearly two hundred interviewees, only two admitted to participating in the uprising. Documents from Salvadoran archives are similarly modest in their contribution to the issue of causality, although they are not irrelevant. And the materials in Dalton's archive are revealing in a distinct way. They challenge us to read the Mármol testimonial with a more critical eye and thereby question its communist-causality approach. According to the reading of Dalton's materials by historian Héctor Lindo-Fuentes, myself, and literary scholar Rafael Lara-Martínez, Dalton injected a lot of his emergent-guerrilla self into the published version of Mármol's testimonial. The original notes from the 1967 interview in Prague seem to offer less support for communist causality than the final published version. Our interpretation is that Dalton's escalating militancy at the time encouraged him to interpret the events of 1932 more from a communist-causality perspective, and so when he compiled the notes from his interview with Mármol into a narrative, he subtly emphasized (presumably unconsciously) those aspects of the story that enhanced the agency of the militant organizations.[27]

The materials from the Comintern Archive offer the most direct look into the militant organizations and their activities leading up to the insurrection. Thus, readings of them stand at the center of historiographical debates over the rebellion. I was the first to gain access to those materials in the early 1990s and offered my interpretation of the 1932 uprising based on them starting with a pair of articles in 1998.[28] My basic claim is that the materials reveal that the organized left, including the Communist Party, the FRTS, and the SRI, was ensconced in highly partisan internal debates over ideology and strategy. Its members thus remained focused on their own affairs, centered mostly in the urban areas, and did not get around to organizing the masses of the western countryside until well into 1931. When they did begin to focus their attention on the west, their members remained divided over objectives, mainly whether or not armed insurrection was viable. The official line of the Communist Party, which coincided with interpretations by the Caribbean Bureau in New York and the Comintern in Moscow, was that El Salvador was not ready for armed insurrection, and thus any attempt to organize a revolt at that time would be counterproductive to the long-term prospects of socialist revolution. Adherents of the party line accused their militant counterparts of being bad Marxist-Leninists, calling them "putchkists" and saying that they held "petit bourgeois" delusions.

My reading of the evidence contends that even those radicals who advocated for insurrection had insufficient time, staffing, or knowledge of the western countryside to have made the inroads necessary to organize an uprising on the scale of 1932.[29] In particular, almost every member of the militant organizations was an urban ladino, whereas the overwhelming majority of residents in the western countryside, especially in those regions at the center of the insurrection, were Indian. The documents in the Comitern Archive are notably devoid of references to the ethnic dimensions of the western countryside.

The Comintern materials lack evidence relating directly to the details of organizing in the west, so they remain limited in what they can tell us—and that absence is revealing in and of itself. Whatever may have been going on in the western countryside, it was not preoccupying the leaders of the radical organizations, nor was it dominating their correspondence with New York and Moscow. Furthermore, in the final weeks and days leading up to the insurrection, the leaders of the various organizations, including Farabundo Martí, were in San Salvador, trying desperately to cobble together an organizational strategy, and none of them demonstrated deep or intimate awareness of conditions in the west.

Thus, I have argued that the causal agency for the 1932 uprising should be pushed away from the militant left and its official organizations and towards the western masses and their distinct social organizations, perhaps the remaining indigenous community structures, such as the co-fradías. Evidence of those subjects remains thin, so we still face serious limitations. But my reading of the Comintern materials suggests the need for it. Subsequently, I believe we should place special emphasis on available evidence that shows the long-standing organizational autonomy of the western masses, especially in those municipalities where the uprising actually occurred. I refer here to the history of ethnically based electoral battles between Indians and ladinos in Nahuizalco from the mid-1880s to 1932 (see chapter 3), as well as to the rapidly shifting patronage alliances of the Indian leader José Feliciano Ama and his supporters in Izalco. As described in chapter 5, Ama made an alliance with the PND under Meléndez-Quiñónez in the early 1920s, apparently serving as a local leader of the Liga Roja. In the 1931 presidential election, Ama and his supporters threw their weight behind the candidacy of Alberto Gómez Zárate, even though the local populist landowner Arturo Araujo would seem to have offered them a more ideologically favorable alternative. Only after Gómez Zárate's defeat did Ama and his supporters form an alliance with the Communist Party (see chapter 6). I believe that evidence suggests that the uprising had roots in distinct forms of local organizing. In particular, whatever the reasons for which Ama and his supporters formed a link with the PCS, it would be myopic to argue that it was based on a substantive understanding or appreciation of what the members of the Communist Party stood for and ultimately hoped to achieve. Instead, their alliance would have grown out of their own interpretations of their immediate surroundings and their belief that the Communist Party was their next best hope for an external ally to replace their most recent and failed contact, Gómez Zárate. It is also evident from the materials in the Comintern Archive that the leaders of the radical left who advocated for insurrection considered themselves to be the coordinators of the insurrection, and so when they described affairs to the Caribbean Bureau in New York, they appeared to be in charge, regardless of their actual command of the events as they unfolded in the western countryside.

My views stand in contrast, to some degree, to the interpretations offered by Gould and Lauria-Santiago in *To Rise in Darkness,* the most substantive rendering of 1932.[30] In addition to having access to the materials in the Salvadoran archives and their interviews with western residents,

Gould and Lauria-Santiago also acquired the Comintern materials, although they did not have access to Dalton's papers or our rereading of them at the time they wrote their book. *To Rise in Darkness* advances a moderately counter-revisionist argument, to the extent that it shifts some attention back towards the formal organizations of the militant left. Notably, Gould and Lauria-Santiago tweak one of the long-standing centerpieces of communist causality by accepting the Communist Party's limited role. But in its stead they elevate the SRI, and to a lesser extent the FRTS, by endowing them with greater organizational capacity and success in the western countryside. Gould and Lauria-Santiago are nuanced in their interpretations, specifically opposing the "general tendency to deny subaltern agency in the movement." Certainly, one of their most prominent contributions is their claim that local residents in the west made the radical organizations, especially the SRI, their own and pushed their leaders towards radical militancy faster and in ways that they would not necessarily have chosen on their own. As they put it, "The campesinos of central and western El Salvador took advantage of the unfixed, nonsectarian position of the SRI to recreate it in their own image." They add that "the largely peasant and rural worker movement transformed the SRI from an organization designed to defend the left and the labor movement against political persecution into a radical social movement."[31]

The subtlety of that argument represents a significant advance in the historiographical development of the uprising. Nevertheless, Gould and Lauria-Santiago often push the focus back towards the leadership of the radical organizations and credit them with making organizational inroads among the rural people in the west. Those leaders supposedly bridged the rural-urban and ladino-indigenous divides. In support of those arguments they cite uncritically statements made by leaders of the radical organizations that portray their organizational autonomy over the western masses, like Mármol in his testimonial and others in the Comintern records, such as the leader who claimed that "the masses only follow the PCS."[32]

It is in their reading of some of the evidence, especially the materials in the Comintern Archive, that I diverge with Gould and Lauria-Santiago. The Comintern Archive provides the only references to the numbers of possible supporters and members of the radical organizations. Those

numbers diverge wildly and need to be viewed with skepticism. On the
one hand, various members of the radical organizations bemoan their lack
of support and their limited ability to organize due to persecution, a lack
of resources, and so forth. The Central Committee of the Communist
Party in fact revealed that at its height the party had only five hundred
members, the majority of whom lived and worked in San Salvador. On
the other hand, various informants from the radical organizations claim
in their correspondence with New York or Moscow that they had many
thousands of adherents, either actual members or allied supporters, especially throughout the western countryside. It strikes me that these claims
are often made by people trying to present an image of organizational
strength to their superiors in New York and Moscow. One of the main
incentives for doing so emerged in late 1931, when the leaders of the
radical organizations realized that an armed insurrection was brewing in
the west and that they were unable to stop it. They began making desperate pleas to the Caribbean Bureau to send money, weapons, and fighters to
assist them, a sure incentive to make fantastic claims about the number of
their supporters and their organizational control over them in hopes of
receiving a positive response from New York. Similarly, even before the
reality of a rebellion was clear to them, the leaders of the radical organizations had incentive to make claims about their organizational success
among the masses in order to appear capable before their superiors in New
York and Moscow. Whenever numerical claims are cited, like the SRI's
claim of recruiting 500 new members in the Zaragosa region in November
1931, or the claim by the FRTS that it had 1,700 union members in Nahuizalco in September 1930, I remain suspicious. I believe that a closely
contextualized reading of the documentation is necessary.[33]

Gould and Lauria-Santiago tend to discredit those individuals who
play down the organizational capacity of the radical organizations and
boost the legitimacy of those who claim the opposite. An example of the
former is Jorge Fernández Anaya, the Mexican communist who was sent
by the Comintern to El Salvador in 1929 to assist the radicals in the labor
movement in their organizational efforts. He was a strong adherent of the
so-called party line that held that El Salvador was not ready for an insurrection, and thus most of his correspondence provides support for that
claim. Gould and Lauria-Santiago suggest that he suffered from feelings of

inadequacy about his ideological views vis-à-vis his superiors in New York and Moscow, and thus his interpretations need to be questioned.[34] On the other side of the argument, Gould and Lauria-Santiago cite a 1936 document from the self-identified Santa Ana comrades, who provided their superiors in New York with a historical summary of the insurrection. Ironically, the comrades blamed the uprising's failure on Anaya and his supporters in the party, even though they were anti-insurrectionary. By contrast, the comrades bolstered the image of their fellow countrymen, Farabundo Martí and his supporters in the SRI, and attributed to them whatever positives could be gleaned from the events. Gould and Lauria-Santiago read this document as evidence of "the emergence of the SRI as the leading organization of the left, displacing the FRTS."[35] I think the document needs to be read in an alternative light, as an attempt by the Santa Ana comrades, probably former members of the SRI and supporters of Martí, to revise the narrative of past events to serve their contemporary political needs. They stated explicitly that they were competing with rival factions in San Salvador for leadership of the left and recognition from the Comintern. They used the story of the uprising to promote themselves, which they believe necessitated disparaging Anaya and his supporters, and thus whatever they say about the uprising needs to be read through that self-serving lens.[36]

These debates over the uprising of 1932 are similar to historiographical debates over the nature and origins of the revolutionary upsurge in the 1970s and 1980s. Did the organizational impetus for that upsurge rest with the radical organizations and their leaders, who originated in intellectual circles in San Salvador, or with peasants who developed their consciousness and militancy autonomously and then approached the radical organizations in search of allies? Or was it some subtle, dialectic combination of the two? Just as in the case of 1932, answers to those questions have evolved along a continuum, with many focusing on the radical organizations and their leaders, and countervailing challenges trying to shift the focus to the countryside and its inhabitants. More research is forthcoming, and invariably the debate will be enriched by these added contributions.[37]

These historiographical debates are important to unraveling the story of El Salvador's past, but ultimately they are detailed and highly specific,

and they need not mask a common appreciation by all scholars of 1932:
the uprising represented a massive statement by El Salvador's subaltern
and popular sectors, urban and rural alike, that the status quo was unsat-
isfactory.[38] Some of the rebels may have believed the uprising had a genuine chance to succeed, whatever success meant to them. Others, especially
leaders in the radical organizations, made clear in their writings that they
believed the uprising was doomed to fail and that whoever participated in
it was likely to die, but they joined up anyway. Brave or foolhardy, clear or
confused, the rebels forced onto the bargaining table the needs of El Salvador's poor. The next questions were, how was the event interpreted at the
time, and what did policymakers do in response?

The Aftermath of 1932: The Military Shapes a Policy toward the Countryside

The military's overwhelming response to the uprising had many tragic
consequences, but one stands out for our present purposes. Not only did
the massacre result in mass murder, but by so thoroughly devastating the
organizational basis for the uprising, it also hindered the rebels' ability to
shape the post-uprising narrative. Most of the rebels were killed or otherwise silenced in the aftermath such that their first-person accounts were
lost forever. We know very little about what motivated them, how they
organized the rebellion, and what they hoped to achieve by it. Even within
the Communist Party, the debilitating crackdown caused competing and
contradictory narrative threads to take hold among its surviving members.
One of those threads disavowed any party involvement with the uprising;
another credited party leaders with organizing the rebellion, but only for
the sake of delivering a stern lesson to them about the errors of acting
rashly. Subsequently, the process of imbuing the 1932 uprising with meaning was left to those who had the freedom and power to speak, governing
military officials paramount among them. The version of events that they
promoted thus played a disproportionately large role in establishing enduring discourses about the events of 1932. Hence, for those who were
inclined to distrust the military officials' narrative, the publication of
Miguel Mármol's testimonial version of the events in 1972 was a major
event.

Military leaders used the term *communist* to refer to the rebels, but they did not harbor illusions that El Salvador was infested with communists by the thousands, or that an international communist conspiracy was responsible for the rebellion. Instead, they looked for explanations in the internal conditions of their own country, recognizing that the overwhelming majority of participants in the uprising were desperately poor, rural inhabitants who were struggling under the burdens of the Great Depression. Military leaders reasoned that if the poverty of the campesinos could be alleviated, the communists' message would fall upon deaf ears and future episodes of insurrection would be prevented. To that end, shortly after the massacre, spokespersons began to publicize informally the government's intention to initiate a reform program in the countryside. Martínez was the program's public face, and while his exhortations cannot be taken to speak for the military as a whole—a large and sprawling institution—they do represent the public posture of the government and shed light on the thoughts and ideas of the main decision makers. In his February speech before the National Assembly, Martínez proclaimed that the causes of the rebellion would be eradicated if the lives of working people were improved:

> It was painful for my Government to have had to use such severe measures of military repression . . . but they were indispensable to protect society, property and family. . . . This exacting work does not have to reoccur. It is up to the Government and the leading classes of society to unite before this urgent necessity and assure the country a tranquil and prosperous future for everyone. We must study and resolve without delay the problems that exist between capital and labor. . . . [The goal of] official activity is to improve the condition of the working classes; to establish just relations between capital and labor; to create secure employment; and to improve the standards of living and subsistence. . . . In El Salvador there is only one justice, equal for everyone, poor and rich, knowledgeable and ignorant.[39]

Five months later, in a July 1932 interview with one of San Salvador's daily newspapers, Martínez stated that "his greatest preoccupation during these days is an improvement in the condition of the proletariat."[40] In another interview, he linked the "protection of the campesino" to the "liberation of the nation from Bolshevism"[41]

Military leaders rested their approach on the belief that El Salvador was comprised of three main social groups: the rural working class (broadly lumped together under the term *campesinos,* or peasants), the landowners, and the military. Each group was an integral, albeit unequal, partner in Salvadoran society. Campesinos provided labor; landowners offered knowledge and skills; and the military represented honor and order. This ideology operated on a step-by-step logic: progress was the goal, but progress required order; order derived from social harmony, and harmony came about only when landowners and laborers got along. Thus military leaders defined as their fundamental goal the harmonization of relations between capital and labor.

The Martínez regime presented a comprehensive summary of its ideological approach in a lengthy article published in the editorial section of the official newspaper. The article was published in February 1933, by which time, as will be presented below, many policies already had been enacted. But, in the first year after the rebellion, the urgent need for action sometimes meant that the formulation of ideology, its public presentation, and policy making happened at uneven rates. The article first called for the improvement in the lives of the working class:

> Our population must recognize that the rights of the proletarian sector are an undeniable national imperative. . . . If we desire to continue to live in a harmonious society with guarantees . . . we must resolve the conflict between capital and labor. . . . Our social stability depends upon granting rights to the proletariat.

Next, the article drew upon the example of Europe's corporatist states:

> This same problem, but in larger, graver proportions, presented itself in Austria, Italy, Romania and other Balkan countries. . . . The governments of these countries, before the multitudinous clamor of the lower class, instigated an immediate revision of the administrative systems of work. They regulated salaries to be in accord with living costs; they distributed land that was owned by the state; they built extensive neighborhoods of

low-cost housing; ultimately, they brought to the proletariat conditions of well-being and opportunities for subsistence. . . . But here, amongst us, the proletarian workers, by virtue of force and never-ending work, are fundamentally denied the riches produced for others.

Finally, the article announced that the national state would assume an unprecedented and active role in the dissolution of social conflict:

> It is precisely the moment to confront our problem with a completely new initiative. The times have changed, almost radically, and they have forced us to examine the future functioning of our institutions. . . . Today there is profound satisfaction in the initiation . . . of a great project of restoration and aid for the same [campesino] class that suffers from the absence of all necessities.[42]

The article was a call to action, but what type of action? Who did military leaders identify as the exploiter of labor? Who were the "others," according to the article, who denied the workers their rightful riches? Military leaders could not avoid the evident causal relationship between the poverty of the campesinos and the wealth of the landowners. The minister of war described the rebellion as a product of "that old problem . . . the struggle between the classes."[43] But military leaders did not consider the upper class as a whole to be responsible for the plight of the peasantry; to have thought so would have been an ideological contradiction, because they rejected class struggle, believing that class differentiation was a natural and proper condition for society. They considered private property to be a basic feature of society, and Martínez repeatedly emphasized his commitment to it, as in one speech in which he proclaimed that "the private economy is the base . . . upon which rests the prosperity of our nation."[44]

Rather than the upper class as a whole bearing responsibility for the poverty of the peasantry, military leaders blamed individuals. They believed that certain irresponsible and, as General Castaneda Castro, the minister of war, put it, "unscrupulous" elites caused disharmony.[45] They were the ones who refused to respect the humanity of their workers by overworking them, paying them in fichas rather than in legal currency, and expropriating their subsistence crops. The governor of La Libertad expressed this belief shortly after the rebellion in a comment that appeared in one of the main newspapers: "The landowners have inflicted upon the campesinos a series of abuses . . . but if we look closely we will recognize these as isolated phenomena. . . . Now is not the hour to place blame on this or that social or political sector."[46] In other words, the problem was with individuals, not an entire social class.

In their internal correspondences, military leaders disparaged "unscrupulous" elites. In April 1932, M. A. Bolaños, the commander of Ahuachapán Department, singled out Antonio Salaverría as one of the most abusive landowners in the region. The particular act that caught Bolaños's eye was Salaverría's decision to close a road that peasants had been using for many years as a pathway. Bolaños denounced Salaverría as being typical "of the rich [*ricos*] who are the principal source of discontent amongst the campesinos, and I suggest that orders be given to cease such abominable abuses."[47] Years later, in response to similar events in his own department, Colonel Julio César Calderón, the governor of Sonsonate, echoed Bolaños's sentiments. After negotiating a land dispute between a group of peasants and a nearby landowner, in which he sided with the peasants, Calderón described his actions as part of a new era of government: "The problem is that in past times these [landowners] have been part a nefarious group here in Sonsonate that has allied with Governors and Comandantes and has caused much damage. . . . But now, myself and the current Comandante are apart from that group, or better said, we have pushed these individuals off to the margins."[48] An ongoing problem of landowners charging exorbitant rents and expropriating the crops of their renters prompted Calderón to write that "large landowners [*terratenientes*] without scruples and without conscience are [inflicting] injustices on their impoverished renters."[49]

The manner in which local elites appealed to the military leaders in government reveals the extent to which the reformist rhetoric had taken effect. When local bosses wanted something from the government, they used a distinctly philanthropic language meant to appeal to military leaders' reformist side. A 1933 example from Juayúa is representative. The incumbent alcalde wanted to ensure that the national government accepted the candidacy of Máximo Jerez, a long-standing political player in the municipality, for alcalde in the forthcoming election. The incumbent submitted his request in the form of a report describing Jerez's beneficent policies towards the peasantry.

> I have already informed you that since April the number of men without work is between 1,000 and 1,500. . . . People without work become vagrants in search of something and will easily take the path of crime. The coffee growers cannot provide work for all of them, because there is no money, actually coffee is almost worthless in these days. . . . The only coffee growers that have *mozos* working for them are: Agustín Alfaro, Máximo Rauda Salaverría and Dr. Máximo Jerez. . . . The humanism of the patrons decidedly influences the general well-being of the proletariat, and a prudent life extends from work on the fincas. Problems arise when patrons squander their money when they receive it without attending to their labors. . . . Dr. Jerez maintains an office that distributes cereal grains to his *colonos*. He gives them on credit an *arroba* of corn per week. . . . This form of providing sustenance to the *colono* and his family lessens the weight of hatred and desperation and causes the *colono* to see that the patron is on his side.[50]

Another petition from a group of wealthy sugar growers near San Salvador is equally revealing. The growers wanted the government to build a distillery for them. In hopes of getting a positive response to their request, they appealed directly to military leaders' interpretation of the 1932 rebellion and then insisted that their proposal was good for working people because it would generate jobs. The petition reads:

> The State that with great difficulty in January of last year confronted the communist convulsion, which was based upon hunger and poverty, and threatened to destroy the social organism; The State that is motivated by the desire for social improvement and distributes parcels of state-owned land and builds cheap housing to elevate the standard of living of the proletariat, should resolve this dilemma. It should decide whether it wants to opt for deindustrializing the nation and throwing the masses to the most cruel and absolute hunger and misery, or on the contrary, if it is sincere in aspiring to create new centers of work to augment the riches of the public and lessen the poverty of the individual.[51]

The Reform Idea in Practice

With its specific ideological approach as a guide, the Martínez government instituted a reform program. It had clear boundaries. It would not extend to politics, and at its heart lay a commitment to private property and a belief that the resources necessary to advance the cause of reform would be given voluntarily by landowners. Any redistribution of goods from landowners to peasants would occur by "mutual compensation," meaning that the government would purchase the resources from the landowners at market price.[52] Any suggestions to the contrary were suppressed immediately. Napoleón Viera Altamirano discovered this in 1932 during his tenure as director general of contributions, a position that placed him at the forefront of the financial side of the reform program. He believed that in order for the reforms to have a lasting impact, they had to be substantial and had to occur immediately. Viera Altamirano contended that the state needed to expropriate land in order to redistribute it to campesinos. Colleagues in his department denounced him, and he was forced to resign shortly thereafter. He was later expelled from the country for remarks made against Martínez.[53]

The Martínez regime also rested the success of its campaign on its ability to monopolize the voice of rural labor. It did not seek to incorporate rural workers into the state as an equal partner in the political system. Rather, it sought to isolate them by destroying any trace of independent organization—a process greatly facilitated by the response to the 1932 uprising. The only groups that could have challenged the military's hold over rural workers, the FRTS and the PCS, had been decimated. For example, the records of the PCS in the Comintern Archive more or less end at 1932, suggesting that organization was weak and surviving communists had difficulty maintaining contact with the Comintern or the Caribbean Bureau. Miguel Mármol confirms this point. In his testimony, he described the party as being in a state of ruin throughout most of the 1930s. The few surviving members who managed to form small party cells suffered from bitter internal disagreements and ongoing harassment by the security forces.[54] According to Mármol, organization among the campesinos was nonexistent.[55] Even the nonradical labor organizations (the mutual aid societies and workers' co-ops) had been shut down during the matanza. To reopen, each had to obtain a license from the government. Only those groups that were strictly urban in their orientation and able to provide clear anticommunist credentials were allowed to reopen, such as the Sociedad de Obreros in Quetzaltepeque and the Sociedad Unión Mutualista de Obreros in Sonsonate.[56] The Barbers' Union (Sociedad Mutualista "Union de Barberos") in San Salvador, however, had difficulty fighting off accusations of communist influences.[57] It appears that government was quite successful in its bid to quell independent labor organizing. Evidence reveals the occurrence of only three work stoppages between 1932 and 1939, and none of them involved rural workers; two of the strikes were by meat cutters, the other was by coffee washers at a coffee processing plant (*beneficio*).[58] The military thus preserved its position as the primary spokesperson for rural labor through sheer force.

The Martínez government developed a multifaceted reform program that, at its most ambitious level, sought to make land and housing available to peasants and urban workers at affordable prices. At a more immediate level, the program was designed to put more bread on the peasants' tables by encouraging landowners to lower or even abolish rents and pay their workers in a timely fashion with legal currency. The highest-ranking members of government, including the president and the minister of government, directed the process. Governors were the point men; local police and comandantes were on the front line, reporting abuses and identifying areas of need. These functionaries acted under the authority of a new administrative department, appropriately named Mejoramiento Social (Social Betterment).[59]

The military's first action was to enforce the abolition of fichas, the coupons that many landowners used to pay their workers in place of legal currency. Fichas had value only in the stores located on the plantation, and since the stores were owned by the landowners themselves, their goods were often overpriced. Fichas had been outlawed in 1920, but the law had not been enforced. The government actually began its campaign against fichas before the 1932 rebellion, indicating that it had anticipated the need for reform. On January 19, 1932, General Martínez ordered the departmental governors to "make it clear to the landowners in your department, principally the coffee growers, that in conformity with . . . the law of 1920 they are prohibited from paying workers in fichas, which allows the landowners to establish monopolies over the sale of primary goods and charge excessively high prices."[60] The campaign was put on hold during the rebellion, but afterwards the government renewed its efforts. Martínez ordered his governors to "proceed with investigations to determine which haciendas or fincas continue to pay their workers in fichas and report them to me."[61] Numerous reticent plantations were singled out, and the government ordered the culpable owners to cease their practices. [62] For example, in response to reports that the finca "El Sunza" near Izalco continued to pay its workers in fichas, Martínez ordered the alcalde of Izalco to ensure "that the defrauding of the workers is ended at once."[63] At this time, however, the military's actions seldom went beyond verbal or written threats, and fichas continued to be used throughout the 1930s.

The government also directed an assault on the institution of *terraje,* the rent paid by tenant farmers to their landlords. The military estimated that in a standard terraje relationship a campesino traded one or two weeks of labor per month in exchange for the access to a parcel of land to plant subsistence crops. The campesino satisfied his debt to the landowner in cash or more typically in crops. Military leaders considered the standard terraje arrangement to be demanding enough, if not overly so, and in the hands of an abusive landowner it became a powerful tool of exploitation.[64] The landowner could arbitrarily alter the terraje agreement by raising the rent or increasing the amount of labor owed to the plantation. Once a campesino had his crops in the ground, he was in a vulnerable position. In one example, a group of workers from the hacienda "Copapayo" near Armenia denounced both the administrator and the owner for arbitrarily raising the rent. As the laborers put it, "Last April we met with the administrator in order to receive our lands . . . then, after we had already prepared and planted the soil, he came around punishing us unjustly by changing the agreement in favor of the hacienda." The governor ordered that the agreement be changed back and announced that he would be "taking appropriate actions against the hacienda's administrator."[65]

As a short-term solution to terraje, the government proposed that landowners abolish it and make land available to campesinos for free. Departmental governors received orders to survey the large plantations and compile a list of those with underutilized land.[66] The national government

then contacted the owners of those properties and asked them to participate. Military leaders appealed to them on grounds of "increasing the production of primary products, such as corn and beans, in order to avoid a
crisis in agricultural [production]."[67] Property owners were under no obligation to participate beyond their own spirit of beneficence. Presumably,
the only motive to agree to the program would have been to gain favor
with the military. Not surprisingly, only a small fraction of landowners
participated, regardless of the fact that the government publicly celebrated
as model citizens those who did.[68]

One of the government's main reform initiatives was to buy private
estates at market value and divide the land into small plots to be sold at
low interest rates to poor families. In a 1933 interview, General Martínez
outlined the ideals of the program: "The son of the campesino will be
born under his own roof; his son will not be the tenant of the landowner,
but will be the owner of his own garden which the father paid for with the
same money that would have been given to cover the rent for that same
piece of beloved land. The division of the land has been carried out in
France, the most organized country in the world. The ownership of the
soil has made Costa Rica an exemplary nation, a model of civility."[69] Land
for the program would come from one of two sources, either properties
already owned by the government or private land that Mejoramiento Social would buy at market price. The land would be divided and sold to
needy campesinos on long-term, low-interest mortgages. A similar plan
was applied to a housing program in which working-class homes would be
constructed and sold to poor families at low mortgages.[70]

To build homes or buy land, Mejoramiento Social needed money.
Since the government was in a financial crisis, so too was the program.
During its first year, Mejoramiento Social did little more than accumulate
funds. The principal source of revenue was a small tax increase on ciga-
rettes and alcohol.[71] Other money came directly from the government, as
in late 1933 when the ministry of planning diverted 25,000 colones to the
program. (The government's total budget for 1933–1934 was just under
18 million colones.)[72] As another source of funds, the government created
the Cédula Patriótica (Patriotic Card). Martínez described its goal as "creating an effective harmony between the different social classes. It is necessary to elevate the living conditions of humble people [and] avoid misery,

the raw material of agitators."[73] The government sold Cédulas to the general public for 40 colones each, with the profits going directly to Mejoramiento Social. The Cédula brought with it certain privileges, such as foregoing the need to acquire other forms of identification. The government also granted Cédula holders the exclusive right to bear firearms. However, this perquisite was abandoned in 1936 when too many people were found to be carrying weapons in public.[74] By July 1934, the Cédula program had garnered Mejoramiento Social a meager 23,000 colones.[75]

While Mejoramiento Social was building up its funds, other government functionaries busied themselves accumulating complaints against the corrupt and illegal actions of landowners. The frequency with which the denunciations arrived suggests both the desperation of the campesinos and their willingness to turn to the military-led government for respite. Some of the cases revealed clear examples of illegal activity, such as that of Copapayo, mentioned above. However, many of the complaints did not arise from specifically illegal acts, but rather from the standard relations of exploitation. A case from Chalatenango Department is representative. In July 1932, the campesino workers on the hacienda "Peñañalapa" denounced their landowner, Ulloa Morazán, for charging overly high rent. As evidence they presented written receipts signed by the administrator of the hacienda. When questioned by the governor, Ulloa confirmed that he charged a high rent but argued that it was justified "by the exceptionally good fertility of his soil." The governor found himself in a difficult position. Unable to disprove Ulloa's claim, he accomplished nothing more than receiving "a promise of suspension of hostilities on behalf of all parties involved."[76] The case of Peñañalapa highlights the dilemma of the reform initiative. To improve the lives of those workers who were not subjected to illegal deeds, military leaders had either to infuse their reform program with enormous sums of money and create alternatives for the rural workers or resort to extralegal measures. Neither alternative came to pass.

In mid-1933, Mejoramiento Social had accumulated over 300,000 colones, enough to begin taking action. One of its first acts was to purchase the finca "La Bemeja" in San Salvador as a site for the construction of one thousand working-class houses. The government also bought and began to build homes on a piece of property in La Libertad City.[77] At the same time, Mejoramiento Social began parceling out rural properties. It started with three government-owned haciendas: "Zapotitán," "Santa Rosa," and "Chiquirín." Zapotitán was one hundred manzanas in size, sixty of which were divided into twenty plots and set aside for large families, while the rest of the hacienda was divided into plots of one-quarter manzana each, to be sold to families with few or no children. Santa Rosa was somewhat larger. It was divided into 519 parcels, although the size of each plot was not announced. The overall size of Chiquirín was not announced. After distributing these first three properties, Mejoramiento Social turned to private land. It purchased five haciendas: "Metalío," near Acajutla in Sonsonate Department; an unnamed hacienda near Chiltiupán in La Libertad Department; "El Encantado" in La Unión Department; an unnamed hacienda in San Miguel Department; and another unnamed hacienda in Ahuachapán Department. Excluding the piece in Ahuachapán, the properties totaled less than four hundred manzanas and ranged in cost from 1,500 to 19,000 colones. The property in Ahuachapán was larger; it sold for 90,000 colones. The size of the parcels for these properties was not announced.[78] In mid-1935, Mejoramiento Social purchased its last property, "San Carlos," in Mejicanos, for a reported 240,000 colones, as the site for a working-class neighborhood.

After its purchase of San Carlos, Mejoramiento Social ran out of money and placed a moratorium on further purchases. According to the minister of government, the program had spent a total of 2 million colones on its projects.[79] The government toyed with the idea of raising taxes on alcohol even further to augment the program, but it ultimately rejected the idea for reasons not made clear by the available sources. Mejoramiento Social was effectively dead.[80] Overall, the program oversaw the construction of some two hundred homes and parceled out not less than nine modestly sized haciendas.[81] In total, some one thousand families benefited. Military leaders publicly praised the program. Martínez made it a tradition during his annual speech before the National Assembly to hail Mejoramiento Social's achievements. But military leaders knew that the program had fallen short of its goals. In 1934, Pío Romero Bosque offered a salient critique of it during an interview with the U.S. military attaché in Costa Rica, saying that "although beyond a doubt Martínez's intentions were of the best, his schemes were little more than dreams, because in order to give all the poor people a piece of land, about half the country would have to be divided up. In regard to the thousand *casas baratas* [cheap houses] . . . a thousand houses is not a drop in the bucket. . . . These problems are ones which cannot be solved in a year or two, but will require much time and study to work out."[82] Nevertheless, the reform program captured the attention of the landowners, who according to U.S. Chargé McCafferty, "would undoubtedly like to see the return of civilian government because they could control it more effectively in their own interests as the Martínez regime, in their opinion, has been too solicitous for the welfare of the lower classes."[83]

Regardless of the diminution of Mejoramiento Social, the government pressed forward with other elements of its reform program. In the process it incited a confrontation with coffee growers in 1935. The conflict erupted when the growers proposed that the value of the colón be allowed to deflate to its market value. When Martínez took power in 1932, he allowed the value of the colón to float because, until then, it had been buoyed artificially by the government. In just a few months it lost 50 percent of its value, declining from 2:1 against the U.S. dollar to 3:1. After the government opened a national bank in 1934, the colón stabilized at 2.5:1 and Martínez froze it at that value. The coffee growers, led by the Coffee Growers' Association (Asociación Cafetalera), proposed that the colón deflate, which by that time would have put its value at approximately 4:1.[84] The government opposed the deflation for reasons both economic and social. Currency devaluation would have helped coffee growers by making Salvadoran exports cheaper in international markets. However, the coffee growers' gains would come at the expense of both the government and the working class. A devalued colón would weaken mass purchasing power, and thus imports would likely drop, which would reduce import duties, still the government's main revenue.[85]

The conflict over deflation lasted nearly four months. The government eventually rejected the proposal and maintained the exchange rate at 2.5:1.[86] Unfortunately, the sources do not provide information on how the decision was reached in government circles; we lack such things as notes of committee meetings and transcripts of negotiations between the government and representatives of the coffee growers. However, a spirited public debate aired in the editorial pages in daily newspapers, especially

Diario Latino. Dozens of editorials and articles appeared, the vast majority of which opposed the landowners' position in no uncertain terms. Considering that the government practiced press censorship at the time, the predominance of favorable articles reflects military leaders' attempt to generate popular support through control over the mass media.[87]

The notable feature of the editorials is the explicit anti-elite language used to denounce the coffee growers. That the government would allow public use of such strong language reveals the rhetoric that military leaders wanted to attach to their reform program. One editorial asked, "Why should we sacrifice our entire population in order to protect a minority that does not account for more than five percent of our population? Away with luxury items: away with silks, away with cars . . . away with things from abroad, because superfluous things should be done away with in this time of anguish. Our government knows our suffering and it will lessen the pains of the people. . . . We have faith in it."[88] Another article claimed that "the irrational reduction of the purchasing power of the masses is a measure that in very short time would manifest itself as a disastrous measure."[89] A third editorial stated that "we have to establish norms of cooperation among all productive sectors in this society; without capricious privileges; where one can feel the protection of the state is equal for everyone."[90] A fourth editorial was perhaps the most inflammatory. It was ostensibly written by an *obrero* (laborer), who reproached the coffee growers: "Where are the coffee growers coming from? What is the so-called coffee industry? If we apply the term 'industry' to coffee, should we not also apply it to corn, rice and beans, and, therefore, have a 'grain industry' in this country as well? . . . Why is coffee in economic crisis? Because there is no demand for it."[91]

Another editorial proposed that the coffee growers reduce the terraje in exchange for a deflated colón. The editorial was from a smallholder in Usulután Department: "In the pages of *Diario Latino* we are seeing much discussion on the attempt to rebuff the proposed increase in the cost of goods of primary necessity. . . . We all know that the producer of these cereal goods is not the landowner but the renters, who always have to pay to the landowner the value of the land whether the crop comes in or not. . . . The protective measure should be to reduce the price of the terraje, thereby lending aid to the small farmers who could then take advantage of their crops."[92] In essence, the editorial informed the coffee growers that they should not have it both ways; they could not deflate the wages of the campesinos and retain the same rates of terraje.

In the wake of its victory over the coffee growers, the government pressed its agenda. Government officials began referring to their efforts as the era of "National Reconstruction." As General José Trabanino, the governor of La Libertad Department, put it, "the concerted effort of National Reconstruction is to protect, in a tangible manner, the Salvadoran campesino whose ideology sustains the government."[93] Some government officials even referred to their reforms as revolutionary: "In creating a feeling of solidarity and a better existence," one said, "the government of El Salvador is sustaining a revolutionary criteria."[94] A Mexican journalist, presumably influenced by the Mexican Revolution, wrote an article that appeared in *Diario Latino* and employed a similarly revolutionary discourse to describe the Martínez regime: "In El Salvador . . . the centuries of social misery have been a product, it is the undeniable truth, of the glacial indifference of the rich . . . toward the pain of the poor. . . . The government of Maximiliano Hernández Martínez is a rare thing in Central America—a true social revolution from above for those below."[95]

After 1935, military leaders became even more aggressive in their defense of working people. When a rumor began circulating that coffee and sugarcane growers intended to cut wages, General José Tomás Calderón, the minister of government, sent a circular to all the alcaldes in the nation, ordering them to tell the growers in their jurisdiction to "not lower the wages of their workers."[96] At the same time, certain high-ranking officials in the government, such as the governors of La Libertad and Chalatenango, General Trabanino and Colonel Francisco José Rivas, emerged as particularly visible proponents of social reform. Trabanino, for instance, involved himself in a variety of activities. He advocated the formation of worker cooperatives, he worked toward the creation of a minimum wage, and, in one of his more ambitious initiatives, he proposed the creation of a national health-care system for working people.[97] Colonel Rivas used personal connections with the landowners in his department to encourage them to help their workers. He often spent weekends traveling around Chalatenango Department and meeting with landowners "to encourage," as he put it, "the large landowners [*terratenientes*] to participate . . . in the noble efforts to advance the well-being and forward progress of the proletarian class." Rivas pressured the landowners by distributing broadsides that challenged them to volunteer their support to the reform campaign. One broadside read, "The Supreme Government calls upon you gentlemen; it asks of you that when the workers come each year to cultivate the lands that you offer them every cooperation in their necessities . . . you agriculturists know that such demonstrations will produce a healthier worker . . . and will raise the moral and cultural level of the Fatherland. . . . People of Chalatenango, help the poor people!"[98]

Like Rivas and Trabanino, other departmental governors carried on in defense of working people, typically by investigating alleged abuses by landowners. In a representative case from October 1939, a group of campesinos from Tacuba denounced the landowner Rogelio Magaña for reducing and withholding their wages. The departmental governor launched an investigation and interviewed the plaintiffs. The governor concluded that the request of the campesinos was just, an opinion shared by the minister of labor, who had read the governor's report. The minister ordered the governor to "use what means are necessary to ensure that the debts owed to the campesinos are canceled. . . . This government is energetically interested in bringing a sense of well-being and calm to the homes of the rural poor, and for this there must be harmony between worker and owner."[99]

The military was quick, however, to suppress any activity that went beyond the strict limits of its program. In April 1939 a rumor circulated among some rural laborers in La Libertad Department that the government intended to guarantee a pay raise as well as a minimum wage for all rural workers. Fearing a popular uprising when the truth became known, the government stepped in: "The happiness of the campesinos could prejudice social order," declared the commander of La Libertad, "for that reason I have ordered the capture of those persons responsible for advancing such speculations."[100]

The Military and Indians: The Reform Program in the West

The reform program was national in scope, but it took on special salience in the western departments. The west, of course, had been the site of the 1932 rebellion and the subsequent mass killings by the military. Moreover, the ethnic makeup of the west presented a unique dynamic. The western peasantry was predominantly Indian, and relations between capital and labor there took on a distinctly ethnic tone. A study of the military's approach to the western region provides an enlightening window on its broader approach to reform. The military's specific negotiation of the ethnic dynamic in the west also reveals much about the way it dealt with its most humble citizens. This look at the west shows the subaltern population of indigenous peasants continuing to insert its demands into the public arena, for consideration by the institution that had just committed widespread killings in the region. Ironically, the Indians of the west found in the military an ally that they hoped to enlist in their ongoing conflicts with local elites. Indigenous individuals and communities had regularly submitted petitions to the government over the past decades. The archival record contains many documentary examples of indigenous people throughout the nation using the customary channels of communication to make requests of the government and enlist its support in one cause or another. Thus, this specific focus on the relations between the government and western Indians in the period from 1931 to 1940 is not meant to imply that there was something unprecedented in these examples. Rather, it is a particularly revealing microcosm because it reveals the complex dynamics of military rule in the wake of the 1932 uprising and massacre.

Noting the brutality of the mass killings by the government, scholars and laypersons alike have contended that the year 1932 marked the end of indigenous culture in El Salvador. The military supposedly targeted Indians during the repression and thereafter effectively outlawed Indian culture, which forced Indians to abandon their ethnic identity and become part of the homogenous "mestizo" peasantry. "All those of strongly Indian cast of features . . . were considered guilty," noted historian Thomas Anderson in his classic study of 1932.[101] Another scholar, Michael McClintock, later concluded that "the massacre mark[ed] and end to Indian culture in El Salvador."[102]

Other research challenges the assumption that Indian identity disappeared after 1932 and that the Martínez regime sought specifically to eradicate indigenous identity. The authors of this research point out that the decline in indigenous culture preceded the Martínez era and that the

Martínez government adopted a more complicated approach to ethnicity.[103] As one example, historians Jeff Gould and Aldo Lauria-Santiago concluded that the activities of the Martínez government "suggest that only a few months after the massacres the regime did not have the ethnocidal intentions often imputed to it by militants."[104] Political scientist Virginia Tilley's research in birth records reveals that Indian populations did not decline after 1932. She shows that it was customary between the 1860s and the 1950s for municipal officials to denote the ethnicity of newborns in the birth registry—even though it is an admittedly vague and imperfect method. Tilley sampled births every five years between 1900 and 1950 for all municipalities in the departments of Sonsonate and Ahuachapán, the heart of the massacre zone. Tilley also sampled births from a variety of municipalities in the departments of San Salvador, Morazán, La Paz, and Cuscatlán. Assuming that the criteria that local officials employed to distinguish between Indians and ladinos remained somewhat constant over time, however vague and imprecise they were, the results indicate not only that the percentage of Indian populations remained steady after the 1932 matanza, but also that they increased in some municipalities, most strikingly in Izalco, a major center of Indian population and a primary target of the military repression. A notable feature of Tilley's research is that "Indian-ness" continued to be recognized by public officials after the rebellion, and Indians themselves continued to embrace their identity publicly and even to make appeals to the government based upon that identity.[105]

The ethnicity of the rebels in 1932 and the potentially racist motives behind the massacres remain difficult to determine, owing to lack of definitive evidence.[106] Indians almost certainly constituted a majority of the rebels, although ladinos participated in the revolt as well. Ladinos definitely participated in the crackdown and used ethnicity to identify their enemies. For example, a few days after the revolt, the ladino-led municipal government of Izalco identified the indigenous cofradías as places where "Indians engage not only in celebration, but also contrive illegal acts that are prejudicial to the honorable citizens of the city."[107] A later report from the governor of Sonsonate Department identifies Indians as having been the "communists" (i.e., rebels) in 1932: "The Protestants [missionaries] have cooperated in the extinction of the communist ideas above all in those populations predominated by the indigenous element."[108] Assuming that Indians constituted the majority of the rebels, and that the military directed the brunt of its attack against rebellious communities, the military likely targeted Indian communities during the repression. If so, the military's policies toward the Indians after the rebellion appear all the more paradoxical.

Military leaders believed the need for reform took on particular urgency in the wake of the rebellion. Incensed ladinos were going out of their way to crack down on Indians, exacerbating an already tense situation. The vehemence of the ladinos is evident in the rabidity of their discourse. For ladinos, the uprising confirmed in stark terms the stereotypical qualities of Indians: latent violence and a brutish disregard for civilization. One ladino coffee planter from Juayúa claimed in an interview with the British chargé d'affaires that he had lived among his Indian employees for twenty-five years and had paid and treated them well. He purported to have given them parcels of land for free so they could grow subsistence crops, and yet "it was the same Indians that came that Sunday night meaning to chop . . . [me] up with their machetes. . . . their rage is something which lies always latent in their blood and flames out on very little provocation."[109] An editorial in *Diario La Prensa* called for the death of Indians. The editorial proposed that the problems of insurrection would be solved if all the machetes in the west were confiscated: "The machete is the weapon of those Indians affiliated with red communism. . . . It is shameful that in a country such as ours with pretensions of culture and civilization, the authorities have done nothing to prevent the barbaric custom of allowing the free porting of machetes." The editorial recognized that such a policy would require drastic action: "'Felled machete, dead Indian,' says the saying. And it is true. The Indian . . . only retires his machete when he dies."[110]

Even some ladinos who were more moderate in their views considered Indians to be savages desperately in need of assistance. Adolfo Herrera Vega, a ladino from Izalco, presented that point of view in a brief book entitled (in translation) *The Western Indian of El Salvador and His Social Incorporation into the School.* Herrera proposed that Indians could be saved from their "barbarism" by being incorporated into the public schools:

"The Indian has a body and a heart, and, therefore, should not be abandoned, but saved through education." But Herrera's descriptions of the Indian retained the standard stereotypes: "Their licentiousness is without end. . . . Fanaticism, alcoholism and prostitution exist in ostentatious abundance. . . . Mothers sell their daughters, brothers their sisters." When the Indian children are brought to school, Herrera claimed, "they arrive filled with the imprint of the environment in which they were raised; they speak little; to each question they respond with monosyllables, if at all. . . . Intelligent? They are not." Herrera went on to argue that the poverty of the Indians was of their own making: "We find our Indian [*nuestro indio*] afflicted with moral and economic poverty. The second is the consequence of the first."[111]

When the ladino authorities regained control of their municipalities after the repression, they began a widespread campaign of terror against Indians. The ladinos believed that the rebels had intended to eliminate them, largely because the main targets of the rebels had been recognized symbols of ladino power, such as the municipal hall and the properties and bodies of locally prominent people.[112] The ladinos responded by attacking the material and symbolic life of Indian society.

The ladinos of Izalco led the charge. They attempted to eliminate the two Indian communities' rights to irrigation and drinking water. Water had been a repeated source of discord between ladinos and Indians in Izalco, triggering at least three major conflicts in the prior two decades.[113] A resolution passed by the municipal council just a few days after the rebellion reads:

> Agriculture has met with many difficulties, owing to the monopoly of irrigation water by the Indian element; they have always put every obstacle before the ladino element, which is dedicated to planting cereal crops during the dry season by use of irrigation water. Owing to the recent events that have occurred in this city, in which the Indian elements were mixing with Communism, the Municipality makes the following accords. . . . From this date forward the Municipality will be in charge of all irrigation waters; it reserves the right to determine which lands will be allowed to receive irrigation water; any rights of the Indians to receive irrigation water are hereby revoked.[114]

Next, the Izalqueños attempted to undermine indigenous religious practices. The municipal government requested that the national government
remove all the religious relics (*imagenes*) from the cofradías and refuse the
Indians access to them.[115] The Izalqueño ladinos also were reported to be
randomly beating Indians, throwing them in jail, and making them pay a
fine to be released. Members of Izalco's Civic Guard were identified as
participating in these activities.[116]

The government sought to abate the abuses in Izalco. Having received
reports of various ladino transgressions against Indians, President Martínez sent Izalco's municipal government an unmistakably clear message:
"I am informed that the municipal authorities of Izalco are undertaking
injustices against the Indigenous class. I hereby serve orders to you to put
an end to such activities."[117] A few days later, the Indians sent a denunciation accusing the municipal secretary of a variety of abuses, prompting
General Castaneda Castro, the minister of government, to call publicly for
the secretary's resignation and privately to order the municipal council to
depose him.[118] The authorities of Izalco resisted the order, insisting that
the secretary was "honorable and competent."[119] But the minister persisted
and the secretary resigned.

Similar tensions played out in Nahuizalco. In February 1932, not
more than two weeks after the military withdrew from the town, correspondence reached San Salvador reporting manifest abuses by local officials. The military sent Lieutenant Enrique Uribe to Nahuizalco to assess
the situation. Uribe presented himself to the municipal officials as the village's new subcommander, but his actual mission was to conduct a "secret
investigation" into the actions of Nahuizalco's ladinos.[120] Indeed, shortly
after he arrived, Uribe discovered that ladino officials were terrorizing the
region with "arbitrary and violent actions." After the military withdrawal
in early February, paramilitary bands roamed the surrounding environs in
search of "communists." The greater portion of the bands was comprised
of members of the Civic Guard, who were joined by other local ladinos as
well as some soldiers. Members of the gangs referred to their activities as
"patriotic service." Uribe learned that the bands initially conducted themselves "as they should," meaning that they patrolled the village in accordance with their orders, but their behavior quickly degraded: "The [local]
authorities prior to my arrival . . . applied justice in a manner so poorly

interpreted that the medicine became worse than the sickness afflicting the patients." Uribe continued, "No one has escaped their criteria; far from establishing harmony and tranquility in the region, they have sowed the seeds of terror and dread, in not only the Indians but amongst some ladinos as well. In regard to their treatment of the Indians these local officials have discredited the name of the Supreme Government as well as the honorable citizens of this community." Thus, a military officer on a special mission for the military linked the plight of the Indians to the reputation and good name of the military government.

It is not clear whether Uribe had the authority to exceed his status as an observer and intervene in these affairs, but he did so nonetheless: "I am undertaking the position of returning harmony, tranquility and well-being to this locality. Under my authority I have ordered a stop to all pillage, and have placed the Guardia Cívica and other local authorities under a strict regimen of discipline. . . . I have also ordered that any individual suspected of communism is to be reported to . . . the head of the Guardia Cívica who will then report directly to this comandancia." Not surprisingly, Uribe's actions antagonized ladino officials, who tried to get rid of him by denouncing him before the national government, accusing him of accepting bribes from prisoners in exchange for freedom. They demanded the national government remove him from the village. The government responded by sending to Nahuizalco an investigative team that determined the accusations to be false. It is not clear what impact Uribe's actions eventually had on local affairs in Nahuizalco, but a few months later the military government ousted the town's municipal secretary due to his discriminatory policies against Indians.[121]

The national government also intervened on behalf of private Indian individuals. In August 1932, Elena Mojica, an Indian from Sonzacate, appealed directly to President Martínez for protection against the local authorities, whom she accused of excessive repression. She did not hide her family's ties to political activism and appealed directly to the suffering she and her family had endured:

Mr. President . . . During the Communist uprising, three of my sons, a nephew, and my husband paid with their lives for the grave error of wanting to implant an unnecessary system amongst us. Without entering into a discussion of their innocence or guilt, the civil authorities of this locality gave a most rude blow to my life, filling it with martyrs. For reasons of wickedness or ignorance . . . [these officials] did not know how to translate the orders of the superior government . . . and thereby committed every class of abuse and exaction on defenseless people. The then-Alcalde ordered in clear Spanish that my home be sacked, causing my possessions to be decommissioned. I am asking for the return of my possessions.[122]

Martínez ordered the governor of Sonsonate Department to arrange the return of her belongings.

Although the national government did not select Indians for political office in ladino-controlled municipalities, it did reject certain ladino candidates on account of their abusive stance toward Indians. In November 1933, when the military was compiling a list of candidates for the forthcoming municipal elections, a political network in Nahuizalco put forth the name of Ismael Domínguez for alcalde. The governor, Colonel José Calderón, described Domínguez as "a good collaborator who is helping our Party," but rejected his candidacy because "said individual expropriated the property of a poor Indian which was recovered thanks to my intervention . . . but I fear that as Alcalde he would commit other ungrateful acts."[123]

The national government not only reacted to ladino abuses, but also on some occasions made gestures toward actively assisting Indians. In September 1932 the government opened the Rafael Campos Indian School on a piece of government-owned property located between Izalco and Sonsonate. The government financed the building of the school in part with 'voluntary" donations that it solicited from the surrounding municipal governments.[124] The school's statutes describe its long-term goal as "improving the social, moral, intellectual, and economic life of the Indigenous class of Sonsonate Department." The school, however, had a more pressing objective: "to offer immediate aid to the children who have been left orphaned as a result of the revolt which occurred in January of this year."[125] Probably, the inherent purpose of the school reflected the widely held belief that, through education, the Indians could be redeemed from the ignorance that left them vulnerable to radical alternatives.[126] Whatever the school's actual goal, Indians found an ally in its director, Lieutenant Alfonso R. Muñoz. On one occasion, Muñoz directly appealed on Indians' behalf to the military commander in Sonsonate:

> From Nahuizalco there have come some Indian women [*inditas*], widows
> of executed Communists, who inform me that the Alcalde of Nahuizalco
> is forcefully demanding that they pay their electricity bills in full. . . .
> Given that these people are abandoned, it seems to me that they should
> not be required to make this payment in full, but little by little as they are
> capable. Moreover, these people have a terrible fear of the authorities,
> which lends credence to reports of the bad conduct of the Alcalde.

Muñoz then suggested that the military come to the defense of the Indians: "We, that is you and I, should see ourselves as the front line in the elimination of the fear of these people. . . . We should also ensure that the demands for payment of the electricity bill are not demanded from the Indians in any way different than from the ladinos."[127]

Muñoz's behavior, and other examples of military leaders' support for Indians, created an image of the government as a potential bulwark against ladino abuse. Indians repeatedly solicited departmental- and national-level officials to come to their assistance. "Consistently," reported the governor of Sonsonate, "they, in greater part Indians, come to me to present their complaints."[128] Even in the eastern reaches of the country, in Morazán Department, Indian communities considered governing officials favorable enough to Indian issues to present them with denunciations of abusive ladinos. One Morazán community protested against the excessive roadwork imposed upon them by municipal authorities. The Indians claimed that "because we are Indians, they forget that we are human beings and that we belong to the same humanity [*humanidad*] that they do and that we too should enjoy all the legal rights of free republican people."[129]

The ethnicity-based conflicts between Indians and ladinos at the local level normally revolved around the same issues that had motivated antagonism prior to the rebellion. In Izalco, for example, conflicts over rights to water were interminable. In February 1933, the Community of Indians of Asunción Izalco asked President Martínez to force the ladinos to restore their water rights: "We ask General Martínez to grant us rights to water which have always been managed by the Community of Indians of Asunción Izalco; we have been forced to cede our rights. . . . We ask that we be allowed to function with said waters by the prior customs that date back to our ancestors."[130] The ladinos responded to the Indians' demand by describing them as abusive and denouncing them as communists and "enemies of public order." They claimed that the Indians "have been given every class of assistance in regard to the irrigation of their lands, yet they continue to commit abuses and place obstacles in the way of the large landowners [*terratenientes*] and public service. Various Indians . . . have undertaken a campaign of disobedience to local authority . . . and are sabotaging irrigation facilities."[131] It is not known whether the government aided the Indians in their claim to water, but it recognized that the ladinos' attempt to portray the Indians as communists was diversionary. When the ladinos later claimed that the Indians were about to instigate a "communist uprising," the governor of Sonsonate dismissed the accusation and described the actual issue as "Indian discontent caused by civilian ladinos who beat and threaten them." He encouraged the minister of war to "take active measures to prevent such abuses."[132]

Indian requests before the national government were not always motivated by ladino improprieties. Sometimes Indians simply requested the presence of a neutral third party. For example, in 1935, a group of Izalqueño Indians belonging to the Cofradía del Niño Dios, asked the government to arbitrate an internal dispute. The members proclaimed that another individual, the widow of a former member, appropriated the *imagenes* of the cofradía and refused to return them, leaving the cofradía unable to conduct its annual celebration. The government agreed to the request, and the governor of Sonsonate oversaw the negotiations, although his ruling on the matter is unknown.[133]

Despite the military government's sympathy toward the Indians, it placed strict limitations on the methods by which Indians could present their demands. Petitions and written or verbal denunciations were acceptable; collective action was not. When a group of Izalqueño Indians was suspected of organizing subversive activities in 1936, fifteen of them were arrested by the Guardia Nacional and subjected to what the documentation eerily defines as "interrogation."[134] Later, in 1938, another group of Izalqueño Indians landed in jail when they took a grievance too far. The conflict began when fifty Indians from Izalco marched to the governor's office in Sonsonate City. Standing below the governor's window, they demanded that he chastise a local ladino, Braulio Sandoval, for closing a walking path that community members traditionally used. The governor arranged a conference between Sandoval and the Indians despite his misgivings about the Indians' aggressiveness, which he referred to as a "violent act." In the meeting, however, the Indians supposedly failed to demonstrate "prudence," and instead of "employing indirect persuasion, they resorted to threats." According to the governor, "[the Indians'] unlawful conduct brings back memories of the reprehensible communist events which leave me still with a bad aftertaste." After the meeting the Indians returned to the governor's office, prompting the governor to address them as a group. When one of the Indians "responded in an ironic manner," the governor called in the police and had them jailed.[135] Similarly, in Santo Domingo de Guzmán, the governor called in the Guardia when, following the local election of 1939, the Indians attempted to prevent ladinos from assuming control of the municipal government.[136] Thus, the government defended Indians on its own terms. When Indians exceeded the acceptable limits of appeal, they were quickly suppressed.

Despite the limits it placed on collective action and the infirmity of its overall reform program, the military government created a space in which Indians found refuge from ladino abuse. In particular, it ignored ladino objections and permitted the cofradías to celebrate their annual religious festivals.[137] The cofradías survived and continued to function publicly and elect their own political leaders. For example, at the end of 1932, and again at the end of 1933, the "Alcalde of the Municipality of Indians of Asunción Izalco" requested recognition by the departmental governor of the traditional "appointment of the elected candidates to their respective offices of this municipality."[138] This is the same language and manner in which Indian communities had been electing officials for decades, if not longer.[139] Notably, it is not the behavior of a community trying hastily to abandon or hide its collective ethnic presence.

The military's policies towards the Indians of western El Salvador are emblematic of the military's overall reform program. The military did not allow Indians to compete for control over the formal municipal government, which continued to be reserved for ladinos. Neither did the military expand the material resources available to Indian communities through such policies as land reform. For the most part, the military defended the Indians on the same grounds that it supported peasants throughout the entire country, as workers whose presence was essential to the progress of the nation. It did not seek to democratize power or even to promote social equality. Nevertheless, its reforms showed tangible results in the west. Indians survived after 1932 in part due to their own will and determination to live, but also because they had some help from the military and local military officials, whose reports typically made clear that they considered it to be their responsibility to assist Indians. "I have attended to the complaints of the poor *naturales* [Indians]," wrote the governor of Sonsonate in 1938, "procuring the reestablishment of their rights and persuading them that the authorities, far from being hostile, want to extend to them guarantees as honorable and peaceful citizens for whom justice will be extended."[140] In particular, the military reprimanded abusive officials and created an atmosphere in which being "Indian" remained possible. Perhaps the most revealing evidence is the reaction of the Indians themselves. Regardless of what they thought about the military, they recognized the role it intended to play and used it as a line of defense against ladino assaults.

The Limits of Reform: The Battle over the Finca-Owned Stores

For the duration of its reform campaign the Martínez government played a nagging zero-sum game. The advance of the worker seemingly required the expense of the landowner, and the defense of the landowner ensured the continued subjugation of the worker. For seven years the government endeavored to balance the interests of capital and labor. After its victory in 1935 in the deflation debate, it became steadily more confident and rhetorically boisterous in its actions. In 1939 the government launched its most ambitious proposal to date and in the process surpassed the limits of acceptable reform.

In August 1939, the government renewed its battle against fichas. Its first campaign in 1932 had failed because it did not sanction resistant landowners. In 1939, military leaders approached the problem with an aggressive stance and a more comprehensive interpretation of the problem. They determined that the problem resided not only with fichas, but also with the institution of the finca-owned store, because even on those fincas where workers received their wages in legal currency, the landowners still controlled the laborers' purchasing power via the stores. Military leaders learned that landowners maintained a commercial monopoly for their stores by refusing to allow outside merchants onto the fincas and also by preventing their workers from leaving the fincas on payday. Thus, military leaders concluded that the institution of the finca-owned store had to be abolished.

In September 1939, the national government notified every municipality that finca-owned stores were to be closed.[141] One notice reads, "I am informing you to do what is necessary to ensure that Señor Canessa stops immediately the commissary that is functioning in his hacienda San Ambrosio, property of his sister Lydia Canessa; see to it that all the *tiquestes* [fichas] are collected and liquidated into cash for the people who are carrying them."[142] Military leaders appealed to article 55 of the constitution, which prohibited monopolies over commerce, and justified their actions on the grounds of protecting capitalism and free enterprise. They actually characterized the stores as being identical to "the system of commissaries also used in Soviet Russia; a system that we should not allow to be implanted in our soil owing to its unjust and unsuitable qualities."[143] In other words, in an ironic twist, the national government was accusing plantation owners of practicing communism. The Guardia Nacional patrolled the departments to ensure that landowners complied with the orders.

Independent merchants stood to gain the most from the government's decision. Their organization, the Cámara de Comerciantes en Pequeño (Chamber of Small Commerce), thanked the government in a letter that articulates the situation:

> There would have been nothing more logical and beneficial for the campesinos in general than for the *patronos* to have allowed the establishment of small independent shops, but disgracefully they did not. The worker of the fincas and haciendas was forced to watch the fruits of his labor be ungratefully absorbed by the store of the *patron* which charges prices that are so exaggerated that for the same amount of money the worker could buy the same product many times over somewhere else, but the jefes will not allow them to do so. Therefore, this Chamber furiously applauds the disposition of the Government for its effort to stimulate the goodwill of the masses in the countryside."[144]

The swift action of the government caught landowners off-guard. When the order was first handed down, many landowners sent letters of appeal asking that they be allowed to keep their stores open a few more weeks in order to liquidate their merchandise. Most of these requests were granted. But by the middle of October 1939, the military determined that the shutdown of the stores was complete; success seemed assured.

The initial compliance of the landowners quickly gave way to determined opposition. The landowners organized and initiated an intense lobbying campaign to force the government to reverse its policy. The Coffee Growers' Association led the charge. In addition, some of El Salvador's most prominent landowners, including Guirola from Santa Tecla, Alvarado from San Salvador, and Regalado from San Julián, actively lobbied the government. They argued that the finca-owned stores benefited workers by providing desperately needed primary goods that laborers could not acquire elsewhere. A letter from the Coffee Growers' Association summarizes the argument and represents the hundreds of similar letters sent to the government during the months of November and December 1939:

> The suppression of the stores does not constitute a measure of protection in favor of the workers; in truth, the stores, far from prejudicing workers, are an element of cooperation by supplying necessities. . . . Now the workers of fincas will have to travel very far to urban centers in order to acquire the items they need. As many fincas are located far away, the worker will have to devote a day, or part of it, just to this one task. . . . There are some stores that exploit workers, but these are exceptions and can be monitored by the public powers. . . . It is unjust to prejudice all the stores, as well as the finqueros and the campesinos, for the actions of a few.[145]

In addition to their own letters, landowners sent letters supposedly written by their laborers detailing the hardships that the policy had inflicted on them. The landowners supplemented their letters with telephone calls and personal meetings. In their written correspondence, government officials mentioned those calls and meetings but unfortunately did not describe their contents in detail.

The lobbying went on for months. Unfortunately, the sources do not provide insight into the reactions of military leaders. What is known, however, is that in April 1940, the national government suddenly reversed its policy and allowed the stores to reopen. The reversal was not announced; one day the stores simply reappeared. When the Chamber of Small Commerce discovered what was occurring, it sent the government the following note:

> The evil on the fincas is renewed. . . . The stores were only closed for a short while, but as of today they have reopened . . . causing a natural disgust amongst the campesinos who once again have to watch the fruits of their modest work return to the landowners' coffers. . . . There is no more obvious test of the presence of justice for the countryside worker than when he is not forced to buy in the store of his boss . . . but has the liberty to choose what he wants . . . without fear of censorship, control or loss of his job.[146]

Despite the absence of specific sources, the nature of the conflict over the finca-owned stores is clear. The government challenged the coffee growers; the coffee growers resisted; and the government capitulated. In more ways than one, this chain of events is emblematic. On the one hand, the events demonstrate the national government's commitment to reform and the growing resolve with which military leaders carried out reformist policies. The order to close the finca-owned stores represented the first time that the Martínez government went beyond the "voluntary will" of the landowners and proactively struck at their economic resources. On the other hand, the national government's defeat illustrates the limits of reform. Until 1939, the national government had enacted mild policies with a boisterous rhetoric. It is not clear to what extent the mildness of the policies was a product of the military's own ideological approach or concern over the potential reaction of landowners. But by 1939 the national government either had changed its beliefs or become more confident in its strength. The new and more aggressive policies, however, crossed the line of acceptability. The coffee growers quashed them, demonstrating that any policy that would work to the long-term detriment of the landowners, regardless of its broader social importance, was disallowed.

*   *   *

It is a great irony, although one not unsurpassed in the history of reform movements in Latin America, that the Salvadoran military, so famous for its abuses, enacted a social reform program after committing mass killings. The skeptic might argue that the military's ideology was nothing more than rhetoric and is policies were inconsequential. Indeed, the military's support of the peasantry did not go beyond the basics. Mejoramiento Social lacked money and was unable to purchase more than a few isolated properties. The voluntary will of the landowners was not forthcoming, and the military lacked the ability, if not the desire, to gain access to those resources by initiating more coercive measures, such as taxation or expropriation. Moreover, it remains pure speculation as to whether the military regime's reforms would have resulted in any meaningful change even if they had been fully funded and implemented. There is no indication that the military intended to deal with such crucial issues as political power, democratic reform, or the long-term economic well-being of the peasantry.

But it would be inaccurate to dismiss the role of the military out of hand, for such a dismissal would contradict the evidence. The military's policies were based on a concise and coherent ideology, whether sound or flawed in its approach. And the military's actions were both evident and concrete. As just one example, the military maintained the exchange rate in 1935 in clear opposition to export-oriented landowners. In many other individual cases, the military came to the defense of peasants in their battles against the illegal or unscrupulous acts of landlords. The military's support for Indians is one of the more tangible variations of its defense of the peasantry. A confirmation that Martínez's reform program was having some impact comes from a surviving member of the Communist Party after the repression of 1932. In the course of an investigation by the Caribbean Bureau in New York in late 1932, the reformist posture of the Martínez regime was described as a threat: "It did not come out and tell the masses that it, the Martínez government, stands with the rich against the poor. On the contrary, it tried to pose as champion of the masses, tried to pose as a national government, a government of all classes. . . . Since he kept promising them things and making gestures, the tendency was for the masses to believe in him."[147] Regardless of its success or failure, Martínez's reform program set some important precedents that succeeding military regimes would follow: social reforms are necessary, the national government must take the lead in implementing them because elites have little incentive to do so, and, furthermore, the military was best suited to lead the cause of reform because of its neutral position between capital and labor.

CONCLUSION

El Salvador's modern political history can be divided into two eras, those before and after the 1931 coup that brought General Maximiliano Hernández Martínez to power. Before Martínez, El Salvador's political system was marked by a series of dictatorships, led by both civilians and military officers, that was defined by relentless competition between rival patron-client networks. In time, and especially after the onset of the coffee economy in the late nineteenth century, the rivalries gave way to a more centralized, albeit no less dictatorial, system. The only political respite came during a brief period of reformism between 1927 and 1931 under the administrations of Pío Romero Bosque and Arturo Araujo. After the 1931 coup, the modern military regimes took a hold that lasted for the next five decades. In fact, the real power of the military lasted even longer, until the end of the civil war in 1992.

One of the central arguments of this study is that El Salvador's political system exhibited a marked degree of continuity between those two eras. Martínez based his system on past structures, serving as a bridge between the patron-client dictatorships of the nineteenth and early twentieth centuries and the modern military regimes of the latter part of the twentieth century. In response to the democratization and reformism of his two predecessors, Martínez adhered to tradition and rolled the political system back to its prereformist mode. He ensured that elites were safely in control of political office in the municipalities, and he promoted an export-based economy built around production on privately owned estates. He also channeled all things political through the increasingly powerful central state, just as his predecessors in the Meléndez-Quiñónez dynasty had sought to do between 1913 and 1926.

The preexisting system on which Martínez built his political edifice was characterized by patronage and clientelism. It was an informal system guided by a body of unwritten rules handed down over time through learned behavior and oral tradition. Although informal, those rules exhibited a traceable and coherent pattern, as revealed in the extant archival record. The present study has shown how that system functioned. It picked up the documentary trail in the 1840s and 1850s, as El Salvador embarked on its path of independent nationhood, and ended in 1940, when the Martínez regime had consolidated power and the archival record trails off.

In the aftermath of decolonization from Spain and the demise of the United Provinces of Central America, local elites, who were part landowner, part military strongman, and part governing official, commanded their respective municipalities. I applied the term *political bosses* to them. The base of a boss's power was his body of supporters—friends, family, laborers, dependent clients, ethnic kinsmen, and so on—which he used as leverage in forming alliances with other bosses, thereby creating a patronage network. These networks propelled their leaders into power, in competition with rivals who were looking to do the same. Once in command of their localities, local bosses could enter into patronage relationships with superiors at the departmental and national levels who were building their respective political networks in hopes of competing for higher-level offices. The local bosses, who were sometimes referred to as subalterns (*subalternos*), were expected to produce the political capital (votes) or the raw materials (manpower, food, money, or guns) to promote their superiors' advance up the political ladder. In return, locals either rode their patrons' coattails up the ladder or stayed at home and used their alliances to help them in local political battles.

In the pre-coffee era, this system functioned in a decentralized manner. Politics consisted of factional conflicts between regional networks based primarily in the departmental capitals. Political fortunes rose and fell in accordance with the formation and breaking of patronage alliances. The conflagrations between networks often turned violent, taking the form of coups and civil wars. The conflicts were essentially interdepartmental disputes, but occasionally they spilled over into neighboring countries in networks' unending search for allies and support, which gave the clashes an interstate dimension.

After the arrival of the coffee economy in the latter third of the nineteenth century, the political system functioned in the same way, but in a more centralized form. Revenues from the sale of coffee allowed whoever was in control of government to consolidate authority and invest in building up the power of the state, ultimately securing its base of control. One of the more important aspects of the process of state-formation was the professionalization of the military, whereby the army became a more obedient arm of the central government. One of the army's main contributions to politics after 1880 was in disciplining recalcitrant local bosses who resisted incorporation into the centralized system for fear of losing their cherished local authority. As was demonstrated by the case of General Rivas in Tacuba, centralization had limits, even into the 1920s.

Over time this process of centralization resulted in the elimination of regional factionalism. An important date in this process was 1898, the year of the last successful overthrow of a sitting president until the military coup of 1931. After 1898, political factions no longer came to power militarily, from outside the network, but rather from within it, by negotiating and jockeying for position. Far from undermining the system of patronage and clientelism, centralization reinforced it. The elimination of factionalism resulted in the formation of one primary patronage network that functioned in the same way as its many predecessors. This network took its most visible form during the era of the Partido Nacional Democrático (PND) under the direction of Jorge Meléndez (1919–1923) and Alfonso Quiñónez (1923–1927). As with any centralized, nondemocratic system, incumbents risked alienating high-ranking aspirants by choosing someone else as their successor. The Meléndez-Quiñónez dynasty faced two such challenges, first by Tomás Palomo in 1919 and then by Miguel Molina in 1923. Palomo and Molina each tried to take their bids for the presidency outside the system by mobilizing a base of independent electoral support. It is not apparent that either candidate wanted genuine political reforms; rather, they seemed to be looking only for a way around the nepotistic stranglehold of the Meléndez-Quiñónez family. A more genuine attack on the system came during the administrations of Pío Romero Bosque (1927–1931) and his successor, Arturo Araujo (March 1931 to December 1931). Nevertheless, the structures of the PND survived, and when General Martínez took power in 1931, he rejected Romero Bosque's democratic reforms and reinforced the old way of doing things. He named the national network "Partido Nacional Pro-Patria," but for all intents and purposes it was the same entity that had existed as the PND.

Although political life in El Salvador was defined by hierarchy and exclusivity, the working poor participated in it and thereby shaped the nation's political trajectory. Elites may have been powerful, but they did not force the poor to do their bidding uncontested. The poor bargained, negotiated, and inserted their interests into the system. Among other examples of this, Indian communities competed for municipal office in western El Salvador between the 1880s and the 1930s. In 1932 they rose up in a definitive expression of mass discontent. After 1932 they struggled to maintain their collective integrity vis-à-vis local ladinos, and they often enlisted the support of the national government in the process.

Other references to smaller, but still important, episodes of negotiation survived into the historical record as well. Among them is the case of the indigenous rebellions of the early 1830s, highlighted by the insurrection in the San Vicente region led by Anastasio Aquino between 1832 and 1833. Unfortunately, evidence from those events is too sparse to support the kind of methodological inquiry that scholars of other Latin American countries have performed for similar-sounding events during roughly the same time period.[1]

Notwithstanding the limitations of the historical record, it appears that El Salvador did not experience a particular moment of mass-based civic republicanism. In other words, El Salvador stands out from the Cauca region in Colombia in the 1840s and 1850s, or the Huanta region in Peru in the 1820s, or the urban environs of Santiago, Chile, in the 1840s and 1850s. The scholars who have conducted research on those places and times have demonstrated that they were sites of mass-based activity when poor people, both urban and rural, broadened the inclusiveness of citizenship and injected it into the broader national discourse.[2] In particular, this research reveals that elites in those countries responded to mass political action in diverse and unpredictable ways. For example, James Sanders shows that the opening in the Cauca region in Colombia in the 1840s and 1850s came about as a consequence of intra-elite rivalries. One group of elites encouraged the masses to take up the cause of civic republicanism and granted them new rights in return for their support in the elites' internecine battles. But when the masses proved too adept and independent in their political endeavors, and their definition of civic republicanism got out of hand, the elites closed ranks and retracted the rights and guarantees. Cecilia Méndez shows that in Peru, in the aftermath of the Huanta rebellion in the 1820s, early republican liberal leaders responded differently to peasant autonomy and militancy. Instead of retracting rights from the plebeians and poor, as Colombian elites did, a faction of Peruvian elites employed the concept of citizenship in hopes of attracting the former rebels and other peasants to them as constituents. The elites were able to consider this strategy because the rebels had been so effective at defining citizenship and advancing their interpretation of it into the broader body politic. This circumstance endowed Peruvian political conflicts with particular qualities—the predominance of multiclass and multiethnic networks in competition, rather than interclass or interethnic rivalries. As Méndez puts it, "the fiercest political antagonisms of the early caudillo period occurred not between the national ruling elites and the peasants, but rather between the various political factions competing for control of the state."[3]

In the absence of a comparable moment of mass-based civic republicanism, Salvadoran elites seem to have been less concerned about mass uprisings than might otherwise be expected. As Méndez showed in the case of Peru, elite Salvadorans seem to have been more interested in mobilizing the masses, albeit safely, as part and parcel of their incessant battles for control over government. While I cannot say so with certainty, this could explain why we see in El Salvador a steady and consistent advance of legal and voting rights for all citizens along with an unrelenting rhetoric in support of democracy and mass suffrage. From the first national charter in 1841, all adult men were given equal rights before the law, regardless of ethnicity or any other social category. Admittedly, various barriers to officeholding existed, such as minimum wealth requirements, and elections remained indirect for the first three decades of El Salvador's history. But by the 1870s, El Salvador's political system was wide open. Rarely did elites feel the need to proclaim publicly their opposition to mass democracy, and rarely if ever did they do so in their internal correspondence. When political bosses disparaged democracy, they usually did so as a way of criticizing aspiring bosses who wanted to oust the incumbents. Particular events, such as the 1932 uprising, did result in some elites calling publicly for mass murder. Less extreme, but still hierarchical, expressions were made at other times, such as in the 1913 newspaper editorial by Reyes Guerra that disparaged the secret vote and even mass suffrage, and in Francisco Galindo's 1874 catechism, which distinguished between *"el pueblo"* and *"el populacho."* Such expressions are to be expected in an agricultural nation defined by disparities in wealth. But they seem to have been infrequent, or at least not the central issue in political discourse.

Rather, El Salvador in the nineteenth century seems to mimic Méndez's characterization of early republican Peru, where instead of relentless class conflict, politics seems to have revolved around rival political factions competing for control over the state and anxious to have the masses involved. In the midst of that factionalism, El Salvador's masses participated in various ways. Sometimes they did so as lackeys, under the thumb of domineering elites, but at other times they did so in more autonomous and complicated ways, as when the indigenous communities of Nahuizalco and Cuisnahuat competed for control over municipal government beginning in the 1880s. They proved to be just as adept as their ladino counterparts at monopolizing polling stations, in accordance with the informal rules of politics.

By force of repetition over time, the informal rules of politics in El Salvador assumed their own institutionalized character. One of those rules was that no one held office without being elected. So no matter how manipulated or predetermined elections may have been, they occurred regularly and mostly on schedule. And during elections, people voted, often in droves. A second informal rule was that politics, especially the electoral process, was accompanied by a democratic discourse. That discourse celebrated free suffrage and popular will. The exceptions to this rule came when challengers accused incumbents of being nondemocratic. The challengers did not want to change the way the system operated; they simply wanted a turn in office. When incumbents were confronted by that accusation, they sometimes responded by criticizing democracy and associating it with mob rule. But mostly, and with impressive consistency, political bosses across the spectrum of time and space adhered to a strict rhetorical defense of democracy. In fact, one of the challenges in studying politics in El Salvador, even though it is a small country, is to appreciate the scale at which those informal rules operated. Many thousands of elections occurred during El Salvador's first century of independence, and tens of thousands of different people ran for office or administered those elections, and many hundreds of thousands of people voted. Throughout it all, every political player demonstrated that he understood the informal rules of the game and adhered to them with steadfast determination. Only on the rarest occasion did anything approaching a genuinely competitive election take place in El Salvador. And almost never, in all of their correspondence relating to politics and elections, did political players reveal that they shared a mutual understanding of the disconnect between what they were saying and what they were doing. If nothing else, the long-standing operation of those informal rules implanted a stubborn tradition of authoritarianism in the collective consciousness of Salvadorans and in their political structures. Changing those rules, as Pío Romero Bosque discovered in the late 1920s, was not an easy task, because it involved re-shaping the nation's political identity and the understanding that its people had of how things were supposed to happen.

The political reform campaign that took place in El Salvador in the late 1920s, and the response of the military and the elites to it, invites an edifying comparison with neighboring Nicaragua during the same time period. Research by historian Michel Gobat reveals that a core sector of Nicaragua's landed elites, the so-called Conservatives, responded to the U.S. democratization campaign of the late 1920s with an atypical embrace of authoritarian corporatism and a call "for greater state intervention in the economic and social spheres, [which] represented an important break with their previous defense of a laissez-faire state."[4] The United States took the campaign seriously, and it created the Guardia Nacional to back it. In conjunction with the U.S. Marines, the Guardia effectively weakened the traditional rural powerbase of many elite Conservative strongmen. In the process, they took away one of the main political strategies of the rural poor—playing rival patron-client networks off one another to gain advantage. The Guardia Nacional soon became the lone channel through which peasants could pursue their desires. As for the Conservative elites, even though they had been staunch supporters of the United States and had touted the merits of its political and economic systems, they responded to the democratization campaign with authoritarian-style corporatism. They believed corporatism would allow them to attract support from alternative constituencies, such as urban workers, who were more amenable to corporatist-style organizing. What they ended up with, much to their surprise and chagrin, was Anastasio Somoza, head of the Guardia Nacional, who used those same corporatist organizational strategies to build up a personalistic dictatorship that worked to the detriment of Conservative elites. Not surprisingly, those elites, including the Chomorro family, then became staunch adversaries of the Somoza regime and even sided with the revolutionary Sandinstas in the campaign against Somoza in the 1970s.[5]

By comparison, the Salvadoran elites never embraced a corporate authoritarianism and instead remained steadfastly committed to economic libertarianism. It would seem that a main difference between the two countries was that the power of regional strongmen in El Salvador had already been broken when the democratization campaign was undertaken in the late 1920s. In the two or so decades prior to Romero Bosque's political reforms, the central state—coincidentally under the direction of fellow landed elites, the Meléndez-Quiñónez family—had waged a campaign against municipal autonomy and had enlisted the military and the security forces, such as the Guardia Nacional, in the process. So when Pío Romero Bosque undertook his reforms, elites did not have to respond with new statist political strategies to gain the support of unaffiliated urban constituents. They had already come to terms with the new order, and they believed that the necessary strategy was simply to make sure that the ideological orientation of the central government remained true to properly libertarian ideologies. Furthermore, the Romero reforms did not last long enough to threaten elite interests. Araujo was ousted in less than one year, and evidence from the municipal level reveals that the democratic reforms had made few inroads against the elite stalwarts who had held power since the days of the PND under Meléndez-Quiñónez. When the military took power and began to tout the need for social reforms, elites were ready to react, once again, by touting the necessity of economic libertarianism. With each passing year, they simply became more and more committed to that position, especially as the rhetoric and reality of reformism became more pronounced under a succession of military-led governments.

Even though both Nicaragua and El Salvador ended up with an authoritarian militarism, a comparison of the two cases reveals the need to appreciate the role of contingency in explaining each nation's political story. Maybe El Salvador was structurally conditioned for authoritarianism, and maybe it developed a distinct political culture of authoritarianism. But at various moments in the nation's history, divergent outcomes were possible. What if the United States had played an active role in the democratization campaign in El Salvador in the 1920s, as it did in neighboring Nicaragua? What if the 1932 uprising had not happened, or the military had responded to it in a more measured way? What if the process of state centralization had been less successful in the 1910s and 1920s, such that the democratization campaign of the late 1920s was the mechanism to break the power of regional strongmen? Each of these questions represents a counterfactual that cannot be answered; however, similar variables were in play in Nicaragua and produced a divergent outcome there, suggesting that something different could have happened in El Salvador. As one example, it is possible that under divergent conditions, Salvadoran elites, or some faction of them, could have supported a statist corporatism, and if so, it is possible that the nation's long-term political outcomes would have developed differently. Perhaps elites would have been less united and thus less able to resist reformism or revolution. Had that happened, El Salvador might have avoided its civil war—or the war might have come even earlier, and El Salvador's rebels would have been the precursor to Nicaragua's Sandinistas, instead of the other way around.

In addition to the work by Gobat, research by other scholars, such as Peter Guardino, Justin Wolfe, and Consuelo Cruz, among others, emphasizes the need to see the contingent nature of political history. Their work shows us, for example, that social classes do not behave in predictable or predetermined ways, that nations are not destined to produce particular political outcomes, and that people make strange decisions because they cannot predict the future and they interpret the past from their unique perspectives. Thus, to understand why a nation and its people do what they do, we have to study them and their actions in close detail and place contingency at the forefront of our analysis. I have tried to do that in the present study.

Although a main argument of this study is that El Salvador exhibited a strong political continuity, a second major legacy of the Martínez era was the injection of reform, or at least the idea of reform. He built upon the example of his two predecessors between 1927 and 1931 and began to consolidate the notion that government was supposed to be there for the common person, particularly to protect them from predatory, landowning elites. Martínez's reform program was called Mejoramiento Social, and its stated goal was the easing of pressure on the nation's poor. It espoused, among other things, buying up land and redistributing it to poor families on favorable terms, building affordable housing, and forcing elites to pay their workers in legal currency rather than local scrip. In the process, Martínez set a governing precedent to which each of his military successors would adhere for the next fifty years.

Ironically—or perhaps not—Martínez launched this reform program in the wake of a massive government crackdown on rebellious peasants in the western countryside. The military killed thousands, perhaps tens of thousands of people in a roughly two-week span, and thereafter it tolerated no form of autonomous rural organizing. All the while, Martínez's government wooed the masses, especially residents in the western region, with promises of reform and protection from vengeful local elites. Additionally, and consistent with his predecessors, Martínez celebrated the virtues of democracy and defined El Salvador as a modern, democratic republic. In so doing, Martínez established as a cornerstone of his governing strategy a complex mixture of reform and repression.

An apparent causal relationship exists between the peasant uprising of 1932 and Martínez's promotion of reform. Martínez was explicit on many occasions about his belief that dead and rebellious peasants did not promote economic productivity and national stability. Furthermore, he clearly said that the best way to prevent peasants from rebelling, which he and other government officials commonly defined as becoming a "communist," was to enact social and economic reforms. If nothing else, then, it seems apparent that the actions of the rebels in 1932 had an impact on the political arena in El Salvador.

Elites did not find Martínez's reforms too threatening, although they opposed some, such as Martínez's attempt to make them stop paying their workers in coupons (fichas) rather than legal currency, his effort to end the commercial monopoly of the finca-owned stores, and his refusal to allow the value of the national currency to float freely on the open market to the benefit of exporters. At the very least, elites did not like the precedent Martínez was setting, and indeed, in time they found themselves confronted by military officers who were more vigorously supportive of reform.

Another consequence of this study, then, is the need to see military–elite relations as complex and subject to conflicting narratives. At the center of the contest between elites and the military was the validity of social and economic reformism. Most elites insisted that El Salvador's development hinged on the degree to which government remained loyal to economic libertarianism. By contrast, many ruling officers believed that approach was a recipe for disaster (and the revolts in Cuba in 1959 and Nicaragua in 1979 would prove that to be a legitimate concern). Many officers advocated reformism as the way to avoid rebellion. However modest their plans might have been, and however expedient their embrace of reformism, they nevertheless made it a cornerstone of government. In the process they irked the libertarian sensibilities of their elite counterparts from the Martínez era onward.

Martínez left a complicated legacy for his reformist successors. After all, his regime murdered thousands of his countrymen. Subsequent governing officials found that fact hard to reconcile with their desire to promote themselves as modernizing reformers committed to social and economic development. No one celebrated the massacres of 1932 during the Martínez era, nor did anyone build monuments to Martínez after his downfall in 1944. Only on rare occasion did an obstinate voice appear on an editorial page, calling on Martínez to initiate the mass murder of peasants or Indians in the name of national development. For the most part, everyone seemed to want to forget what happened in 1932. Once Martínez had been ousted, it would be a long while before anyone overtly referred to him or his regime as a model. In fact, most of Martínez's successors purposely distanced themselves from his complicated legacy. The so-called revolutionary officers of 1948 rejected him as a backward-looking dictator and instead drew inspiration from the officers Martínez executed in April 1944 after their failed coup attempt. The "revolutionaries" portrayed those officers as martyrs of middle-class reformism who embodied El Salvador's hope for modernizing progress.

Even though none of the military governments after 1944 embraced Martínez openly, all of them followed his pattern of rule. In particular, each of them embraced the reform/repression dichotomy that the Martínez regime had exemplified. In the face of any perceived threat from peasants or urban workers, they quickly turned to violence and repressed without quarter. But all the while they presented themselves as modernizing reformers, hailed the virtues of democracy, and even pushed through some reformist programs. For example, the "revolutionary" officers wrote a new constitution in 1950 that not only gave women the right to vote and established the secret ballot, but also empowered the government to expropriate private property in the name of social justice. Those officers had neither the willingness nor the ability to act on their new legal right, but they took the rhetoric of reform to unprecedented levels. Even the self-declared conservative, anticommunist leaders who came to power in the coup of January 1961 pushed the cause of modernizing reform. They opened up the political system, passed labor laws for urban workers, and eventually attempted a land reform program. In both word and deed, they far exceeded anything that their "revolutionary" predecessors did. But they also oversaw the creation of ORDEN, a massive rural paramilitary organization that terrorized anyone who questioned the system or tried to mobilize against it.

Martínez's successors also followed his politics. Research into the day-to-day functioning of politics after 1944 remains hindered by a lack of evidence, but all indications point to practices that bear a strong resemblance to Martínez's. Each military regime approved the slate of candidates for municipal office and for the National Assembly, and they oversaw noncompetitive elections that naturally produced unanimous results. A brief window of respite opened up in the mid-1960s in response to the political reforms put through by Presidents Julio Adalberto Rivera (1962–1967) and Fidel Sánchez Hernández (1967–1972). A main beneficiary of those reforms was the centrist Christian Democratic Party, which made strong showings in both municipal elections and deputy elections for the National Assembly. But whenever the regime was threatened with ouster by popular vote, as occurred in the presidential elections of 1972 and 1977, it quickly clamped down on the reforms, stole elections, and increased repression against suspected adversaries. And so, regardless of whether it was the Partido Pro-Patria (1931–1944), the Partido Revolucionario de Unificación Democrática (1948–1960), or the Partido de Conciliación Nacional (1961–1979), each military government had a political machine that it used to dominate politics and control elections, in the tradition of its civilian predecessors.[6]

The integration of military politics into national politics was another precedent set during the Martínez era. Martínez came to power as part of a youth movement, when a group of disgruntled young officers organized themselves and overthrew the government in 1931. Once Martínez entrenched himself in power, he became the target of renewed youth activities inside the military. These movements emerged because young officers wanted a shot at holding office, not necessarily because they opposed their senior officers' dictatorial ways and wanted to do politics more democratically. By monopolizing government, Martínez and his cronies blocked the ascent of many young and aspiring officers. Constantly throughout his reign, Martínez had to stifle conspiracies from within the officer corps. A cyclical pattern had begun. Younger officers who wanted a turn in office portrayed the older officers in power as out-of-touch authoritarians while touting themselves as modernizing reformers. All of them adhered to the informal rules of politics by celebrating democracy and defining popular will as the arbiter of government action. Once in office, however, the new leaders became entrenched and thereby inspired their underlings to accuse them of betraying the spirit of modernization. And so the pattern went on, until the civil war of 1980 to 1992.[7]

This complex amalgamation of reform/repression, military–elite relations, and internal military politics came to a head in October 1979, when a military coup overthrew El Salvador's sitting president, General Carlos Romero. In his place, a governing junta came to power, consisting of two officers and three civilians. It was hardly a novel event in El Salvador's modern political history, as coups and attempted coups had been commonplace. Admittedly, though, nearly eighteen years had passed since the last successful coup in January 1961, and, ironically, General Romero was the political heir of that particular coup. The officers who came to power in 1961 had created a new party as their political machine, the Partido de Conciliación Nacional (PCN, the National Conciliation Party). A series of four officers served as president under its auspices between 1962 and 1979, with General Romero, who stepped up in 1977, being the last.

However, the coup of 1979 occurred when El Salvador was going through a particularly intense and unstable moment in its history. Just four months prior, in July 1979, the Somoza regime in neighboring Nicaragua had fallen to the revolutionary Sandinistas, bringing international attention and a new wave of geopolitical intensity to the isthmus. El Salvador's radical left viewed the events in Nicaragua with hope; the conservative right viewed them with fear; and everyone in between hoped to avoid the type of polarized implosion that Nicaragua had just suffered.

But October 1979 was almost too late to stop El Salvador from descending into war. Guerrilla organizations were well established and engaging the government's security forces in violent clashes almost daily. As many as a thousand people died each month, most of them innocent civilians who perished in brutal and mysterious ways at the hands of government security forces and paramilitary bands—the so-called death squads. Rumors circulated constantly of an impending coup by hardline rightists who believed that the solution to El Salvador's problems was even more killing, and they looked to the example set by General Martínez in 1932.

The architects of the 1979 coup came to power promising to implement widespread social and economic reforms that would stave off extremists on the right and the left. The coup was avidly supported by the U.S. government—some even contend that it was organized by the U.S. embassy—which desperately wanted a stable political center in power. The reformist spirit of the first junta suffered a series of blows, including the resignation of its three civilian members in early 1980 and various machinations by conservatives, both civil and military, who sought to limit the extent of reform. Nevertheless, the officials who governed El Salvador between 1979 and 1982 in a series of three juntas delivered on the promise of reform. The reforms may have been watered down relative to progressives' initial hopes, but the fact remains that they were the most far-reaching in Salvadoran history. Three of the more substantial reforms were the nationalization of banks, the nationalization of the export trade (including coffee), and a massive land reform. The latter was to occur in three stages over just a few years, with the ultimate goal being the expropriation (albeit with compensation) of most of the nation's largest properties and its distribution to poor families in the form of cooperatives and privately held plots.[8]

The tone and spirit of the coup was captured well by one of the original junta members, Colonel Jaime Abdul Gutiérrez, in a speech in the National Stadium in October 1981, on the second anniversary of the coup. Gutiérrez was then serving as vice president of the junta and commander in chief of the armed forces. In his roughly thirty-minute speech before a large crowd, he sounded every bit the reformist firebrand. Naturally, he included the requisite dose of anticommunism and accused the guerrillas of being terrorists and enemies of the state. But he also attacked intransigent rightists in both civilian and military forms. He accused them of being the main problem in El Salvador and of creating the conditions that allowed communists to gain an organizational foothold. He accused them of hoarding wealth, paying their workers poorly, and using unrestrained violence to keep labor in its place. Gutiérrez declared that "we leaders of the liberation movement of October 15 decided this time to set forth with determination the need for structural change as measures leading to an equal distribution of the national wealth." He cited as precedent the military reformers who had come to power in the coups of 1931, 1948, and 1961. The only problem with those predecessors, Gutiérrez insisted, was that they did not take reformism far enough. But at least they began the process that ended the era of "government by the great families . . . when any distinction between public and private interest was impossible and government institutions were conceived and managed as private preserves." In the process, he even tried to rehabilitate the name of General Martínez, not for his willingness to massacre thousands of people in the battle against communism, but because he weakened elite hegemony by implementing "fundamental changes" that "correct[ed] the excesses which had given rise to an extremely liberal concept of the State."[9]

Naturally, the guerrillas dismissed the coup and its reform program as a vacuous, desperate attempt to prevent real revolutionary change. They accused junta members of being lackeys of the United States, and they insisted that the reforms were poorly designed and inadequate to compensate for the ongoing slaughter by the state's security forces. As Gersón Martínez, a high-ranking guerrilla commander, put it in an interview nearly thirty years later, "The 1979 coup, with its purely counterinsurgent tendencies, had a well-defined goal: take away the guerrillas' momentum, drain the water away from the fish, take away the water from the guerrilla, diminish social support for the guerrilla."[10] Indeed, despite the reforms, mass killings continued unabated; nearly one thousand people died every month in politically related violence for nearly four years after the coup. High-profile assassinations, such as those of Archbishop Óscar Romero in March 1980, Enrique Alvarez in November 1980, and the two U.S. advisers to the land reform, Michael Hammer and Mark Pearlman, in January 1981, symbolized the broader campaign of terror.[11]

The left had good reason to oppose the reforms, and especially the appearance of the likes of Colonel Gutiérrez as spokespeople for social justice. Leftists accurately recognized the steady march to the right of each of the three successive juntas, symbolized by the resignation of the first junta's progressive civilians. They also accused the juntas of being unable or unwilling to stop the slaughter. Colonel Gutiérrez was, after all, a conservative stalwart in government, responsible for much of the stonewalling against far-reaching reform. Gutiérrez and other high-ranking officers bemoaned the ongoing killings by both paramilitary death squads and army troops, claiming they were doing their best to stop them. But it seems likely that these leaders were responsible for or at least indifferent to their perpetration. From the left's perspective, the 1979 coup was just a new wine in the old bottle of a conservative military-oligarchic dictatorship.

The left may have dismissed the post-1979 reforms as right-wing ploys, but conservative elites did not like them either. In fact, they hated them, seeing them as almost worse than a Sandinista-type revolution. In their minds, the reforms were nothing short of theft, and the reforms' architects were thieves hiding under the cover of government. The elites believed they had a right to their wealth and that the reformists were trampling the free market, El Salvador's only hope of escaping the growing crisis. Memoirs by economic elites and right-wing political activists make explicit the conservative animosity for the 1979 coup and all the actors complicit in it. From the elites' perspective, the coup brought together a murderer's row of political opportunists, including reformist military officers, the centrist politicians of the Christian Democratic Party, the U.S. government under President Jimmy Carter and his human rights–based foreign policy, the Jesuit priests at the Central American University (UCA) in San Salvador, and many other reform-minded organizations throughout El Salvador. These memoirists unleash vitriol in their descriptions of those actors and the reforms. For example, Luis Escalante Arce, a banker and member of one of El Salvador's wealthiest families, describes the 1979 coup in his 1986 memoir as having "intensified in El Salvador a long period of decadence and corruption." He says the subsequent reforms were inspired by "the vigorous ideological influence of Cuban sovietism" and that the two army officers who sat on the junta, including the conservative Colonel Gutiérrez, were "revolutionary statists who listened obediently to the voice of a foreign ambassador and of certain Jesuit priests who wanted to lead him down the path to Marxism."[12] Like Escalante Arce, David Panamá Sandoval and Ricardo Valdivieso Oriani were wealthy conservatives. They owned land and helped co-found the new conservative political party, the Alianza Republicana Nacionalista (ARENA, the Nationalist Republican Alliance), in 1980 alongside the notorious politician and paramilitary architect Roberto D'Aubuisson. In his 2005 memoir, Panamá Sandoval calls U.S. foreign policy makers under Carter a bunch of *"ineptos, ilusos o idiotas."*[13] For his part, Valdivieso Oriani borrows from 1950s-style McCarthyism to say in his 2008 memoir that the U.S. State Department was infested with communists and that in the late 1970s and early 1980s, Washington, DC, "was the beachhead of the Soviet Union's Marxist-Leninist imperialism throughout the entire Western Hemisphere." He goes on to say that it is "curious that during this time of the cold war, the North Americans never realized that its enemy was inside the halls of their own government."[14] A matriarch of a wealthy family, who granted an interview to a North American academic in the 1990s under the pseudonym Monica Nuñez, blames the U.S. government for the war, saying that "the Americans were the ones who really stirred things up here." President Carter, she insists, figured that land reform "was the way to head off a revolution here. But in the end the land reform laws he and his advisers pushed on us led to our civil war. We paid for Carter's experiments. We were his guinea pigs."[15]

Elite sentiments about the post-1979 reforms are so strong that they have produced a rift in conservative circles between those who claim they resisted them and their counterparts who supposedly collaborated with them. Orlando de Sola was a landowner who lost two properties in the land reform and also was one of ARENA's early supporters. He claims that he resisted the reforms at great personal cost, and he accuses none other than the first ARENA president, Alfredo Cristiani (1989–1994), of collaborating with the reformers. De Sola refers to himself as an *agrarista,* or coffee grower, whereas Cristiani was a *beneficiador-exportador,* or processor and exporter. Even though he knew Cristiani from childhood and their families were close, he opposed Cristiani's ascent through the ranks of ARENA because of the choices he made after 1979. De Sola accuses Cristiani of "selling out coffee growers" and "sacrificing producers" to make money, because while landowners like him were losing their lands to the agrarian reform, Cristiani, in his role as president of the Asociación de Beneficiadores y Exportadores de Café (Abecafé), sold to the government's new export control board "instead of resisting it." De Sola even criticizes D'Aubuisson for being too soft on the reforms, saying that "a difference that I had with D'Aubuisson was the agrarian reform, which I wanted to classify as negative, but he refused to do so." De Sola claims that he had a falling-out with D'Aubuisson and ARENA over these issues, especially after D'Aubuisson picked Cristiani to be the presidential candidate in 1989 after his own failed bid for the presidency in 1984. De Sola claims that the rise of people like Cristiani sold ARENA out to the "*neoliberales,*" as opposed to the "*liberales clásicos*" like him.[16]

Elite memoirists like Escalante Arce, De Sola, Panamá Sandoval, Valdivieso Oriani, and others consider the 1979 reforms to be the culminating moment in a long history of conflict between elites and military reformers. As evidence they cite a litany of prior reforms or attempted reforms that the military governments imposed on them. Those reforms include, among others, the attempted land reform in 1976; the land-reform congress in the National Assembly in 1970; aspects of the 1968 education reform; the political reforms in the mid-1960s that allowed for proportional representation in the National Assembly; the embrace of the Alliance for Progress in the 1960s and its modernization-theory mantra accusing large landowners of being a barrier to development; and the 1950 constitution that empowered the state to expropriate private property for the common good. And when it comes to discussing the civil war, elite memoirists barely mention the army, as if twelve years of almost daily combat against leftist guerrillas were merely a side item to the more central mission of preserving the free market and private property. At the very least, elite memoirists do not portray the military as their historic benefactor and ally. Rather, they see the military in a more suspicious light, describing officers as willing to sacrifice elites and free-market capitalism for personal aggrandizement or institutional survival.

Not surprisingly, when military officers penned their memoirs, they had few positive things to say about the elites. In particular, they believe elites sold them out at the negotiating table in 1992 by allying with their former enemy, the guerrillas, in a sort of civilian cabal plotting to destroy the military. As just one example, General Orlando Zepeda, former vice minister of defense, claims in his 2008 memoir that of the stakeholders in the peace negotiations, "the military sector was the most affected." He characterizes the forced retirements and decommissioning of nearly two hundred officers in the wake of the Chapultepec Peace Accords as "an unjust and humiliating process." He critiques elites and the "monopolies and privileges of the big enterprises" and says El Salvador's "true problem rests in its unjust distribution of wealth and benefits that emerges from the cultivation of land that remains in the hands of a few large landowners." He then says that elites, through ARENA, banded together with the FMLN at the end of the war to "demilitarize society."[17]

A reader might look upon these rhetorical jousts between elites and officers with skepticism. After all, elites fared well under military rule, and they came out of the civil war with most of what they wanted—libertarian capitalism and sanctity for private property. The military did not suffer too badly either until the end of the civil war. It commanded large portions of the state's budget for decades, especially during the conflict, and many individual officers made out handsomely before, during, and after it. And almost every one of the officers who was decommissioned, frankly, deserved it, having committed a range of human-rights abuses or acts of graft, or both. A healthy dose of doubt is thus warranted.

But too much skepticism would be contrary to the evidence. However much elites and officers might propagandize their respective views, the fact remains that their rhetorical positions express the way they see themselves and want to be seen by others. The elites believe themselves to be an aggrieved minority that has suffered threats and abuses not only from so-called terrorists on the left, but also from centrist reformists, civilians and officers alike. They believe those reformists have blamed them for society's ills and have targeted their wealth as the solution. Elites see themselves as responsible for whatever level of development El Salvador has achieved, going all the way back to the privatization decrees of the 1880s, and that by targeting them and their wealth, revolutionaries and reformers are dooming El Salvador to perpetual backwardness and underdevelopment. The elites contend that they worked hard for their wealth, and in the process of acquiring it they served their nation, so they have a right to keep it.[18]

The military—despite its assaults on autonomous labor organizing, which allowed elites access to labor on beneficial terms—did not see itself as simply the elites' Praetorian Guard. As one of the more publicly outspoken officers, General Mauricio Vargas, put it in a 2010 interview, the military was not the "guardian of the plantations. . . . We had our own institutional and constitutional mission."[19] Instead, military leaders, especially those who sat in government positions, considered themselves modernizing reformers who believed that one of the necessary defenses against communism was the modernization of society. They interpreted modernization in various ways, but included among them was the use of state power to diversify the economy and broaden access to the nation's wealth. They reasoned that the state had to play an active role in these endeavors because elites had little incentive to alter the status quo and venture into risky alternative investments.

To conclude, I believe the evidence suggests that El Salvador had a distinct political culture in which a discourse of democracy and reformism resided amidst authoritarian practices. Borrowing from Consuelo Cruz's comparative analysis of Nicaragua and Costa Rica, it is entirely possible that this culture in El Salvador, if it indeed existed, functioned as a bulwark against genuine democratization over the long run. That culture may owe its origins to El Salvador's structural conditions; in other words, El Salvador may have been materially predetermined to have an authoritarian political system that would naturally produce an authoritarian culture. But if Cruz's scholarship provides guidance, then it is also possible that El Salvador has struggled so much to achieve democracy, to say nothing of a more well-balanced distribution of wealth (á la Costa Rica), because its political culture functioned as an autonomous variable and determined the way Salvadorans viewed themselves and the policy choices they made. When it came time, for example, to privatize land in the early 1880s, the long-term outcome was not more egalitarianism, as could have been the case had people chosen to enact the policies differently, but rather a highly uneven distribution of wealth with an ever-expanding pool of desperate rural inhabitants. Subsequently, they had few alternatives when their situation declined even further, as it did during the Great Depression, and so some of them chose to rise up in violent rebellion. That rebellion, in turn, was met not with responsible justice, but rather with a brutal military slaughter. Rather than acknowledge that the extant structures of society might bear some responsibility for poor people's desperation, elites responded with an ever more determined ideology of economic libertarianism and reactionary politics.

I followed a different methodology than Cruz in that I did not dissect political rhetoric throughout El Salvador's history going all the way back to the Spanish Conquest. However, I did examine the way politics was practiced over a few decades in the late nineteenth and early twentieth centuries, and I evaluated the discourse that accompanied the practice of politics. Thus, I can respond to Cruz's "blunt questions. . . . Are their [political actors'] actions consistent with their words? In the crudest terms, do they adhere, do they deliver?"[20] To each of those questions, the evidence responds with a resounding no.

Regardless of whether El Salvador had a political culture of authoritarianism, and regardless of whether that culture functioned as an autonomous variable, the evidence shows clearly that politics in El Salvador functioned in an authoritarian manner. That system eventually took the form of a relationship between landed elites and governing military officers. In this regard, the evidence suggests that the prevailing comparative scholarship is correct: a defining feature of El Salvador's modern history is the unity of its elite sector and the durability of the elite–military alliance, however complex and diverse it may have been.[21]

APPENDIX

Table A1. The Presidents of El Salvador, 1840–1944

General Francisco Morazán	June 8, 1839, to February 16, 1840
José María Silva	February 16, 1840, to May 20, 1840
Antonio José Cañas	May 20, 1840, to September 20, 1840
Norberto Ramírez	September 20, 1840, to January 7, 1841
Juan Lindo*	January 7, 1841, to February 1, 1842
General José Escolastico Marín	February 1, 1842, to April 13, 1842
Juan J. Guzmán	April 13, 1842, to June 30, 1842
Dioniso Villacorta	June 30, 1842, to July 19, 1842
General José Escolastico Marín	July 19, 1842, to September 26, 1842
Juan J. Guzmán	September 26, 1842, to January 26, 1843
Pedro Arce	January 26, 1843, to March 8, 1843
Juan J. Guzmán	March 8, 1843, to January 31, 1844
Fermín Palacios	January 31, 1844, to February 1, 1844
General Francisco Malespín	February 1, 1844, to May 9, 1844
Joaquín Eufrasio Guzmán	May 9, 1844, to June 16, 1844
General Francisco Malespín	June 16, 1844, to October 25, 1844
Joaquín Eufrasio Guzmán	October 25, 1844, to February 16, 1845
Fermín Palacios	February 16, 1845, to April 22, 1845
Joaquín Eufrasio Guzmán	April 22, 1845, to February 1, 1846
Fermín Palacios	February 1, 1846, to February 21, 1846
Eugenio Aguilar	February 21, 1846, to July 12, 1846
Fermín Palacios	July 12, 1846, to July 21, 1846
Eugenio Aguilar*	July 21, 1846, to January 31, 1848
Tomás Medina	February 1, 1848, to February 3, 1848
Félix Quirós	February 3, 1848, to February 7, 1848
Doroteo Vasconcelos*	February 7, 1848, to January 26, 1850
Ramón Rodríguez	January 26, 1850, to February 1, 1850

Table A1. (*continued*)

Miguel Santín del Castillo	February 1, 1850, to February 4, 1850
Doroteo Vasconcelos	February 4, 1850, to January 12, 1851
Francisco Dueñas	January 12, 1851, to March 1, 1851
Félix Quirós	March 1, 1851, to May 13, 1851
Francisco Dueñas*	May 13, 1851, to February 1, 1854
Vicente Gómez	February 1, 1854, to February 13, 1854
José María San Martín	February 15, 1854, to September 26, 1854
Mariano Hernández	September 26, 1854, to November 13, 1854
José María San Martín*	November 13, 1854, to February 1, 1856
Francisco Dueñas	February 1, 1856, to February 12, 1856
Rafael Campo	February 12, 1856, to May 16, 1856
Francisco Dueñas	May 16, 1856, to July 16, 1856
Rafael Campo*	July 16, 1856, to January 31, 1858
Lorenzo Zepeda	January 31, 1858, to February 7, 1858
Miguel Santín del Castillo	February 7, 1858, to June 24, 1858
General Gerardo Barrios	June 24, 1858, to September 20, 1858
Miguel Santín del Castillo	September 29, 1858, to January 9, 1859
Joaquín Eufrasio Guzmán	January 9, 1859, to February 15, 1859
José María Peralta	February 15, 1859, to March 9, 1859
General Gerardo Barrios	March 9, 1859, to December 15, 1860
José María Peralta	December 15, 1860, to February 9, 1861
General Gerardo Barrios*	February 9, 1861, to October 26, 1863
Francisco Dueñas*	October 26, 1863, to April 1, 1871
General Santiago González*	April 1, 1871, to May 1, 1872
Manuel Méndez	May 1, 1872, to July 9, 1872
General Santiago González*	July 9, 1872, to February 1, 1876
Andrés Valle	February 1, 1876, to April 30, 1876
Rafael Zaldívar*	April 30, 1876, to April 6, 1884
Angel Guirola	April 6, 1884, to August 21, 1884
Rafael Zaldívar	August 21, 1884, to May 15, 1885
General Fernando Figueroa	May 15, 1885, to June 18, 1885
José Rosales	June 18, 1885, to June 22, 1885
General Francisco Menéndez*	June 22, 1885, to June 22, 1890
General Carlos Ezeta*	June 22, 1890, to June 9, 1894
General Rafael Gutiérrez*	June 9, 1894, to November 13, 1898
General Tomás Regalado*	November 13, 1898, to February 28, 1903
Pedro José Escalón*	March 1, 1903, to February 28, 1907
General Fernando Figueroa*	March 1, 1907, to February 28, 1911

Manuel Enrique Araujo*	February 28, 1911, to February 8, 1913
Carlos Meléndez*	February 9, 1913, to August 28, 1914
Alfonso Quiñónez Molina	August 28, 1914, to February 28, 1915
Carlos Meléndez*	February 28, 1915, to December 21, 1918
Alfonso Quiñónez Molina	December 21, 1918, to February 28, 1919
Jorge Meléndez*	February 28, 1919, to February 28, 1923
Alfonso Quiñónez Molina*	February 28, 1923, to February 28, 1927
Pío Romero Bosque*	February 28, 1927, to February 28, 1931
Arturo Araujo	February 28, 1911, to December 2, 1931
General Maximiliano H. Martínez*	December 2, 1931, to August 28, 1934
General Andrés Menéndez	August 28, 1934, to February 28, 1935
General Maximiliano H. Martínez*	February 28, 1935, to May 8, 1944

Sources: Hernández, *Biografías de vicentinos,* 173–177; and Taplin, *Middle American Governors,* 96–103.

Note: An asterisk (*) denotes a president who remained in office for more than twelve months consecutively.

**Table A2. Political Continuity under the PND, 1920–1927,
San Vicente and Ahuachapán Departments**

San Vicente Department

Municipality	Did any officials serve in more than one administration for the elections of 1920, 1921, 1923, or 1925? If so,who were they, and in which years were they elected?	Did any different persons bearing the same surname appear more than once? If so, what was the name, and in which years did it appear?
Apastepeque	No	Vega 1920, 1921
Guadalupe	Miguel Menjívar 1920, 1923 José Obulio Hernández 1921, 1925 Guadalupe Montoya 1921, 1925	Platero 1920 (2x) Marroquín 1920, 1923 Rodríguez 1920, 1923 Henríquez 1921, 1923 1925 (2x) Cerritos 1921, 1923
San Cayetano	José Coreas 1920, 1923 Vicente Flores, 1920, 1923	Fernández 1920, 1921
San Estebán	Rubén Acevedo 1920, 1925 José Vicente 1921, 1925	Durán 1921 (2x), 1925 Acevedo 1920 (2x), 1925 Aguilar 1923 (2x)
San Idelfonso	Francisco Panameño 1920, 1923	Marín 1920, 1921, 1923 Artiga 1920, 1923 Amaya 1920, 1923 Panameño (1920, 1923), 1921
San Lorenzo	Mateo Merino 1920, 1923	Acevedo 1923, 1925
San Sebastián	Fidel Burgos 1920, 1923 Alberto Rodríguez 1920, 1923	Barahona 1920 (2x), 1921 (2x) Alfaro 1921, 1923, 1925 Burgos (1920, 1923), 1921
San Vicente	José María Arévalo 1920, 1923 Cárlos Vidal 1920, 1923 Guadalupe Cañas 1920, 1923 Constantino Ticas 1920, 1923 Miguel Lara Iraheta 1920, 1925 José Luís Ticas 1921, 1925	Ticas (1920, 1923), 1921, 1925 Castillo 1920, 1921

Santa Clara	Florentino Flores 1920, 1923	Cerritos 1920, 1921, 1923 Merino 1923, 1925
Santo Domingo	No	Meléndez 1920, 1921, 1923, 1925
Tecoluca	Coronado Choto 1920, 1923	Corpeño 1920, 1921 Cañas 1920, 1921 Choto (1920, 1923), 1921 Flores 1920, 1923 Rodríguez 1923 (2x)
Verapáz	Manuel Durán 1920, 1923	Durán (1920, 1923), 1921

Sources: List of municipal officials elected in San Vicente Department in December 1920, compiled by Governor of San Vicente Department, December 14, 1920, AGN, MG, SSV, 1923, Box 3; List of municipal officials elected in December 1921, found in AGN, MG, 1915, Box 1; List of municipal officials elected in December 1923, AGN, MG, 1923, Box 4; and List of municipal officials elected in December 1925, AGN, MG, unclassified box.

Key: The symbol (2x) means that the surname appeared twice in the same year. When two years are listed together in brackets (1920, 1923), it means that in those years the surname is represented by the same person. The maternal surnames rarely were listed in the documents.

Ahuachapán Department

Municipality	Did any officials serve in more than one administration for the elections of 1920, 1921, 1923, or 1925? If so, who were they, and in which years were they elected?	Did any different persons bearing the same surname appear more than once? If so, what was the name, and in which years did it appear?
Ahuachapán City	No	Padilla 1920, 1921 Calderón 1920, 1921 Arriaza 1920, 1923 Avelar 1920, 1925 Contreras 1925 (2x) Rodríguez 1921, 1923
Apaneca	No	Morán 1920, 1921 Mata 1920, 1925
Ataco	Porfirio García 1920, 1923 Antonio Hernández 1920, 1925	Cardona 1920 (2x) Aguirre 1920, 1923 Arévalo 1921 (2x), 1925

Table A2. (*continued*)

Atiquizaya	Simeón Vega 1920, 1923	Ortíz 1920, 1921
	Isidro Góchez 1921, 1925	Góchez 1920, 1921, 1925 (2x)
Guaymango	Valeriano Valencia 1920, 1923	Castañeda 1920 (2x), 1921, 1923
	José Alvarenga 1921, 1925	Monroy 1920, 1921
Jujutla	Luís Rivera 1920, 1921	Martínez 1920, 1925
	Eligio de Mata 1920, 1925	Ibañez 1921, 1923
	Daniel Girón 1920, 1925	
El Refugio	Miguel Rodríguez 1920, 1923	Rodríguez 1920, 1923 (2x)
	Eugenio Castro 1921, 1925	Vega 1920, 1923
San Francisco	Domingo Tobar 1920, 1923	Arévalo 1920, 1923 (2x)
	Felícito Fajardo 1920, 1923	Alvárez 1921, 1925
		Castillo 1921, 1925
San Lorenzo	No	Rodríguez 1920, 1921, 1925
		Sermeño 1920, 1923
San Pedro Pustla	Estebán Montenegro 1920, 1923	Quezada 1920, 1925
	Celso Castañeda 1921, 1925	Padilla 1921, 1923
Turín	Santiago Chicas 1920, 1925	Canizález 1920, 1923
		Chicas (1920, 1925), 1921

Sources: List of municipal officials elected in Ahuachapán Department in December 1920, compiled by Governor of Ahuachapán Department, January 12, 1921, AGN, MG, unclassified box; List of municipal officials elected in December 1921, found in AGN, MG, 1915, Box 1; List of municipal officials elected in December 1923, AGN, MG, 1923, Box 4; and List of municipal officials elected in December 1925, AGN, MG, unclassified box.

Key: The symbol (2x) means that the surname appeared twice in the same year. When two years are listed together in brackets (1920, 1923), it means that in those years the surname is represented by the same person. The maternal surnames rarely were listed on the documents. Tacuba was excluded for reasons discussed at the end of chapter 5.

Explanatory Summary: The material contained in Table A2 is admittedly sprawling and difficult to comprehend at first glance. The evidence represents surveys of the officials elected to municipal office in Ahuachapán and San Vicente departments between 1920 and 1927, during the era of the Meléndez-Quiñónez dynasty and their political party, the PND. The simple appearance of the various names and the dates behind them on these lists shows the continuity that occurred in local officeholding under the PND. Basically, once a local political network, represented by the individuals on this list, got into local power under the PND, it stayed there and held office for many consecutive elections. I interpret this information as evidence of the centralizing consolidation of the patronage system under the PND.

**Table A3. The Transition to Pío Romero Bosque in the Elections of
December 1927, San Vicente and Ahuachapán Departments**

San Vicente Department

Municipality	Did any officials elected in 1927 serve in an administration from 1920, 1921, 1923, or 1925? If so, who were they, and in which years had they also served?	Did any persons bearing the same surname as one of the officials from 1927 serve in prior administrations? If so, what was the name, and in which year(s) did they serve?
Apastepeque	Jesús Vega 1921 Jesús Cubías 1921	No
Guadalupe	Miguel Menjívar 1920, 1923 Magdeleno Chávez 1921, 1927	Henríquez 1921, 1923, 1925 (2x)
San Cayetano	Vicente Flores 1920, 1923	No
San Estebán	Joaquín Rivera 1920	Acevedo 1920 (2x), 1925
San Idelfonso	No	Artiga 1920 Marín 1920
San Lorenzo	Domingo Ponce 1923	Cubías 1921, 1923
San Sebastián	Pedro Juan Alfaro 1921	Alfaro 1923, 1925 Guzmán 1921 Barahona 1920 (2x), 1921 (2x)
San Vicente	No	No
Santa Clara	Gregorio Ramos 1920	No
Santo Domingo	No	Quintanilla 1921 Platero 1921
Tecoluca	Bonifacio Choto 1921	Ortíz 1921 Choto 1920, 1923
Verapáz	Moisés Alfaro 1921	Lozano 1920 García 1925

Source: List of municipal officials elected in San Vicente Department, December 1927, AGN, MG, SSV, 1927, Box 1, compared to data in Table A2.

Table A3. (*continued*)
Ahuachapán Department

Municipality	Alcalde	Had the alcalde served in any of the administrations that came to power in 1920, 1921, 1923, or 1925? If so, when?	Did any person bearing the alcalde's surname serve in those prior administrations? If so, who, and when?
Ahuachapán	Rigoberto Pinel	No	No
Apaneca	Israel Rodríquez	No	No
Ataco	Angel Arévalo	No	Teodoro Arévalo 1921 José Antonio Arévalo 1921 Vicente Ortíz Arévalo 1925
Atiquizaya	Antonio Luna	No	No
Guaymango	Rosalio Castañeda	No Rómulo Castañeda 1923	Antonio Suriano Castañeda 1921 Miguel Valiente Castañeda 1921 Máximo Castañeda 1923
Jujutla	Mariano Aguirre	No	Emilio Aguirre 1923
El Refugio	Benjamín Cárcamo	No	José Cárcamo 1923
San Francisco	Carlos Doral	No	No
San Lorenzo	Baudilio Luna	No	Emigdio Luna 1925
San Pedro Pustla	Adolfo Padilla	Yes, 1921	No
Turín	Germán Molina	No	No

Source: List of alcaldes elected nationwide in December 1927, *Diario del Salvador,* December 14, 1927, 5, compared to data in Table A2.

Note: The municipality of Tacuba was excluded for the reasons discussed at the end of chapter 5.

Explanatory Summary: The material contained here in Table A3, like that in A2 above, is sprawling and difficult to comprehend at first glance. The evidence represents surveys of the officials elected to municipal office in Ahuachapán and San Vicente departments in December 1927, in the first elections held under the new administration of Pío Romero Bosque. The goal of the survey was to determine whether there was any significant changeover in local of-ficeholding in the transition from Meléndez-Quiñónez and the PND to Romero Bosque. Using common surnames as a rough indicator of kinship relations, the appearance of the names on these lists suggests a continuity in office-holding. Basically, Romero Bosque had only limited success in bringing about changeover in local office, suggesting that the patronage networks that dominated municipal office under the PND continued to do so.

Table A4. The Transition to Pío Romero Bosque in the Elections of December 1929, Ahuachapán Department

Municipality	Did any officials serve in more than one administration for the elections of 1920, 1921, 1923, or 1925? If so, who were they, and in which years were they elected?	Did any different persons bearing the same surname appear more than once? If so, what was the name, and in which years did it appear?
Ahuachapán	Rafael Rivas 1923	Calderón 1920, 1921, Equizabel 1920
Apaneca	Luís Melgar 1923 Nicolás Herrera 1923	No
Ataco	Toribio Chávez 1923 Tomas Hernández 1921, 1925 Gregorio Alvarado 1920	No
Atiquizaya	Simeón Vega 1920, 1923	Noyola 1920
Guaymango	Valerianco Valencia 1920, 1923	García 1921
Jujutla	Venancio Urutia 1923	No
El Refugio	No	Avévalo 1920
San Francisco	Abrahám Ruíz 1921	No
San Lorenzo	No	Cárcamo 1923
San Pedro Pustla	Carlos Tadeo Jiménez 1920 Celso Castañeda 1921, 1925	No
Turín	No	Betancourt 1920 Flores 1920 Canizales 1920, 1923

Source: List of municipal officials elected in Ahuachapán Department, December 1927, AGN, MG, unclassified box.

Note: The municipality of Tacuba was excluded for the reasons discussed in chapter 5.

Explanatory Summary: The material contained here in Table A4, like that in A3 above, is sprawling and difficult to comprehend at first glance. The evidence represents surveys of the officials elected to municipal office in Ahuachapán Department in December 1929, under the administration of Pío Romero Bosque. The goal of the survey was to determine if any more changeover in local officeholding occurred during the transition from Meléndez-Quiñónez and the PND to Romero in 1929 than had occurred in 1927. Using common surnames as a rough indicator of kinship relations, the appearance of the names on these lists suggests that a degree of continuity in officeholding similar to that of 1927 typified the elections of 1929 as well. Basically, Romero continued to have limited success in bringing about changeover in local office, suggesting that the patronage networks that dominated municipal office under the PND continued to do so.

Table A5. Alcaldes Elected in 1937, 1939, and 1941, Departments of Sonsonate, Ahuachapán, and San Miguel

Sonsonate Department

	Alcalde Elected by Year		
Municipality	1937	1939	1941
Sonsonate	Abraham Castillo	Héctor Salaverría	Héctor Salaverría
Sonzacate	Francisco Portillo	Hipólito Rosa	Francisco Portillo
Nahuilingo	Eduardo Valenzuela	Pablo Rodríguez	Rodrigo González
Nahuizalco	Rodolfo Brito	Juan Mendoza	Fernando Martínez
Santo Domingo	Pedro Ramos	Manuel Candel	Manuel Candel
San Antonio	Jacinto Gudiel	Jerónimo Menéndez	Jacinto Gudiel
Acajutla	Juan Escobar	Juan Escobar	Juan Escobar
Juayúa	José Mata	José Mata	José Mata
Salcoatitán	Antonio Salaverría	Manuel Canales	Fernando Alarcón
Masahuat	Juan Cardona	Abelardo Larín	Abelardo Larín
Izalco	Carlos Salazar	Paulino Herrera	Carlos Salazar
Cuisnahuat	Lino Ruiz	Santos Hernández	Pablo Martínez
Caluco	Estebán Leonor	Manuel Guillén	Estebán Leonor
Ishuatán	Pablo de Leon	Félix Rivera	Ramón Peña
San Julián	Alberto Englehard	Salvador Díaz	Carlos García
Armenia	Alfredo Morán	Manuel Recinos	Manuel Recinos

Additional Linkages, by municipality (includes persons bearing the same surname, or the same person serving in more than one administration, who are not contained in above list): *Sonsonate*: none; *Sonzacate*: Francisco Portillo (elected alcalde in 1937 and 1941) was also elected to municipal council in 1939; *Nahuilingo*: surname González appears in 1939 and 1941; *Nahuizalco*: surnames Brito and Martínez appear in 1937 and 1939, Juan Contreras (elected to municipal council in 1939) is cousin and political ally of Rodolfo Brito (elected alcalde in 1937) as mentioned in chapter 3; *Santo Domingo*: none; *San Antonio*: none; *Acajutla*: not necessary; *Juayúa,* not necessary; *Salcoatitán*: surname Canales appears in 1937 and 1939, surname Alarcón appears in 1939 and 1941; *Masahuat*: surname Santos appears in 1937 and 1939; *Izalco*: surnames Martínez and Alvarez appear in 1937 and 1939; *Cuisnahuat*: Pablo Martínez (elected alcalde in 1941) elected to municipal council in 1937, surname Hernández appears in 1937 and 1939; *Caluco*: Manuel Guillén (elected alcalde in 1939) elected to municipal council in 1937; *Ishuatán*: surname Rivera appears in 1937 and 1939; *San Julián*: Carlos García (elected alcalde in 1941) elected to municipal council in 1937, surnames Barrientos, Rivera, and Díaz appear in 1937 and 1939; *Armenia*: none.

Ahuachapán Department

	Alcalde Elected by Year		
Municipality	1937	1939	1941
Ahuachapán	José Morán	Alfonso Borja	Alfonso Borja
Atiquizaya	José Cárceres	Juan ?	Angel Castro
Tacuba	Alberto Linares	Rogelio Doratt	Rogelio Doratt
Ataco	Victor Pineda	Victor Pineda	Victor Pineda
Apaneca	José Román	Israel Rodríguez	Jorge Luna
Turín	Antonio Flores	José Matute	José Matute
San Francisco	Humberto Doratt	Mariano Ruiz	Carlos Doratt
San Pedro Puxtla	Narciso Pérez	Narcisco Pérez	Erasmo Castro
Guaymango	José Torrente	Atilio Castro	Andrés Ruiz
San Lorenzo	Marcial Cárcamo	Rafael Perdomo	Rafael Perdomo
Jujutla	Rafael Morán	Francisco Carranza	Francisco Carranza
El Refugio	José Zepeda	José Zepeda	José Zepeda

Additional Linkages, by municipality: *Ahuachapán*: Miguel Chacón elected in 1937 and 1939, Juan Herrera elected in 1937 and 1939; *Atiquizaya*: surnames Cárcamo and Ibarra appear in 1937 and 1939; *Tacuba*: surname Magaña appears in 1937 and 1939; *Ataco*: not necessary; *Apaneca*: Jorge Luna (elected alcalde in 1941) elected to municipal council in 1939, and another person bearing surname Luna elected in 1937; *Turín*: surname Flores appears in 1937 and 1939; *San Francisco*: Atiliano Córtez elected in 1937 and 1939; *San Pedro Puxtla*: surname Castro appears in 1937 and 1941; *Guaymango*: José Torrente (elected alcalde in 1937) elected to municipal council in 1939; *San Lorenzo*: surname Sermeño appears in 1937 and 1939; *Jujutla*: Francisco Carranza (elected alcalde in 1939 and 1941) elected to municipal council in 1937; *El Refugio*: not necessary.

San Miguel Department

	Alcalde Elected by Year		
Municipality	1937	1939	1941
San Miguel	José Luís Silva	José Luís Silva	Alfonso Gustave
Chinameca	Rosendo Vásquez	José Recinos	José Recinos
Sesori	Daniel Bernal	Atilio Villafuerte	Atilio Villafuerte
Ciudad Barrios	Claudio Portillo	Mónico Quintero	Carlos Guerra
Nuevo Eden	Manuel Jerez	Cornado Márquez	Cornado Márquez
Uluazapa	Manuel Gómez	Fidel Benavides	Fidel Benavides
Moncagua	Rodrigo Palacios	Valentínn Alegría	Atilo Loza
Chirilagua	Rubén Rivera	Alberto Grimaldi	Alberto Grimaldi
Carolina	Isidoro Guzmán	Francisco Protillo	Francisco Portillo

Table A5. (*continued*)

Comacarón	Marcos Martínez	Nicolás Bustillo	Nicolá Bustillo
Chapeltique	Joaquín Carballo	Marcelo Ortíz	Marcelo Ortíz
San Luis Reina	Clemente Salmerón	Julio Aguirre	Julio Aguirre
San Gerardo	Luís Araujo	Enrique Rosa	Enrique Rosa
San Antonio	Tomás Aguilar	José Guevara	José Guevara
Quelapa	Isabel Privado	Abel Ramírez	Abel Ramírez
El Transito	Gonzalo Alvarado	Alberto García	Rafael Gómez
San Rafael Oriente	Lino Serpas	José Amaya	José Amaya
Nueva Guadalupe	Rodrigo Benavides	José Ulloa	Ovidio Zelaya
Lolotique	José Cruz	José Cruz	Raúl Molina
San Jorge	Eleazar Quintanilla	Eleazar Quintanilla	Celestino Campos

Additional Linkages, by municipality: *San Miguel*: none; *Chinameca*: Fernando Pacheco elected in 1937 and 1939; *Sesori*: surnames Guzmán, Bernal, and Argueta appear in 1937 and 1939; *Ciudad Barrios*: surname de la O. appears in 1937 and 1939; *Nuevo Eden*: Dolores Alfonso served in 1937 and 1939; *Uluzapa*: none; *Mancogua*: surname Loza appears in 1937 and 1939; Rubén Rivera (elected alcalde in 1937) also elected to municipal council in 1939, José Campos and Alonso Avilez elected in both 1937 and 1939; *Carolina*: surname Guzmán appears in 1937 and 1939; *Comacarón*: none; *Chapeltique*: surnames Alvarez and Portillo appear in 1937 and 1939; *San Luis*: surname Ramos appears in 1937 and 1939; *San Gerardo*: surname Padilla appears in 1937 and 1939; *San Antonio*: surname Guevara appears in 1937 and 1939; *Quelapa*: surnames Privado and González appear in 1937 and 1939; *El Transito*: none; *San Rafael*: none; *Nueva Guadalupe*: Indalecio Lovo elected in 1937 and 1939, surname Zelaya appears in 1937, 1939, and 1941, surname Funes appears in 1937 and 1939; *Lolotique*: none; *San Jorge*: Celesino Campos (elected alcalde in 1941) also elected to municipal council in 1937.

Sources: List of municipal officials from election of December 1937, AGN, MG, 1938 unclassified paquete; List of municipal officials selected in December 1939, AGN, MG, 1939, unclassified paquete; List of municipal officials selected in December 1941, AGN, MG, 1942, unclassified paquete, Folder #181.3.

Note: Elections after 1935 occurred every two years, and after 1939 the municipal officials were appointed directly by the government without a corresponding election.

Explanatory Summary: As in tables A2, A3, and A4 above, the evidence contained in this table surveys municipal officeholders over successive elections to determine whether changeover in office was occurring. The focus in the table itself is solely on the position of alcalde (with additional officers described in the paragraph below them), and the "elections" are between 1937 and 1941, under the regime of General Martínez, in three departments—San Vicente, Ahuachapán, and San Miguel. By this time, municipal elections had been abandoned in favor of direct appointment by the central government. Here again, the goal is to determine whether there was any significant changeover in office, or if the same people tended to hold office year to year. The repeated appearance of the same individuals (or people bearing the same surname) suggests that there was very little turnover in office. In short, once a local political network earned the favor of the central administration under Martínez, they held local office without interruption.

NOTES

Introduction

1. General Martínez's full surname was Hernández Martínez, but he went by his maternal name only.

2. Stanley, *Protection Racket State*. See also Baloyra, *El Salvador in Transition*; Byrne, *El Salvador's Civil War*; Cabarrús, *Génesis de una revolución*; Castro Morán, *Función política*; Dunkerley, *The Long War*; Gordon, *Crisis política*; Grenier, *Emergence of Insurgency*; C. McClintock, *Revolutionary Movements*; Pearce, *Promised Land*; Serpas, *La lucha por un sueño*; and Williams and Walter, *Militarization and Demilitarization*. All of these works are rife with nuance and sophistication, although they tend to advance the oligarchy-military alliance as a prevailing feature of twentieth-century El Salvador. That argument is exemplified by comparativist scholars who explain El Salvador's uniqueness vis-à-vis its neighbors, including Nicaragua and Costa Rica, according to the unity of its elites and their close alliance with the military. See, for example, Brockett, *Political Movements*; Dunkerley, *Power in the Isthmus*; Goodwin, *No Other Way Out*; Mason, *Caught in the Crossfire*; Paige, *Coffee and Power*; and Wickham-Crowley, *Guerrillas and Revolution*.

3. Dalton, *El Salvador,* and *El Salvador: monografía*. Some other examples of the emergent counternarrative include Arias, *Farabundo Martí*; Browning, *El Salvador*; Carpio, *Secuestro y capucha*; Dalton, *Miguel Marmol*; Domínguez Sosa, *Ensayo histórico*; and Menjívar, *Acumulación originaria*. See also Gould and Lauria-Santiago, *To Rise in Darkness*; Lauria-Santiago, *Agrarian Republic*; and Lindo-Fuentes, Ching, and Lara-Martínez, *Remembering a Massacre*; as well as Ching, "In Search of the Party," in which I place the organizational impetus of the 1932 uprising in peasant autonomy.

4. See, for example, Guardino, *Time of Liberty*; C. Méndez, *Plebian Republic*; Salvatore, *Wandering Paysanos*; Sanders, *Contentious Republicans;* and J. Wood, *Society of Equality*.

5. Guardino, *Time of Liberty,* 168.

6. Holden, *Armies without Nations,* 20.

7. Tilly, *Democracy.* See also Geddes, *Politician's Dilemma.*

8. Historian Aldo Lauria-Santiago describes the archival system in El Salvador in "Historical Research."

9. Descriptions of the Comintern archive can be found in Ching and Pakkasvirta, "Latin American Materials"; and Ching, "Central Americanist."

10. My use of the term *public sphere* is naturally drawn from Habermas, *Structural Transformation.* But I use the term broadly, to include a more extensive swath of society than Habermas's community of bourgeois citizens participating in their rational-critical debate. For discussions of the limits of Habermas, see Calhoun, "Introduction: Habermas and the Public Sphere"; for a distinctly Latin American setting, see J. Wood, *Society of Equality,* 7–8.

11. Wunthrow, *Communities of Discourse.*

12. Salvatore, *Wandering Paysanos*; and J. Wood, *Society of Equality.* See also Scott, *Domination and the Arts.*

13. Bushnell and Macaulay, *Emergence of Latin America*; Dym, *Sovereign Villages*; Lindo-Fuentes, *Weak Foundations;* Gudmundson and Lindo-Fuentes, *Central America*; and Lauria-Santiago, *Agrarian Republic.*

14. Bulmer-Thomas, *Political Economy*; Lindo-Fuentes, *Weak Foundations*; and Lauria-Santiago, *Agrarian Republic.*

15. For evidence of the stark inequities in landholding, especially of crucial coffee-growing lands, see Asociación Cafetalera de El Salvador, *Primer censo nacional.*

16. Lindo-Fuentes, Ching, and Lara-Martínez, *Remembering a Massacre*; Gould and Lauria-Santiago, *To Rise in Darkness*; Alvarenga, *Cultura y ética*; Almeida, *Waves of Protest.*

17. Bethell and Roxborough, *Latin America*; and Rock, *Latin America in the 1940s.*

18. Parkman, *Nonviolent Insurrection.*

19. Lindo-Fuentes and Ching, *Modernizing Minds*; Holden, *Armies without Nations*; Turcios, *Autoritarismo y modernización;* Williams and Walter, *Militarization and Demilitarization*; Stanley, *Protection Racket State*; and Guevara, "Military Justice."

20. Lindo-Fuentes and Ching, *Modernizing Minds*; and Almeida, *Waves of Protest.*

21. Byrne, *El Salvador's Civil War*; Brockett, *Political Movements.*

22. Gudmundson, *Costa Rica before Coffee*; and Yarrington, *Coffee Frontier.*

23. Colindres, *Fundamentos económicos.*

24. Tilley, *Seeing Indians.* See also Gould's *To Die in this Way* for seminal

treatment of a nation writing its indigenous population out of its history. See Gould and Lauria-Santiago, *To Rise in Darkness,* for a specifically Salvadoran look at the process. See also Euraque, Gould, and Hale, *Memorias del mestizaje.*

25. The slanted geographic position of El Salvador can be confusing to people unfamiliar with local customs relating to directions. One might expect that locals in a nation on the Pacific Ocean would refer to the ocean as the west, but in fact Salvadorans say it is to their south, that Guatemala is to their west, Honduras to the north, and the Gulf of Fonseca to the east.

26. Drake, *Between Tyranny and Anarchy,* 4.

27. Ibid. This reliance on Drake's functionalist definition of democracy is not meant to ignore more qualitative definitions, such as that provided by Gerardo Munck. He insists that definitions of democracy go beyond process and take into account the relationship between elected officials and their electorate, and whether or not voters actually have a say in the making of the policies by which they are expected to abide. See Munck, *Regimes and Democracy,* especially 30.

28. Acemoglu and Robinson, *Economic Origins.* See also Friedman, *Moral Consequences.*

29. See, for example, Williams, *States and Social Evolution*; and Mahoney, *Legacies of Liberalism.*

30. The term *weak foundations* is borrowed from Lindo-Fuentes, *Weak Foundations.*

31. This discussion of the debates over development is based on Lindo-Fuentes and Ching, *Modernizing Minds,* as well as conversations with Salvadoran historian Knut Walter.

32. Tilly, *Democracy.*

33. Even the heralded democracy of Costa Rica exhibited much electoral chicanery well into the twentieth century. See Lehoucq and Molina, *Stuffing the Ballot Box.*

34. Forment, *Democracy in Latin America.*

35. For this debate over socioeconomic structures and the role of coffee in the rise of authoritarianism in Central America, see Williams, *States and Social Evolution.*

36. See Gobat, *Confronting the American Dream,* especially chapter 8.

37. Yashar, *Demanding Democracy.*

38. Acemoglu and Robinson, *Economic Origins,* xii.

39. Similar discussions of this divide between formal and informal rules can be found in Drake, *Between Tyranny and Anarchy*; Helmke and Levitsky, *Informal Institutions*; and Whitehead, "Miners as Voters."

40. Mallon, *Peasant and Nation,* 15.

41. See, for example, Forment, *Democracy in Latin America*; Guardino, *Time of Liberty*; Munck, *Regimes and Democracy*; Myers, "Languages of Politics"; Posada-Carbó, *Elections before Democracy*; Sábato, "On Political Citizenship"; Sanders, *Contentious Republicans*; Warren, *Vagrants and Citizens*; Wolfe, *Everyday Nation-State*; and J. Wood, *Society of Equality*. Posada-Carbó points out that elections in Latin America did not grow organically from within, but were thrust upon the region in 1809, and thus the referent points were external, mostly from the United Kingdom, France, and the United States. Nevertheless, Latin Americans actively and rapidly embraced the language of democracy, and sometimes even the practices (*Elections before Democracy*, 4). Forment observes a surprisingly wide franchise in some areas of Latin America as early as the 1810s. He further claims that many Latin American nations had a wider franchise than the United States or Western Europe at that time: "The democratic tradition in Latin America is far more robust than most scholars have claimed" (*Democracy in Latin America*, xi). Forment thus contends that the authoritarian separation commonly ascribed to Latin America vis-à-vis the United States or United Kingdom was more a phenomenon of the twentieth century than the nineteenth.

42. Myers, "Languages of Politics," 37.

43. Ibid., 10, 11, and 20.

44. Sábato, "On Political Citizenship," 1299.

45. Ibid., 1303. See also Eiss, *In the Name of El Pueblo*, and Grandin, "Liberal Traditions."

46. Drake, *Between Tyranny and Anarchy*, 32–35.

47. See, for example, Schmidt, "Discursive Institutionalism," and Hall and Taylor, "Political Science." For an applied example in the Central American context, see Lehoucq and Molina, *Stuffing the Ballot Box*.

48. R. Scott, *Institutions and Organizations*, 57. Such a claim resembles the commonly used concept of "habitus," made famous by the French theorist Pierre Bourdieu in *The Logic of Practice*. See also Holden, *Armies without Nations*, 28, note 10, for use of the concept in a Central American context.

49. Holden, *Armies without Nations*, 19.

50. Helmke and Levitsky, *Informal Institutions*, 7, 21, and 25.

51. Guardino, *Time of Liberty*, 73.

52. Cruz, *Political Culture*, 9.

53. Guardino, *Time of Liberty*, 73.

54. Cruz, *Political Culture*, 7.

55. Myers, "Languages of Politics," 35.

56. Ibid., 37.

57. The quote is drawn from Hendrick Hertzberg's review of Amanda Forman's *A World on Fire*. See Hertzberg, "Over There," 62. For a similar reference to the U.S. South in a comparative context, see Sanders, *Contentious Republicans*, 188.

58. As just a small sample of said scholarship, see Bender, *Toward an Urban Vision*; Earle, *Jacksonian Antislavery*; and McCoy, *Elusive Republic*.

Chapter 1.   The Rules

1. Asamblea Nacional, "Elección de 1895," AGN, MG, unclassified box.

2. Rivera owned coffee fincas in Juayúa and Salcoatitán and a cattle ranch near Sonsonate City. He served in various electoral posts in Sonsonate City, including regidor in 1888, alcalde in 1891, regidor in 1897, and síndico in 1909 and 1911. He also was a Sonsonate Department deputy to the National Assembly in 1912. See "Catalogo de Municipalidad" and "Libro de actas de elecciones por autoridades de altos poderes, 1908–," AMS, unclassified boxes. See also "Lista de Propietarios," Departamento Sonsonate, 1917, AGN, MG, SS, unclassified box.

3. Abrahán Rivera, Sonsonate, to Prudencio Alfaro, San Salvador, January 16, 1895, AGN, MG, 1895, Box 1.

4. Asamblea Nacional, "Elección de 1895," AGN, MG, unclassified box. Including Izalco and Armenia, Alfaro won the department by a total of 3,824 votes to 1,003. Carlos Meléndez took Armenia, and a third candidate, Estanislau Pérez, won Izalco.

5. "Rectificaciones," *Diario Oficial,* January 25, 1895, 137.

6. "Las elecciones a Altos Poderes," *Diario Oficial,* January 30, 1895, 161–62.

7. Ibid.

8. If we estimate El Salvador's population at the time as 1 million people, with roughly half being male, and half of those men being of voting age, then the maximum number of eligible voters was around 250,000; thus 60,000 voters represents around 40 percent of eligible voters, and probably more. One reason to assume that there had not been widespread stuffing of the ballot boxes is that the total number of voters in this election was relatively consistent with other national elections that occurred in the decade or so before and after this election. It would have been difficult for ballot-box stuffers to have been so careful in their results as to make it appear that the only change in the number of voters was natural demographic growth.

9. Lovell and Lutz, *Demography and Empire.*

10. For examinations of the evolution of creole nationalism and the formation of an American political identity vis-à-vis Spain, see Adelman, *Sovereignty and Revolution*; Brading, *First America*; Grandin, "Liberal Traditions"; and Burkholder, *Spaniards in the Colonial Empire.*

11. The available literature on Bolívar, including studies on him and compilations of his writings, is vast. A series of articles in the *Hispanic American*

Historical Review 63, no. 1 (1983) offers a good overview, especially the piece by Simon Collier, "Nationality, Nationalism, and Supranationalism."

12. Lecuna and Bierck, *Selected Writings of Bolívar* 1:184.

13. Ibid., 191.

14. Throughout Latin America, in the aftermath of independence from Spain and the corresponding rejection of monarchism, a liberal ideology temporarily prevailed, and leaders like Bolívar looked to the United States, France, and the United Kingdom as the countries that had spawned liberalism and were most active in putting it into practice. I am not trying to suggest here that the political leaders in these countries were necessarily any more adept at merging the letter and the spirit of liberalism. As Bernard Manin points out in *The Principles of Representative Democracy,* the original representative governments in Europe and America were designed specifically to reject democracy. However, as various scholars have pointed out, in the United States the breakdown of the colonial order fostered an ideology of revolution and liberty that eventually became institutionalized and served as the foundation upon which modern democracy was built, even if this ideology did not elicit much of a tangible outcome in the immediate aftermath of independence. On the United States, see G. Wood, *Radicalism of the American Revolution.* For good comparative analyses of the United States and Latin America, see Langley, *Americas in the Age of Revolution;* Fukuyama, *Falling Behind*; and Grandin, "Liberal Traditions."

15. For a similar discussion of Bolívar as symbolic of this distinct political trend in the former Spanish America, see Grandin, "Liberal Traditions," 72–73.

16. See Dym, *Sovereign Villages.* See also Karnes, *Failure of Union*; Rodríguez, *Cádiz Experiment*; Torres-Rivas, *Historia general de Centroamérica* 3; Woodward, "Liberal-Conservative Debate," in Peloso and Tenenbaum, *Liberals, Politics, and Power*; and Wortman, *Government and Society.*

17. See Dym, *Sovereign Villages,* 205.

18. A copy of the 1824 Constitution is found in Gallardo, *Cuatro constituciones.*

19. For a comparable debate in Colombia (New Granada), see Sanders, *Contentious Republicans.*

20. Guardino, *Time of Liberty,* 169.

21. Rodríguez, *Cádiz Experiment*; and Dym, *Sovereign Villages.* Both provide good analyses of the similarities and differences between the two constitutions. The voting lists of elections in Sonsonate City in the 1820s and 1830s are located in AMS, unclassified boxes marked "elecciones," 1820–29 and 1830–39. For a discussion of the European models and the 1812 Cádiz Constitution, see Fitzgerald, *Constitutions of Latin America,* x.

22. Stephens, *Incidents of Travel* 2:127.

23. Vega, Campo, and Gómez were actively involved in Sonsonate politics during the federation. Each of them served as electors from the department and at various times served in the Federal Assembly. After the fall of the federation, Campo served in the National Assembly as a senator in 1841 and a deputy in 1842; he ran for president on numerous occasions during the 1840s. Gómez served several terms in the National Assembly. He was also vice president and president of the republic. Vega remained in Sonsonate and participated actively in departmental politics. See the voting lists and elections results from Sonsonate in AMS, in unclassified boxes marked "elecciones," dated by decade. Gerardo Barrios served in the Federal Assembly for two years starting in 1834. He went on to hold numerous offices in El Salvador before eventually becoming president. Barrios was one of the most influential political figures in nineteenth-century El Salvador. See López Vallecillos, *Gerardo Barrios*.

24. Manuel Gómez to Cámara de Diputados, February 5, 1849, AGN, PB.

25. See Gallardo, *Cuatro constituciones*, for a copy of the 1841 constitution. The quote is drawn from title 4, article 13. The references to *"hacendados y propietarios"* are found in numerous instances throughout the records relating to Sonsonate City and San Vicente City. For specific examples, see Circular to alcaldes of San Vicente Department from governor of San Vicente, December 29, 1849, AGN, MG, SSV, 1849, unclassified box; and voting list from Sonsonate City dated March 31, 1841, AMS, box titled "elecciones, 1840–49."

26. See Sanders, *Contentious Republicans,* especially 172–89; and Appelbaum, *Muddied Waters.* For a look at the case of elite retraction of initial electoral advances in Mexico, see Guardino, *Time of Liberty,* and Warren, *Vagrants and Citizens.*

27. Wolfe, *Everyday Nation-State,* 188.

28. On El Salvador, see Gundmundson and Lindo-Fuentes, *Central America*; and Herrera, "¿Liberales contra conservadores?". On Guatemalan conservatism, see McCreery, *Rural Guatemala*; Sullivan-González, *Piety, Power, and Politics*; and Woodward, *Rafael Carrera.* Even in those countries where the liberal-conservative divide was more pronounced, research shows rival elites to have held common views on key issues like economic production. See Gobat, *Confronting the American Dream*; Guardino, *Time of Liberty*; and Wolfe, *Everyday Nation-State.*

29. For this comparison, see Sanders, *Contentious Republicans,* especially 172–89. See also C. Méndez, *Plebian Republic,* for another case study.

30. Dym, *Sovereign Villages,* 205.

31. Ibid., 146.

32. For Mexico, for example, see Guardino, *Time of Liberty,* 164.

33. Galindo, *Cartilla del ciudadano.* A similar use of the term *populacho* in Mexico is revealed by Stevens, *Origins of Instability,* 36.

34. Gary Nash noted the importance of the oral vote in restricting franchise in colonial America. See Nash, "Transformation of Urban Politics."

35. Letter from Frederick William Taylor, San Salvador, to family, Los Angeles, CA, January 11, 1927, FWTP, Box 3, Folder 1. Taylor was an American hired by the Salvadoran government to serve as director general of agriculture between 1923 and 1927. He had an office in the Palacio Nacional and had close contact with most high-ranking members of government.

36. This is a description of a typical direct election. Indirect elections functioned in the same manner, except that they occurred in two rounds. In the first round in the cantón, the election resembled a direct election, as the mass voters gathered to vote for electores. The second round of voting occurred in the *cabildo,* but it was a very small affair, with only the handful of electores participating.

37. The descriptions of municipal officials are found in the Ramos Municipales, the municipal legal codes. See Ley de Ramo Municipal, AGN, MG, 1908, Box 1; and Proyecto de Ley Municipal, AGN, MG, 1925, Box 5. See also Lardé y Larín, *Recopilación de leyes.*

38. The nullification cases have been placed in a separate collection, Colección de Nulos (CN), in the AGN.

39. For elites making this claim about politics being dirty business, see, for example, Valencia and Martinez, "Plática con Orlando de Sola." See also Rosenberg, *Children of Cain,* chapter 4, "The Laboratory." See also analyses of the 1931 presidential election, in which none of the candidates or parties seemed to represent specifically elite interests, such as that by Gould and Lauria-Santiago, *To Rise in Darkness.*

40. Roniger, "Caciquismo and Cornelismo." In addition to studying patronage in Mexico and Brazil, Roniger provides a good overview of the historiography of patronage.

41. The term "leader on horseback" is from Wolf and Hansen, "Caudillo Politics," 169. For further discussion of the historiography of caudillismo and patronage, see Quintana, *Maximino Avila Camacho.*

42. See Roniger, "Caciquismo and Cornelismo"; Graham, *Patronage and Politics*; Nunes Leal, *Coronelismo*; Eisenstadt and Lemarchand, *Political Clientelism*; Hamill, *Caudillos*; Lynch, *Caudillos in Spanish America*; Martz, *Politics of Clientelism*; Holden, *Armies without Nations,* 18–21; Bieber, *Power, Patronage, and Political Violence*; and Quintana, *Maximino Avila Camacho.*

43. Chalchuapa, Nulo, 1919, AGN, CN, Box 4.

44. Wolfe, *Everyday Nation-State,* 199.

45. As just a few examples, see Guardino, *Time of Liberty*; Sanders, *Contentious Republicans*; Wolfe, *Everyday Nation-State*; Wood, *Society of Equality*; C. Méndez, *Plebian Republic*; Salvatore, *Wandering Paysanos*; Warren, *Vagrants and Citizens*; Sábato, *The Many and the Few*; and McCreery, *Rural Guatemala.*

46. After their successful coup in 1890, Generals Carlos Ezeta and Antonio Ezeta doled out dozens of military promotions explicitly for services rendered during the coup. This will be examined in greater detail in chapter 3. The documents relating to the promotions are scattered throughout AGN, MG, 1891, Box 10.

47. Idelfonso Espinoza, Tejutepeque, to governor, Sensuntepeque, Cabañas Department, February 17, 1933, AGN, FA, Box 6, folder "persecusión criminal, 1933."

48. As just one example, see the editorial in the liberal newspaper *La Unionistsa,* May 14, 1895, 1. For a more extensive discussion, see Herrera, "¿Liberales contra conservadores?".

49. See, for example, Sanders, *Contentious Republicans;* Munck, *Regimes and Democracy;* J. Wood, *Society of Equality;* Warren, *Vagrants and Citizens;* Myers, "Languages of Politics"; Forment, *Democracy in Latin America;* Sábato, "On Political Citizenship"; Whitehead, "Miners as Voters"; Warren, "Elections and Popular Participation"; Peloso, "Electoral Reform," in Peloso and Tenenbaum, *Liberals, Politics, and Power;* and Posada-Carbó, *Elections before Democracy.* Luis Roniger points out that this debate had been going on among Brazilian historians, with the traditional approach being offered by Victor Nunes Leal and the revisionist line being taken by P. Carmack and M. I. Pereira. See Roniger, "Caciquismo and Cornelismo," 79.

50. For works that contend that there was widespread franchise, see Nash, "Transformation of Urban Politics"; Foster, *Their Solitary Way,* especially appendix A, "The Massachusetts Franchise in the Seventeenth Century"; and Brown, "The Controversy over the Franchise." Brown offers a good overview of the historiographical debate. For a work that challenges the idea of a broad franchise, see the rebuttal to Brown by Wall, "The Franchise in Seventeenth-Century Massachusetts."

51. Rouquié, *The Military and the State,* 35.

52. From Sala Municipal, Sonsonate City, to surrounding municipalities, December 9, 188?, AGN, MG, Box "Política 1882, 84, 86, 87, 88."

53. For reference to the landholdings and prominence of the Barrientos and Castillo families, see "Personas notables del departamento de Sonsonate," 1897, AGN, MG, SS, unclassified box; "Nomina de las señoras y señoritas honorables de esta ciudad," Izalco, October 28, 1904, AGN, MG, SS, Box 3; "Listas de los agricultores principales agricultores de la ciudad y jurisdición de Izalco," March 8, 1912, AGN, MG, SS, Box 3; *Directorio comercial,* 508–9.

54. Junta Electoral, Santa Ana, October 1841, AGN, PB; Junta Electoral, Sonsonate, December 12, 1841, AMS, Box "Eleccions, 1840–9"; Junta Electoral, Sonsonate, December 11, 1842, AMS, Box "Eleccions, 1840–9."

55. For a description of Campo's political activities, see Bancroft, *History of Central America* 3:397; Gallardo, *Papeles históricos* 1:87; and López Vallecillos, *Gerardo Barrios* 1:260–82, 382, 394. For Campo's electoral activities, see lists of electoral participants and voting results in Sonsonate City in AMS, Boxes "Elecciones" 1840–9, 1850–9, 1860–9, 1870–9. See also "Catalogo de municipalidad, Ciudad de Sonsonate," AMS.

56. Article 64 of the 1841 Constitution. The law was dropped in the 1864 charter. See Gallardo, *Cuatro constituciones.*

57. Elections took place in May, August, and December of 1841. See elections records in AMS, Box "Elecciones, 1840–9."

58. Junta de Elección, Atiquizaya, August 14, 1841, AGN, PB; Junta de Elección, San Antonio, December 3, 1843, AMS, Box "Elecciones, 1840–9"; Junta de Elección, Sonzacate, December 3, 1843, AMS, Box "Elecciones, 1840–9"; Junta de Elección, Santa Catarina Masahuat, December 4, 1853, AMS, "Box Elecciones 1850–9."

59. The results are found grouped together in a packet marked "Elección de Altos Poderes, 1891," AGN, MG, unclassified box.

60. The Office of the Government, San Salvador, to the governor of San Vicente Department, February 14, 1852, AGN, SSV, 1852, unnumbered box.

61. Junta Electoral, Sonsonate, December 11, 1864, AGN, MG, unclassified box.

62. As mentioned previously, see Gudmundson and Lindo-Fuentes, *Central America,* for a discussion of the limited relevance of these ideological distinctions in the case of El Salvador.

63. The term *hombres conservadores* is found in *La Gaceta,* November 30, 1849. The term *instituciones liberales* is from *La Gaceta,* December 14, 1849.

64. *La Gaceta,* September 15, 1848.

65. *La Gaceta,* August 31, 1849.

66. *La Gaceta,* December 14, 1849.

67. *La Gaceta,* December 7, 1849.

68. *La Gaceta,* March 4, 1853.

69. *La Gaceta,* March 18, 1853.

70. *La Gaceta,* April 8, 1953.

71. Herrera, "¿Liberales contra conservadores?," 179–80.

72. The successive quotations are located in San Vicente City, Nulo, 1866, AGN, CN, Box 1; Atiquizaya, Nulo, 1874, AGN, CN, Box 1; Juan Chico and others, Polorós, to Supreme Gobierno, AGN, MG, 1892, Box 4; and San Cristobal, Nulo, 1925, AGN, CN, Box 4.

73. Ramón Bautista, Alegría, to departmental governor, November 3, 1927, AGN, MG, unclassified box.

74. Materials relating to the political battles between Bautista and Iglesias, and lists of municipal officials in Alegría for the period 1890–1938, are found in Ramón Bautista to minister of government, December 31, 1893, AGN, MG, 1893, Box 5; José Parker, Usulután City, to minister of government, December 30, 1893, AGN, MG, 1893, Box 10; Usulután Department, Nulo, 1893, AGN, CN, Box 1; List of Elected Officials, Usulután Department, December 28, 1896, AGN, MG, unclassified box; Letter from departmental governor, Usulután City, to minister of government, December 14, 1907, AGN, MG, unclassified box; List of Elected Officials, Usulután Department, December 1921, AGN, MG, 1915, Box 1; List of Elected Officials, December 1923, AGN, MG, 1923, Box 4; List of Municipal Officials 1927, *Diario del Salvador*, December 14, 1927; Ramón Bautista, Alegría, to departmental governor, November 3, 1927, and November 5, 1927, AGN, MG, unclassified box; Alegría, Nulo, 1929, AGN, CN, Box 6; Alegría, Nulo, 1931, AGN, CN, Box 9; List of Elected Officials, December 1937, AGN, MG, unclassified paquete, 1938. References to the landholdings of Bautista and Iglesias are found in R. Montoya, "Personas Notables de Usulután," to minister of government, January 22, 1897, AGN, MG, unclassified box; List of coffee growers, Usulután Department, 1926, AGN, MG, 1926, Box 5; and *Directorio comercial*, 580.

75. Enrique Molina and others, to Prudencio Alfaro, minister of government, December 14, 1895, AGN, MG, 1895, unclassified box.

76. Governor of San Vicente, "Libro en que se copia las partidas notas que ponen a las autoridades del departamento," entry for May 7, 1845, AGN, MG, SSV, 1845, unclassified box.

77. Villavicencio, San Miguel, to minister of government, January 15, 1895, AGN, MG, unclassified box.

Chapter 2.   National-Level Networks in Conflict in the Nineteenth Century

1. Graham, *Patronage and Politics,* 42. See also Bieber, *Power, Patronage, and Political Violence.*

2. A discussion of the influence of the Haitian Revolution on the consciousness of elites throughout Latin America can be found in Langley, *Americas in the Age,* especially part 2. See also Adelman, *Sovereignty and Revolution.*

3. Graham, *Patronage and Politics,* 79.

4. For a comparison between Colombia, Mexico, and Brazil, see Sanders, *Contentious Republicans,* 188.

5. Lindo-Fuentes, *Weak Foundations,* 50.

6. Ibid., 201; Williams, *States and Social Evolution,* 203.

7. Evidence of the alliance is found in a letter detailing the transfer of weapons from San Miguel to San Vicente. See Casa de Gobierno, San Salvador, to governor of San Vicente, June 2, 1845, AGN, MG, SSV, 1845, unclassified box.

8. "Libro en que se copia las partidas notas que ponen a las autoridades del Departamento," March 27, 1845, AGN, MG, SSV, 1845, unclassified box.

9. Ibid.

10. For descriptions of Marín, Miranda, and their political alliances, see Hernández, *Biografías de vicentinos,* 43–44, 59–66, 71–75, 81–82.

11. "Libro en que se copia las partidas notas que ponen a las autoridades del Departamento," 1845, April 12 entry, AGN, MG, SSV, 1845, unclassified box.

12. Ibid., March 27 entry.

13. Ibid., April 8 entry.

14. Ibid., May 7 entry.

15. Vasconcelos's letters are grouped together in a packet in AGN, PB.

16. Córtes, *Biografía del Capitán General Gerardo Barrios,* 53.

17. "Libro en que contan las comunicaciones que se dirigen al Ministro, Departamento de San Vicente," 1852, October 14 entry, AGN, MG, SSV, 1852, unclassified box.

18. Ibid., August 16 entry. Dueñas's suspicions about the looming revolt are described in the August 6 entry.

19. Ibid., October 9 entry.

20. Ibid., October 25 entry.

21. López Vallecillos, *Gerardo Barrios* 1:278. This work is particularly valuable for historians. While trying to construct a narrative history, López Vallecillos ended up reprinting many of his documents in their entirety. Some of these materials are no longer available in original form.

22. Hernández, *Biografías de vicentinos,* 45–49; López Vallecillos, *Gerardo Barrios* 1:315; 2:21.

23. López Vallecillos, *Gerardo Barrios* 1:302 and 310.

24. Gallardo, *Papeles históricos* 3:68

25. López Vallecillos, *Gerardo Barrios* 2:11.

26. Printed in *Gaceta del Salvador,* April 4, 1863, and reprinted in López Vallecillos, *Gerardo Barrios* 2:358. For a reprint of the order to confiscate the properties, see Gallardo, *Papeles históricos* 3:49.

27. See sections "Emprésito" and "Gobernadores" in Gallardo, *Papeles históricos* 3, part 2.

28. The letter is from April 7, 1863, and is reprinted in ibid., 163.

29. López Vallecillos, *Gerardo Barrios* 2:382–90.

30. Gallardo, *Papeles históricos* 3:95–96; Cardenal, *El poder eclesiástico,* 100–101.

31. *Diario Oficial,* May 7, 1890.

32. Castañeda, *General Menéndez,* 128; Gallardo, *Papeles históricos* 3:96; Ezeta's reference to the junta is reprinted in *El 22 de junio,* 27.

33. Joaquín Bran, Sonsonate, to ministro general, June 12, 1894, AGN, MG, 1894, Box 5.

34. San Vicente to ministro general, June 12, and June 13, 1894, AGN, MG, 1894, Box 5.

35. Laragoza to inspector general, June 8, 1894, AGN, MG, 1894, Box 5.

36. Angulo, Usulután, to ministro de hacienda, June 8, 1894, AGN, MG, 1894, Box 5.

37. Gómez, Sonsonate, to ministro general, June 13, 1894, AGN, MG, 1894, Box 5.

38. San Miguel to ministro general, June 10, 1894, AGN, MG, 1894, Box 5.

39. For claims on Ezeta's loans in 1890, see Manuel Sol and other citizens to ministro de hacienda, August 30, 1894, AGN, MG, unclassified box.

40. Ibid.

41. Zacatecoluca to ministro general, June 10, 1894, AGN, MG, 1894, Box 5.

42. Hurtado to minister of war, December 26, 1894, AGN, MG, unclassified box.

43. Each declaration of promotion contained the same wording quoted above. The documents relating to the promotions are stored together in AGN, MG, 1891, Box 10.

44. On General Rivas, see also Lauria-Santiago, *Agrarian Republic,* 115–19 and 124–26; Lauria-Santiago, "Los indígenas de Cojutepeque"; and Alvarenga Venutolo, *Cultura y ética,* 50–61. Both Lauria-Santiago and Alvarenga Venutolo base their analyses on some of the same sources employed here, but with variations in argument. Lauria-Santiago emphasizes the autonomy and power of the peasantry from Cuzcatlán as the driving force behind Rivas, and Alvaregna Venutolo stresses the political conflagrations of the mid-1880s.

45. Castañeda, *General Menéndez,* 103.

46. José María Rivas to minister of war, February 7, 1875, AGN, PB. Rivas's opposition to Barrios also is described in a letter from Lozano, governor of La Paz, to Irungaray, September 2, 1863, reprinted in Gallardo, *Papeles históricos* 3:96.

47. Rivas's support for Menéndez is described in a letter from Menéndez in the *cuartel* of Santa Ana in 1885. The letter is reprinted in Castañeda, *General Menéndez,* 49. See also Cardenal, *El poder eclesiástico,* 127–28.

48. Castañeda, *General Menéndez,* 106.

49. Ibid., 116.

50. Rivas's revolt of 1890 is described in a solicitation from the mother of a son who was killed on January 1, 1890, while defending Sensuntepeque against

Rivas' soldiers: ? to minister of war, January ?, 1890, AGN, MG, 1890, Box 6. The revolt is also made clear in a letter from the municipal authorities of San Juan Tepezontes, who were denouncing a group of citizens from that village who joined up with Rivas during the revolt. See González, San Juan Tepezontes, to minister of government, January 17, 1890, AGN, MG, 1890, Box 1. The post-revolt upheavals in Cuscatlán are made evident in the numerous election nullifications arriving from the department. See Cuscatlán Department, Nulo, 1890, AGN, CN, Box 1. The revolt is also mentioned in Castañeda, *General Menéndez,* 121. An order to extend the state of siege in the departments of Cuscatlán and Cabañas owing to the post-revolt anarchy is found in Romero to minister of government, April 18, 1890, AGN, MG, 1890, Box 1.

51. Villavicencio's alliance with Ezeta is described in a telegram from Ezeta to Colonel Ceballos of San Martín. It reads, "General Horacio Villavicencio is in accord with us. You can now fraternize with him without fear of exposing us." Ezeta to Ceballos, June 23, 1890, AGN, MG, 1890, Box 5.

52. Rivas's attack on San Salvador is described in a denunciation from a group of citizens in the municipality of Juyaque. The denunciation is against a another group of persons from the village who went to join up with Rivas, but had only gotten as far as Nueva San Salvador before Antonio Ezeta recaptured the capital. Ines Herrera and others to Supremo Poder Ejecutivo, October ?, 1890, AGN, MG, unclassified box. The events are also described in *El 22 de junio,* 21–32.

53. *El 22 de junio,* 21.

54. Taylor to family, August 5, 1924, and September 12, 1924, FWTP, Folder 1.

55. "Libro en que se copia las partidas notas que ponen a las autoridades del Departamento," 1845, April 1 entry, AGN, MG, SSV, 1845, unclassified box.

56. "Libro en que contan las comunicaciones que se dirigen al Ministro, Departamento de San Vicente," 1852, September 11 entry, AGN, MG, SSV, 1852, unclassified box.

57. A decree published in *La Gaceta del Salvador* on August 11, 1854, announced the formation of the town of Nueva San Salvador on the "llanos de Santa Tecla" (the plain or flatland of Santa Tecla). The municipality was officially renamed "Santa Tecla" in 2003, but that name seems to have been in use alongside "Nueva San Salvador" for more than a century.

58. López Vallecillos, *Gerardo Barrios* 1:293–95.

59. Gallardo, *Papeles históricos* 3:79–82.

60. The decree that divided San Miguel was published in *El Constitucional,* June 22, 1865, reprinted in López Vallecillos, *Gerardo Barrios* 2:471.

Chapter 3.   *Building Networks at the Local Level*

1. Baltazar Estupinian, Chinameca, San Miguel Department, to José Larreynaga, December 22, 1873, in Gallardo, *Papeles históricos* 3:452.

2. Comandancia Departamental, San Vicente, to minister of war, March 29, 1915, AGN, MG, 1915, Box 1.

3. Thompson, *Rainbow Countries*, 245.

4. For a comparative examination of coffee economies, see Roseberry, Gudmundson, and Samper Kutschbach, *Coffee, Society, and Power*. Costa Rica is the exemplary case of a nation in which smallholders responded to the opportunities offered by coffee. See also Gudmundson, *Costa Rica before Coffee*; and Samper, *Generations of Settlers*. See Yarrington, *Coffee Frontier*, on Venezuela.

5. See Williams, *States and Social Evolution,* chapter 6; and Lindo-Fuentes, *Weak Foundations,* 116–19, 159–67.

6. See Lauria-Santiago, "Agrarian Republic," chapters 5 and 6, especially pages 261–88.

7. Lauria-Santiago, "Agrarian Republic," 289. See also 242 for examples of peasants selling off their plots to speculators.

8. For land figures, see Lauria-Santiago, *Agrarian Republic*; and Lindo-Fuentes, *Weak Foundations*.

9. On indigo production in El Salvador, see Fernández, *Pintando el mundo*; Lauria-Santiago, *Agrarian Republic*; Lindo-Fuentes, *Weak Foundations*; and Rubio Sánchez, *Historia del añil*.

10. Lindo-Fuentes, *Weak Foundations,* 83–87.

11. Lauria-Santiago, "Agrarian Republic," 87–88.

12. Dionisio Coto, Tepetitán, to governor of San Vicente, August 26, 1852, AGN, MG, SSV, 1852, unclassified box.

13. Fernández, *Pintando el mundo*.

14. From "Libro en que se copian las notas que se dirigen al Gobierno Supremo en el presente año, 1855," governor of San Vicente, AGN, MG, SSV, 1855, unclassified box.

15. As John Tutino points out, the existence of debt also reflects the likelihood that laborers had a degree of secure subsistence and that the landowners needed to resort to coercive measures to force laborers out of their subsistence. See Tutino, *Insurrection to Revolution,* 296.

16. From a Libro de sentencias, 1878, AMS, 1870–79, unclassified box.

17. The dozens of cases are found in "Libros de sentencias," which are scattered throughout unclassified boxes in AMS, dated 1860–69, 1870–79, and 1880–89.

18. Transito Gaetán, Santiago de María, to minister of government, November 28, 1927, AGN, MG, unclassified box.

19. San Antonio Masahuat, Nulo, 1903, AGN, CN, Box 3.

20. Giddens, *Profiles and Critiques,* 199. See also James Scott's *Weapons of the Weak* and *Domination and the Arts.*

21. Alvarenga Venutolo, "Reshaping the Ethics," 103–16; and Alvarenga Venutolo, *Cultura y ética,* 117–24.

22. For studies of mass/peasant movements in the nineteenth century, see Lauria-Santiago, *Agrarian Republic,* "Agrarian Republic," and "Land, Community, and Revolt"; and Kincaid, "Peasants into Rebels."

23. Transito Gaetán, Santiago de María, November 28, 1927, AGN, MG, unclassified box. The role of liquor is also referred to in a case from Santa Catarina Masahuat, Sonsonate Department. See, Rafael ?, to departmental governor, December ?, 189?, AGN, MG, SS, Box 3.

24. Luis Cotera, Santa Lucia, to departmental governor, San Vicente, February 5, 1852, AGN, MG, SSV, 1852, unclassified box.

25. The career of General Rivas is discussed in Lauria-Santiago, "Agrarian Republic," chapter 8; Lauria-Santiago, *Agrarian Republic,* 115–19, 124–26; and Alvarenga Venutolo, *Cultura y ética,* 46–61. Alvarenga Venutolo refers to Rivas's relations with his Indian supporters as "a consensual system of domination."

26. Lauria-Santiago, "Land, Community, and Revolt," 520.

27. See Guardino, *Time of Liberty*; and Sanders, *Contentious Republicans.*

28. See Lauria-Santiago, *Agrarian Republic*; "Agrarian Republic," especially chapter 8; and "Land, Community, and Revolt."

29. Salvatore, *Wandering Paysanos,* 10.

30. See Ching, "In Search of the Party"; and Lindo-Fuentes, Ching, and Lara-Martínez, *Remembering a Massacre.*

31. See Lauria-Santiago, *Agrarian Republic.*

32. Libro en que contan las comunicaciones que se dirigen al Ministro, Departamento de San Vicente, 1852, entries from April 7, June 22, August 6, and September 11, AGN, MG, SSV, 1852, unclassified box.

33. Idelfonso Espinoza, Tejutepeque, February 17, 1933, to departmental governor, Sensuntepeque, February 17, 1933, AGN, FA, Box 6.

34. J. T. Osorio, Sensuntepeque, to departmental governor, Sensuntepeque, February 16, 1933, AGN, FA, Box 6.

35. Atiquizaya, Nulo, 1874, AGN, CN, Box 1; and *Directorio comercial,* 29–31.

36. Comandante Departamental, Usulután City, to Rubén Rivera, San Salvador, December 18, 1899, AGN, MG, unclassified box.

37. The family relations of the elite of Juayúa are drawn from a variety of sources. For relations between the Cea and Salaverría families, see Juayúa, Nulo, 1891, AGN, CN, Box 1. For the arrival of Jerez and his marriage into the Salaverría family, see the inaugural copy of the *revista* "Lempa," July 1934, 15, in AGN, MG, 1934, Box 4. For land wealth of all the families and the finca belonging to Jerez's wife, see report of coffee production from Alcaldía Municipal de Juayúa to departmental governor, June 18, 1926, AGN, MG, 1926, Box 5. For a lengthy description of social elite of Juayúa and its intermarriage, see *Diario La Prensa,* January 18, 1936, 5.

38. Ahuachapán City, Nulo, 1888, AGN, CN, Box 1.

39. Juayúa, Nulo, 1891, AGN, CN, Box 1.

40. Pedro Aparicio, Chinameca, to minister of government, May 26, 1911, AGN, MG, 1911, Box 3, "Notas varias, mayo."

41. Dario Rivera and others, Izalco, to departmental governor, June 27, 1921, AGN, MG, 1921, Box 3.

42. For a case of an uncle of the alcalde being elected to a council, see Olocuilta, Nulo, 1892, AGN, CN, Box 1. For a father-son team in politics, see San Cayetano Istepeque, Nulo, 1911, AGN, CN, Box 4. For another father-son team, see Santiago de María, Nulo, 1934, AGN, CN, Box 10.

43. Nomina de los capitalistas de este Departamento expresando aproximadamente el capital de cada uno, 1893, governor of La Libertad, AGN, MG, unclassified box.

44. See lists of coffee growers, Sonsonate Department, 1926, AGN, MG, 1926, Box 5.

45. Santiago Texacuangos, Nulo, 1909, AGN, CN, Box 3.

46. For just one example, see police report on investigation of a political meeting in Santa Ana in Pedro Aviles to minister of government, December 4, 1919, AGN, MG, unclassified box.

47. Lislique, Nulo, 1891, AGN, CN, Box 1.

48. Santa Clara, Nulo, 1888, AGN, CN, Box 1. For list of land, see *Directorio comercial,* 422–23.

49. Uluazapa, Nulo, 1897, AGN, CN, Box 2.

50. See Holden, *Armies without Nations,* 21 and 27.

51. See Casa de Gobierno, San Salvador, to Cojutepeque, February 5, 1849, AGN, PB. For another case, see Casa de Gobierno to governor of San Vicente, January 4, 1863, AGN, PB.

52. La Union, Nulo, 1899, AGN, CN, Box 2.

53. Alcalde, Apopa, to minister of government, April 21, 1895, AGN, MG, 1895, Box 10. For land wealth of Merino and Duque, see *Directorio comercial,* 694–97.

54. Santa Elena, Nulo, 1914, AGN, CN, Box 4. For land wealth of Lozanos, see *Directorio comercial,* 547.

55. Juntas de Elecciones, 1886 and 1891, AGN, MG, SS, Box "Política 1890–99, 1900–1908"; Juayúa, Nulo, 1891, AGN, CN, Box 1, see remaining elections for dominance of Cea, Mata, and Salaverría families. For the land wealth of Mata, Cea, Salaverría, and Mendoza, and the conspicuous absence of Colonel Pérez, see list of coffee growers Sonsonate Department, 1926, AGN, MG, 1926, Box 5; "Directorio comercial, Agricola y Industrial de la Ciudad de Juayúa," 1917, AGN, MG, SS, Box 6; and *Directorio comercial,* 528–29.

56. For mention of Rivas's alliances with local coffee growers, see Director General de la Guardia Nacional to minister of government, October 22, 1921, AGN, MG, 1922, unclassified paquete; List of Municipal Officials, Ahuachapán Department, January 12, 1921, AGN, MG, unclassified box; List of Municipal Officials, December 1921, AGN, MG, 1915, Box 1; List of Municipal Officials, December 1923, AGN, MG, 1923, Box 4; List of Municipal Officials, December 1925, AGN, MG, unclassified box; List of Municipal Officials, December 1927; *Diario del Salvador,* December 14, 1927, 5; List of Municipal Officials, December 1929, AGN, MG, unclassified box. For lists of landowners in Tacuba in order to show landholdings of Rivas's allies, see *Directorio comercial,* 17; and Ministerio de Agricultura, Departamento de Ahuachapán, 192?, AGN, MG, unclassified box.

57. The quotes are drawn from Jucuapa, Nulo, 1897, AGN, CN, Box 2; and Rafael Hidalgo, Jucuapa, to minister of government, March 2, 1898, AGN, MG, 1898, Box 14. For the imposition of a member of the Castro clan, see Rufino Castro, alcalde, Jucuapa, to minister of government, December 16, 1893, AGN, MG, 1893, Box 8. For the land wealth and social status of the families involved, see Lista de Notables, Departamento Usulután, January 22, 1897, AGN, MG, unclassified box; List of coffee growers, Jucuapa, 1926, AGN, MG, 1926, Box 5; List of Municipal Officials, Usulután Department, governor of Usulután to minister of government, December 14, 1907, AGN, MG, unclassified box, *Directorio comercial,* 568–69.

58. For a discussion of Indian demographics, see Tilley, *Seeing Indians*; and Ching and Tilley, "Indians, the Military"; Lauria-Santiago, "Agrarian Republic," 205–13; and Chapin, *La población indígena.*

59. Donghi, "Economy and Society," 322–26.

60. On Izalco, see Lauria-Santiago, "Land, Community, and Revolt."

61. For good discussions of ethnicity and ethnic identity in El Salvador, see Lauria-Santiago, *Agrarian Republic,* especially 57–63; Tilley, *Seeing Indians*; Gould and Lauria-Santiago, *To Rise in Darkness*; and Euraque, Gould, and Hale, *Memorias del mestizaje,* part 4.

62. Cardenal, *El poder eclesiástico,* 147–59. For a good examination of a contemporary Indian community in Morazán, see Amaya, *Historia de Cacoapera.* For the classic examination of Central American Indians, see Adams, *Cultural Surveys.*

63. Común de Indígenas, Juayúa, to minister of government, July 22, 1867, AGN, MG, unclassified box.

64. Abrahán Monsón, Izalco, December 9, 1888, and December 23, 1888, AGN, MG, SS, Box "Política, 1890–1899, 1900–1908."

65. See Guardino, *Time of Liberty,* 233.

66. Wolfe, *Everyday Nation-State,* 165.

67. For the population of Indians in Nahuizalco, as well as in the rest of Sonsonate Department and in other western departments, see Ching and Tilley, "Indians, the Military." For even more complete data, see Tilley, *Seeing Indians.*

68. The following description of politics in Nahuizalco appeared in slightly altered form in Ching, "In Search of the Party." See also Gould and Lauria-Santiago, *To Rise in Darkness,* 47–48; and Alvarenga Venutolo, *Cultura y ética,* 306–22.

69. For the information from 1858, see López, *Estadística general,* 160–62. For population figures from 1900, see Informe, governor of Sonsonate Department, January 12, 1903, AGN, MG, unclassified box. For the privatization of the communal land and the predominance of smallholding in general, see Lauria-Santiago, *Agrarian Republic,* especially 148 on Nahuizalco. For the lists of fincas and their ladino owners, see *Directorio comercial,* 494–96. The 1913 survey is from Cerridos, Sonsonate City, to minister of government, September 20, 1913, AGN, MG, SS, Box 5. A 1934 survey shows substantial smallholding in corn and bean production and lists the agriculturists by name; most of them bear typically Indian surnames. See the survey dated July 13, 1934, in AGN, MG, SS, Box 3.

70. The description is taken from Aldo Lauria-Santiago, "Agrarian Republic," 514–19, which is based on the records of the official investigation of the rebellion. A description of the rebellion is also contained in the 1913 survey from Cerridos, Sonsonate City, to minister of government, September 20, 1913, AGN, MG, SS, Box 5.

71. Cardenal, *El poder eclesiástico,* 127.

72. The issue of rebels in militia uniforms is drawn from Lauria-Santiago, "Agrarian Republic," 514–19, and also from discussions with Lauria-Santiago himself, who described the evidence in greater detail. I would like to thank Aldo for sharing this information with me.

73. Junta de Elección, Nahuizalco, 1887, AGN, MG, SS, Box Política 1890–1899, 1900–1908; Nulo, 1894, AGN, CN, Box 1.

74. Gould and Lauria-Santiago, *To Rise in Darkness,* chapter 3.

75. The landholdings of the Brito and Valdéz families are found in Lista de Agricultores Principales, Nahuizalco, March 8, 1912, AGN, MG, SS, Box 3; and in *Directorio comercial,* 494–96.

76. Juan Aviles, Nahuizalco, to minister of government, December 23, 1896, AGN, MG, 1896, Box 5.

77. Junta de Elección, Nahuizalco, December 1901, AGN, MG, SS, Box "Política 1890–1899, 1900–1908."

78. Junta de Elección, Nahuizalco, December 14, 1903, AGN, MG, SS, Box "Política, 1890–1899, 1900–1908."

79. From minister of government to governor of Sonsonate Department, April 26, 1926, AGN, MG, 1926, Box 2.

80. From Juan Aviles to minister of government, December 23, 1896, AGN, MG, 1896, Box 5; see also Nulo, Nahuizalco, December 14, 1923, AGN, CN, Box 5; and the *Lista de electos,* Sonsonate Department, from departmental governor of Sonsonate to minister of government, December 13, 1923, AGN, MG, 1923, Box 4. See also the report by Pedro Lúe, Nahuizalco, to Ismael Fuentes, Secretario General del Comité Quiñonista, San Salvador, February 24, 1919, IFP. This latter document, which describes a local conflagration between supporters of Alfonso Quiñónez Molina and Tomás Palomo in the run-up to the 1920 presidential election, suggests that Indians were linked to and participated in broader national-level patronage-based networks.

81. The reference to Rodríguez is found in a note from the governor of Sonsonate Department to the minister of government, September 9, 1926, AGN, MG, 1926, Box 6. The letter from the three ladinos (Leonidas Durán, Manuel González, and Alfredo Alvarado) is transcribed in minister of government to governor of Sonsonate Department, April 26, 1926, AGN, MG, 1926, Box 2. The letter stated that Antonio Contreras had been made alcalde and Rodolfo Brito had been appointed as judge, and reads, "as Judge he engages in every class of abuse and venality; he is a heavy burden upon the poor and Indian peoples." The letter also claimed that Contreras and Brito ensured that only their friends and family members were appointed to the police force.

82. Nulo, December 1927, Nahuizalco, AGN, CN, Box 5. Also cited in Alvarenga Venutolo, *Cultura y ética,* 310–11.

83. For example, between December 1929 and January 1932, five nullification requests originated from Nahuizalco. The respective dates are December 1929, August 1930, September 1930, December 1930, and January 1932. See AGN, CN, Boxes 7 and 9.

84. Request for nullification of Pedro Mendoza as regidor, September 9, 1930, Nahuizalco, AGN, CN, Box 7.

85. Nullifcation request for December 1929 municipal elections, Nahuizalco, AGN, CN, Box 7.

86. Nullification request for January 1932 municipal elections, Nahuizalco, AGN, CN, Box 9.

87. The information and quotes from 1858 are found in López, *Estadística general,* 188–89. The population figure from 1900 is found in an Informe, governor of Sonsonate department, January 12, 1903, AGN, MG, unclassified box. The 1913 survey is found in Cerridos, Sonsonate City, to minister of government, September 20, 1913, AGN, MG, SS, Box 5. For the lack of haciendas, see also *Directorio comercial,* 524–25.

88. Cuisnahuat, Nulo, 1900, AGN, CN, Box 2.

89. Ibid.

90. The case of Tonalá is found in Juan Mathé to Supremo Poder Ejecutivo, April 1890, AGN, MG, SS, unclassified box. For the 1858 report, see López, *Estadística general,* 188–89.

91. Specific figures on the land distribution in Cuisnahuat are not available. For a broad description of landholding both before and after the privatization process, see Lauria-Santiago, *Agrarian Republic.* For a specific example, see the list of land titles in Izalco, August 26, 1896, AGN, MG, SS, unclassified box. The list identifies 248 people, almost all of them Indian *comuneros,* who received plots during the privatization process. The vast majority of the plots are less than five manzanas in size. However twenty-nine of the recipients received more than ten manzanas, and two people received twenty-five manzanas.

92. For internal politics within indigenous communities, particularly in the midst of privatization, see Dore, *Myths of Modernity*; Guardino, *Time of Liberty*; Lauria-Santiago, *Agrarian Republic*; McCreery, *Rural Guatemala;* and Wolfe, *Everyday Nation-State.*

93. Junta de Elección, Cuisnahuat, December 10, 1900, AGN, MG, SS, Box "Política 1890–99, 1900–08."

Chapter 4.   Municipal Elections and Municipal Autonomy, ca. 1880–1930

1. It is impossible to provide a comprehensive list of these scattered records. However, substantial groups of them are stored together. For a large collection from Sonsonate Department for the period 1885 to 1910, see AGN, MG, SS, Box "Política 1890–1899, 1900–1908." For earlier results from Sonsonate, see boxes in AMS marked "elecciones," dated by decade. Results from San Vicente Department can be found in the annual logbooks of the departmental governor, who recorded election results there at least during the period 1845 to 1870; AGN, SSV.

Lists of results from Ahuachapán Department can be found AGN, MG, Box "1882, 84, 86, 87, 88."

2. Junta Electoral, Nahuilingo, May 31, 1840, AMS, Box "Elecciones, 1840–9."

3. Junta Electoral, Villa Santa Clara, to Gobierno Supremo, January 3, 1843, AGN, MG, SSV, 1852, unclassified box.

4. Junta de Elección, Sonsonate City, December 18, 1864, AMS, Box "Elecciones, 1860–9."

5. Junta de Elecciones, Nahuizalco, December 14, 1908, AGN, MG, SS, Box "Política 1890–1899, 1900–1908."

6. San Miguel City, Nulo, 1854, AGN, CN, Box 1.

7. Junta Electoral, Ishuatán, December 16, 1889, AGN, MG, SS, Box "Política 1890–1899, 1900–1908."

8. Junta Electoral, Acajutla, December 16, 188?, AGN, MG, unclassified box.

9. Junta Electoral, Sonsonate City, 1849, AMS, Box "Elecciones, 1840–9."

10. Graham, *Patronage and Politics,* 74. For a discussion of this same issue in the context of Mexico, see Tutino, *Insurrection to Revolution,* especially 18.

11. The rules are set forth in the constitutions and the Ramos Municipales. For the constitutions, see Gallardo, *Cuatro constituciones.* For copies of the Ramo Municipal, see Ley de Ramo Municipal, AGN, MG, 1908, Box 1; Proyecto de Ley Municipal, AGN, MG, 1925, Box 5; and Lardé y Larín, *Recopilación de leyes.*

12. Reference to the two-year wait is made in Leonicio Rodríguez, Zacatecoluca, to governor, San Vicente Department, December 23, 1849, AGN, MG, SSV, 1849, unclassified box.

13. Roberto Ramírez and others, Jayaque, to Gobierno Supremo, October 25, 1890, AGN, MG, unclassified box.

14. Yaloaiquen, Nulo, 1889, AGN, CN, Box 1.

15. Jocoro, Nulo, 1885, AGN, CN, Box 1.

16. Santa Ana City, Nulo, 1911, AGN, CN, Box 4. For references to the land wealth of the leaders, see *Directorio comercial,* 428–31.

17. Atiquizaya, Nulo, 1873, AGN, CN, Box 1.

18. San Francisco Chinameca, Nulo, 1903, AGN, CN, Box 3.

19. Jayaque, Nulo, 1891, AGN, CN, Box 1.

20. Just a few examples of this widely used practice are found in Santiago Nonualco, Nulo, 1898, AGN, CN, Box 2; Santa Elena, Nulo, 1899, AGN, CN, Box 2; and Santa Elena, Nulo, 1907, AGN, CN, Box 3.

21. Chapeltique, Nulo, 1891, AGN, CN, Box 1. The same situation occurred in Armenia, Nulo, 1897, AGN, CN, Box 2.

22. Mercedes, Nulo, 1908, AGN, CN, Box 3; Tonatapeque, Nulo, 1899, AGN, CN, Box 3.

23. Examples of these practices are found in Usulután City, Nulo, 1891, AGN, CN, Box 1; and Santa Clara, Nulo, 1898, AGN, CN, Box 2. For a case of the directorio accepting votes in the middle of the night, see San Pedro Perulapa, Nulo, 1899, AGN, CN, Box 2. For a case of the directorio counting the votes in private and nullifying votes for the opposition, see Soyopango, Nulo, 1907, AGN, CN, Box 3.

24. San Miguel City, Nulo, 1899, AGN, CN, Box 2.

25. Francisco Pimentel, director de policía, Santiago de María, to minister of government, December 12, 1927, AGN, MG, unclassified box.

26. The nullification cases have been placed in a separate collection, Colección de Nulos (CN), in the AGN.

27. See records relating to Izalco in the 1890 and 1900 collection of election records from Sonsonate Department, found in AGN, MG, SS, Box "Política 1890–1899, 1900–1908."

28. The respective quotes are taken from San Miguel City, Nulo, 1897, AGN, CN, Box 2; and Jocoro, Nulo, 1898, AGN, CN, Box 2.

29. Quote is taken from Santa Rosa, Nulo, 1919, AGN, CN, Box 4. For similar cases, see Ishuatán, Nulo, 1892, AGN, CN, Box 1; and Perulapia, Nulo, 1920, AGN, CN, Box 4.

30. References to "gambler" are found in Santa Rosa, Nulo, 1919, AGN, CN, Box 4; and Perulapia, Nulo, 1920, Ibid. References to *vago* are found in Chilanga, Nulo, 1897, AGN, CN, Box 2; and in Santa Clara, Nulo, 1898, AGN, CN, Box 2. The reference to *loco* is from San Miguel City, Nulo, 1854, AGN, CN, Box 1. The reference to "dishonorable" is found in La Union City, Nulo, 1919, AGN, CN, Box 4.

31. The quote is taken from Santa Rosa, Nulo, 1919, AGN, CN, Box 4. Reference to "honor" is found in El Rosario, Nulo, 1900, AGN, CN, Box 3.

32. Ishuatán, Nulo, 1898, AGN, CN, Box 2.

33. For analyses of violence in El Salvador, see Alvarenga Venutolo, *Cultura y ética*; and Holden, *Armies without Nations*.

34. Supremo Gobierno to departmental governor of San Miguel, September 21, 1846, AGN, PB.

35. Ahuachapán City, Nulo, 1848, AGN, CN, Box 1.

36. San Antonio Masahuat, Nulo, 1903, AGN, CN, Box 3.

37. Mercedes, 1907, Nulo, AGN, CN, Box 3.

38. Juayúa, Nulo, 1911, AGN, CN, Box 4.

39. Rosario de Mora, Nulo, 1911, AGN, CN, Box 4; *Directorio comercial*, 708.

40. Director general de la Guardia Nacional to minister of government, October 22, 1921, AGN, MG, 1922, unclassified paquete.

41. For the electoral history of San Sebastián during the period 1891 to 1897, see Carlos Caballos, governor of San Vicente, to minister of government, February 27, 1890, AGN, MG, 1890 Box 1; Geronimo Abarca, San Sebastián, to minister of war, December 16, 1894, AGN, MG, 1894, Box 3; Informe del Gobernador de San Vicente en relato a las sucesos en San Sebastián, June 4, 1897, AGN, FA, Box 3.

42. Williams, *States and Social Evolution,* 266–68.

43. Lindo-Fuentes, *Weak Foundations,* 111–12. The figures from 1890s include only 1890–96.

44. Walter, "Trade and Development," cited in Williams, *States and Social Evolution,* 222.

45. Lindo-Fuentes, *Weak Foundations.*

46. From a sixty-six-page report from the minister of the interior to the National Assembly. The report is not dated, but internal references suggest that it was presented to the newly ordained assembly in February 1902, AGN, MG, 1901, Box 4.

47. Lardé y Larín, *Origines de la Fuerza.*

48. Alvarenga Venutolo, *Cultura y ética,* 145–46.

49. Ibid., 156–68.

50. See, for example, Alvarenga Venutolo, *Cultura y ética,* 143–44; Holden, *Armies without Nations,* 58–67; Williams, *States and Social Evolution*; Guidos Véjar, *El ascenso*; M. McClintock, *American Connection*; Dunkerley, *Power in the Isthmus*; Burns, "Modernization"; and Anderson, *Matanza.*

51. Gobat, *Confronting the American Dream,* especially chapter 8.

52. Castañeda, *General Menéndez,* 58–59. For a descriptions of the deputies who made up the assembly of 1886, see García, *Asamblea Nacional.*

53. For an insider's look at the process of presidential succession between 1898 and 1913, see the memoirs of Enrique Córdova, *Miradas retrospectivas.* See also the dispatches of the U.S. legation in San Salvador for the period 1910 to 1914, USNA, RG 59, 816.00/118 to 816.00/190. For secondary accounts of the transfers, see Ministerio de Educación, *Historia de El Salvador*; White, *El Salvador*; and Cárdenal, *El poder eclesiástico.*

54. Thomas Dabney, chargé d'affaires ad interim, San Salvador, to U.S. secretary of state, October 29, 1910, USNA, RG 59, 816.00/119.

55. Villavicencio's political machinations generated a copious amount of appeals to the government on the part of Regalado affiliates. See, for instance, Nulo, San Vicente, 1898, AGN, CN, Box 1; Nulo, Tonatepeque, 1899, AGN, CN, Box 2; Abel Magaña, San Francisco de Gotera, to minister of the interior, Septem-

ber 20, 1989, AGN, MG, 1898, Box 14; Teófilo Muñoz, Jocoro, to governor of Morazán Department, September 20, 1898, AGN, MG, 1898, Box 14; Braulio Magaña, Ahuachapán to Tomás Regalado, February 22, 1988, AGN, MG, unclassified box; and Comandante Departamental, Usulután, to Rubén Rivera, San Salvador, December 18, 1899, AGN, MG, unclassified box.

56. For the defeat of Villavicencio, see Córdova, *Miradas retrospectivas,* 20–21.

57. The opposition to Figueroa, and especially the conflicts between him and Barahona, are described at length in Córdova, *Miradas retrospectivas, 36–55.*

58. Córdova bore witness to the revolt in 1907 and his arrival to Sonsonate. See *Miradas retrospectivas,* 50. Alfaro's activities also are described by U.S. legation officers. See U.S. chargé to U.S. secretary of state, October 26, 1910, 816.00/118; Heimke to U.S. secretary of state, July 3, 1911, 816.00/132; and Heimke to U.S. secretary of state, September 27, 1911, 816.00/134; all are in USNA, RG 59.

59. Alfaro, *Protest of Dr. Prudencio Alfaro.*

60. Illegible signature of U.S. embassy officer, San Salvador, to U.S. secretary of state, October 5, 1910, USNA, RG 59, 816.00/116.

61. Ibid.

62. For studies of the political situations in turn-of-the-century Argentina, Uruguay, and Mexico, see, for example, Rock, *Politics in Argentina*; Knarr, *Uruguay and the United States*; and Knight, *Mexican Revolution.*

63. Alfonso Reyes, "Sufragio universal"; the quotations are drawn from 285.

64. R. Angulo, Usulután to minster of government, December 11, 1892, AGN, MG, 1897, Box 3.

65. San Juan Nonualco to minister of government, December 1, 1896, AGN, MG, unclassified box.

66. Jesús Ungo, Chalatenango, to minister of government, January 24, 1895, AGN, MG, unclassified box.

67. Governor of Sonsonate to Flores, alcalde of Nahuizalco, December 22, 1899; governor of Sonsonate to minister of government, December 26, 1899; and Alcalde of Nahuizalco to governor of Sonsonate, December ?, 1899; stored together in AGN, MG, unclassified box.

68. The dispute between Tecapa and the military is found in the transcript of the Libro de Actas of Tecapa, December 2, 1889 (which contains a reprint of the letter of November 30, 1889, to Tecapa from General Castañeda), AGN, MG, unclassified box; and Ramón Bautista to minister of war, December 3, 1889, AGN, MG, 1889, Box 2.

69. Telegram from governor of Usulután to president of the republic, December 31, 1889, AGN, MG, 1889, Box 2.

70. From ?, the owner of hacienda "La Mizata," to Baltazar Estupián, minister of government, August 12, 1921, AGN, MG, unclassified box.

71. Vicente Sol to the minister of government, November 5, 1921, AGN, MG, unclassified box. Patricia Alvarenga Venutolo cites similar cases from the Sección Juridica in the AGN. See Alvarenga Venutolo, "Reshaping the Ethics," 158.

72. Peloso and Tenenbaum, *Liberals, Politics, and Power,* 2.

73. Gallardo, *Cuatro constituciones.*

74. Castañeda, *General Menéndez,* 72.

75. Annual report from minister of the interior, read before the national assembly in February 1902, AGN, MG, 1901, Box 4.

76. In Peloso and Tenenbaum, *Liberals, Politics, and Power,* 286.

77. From the municipal council and "Asamblea vecinos del Pueblo de San Juan Nonualco," to minister of government, November ?, 1896, AGN, MG, unclassified box.

78. The related documents are bound together with the police report dated July 24, 1900, AGN, MG, unclassified box.

79. Telegram from governor of Ahuachapán to minister of government, 1891, AGN, MG, 1891, Box 7.

80. Alvarenga Venutolo, "Reshaping the Ethics," 166–67. All the accounts are from *Diario del Salvador:* see August 9, 1906, 1; August 10, 1906, 1; March 19, 1910, 4; February 10, 1912, 4; March 25, 1912, 4; April 14, 1910, 1; and September 10, 1912, 1.

81. Sabas Cantor, Oratorio, to governor of Cuscatlán Department, January 14, 1917, AGN, MG, 1917, Box 1.

82. Francisco ?, Cojutepeque, to minister of government, January 15, 1917, AGN, MG, 1917, Box 1.

83. Office of the departmental governor of San Miguel to minister of government, January 5, 1920, AGN, MG, 1920, Box 5; and minister of government to director of the Guardia Nacional, November 9, 1920, AGN, MG, 1920, Box 2. The clash in Santa Ana also was reported by the U.S. chargé in his report to Washington. He stated that the clash resulted in the death of two policemen and two guardias, in addition to a number of wounded: Arnold to secretary of state, November 18, 1920, USNA, RG 59, 816.00/297; Acta oficial de la Municipalidad de Berlín, May 20, 1921, AGN, MG, unclassified box; minister of war to minister of government, May 11, 1921, AGN, MG, 1921, *Notas Varias,* unclassified paquete; director general of the Guardia Nacional to governor of Sonsonate Department, November 13, 1918, AGN, MG, SS, Box 3; and director general of the Guardia Nacional to the minister of government, October 22, 1921, AGN, MG, *Notas de la Guardia Nacional, octubre 1921,* unclassified paquete.

84. Justo Preza and others, San Martín, to minister of government, November 16, 1919, AGN, MG, unclassified box.

85. Municipal act of the municipal council of Jiquilisco, February 14, 1920, AGN, MG, 1920, Box 1.

86. Comandante of San Vicente Department to minister of war, March 29, 1915, AGN, MG, 1915, Box 1.

87. Director general of the Guardia Nacional to minister of government, October 22, 1921, AGN, MG, 1922, unclassified paquete.

88. Ibid.

Chapter 5.   *The Network of the State*

1. Williams, *States and Social Evolution,* 220.

2. Graham, *Patronage and Politics,* 7 and 272. Additional scholarship has suggested the salience of a similar line of inquiry for Central America. In his exploratory article on state formation in Central America, Robert Holden suggests that state centralization reinforced traditional patronage relations, resulting in the creation of "clientelist states." See Holden, "Constructing the Limits," 442.

3. Carlos Meléndez served as a regidor in San Salvador in 1890 and 1901. Quiñónez served as a regidor in 1899 and in 1904. See "Nomina de los alcaldes y municipalidades de la ciudad de San Salvador desde el año de 1889 hasta 1972," AGN, MG, unclassified box. A biography of Quiñónez, showing his various administrative positions, was compiled by the British Legation. See Harrington, Guatemala, to Foreign Office, April 24, 1928, PRO, FO 371/12749, A 3214/3214/8.

4. The census from 1929 is found in AGN, MG, 1929, Box 1.

5. *Directorio comercial,* 625–708.

6. Contained in a report from U.S. Consul in San Salvador to U.S. secretary of state, March 31, 1920, USNA, RG 84, Section 865.81 Sugar.

7. Ruhl, *Central Americans,* 197. For a meeting with Quiñónez, see Mitchell-Hedges, *Land of Wonder and Fear,* 153.

8. Frederick William Taylor to Marion, September 9, 1923, FWTP, Box 3, Folder 1.

9. ? Durán, Sensuntepeque, to Cecilio Bustamante, San Salvador, October 12, 1914, AGN, MG, 1914, Box 2.

10. Alcalde of El Refugio to minister of government, December 12, 1914, AGN, MG, 1914, Box 2.

11. Gabriel ?, Apastepeque, to governor of San Vicente Department, December 14, 1913, AGN, SSV, 1913, Box 3.

12. Lang to U.S. secretary of state, January 2, 1915, USNA, RG 59, 816.00/198.

13. As examples of these other cases: In 1914 the governor of San Vicente reported that one of his municipalities pointed out that one of the candidates selected by the national committee of the Club Melendista for the deputy position was from a neighboring department and therefore could not legally represent the department. The governor recommended that the national government select another candidate. See Gonzalo Ayala to president of the republic, December 30, 1914, AGN, SSV, 1915, Box 2. See also the telegram from the alcalde of Idelfonso to governor of San Vicente Department, January 10, 1916, AGN, SSV, 1916, Box 1. This letter refers to the candidates that the national committee selected for the forthcoming municipal election.

14. *Diario Oficial,* August 29, 1914, contained in Henry F. ?, U.S. Chargé, San Salvador, to U.S. secretary of state, September 7, 1914, USNA, RG 59, 816.00/24.

15. The pamphlet ostensibly was a letter from Jorge to one Dr. Bolaños, written on September 14, 1917. But more than likely, given that the pamphlet is just under one hundred pages long, it was intended as a piece of government propaganda. See *Orientaciones económicas del Sr. Presidente Meléndez*—the copy I found is in the Fundación Gallardo, Santa Tecla.

16. Córdova, *Miradas retrospectivas,* 109–33.

17. Ibid., 135–36.

18. Arnold to U.S. secretary of state, July 13, 1918, USNA, RG 59, 816.00/211.

19. Córdova, *Miradas retrospectivas,* 161.

20. Ibid., 144.

21. Arnold, to U.S. secretary of state, December 10, 1918, USNA, RG 59, 816.00/230.

22. Córdova, *Miradas retrospectivas,* 145; Arnold to U.S. secretary of state, December 10, 1918, USNA, RG 59, 816.00/213. For municipal conflicts between Quiñonistas and Palomistas, see Nulo, Guadalupe, 1918, AGN, CN, Box 4; and Nulo, Tecoluca, 1918, AGN, CN, Box 4.

23. A relative of Fuentes has put together a webpage that includes a brief biography and reproductions of some of his writings, along with the obituary from a local newspaper in 1934. See http://www.oocities.org/es/hugolindosv /Ismael.htm.

24. Pedro Lúe, Nahuizalco, to Ismael Fuentes, San Salvador, February 24, 1919, IFC.

25. Córdova, *Miradas retrospectivas,* 150. It also is likely that Palomo recognized the futility of continuing, given Quiñónez's dominance in the municipal elections.

26. Martínez's candidacy is reported in Córdova, *Miradas retrospectivas,* 156; and in Arnold to U.S. secretary of state, December 26, 1918, USNA, RG 59, 816.00/220.

27. Guidos Véjar, *El ascenso,* 108–9.

28. Calixto Rodríguez, San Sebastián, to governor of San Vicente Department, January 14, 1919, AGN, MG, SSV, 1919, Box 5.

29. Manuel Burgos, Verapáz, to governor of San Vicente Department, January ?, 1919, AGN, MG, SSV, 1919, Box 5.

30. Arnold to U.S. secretary of state, January 16, 1919, USNA, RG 59, 816.00/235.

31. Ibid.

32. Arnold to U.S. secretary of state, April 2, 1919, USNA, RG 59, 816.00/236.

33. Araujo's conflict of March 1920 is reported in Arnold to secretary of state, March 10, 1920, USNA, RG 59, 816.00/248; Córdova, *Miradas retrospectivas,* 169; and in Alfonso Quiñónez, San Salvador, to Ismael Fuentes, Madrid, March 24, 1920, IFC.

34. Jorge Meléndez describes the invasion of May 1920 for Ismael Fuentes in Meléndez, San Salvador, to Fuentes, Madrid, June 1, 1920, IFC. The invasion is also reported in Arnold to U.S. secretary of state, May 13, 1920, 816.00/262, and May 14, 1920, 816.00/263, both in USNA, RG 59; and in Medhurst to Curzon, Foreign Office, May 7, 1920, A 3730/98/8, and May 14, 1920, A 4294/98/8, both in PRO, FO 371/4443. Araujo's return to El Salvador is reported in Schuyler to secretary of state, January 7, 1924, USNA, RG 59, 816.00/527.

35. See Bernal, San Francisco, to Fuentes, San Salvador, March 28, 1919, IFC.

36. See, for example, ibid.; and Galdámez, San Salvador, to Fuentes, San Salvador, March 29, 1919, IFC.

37. Fermín Velasco, Sensuntepeque, Cabañas Department, to Arturo Arguello, San Salvador, April 30, 1921, AGN, MG, 1921, unclassified paquete, "notas varias."

38. Manuel Funes, Chinameca, to Horacio Villavicencio, governor of San Miguel Department, April 20, 1920, AGN, FA, Box "C no. 2."

39. Gustavo ?, Ataco, Ahuachapán Department, to "correligionarios y amigos," June 22, 1921, AGN, MG, unclassified box.

40. Ibid.

41. Governor of Ahuachapán to the minister of government, July 1, 1921, AGN, MG, unclassified box.

42. Meléndez, San Salvador, to Fuentes, Madrid, November 5, 1919, IFC. See also Alfonso Quiñónez describing the recent municipal elections, in Quiñónez, San Salvador, to Fuentes, Madrid, December 27, 1919, IFC; the letter from

an illegible signature in Usulután City on letterhead from the Dirección General de Sanidad de San Salvador to Fuentes, Madrid, October 18, 1921, IFC; and Miguel ?, San Salvador, to Fuentes, Madrid, August 11, 1920, IFC.

43. Ayala, governor of Chalatenango Department, to minister of government, December 27, 1921, AGN, MG, 1921, Box 3.

44. José Posada, Santa Tecla, to Baltazar Estupinian, August 27, 1920, AGN, MG, 1920, Box 2.

45. Contained in a *solicitud* for nullification of municipal election of December 1920 in the municipality of Nueva Esparta, La Unión Department. The date of the request is May 29, 1921, and the solicitor is Bernardo Escobar, alcalde. See Nulo, Nueva Esparta, 1921, AGN, CN, Box 4. For other examples, see Joaquín Chávez, Santiago de Maria, April 20, 1924, AGN, MG, unclassified box; and the request from Rafael Enríquez of Ilobasco, which is reprinted in Jorge Meléndez to minister of government, January 13, 1920, AGN, MG, 1920, Box 5.

46. Jorge Meléndez to minister of war, December 15, 1920, AGN, MG, unclassified box.

47. Minister of war to minister of government, December 4, 1920, AGN, MG, unclassified box.

48. Director General de Policia to minister of government, April 13, 1922, AGN, MG, unclassified box.

49. Córdova left the government after Meléndez's election, and thus this comment comes from his position as an outside observer, rather than as a government insider. Córdova, *Miradas retrospectivas,* 200.

50. Palomo's departure from politics and his eventual death are reported in Jay, San Salvador, to Fletcher, undersecretary of state, May 17, 1921, USNA, RG 59, 816.00/358.

51. Arnold to U.S. secretary of state, March 10, 1920, USNA, RG 59, 816.00/248.

52. Schuyler to U.S. secretary of state, May 15, 1922, USNA, RG 59, 816.00/392.

53. Peña Trejo's memoir was published in twenty-two installments between the months of April and June 1964 in *Diario Latino* under the title "Narración histórica de la insurrección militar del 2 de diciembre de 1931." I found the memoir in an unclassified book of press clippings for the year 1931 in AGN, MG, unclassified box. Peña Trejo's discussion of the year 1918 as a watershed is found in installment 4, "Ascensos militares hasta 1912"; and his discussion of payment and the policies of Meléndez and Quiñónez is found in installment 7, "Reseña economia," and installment 8, "Reseña economia 1923–1931."

54. "Mensaje dirigido a la Asamblea Nacional por el Señor Presidente de la República, don Jorge Meléndez, en la aperatura de las sesiones ordinarias de 1920." San Salvador: Imprenta Nacional, 1920.

55. Alfonso Quiñónez describes the conflict in the military school and the resignation of General Llanos in Quiñónez, San Salvador, to Fuentes, Madrid, March 24, 1920, IFC.

56. Arnold to U.S. secretary of state, March 2, 1920, USNA, RG 59, 816.00/246.

57. Medhurst to Curzon, Foreign Office, May 14, 1920, PRO, FO 371/4442, A 4294/98/8.

58. The revolts are described in Scott to Curzon, Foreign Office, February 18, 1920, A 1750/1239/8, and May 26, 1922, A 3911/1239/8, both in PRO, FO 371/7199; Schuyler to U.S. secretary of state, May 22, 1922, USNA, RG 59, 816.00/394; and Gywnn, Guatemala, March 26, 1926, G-2 Military Reports, Box 764, Folder 3020, "Revolutionary Movements." A transcript of President Meléndez's speech before the National Assembly in which he addresses the issue of the revolt in the military school is found in Hewes, to U.S. secretary of state, February 22, 1923, USNA, RG 84, Volume 71.

59. For examples of the revisionist argument, see Alvarenga Venutolo, *Cultura y ética*; and Gould and Lauria-Santiago, *To Rise in Darkness*.

60. For examples of elite splits creating bargaining space for subaltern actors, see Sanders, *Contentious Republicans*; Gobat, *Confronting the American Dream*; and Yashar, *Demanding Democracy*.

61. Traditional arguments portray ORDEN as a creature of the military regimes and the U.S. counterinsurgency doctrine. Even though its roughly one hundred thousand members were poor peasants, the traditional view describes it as a wing of the national security state, dedicated to terrorizing opponents and committing brutal acts of violence in the name of anticommunism and nationalism. A revisionist view claims that the story is more complex and says that poor peasants joined ORDEN for diverse reasons, such as economic survival, and that some of them had little in common with the military regime or the United States. For summaries of the debate, see Mazzei, *Death Squads*; and for a particular example of the revisionist view, see Todd, *Beyond Displacement,* especially 40.

62. Conflicts between the Liga Roja and elements of the military in Nahuizalco and Chalatenango are described in *Diario del Salvador,* September 16, 1918, 20; in Jujutla and Turín in *Diario del Salvador,* December 10, 1918, 2; and in Juayúa in *Diario del Salvador,* August 3, 1918, 2. I drew all of these citations from Alvarenga Venutolo, "Reshaping the Ethics," 280–86.

63. Nulo, Yayantique, 1921, AGN, CN, Box 4.

64. Francisco Gutiérrez, San Salvador, to Jorge Meléndez, January 13, 1920, AGN, MG, 1920, Box 5.

65. Minister of war to minister of government, December 29, 1921, AGN, MG, unclassified box.

66. Hoja suelta of the Liga Roja of Santa Ana, signed by Rodolfo Lara, Secretary, April 2, 1921, AGN, MG, unclassified box.

67. *Diario del Salvador,* December 11, 1920, cited in Alvarenga Venutolo, "Reshaping the Ethics," 275. The translation is by Alvarenga Venutolo. Alvarenga Venutolo also cites other manifestations that were described in the *Diario del Salvador.* See November 29, 1922, 5; and December 6, 1922, 5. The processions also were noted by the U.S. chargé: see Hewes, to U.S. secretary of state, December 15, 1922, USNA, RG 59, 816.00/458. The Liga also was a very visible element in a 1920 rally to show support for the government during the Araujo invasion. See Arnold, to U.S. secretary of state, May 13, 1920, USNA, RG 59, 816.00/262.

68. The increasing interest on the part of the U.S. can be attributed to recent changes in U.S. policy regarding recognition of governments in Central America. The changes were in large part the by-product of the Panama Canal and the desire of the U.S. government for stability in the surrounding region. British interest intensified due to their increasing financial investments in the nation, particularly the British-owned Salvador Railway Co. For good discussions of international involvement in Central America in the early twentieth century, see Salisbury, *Anti-Imperialism*; and LaFeber, *Inevitable Revolutions.*

69. Hewes to U.S. secretary of state, December 27, 1922, USNA, RG 59, 816.00/466.

70. Scott to Curzon, Foreign Office, January 5, 1922, PRO, FO 371/8434, A 689/158/8.

71. Hewes to U.S. secretary of state, October 20, 1922, USNA, RG 59, 816.00/437. For another reference to the members of the Liga as Indians, see Hewes to U.S. secretary of state, January 19, 1923, USNA, RG 59, 816.00/479.

72. Hewes to U.S. secretary of state, October 29, 1922, USNA, RG 59, 816.00/467.

73. Salvador Sol's property holdings are reported in the *Directorio comercial,* 477–78 and 636. For the position of the Sol family in the broader coffee economy, see Williams, *States and Social Evolution,* 279.

74. *Diario del Salvador,* September 16, 1918, 2, cited in Alvarenga Venutolo, "Reshaping the Ethics," 280.

75. Alvarenga Venutolo inaccurately describes Brito as an Indian as part of her argument that the Liga Roja was a populist institution. Alvarenga Venutolo, "Reshaping the Ethics," 280.

76. The documents relating to Nueva Concepción are transcribed in A. Gómez Zárate, minister of war, to minister of government, September 20, 1923, AGN, MG, 1923, unclassified paquete. For the agricultural production of the region in comparison to other regions, and for reference to the landholdings of the Parrillas, see *Directorio comercial,* 135.

77. Nulo, Yayantique, 1921, AGN, CN, Box 4; and *Directorio comercial,* 287.

78. *El Espectador,* September ?, 1930, in Pío Romero Bosque to minister of government, December 21, 1930, AGN, MG, unclassified box. See also Pinto, governor of Santa Ana Department, to minister of government, December 27, 1930, AGN, MG, unclassified box; and *Directorio comercial,* 456–57. See also the lists of coffee growers for Chalchuapa from the year 1926 in "Nomina de los cultivadores de café en la jurisdicción de Chalchuapa," AGN, MG, 1926, Box 5. According to a 1943 list of local landowners, Portillo held the status of "*agricultor en grande.*" See the unclassified lists of property owners from April 1943 in AGN, MG, 1943, unclassified paquette.

79. See the collection of materials contained in the pre-electoral denunciation from Colón, November 1929, AGN, CN, Box 6.

80. See the collection of materials contained in the pre-electoral denunciation from Tenancingo, October, 1929, AGN, CN, Box 6. For the landholdings of Barriere, see *Directorio comercial,* 82.

81. Historian Carlos Gregorio López Bernal found that reference. See López Bernal, *Tradiciones inventadas,* 190.

82. See Ching, "In Search of the Party."

83. Schuyler to U.S. secretary of state, July 12, 1923, USNA, RG 59, 816.00/505.

84. Schuyler to U.S. secretary of state, April 8, 1925, USNA, RG 59, 816.00/558.

85. Alvarenga Venutolo, "Reshaping the Ethics," 285–86.

86. Schuyler to U.S. secretary of state, July 12, 1923, USNA, RG 59, 816.00/505.

87. These events are described in the documents relating to the occurrences, which are transcribed in A. Gómez Zárate to minister of government, September 20, 1923, AGN, MG 1923, unclassified paquete.

88. Schaefer to U.S. secretary of state, January 6, 1922, USNA, RG 59, 816.00/369.

89. Hill to Foreign Office, February 13, 1936, PRO, FO 371/19771, A 1261/1261/8.

90. The broadside/periodical was entitled *La Tribuna* and is found in Hewes to U.S. secretary of state, December 12, 1922, USNA, RG 59, 816.00/457.

91. From the broadside/periodical of the Molina campaign, *El Constitucional,* December 5, 1922, in Hewes to U.S. secretary of state, ibid.

92. According to the U.S. chargé who was monitoring the elections, Quiñónez had made some limited appeals to workers during the 1918 campaign. And, of course, there was the campaign of the infamous prolabor landowner Arturo

Araujo in 1918. For reference to the campaign and its appeals to workers, see Hewes to U.S. secretary of state, November 3, 1922, USNA, RG 59, 816.00/442.

93. These complaints are described in Hewes to U.S. secretary of state, December 20, 1922, 816.00/461; December 22, 1922, 816.00/463; and December 22, 1922, 816.00/464, all in USNA, RG 59.

94. Nicolás Durán, Alcalde, Verapáz, to governor of San Vicente Department, December 1, 1922, AGN, MG, SSV, 1922, Box 4.

95. One of the broadsides denouncing the activities of the Liga Roja is in Hewes to U.S. secretary of state, December 12, 1922, USNA, RG 59, 816.00/457.

96. Scott to Curzon, December 30, 1922, PRO, FO 371 8434, A 396/158/8.

97. Hewes, to U.S. secretary of state, January 5, 1923, 816.00/475.

98. Transcripts of the trial and descriptions of those accused of killing Escalante appeared approximately every two days in *Diario La Prensa* between August 29, 1927, and November 25, 1927. In *Diario Latino,* see August 29, 1927, 1, for an extended description of the events; and also August 31, 1927, 1; September 2, 1927, 1; and September 3, 1927, 1. The same newspaper picked up the story again in articles on April 30, 1928; September 4, 1928; October 11, 1929; and November 12, 1929. See also *Diario del Salvador,* September 9, 1927, and August 18, 1928, 8.

99. Hewes to U.S. secretary of state, January 5, 1923, USNA, RG 59, 816.00/471.

100. Schuyler to U.S. secretary of state, December 29, 1923, USNA, RG 59, 816.00/526.

101. Hewes to U.S. secretary of state, January 12, 1923, USNA, RG 59, 816.00/478.

102. Hewes to U.S. secretary of state, January 19, 1923, USNA, RG 59, 816.00/479.

103. Unos vecinos de Quetzaltepeque, Chalatenango Department, to minister of government, September 25, 1923, AGN, MG, 1923, Box 3.

104. Gabino Jovel, El Cármen, La Unión Department, to minister of government, October 9, 1923, AGN, MG, unclassified box.

105. Quiñónez to minister of government, December 19, 1925, AGN, MG, unclassified box.

Chapter 6.   *Facing the Leviathan*

1. Frederick William Taylor to Marion, November 20, 1926, FWTP, Box 3, Folder 1.

2. Caffery to U.S. secretary of state, April 26, 1927, USNA, RG 59, 816.00/629.

3. A noteworthy exception to this absence is Gould and Lauria-Santiago, *To Rise in Darkness*. The section of that book dealing with the late 1920s is based on archival work in the AGN, which was conducted in the late 1980s mainly by Lauria-Santiago, outside the realm of his dissertation topic, and eventually became *An Agrarian Republic*. The main objective of *To Rise in Darkness* with regard to the Romero reforms is to set the stage for the 1932 insurrection. Nevertheless, many of its findings support the claims made here. See also Alvarenga Venutolo, *Cultura y ética*; and Wilson, "Crisis of National Integration."

4. A mild attempt at reform had been made by President Manuel Enrique Araujo (1911–1913), but his reforms did not venture into the political realm. See Chasteen, "Manuel Enrique Araujo."

5. From a general biographical description of Pío Romero Bosque in *Diario del Salvador,* January 1, 1929, 1; and from A. W. Bloor, U.S. Military Attaché, July 5, 1927, WNRC G-2 Military Reports, Box 764, Folder 3110.

6. From the list of notables in La Paz Department, José Gutiérrez, Zacatecoluca to Dr. R. Reyes, San Salvador, January 20, 1897, AGN, MG, unclassified box.

7. For references to Romero Bosque's landholdings, see Pío Romero Bosque to Dr. Arturo Argüello, subsecretary of government, February 17, 1920, AGN, FA, Box "C, no. 2"; and *Directorio comercial,* 674.

8. Romero Bosque's family ties are discussed in Caffery to U.S. secretary of state, March 3, 1927, USNA, RG 59, 816.00/615; and May 28, 1927, 816.00/642. Julio Mejía would be given the position as chief of protocol in Romero Bosque's administration.

9. Pío Romero Bosque, minister of war, to minister of government, December 23, 1921, AGN, MG, unclassified box.

10. Engert to U.S. secretary of state, July 6, 1925, USNA, RG 59, 816.00/561.

11. Caffery to U.S. secretary of state, August 14, 1926, USNA, RG 19, 816.00/585; and August 19, 1926, 816.00/588.

12. Caffery to U.S. secretary of state, December 10, 1926, USNA, RG 59, 816.00/601.

13. Caffery to U.S. secretary of state, March 3, 1927, USNA, RG 59, 816.00/615.

14. For one brief discussion of reformism and its origins, see Huntington, *Third Wave,* 127. For a more specific discussion of the "public demand for reform," as well as reference to some of the various theories on the origins of reform, see Geddes, *Politician's Dilemma,* especially 93–98 and 184–86. The reformist

program in Peru in the 1960s under General Velasco Alvarado is a notable example. For discussion of it, see Rouquié, *Military and the State,* especially chapter 10; and Philip, "The Soldier as Radical."

15. The speech before the assembly of February 1930 can be found in Schott to U.S. secretary of state, February 21, 1930, USNA, RG 84, Section 803.

16. See Gould and Lauria-Santiago, *To Rise in Darkness,* 41–44; Alvarenga Venutolo, *Cultura y ética,* chapter 6; and Ministerio de Educación, *Historia de El Salvador* 2:110–25.

17. For discussions of and debates over the growth of the labor movement in El Salvador in the 1920s, see Ching, "In Search of the Party"; Gould and Lauria-Santiago, *To Rise in Darkness,* chapter 2; Alvarenga Venutolo, *Cultura y ética,* chapters 6 and 7; Almeida, *Waves of Protest,* chapter 2; and Larín, *Historia del movimiento.*

18. Gould and Lauria-Santiago, *To Rise in Darkness,* 40. As just one example of the distinction between urban and rural actors in a political system, see Guardino, *Time of Liberty,* in which he compares the urban poor in Oaxaca City with the indigenous communities in the surrounding highlands.

19. From Trinidad Romero to Consejo Directivo de la FRTS, January 1929, AGN, MG, 1929, Box 16. There was one editorial published in the *Diario del Salvador* in 1927 in which the anonymous author argued that "Bolshevism" was threatening Central America and that the government should "castigate it severely." See *Diario del Salvador,* September 23, 1927, 3. But this was an isolated example. When labor issues were addressed in editorials, which was not often, it was much more common to find the editorialist hailing the conspicuous lack of radicalism among El Salvador's working class. See, for example, *Diario del Salvador,* June 29, 1925, 3; and February 10, 1928, 3.

20. Andino, *Padre de la democracia.*

21. Córdova, *Miradas retrospectivas,* 252.

22. Gobat, *Confronting the American Dream,* chapter 8. For an argument similar to Gobat's on this matter, see Schroeder, "Cultural Geographies."

23. Caffery to U.S. secretary of state, December 10, 1926, USNA, RG 59, 816.00/601.

24. See Caffery to U.S. secretary of state, April 25, 1927, USNA, RG 59, 816.002/43; and June 7, 1927, 816.00/52.

25. The verbal disputes between Quiñónez and Romero are described in Harrington to Foreign Office, October 15, 1927, PRO, FO 371/11971, A 7516/37/8; Caffery to U.S. secretary of state, April 5, 1927, USNA, RG 59, 816.002/42, and April 5, 1927, 816.00/625; and *Diario Latino,* June 7, 1927, 1.

26. Caffery to U.S. secretary of state, June 7, 1927, USNA, RG 59, 816.002/52.

27. A table showing that the Meléndez and Quiñónez administrations operated under a state of siege for almost their entire duration can be found in Suter, *Prosperität und Krise,* 678.

28. *Diario Latino,* June 11, 1927, 1; also described in A. W. Bloor, U.S. Military Attaché, July 26, 1927, WNRC, G-2 Military Report #94, Box 764, Folder 3110.

29. The transcripts of the debate are found in *Diario del Salvador,* June 9, 1927, 1. The debate also was played out in the editorial pages of *Diario Latino*: see June 11, 1927, 1; and June 14, 1927, 8.

30. A. W. Bloor, U.S. Military Attaché, July 26, 1927, WNRC, G-2 Military Report #94, Box 764, Folder 3110. Quiñónez's resignation also was reported in Caffery to U.S. secretary of state, July 16, 1927, USNA, RG 59, 816.00/646.

31. To repeat the citation from the last chapter: Transcripts of the trial and descriptions of those accused of killing Escalante appeared approximately every two days in *Diario La Prensa* between August 29, 1927, and November 25, 1927. In *Diario Latino,* see August 29, 1927, 1 for an extended description of the events; and also August 31, 1927, 1; September 2, 1927, 1; and September 3, 1927, 1. The same newspaper then returns to the story in articles on April 30, 1928; September 4, 1928; October 11, 1929; and November 12, 1929. See also *Diario del Salvador,* September 9, 1927; and August 18, 1928, 8.

32. Evidence of the coup of December 1927 is found in Córdova, *Miradas retrospectivas,* 246–47; Cohen, Costa Rica, December 8, 1927, WNRC, G-2 Military Report #189, and December 8, 1927, Report #190; *Diario Latino,* December 12, 1927, 1, December 17, 1927, 1, December 19, 1927, 1, December 20, 1927, 1, and December 27, 1927, 1; Dickson to U.S. secretary of state, December 6, 1927, December 8, 1927, December 13, 1927, December 14, 1927, and December 19, 1927, all from USNA, RG 84, Section 800; and the succession of reports from the U.S. legation dated between December 6, 1927, and January 13, 1927, USNA, RG 59, 816.00/675 to 816.00/692.

33. Meléndez's presence and business ventures in Costa Rica are described in *Diario del Salvador,* November 8, 1928, 8; and October 21, 1928, 1.

34. The conversation between Muse, the former chargé, and Quiñónez is contained in a report from Herrick, Paris, to U.S. secretary of state, February 28, 1928, USNA, RG 84, Section 800; see also RG 59, 816.00/710.

35. As reported in Caffery to U.S. secretary of state, April 25, 1928, USNA, RG 84, Section 820.

36. The text of Romero Bosque's speech is found in *Diario Latino,* June 25, 1927, 1.

37. *Diario del Salvador,* August 13, 1927, 3.

38. *Diario del Salvador,* October 22, 1927, 3.

39. As reported in Caffery to U.S. secretary of state, September 5, 1927, USNA, RG 84, Section 800.

40. *Diario del Salvador,* September 6, 1927, 2.

41. *Diario Latino,* November 25, 1927, 1.

42. Ramón Bautista, Alegría, to governor of Usulután Department, November 3, 1927, AGN, MG, unclassified box.

43. J. V. Maza and others, San Julián, to governor of Sonsonate Department, November 18, 1927, AGN, MG, unclassified box.

44. *Diario del Salvador,* December 2, 1927, 7. An almost identical comment from San Sebastián was printed in *Diario del Salvador* on November 15, 1927, 8. For a similar comment from Quezaltepeque, see *Diario del Salvador,* November 25, 1927, 7; and from Izalco, see *Diario del Salvador,* December 7, 1927, 3.

45. *Diario Latino,* October 28, 1929, 8.

46. Isaac Olivo Raymundo, Armenia, to Pío Romero Bosque, November 26, 1927, AGN, MG, unclassified box.

47. Handbill of Club Patriótica Pío Romero Bosque, Atiquizaya, November 27, 1927, AGN, MG, unclassified box.

48. Manuel González, San Agustín, to minister of government, November 19, 1927, AGN, MG, unclassified box.

49. Abrahán Peña, Ishuatán, to minister of government, October 22, 1927.

50. For other examples, see Rómulo Castañeda, Guaymango, to Pío Romero Bosque, November 24, 1927, AGN, MG, unclassified box; Pío Romero Bosque to minister of government, December 5, 1927 (regarding a case from Ahuachapán City), AGN, MG, unclassified box; Adán Soto, San Buenaventura, to minister of government, December 2, 1927, AGN, MG, unclassified box; Transito Gaetán, Santiago de María, to minister of government, November 28, 1927, AGN, MG, unclassified box; Joaquín Rivera, Jucuapa, to Trinidad Romero, San Salvador, November 27, 1927, AGN, MG, unclassified box; Bonifacio Baires, Berlín, to Pío Romero Bosque, November 7, 1927, AGN, MG, unclassified box; L. ?, Usulután, to Manuel Vicente, San Salvador, November 25, 1927, AGN, MG, unclassified, box; Gonzalo Hernández, San Vicente City, to minister of government, December 5, 1927, AGN, MG, unclassified box; J. Antonio Cienfuegos, Sonsonate, to Pío Romero Bosque, November 17, 1927 (regarding a case from Santa Catarina Masahuat), AGN, MG, unclassified box; Lisandro Larín, Sonsonate, to minister of government, October 31, 1927, AGN, MG, unclassified box; and J. Angel de León, San Julián, to minister of government, November 18, 1927, AGN, MG, unclassified box.

51. Moisés Jiménez, San Pedro Pustla, to minister of government, October 29, 1927, AGN, MG, unclassified box.

52. Horacio Villavicencio, San Vicente, to Pío Romero Bosque, November 7, 1927, AGN, MG, unclassified box.

53. Interview with Minister of Government Manuel Mendoza, *Diario Latino,* November 25, 1927, 1.

54. Dickson to U.S. secretary of state, November 28, 1927, USNA, RG 59, 816.00/673.

55. Interview with Minister of Government Manuel Mendoza, *Diario Latino,* November 25, 1927, 1.

56. Telegram from Raul F. Munguia, Usulután, to minister of government, December 7, 1927, AGN, MG, unclassified box.

57. *Diario del Salvador,* December 2, 1927, 2. For other examples from *Diario del Salvador,* see November 24, 1927, 8; November 25, 1927, 7; November 29, 1927, 7; December 6, 1927, 6 and 7; December 10, 1927, 1. See also *Diario Latino,* November 23, 1927, 1; November 26, 1927, 1; December 1, 1927, 3; and December 10, 1927, 1.

58. The circumstances under which the interview was conducted are vague. It appears to have been inspired by Claramount Lucero himself, who in the later stages of his life had the desire to record his story for posterity. A copy of the tape of this interview is in the hands of Knut Walter, a Salvadoran historian. I would like to thank Dr. Walter for sharing the information on the tape with me.

59. Horacio Villavicencio, San Vicente, to minister of government, December 3, 1927, AGN, MG, unclassified box.

60. Benjamín Membreño, Director of Police of Atiquizaya, to minister of government, December ?, 1927, AGN, MG, unclassified box.

61. Francisco Pimentel, Director of Police, Santiago de María, to minister of government, December 12, 1927, AGN, MG, unclassified box.

62. *Diario del Salvador,* June 14, 1929, 1.

63. Ibid.

64. Buell, Raymond Leslie, "Progress in Central America," *News Bulletin* 9, no. 39 (August 1, 1930): 1–2. A copy of this is located in the WNRC, G-2 Military Reports, Box 764, Folder 3110.

65. *Diario del Salvador,* May 2, 1927, 3; *Diario Oficial,* March 28, 1927; and Caffery to U.S. secretary of state, March 30, 1927, USNA, RG 59, 816.00/624, and April 22, 1927, 816.00/627, and April 26, 1927, 816.00/629.

66. *Diario Latino,* November 25, 1927, 1.

67. Ibid.

68. Nulo, Jiquilisco, 1927, AGN, CN, Box 5.

69. Nulo, Nahuizalco, 1927, AGN, CN, Box 5.

70. Nulo, Ataco, 1929, AGN, CN, Box 7.

71. Nulo, Santa Maria, 1929, AGN, CN, Box 6.

72. Nulo, Tecoluca, 1929, AGN, CN, Box 6.

73. Nulo, Juiquilisco, 1929, AGN, CN, Box 7.

74. B. Bertrand, governor of Chalatenango, to minister of government, January 9, 1930, AGN, MG, unclassified box.

75. Schuyler to U.S. secretary of state, April 8, 1925, USNA, RG 59, 816.00/557.

76. Caffery to U.S. secretary of state, August 14, 1926, USNA, RG 59, 816.00/585.

77. Caffery to U.S. secretary of state, March 3, 1927, USNA, RG 59, 816.00/615.

78. From Peña Trejo's memoir, "Narración histórica." Peña Trejo's lauditory discussions of Romero Bosque are found in installment 3, "Renovación de los cuadros de oficiales del ejército," and installment 8, "Reseña economica 1923 a 1931."

79. A translation of the amnesty can be found in *Diario del Salvador,* August 8, 1928, 8.

80. *Diario Latino,* September 4, 1928, 1.

81. Ibid.

82. *Diario Latino,* September 13, 1928.

83. Menéndez's career biography can be found in Schott to U.S. secretary of state, May 20, 1930, USNA, RG 59, 816.002/121; and May 22, 1930, 816.002/123.

84. Schott to U.S. secretary of state, July 23, 1930, USNA, RG 59, 816.00—Presidential Campaigns 1931/9.

85. Interview between Pío Romero Bosque and Mr. Cohen, a clerk in the military attaché's office in Costa Rica, during the time that Romero Bosque was in exile in Costa Rica. See G-2 Military Report #2,318, February 23, 1934, in USNA, RG 59, 816.00/941.

86. Stadler, of the British legation, also indicated that Romero Bosque was changing governors who were suspected of or found to be engaging in partisan politics. See Stadler to Foreign Office, December 23, 1930, PRO, FO 371/15072, A 346/201/8.

87. *Diario del Salvador,* September 17, 1929, 4.

88. *Diario Latino,* November 26, 1930, 1; see also Robbins to U.S. secretary of state, December 3, 1930, USNA, RG 59, 816.00/777.

89. *Diario Latino,* November 27, 1930, 1.

90. Dickson to U.S. secretary of state, January 11, 1928, USNA, RG 59, 816.00/700.

91. *El Dia,* January 17, 1929, translation carried in Lambert to U.S. secretary of state, January 19, 1929, USNA, RG 59, 816.00/740.

92. This process of identifying the various candidates and then gathering them together is described in detail in a series of exchanges between Lisandro Larín, the governor of Sonsonate, and officials in San Salvador, and between Larín and the municipalities in his department. See Larín to minister of government, November 20, 1929; Larín to minister of government, November 21, 1929; Larín to minister of government, November 30, 1929; Larín to minister of government, December 5, 1929; and Circular from Larín to Alcaldes Municipales de todo el Departamento, December 5, 1929; all of these are bound together in AGN, MG, SS, unclassified box. The mixed directorios are also discussed in the *Diario Oficial,* December 8, 1929; and in Schott to U.S. secretary of state, December 14, 1929, USNA, RG 59, 816.00/764. A list sent to San Salvador from the governor of San Vicente, for instance, contains the names of the members of the directorio in each municipality and their political affiliations. See "Nomina de las personas que integran los Directorios de Elecciones en el departamento," 1930, AGN, MG, SSV, 1930, Box 6.

93. Lisandro Larín to minister of government, December 6, 1929, AGN, MG, SS, unclassified box.

94. Separate polling places were actually established in a presidential decree printed in the *Diario Oficial,* December 31, 1930. Mention of the various parties being allowed to have observers at the voting tables of opposing directorios is made in Larín, governor of Sonsonate Department, to alcalde of Sonsonate, January 9, 1931, AGN, MG, SS Box 4.

95. The map of San Salvador showing the various sites for the directorios was found in AGN, MG, unclassified box. The process of selecting locations for the separate directorios in the municipality of El Refugio (Ahuachapán Department) is described in the memo from Francisco Acosta, governor of Ahuachapán, January 8, 1931, AGN, MG, unclassified box.

96. Schott to U.S. secretary of state, December 6, 1929, USNA, RG 59, 816.00 General Conditions/6.

97. From Peña Trejo's memoir, "Narración histórica." Peña Trejo's discussion of the electoral procedures under Romero Bosque are found in installment 10, "Elecciones de los supremos poderes en 1931."

98. See *oficio* from the governor of La Libertad, January 2, 1931, AGN, MG unclassified box; and a similar *oficio* from governor of Cuscatlán, January 11, 1931, AGN, MG, unclassified box.

99. Reprinted in *Diario del Salvador,* July 28, 1929, 1. This was in reference to the deputy elections of January 1930. For a similar example regarding municipal elections of December 1929, see *Diario del Salvador,* November 19, 1929, 1.

100. This was in a personal letter from Pío Romero Bosque to Luís Busta-mante that Romero Bosque released to the press; see *Diario del Salvador,* July 11, 1929, 1. For another example, see Romero Bosque's interview in *Diario del Salvador,* June 14, 1929, 1.

101. An example of one of these declarations from Sonsonate Department can be found in Larín, governor of Sonsonate, to alcaldes of Sonsonate Depart-ment, December 5, 1929, AGN, MG, SS, unclassified box.

102. *Oficio* of President Romero Bosque, April 22, 1930, AGN, MG, un-classified box.

103. Jesús Miranda to Pío Romero Bosque, March 4, 1930, AGN, MG, SSV, 1930, Box 5.

104. Valentín Flores, Panchimalco, to minister of government, Septem-ber 19, 1929, AGN, MG, 1929, Box 19.

105. Manuel Mendoza to Valentín Flores, Panchimalco, September 20, 1929, AGN, MG, 1929, Box 19. For a large number of similar exchanges see AGN, FA, Box 3.

106. *Oficio* of President Romero Bosque, April 22, 1930, AGN, MG, un-classified box.

107. See, for example, the extensive debate over the election in Armenia in which Enrique Córdova, a presidential candidate in 1931, played a significant role in the process. Some of the case is found in Larín to minister of government, April 25, 1930, AGN, MG, SS, Box 2; other portions of the case can be found under a memo from the Ministry of Government dated April 8, 1930, in AGN, MG, SS, Box 1. The issue is discussed extensively in relation to the municipal elections of 1930 in Velado, Chalchuapa, to minister of government, March 7, 1931, AGN, MG, unclassified box.

108. There was in fact a seventh candidate of sorts, Prudencia Ayala, who was not allowed to stand as a candidate, by order of the Supreme Court, on the grounds that she was a woman. Little is known about Ayala. I found the first two copies of a periodical, *Redención Femenina,* that she founded in June 1930 as the mouthpiece for her campaign. A review of their contents suggests that she consid-ered herself to be a sincere feminist and a mild socialist. The copies of *Redención* can be found in AGN, MG, 1930, Box 7. Prior to 1930, Ayala worked as a for-tune teller in San Salvador, and I have come across some advertisements promot-ing her services in the pages of *Diario Latino.* See, for example, April 23, 1928, 3; and May 22, 1928, 2. For a brief description of Ayala's experience with the Su-preme Court, see Ministerio de Educación, *Historia de El Salvador* 2:156–57.

109. Antonio Vilanova, a member of one of El Salvador's leading coffee-growing families, made some noise about campaigning as the candidate of the coffee planters but never put his ideas into action. Comments on his campaign

and the lack of differences between the candidates can be found in Schott to U.S. secretary of state February 3, 1930, USNA, RG 59, 816.00/767; see also February 25, 1930, 816.00/768; January 3, 1930, 816.00 General Conditions/8; and February 25, 1930, 816.00 General Conditions/12. The platforms of the candidates are discussed in Andino, *Padre de la democracia*. See also Córdova, *Miradas retrospectivas,* 247–56.

110. The broadside is dated July 1930 and is found in AGN, MG, unclassified box.

111. The report on this speech and transcriptions of it are found in Benjamín Arrieta Rossi, governor of San Salvador Department, to minister of government, June 27, 1930, AGN, MG, unclassified box.

112. In a letter to the minister of government, the president of Araujo's Partido Laborista campaign in San Salvador denied that party organizers were making such claims and referred to land redistribution as "Bolshevik and something that amazes us for its fatal and impractical qualities." See José ?, Presidente Comité Capitalino "Pro Araujo," to minister of government, July 4, 1930, AGN, MG, unclassified box. The British chargé made mention of Araujo's denials and also reported that "Araujo's canvassers dispensed much propaganda amongst the Indian plantation laborers and poorer classes in general." See Rogers to Henderson, January 25, 1931, PRO, FO 371/15072, A 850/201/8.

113. *El Espectador,* May 6, 1930, 1; this copy was found in AGN, MG, unclassified box.

114. RGASPI, 495:119:4, 21; and 495:119:10, 117.

115. From Peña Trejo's memoir, "Narración histórica." Peña Trejo's discussion of Araujo's campaign is found in installment 9, "Campaña electoral de 1930."

116. See the speech from Guazapa in Benjamín Arrieta Rossi, governor of San Salvador Department, to minister of government, June 27, 1930, AGN, MG, unclassified box.

117. Most of the denunciations and Mendoza's responses are bundled together in AGN, MG, 1931, Boxes 3 and 6.

118. Manuel Mendoza to alcalde of Izalco, January 9, 1931, AGN, MG, 1931.

119. Robbins to U.S. secretary of state, January 16, 1931, USNA, RG 59, 816.00/791.

120. Manifesto of Arturo Araujo, *Diaro Oficial,* March 25, 1931, found in Robbins to U.S. secretary of state, March 27, 1931, USNA, RG 59, 816.00/801 (Translation by Robbins).

121. Some of these have been cited above, but as a summary of some of the main ones, see *Diario Latino,* December 3, 1929; August 12, 1930; and January 21, 1931. See also *Diario del Salvador,* March 22, 1927; May 16, 1927; August 13,

1927; October 22, 1927; November 12, 1927; November 25, 1927; and December 2, 1927.

122. Putnam, *Making Democracy Work,* 167, 177; see pages 167–81 for Putnam's discussion of this issue.

Chapter 7.   *Politics under the Military Regime, 1931–1940*

1. Brannon, *Breves consideraciones,* 18. (A quintal is 46 kilograms.)

2. Bulmer-Thomas, *Political Economy,* 50 and 328.

3. Schott to U.S. secretary of state, August 24, 1930, USNA, RG 59, 816.00/773. The British legation especially commented on financial issues. See, for example, Watson, Guatemala, to Henderson, Foreign Office, February 25, 1930, PRO, FO 371/14210, A 2140/2106/8; Rodgers to Henderson, May 19, 1930, PRO, FO 371/14212, A 4169/4169/8; Murray-Simpson to Henderson, August 18, 1930, PRO, FO 371/14212, A 5852/4169/8; Stadler to Henderson, October 30, 1930, PRO, FO 371/14212, A 7601/4169/8.

4. See Murray-Simpson to Henderson, August 18, 1930, PRO, FO 371/14212, A 5852/4169/8.

5. Stadler to Henderson, October 18, 1930, PRO, FO 371/14212, A 7284/4169/8.

6. These petitioners are described in Rodgers to Henderson, January 27, 1931, FO 371/ 15072, A 1156/201/8; and in *Diario La Prensa,* July 16, 1931, in unclassified folder of press clippings for the year 1931, in AGN, MG, unclassified box.

7. Rodgers to Henderson, April 15, 1931, PRO, FO 371/15702, A 3124/20/8.

8. Enrique Córdova describes the Consejo Económico in *Miradas retrospectivas,* 261–64.

9. The demonstration and the crackdown are described by Córdova in *Miradas retrospectivas,* 268–77. Córdova was then serving as rector of the National University. See also *Diario Latino,* July 11, 1931; *El Dia,* July 11, 1931; and *Diario Patria,* July 11, 1931, all in unclassified book of press clippings for the year 1931, in AGN, MG, unclassified box; Rodgers to Henderson, July 13, 1931, PRO, FO 371/15072, A 4781/201/8; Finley to U.S. secretary of state, July 15, 1931, USNA, RG 59, 816.00/808; and Peña Trejo, "Narración histórica," installment 11, "Incidentes en el gobierno del ingeniero Araujo."

10. A description of this plan was found in *Diario Latino,* April 27, 1931, 1. Up to that point, Masferrer had had a rather raucous tenure in the assembly, at

one point standing up during a session and accusing some of his fellow deputies of being hostile to the working class. See *Diario Latino,* April 17, 1931, 1.

11. This was reported in Finley to U.S. secretary of state, August 8, 1931, USNA, RG 59, 816.00/811. The proposal had not yet been made public. Finley drew his information from interviews with members of the government whom he does not name.

12. Descriptions of the coup based on primary evidence include Anderson, *Matanza,* 79–88; Elam, "Appeal to Arms," 27–33; Williams and Walter, *Militarization and Demilitarization,* chapter 2; and Grieb, "The United States and the Rise." For descriptions from U.S. and British legations, see USNA, RG 59, 816.00/820 to 816.00/825 and 816.00 Revolutions/7 to 816.00 Revolutions/98; and PRO, FO 371/15812 A 9/9/8, A 11/9/8, and A 196/9/8.

13. Michael McClintock posits the conspiracy perspective. See M. McClintock, *American Connection,* 106–9. Peña Trejo argues in "Narración histórica" that there was no conspiracy. Elam argues likewise, based on his 1964 interview with Joaquín Castro, one of the eleven members of the directorate: Elam, "Appeal to Arms," 31. Kenneth Grieb, in "The United States and the Rise," also rejects the conspiracy theory.

14. Williams and Walter, *Militarization and Demilitarization,* chapter 2.

15. Krehm, *Democracies and Tyrannies,* 25. Krehm describes his general experience in El Salvador during the time of Martínez in pages 2–27. Another description of Martínez's religious outlook, based on interviews with people close to him, is found in Astilla, "Martínez Era," 43.

16. Shepherd, San Salvador, to Foreign Office, December 4, 1933, PRO, FO 371/16560, A 8750/706/8.

17. Grieb, "The United States and the Rise," 159. As Grieb indicates, Caffery had formerly headed the legation in El Salvador in 1928. He arrived in El Salvador as the special envoy on December 19, 1931.

18. As reported in *Diario Latino,* July 11, 1931, in unclassified book of press clippings, in AGN, MG, unclassified box.

19. Report from A. R. Harris, Military Attaché, December 12, 1931, USNA, RG 59, 816.00 Revolutions/50.

20. For discussions of Fonseca and Molina, see McCafferty to U.S. secretary of state, April 2, 1932, USNA, RG 59, 816.00 General Conditions/29.

21. From the text of Martínez reprinted in Curtis, San Salvador, to U.S. secretary of state, December 5, 1931, USNA, RG 59, 816.002/136.

22. Memo from U.S. Chargé, San Salvador, to U.S. secretary of state, December 11, 1931, USNA, RG 59, 816.00/821.

23. Minister of war to minister of government, January 27, 1932, AGN, MG, unclassified box.

24. The memo is contained in a circular from the governor of Sonsonate to the alcaldes of Sonsonate Department, December 8, 1931, AGN, MG, SS, Box 4.

25. Martínez's declaration on the laboristas is found in *Diario Latino,* December 18, 1931; his declaration on the communists is found in *Diario Patria,* December 12, 1931; both are located collection of press clippings in AGN, SI, Capitulo 1, Caja 17.

26. Salvador Castaneda Castro, to departmental governors, February 1, 1932, AGN, SI, Capitulo 1, Caja 7, "Censura de Prensa, 1932–1937."

27. On Gómez's political activities, see McCafferty, San Salvador, to U.S. secretary of state, January 19, 1932, USNA, RG 59, 816.00/827. In the opinion of the U.S. chargé, Gómez was putting himself in position to be appointed president in the event that Martínez was forced to resign.

28. Córdova, *Miradas retrospectivas,* 281, 285, and 301.

29. For Claramount Lucero's political activities, see *Diario Latino,* January 3, 1932, in a collection of press clippings in AGN, SI, Capitulo 1, Caja 17. See also McCafferty, San Salvador, to U.S. secretary of state, January 12, 1932, USNA, RG 59, 816.00/824.

30. Joaquín Valdés claimed this in a memo to the U.S. chargé, contained in the report by U.S. Chargé to U.S. secretary of state, December 11, 1931, USNA, RG 59, 816.00/821.

31. As announced in *Diario Latino,* December 12, 1931, in a collection of press clippings in AGN, SI, Capitulo 1, Caja 17.

32. The initial postponement is described in McCafferty to U.S. secretary of state, January 16, 1932, USNA, RG 59, 816.00 General conditions/27. The additional postponements are reported in *Diario del Salvador,* January 19, 1932, in a collection of press clippings, AGN, SI, Capitulo 1, Caja 17.

33. Uceda, San Julián, to governor of Sonsonate Department, January 7, 1932, AGN, MG, SS Box 2. For another example, see Aquilino Pineda, Guaymango, to governor of Ahuachapán Department, December 31, 1931, AGN, MG, SS, Box "Gobernación Sonsonate y Ahuachapán." A denunciation of Araujistas in Chalatenango Department after the election was reported in General Francisco Choto, governor of Chalatenango, to minister of government, May 30, 1932, AGN, MG, unclassified box. Requests that employed the specter of communism, rather than laborism, can be found in Elias ?, Masahuat, to governor of Sonsonate Department, January 9, 1932, AGN, MG, SS, Box 2; and "unos vecinos," Nahuilingo, to governor of Sonsonate Department, AGN, MG, SS, Box 2. Some other denunciations, which did not identify Araujistas specifically, are reported in *Diario Latino,* January 7, 1932; January 9, 1932; January 11, 1932; and January 19, 1932; and *Diario Patria,* January 13, 1932; all are located in a collection of press clippings in AGN, SI, Capitulo 1, Caja 17.

34. The strong showing of the communist candidate in San Salvador was reported in *Diario Latino,* January 5, 1932. The newspaper *Diario Patria* hailed the communists for their ordered behavior during voting, in contrast to the other parties: *Diario Patria,* January 4, 1932. *Diario Patria* also reported some police repression of communist candidates: December 12, 1931. All of these reports are found in a collection of press clippings in AGN, SI, Capitulo 1, Caja 17. The participation of the communists in the elections also is presented in detail in the reports from the Communist Party: see Ching, "In Search of the Party." Some scholars have contended that Martínez allowed the PCS to participate in the election in order to surreptitiously draw them out of hiding and then crush them. See Alvarenga Venutolo, *Cultura y ética*; and M. McClintock, *American Connection*. As of October 1931, the army had a detailed list of the persons it believed to be affiliated with the Communist Party. When this list is compared to records from the PCS itself, it turns out to be quite accurate. See Ching, "In Search of the Party."

35. For Claramount Lucero's political activities, see *Diario Latino,* January 3, 1932, in a collection of press clippings in AGN, SI, Capitulo 1, Caja 17. See also McCafferty, San Salvador, to U.S. secretary of state, January 12, 1932, USNA, RG 59, 816.00/824.

36. As reported in Curtis to U.S. secretary of state, December 28, 1931, USNA, RG 59, 816.00/822.

37. Telegram from Alberto Engelhard, alcalde of San Julián, to governor of Sonsonate Department, January 9, 1932, AGN, MG, SS, Box 1.

38. McCafferty, San Salvador, to U.S. secretary of state, January 19, 1932, USNA, RG 59, 816.00/826.

39. *Diario Patria,* January 11, 1932, in a collection of press clippings in AGN, SI, Capitulo 1, Caja 17.

40. From the diary of Henry Stimson, January 25, 1932, entry. Yale University Manuscripts Collections, cited in Astilla, "Martínez Era."

41. A good discussion of financial issues under Martínez can be found in Astilla, "Martínez Era," 49. Astilla also points out that El Salvador was not the first country to default on its foreign loans during the Great Depression. Bolivia, Peru, and Chile had all defaulted in 1931 (100). Martínez resumed payment on the loan in August 1932, after negotiating a deal with the bondholders whereby the government would pay only 15 percent towards it in 1932 and 20 percent in 1933, rather than the prior arrangement of 70 percent. See Watson, Guatemala, to Foreign Office, January 2, 1933, PRO, FO 371/16559, A 513/513/8.

42. Martínez's payment of the military is described in Peña Trejo, "Narración histórica," installment 22, "Situación de la tesoreria general de la república." See also Shepherd to Simon, December 4, 1933, PRO, FO 371/16560, A

8750/706/8; and Watson, Guatemala, to Foreign Office, ibid.; and Shepherd to Foreign Office, December 4, 1933, PRO, FO 371/16560, A 8750/706/8.

43. McCafferty, San Salvador, to secretary of state, April 16, 1932, USNA, RG 59, 816.20/31.

44. The reports on Aguirre are provided by Rodgers, San Salvador, to Foreign Office, May 10, 1932, PRO, FO 371/15814, A 3133/9/8; Rodgers, San Salvador, to Foreign Office, July 15, 1932, PRO, FO 371/15814, A 4276/9/8; and Annual Report 1933, in Birch, Guatemala, to Foreign Office, January 20, 1934, PRO, FO 371/17499, A 1215/1215/8. Miguel Mármol also commented on Aguirre's conspiracy: see Dalton, *Miguel Marmol,* 431.

45. Ibid. (The information on Valdés is contained in the same reports as that of Aguirre.)

46. The November revolt is discussed in McCafferty to U.S. secretary of state, November 39, 1932, USNA, RG 59, 816.00 Revolutions/173.

47. See, for example, the case of the political conflicts in the municipality of Soyapango in July 1932, as described in *Diario del Salvador,* July 6, 1932, and July 12, 1932. Another example of local political violence occurred in Usulután City in October 1932. The perpetrators were local affiliates of Enrique Córdova's party who stoned the home of a local rival, resulting in a brief military intervention. See Pedro Novoa, Usulután City, to Teninete Joaquín Meléndez (a brother of one of the perpetrators), San Salvador, October 3, 1932, AGN, SI, Capitulo 1, Caja 7.

48. From a collection of election returns from the 1933 deputy elections, AGN, MG, 1933, Box 1, Folder "Formación Directorios." The four municipalities with opposition candidates were Chalchuapa, San Marcos, Cojutepeque, and San Miguel, of Ahuachapán, San Salvador, Cuscatlán, and San Miguel Departments respectively.

49. The case of the teacher/spy is contained in José Cruz Peñate to General Felipe Ibarra, August 18, 1932, AGN, MG, SS, Box 2. The term *oreja* is found in Colonel Julio César Calderón, governor of Sonsonate Department, to General José Tomás Calderón, July 22, 1935, AGN, MG, SS, Box "Política, 1930–9."

50. Dalton, *Miguel Marmol,* 329–54. His arrest is described in pages 351–53.

51. The case against Abullarde is contained in a police report from the director of police in Santa Ana, June 27, 1933, AGN, MG, unclassified box.

52. The minister's comments are contained in Annual Report 1933, Birch, Guatemala, to Foreign Office, January 20, 1934, PRO, FO 371/17499, A 1215/1215/8.

53. Calderón mentions his agents on repeated occasions. See Colonel Calderón to President Martínez, October 14, 1936, MG, SS, Box 2; Colonel Calderón to General José Tomás Calderón, July 22, 1935, AGN, MG, SS, Box "Política,

1930–9"; and Colonel Calderón to minister of government, September 19, 1938, AGN, MG, 1938, Folder "Comunismo, Bolcheviquismo y terrorismo."

54. See Annual Report 1934, Birch, Guatemala, to Foreign Office, February 1, 1935, PRO, FO 371/18660, A 1752/825/8; and Shepherd, San Salvador, to Foreign Office, December 4, 1933, PRO, FO 371/16560, A 8750/706/8.

55. Molina's response to the election is described by Córdova, *Miradas retrospectivas,* 311–12. Córdova writes that Molina did not publicly announce that he was resigning because of Martínez's decision to run. Rather, he told this to Córdova later.

56. Manuel Mendoza to General José Tomás Calderón, April 23, 1934, AGN, MG, 1934, Box 7. Mendoza's police troubles also were commented on by the U.S. chargé: see McCafferty, San Salvador, to secretary of state, January 4, 1934, USNA, RG 59, 816.00/934.

57. The political activity and the exile of Romero Bosque and Claramount Lucero are discussed in Harris, Costa Rica, August 30, 1933, WNRC, G-2 Military Report, #2166, Box 763, Folder #1000-3800; McCafferty, San Salvador, to secretary of state, January 4, 1934, USNA, RG 59, 816.00/934, Box 5506, Folder #3; Annual Report 1933, Birch, Guatemala, to Foreign Office, January 20, 1934, PRO, FO 371/17499, A 1215/1215/8; and Annual Report 1934, Birch, Guatemala, to Foreign Office, February 1, 1935, PRO, FO 371/18660, A 1752/825/8. The interview with Pío Romero Bosque is found in Harris, Military Attaché, Costa Rica, G-2 Military Report, # 2318, February 23, 1934, USNA, RG 59, 816.00/941.

58. From Harris, Military Attaché, Costa Rica, G-2 Report, #2318, February 23, 1934, USNA, RG 59, 816.00/941.

59. McCafferty, San Salvador, to secretary of state, January 4, 1934, USNA, RG 59, 816.00/934.

60. McCafferty, January, 4, 1934, ibid.

61. Dalton, *Miguel Marmol,* 373.

62. Annual Report for Central America, 1933, Birch, Guatemala, to Foreign Office, January 20, 1934, FO 371/17499, A 1215/1215/8.

63. The coup is described in Goldie to Foreign Office, January 31, 1934, PRO, FO 371/17488, A 1435/575/8; and in Lane to secretary of state, January 25, 1934, USNA, RG 59, 816.00/933. The government's denunciation is found in *Diario La Prensa,* February 16, 1934, 1.

64. From A. R. Harris, Military Attaché, December 12, 1931, USNA, RG 59, 816.00 Revolutions/50.

65. Goldie, San Salvador, to Foreign Office, January 31, 1934, PRO, FO 371/17488, A 1435/575/8.

66. The list of political enemies is found in G-2 Military Reports, WNRC, Box 764, Folder 3000-4000.

67. Hill to Foreign Office, "Report on Leading Personalities in the Republic of El Salvador," February 13, 1936, PRO, FO 371/19771, A 1261/1261/8.

68. Goldie, San Salvador, to Foreign Office, January 31, 1934, PRO, FO 371/17488, A 1435/575/8.

69. From an interview with Pío Romero Bosque contained in Harris, Military Attaché, Costa Rica, G-2 Military Report, # 2318, February 23, 1934, USNA, RG 59, 816.00/941.

70. Annual Report 1934, Birch, Guatemala, to Foreign Office, February 1, 1935, PRO, FO 371/18660, A 1752/825/8.

71. The guidelines for Pro-Patria's organization are contained in Enecón Paredes to departmental governors, August 16, 1933, AGN, MG, SS, Box "Política, 1930–9." This box contained most of the Pro-Patria materials. Another collection of Pro-Patria materials was found in an unclassified box in the Ministerio de Gobernación collection in AGN.

72. From a survey of all the societies, organizations, and clubs in the nation, conducted between June and August 1940, AGN, MG, unclassified box.

73. The list of moneyed citizens is from a comprehensive list of the financial holdings of every well-to-do citizen in El Salvador. The list was compiled by the government in 1943. The lists are stored together in a folder in AGN, MG, 1943, unclassified paquete. For a list of the landowners in Nahuizalco from 1924, see *Directorio comercial,* 494–96. See also "principal ganaderos," Department Sonsonate, Municipality Nahuizalco, June 7, 1935, AGN, MG, SS, Box 3; and for a list of coffee growers in Nahuizalco from 1926, "nomina de las personas cultivadoras de café en la villa de Nahuizalco," AGN, MG, 1926, Box 5.

74. Larín was elected alcalde in 1916 and again in 1935. From "Catalogo de municipalidad," AMS.

75. Herrera's properties are listed in *Directorio comercial,* 477–80. His role as auditor is found in *Diario del Salvador,* July 22, 1932, and July 28, 1932. In the latter report, it is evident that Herrera was supported by Martínez. Herrera's role as auditor also is discussed in McCafferty, San Salvador, to secretary of state, July 22, 1932, USNA, RG 59, 816.00 Revolutions/171.

76. A list of coffee growers for Juayúa for 1926 is found in Redaelli to governor of Sonsonate Department, June 18, 1926, AGN, MG, 1926, Box 5; see also *Directorio comercial,* 528–29.

77. Extensive lists can be found in AGN, MG, 1934, Box 2. The reports and communications sent between the various levels of the party can be found in AGN, MG, various unclassified packets dated 1937 to 1943; in AGN, MG, SS, Box "Política, 1930–39"; and in AGN, MG, SS, "Caja 2.2, 1895–1937."

78. From a copy of Pro-Patria's organizational mandate, from Enecón Paredes, San Salvador, to departmental governor of Sonsonate, August 16, 1933, AGN, GS, Box "Política, 1930–9." Along with this document are various communications between the national and departmental levels demonstrating the functioning of the various levels of the party.

79. The organization of Pro-Patria in Sonsonate is found in Paredes to governor of Sonsonate Department, December 15, 1933, AGN, MG, unclassified box; memo from departmental delegation, Sonsonate, to president of Pro-Patria, San Salvador, October 6, 1934, AGN, MG, unclassified box; and Guzmán, Sonsonate, to president of Pro-Patria, San Salvador, December 31, 1934, AGN, MG, unclassified box. Reference to the women's committees is found in Samayo, San Salvador, to president of Sonsonate's departmental delegation, September 13, 1934, AGN, MG, unclassified box.

80. Contained in Enecón Paredes (member of the Consejo Supremo), San Salvador, to governor of Sonsonate, November 4, 1933, AGN, MG, SS, Box "Política 1930–9."

81. Guillermo Barrientos, San Julián, to José Santos Zepeda, November 6, 1933, AGN, MG, unclassified box. Zepeda's position on the *directiva* of the departmental delegation is found in "nomina de las personas que forma la Directiva del Comite, "Pro Patria," Sonsonate, July 22, 1934, AGN, MG, unclassified box.

82. This list is contained in José Santos Zepeda to president of the Partido Nacional, San Salvador, November 7, 1933, AGN, MG, unclassified box.

83. *Diario La Prensa,* January 14, 1932, and *Diario Latino,* January 14, 1932. Both are found in a collection of press clippings in AGN, SI, Capitulo 1, Caja 17.

84. Telegram Circular #1, from General José Tomás Calderón, January 3, 1935, AGN, MG, SS, Box "Política, 1930–9."

85. The proposals by the Sonsonate delegation are found in Joaquín Guzmán, Sonsonate, to president of Pro-Patria, November 13, 1934, AGN, MG, unclassified box; and Lisandro Larín, Sonsonate, to president of Pro-Patria, December 30, 1934, AGN, MG, unclassified box.

86. Telegram Circular #2, from General José Tomás Calderón, January 3, 1935, AGN, Ministerio de Gobernación, Gobernación Sonsonate, Box "Política, 1930–9."

87. Telegram Circular #7, from General José Tomás Calderón, January 3, 1935, AGN, Ministerio de Gobernación, Gobernación Sonsonate, Box "Política, 1930–9."

88. From Pedro Ramos, alcalde of Santo Domingo de Guzmán, January 11, 1935, AGN, MG, SS, Box 1. A great number of these reports can be found in AGN, MG, SS, Box 1.

89. Contained in memo from Alex Cohen, U.S. Military Attaché Office, Costa Rica, March 14, 1935, WNRC, G-2 Military Report #2,784, Box 763, Folder 1000-3800.

90. From Juan Vidal, departmental comandante of Cabañas, to governor of Sonsonate, January 14, 1935, AGN, MG, SS, Box 1.

91. Telegram from Juayúa to Sonsonate, January 14, 1935, AGN, MG, SS, Box 1.

92. Contained in Annual Report 1935, Birch, Guatemala, to Foreign Office, January 23, 1936, PRO, FO 371/19771, A 1281/1281/8.

93. Gabino Mata Jr. to Julio C. Calderón, governor of Sonsonate, November 11, 1937, AGN, MG, SS, Box 2.2.

94. Gabino Mata Jr. to Julio C. Calderón, governor of Sonsonate, November 22, 1937, AGN, MG, SS, Box 2.2.

95. Humberto Portillo and others, Cacaopera, Morazán Department, to minister of government, November 14, 1937, AGN, MG, 1937, unclassified paquete.

96. From the list of Pro-Patria affiliates in Izalco, December 27, 1938, AGN, MG, 1938, unclassified paquete; and the list of municipal officials selected for Izalco in December 1939, AGN, MG, 1939, unclassified paquete.

97. Hermogenes Alvarado Jr. to governor of Ahuachapán Department, December 2, 1937, AGN, MG, 1937, unclassified paquete.

98. Jesús Rivas, Guazapa, to minister of government, December 12, 1937, AGN, MG, 1937, unclassified paquete.

99. See the municipal election of December 1937, AGN, MG, 1938, unclassified paquete.

100. Molina, president of local committee of Juayúa, to governor of Sonsonate Department, November 8, 1937, AGN, GS, "Caja 2.2, 1895–1937."

101. Salvador Abrego, president of directorio, San Martín, to minister of government, December 12, 1937, AGN, MG, 1937, unclassified paquete.

102. Orellana, Alcalde, and Arévlo, Comandante, Jucuarán, Usulután Department, to minister of government, December 6, 1937, AGN, MG, 1937, unclassified paquete.

103. Message to local authorities of Izalco?, contained in decoded telegram from governor of Sonsonate to minister of government, December 4, 1937, AGN, MG, SS, "Caja 2.2., 1895–1937."

104. In the new political constitution of 1939, the government officially abolished municipal elections and instead appointed all municipal officials. Of course, this did not change the actual practice of local politics, for by that time all municipal officials were coming into office as preapproved candidates of Pro-Patria, and local elections were nothing more than farcical validations of Pro-Patria's decisions.

105. The properties of the Mata and Salaverría families and of Jerez and Redaelli are found in the following: Personas notables del Departamento de Sonsonate, 1897, AGN, MG, SS, unclassified box; *Directorio comercial,* 528–29; "agricola e industrial de la ciudad de Juayúa," December 13, 1917, AGN, MG, SS, Box 6; list of coffee growers in Redaelli to governor of Sonsonate Department, June 18, 1926, AGN, MG, 1926, Box 5. The intermarriages between the Mata and Salaverría families are found in a journalist's lengthy description of the municipality and its leading families during an annual rodeo fair in 1936: see *Diario Latino,* January 18, 1936, 5. Information on Emilio Redaelli was found in Lista de electos, Departamento Sonsonate, 1924–1927, governor of Sonsonate Department to minister of government, December 13, 1923, AGN, MG, 1923, Box 4; and in J. Méndez, *Sucesos comunistas,* 73–75. Redaelli's obituary is found in the Libro de Actas, March 16, 1932, Municipal Archive of Juayúa (AMJ). Information on Jerez is found in the journal *Lempa* 1:1 (July 1934), AGN, MG, 1934, Box 4.

106. The decree was published in *Diario Latino,* June 17, 1935, and can be found in Gassaway, San Salvador, to secretary of state, June 22, 1935, USNA, RG 59, 816.00B/74.

107. José Antonio Morán, comandante of the Third Company of the Guardia Nacional, to the governor of Sonsonate Department, October 18, 1936, AGN, MG, SS, Box 2.

108. Dalton, *Miguel Marmol,* 387 and 396.

109. Quoted from the decree that abolished the university's autonomy, February 2, 1932, contained in McCafferty, San Salvador, to secretary of state, February 5, 1932, USNA, RG 59, 816.00/845.

110. McCafferty, San Salvador, to secretary of state, February 5, 1932, USNA, RG 59, 816.00/845.

111. Gassaway, San Salvador, to secretary of state, June 22, 1935, USNA, RG 59, 816.00B/74.

112. See, for example, Francisco Marroquín, inspector general of police, to director of police, March 9, 1935, AGN, MG, unclassified box.

113. The comments on the intellectuals are drawn from "Bosquejo biográfico del intelectualidad salvadoreña," AGN, SI, Capitulo 1, Caja 7, "Censura de Prensa, 1932–1937."

114. Examples of each list can be found in AGN, Ministerio de Gobernación, 1943. For the lists of merchants, see Folder #070, "Comercio." For the lists of professionals, see Folder #010, "Asuntos Gremiales." The lists of wealthy people are held together in an unclassified folder.

115. Information on the coup is found in Corrigan, San Salvador, to secretary of state, October 8, 1935, USNA, RG 59, 816.00B/75; and Birch, Guatemala, to Foreign Office, January 23, 1936, PRO, FO 371/19771, A 1281/1281/8.

The Consejo de Guerra is described in *Diario Latino,* August 19, 1936, 1, and August 20, 1936, 1.

116. Information on the coup is found in Hill, San Salvador, to Foreign Office, November 2, 1936, PRO, FO 371,19772, A 9292/2005/8; Gassaway, San Salvador, to secretary of state, November 3, 1936, USNA, RG 59, 816.00B/76, Box 5508, Folder #1; and *Diario Latino,* November 2, 1936, 1.

117. Contained in Annual Report 1937, Birch, Guatemala, February 3, 1938, PRO, FO 371/21431, A 1500/1500/8.

118. Miguel Mármol describes both the coup leaders' appeal to the Communist Party and the destinations of the exile: see Dalton, *Miguel Marmol,* 393–94.

119. The coup is described in Hill, San Salvador, to Foreign Office, January 13, 1939, PRO, FO 371/22727, A 1115/53/8.

120. The drafts of the constitution can be found in AGN, MG, 1939, Folder "Asamblea Constituyente." The final constitution did not deviate from the draft: see Gallardo, *Cuatro constituciones,* 603–4.

121. The guidelines for constitutional reforms are described in two memos from Caffrey, San Salvador, to secretary of state, March 30, 1927, and May 3, 1927, USNA, RG 59, 816.00/624, and 816.00/630.

122. Telegram from Antonio Galdámez, departmental governor of Usulután, to ministry of government, July 17, 1938, AGN, MG, 1938, Folder "Asuntos Políticos—General." Reports from all the other municipalities are contained in the same folder.

123. A copious number of reports regarding public rallies and parades is found in the folder "Asuntos Políticos—General," AGN, MG, 1938.

124. Contained in Colonel Calderón, governor of Sonsonate Department, to minister of government, September 19, 1938, AGN, MG, 1938, Folder "Comunismo, Bolcheviquismo y terrorismo."

125. Luna, "Analisis de una dictadura," 50.

126. From the text of the assembly's ruling on the State of Siege, December 9, 1938, AGN, MG, 1938, Folder #302.

127. See the two memos from Juan Cóbar, governor of Cabañas Department, October 24, 1938, and November 3, 1938, AGN, MG, 1938, Folder #210.

128. "Asuntos Políticos: Pláticas del Señor Presidente de la Republica," October 12, 1940, AGN, MG, 1941, unclassified paquete.

129. Ibid., October 15, 1940.

130. Ibid., July 2, 1941.

131. Ibid., December 11, 1940.

132. Ibid., April 29, 1941.

133. Ibid., February 11, 1941.

134. Ibid., July 29, 1941.

135. Ibid., May 13, 1941.

136. Ibid., July 2, 1941.

137. Ibid., April 1, 1941.

138. Ibid., July 15, 1941.

139. Ibid., May 13, 1941.

140. Ibid.

141. Ibid.

142. Ibid., April 29, 1941.

143. Ibid., August 26, 1941.

144. Ibid., February 25, 1941.

145. Harris, Military Attaché, Costa Rica, G-2 Military Report, #2318, February 23, 1934, USNA, RG 59, 816.00/941.

Chapter 8.   Populist Authoritarianism, 1931–1940

1. From Dalton's poem, "All," in Dalton, *Poems,* 42. The original Spanish reads "Todos nacimos mitad muertos en 1932," in Dalton, *Historias prohibidas.*

2. The first reports of disturbances appeared in the pages of *Diario Latino* on January 21, 1932. Details of the main rebellion were described in subsequent issues of *Diario Latino,* as well as in *Diario La Prensa.* The original volumes of these newspapers are missing from the National Library in San Salvador; however, a collection of press clippings exists in AGN, SI, Capitulo 1, Caja 17.

3. From the governor of Sonsonate Department to the national accountant's office, February 4, 1932, contained in *Notas del Ministerio de Gobernación,* February, 1932, AGN, MG, unclassified box.

4. MacNaught, "Horrors of Communism," 25.

5. Zamosc, "Landing that Never Was," 143. The article by Zamosc is a reprint of the reports of two Canadian commanders on-site in El Salvador in 1932. The reports were forwarded to the Foreign Office in London and stored in the Public Record Office. See Hose, Chief of Naval Staff, Ottawa, to Commander in Chief, America and West Indies Station, Bermuda, April 20, 1932, PRO, FO 371/15814, A 4077/9/8.

6. RGASPI, 495: 114: 4, 61. Other firsthand accounts of the rebellion and its aftermath include Dalton, *Miguel Mármol,* and J. Méndez, *Sucesos comunistas.* The reports of the British minister also contain a brief description of the aftermath in Izalco; see Rodgers, San Salvador, to Foreign Office, February 12, 1932, PRO, FO 371/15813, A 1243/9/9, 6.

7. Libro de Actas, February 6, 1932, AMI. Similar statements can be found in the Libro de Actas in the municipal archives in Tacuba, Juayúa, Nahuizalco, and Salcoatitán.

8. Alcalde of Tacuba to comandante of Ahuachapán Department, January 27, 1932, AGN, MG, unclassified box.

9. Telegram from Máximo Jerez, alcalde of Juayúa, to governor of Sonsonate Department, June 18, 1932, AGN, MG, SS, Box 1.

10. The formation of the Guardia Cívica is discussed in *Diario del Salvador,* January 25, 1932, AGN, SI, Capitulo 1, Caja 17. Lengthy reports discussing the formation of the Guardia Cívica are contained in the quarterly *informes* of the departmental governors for the first four months of 1932. They are dated April 1932 and are bound as a group in AGN, MG, in an unclassified box.

11. On the issue of the guardias burning and burying cadavers, see the letter from the alcalde of Armenia to the governor of Sonsonate Department, February 3, 1932, AGN, MG, SS, Box 4.

12. The formation of the Comités de Defensa Social is addressed in two memos from the governor of Sonsonate Department. The first was sent to the president of the Comité de Defensa Social, San Salvador, February 3, 1932, and the second was sent as a circular to the acaldes of Sonsonate Department, February 5, 1932. Both memos are located in a collection of telegrams found in AGN, MG, SS, Box 3. The issue of voluntary contributions and the role of the *comités* in soliciting them is discussed in a telegram from the Governor of Sonsonate to the President of the Comité de Defensa Social, San Salvador, February 20, 1932, AGN, MG, SS, Box 3 (from the collection of telegram dispatches); the issue also was reported in *Diario del Salvador,* August 1, 1932. For an alternative view of the Guardia Cívica and its relationship to the military, see Alvarenga Venutolo, "Reshaping the Ethics," 365–78.

13. The documentation for the Huizúcar case is gathered into a single packet located in AGN, FA, Box 2. For quotations I will cite the individual documents.

14. From Vicente Platero, alcalde of Huizúcar, to the governor of La Libertad Department, March 9, 1932, AGN, FA, Box 2.

15. From the governor of La Libertad to the minister of government, March 17, 1932, AGN, FA, Box 2.

16. Ibid.

17. "List of Communists," from director general of the police to the minister of government, October 27, 1931, AGN, MG, unclassified box.

18. RGASPI, 495:119:4, 55. For a second mention of this same figure, see RGASPI, 495:119:4, 5.

19. "Mensaje del Señor Presidente de la República, leido ante la Asamblea Nacional, en el acto de la apertura de su periodo de sesiones ordinarias, el día 4 de

febrero de 1932," published as a booklet by the Imprenta Nacional, found in AGN, in a collection of bound and unclassified presidential addresses.

20. For a discussion of the information contained in the PCS records as they relate to the rebellion of 1932, see Ching, "Archivos de Moscú," and "In Search of the Party."

21. A comparative example in which an urban-oriented party failed to build ties to Indian populations in the countryside is the APRA party in Peru, although it was more reformist and less radical in its orientation than was the PCS. See Davies, "*Indigenismo*." See also Klaiber, "Popular Universities," 703.

22. Anderson, *Matanza*. Another contemporary contribution to this foundational historiography is Arias, *Farabundo Martí*.

23. For discussion of the communist-causality argument, see Lindo-Fuentes, Ching, and Lara-Martínez, *Remembering a Massacre*.

24. Dalton, *Miguel Mármol*.

25. Alvarenga Venutolo, *Cultura y ética*, 276.

26. Pérez Brignoli, "Indians, Communists."

27. Lindo-Fuentes, Ching, and Lara-Martínez, *Remembering a Massacre*.

28. For initial descriptions of the Comintern archives, see Ching, "Central Americanist"; and Ching and Pakkasvirta, "Latin American Materials." For the 1998 articles, see Ching, "In Search of the Party"; and Ching and Tilley, "Indians, the Military."

29. In addition to the two articles from 1998, see also Lindo-Fuentes, Ching, and Lara-Martínez, *Remembering a Massacre*; and Ching, Tilley, and López Bernal, *Las masas, la matanza*.

30. Some of my initial assessments of their work can be found in Ching, Review of *To Rise in Darkness*.

31. Gould and Lauria-Santiago, *To Rise in Darkness*, 198, 91, 88.

32. Ibid., 141.

33. Ibid. Gould and Lauria-Santiago cite numerical statistics in various places, but see 134 for the Zaragosa reference, and 83, 84, and 87 for their use of the document citing 1,700 union members in Nahuizalco. I find their two maps on 84 and 86, showing the location, spread, and influence of radical organizations throughout the western countryside, lacking in substantiation.

34. Ibid., 79–83.

35. Ibid., 89.

36. For an elaboration of this point, see Lindo-Fuentes, Ching, and Lara-Martínez, *Remembering a Massacre*, 197–200. For a transcription of an English translation of a major portion of the document, see 314–20.

37. For a brief discussion of this rather sprawling debate, see William Stanley's 2000 review of Grenier's *Emergence of Insurgency*. For a few additional

examples, see Binford, "Peasants, Catechists"; Chávez, "Pedagogy of Revolution"; and Pearce, *Promised Land*. For some interesting claims about the autonomy of peasant organizing in the region of Suchitoto in the early 1970s, see the testimonial by Fidel Recinos (nom de guerre Raúl Hercules) in Rico Mira, *En silencio,* chapter 2, especially 256. Héctor Lindo-Fuentes and I also interviewed Recinos regarding peasant mobilization for *Modernizing Minds,* 221–22.

38. As one example of the implications of the debate, see Paul Almeida's use of the case of 1932 in support of his broader thesis in *Waves of Protest*. As I suggested in a review of the book, if he employs a more communist-causality approach in his argument about 1932, and then uses that argument as part of an edifice of a broader thesis, and if communist causality is open to debate, then potentially the broader thesis is at risk. See Ching, Review of *Waves of Protest*. That said, Almeida's work is impressive, and it influenced Héctor Lindo-Fuentes and me greatly for *Modernizing Minds*. An interesting example of a juxtaposition of arguments about 1932 appears in *Revista 1857,* no. 12, enero–abril, 2012, put out by the Partido Socialista Centoamericana. I would like to thank Carlos Gregorio López Bernal for bringing the copy of *Revista 1857* to my attention.

39. "Mensaje del Señor Presidente de la República," February 4, 1932.

40. *Diario del Salvador,* July 26, 1932.

41. From an interview granted to *Diario del Salvador,* February 11, 1933.

42. *La República,* February 9, 1933, reprinted in *Diario del Salvador,* February 10, 1933, 1.

43. In an interview in *Diario del Salvador,* January 21, 1933, 1.

44. As quoted from Martínez's speech read before the National Assembly, reprinted in *Diario La Prensa,* February 15, 1937, 1.

45. The term "unscrupulous" was used by the minister of government, General Castaneda Castro, in a circular to the fourteen departmental governors, September 22, 1932, AGN, MG, 1932, Box 8.

46. From an *informe* from the governor of La Libertad Department to President Martínez, February 8, 1932, reprinted in *Diario Latino,* February 10, 1932.

47. Contained in a memo from Joaquín Valdés, office of the ministry of war, to the minister of government, April 21, 1932, AGN, MG, unclassified box.

48. Julio César Calderón, governor of Sonsonate, to José Tomás Calderón, minister of government, July 17, 1935, AGN, MG, SS, Box 3.

49. Julio César Calderón, governor of Sonsonate Department, to the minister of government, November 10, 1938, AGN, MG, 1938, Folder 210.

50. José María Rivas, Juayúa, to governor of the Sonsonate Department, August 23, 1933, AGN, MG, SS, Box 3.

51. J. Antonio Vilanova, José Peralta, and R. Aguilar, on behalf of the Comisión de Defensa de la Industria Azucarera, to minister of fomento, July 13, 1933, AGN, MG, 1933, Box 2.

52. The reference to mutual compensation is found in the February 1933 *La República* editorial, reprinted in *Diario del Salvador,* February 10, 1933, 1.

53. The case against Viera Altamirano is found in AGN, SI, volume 16. The expulsion of Viera Altamirano is found in a note from the Comisionado de Minas to the minister of government, February 1, 1939, AGN, MG, 1939, unclassified paquete, Folder "conducta de individuos." This case of Viera Altamirano is interesting and complex. He went on to be the founder and editor of the steadfastly conservative newspaper *Diario de Hoy* in 1936. Furthermore, he was a notorious free-market libertarian, so it is difficult to imagine that he would have pushed the government to expropriate private property. It is possible that the conflict as it appears in the documentation being consulted masks some other conflict between him and the government.

54. See Lindo-Fuentes, Ching, and Lara-Martínez, *Remembering a Massacre*; and Gould and Lauria-Santiago, *To Rise in Darkness*.

55. Dalton, *Miguel Marmol.* The state of the post-1932 Communist Party is described in 329–400. The comment on the absence of organization amongst the peasantry is on 397.

56. For the Sonsonate group, see governor of Sonsonate Department to Colonel Coronado Montalvo, director of police, June 23, 1932, AGN, Ministerio de Gobernación, Gobernación Sonsonate, Box 2; for the Quetzaltepeque group, see letter to the governor of La Libertad, October 14, 1932, AGN, Unclassified Ministerio de Gobernación.

57. For the request from the Barbers' Union, see director of police to minister of government, December 13, 1932, AGN, Unclassified Ministerio de Gobernación. For its problems, see *Diario del Salvador,* January 17, 1933, and February 4, 1933.

58. For the meat cutters' strikes, see *Diario del Salvador,* July 7, 1932; and the case enclosed in Director general of police to minister of government, July 26, 1939, AGN, MG, 1939, unclassified paquete, Folder "Huelgas." For the *beneficio* strike, see *Diario La Prensa,* January 12, 1934.

59. For further analyses of Mejoramiento Social and the military's reform program, see Williams and Walter, *Militarization and Demilitarization,* especially chapter 2. See also Parkman, *Nonviolent Insurrection.*

60. The quote is taken from Salvador Castaneda Castro, minister of government, to governor of Sonsonate Department, July 19, 1932, AGN, MG, SS, Box 2. The anti-ficha campaign was reported in *Diario Latino,* January 26, 1932.

61. President Martínez to governor of Sonsonate Department, September 30, 1932, AGN, FA, Box 3.

62. For a list of some of the plantations, see President Martínez to governor of Sonsonate Department, October 20, 1932, AGN, FA, Box 3.

63. From the governor of Sonsonate to the alcalde of Izalco, September 30, 1932, AGN, MG, SS, Box 2.

64. The military's perspective on terraje is expressed in an editorial in *Diario Latino* for which General Castaneda Castro, minister of government, provided the statistics. *Diario Latino,* February 5, 1932.

65. The complaint is contained in a memo from President Martínez to the governor of Sonsonate Department, September 8, 1932, from "Correspondencia del Ministerio de Gobernación, 1930–1935"; the resolution is found in a memo from the governor of Sonsonate to President Martínez, September 30, 1932; both are located in AGN, MG, SS, Box 2.

66. For two examples of the list of landowners with available land, see memo from Máximo Jerez, alcalde of Juayúa, to governor of Sonsonate Department, May 2, 1932, AGN, MG, SS, Box 2; and memo to the governor of Sonsonate Department, March 9, 1932, AGN, MG, 1932, Box 7. Examples of the government's requests for surveys and petitions to the landowners appear repeatedly throughout the 1932 records. For just a few examples, see telegram circular from the minister of government to the departmental governors, March 11, 1932, AGN, MG, SS, Box 1; and the collection of *informes* from the departmental governors for the first quarter of 1932, bound as a group, all dated from late April, in AGN, MG, unclassified box.

67. As stated in the memo from the governor of Sonsonate Department to the minister of agriculture, March 31, 1932, AGN, MG, SS, Box 2.

68. Roberto Candel of Sonsonate City was one of the few landowners who participated in the program. He received the following letter of thanks from the departmental governor: "I understand that you have spontaneously dedicated 20 to 25 manzanas of land . . . for the cultivation of primary products, foregoing payment or remuneration of any kind. This altruism of yours has been brought to my attention, and it gives me great happiness to see such praiseworthy generosity; and I hope that the other landowners will imitate your action." Departmental governor of Sonsonate to Roberto E. Candel, Sonsonate City, March 9, 1932, AGN, MG, 1932, Box 7.

69. *Diario del Salvador,* February, 11, 1933, 1.

70. The terms of Mejoramiento Social and the debate in the National Assembly over its creation were reprinted in *Diario del Salvador,* July 9, 1932, and August 18, 1932.

71. *Diario del Salvador,* September 15, 1932, 3; *Diario La Prensa,* May 8, 1934.

72. From two examples of a Record of Transfer of Funds from the Ministry of Hacienda to Mejoramiento Social, September 20, 1933, and December 6, 1933, AGN, MG, unclassified box. The government's budget figure came from

Goldie, San Salvador, to Simon, London, July 11, 1934, PRO, FO 371/17495 A 61591/109/8.

73. Cited in Alvarenga Venutolo, *Cultura y ética,* 330. The regulations of the Cédula program are found in AGN, MG, 1933, Box 10. It is also reported in *El Comercio,* October 21, 1934, 2a, found in AGN, MG, 1934, Box 9.

74. The privilege of bearing firearms under the Cédula program was never officially discussed. But it is clear that the government allowed Cédula holders to do so. In the 1935 presidential election, the minister of government ordered that no weapons would be allowed in the voting areas, "even for those people who hold a Cédula Patriótica." See telegram circular from General Calderón, January 3, 1935, AGN, MG, SS, Box "Política, 1930–9." In another case, a Cédula holder lent his weapon to a friend who was later arrested for drunkenness. The director of police chastised the Cédula holder for lending out his weapon, telling him that the privilege is only for the Cédula holder himself, not his friends. See director general of police to minister of government, October 31, 1933, AGN, MG, 1933, Box 10. The abolition of the right to bear weapons under the Cédula program is found in *Diario Oficial,* October 31, 1936. In 1940 the government still found Cédula holders claiming the right to bear arms with their Cédula card; see minister of hacienda to minister of government, April, 22, 1940, AGN, MG, folder, "Cédula Patriótica."

75. *La República,* July 12, 1934, found as a clipping in AGN, MG, 1934, Box 7.

76. The case of Peñañalapa is addressed in a memo from President Martínez to minister of government, July 12, 1932, AGN, MG, unclassified box. Other examples, from La Libertad Department, are found in the memo from the minister of war to the minister of labor, July 20, 1932, in "notas del Minsiterio de Guerra," July to December, 1932, AGN, MG, unclassified box. For the case of Armenia, see the memo from President Martínez to the governor of Sonsonate Department, September 8, 1932, from "Correspondencia del Ministerio de Gobernación, 1930–1935," AGN, MG, SS, Box 2. For later examples from La Libertad Department, see *Diario La Prensa,* August 22, 1934, 1.

77. *Diario La Prensa,* May 16, 1934, 1, and July 26, 1934, 1.

78. The information on the activities of Mejoramiento Social was accumulated from a variety of sources. For a summary from President Martínez, see his 1934 speech before the assembly, reprinted in *Diario La Prensa,* February 13, 1934, 1. On the housing project, see *Diario La Prensa,* May 16, 1934, 1, and July 25, 1934, 1; and McCafferty, San Salvador, to secretary of state, October 31, 1932, USNA, RG 59, 816.00 General Conditions/37, Box 5508, Folder #2. On land redistribution, see *Diario La Prensa,* May 8, 1934, 1, August 15, 1934, 1, August 28, 1934, 5; *Diario Latino,* May 14, 1935, 8, August 14, 1935, 1, and

January 20, 1936, 7. Also, on the issue of land, see the following three reports from McCafferty, San Salvador, to secretary of state, all located in USNA, RG 59: November 30, 1932, 816.00 General Conditions/38, Box 5508, Folder #2; December 31, 1932, 816.00 General Conditions/39, Box 5508, Folder #2; and September 4, 1932, 816.00 General Conditions/59, Box 5508, Folder #4.

79. *Diario Latino,* April 16, 1936, 1.

80. On the end of Mejoramiento Social and the discussion over its lack of funds, see *Diario Latino,* August 15, 1935, 7. Mejoramiento Social continued to distribute the lands which it had already purchased; see *Diario Latino,* July 10, 1937, 11, and July 26, 1937, 1.

81. The references to the nine haciendas and the approximately two hundred houses are summarized from all the references I was able to find. At least one other work has made a substantially higher prediction: 22 haciendas totaling over 50,000 manzanas by 1950, and 332 houses constructed (Ministerio de Educación, *Historia de El Salvador* 2:155). But the source of that is not clear.

82. Interview with Pío Romero Bosque in San José, Costa Rica, following his exile by Martínez, February 23, 1934, USNA, RG 59, 816.00/941, Box 5506, Folder #3.

83. McCafferty, San Salvador, to secretary of state, January 4, 1934, USNA, RG 59, 816.00/934, Box 5506, Folder #3.

84. The coffee growers' position and the actions of the Coffee Growers' Association are described in *Diario Latino,* June 28, 1935, 6.

85. The economic policies of the Martínez regime are discussed in the journal *Lempa* 1 (July 1934), found in AGN, MG, 1934, Box 4. See also Bulmer-Thomas, *Political Economy,* 72. The issue of the deflation is presented repeatedly in the pages of *Diario Latino* during the months of June, July, and August 1935. Also, the British minister made some well-informed reports on the issue; in particular see Shepherd, San Salvador to Foreign Office, September 9, 1933, PRO, FO 371 16559, A 6871/386/8. On the deflation of the colón prior to 1934, see Shepherd, San Salvador to Foreign Office, August 28, 1933, PRO, FO 371 16559, A 6669/386/8.

86. The government's opposition to the deflation was presented in *Diario Latino,* July 12, 1935, 8, and July 13, 1935, 1.

87. Evidence of the military's extensive censorship campaign can be found in folder "censura de prensa, 1932–7," AGN, SI, Capitulo 1, Tomo 7, and in the folders of "censura de prensa," for the years 1937–1944 in AGN, MG.

88. *Diario Latino,* June 28, 1935, 3.

89. *Diario Latino,* July 4, 1935, 9.

90. *Diario Latino,* July 16, 1935, 3.

91. *Diario Latino,* June 28, 1935, 3.

92. *Diario Latino,* August 21, 1935, 3.

93. From Vásquez, governor of La Unión, to minister of government, October 4, 1935, AGN, MG, 1936, Box 3. See also the annual *informe* from General Calderón, governor of Sonsonate, December 31, 1938, 1, in a collection of *informes,* AGN, MG, SS, Box 5.

94. *Diario La Prensa,* November 19, 1937, 1.

95. *Diario Latino,* August 25, 1936, 3.

96. The circular was reprinted in *Diario La Prensa,* November 11, 1937, 1. For mention of the slump in prices and the rumor of wage cuts, see Hill, San Salvador to Foreign Office, March, 24, 1938, PRO, FO 371/21431, A 2894 /586/8, 8.

97. See *Diario Latino,* August 16, 1935, 4; August 17, 1935, 10; February 5, 1936, 1; and March 6, 1936, 6.

98. See the two memos from Francisco José Rivas, governor of Chalatenango, both dated May 16, 1939. The first is to the minister of government and is located in AGN, MG, 1939, unclassified paquete; the second is from minister of agriculture to ?, AGN, MG, 1939, folder, "circular colecciones annual, 1939."

99. The case is stored together under Vásquez to minister of government, October 12, 1939, AGN, MG, Box "Gobernación Sonsonate y Ahuachapán." For a case from La Unión in which the government sided with campesinos to stave off an expansion-oriented landowner, see governor of La Unión to the minister of government, October 4, 1935, AGN, MG, 1936, Box 3. In December 1937, the government launched an investigation into the practice of the Laggeneger and Sandoval Company in Sonsonate for forcing their workers to rent dilapidated, unsanitary shacks. See the lengthy memo from the minister of government to the governor of Sonsonate, December 20, 1937, AGN, MG, SS, Box 3; and the initial complaint in AGN, SS, Box 4. For the government's rebuke of an abusive landowner in San Miguel Department, see memo from Ignacio Vásquez to minister of government, March 10, 1936, AGN, MG, unclassified box. For another example of rebuking landowners, see memo from Julio César Calderón, governor of Sonsonate Department, to minister of government, November 10, 1938, AGN, MG, 1938, folder 210. For the report on the successful reduction in the terraje on a hacienda near the town of Jiquilisco, see *Diario Latino,* July 10, 1935, 1. For a case from Sonsonate Department (hacienda "Santa Emilia"), in which the owner was delinquent in paying his workers and the governor came to the workers' aid, see memo from José Tomás Calderón, minister of government, to director general of policía, August 14, 1939, AGN, MG, 1939, folder "Protección de intereses—general."

100. From minister of war to minister of government, April 20, 1939, AGN, MG, Folder 300.

101. Anderson, *Matanza,* 170. See also Alvarenga Venutolo, *Cultura y ética.* 326.

102. M. McClintock, *American Connection,* 112.

103. See, for example, Ching and Tilley, "Indians, the Military."

104. Gould and Lauria-Santiago, *To Rise in Darkness,* 253. See also Peterson, "Remains Out of Place."

105. Tilley, *Seeing Indians.* A concise summary of Tilley's birth-record data can be found in Ching and Tilley, "Indians, the Military." Brandt Peterson posed some challenging and good questions to me about the legitimacy of using those birth records in that manner. I appreciated his insights during the New York International Forum, "El Salvador 1932: Historical Memory, Justice, Identity, and Indigenous Peoples' Rights," New York, NY, October 11–14, 2004.

106. The limitations of the sources that were available as of 1993 are described very well in Pérez Brignoli, "Indians, Communists." On questions of the ethnicity of the rebels and the nature of ethnicity in the motivations for the rebellion, see Gould and Lauria-Santiago, *To Rise in Darkness*; and Tilley, *Seeing Indians.*

107. Libro de Actas, February 4, 1932, AMI.

108. *Informe* from the governor of Sonsonate Department to the minister of government, August 31, 1938, AGN, MG, SS, Box 5.

109. From Rodgers, San Salvador, to Foreign Office, February 12, 1932, PRO, FO 371/15813. A 1243/9/8.

110. *Diario La Prensa,* January 29, 1932, in collection of press clippings, AGN, SI, Capitulo 1, Caja 17.

111. Herrera Vega, *Indio occidental,* excerpts taken from 69, 70, 74, and 75.

112. For accounts of the targets of the rebellion, see MacNaught, "Horrors of Communism"; and Méndez, *Sucesos comunistas.*

113. The three episodes are found in the following: Community of Indians of Izalco to the president of the republic, October 24, 1907, AGN, MG, 1907, Box 1; Representatives of the Común de Indígenas to the president of the republic, July 18, 1925, AGN, MG, 1925, Box 10; Representative Indians to the governor of Sonsonate Department, March 7, 1929, AGN, MG, SS, unclassified box.

114. Libro de Actas, February 3, 1932, AMI.

115. Ibid.

116. The various abuses were reported in *Diario del Salvador,* September 13, 1932.

117. Martínez's message was contained in a memo sent from the governor of Sonsonate Department to the alcalde of Izalco, September 7, 1932, Unclassified Gobernación Sonsonate, 1932, in AGS, unclassified box.

118. *Diario del Salvador,* September 14, 1932.

119. Libro de Actas, September 15, 1932, AMI.

120. From Enrique Uribe, sub-comandante local, Nahuizalco, to comandante of Sonsonate Department, March 4,1932, AGN, MG, SS, Box 3.

121. *Diario del Salvador,* September 13, 1932.

122. Maximiliano Hernández Martínez, San Salvador, to the governor of Sonsonate Department, August 8, 1932, AGN, MG, unclassified box.

123. Calderón, governor of Sonsonate, to General Martínez, San Salvador, November 16, 1933, AGN, MG, SS, Box "Política, 1930–9."

124. A collection of telegrams related specifically to solicitation of funds for the school, and documents relating to the inaugural celebration of the school in August 1932, are found in Gobernación Sonsonate, AGS, unclassified box, 1932. See also Libro de Actas, August 29, 1932, AMI.

125. From the statutes of the Rafael Campos Indian School, contained in a memo from Arévalo, subsecretary for the ministry of government, September 2, 1932, AGN, MG, unclassified box.

126. The previously mentioned book by Herrera Vega stands as an example of this belief; see Herrera Vega, *Indio occidental.* In 1933 the government solicited opinions from dozens of local officials as part of an initiative to decrease criminality and delinquency. A common theme in the responses was a need for education as a means to instill the population with values and civility. One local respondent effectively summarized the general arguments when he opined that "various vices exist in this incipient society, and all of them are a consequence of a lack of instruction and culture. . . . This lack of culture induces individuals to look for other entertainment, such as the cantina, gambling." The entire investigation is found in AGN, FA, Box 6; the quote is from Rafael ?, alcalde of ?, Cabañas Department, to governor, Sensuntepeque Department, February ?, 1933.

127. From Lieutenant Alfonso R. Muñoz, Director, Rafael Campos Indian School, to General Felipe Ibarra, Sonsonate, October 14, 1932, AGS, unclassified box. For a similar description of the Rafael Campo School and its director, see Gould and Lauria-Santiago, *To Rise in Darkness,* 253.

128. From the Informe Cuatrimestral de la Gobernación Política, Departamento Sonsonate, meses enero a abril, May 20, 1936, AGN, MG, SS, unclassified box.

129. Denunciation presented to the Supreme Court of Justice by Candelario Martínez and others from the municipality of Guatajuayaque, Morazán Department, December 1, 1934, AGN, MG, 1934, Box 1.

130. Community of Indians of Asunción Izalco to General Maximiliano Hernández Martínez, February 26, 1933, AGN, MG, SS, Box 2.

131. Copy of the entry of the Libro de Actas, February 5, 1934, AGN, MG, 1934, Box 8.

132. Telegram from José Tomás Calderón, governor of Sonsonate Department, to minister of government, July 4, 1935, AGN, MG, unclassified box. See also minister of war to minister of government, July 8, 1935, AGN, MG, 1935, Box 8.

133. "Diligencias sobre exigir a la indígena, 1935," AGN, MG, SS, Box 2.

134. Captain Morán, comandante of the Third Company, Sonsonate, to governor of Sonsonate Department, October 18, 1936, AGN, MG, SS, Box 2.

135. Julio César Calderón, governor of Sonsonate Department, to minister of government, November 23, 1938, AGN, MG, 1938, Folder 210.

136. Julio César Calderón, governor of Sonsonate Department, to minister of government, December 20, 1939, AGN, MG, 1939, folder "Seguridad pública—general."

137. Maximiliano Hernández Martínez to the governor of Sonsonate Department, November 19, 1932, AGS, unclassified box.

138. Manual Pasín, Izalco, to governor of Sonsonate Department, January 2, 1933, AGN, SS, Box 3; and Jesús ?, Izalco, to governor of Sonsonate Department, December 27, 1933, AGN, SS, Box 3.

139. For numerous examples of Indian *solicitudes,* including some reprinted in their entirety, see Lauria-Santiago, "Agrarian Republic."

140. *Informe* from the governor of Sonsonate Department to the minister of government, August 31, 1938, AGN, MG, SS, Box 5.

141. The documents relating to the 1939–1940 campaign against the finca-owned stores are gathered together in AGN, MG, 1940, unclassified paquete, Folder "Tiendas en Fincas."

142. Minister of government to departmental governor, Usulután, September 19, 1940, AGN, MG, 1940, folder "Tiendas en Fincas."

143. Minister of government to Amadeo Canessa, October 4, 1939, AGN, MG, 1940, Folder "Tiendas en Fincas."

144. Arturo Sánchez, secretary of the Cámara de Comerciantes en Pequeño, to minister of government, December 5, 1939, AGN, MG, 1940, Folder "Tiendas en Fincas."

145. Alvarez, secretary of the Coffee Growers' Association, December 1, 1939, AGN, MG, 1940, Folder "Tiendas en Fincas."

146. Arturo Sánchez, secretary of the Cámara de Comerciantes en Pequeño, to minister of government, December 24, 1940, AGN, MG, 1940, Folder "Tiendas en Fincas."

147. RGASPI, 495:119:1, 15.

Conclusion

1. See, for example, Guardino, *Time of Liberty*; C. Méndez, *Plebian Republic*; Salvatore, *Wandering Paysanos*; Sanders, *Contentious Republicans*; and Wolfe, *Everyday Nation-State*.

2. See Sanders, *Contentious Republicans*; C. Méndez, *Plebian Republic*; and J. Wood, *Society of Equality*.

3. C. Méndez, *Plebian Republic*, 242.

4. Gobat, *Confronting the American Dream*, 226.

5. See also Walter, *Regime of Anastasio Somoza*.

6. On the structure of politics under the military, the reformism of the 1960s, and the eventual rejection of those reforms, see Almeida, *Waves of Protest*; Castro Morán, *Función política*; García Guevara, "Military Justice and Social Control"; Lindo-Fuentes and Ching, *Modernizing Minds*; Stanley, *Protection Racket State*; Turcios, *Autoritarismo y modernización*; Webre, *José Napoleón Duarte*; and Williams and Walter, *Militarization and Demilitarization*.

7. For an impressive analysis of the internal workings of military politics, see Bosch, *Salvadoran Officer Corps*.

8. For insider analyses of the 1979 coup, see Majano, *Una oportunidad perdida*; and Menjívar, *Tiempos de locura*.

9. Gutiérrez, *Message from the Vice President*, 1 and 6.

10. "Entrevista con Gerson Martínez," *El Faro*, n.d., http://archivo.elfaro .net/dlgalp/contrainsurgencia/gm.asp (archived at http://webcache.googleuser content.com/search?q=cache:http://archivo.elfaro.net/dlgalp/contrainsurgencia/ gm.asp). For another postwar rejection of the 1979 coup by another guerrilla commander, Ana Guadalupe Martínez, see del Olmo, "El Salvador: Ana Guadalupe Martinez, 'Commander Mary.'" For contemporary guerrilla analyses of the 1979 coup and the subsequent reforms, see Dixon and Jonas, *Revolution and Intervention*.

11. For an insightful look into the life and death of Alvarez, see Lamperti, *Enrique Alvarez*.

12. Escalante Arce, *Sacrificios humanos*, 212–15.

13. Panamá Sandoval, *Guerreros*, 76.

14. Valdivieso Oriani, *Cruzando*, 72.

15. Gorkin, Pineda, and Leal, *From Grandmothers*, 62.

16. Valencia and Martinez, "Plática con Orlando de Sola," *El Faro*, July 10, 2009, 1:204; see Pyes, *Salvadoran Rightists*, 40, for reference to de Sola's loss of land.

17. Zepeda Herrera, *Perfiles de la guerra*, 28, 248, 263, 278, and 314.

18. For some insights into elite narratives and their historicized sense of self, see Lindo-Fuentes, Ching, and Lara-Martínez, *Remembering a Massacre,* chapter 5; and Lindo-Fuentes and Ching, *Modernizing Minds,* chapter 1.

19. Vaquerano et al., "Sánchez Cerén no hubiera pasado de soldado."

20. Cruz, *Political Culture,* 7.

21. As a sampling of this comparative scholarship, see Wickham-Crowley, *Guerrillas and Revolution*; and Goodwin, *No Other Way Out.* For a longer-term comparative view, see Williams, *States and Social Evolution*; and Mahoney, *Legacies of Liberalism.*

BIBLIOGRAPHY

Archives

El Salvador:
San Salvador
    Archivo General de la Nación
        Ministerio de Gobernación
            Seccíon San Vicente
            Sección Sonsonate
            Collección de Nulos
        Fondo Alcaldía
        Sección Indiferente
Sonsonate
    Archivo Municipal de Sonsonate
    Archivo de Gobernación Sonsonate
Izalco
    Archivo Municipal de Izalco
Juayúa
    Archivo Municipal de Juayúa

Moscow, Russia
Russian State Archive of Social and Political History (the Comintern Archive)
    Fond 495: Opus 119: Communist Party of El Salvador
    Fond 500: Caribbean Bureau of the Executive Committee of the Comintern
    Fond 534: International Red Trade Union
    Fond 539: International Red Aid

United States
National Archives, Washington, DC
    Records Group 59, 1911–1939
    Records Group 84, 1926–1932
Washington National Records Center, Suitland, Maryland
    G-2 Military Reports, El Salvador

UCLA Department of Special Collections
   The Papers of Frederick William Taylor
New York, NY
     Ismael Fuentes Collection, in the personal possession of Dr. Héctor Lindo-
     Fuentes

London, United Kingdom
  Public Record Office
     Foreign Office 371, El Salvador, General Correspondence, 1920–1938

San Salvador Newspapers and Periodicals

El Ateneo de El Salvador
El Día
Diario del Salvador
Diario Latino
Diario La Prensa
Diario Oficial
Diario Patria
El Espectador
La Gaceta del Salvador
La República

Websites and Online Newspapers

El Faro, http://www.elfaro.net
Iniciativa Socialista, www.inisoc.org/anagua.htm
Ismael G. Fuentes, http://www.oocities.org/es/hugolindosv/Ismael.htm

Published Materials and Dissertations

Acemoglu, Daron, and James Robinson. *Economic Origins of Dictatorship and De-*
    mocracy. Cambridge: Cambridge University Press, 2006.
Adams, Richard. *Cultural Surveys of Panama, Nicaragua, Guatemala, El Salvador*
    and Honduras. Detroit: Blaine Ethridge, 1976 [1957].
Adelman, Jeremy. *Sovereignty and Revolution in the Iberian Atlantic.* Princeton:
    Princeton University Press, 2006.

Alfaro, Prudencio. *The Protest of Dr. Prudencio Alfaro*. Santa Ana, El Salvador: n.p., 1913.

Almeida, Paul. *Waves of Protest: Popular Struggle in El Salvador, 1925–2005*. Minneapolis: University of Minnesota Press, 2008.

Alvarenga Venutolo, Ana Patricia. *Cultura y ética de la violencia: El Salvador, 1880–1932*. San José: EDUCA, 1996.

————. "Reshaping the Ethics of Power: A History of Violence in Western Rural El Salvador, 1880–1932." Ph.D. dissertation, University of Wisconsin, 1994.

Amaya, Miguel. *Historia de Cacoapera*. San Salvador: Ministerio de Educación, 1985.

Anderson, Thomas. *Matanza: El Salvador's Communist Revolt of 1932*. Lincoln: University of Nebraska Press, 1971.

Andino, Manuel. *El padre de la democracia: Revelaciones de un periodista sobre la campaña electoral, 1929–1931*. San Salvador: Tipografía La Unión, 1931.

Appelbaum, Nancy. *Muddied Waters: Race, Region and Local History in Colombia, 1846–1948*. Durham: Duke University Press, 2003.

Arias, Jorge. *Farabundo Martí: Esbozo biográfico*. San José: EDUCA, 1972.

Asociación Cafetalera de El Salvador. *Primer censo nacional del café*. San Salvador: Talleres Gráficos Cisneros, 1940.

Astilla, Carmelo. "The Martínez Era: Salvadoran-American Relations, 1931–44." Ph.D. dissertation, Louisiana State University, 1976.

Baloyra, Enrique. *El Salvador in Transition*. Chapel Hill: University of North Carolina Press, 1982.

Bancroft, Hubert Howe. *History of Central America*. 3 vols. San Francisco: The History Company Publishers, 1897.

Bender, Thomas. *Toward an Urban Vision: Ideas and Institutions in Nineteenth-Century America*. Lexington: University of Kentucky Press, 1975.

Bethell, Leslie, and Ian Roxborough, eds. *Latin America between the Second World War and the Cold War, 1944–1948*. New York: Cambridge University Press, 1992.

Bieber, Judy. *Power, Patronage, and Political Violence: State Building on a Brazilian Frontier*. Lincoln: University of Nebraska Press, 1999.

Binford, Leigh. "Peasants, Catechists and Revolutionaries: Organic Intellectuals in the Salvadoran Revolution, 1980–1992." In *Landscapes of Struggle: Politics, Society, and Community in El Salvador,* edited by Aldo Lauria-Santiago and Leigh Binford, 105–25. Pittsburgh: University of Pittsburgh Press, 2004.

Bosch, Brian. *The Salvadoran Office Corps and the Final Offensive of 1981*. Jefferson, NC: McFarland and Co., 1999.

Bourdieu, Pierre. *The Logic of Practice*. Translated by Richard Nice. Stanford: Stanford University Press, 1990.

Brading, D. A. *The First America: The Spanish Monarchy, Creole Patriots, and the Liberal State, 1492–1867*. Cambridge: Cambridge University Press, 1991.

Brannon, Max. *Breves consideraciones sobre la industria cafetalera en México y en El Salvador*. San Salvador: Imprenta Nacional, 1934.

Brockett, Charles. *Political Movements and Violence in Central America*. New York: Cambridge University Press, 2005.

Brown, B. Katherine. "The Controversy over the Franchise in Puritan Massachusetts, 1954–1974." *William and Mary Quarterly* 33, no. 2 (1976): 212–41.

Browning, David. *El Salvador: Landscape and Society*. Oxford: Clarendon Press, 1971.

Bulmer-Thomas, Victor. *The Political Economy of Central America since 1920*. Cambridge: Cambridge University Press, 1988.

Burkholder, Mark. *Spaniards in the Colonial Empire: Creoles vs. Peninsulares?* Malden, MA: Wiley, 2013.

Burns, E. Bradford. "The Modernization of Underdevelopment in El Salvador, 1858–1931." *Journal of Developing Areas* 18, no. 3 (1984): 293–316.

Bushnell, David, and Neill Macaulay. *The Emergence of Latin America in the Nineteenth Century*. New York: Oxford University Press, 1988.

Byrne, Hugh. *El Salvador's Civil War: A Study of Revolution*. Boulder, CO: Lynne Rienner, 1996.

Cabarrús, Carlos Rafael. *Génesis de una revolución*. México: CIESAS, 1983.

Calhoun, Craig. "Introduction: Habermas and the Public Sphere." In *Habermas and the Public Sphere*, edited by Craig Calhoun, 1–48. Cambridge, MA: MIT Press, 1992.

Cardenal, Rodolfo. *El poder eclesiástico en El Salvador, 1871–1931*. San Salvador: UCA Editores, 1980.

Carpio, Salvador Cayetano. *Secuestro y capucha en un país del "mundo libre."* San José: EDUCA, 1979.

Castañeda, Francisco. *El General Menéndez y sus victimarios*. San Salvador: Ministerio de Educación, 1966 [1893].

Castro Morán, Mariano. *Función política del ejército salvadoreño en el presente siglo*. San Salvador: UCA Editores, 1984.

Chapin, Mac. *La población indígena de El Salvador*. San Salvador: Ministerio de Educación, 1990.

Chasteen, John. "Manuel Enrique Araujo and the Failure of Reform in El Salvador, 1911–1913." *South Eastern Latin Americanist* 28, no.2 (September 1984): 1–15.

Chávez, Joaquín. "Pedagogy of Revolution: Popular Intellectuals and the Origins of the Salvadoran Insurgency, 1960–1980." Ph.D. dissertation, New York University, 2010.

Ching, Erik. "Los archivos de Moscú: una nueva apreciación de la insurrección del 32," *Tendencias* (San Salvador, El Salvador) 3, no. 44 (septiembre 1995): 28–31.

————. "A Central Americanist in Russia's Comintern Archive." *Latin American Labor News* 14 (1996): 7–10.

————. "In Search of the Party: Communism, the Comintern and the Rebellion of 1932 in El Salvador." *The Americas* 55, no. 2 (1998): 204–39.

————. "Patronage and Politics under Martínez, 1931–39: The Local Roots of Military Authoritarianism in El Salvador." In *Landscapes of Struggle: Politics, Society, and Community in El Salvador,* edited by Aldo Lauria-Santiago and Leigh Binford, 50–70. Pittsburgh: University of Pittsburgh Press, 2004.

————. Review of *To Rise in Darkness: Revolution, Repression, and Memory in El Salvador, 1920–1932,* by Jeffrey Gould and Aldo Lauria-Santiago. *Hispanic American Historical Review* 90, no. 1 (February 2010): 182–84.

————. Review of *Waves of Protest: Popular Struggle in El Salvador, 1925–2005,* by Paul Almeida. *Journal of Latin American Studies* 41 (2009): 806–9.

Ching, Erik, and Jussi Pakkasvirta. "Latin American Materials in the Comintern Archive." *Latin American Research Review* 35, no. 1 (2000): 138–49.

Ching, Erik, and Virginia Tilley. "Indians, the Military and the Rebellion of 1932 in El Salvador." *Journal of Latin American Studies* 30, no. 1 (1998): 121–56.

Ching, Erik, Virginia Tilley, and Carlos Gregorio López Bernal. *Las masas, la matanza y el martinato en El Salvador: Ensayos sobre el 32.* San Salvador: UCA Editores, 2007.

Colindres, Eduardo. *Fundamentos económicos de la burguesía salvadoreña.* San Salvador: UCA Editores, 1977.

Collier, Simon. "Nationality, Nationalism, and Supranationalism in the Writings of Simón Bolívar." *Hispanic American Historical Review* 63, no. 1 (1983): 37–64.

Córdova, Enrique. *Miradas retrospectivas por el Dr. Enrique Córdova, 1881–1966.* San Salvador: n.p., 1993.

Córtes, Emiliano. *Biografía del Capitán General Gerardo Barrios.* San Salvador: n.p., 1965.

Cruz, Consuelo. *Political Culture and Institutional Development in Costa Rica and Nicaragua: World-Making in the Tropics.* Cambridge: Cambridge University Press, 2005.

Dalton, Roque. *El Salvador.* Havana: Casa de las Américas, 1963.

————. *El Salvador: monografía.* Havana: Enciclopedia Popular, 1963.

————. *Las historias prohibidas del Pulgarcito.* Mexico: Siglo Veintiuno Editores, 1974.

————. *Miguel Marmol.* Translated by Kathleen Ross and Richard Schaaf. Willimantic, CT: Curbstone Press, 1987.

———. *Poems*. Translated by Richard Schaaf. Willimatic, CT: Curbstone Press, 1984.

Davies, Thomas. "The *Indigenismo* of the Peruvian Aprista Party: A Reinterpretation." *Hispanic American Historical Review* 51, no. 4 (November 1971): 626–45.

Directorio comercial. San Salvador: Imprenta Nacional, 1924.

Dixon, Marlene, and Susanne Jonas, eds. *Revolution and Intervention in Central America*. San Francisco: Synthesis Publications, 1983.

Domínguez Sosa, Jorge Alberto. *Ensayo histórico sobre las tribus nonualcas y su caudillo Anastasio Aquino*. San Salvador: Ministerio de Educación, 1964.

Donghi, Tulio Halperín. "Economy and society in post-Independence Spanish America," in *Cambridge History of Latin America* 3, edited by Leslie Bethell, 297–346. Cambridge: Cambridge University Press, 1985.

Dore, Elizabeth. *Myths of Modernity: Peonage and Patriarchy in Nicaragua*. Durham: Duke University Press, 2006.

Drake, Paul. *Between Tyranny and Anarchy: A History of Democracy in Latin America, 1800–2006*. Stanford: Stanford University Press, 2009.

Dunkerley, James. *The Long War: Dictatorship and Revolution in El Salvador*. London: Junction Books, 1982.

———. *Power in the Isthmus: A Political History of Central America*. London: Verso, 1988.

Dym, Jordana. *From Sovereign Villages to National States: City, State, and Federation in Central America, 1759–1839*. Albuquerque: University of New Mexico Press, 2006.

Earle, Jonathan. *Jacksonian Antislavery and the Politics of Free Soil*. Chapel Hill: University of North Carolina Press, 2004.

Eisenstadt, S., and René Lemarchand. *Political Clientelism, Patronage, and Development*. Beverly Hills: Sage Publications, 1981.

Eiss, Paul. *In the Name of El Pueblo: Place, Community, and the Politics of History in the Yucután*. Durham: Duke University Press, 2010.

El 22 de junio: Homenaje a la redentora idea de las más gloriosa revolución de El Salvador. San Salvador: Imprenta Nacional, 1892.

Elam, Robert Varney. "Appeal to Arms: The Army and Politics in El Salvador, 1931–1964." Ph.D. dissertation, University of New Mexico, 1968.

Escalante Arce, Luis. *Sacrificios humanos contra derechos humanos: Relato del secuestro de un banquero salvadoreño*. 2d ed. San Salvador: EDILIT, 1991 [1986].

Euraque, Dario, Jeffrey Gould, and Charles Hale, eds. *Memorias del mestizaje: Cultura política en Centroamérica de 1920 al presente*. Guatemala: CIRMA, 2004.

Fernández, José Antonio. *Pintando el mundo azul: el auge añilero y el mercado centroamericano, 1750–1810*. San Salvador: CONCULTURA, 2003.

Fitzgerald, Gerald, ed. *The Constitutions of Latin America*. Chicago: Henry Regnery, 1968.

Forment, Carlos. *Democracy in Latin America, 1760–1900*. Chicago: University of Chicago Press, 2003.

Foster, Stephen. *Their Solitary Way: The Puritan Social Ethic in the First Century of Settlement in New England*. New Haven: Yale University Press, 1971.

Friedman, Benjamin. *The Moral Consequences of Economic Growth*. New York: Knopf, 2005.

Fukuyama, Frances. *Falling Behind: Explaining the Development Gap Between Latin America and the United States*. New York: Oxford University Press, 2008.

Galindo, Francisco. *Cartilla del ciudadano*. 4th ed. San Salvador: Imprenta Nacional, 1904 [1874].

Gallardo, Miguel, ed. *Papeles históricos*. 3 vols. San Salvador: Imprenta "La Idea," 1964–1974.

Gallardo, Miguel Angel. *Cuatro constituciones federales de Centroamérica y las constituciones políticas de El Salvador*. San Salvador: Tipografía La Unión, 1945.

García, Miguel Angel, ed. *Asamblea Nacional Constituyente de 1885*. San Salvador: Imprenta Nacional, 1936.

García Guevara, Aldo. "Military Justice and Social Control: El Salvador, 1931–1960." Ph.D. dissertation, University of Texas, Austin, 2007.

Geddes, Barbara. *Politician's Dilemma: Building State Capacity in Latin America*. Berkeley: University of California Press, 1994.

Giddens, Anthony. *Profiles and Critiques in Social Theory*. Berkeley: University of California Press, 1982.

Gobat, Michel *Confronting the American Dream: Nicaragua under U.S. Imperial Rule*. Durham: Duke University Press, 2005.

Goodwin, Jeff. *No Other Way Out: States and Revolutionary Movements, 1945–1991*. New York: Cambridge University Press, 2001.

Gordon, Sara. *Crisis política y guerra en El Salvador*. Mexico: Siglo Veintiuno Editores, 1989.

Gorkin, Michael, Marta Pineda, and Gloria Leal. *From Grandmother to Granddaughter: Salvadoran Women's Stories*. Berkeley: University of California Press, 2000.

Gould, Jeffrey. *To Die in this Way: Nicaraguan Indians and the Myth of Mestizaje, 1880–1965*. Durham: Duke University Press, 1998.

Gould, Jeffrey, and Aldo Lauria-Santiago. *To Rise in Darkness: Revolution, Repression, and Memory in El Salvador, 1920–1932*. Durham: Duke University Press, 2008.

Graham, Richard. *Patronage and Politics in Nineteenth-Century Brazil.* Stanford: Stanford University Press, 1990.

Grandin, Greg. "The Liberal Traditions in the Americas: Rights, Sovereignty, and the Origins of Liberal Multilateralism." *American Historical Review* 117, no. 1 (February 2012): 68–91.

Grenier, Yvon. *Emergence of Insurgency in El Salvador: Ideology and Political Will.* Pittsburgh: University of Pittsburgh Press, 1999.

Grieb, Kenneth. "The United States and the Rise of Maximilian Hernández Martínez." *Journal of Latin American Studies* 3, no. 2 (1971): 151–172.

Guardino, Peter. *The Time of Liberty: Popular Political Culture in Oaxaca, 1750–1850.* Durham: Duke University Press, 2005.

Gudmundson, Lowell. *Costa Rica before Coffee: Society and Economy on the Eve of the Export Boom.* Baton Rouge: Louisiana State University Press, 1977.

Gudmundson, Lowell, and Héctor Lindo-Fuentes. *Central America, 1821–1871: Liberalism before Liberal Reform.* Tuscaloosa: University of Alabama Press, 1995.

Guidos Véjar, Rafael. *El ascenso del militarismo en El Salvador.* San Salvador: UCA Editores, 1980.

Gutiérrez, Jaime Abdul. *Message from the Vice President of the Revolutionary Government Junta of El Salvador.* San Salvador: Secretaría de Información de la Presidencia de la República, 1981.

Habermas, Jürgen. *The Structural Transformation of the Public Sphere: An Inquiry into a Category of Bourgeois Society.* Translated by T. Burger and F. Lawrence. Cambridge, MA: MIT Press, 1991.

Hall, Peter, and Rosemary Taylor. "Political Science and the Three New Institutionalisms." *Political Studies* 44, no. 4 (December 1996): 936–57.

Hamill, Hugh, ed. *Caudillos: Dictators in Spanish America.* Norman: University of Oklahoma Press, 1992.

Helmke, Gretchen, and Steven Levitsky, eds. *Informal Institutions and Democracy: Lessons from Latin America.* Baltimore: Johns Hopkins University Press, 2006.

Hernández, Antonio Flores. *Biografías de vicentinos ilustres.* San Salvador: Ministerio de Educación, 1962.

Herrera, Sajid. "¿Liberales contra conservadores? Las facciones políticas en El Salvador del siglo XIX." In *Historia electoral en Centroamérica,* edited by Xiomara Avendaño Rojas, 177–215. Managua: Lea Grupo Editorial, 2011.

Herrera Vega, Adolfo. *El indio occidental de El Salvador y su incorporación social por la escuela.* Santa Ana: Tipografía Comercial de Nicolás Cabezas Duarte, 1935.

Hertzberg, Hendrik. "Over There: A New History of Britain's Role in the American Civil War." *New Yorker,* August 1, 2011, 62–68.

Holden, Robert. *Armies without Nations: Public Violence and State Formation in Central America, 1821–1960.* New York: Oxford University Press, 2004.

———. "Constructing the Limits of State Violence in Central America: Towards a New Research Agenda." *Journal of Latin American Studies* 28, no. 2 (May 1996): 435–459.

Huntington, Samuel. *The Third Wave: Democratization in the Late Twentieth Century.* Norman: University of Oklahoma Press, 1991.

Karnes, Thomas. *The Failure of Union in Central America, 1824–1960.* Chapel Hill: University of North Carolina Press, 1961.

Kincaid, Douglas. "Peasants into Rebels: Community and Class in Rural El Salvador." *Comparative Studies in Society and History* 29, no. 3 (July 1987): 466–94.

Klaiber, S. J. "The Popular Universities and the Origins of Aprimso, 1921–24." *Hispanic American Historical Review* 54, no. 4 (November 1975): 693–715.

Knarr, Jay. *Uruguay and the United States, 1903–1929: Diplomacy in the Progressive Era.* Kent, OH: Kent State University Press, 2012.

Knight, Alan. *The Mexican Revolution.* 2 vols. New York: Cambridge University Press, 1986.

Krehm, William. *Democracies and Tyrannies in the Caribbean.* Westport, CT: Lawrence Hill, 1984.

LaFeber, Walter. *Inevitable Revolutions: The United States in Central America.* New York: W. W. Norton, 1983.

Lamperti, John. *Enrique Alvarez Cordova: Life of a Salvadoran Revolutionary and Gentleman.* Jefferson, NC: McFarland, 2006.

Langley, Lester. *The Americas in the Age of Revolution, 1750–1850.* New Haven: Yale University Press, 1996.

Lardé y Larín, Jorge. *Orígenes de la Fuerza Armada de El Salvador.* San Salvador: Ministerio de Defensa y Seguridad Pública, 1977.

———. *Recopilación de leyes relativas a la historia de los municipios de El Salvador.* San Salvador: Edición del Ministerio del Interior, 1950.

Larín, Aristides Agusto. *Historia del movimiento sindical de El Salvador.* San Salvador: Editorial Universitaria, 1971.

Lauria-Santiago, Aldo. *An Agrarian Republic: Commercial Agriculture and the Politics of Peasant Communities in El Salvador, 1823–1914.* Pittsburgh: University of Pittsburgh Press, 1999.

———. "An Agrarian Republic: Production, Politics, and the Peasantry in El Salvador, 1740–1920." Ph.D. dissertation, University of Chicago, 1992.

———. "Historical Research and Sources on El Salvador." *Latin American Research Review* 30, no. 2 (Spring 1995): 151–77.

———. "Los indígenas de Cojutepeque: La política faccional y el estado en El Salvador, 1830–1890." In *Identidades nacionales y estado moderno en Centroamérica,* edited by Arturo Taracena and Jean Piel. San José: FLACSO/EDUCA, 1995.

———. "Land, Community, and Revolt in Late-Nineteenth Century Indian Izalco, El Salvador." *Hispanic American Historical Review* 79, no. 3 (1999): 495–534.

Leal, Victor Nunes. *Coronelismo: The Municipality and Representative Government in Brazil.* London: Cambridge University Press, 1977.

Lecuna, Vicente, and Harold Bierck , eds. *Selected Writings of Bolívar.* 2 vols. New York: Colonial Press, 1951.

Lehoucq, Fabrice, and Ivan Molina. *Stuffing the Ballot Box: Fraud, Electoral Reform, and Democratization in Costa Rica.* New York: Cambridge University Press, 2002.

Lindo-Fuentes, Héctor. *Weak Foundations: The Economy of El Salvador in the Nineteenth Century.* Berkeley: University of California Press, 1990.

Lindo-Fuentes, Héctor, and Erik Ching. *Modernizing Minds in El Salvador: Education Reform and the Cold War, 1960–1980.* Albuquerque: University of New Mexico Press, 2012.

Lindo-Fuentes, Héctor, Erik Ching, and Rafael A. Lara-Martínez. *Remembering a Massacre in El Salvador: The Insurrection of 1932, Roque Dalton, and the Politics of Historical Memory.* Albuquerque: University of New Mexico Press, 2007.

López, Lorenzo. *Estadística general de la República de El Salvador.* San Salvador: Ministerio de Educación, 1974 [1858].

López Bernal, Carlos Gregorio. *Tradiciones inventadas y discursos nacionalistas: El imaginario nacional de la época liberal en El Salvador, 1876–1932.* San Salvador: Imprenta Universitaria, 2007.

López Vallecillos, Italo. *Gerardo Barrios y su tiempo.* 2 vols. San Salvador: Ministerio de Educación, 1965.

Lovell, George, and Christopher Lutz. *Demography and Empire: A Guide to the Population History of Spanish America, 1500–1821.* Boulder, CO: Westview Press, 1995.

Luna, David. "Analisis de una dictadura fascista latinoamericano: Maximiliano Hernández Martínez, 1931–1944." *La Universidad* 94, no. 5 (September–October 1969): 39–130.

Lynch, John. *Caudillos in Spanish America, 1800–1850.* Oxford: Clarendon Press, 1992.

MacNaught, Roy. "The Horrors of Communism in El Salvador." *Central American Bulletin* 181 (March 1932): 8–10 and 25–27.

Mahoney, James. *The Legacies of Liberalism: Path Dependence and Political Regimes in Central America.* Baltimore: Johns Hopkins University Press, 2001.

Majano, Adolfo. *Una oportunidad perdida: 15 de octubre 1979.* San Salvador: Indole Editores, 2009.

Mallon, Florencia. *Peasant and Nation: The Making of Postcolonial Peru and Mexico.* Berkeley: University of California Press, 1995.

Manin, Bernard. *The Principles of Representative Democracy.* Cambridge: Cambridge University Press, 1997.

Martz, John. *The Politics of Clientelism: Democracy and the State in Colombia.* New Brunswick: Transaction Publishers, 1997.

Mason, David. *Caught in the Crossfire: Revolutions, Repression, and the Rational Peasant.* Lanham, MD: Rowman and Littlefield, 2004.

Mazzei, Julie. *Death Squads or Self-Defense Forces? How Paramilitary Groups Emerge and Threaten Democracy in Latin America.* Chapel Hill: University of North Carolina Press, 2009.

McClintock, Cynthia. *Revolutionary Movements in Latin America: El Salvador's FMLN and Peru's Shining Path.* Washington, DC: United States Institute of Peace, 1998.

McClintock, Michael. *The American Connection, Volume 1: State Terror and Popular Resistance in El Salvador.* London: Zed Books, 1985.

McCoy, Drew. *The Elusive Republic: Political Economy in Jeffersonian America.* Chapel Hill: University of North Carolina Press, 1980.

McCreery, David. *Rural Guatemala, 1760–1940.* Stanford: Stanford University Press, 1994.

Méndez, Cecilia, *The Plebian Republic: The Huanta Rebellion and the Making of the Peruvian State, 1820–1850.* Durham: Duke University Press, 2005.

Méndez, Joaquín. *Los sucesos comunistas en El Salvador.* San Salvador: Imprenta Funes y Ungo, 1932.

Menjívar, Rafael. *Acumulación originaria y desarrollo del capitalismo en El Salvador.* San José: EDUCA, 1980.

———. *Tiempos de locura: El Salvador, 1979–1981.* San Salvador: FLACSO, 2008.

Ministerio de Educación, *Historia de El Salvador.* 2 vols. San Salvador: Ministerio de Educación, 1994.

Mitchell-Hedges, F.A. *Land of Wonder and Fear.* New York: The Century Co., 1931.

Munck, Gerardo. *Regimes and Democracy in Latin America: Theories and Methods.* Baltimore: Johns Hopkins University Press, 2007.

Myers, Jorge. "Languages of Politics: A Study of Republican Discourse in Argentina from 1820–1852." Ph.D. dissertation, Stanford University, 1997.

Nash, Gary. "The Transformation of Urban Politics, 1700–1765." *Journal of American History* 60, no. 3 (December 1973): 605–32.

Olmo, Enrique del. "El Salvador: Ana Guadalupe Martinez, 'Commander Mary,'" *Iniciativa Socialista,* n.d., www.inisoc.org/anagua.htm.

Orientaciones económicas del Sr. Presidente Meléndez. San Salvador: Imprenta Meléndez, n.d.

Paige, Jeffrey. *Coffee and Power: Revolution and the Rise of Democracy in Central America.* Cambridge, MA: Harvard University Press, 1997.

Panamá Sandoval, David Ernesto. *Los guerreros de la libertad.* Andover, MA: Versal Books, 2005.

Parkman, Patricia. *Nonviolent Insurrection in El Salvador: The Fall of Maximiliano Hernández Martínez.* Tucson: University of Arizona Press, 1988.

Pearce, Jenny. *Promised Land: Peasant Rebellion in Chalatenango, El Salvador.* London: Latin American Bureau, 1986.

Peloso, Vincent, and Barbara Tenenbaum, eds. *Liberals, Politics, and Power: State Formation in Nineteenth-Century Latin America.* Athens: University of Georgia Press, 1996.

Peña Trejo, Salvador. "Narración histórica de la insurrección militar de 2 de diciembre de 1931." *Diario Latino,* April–June 1964.

Pérez Brignoli, Héctor. "Indians, Communists, and Peasants: The 1932 Rebellion in El Salvador." In *Coffee, Society, and Power in Latin America,* edited by William Roseberry, Lowell Gudmundson, and Mario Samper Kutschbach, 232–61. Baltimore: Johns Hopkins University Press, 1995.

Peterson, Brandt. "Remains Out of Place: Race, Trauma and Nationalism in El Salvador." *Anthropological Theory* 7, no. 1 (2007): 59–77.

Philip, George. "The Soldier as Radical: The Peruvian Military Government, 1968–1975." *Journal of Latin American Studies* 8, no. 2 (May 1976): 29–51.

Posada-Carbó, Eduardo. *Elections before Democracy: The History of Elections in Europe and Latin America.* Houndmills: Macmillan Press, 1996.

Putnam, Robert. *Making Democracy Work: Civic Traditions in Modern Italy.* Princeton: Princeton University Press, 1993.

Pyes, Craig. *Salvadoran Rightists: The Deadly Patriots.* Albuquerque: Albuquerque Journal, 1983.

Quintana, Alejandro. *Maximino Avila Camacho and the One-Party State: The Taming of Caudillismo and Caciquismo in Post-Revolutionary Mexico.* Lanham, MD: Lexington Books, 2010.

Reyes, Alfonso. "Sufragio universal: el voto secreto y escrito." *El Ateneo de El Salvador* 1, no. 9 (July 1913): 285–90.

Rico Mira, Carlos Eduardo. *En silencio tenía que ser: testimonio del conflicto armado en El Salvador, 1967–2000.* San Salvador: Universidad Francisco Gavidia, 2003.

Rock, David, ed. *Latin America in the 1940s: War and Postwar Transitions*. Berkeley: University of California Press, 1994.

———. *Politics in Argentina, 1890–1930: The Rise and Fall of Radicalism*. Cambridge: Cambridge University Press, 1975.

Rodríguez, Mario. *The Cádiz Experiment in Central America, 1808 to 1826*. Berkeley: University of California Press, 1978.

Roniger, Luis. "Caciquismo and Cornelismo: Contextual Dimensions of Patron Brokerage in Mexico and Brazil." *Latin American Research Review* 32, no. 2 (1987): 71–99.

Roseberry, William, Lowell Gudmundson, and Mario Samper Kutschbach, eds. *Coffee, Society, and Power in Latin America*. Baltimore: Johns Hopkins University Press, 1995.

Rosenberg, Tina. *Children of Cain: Violence and the Violent in Latin America*. New York: Wm. Morrow, 1991.

Rouquié, Alain. *The Military and the State in Latin America*. Berkeley: University of California Press, 1987.

Rubio Sánchez, Manuel. *Historia del añil o xiquilite en Centro América*. San Salvador: Dirección de Publicaciones del Ministerio de Educación, 1976.

Ruhl, Arthur. *The Central Americans: Adventures and Impressions between Mexico and Panama*. New York: Charles Scribner's Sons, 1928.

Sábato, Hilda. *The Many and the Few: Political Participation in Republican Buenos Aires*. Stanford: Stanford University Press, 2001.

———. "On Political Citizenship in Nineteenth-Century Latin America." *American Historical Review* 106, no. 4 (October 2001):1290–315.

Salisbury, Richard. *Anti-Imperialism and International Competition in Central America, 1920–1929*. Wilmington, DE: Scholarly Resource Books, 1989.

Salvatore, Ricardo. *Wandering Paysanos: State Order and Subaltern Experience in Buenos Aires during the Rosas Era*. Durham: Duke University Press, 2003.

Samper, Mario. *Generations of Settlers: Rural Households and Markets on the Costa Rican Frontier, 1850–1935*. Boulder: Westview Press, 1995.

Sanders, James. *Contentious Republicans: Popular Politics, Race, and Class in Nineteenth-Century Colombia*. Durham: Duke University Press, 2004.

Sarmiento, Domingo. *Life in the Argentine Republic in the Days of the Tyrants; or, Civilization and Barbarism*. New York: Collier Books, 1961.

Schmidt, Vivian. "Discursive Institutionalism: The Explanatory Power of Ideas and Discourse." *Annual Review of Political Science* 11 (June 2008): 303–26.

Schroeder, Michael. "Cultural Geographies of Grievance and War: Nicaragua's Atlantic Coast Region in the First Sandinista Revolution, 1926–1934." *Dialectical Anthropology* 36, no. 3–4 (December 2012): 161–96.

Scott, James. *Domination and the Arts of Resistance: Hidden Transcripts*. New Haven: Yale University Press, 1990.

———. *Weapons of the Weak: Everyday Form of State Formation.* New Haven: Yale University Press, 1985.

Scott, Richard. *Institutions and Organizations.* 2d ed. Thousand Oaks, CA: Sage Publications, 2001.

Serpas, Jaime. *La lucha por un sueño: Antecedentes y crónicas completas de la guerra civil en El Salvador.* San Salvador: n.p., 2006.

Stanley, William. *The Protection Racket State: Elite Politics, Military Extortion and Civil War in El Salvador.* Philadelphia: Temple University Press, 1996.

———. Review of *Emergence of Insurgency in El Salvador: Ideology and Political Will,* by Yvon Grenier. *Comparative Politics* 94, no. 1 (March 2000): 214–15.

Stephens, John L. *Incidents of Travel in Central America and Yucatan,* 2 vols. New York: Dover Publications, 1969.

Stevens, Donald Fithian. *Origins of Instability in Early Republican Mexico.* Durham: Duke University Press, 1991.

Sullivan-González, Douglass. *Piety, Power, and Politics: Religion and Nation Formation in Guatemala, 1821–1871.* Pittsburgh: University of Pittsburgh Press, 1998.

Suter, Jan. *Prosperität und Krise in einer Kaffeerepublik: Modernisierung, sozialer Wandel und politischer Umbruch in El Salvador, 1910–1945.* Frankfurt am Main: Vervuert Verlag, 1996.

Taplin, Glen. *Middle American Governors.* Metuchen, NJ: Scarecrow Press, 1972.

Thompson, Wallace. *Rainbow Countries of Central America.* New York: Chantauqua Press, 1927.

Tilley, Virginia. *Seeing Indians: A Study of Race, Nation, and Power in El Salvador.* Albuquerque: University of New Mexico Press, 2005.

Tilly, Charles. *Democracy.* New York: Cambridge University Press, 2007.

Todd, Molly. *Beyond Displacement: Campesinos, Refugees, and Collective Action in the Salvadoran Civil War.* Madison: University of Wisconsin Press, 2010.

Torres-Rivas, Edelberto, and Héctor Pérez-Brignoli, eds. *Historia general de Centroamérica, Vol. 3: de la Ilustración al liberalismo, 1750–1870.* Madrid: Editorial Siruela, 1993.

Turcios, Roberto. *Autoritarismo y modernización: El Salvador, 1950–1960.* San Salvador: Ediciones Tendencias, 1993.

Tutino, John. *From Insurrection to Revolution in Mexico: Social Bases of Agrarian Violence, 1750–1940.* Princeton: Princeton University Press, 1986.

Valdivieso Oriani, Ricardo Orlando. *Cruzando El Imposible: Una saga.* San Salvador: n.p., 2007.

Valencia, Daniel, and Carlos Martinez. "Plática con Orlando de Sola," *El Faro,* July 10, 2009, http://archivo.elfaro.net/secciones/platicas/20090710/Platicas1 _20090710.asp.

Vaquerano, Ricardo, Daniel Valencia, Diego Murcia, and Mauro Arias. "Sánchez Cerén no hubiera pasado de soldado" *El Faro,* January 24, 2010, n.p., http://www.elfaro.net/es/201001/el_agora/977/.

Wall, Robert. "The Franchise in Seventeenth-Century Massachusetts: Dedham and Cambridge." *William and Mary Quarterly* 34 (1977): 453–58.

Walter, Knut. *The Regime of Anastasio Somoza, 1936–1956.* Chapel Hill: University of North Carolina Press, 1993.

———. "Trade and Development in an Export Economy: The Case of El Salvador, 1870–1914." M.A. thesis, University of North Carolina, Chapel Hill, 1977.

Warren, Richard. "Elections and Popular Political Participation in Mexico, 1808–1936." In *Liberals, Politics, and Power: State Formation in Nineteenth-Century Latin America,* edited by Vicent Peloso and Barbara Tenenbaum, 30–58. Athens: University of Georgia Press, 1996.

———. *Vagrants and Citizens: Politics and the Masses in Mexico City from Colony to Republic.* Wilmington, DE: Scholarly Resources, 2001.

Webre, Stephen. *José Napoleón Duarte and the Christian Democratic Party in Salvadoran Politics, 1960–1972.* Baton Rouge: Louisiana State University Press, 1979.

White, Alastair. *El Salvador.* New York: Praeger, 1973.

Whitehead, Laurence. "Miners as Voters: The Electoral Process in Bolivia's Mining Camps." *Journal of Latin American Studies* 13, no. 2 (November 1981): 313–46.

Wickham-Crowley, Timothy P. *Guerrillas and Revolution in Latin America: A Comparative Study of Insurgents and Regimes since 1956.* Princeton: Princeton University Press, 1991.

Williams, Philip, and Knut Walter. *Militarization and Demilitarization in El Salvador's Transition to Democracy.* Pittsburgh: University of Pittsburgh Press, 1997.

Williams, Robert. *States and Social Evolution: Coffee and the Rise of National Governments in Central America.* Chapel Hill: University of North Carolina Press, 1994.

Wilson, Everett. "The Crisis of National Integration in El Salvador, 1919–1935." Ph.D. dissertation, Stanford University, 1970.

Wolf, Eric, and Edward Hansen. "Caudillo Politics: A Structural Analysis." *Comparative Studies in Society and History* 9, no. 2 (January 1967): 169–79.

Wolfe, Justin. *The Everyday Nation-State: Community and Ethnicity in Nineteenth-Century Nicaragua.* Lincoln: University of Nebraska Press, 2007.

Wood, Gordon. *The Radicalism of the American Revolution.* New York: Knopf, 1992.

Wood, James. *The Society of Equality: Popular Republicanism and Democracy in Santiago de Chile, 1818–1851*. Albuquerque: University of New Mexico Press, 2011.

Woodward, Ralph Lee. *Rafael Carrera and the Emergence of the Republic of Guatemala, 1821–1871*. Athens: University of Georgia Press, 1993.

Wortman, Miles. *Government and Society in Central America, 1680–1840*. New York: Columbia University Press, 1982.

Wunthrow, Robert. *Communities of Discourse: Ideology and Social Structure in the Reformation, the Enlightenment, and European Socialism*. Cambridge, MA: Harvard University Press, 1989.

Yarrington, Doug. *A Coffee Frontier: Land, Society and Politics in Duaca, Venezuela, 1830–1936*. Pittsburgh: University of Pittsburgh Press, 1997.

Yashar, Deborah. *Demanding Democracy: Reform and Reaction in Costa Rica and Guatemala, 1870s–1950s*. Stanford: Stanford University Press, 1997.

Zamosc, Leon. "The Landing that Never Was: Canadian Marines and the Salvadoran Insurrection of 1932." *Canadian Journal of Latin American and Caribbean Studies* 21 (1986): 131–47.

Zepeda Herrera, Juan Orlando. *Perfiles de la guerra en El Salvador*. San Salvador: New Graphics, 2008.

INDEX

E R I K   C H I N G

is professor of history at Furman University.

He is the author or coauthor of numerous books and articles on

Salvadoran history, which have received such recognition as

the Alfred B. Thomas Book Award from the Southeastern Council

of Latin American Studies, the Conference on Latin American History

Prize, and the Hubert Herring Prize from the Pacific Coast Council

of Latin American Studies.